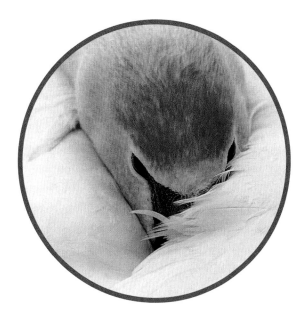

Reader's Digest
Wildlife Watch

Gardens & Parks in Spring

Reader's Digest
Wildlife Watch

Gardens & Parks in Spring

Published by
The Reader's Digest Association Limited
London · New York · Sydney · Montreal

Contents

Wildlife habitats and havens

Animals and plants in focus

Garden watch

Park watch

Introduction

Late February in a park or garden can feel like the depths of winter. Daffodils and tulips may be showing their pointed shoots, but the soil around the green spikes is often frozen hard and glinting with frost. The branches of deciduous shrubs and trees are bare. Herbaceous plants that have died down for the winter are nowhere to be seen. There is a sense of nature on hold.

But then one day all is different. The frost has gone and the sunlight is stronger. You can feel it on your face and smell the earth as the warmth seeps down into the ground, transforming cold clay and grit into living soil. To a gardener, that whiff of warm earth has a heady fragrance, for it is the scent of spring.

The varied, repeated phrases of the song thrush are less commonly heard today, owing to a sharp decline in numbers that may be caused by garden pesticides.

The first crop of young greenfly make a welcome meal for hungry ladybirds, which have spent the winter clustered in sheltered crevices to avoid the frost.

Garden ponds make ideal nurseries for frogs, whose tadpoles develop through the spring months and finally emerge as tiny froglets in early summer.

Green havens

Wildlife is always ahead of the gardener. For instance, male common frogs in garden ponds wake up from their winter's hibernation while the pond is still glazed with ice. The frogs can usually find a little open water around the overwintered stems of iris and other emergent plants. They croak to attract females from their winter quarters on land, and wait for the thaw. Then one night the ice melts and the shallows are full of croaking, splashing activity as the mating frogs fill the water with masses of spawn. Garden ponds are now among the main breeding sites of common frogs in Britain. They have helped to replace wetlands that have been drained to make farmland, and farm ponds that have been abandoned and allowed to silt up.

In much the same way, urban parks and 16 million back gardens have partly taken the place of felled woodlands, cleared scrub and ploughed-up grassland, and now provide living spaces for a surprising variety of native insects, spiders, amphibians, reptiles, birds and mammals. You can see sparrowhawks and tawny owls hunting over city parks and gardens, and every town has its population of urban foxes. Badgers forage through the night, often visiting several gardens in search of scraps before returning to their setts in wooded parks or on patches of wasteland. Park lakes have become havens for water birds, such as coots, moorhens, several species of ducks and geese, and majestic mute swans (see pages 102–107). In rural areas, animals treat gardens as extensions of their wild habitat, but in cities and suburbs the patchwork of green between the buildings is their territory.

Rivals in song

The most conspicuous of this wild population are the birds – although many are not resident all year round. Insect-eating birds, such as swifts, warblers and flycatchers, spend the northern winter in the tropics and subtropics, where insects are to be found throughout the year. In spring they return north to breed, taking advantage of the seasonal boom in insect life and the long days that allow them to hunt for hours on end to feed their hungry broods.

Treetop rookeries in parks and large gardens become centres of raucous activity as the birds renew their pair-bonds and repair their nests.

The predatory aquatic young of dragonflies enjoy a feast as garden ponds become crowded with tadpoles and other small animals.

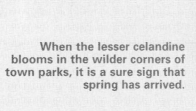

When the lesser celandine blooms in the wilder corners of town parks, it is a sure sign that spring has arrived.

By the time these summer migrants arrive, parks and gardens are alive with birdsong. All-year residents such as the robin, wren, house sparrow, blackbird and song thrush start claiming their territories at the very beginning of the breeding season, just as the buds start to swell on the trees and shrubs. The males compete for the best sites, which are usually in untidy, rather overgrown gardens that never get sprayed with pesticides. In parks they favour areas where the park authorities have deliberately encouraged native vegetation to grow, creating nature reserves rather than recreational open spaces. Neat, well-tended parks and gardens consisting just of bedding plants and mown grass hold few attractions for wildlife.

Older, more experienced birds usually claim the best spots, but only after prolonged disputes that involve rival males duelling with song from before dawn. The chorus reaches a crescendo just before sunrise and continues through the day and into the evening. Perched on rooftops, TV aerials and trees, blackbirds and song thrushes fill the darkening sky with rich, plangent notes, competing with the rumble of traffic. In well-lit towns, robins may sing throughout the night.

Fresh start

As the birds start prospecting for nesting sites, insects are doing the same. Queen wasps that have spent the winter hibernating in attics and garden sheds emerge to look for cavities such as old mouseholes, where they can start new colonies. Soon they are scraping wood shavings from garden fences and benches, and forming them into the wet balls of wood pulp that they use to build their paper palaces.

They may have to dispute nest sites with queen bumblebees, which also favour mouseholes. Bumblebees (see pages 70–73) are among the earliest insects to emerge in spring, but in southern England and Wales they are soon joined by yellow brimstone butterflies, which have often spent the winter hidden beneath the sheltering leaves of ivy growing on walls and trees, and by colourful small tortoiseshells. Before long, other garden butterflies such as the peacock and comma emerge from hibernation too. They are often darker than those that appear in summer, their darker colouring helping them to absorb energy from the weaker spring sun.

In early spring, tawny owls in town parks become very vocal as they form breeding pairs, duetting with sharp *'ke-wick!'* calls and long hoots.

The rapid, piercing song of the wren seems far too loud to come from such a tiny bird. The wren is often the first to begin the dawn chorus, starting to sing while it is still dark.

Spring creates a baby boom among the garden vole population, which is good news for predators such as tawny owls and foxes.

Spring flush

Soon the spring flowers are buzzing with insects of all kinds, eagerly probing the blooms for nectar. Flowers in gardens and parks are rich sources of nectar for adult insects, even though many of the plants are alien to these islands. But the energy-rich nectar is just fuel to keep the insects aloft while they get on with the real business of the season – finding mates and laying their eggs.

Adult insects may feed by sipping nectar from exotic blooms, but the plant-eating caterpillars of butterflies and moths have different requirements. Normally they eat only the foliage of native plants – or cultivated forms of native plants such as cabbages. So while adult butterflies and moths feed in the flower gardens, they lay their eggs on the vegetables, in the hedges or in native trees such as oak and willow. The caterpillars hatch as the spring flush of new leaves appears, giving them plenty of tender young foliage to eat.

Just as the caterpillars are starting to get plump, the newly hatched nestling birds start begging for food. They need protein-rich meals, so many birds that normally eat seeds as adults switch to catching insects in spring. A pair of blue tits rearing a family of ten or more in a garden nestbox will bring caterpillars back to the nest at the rate of one per minute throughout the day and catch many thousands over the whole breeding season. If they have made the mistake of nesting where insects are routinely controlled with chemical pesticides, some chicks may starve in the nest.

Late arrivals

Early in May the swifts return from Africa, often on the same day each year. Swifts spend most of their lives in the air, landing only to breed. At one time they nested in hollow trees, but nearly all the swifts that breed in Britain today nest in the roof spaces of old buildings and hunt over parks and gardens. On fine days they circle high in the air, pursuing small airborne insects with short bursts of rapid wingbeats punctuating long, stiff-winged glides. But when they are not hunting, and especially towards dusk, the swifts swoop around the rooftops in high-speed aerial chases, giving high, screaming calls as their underwings flash in the low light.

As it gets darker the swifts disappear, returning to their nests or circling high into the air, and their place is taken by bats, such as the tiny pipistrelle (see pages 93–96), fluttering noiselessly and aerobatically through the gathering gloom as they target gnats and other small flies with their extraordinary echo-location systems. Meanwhile nectar-feeding moths seek out the spicy fragrance of honeysuckle, which always becomes stronger at nightfall.

In rural gardens swallows often build their nests in open sheds or even house porches, ignoring their human neighbours as they bring insects for their young.

Neat semicircles cut out of rose leaves are the work of the solitary leaf-cutter bee, which rolls the leaf sections into tubular nests for its eggs.

Snake-like slow-worms emerge from hibernation and often appear in garden compost heaps, where they feed on slugs and other garden pests.

Wildlife habitats and havens

- Spring garden activity
- From wild flowers to garden blooms
- Butterflies in your garden
- Urban parks – havens of tranquillity
- Wildlife of a tree hole
- Kew Gardens – a natural treasure trove

Spring garden activity

In this wonderful time of regeneration and renewal, birds are returning from sunnier climes while other animals stir from the long winter months of hibernation – and all of them have mating on their minds.

Hedgehog courtship

After coming out of hibernation and having a good feed, the hedgehog's next priority is to find a mate. Females ready to breed soon attract the attention of males and noisy courtship rituals begin.

The male may approach the female until their noses almost touch, at which point his intended mate generally rebuffs him with a bite or a blow from her paw. Undeterred, the male changes tack and starts circling the female while she turns on the spot, snorting loudly and rhythmically. From time to time, the male gently nudges the female, only to have his advances rejected by a spiky cold shoulder. Such behaviour can continue for several hours, accompanied by continuous snorting by the female, before she lowers her spines and is ready to mate. During this time, the pair may be interrupted by rival males drawn by the commotion.

After mating, the female constructs a nest from leaves and grass, perhaps mixed with scraps of paper and other rubbish, often in a pile of garden litter or under a shed, where she eventually gives birth to her young.

▶ While hibernating over the winter, a hedgehog may lose over a quarter of its body weight. On waking, it immediately trundles around the garden, picking up any slugs, worms and beetles it can find.

Common frogs lay their eggs in clumps, unlike common toads, which lay them in strings. Several female frogs often lay their eggs close together, forming large mats of frogspawn.

Frog reproduction

Amphibians breed in water. Many male common frogs are already living in ponds, having hibernated there during the winter. Most females and young frogs, as well as toads and newts, stay on land. When a female frog reaches a pond, she is grabbed by a male, who hangs on to her until it is time to mate. He can keep his grip for weeks or even months, holding on so tightly that she may be injured and may even drown.

It is not clear exactly what triggers mating, but it usually starts at night when all the frogs in a particular pond move to the shallowest waters. A female generally lays her eggs at around three in the morning. As they are released the male fertilises them. The mass of jelly-coated eggs sinks to the bottom of the pond, where it expands as the jelly absorbs water, eventually rising to the surface as frogspawn. Although the eggs are relatively safe from attack, when they hatch into tadpoles they attract many predators. Few tadpoles reach maturity. The metamorphosis from egg to miniature adult frog usually takes around 12 weeks.

Squirrel's drey

Grey squirrels that live in gardens often survive the winter by raiding bird tables for scraps and nuts. As food becomes less scarce with the arrival of spring, the grey squirrels start preparing for a family. In the fork of a tree, the female builds a domed, football-sized drey to serve as nest and nursery. Constructed from leafy twigs, leaves and grass, snugly lined with moss, shredded bark and dry grass, many dreys have no entrance – the squirrels simply push their way in and out.

Towards the end of her pregnancy, the female chases other squirrels, especially males, away from the drey. The first young grey squirrels of the year are usually born in March. Each litter averages three kittens, as young squirrels are called. They are helpless, blind, naked and deaf at birth and suckle their mother's milk until they are about ten weeks old.

◄ There are few more endearing sights in a spring garden than a family of young grey squirrels at play. However, they are not always welcome because they damage trees and bird feeders and raid birds' nests.

Queen bumblebees

Having slept through the winter in some sheltered place, bumblebees are stirring and their familiar droning starts to reverberate around the garden once more. The first to emerge are usually queens that mated last autumn. These females will spend several weeks gaining strength and building a nesting chamber before laying their eggs.

A queen is often encumbered by an army of tiny reddish or brownish mites that hitch a lift on her fluffy abdomen. Occasionally, the burden is so great that she has difficulty taking off. Once she has prepared a nest, the mites abandon their host and take refuge there, feeding on any scraps of pollen and other food that are left over.

▶ After hibernating all winter, a queen white-tailed bumblebee has to top up her energy reserves quickly, so she visits nectar-rich spring flowers. In the process, she transfers pollen from one to another, helping to pollinate them.

Butterflies emerge

The small tortoiseshell and brimstone butterflies that found suitable winter quarters in and around the garden the previous autumn, start emerging from hibernation almost simultaneously.

Once they have fed on nectar from spring flowers, the females start to search for suitable plants on which to lay their eggs. All butterflies 'taste' using special sense organs on their feet, and the female stamps on a leaf to ensure she has a plant that will supply food for the caterpillars before laying.

Brimstone caterpillars need either alder buckthorn or purging buckthorn, usually in hedges and around woods. The female small tortoiseshell looks for stinging nettles. Patches in gardens are often too small, so she widens her search to waste ground, hedgerows and woodland edges. She lays between 60 and 100 eggs on the underside of the young uppermost leaves. Several small tortoiseshells may use the same plant, forming large clusters of eggs.

In the spring, having recently emerged from hibernation, a male brimstone butterfly needs to drink plenty of nectar before he has the strength to find a mate.

Hawthorn buds

The first green hawthorn buds open quite early in the year. One day the hedges seem bare and the next they are shrouded in a green mist as the young leaves open. In a remarkably short time the tree or bush is fully clothed in bright green leaves. Although hawthorn is often used for hedges, where it is left untrimmed it grows into a medium-sized tree. Old hawthorn trees have wonderfully gnarled and twisted trunks.

Hawthorn provides food for a variety of insects, including caterpillars of the distinctively marked lackey moth. On hatching in spring, the caterpillars cover hawthorn twigs with a whitish, silken web under which they feed. When present in large numbers, they may strip all the leaves from a hedge.

► Clusters of white flower heads on a hawthorn have a sickly sweet scent that attracts myriad insects to sup nectar.

Hawthorn produces a prodigious mass of flowers, mostly in May, which accounts for its alternative name of 'May' or 'May-tree'.

Oak galls

The oak is often considered to be the most English of all trees. It is certainly a haven for wildlife. A huge number of insects, including butterflies, moths, bush crickets, beetles and bugs, as well as spiders and mites, depend on it for survival. Many other creatures, such as squirrels and birds, come to feed, nest and seek shelter among its branches.

In the spring, oaks are plagued by strange growths, known as galls. When a tiny insect known as a gall wasp injects her eggs into an oak tree, she also injects a chemical that makes the tree produce a gall around her egg, effectively isolating it. Oak galls range in size from currant-like growths on oak flowers to much larger marble galls and oak apples. The oak eggar moth also visits the oak to lay her eggs. If large numbers of caterpillars survive, they may strip most of the leaves. If this happens early in the year, the tree can produce a second, tougher crop of leaves.

◄ Young, bright green oak leaves look very different from the wavy-edged, khaki-coloured leaves of high summer. Catkin-like flowers appear in May and June; male catkins are longer than female ones, which are tucked away in the tip of a shoot.

Wren song

The diminutive wren has one of the most delightful of all bird songs – and one of the loudest for the singer's size. Secretive by nature, it spends a good deal of its time hidden away, occasionally darting in and out of a hedge or undergrowth in search of food. Its slender bill is well adapted for prising spiders and insects from cracks in bark and between bricks.

In early spring, the cock wren builds several nests, usually between five and eight but sometimes as many as 12, then lets his mate select one for laying, which she lines with soft feathers. Meanwhile, the male may go off to persuade a second, a third and even a fourth female to occupy his other nests. The females incubate the eggs and usually have sole responsibility for feeding the nestlings. It is only when the chicks are almost ready to fly that the male returns to help feed them. He may take charge of the fledglings and accompany them on forays from the nest.

There is no mistaking the wren, with its cocked tail and tiny, rotund body. It often delivers its loud, rattling song from a conspicuous perch.

Territorial blackbirds

Over the winter, blackbirds and song thrushes will have been feeding in the garden, taking grubs and pulling earthworms from their burrows on mild days. At the onset of spring, males start defending their breeding areas to keep out rivals, although resident blackbirds are often territorial all year. The male, with his bright yellow bill and jet black plumage, is quite distinct from the female, with her dark brown feathers and underparts variably mottled in a darker shade, sometimes with a reddish brown tinge. Dull days are brightened by the male's beautiful melodic, fluting song, which he pours forth from tall trees, chimney stacks or TV aerials, especially at dusk.

Some blackbirds build their nests early, at the end of February or the beginning of March, in a bare hedge or bush. Early laying is a calculated risk – if the chicks do survive, they have a head start on young birds born later in the season. However, clutches of eggs laid at this time are often lost, due either to cold weather or attacks from predators.

Having an early brood means that the parent blackbirds have to work that much harder to find large enough supplies of insects and worms to satisfy their hungry chicks.

Cock robins

Robins establish their territories long before winter begins, and the males defend them energetically when spring, and the breeding season, approaches. Eventually, a male will allow a female of the species to enter and stay on his patch as his mate.

The female constructs a domed nest from grass, dead leaves and moss, sometimes choosing to build in odd places, such as car engines and old cooking utensils. Eggs are laid any time from April to June and the female does all the incubating for 13 or 14 days; both parents then share the feeding of the chicks. The youngsters can fly 13 days after hatching but they don't leave the nest permanently until they are 16 to 24 days old. Robins will often have a second brood and, rarely, a third.

◄ One of the few birds that sings almost all year round, in spring the cock robin warbles with extra vigour. His short, warbling song proclaims his territory and advertises for a mate.

Noisy foxes

Many foxes live and breed in urban areas and frequently visit gardens in search of food. Early in the year, the distinctive, loud, eerie shriek of their mating screams can sometimes be heard on calm, quiet nights.

After mating, as the spring days warm up, the vixen looks for a place to excavate her den, or earth as it is called. In gardens, this may be under a shed or piles of rubble. Here, in March or April, she gives birth to a litter of four or five chocolate-brown cubs. The male brings food for the vixen and cubs, either giving it to his mate or leaving it at the entrance to the den. He is not usually allowed to enter.

Taking advantage of a sunny day in spring, this fox appears to be quite relaxed. Even so, it is sure to be well aware of what is going on nearby and, at the first whiff of danger, it will be off in a flash.

Aquatic insects

During the winter, many aquatic animals retreat to the bottom of the garden pond where the effects of very cold temperatures are moderated. As the temperature of the water slowly rises again in spring, they begin to re-appear at the surface. Many adult pond insects fly from one pool of water to another to lay their eggs, which is how newly created ponds are colonised by aquatic insect life so rapidly.

The great diving beetle, one of the biggest insects in Britain at 35mm (1⅜in) long, is a top predator, feeding on a variety of other insects, tadpoles and even small fish. There is also an array of predatory insect larvae in the pond, including those of damselflies, mayflies, caddis flies, dragonflies and beetles.

Adult pond skaters hibernate away from the water and return to the pond in spring. A pond skater's widely spaced legs spread its weight, so that it doesn't break the surface film and sink.

▶ It is a sign of a healthy garden pond when many damselflies emerge from their aquatic nymphal stage simultaneously. In their strange tandem mating position, pairs are seen later as the female lays her eggs at the water's surface.

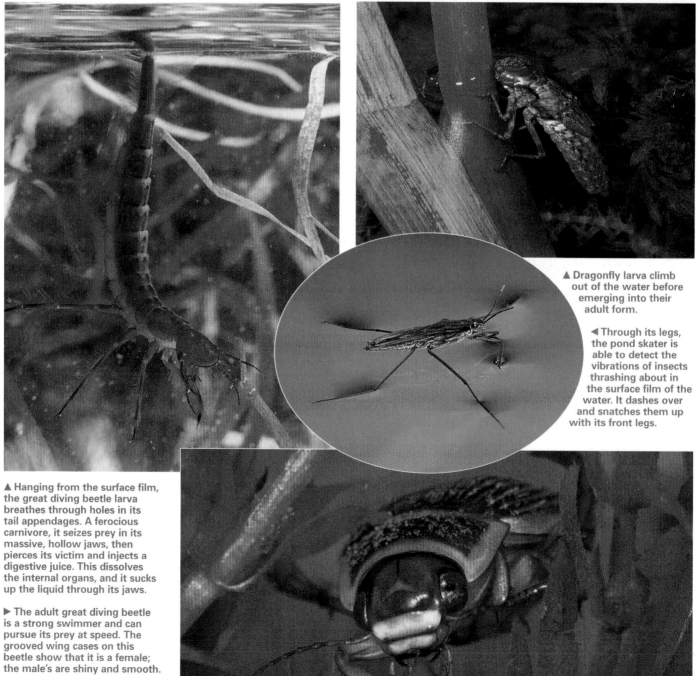

▲ Dragonfly larva climb out of the water before emerging into their adult form.

◀ Through its legs, the pond skater is able to detect the vibrations of insects thrashing about in the surface film of the water. It dashes over and snatches them up with its front legs.

▲ Hanging from the surface film, the great diving beetle larva breathes through holes in its tail appendages. A ferocious carnivore, it seizes prey in its massive, hollow jaws, then pierces its victim and injects a digestive juice. This dissolves the internal organs, and it sucks up the liquid through its jaws.

▶ The adult great diving beetle is a strong swimmer and can pursue its prey at speed. The grooved wing cases on this beetle show that it is a female; the male's are shiny and smooth.

Returning house martins

House martins arrive back in gardens in spring, having made a long and arduous journey from Africa. Some four weeks later, having recouped their strength, they start nest building. The upside-down mud igloos are usually placed under the eaves of buildings, especially houses. How long it takes to build the nest depends on the supply of mud. Maintaining a muddy area in the garden provides the birds with an essential building material. It is estimated that a pair of house martins collects around 1000 or more pellets of mud to complete a nest. The mud is reinforced with roots and grass.

Both parents share the incubation duties and feeding the nestlings. At first, the young remain hidden in the nest, but as they grow they thrust their heads out of the entrance hole. They are encouraged to fly from about 15 days old, but it is not unusual for the young birds to go on roosting in the nest until they leave for Africa in late summer. As many as 14 house martins, the result of two or three broods, have been found sharing one nest.

▶ A house martin is a wonderfully agile flier. It swoops up to the entrance of its nest, then almost stalls in midair to slow itself down enough to grab hold of the lip of the entrance hole with its tiny feet.

In spring, earthworms leave their deep burrows to return to the surface layers of soil. Here they work away, diligently adding minerals to the upper layers of soil where the new growth of plants can utilise it.

Hard-working worms

Earthworms normally live in the top 20–25cm (8–10in) of soil, but when the ground is frozen in winter, they often burrow down as deep as 3m (10ft). When temperatures warm up, they move back to the surface where they work tirelessly as 'nature's little ploughmen', a description given them by Charles Darwin, who made detailed studies of earthworms.

Worms usually stay out of sight, although they do come onto the surface on warm, damp nights to mate. Some types of worm leave telltale worm casts on lawns. These consist of soil the worm has swallowed at depth, passed through its body to extract decaying plant and animal matter, and ejected at the surface.

WILDLIFE WATCH

How can I see spring wildlife in my garden?

● You can encourage wildlife to come into your garden in the spring – plant plenty of nectar-rich, spring-flowering species to attract butterflies, bumblebees and other insects; put up nestboxes and note which birds use them; keep the bird table well stocked with food and fresh water.

● The garden pond is often the focus of attention for much wildlife. Insects are comparatively easy to observe because they are often oblivious to the presence of people.

To watch spawning frogs, which often disappear from view at the first sign of danger, erect a small screen that will hide you and allow a closer approach. However, keep a watchful eye out for cats, the bane of some garden wildlife, as they may learn to use the screen to catch the frogs.

From wild flowers to garden blooms

So bright and beautiful are these heralds of spring, it is not surprising that cultivated varieties of native British grassland and woodland wild flowers now make popular additions to garden flowerbeds.

Bluebell

Hazy-blue, lightly scented carpets of bluebells are a glorious feature of woodlands in spring. A display of bluebells can look lovely in a garden setting too. In the autumn, buy bulbs of the native *Hyacinthoides non-scripta*, which has bells hanging on only one side of its drooping stem, from a reputable wild flower supplier.

Dig in plenty of manure or garden compost to create humus-rich soil that is moist but well draining, and plant the bulbs in natural-looking clumps in areas of light shade, perhaps under some trees. These plants do best if they are not overly exposed to direct sunlight. After flowering, let the leaves die back naturally before cutting them off, to replenish the bulbs for the next spring. Over time, the display will spread.

◀ Bluebells thrive in the moist climate of the British Isles and usually flower in April and May.

▼ Wild pansies flower when there are plenty of bees to pollinate them. The lowest petal is a landing stage for bees coming to collect the nectar. The dark lines on the yellow petals guide them in.

Pansy

Less than two hundred years ago, the wild pansy was no more than a small but attractive wild plant of pastures, cornfields and waste land, but since the early 19th century, it has been extensively hybridised by horticulturalists. The name pansy is derived from the French word *pensée* meaning 'thought', usually with romantic connotations. It was also known as heartsease.

Today, the modern cultivated pansy is one of the best-loved and commonly planted spring bedding plants. It has a long flowering period between April and September, making it a useful addition to any border, and is very popular for window boxes and hanging baskets as well.

Lords-and-ladies

Lords-and-ladies is a curious plant that thrives in woodland, under hedgerows and along banks, most commonly on chalk and limestone soils. It has up to 90 local names, including wild arum and cuckoo pint.

In March and April, lords-and-ladies produces a strange 'bloom'. Tiny male flowers are stacked above female flowers, on the same plant, in a bulge at the top of a long green stem. This swollen part is topped by a long club-shaped structure, called the spadix, which is surrounded by a broad, greenish yellow modified leaf (the spathe).

As the spadix warms up, it emits a putrid smell that attracts flies, bringing pollen from another lords-and-ladies plant. Landing on the spadix, the flies slip down into the bulge where they are held captive by a ring of downward-facing hairs until all the female flowers are pollinated. Only then do the male flowers start releasing pollen, the bristly hairs wither and the flies escape, taking with them some of the male pollen, which they carry to another plant. By autumn, the stem has a mass of bright orange-red berries, which are very poisonous. Grow the cultivated Italian arum in full sun in well-drained soil.

▶ The Italian lord-and-ladies is a striking plant that has big arrow-shaped leaves with creamy-white veins and a yellow spadix. It looks very eye-catching in a garden border and is much sought after by flower arrangers.

Daffodil

Although it used to grow in abundance in woods and orchards, today the truly wild daffodil is rare in most of England, Wales and Scotland, and absent from Ireland. Its flowers are all-yellow, with petals paler than the trumpet. Over the centuries, this prototype has been modified to produce a huge range of colours, from white through shades of yellow to orange.

Among the favourites of all shop-bought bulbs, the daffodil is a reliable, low-maintenance garden flower. Over time, a clump spreads and can persist for decades. Plants often become naturalised, so it can be difficult to tell whether some daffodils are really wild or old garden escapees.

◀ Clusters of golden daffodils brighten up most spring gardens. They are best seen in big displays in informal settings, on grassy banks and under trees.

Grape hyacinth

Wild grape hyacinths are now very rare in their natural dry-grassland habitat. They are confined to a few localities in the Breckland of Suffolk and chalky verges in Cambridgeshire.

Bulbs of the garden grape hyacinth, which originated in eastern Europe, are readily available from garden centres nationwide. Planted in a sunny, well-drained spot in the garden, the grape hyacinth produces sweet, plum-scented, dark blue flowers in April and May. Occasionally, garden grape hyacinths become naturalised on roadside verges.

The imported garden grape hyacinth gives some idea of the stunning spring spectacle that the native species must once have created on the sandy soils of eastern Britain.

Primrose

Genuinely wild primroses have become increasingly scarce because their habitat has been destroyed by farmers uprooting hedges, changing drainage patterns and spraying herbicides, and also by overshading from planted trees. Although there is no real evidence that picking the flowers has done much harm, collectors digging up whole plants, roots and all, almost certainly have.

It may be struggling in the wild, but many different cultivated forms are readily available, making this one of the most popular spring bedding plants. As scented flowers blooming from January to May, they attract a variety of insect pollinators, such as early brimstone butterflies.

▶ One of the first flowers of spring, the primrose grows in charming natural posies, whether natural or cultivated. It was Victorian Prime Minister Benjamin Disraeli's favourite flower.

Pasqueflower

The nodding purple blooms of the pasqueflower make it one of the most attractive native wild flowers. It is also one of the rarest, occupying fewer than 30 scattered sites in England, the most northerly being in West Yorkshire. Other remaining strongholds include the Cotswolds, the Chilterns, Cambridgeshire and Lincolnshire. The main reason for this decline is its preference for undisturbed limestone or chalk grassland, which has become a rare habitat due to modern agricultural practices.

Although a member of the buttercup family, the pasqueflower bears no resemblance to a buttercup. Its glorious bell-shaped flowers bloom above delicate, silvery haired foliage. 'Pasque' refers to Easter, and the main flowering period of the pasqueflower is around Easter time, between April and May.

◀ Although disappearing in the wild, the spectacular purple flowers of the pasqueflower can still be enjoyed in the garden, and most garden centres stock the plant during the spring. Even when not in bloom, the feathery foliage makes it attractive at any time of year.

Cowslip

Once as profuse and familiar as the buttercup is today, wild cowslips have declined dramatically since the 1950s as a result of the extensive use of herbicides and the ploughing up of old grassland. Fortunately, the cowslip has staged a partial recovery since the 1990s and is a fairly common sight on light chalky soils, in meadows, grassland and open woods. The name cowslip comes from a euphemism for cow-pat, a reminder of the pastures where it was once found in abundance.

The cowslip is a dainty addition to any border or wild-flower meadow. It appears in a profusion of different colours. When crossed with the primrose it becomes the polyanthus, a well-known spring bedding plant that occurs in many colours.

Cowslips flower in April and May. Typically, there are between 10 to 30 yellow flowers per stem. Each exudes a sweet, apricot-like scent and produces copious amounts of nectar, which attracts insects.

Wood anemone

In the wild, the wood anemone's attractive, white flowers are often tinged with purple streaks or a pink flush. They cover the floor of ancient woodlands from April to June. One alternative common name for these delicate blooms is windflower, as they tremble in the slightest breeze. Other names include grandmother's nightcap and moggie nightgown (in the Derbyshire dialect a moggie is a mouse, not a cat).

The plant rarely grows from seeds. Instead, it spreads by sending out creeping, underground stems (rhizomes), which it does extremely slowly – about 2m (6½ft) every century. So a mass of wood anemones indicates that the woodland is hundreds of years old.

You can buy dormant rhizomes or plants from most garden centres. Plant them around the bases of deciduous shrubs and trees so the wood anemones can grow naturally through leaf litter in shady surroundings.

◀ As a damp-meadow plant, the snake's-head fritillary looks most natural growing among long grass in wild-flower meadows, but it is also good in sunny borders.

▲ Decaying leaf litter generates a little heat that speeds the growth of the wood anemones as they push their way up through the woodland floor.

Snake's-head fritillary

A most exotic-looking wild flower, this member of the lily family blooms in April and May. Its purple-chequered, bell-shaped flowers hang on stems up to about 45cm (18in) tall. In some colonies, about one third of the blooms are white, not purple. Until the early 20th century, the snake's-head fritillary was quite a common plant in rich soils on river flood plains. Now it is found in only a few locations, including the water meadows at Magdalen College, Oxford, in Cricklade, Wiltshire, and at Stratfield Saye in Hampshire.

You can buy the bulbs from most garden centres. Plant them in late summer in well-drained, moist soil under dappled shade. Left undisturbed, snake's-head fritillary seeds itself.

Sweet violet

In England, sweet violets are common in the wild but are much rarer elsewhere in Britain. Little bunches of deep purple, violet, dark bluish or white flowers, set off against heart-shaped, pale green leaves, appear from March to May. They have a delicious fragrance but, unless you are looking for them, you may easily miss them because they grow in scrub, at the foot of hedges or in woods.

Sweet violets make a welcome addition to the spring garden, preferring those shady areas that can be difficult to fill with colourful plants. Ensure that the soil is free-draining and, if possible, add some organic material, such as leaf mould. Plants should be divided every few years to keep them looking healthy.

Heavily scented sweet violets were much-loved by the Victorians for disguising unpleasant smells. As a result, they are often found growing semi-wild in and around long-established gardens.

WILDLIFE WATCH

How can I grow spring wild flowers?

● Wild-flower seed mixtures and bulbs are available at most garden centres, along with advice on care and planting.

● Use the plant's natural habitat as a guide to where to plant them. For example, woodland species prefer shady sites, whereas grassland flowers can be planted in more exposed, sunnier positions.

● Never attempt to transplant flowers from their natural locations in the wild. Not only will this spoil the enjoyment of others, but the plants may well not survive – and in many cases you will be breaking the law.

Butterflies in your garden

Gaining nourishment by sucking sweet nectar from flowers, butterflies see a garden as a good place to find food. Planting buddleia, aubrieta, hebe and other butterfly-friendly plants will help to attract many common species.

Gardens are an important refuge for butterflies, especially now there are fewer wild-flower meadows and hedgerows for them to feed and breed in. If you sit quietly beside a clump of aubrieta, snowdrops or crocus on a sunny spring day, you should see several different species visiting the flowers to feed. Anemones, too, especially *Anemone blanda*, grape hyacinths and wallflowers can provide lifesaving nectar for butterflies emerging from hibernation.

When butterflies are not feeding, they spend a lot of time sunbathing. Flying is an energetic business and the warmer the butterfly, the more efficient its metabolism. Butterflies often rest in sunny spots, with their wings spread to soak up the sunshine.

▶ The holly blue's underwings are a clear silvery blue with black dots. These butterflies may be seen in the upper branches of holly in spring and ivy in late summer.

Supplying nectar

To attract and sustain butterflies, the gardener needs to grow a wide selection of nectar-rich plants that will flower at different times during spring and summer. Create a colourful display with flowers that give off enough scent to tempt the butterflies into the garden.

They are most attracted to deep red or purple blossoms because they see farther into the infra-red and ultra-violet ends of the spectrum than humans. However, they also feed with relish on the nectar of yellow, blue and white flowers, such as French marigolds, alyssum and mock orange. Double

The small tortoiseshell is a strong flyer and also one of the butterflies most resistant to cold. This one is feeding on early spring catkins.

◀ The orange-tip butterfly visits gardens from the surrounding hedgerows and open woodland. This female lacks the orange patches that the male has on his dark-tipped upperwings.

▶ As well as drinking nectar, butterflies suck up moisture and salts from ponds or puddles, as this peacock is doing.

flowers and those with deep trumpets are not so appealing because it is hard for butterflies to reach the nectar.

Finding shelter

In order to survive the long, cold days of winter, butterflies have to find nooks and crannies in which to hibernate. Various species hibernate at different stages of their development. Small tortoiseshells, peacocks, commas and brimstones hibernate as adult butterflies. An ivy-covered wall or fence is an ideal site for brimstone butterflies to spend the winter, while an unheated garden shed makes a good shelter for small tortoiseshells and peacocks. White species and the holly blue overwinter in the pupal or chrysalis stage. The butterflies known as 'browns' overwinter as caterpillars.

Come the following spring, they carry on where they left off the previous autumn – feeding, pupating or emerging as adults. They still need to find shelter from wind and rain, so on cooler spring days and at night, butterflies seek refuge in leafy trees, shrubs and hedges. Eventually, the adults mate and lay eggs to produce a fresh generation of butterflies later on in the summer.

Friend or foe?

Butterflies perform an invaluable service in pollinating wild and cultivated flowers. The downside for the gardener is that the eggs they lay eggs hatch into hungry caterpillars that can damage plants.

To vegetable growers, the butterflies collectively known as 'cabbage whites' are arch enemies. The caterpillars of large white and small white butterflies can rapidly reduce lush green cabbage leaves to skeletal remains. It is possible to control them by removing the eggs or picking off the caterpillars by hand rather than using poisonous chemicals that also kill beneficial insects. The similar green-veined white and the orange-tip are entirely innocent, as their caterpillars feed only on wild relatives of the cabbage.

▼ Almost every painted lady seen in Britain has just arrived from the Continent or is the offspring of such a migrant.

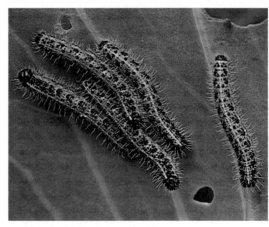

▲ Caterpillars of the large white are usually easy to find on cabbage plants as groups often feed together and cover surrounding leaves with lots of large green droppings.

◀ Large whites are among the most common British butterflies. Those hatched here are joined by migrants from the Continent.

Warning signs

If a garden is surrounded by countryside, expect to see a greater number and variety of butterflies than in a town garden. In some farming areas where crops are sprayed with insecticides and weed killers, however, butterfly numbers are likely to be low. As a consequence of this type of pollution, the numbers of other insects, birds and wild flowers may also be reduced.

Don't be too quick to jump to conclusions. Pollution is not the only reason for seeing fewer butterflies. Numbers are generally lower in cold, wet summers and after long spells of drought. When caterpillars' foodplants wither, there won't be as many butterflies the following year.

Food for caterpillars

Although butterflies mainly visit gardens to feed from flowers, they may breed there as well if supplied with suitable foodplants for their caterpillars. If you have a sunny corner where you can allow a patch of nettles to grow, you may find that small tortoiseshell, peacock and red admiral butterflies will lay their eggs there, and these will develop into spiny caterpillars.

Nettles have a tendency to spread and attempt to take over the garden, but they can be kept in check. One method is to sink a container of some sort in the ground around them. If the nettle patch is too small, however, butterflies will go elsewhere to deposit their eggs. Avoid using insecticides and herbicides in any part of the garden where you want to encourage butterflies to breed.

When can I see common garden butterflies?

- **Small white** (March–May and June–September)
- **Large white** (April–June and July–September)
- **Green-veined white** (April–mid-June and July–September)
- **Brimstone** (February–mid-June and late July–November)
- **Peacock** (March–November)
- **Red admiral** (May–October)
- **Painted lady** (May–October)
- **Comma** (March–June and July–October)
- **Orange-tip** (May–June)
- **Holly blue** (April–early June and July–September)
- **Small tortoiseshell** (March–November)
- **Gatekeeper** (July–September)
- **Meadow brown** (June–September)

JANUARY ● FEBRUARY

All butterflies are in hibernation, although the odd small tortoiseshell may fly briefly on warm days. This species and peacocks often lie up in sheds. Try to avoid disturbing them or they will waste precious energy on awakening.

Some overwintering butterflies, notably the hardy small tortoiseshell, may briefly come out of hibernation if the weather is exceptionally mild in January or February.

USEFUL PLANTS

Here are some plants that are cheap and easy to grow, and will provide nectar for butterflies from March through to November.

- **Aubrieta** Probably the best of the spring butterfly plants, it attracts butterflies emerging from hibernation.
- **Honesty** Another good spring butterfly plant that is particularly attractive to the beautiful orange-tip.
- **Lavender** A good all-round insect plant for feeding both butterflies and bees in the summer months.
- **Marjoram** An excellent summer butterfly plant, which is particularly attractive to butterflies of the brown group, such as gatekeepers and meadow browns.
- **Verbena** A very good all-round butterfly plant, with different varieties providing a rich source of nectar throughout the summer.

- **Scabious** Both annual and perennial varieties will attract a wide range of butterflies in summer.
- **Buddleia** The top butterfly plant, fully deserving its name 'butterfly bush'. Every garden should have one; it will grow almost anywhere.
- **Hebe** A small shrub with long-lasting sprays of purple or white flowers reminiscent of buddleia, although not quite as effective as a butterfly magnet.
- **Sedum** Commonly known as iceplant, this is one of the best late-summer plants to provide nectar for butterflies. *Sedum spectabile* is the best option because some of the other varieties do not look so attractive in the garden.
- **Michaelmas Daisy** This replaces sedum in the autumn, providing food for small tortoiseshells until they start hibernating from late August to early November.

▲ The gatekeeper is similar to the meadow brown, but smaller. It has two white dots in the black eyespot on each upperwing; the meadow brown usually has one.

BUTTERFLY CALENDAR

MARCH ● APRIL

Butterflies that hibernate as adults are first to appear, with the brimstone usually leading the way. Overwintering caterpillars become active and start to feed again. White butterflies emerge from their pupae in April.

◀ The sulphur-yellow brimstone is primarily a woodland and hedgerow butterfly, although it visits sheltered gardens.

▶ These two green-veined white butterflies are mating – their offspring will emerge as butterflies from July to August. The caterpillars do not eat garden plants.

MAY ● JUNE

Migrant painted ladies and red admirals begin to arrive. Holly blue butterflies are often seen now.

Painted ladies migrate to Britain from Europe and replenish their energy by visiting early-summer garden flowers. They lay eggs and the resulting butterflies appear later in the summer – but none survive the English winter.

JULY ● AUGUST

The meadow brown and gatekeeper butterflies now put in an appearance, followed by a second generation of peacocks and small tortoiseshells.

◀ Adult meadow browns are seen only during high summer. They tend to visit flowers that are quite close to the ground, often just above grass level.

▲ Two generations of the peacock are common garden visitors from March to November. The peacock is particularly fond of buddleia.

SEPTEMBER ● OCTOBER

White butterflies, small tortoiseshells and commas are still in evidence until cold weather sets in. Red admirals may be seen feeding on rotting windfall apples and other fruit.

Large white butterflies help to pollinate flowers but their caterpillars do a lot of damage to their foodplants.

▶ Small white butterflies are about half the size of large whites and their caterpillars are pale green rather than black and green.

NOVEMBER ● DECEMBER

All butterflies are now in hibernation, as caterpillars, pupae or adults. The occasional small tortoiseshell may still be active if the weather is warm enough.

Red admirals (right), small tortoiseshells, peacocks and commas enjoy the last sunny days, feeding on late flowers and fruit to build up energy reserves for winter.

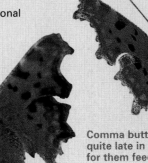

Comma butterflies are still flying quite late in the year. Look out for them feeding on ivy flowers.

Urban parks – havens of tranquillity

An oasis of trees, grass and flowers in the heart of a town or city is a welcoming place of peace for human visitors and wildlife alike – and because the animals that live there are so used to seeing people, many are bolder and more visible than elsewhere.

On the face of it, parks full of beautiful old trees and expanses of grassland, such as those to be found in Windsor and Richmond on the outskirts of London, seem a far cry from the orderly flowerbeds and well-mown lawns that characterise those of the inner cities, such as St James's Park or Kensington Gardens in the centre of the capital. But in any urban park, no matter what its size or location, it soon becomes apparent just how many creatures are taking advantage of the trees, the flowers, the ponds and the rest of the environment. Birds, squirrels, butterflies, ducks and a whole host of insects may all be observed in something like their natural surroundings, while some mammals, such as foxes and deer, have adapted to life side-by-side with the human race.

Park management

The open spaces in many urban parks are manicured to the point of excluding almost any plants except grasses. However, some wild flowers actively thrive on having the surrounding vegetation mown at regular intervals, since it literally cuts down the competition from other herbaceous plants, and leaves the way open for plants such as dandelions, daisies, creeping buttercups and greater plantain to flourish.

Left to grow naturally, without the intervention of mowers or weedkillers, grassland starts to look like an old-fashioned meadow, where wild flowers such as selfheal, and various hawkweeds and mouse-ears add colour to the scene. In spring, there may be drifts of planted crocuses and daffodils to brighten up a dull day. In an urban park, there is very often a flavour of both the wild and the cultivated worlds.

Flying visitors

A large number of birds are found in urban parks throughout the year. The presence of some, such as house sparrows, feral pigeons, collared doves, pied wagtails and carrion crows, is no surprise since they are well known for being quick to take advantage of a variety of different foods and are willing to live alongside people.

There are usually familiar garden birds about, too – blackbirds, song thrushes, robins and chaffinches, for instance. Although these were originally woodland birds, there are plenty of trees and

In urban areas, foxes often stay out of sight until late at night, when there is less traffic about, but occasionally they may be seen in broad daylight, like these cubs, out in the last of the sunshine on a warm evening in late spring.

GREY SQUIRRELS

Grey squirrels were introduced to Britain from North America between 1876 and 1929, and are now widespread. They are notorious for having ousted the native red squirrel from many areas, although that was due in part to the parapox virus, which didn't affect grey squirrels.

The tree-climbing antics of these agile rodents are very entertaining, but they can seriously damage plants and trees since nuts, acorns, beech-mast, fungi, tree bark, leaves, shoots, buds and flowers all form part of their natural diet.

The adaptable grey squirrel is a common sight in most parks. Although sunflower seeds and peanuts are not very good for them, squirrels are often given this food by well-meaning visitors and become quite tame.

PARK LAKES AND BIRD LIFE

Most urban parks are designed with at least one water feature. Some may be small and purely ornamental, but many are large and mature enough to support a wonderful assortment of creatures, most conspicuously birds.

Urban ponds and lakes invariably have their fair share of tame ducks. In the spring, it is not unusual to come across the delightful sight of a duck waddling along beside the pond followed by a string of ducklings.

After generations of interbreeding, it can often be hard to tell what kind of ducks they are. Many look a bit like wild mallards, but their plumage varies from pure white to all-over dark. Search closely and you can usually find at least some pure mallards among their number. A few pochard and tufted duck may also have decided to abandon life in the wild in favour of a more secure existence in the park, being kept an eye on, and perhaps fed, by the park managers.

Canada geese also take the easy option. Having been introduced to Britain from North America during the 17th century, these birds have become so well established that sizeable feral populations now exist. In some urban parks, their grazing puts excessive pressure on the grassland – and the slippery droppings that

they leave behind are distinctly unpleasant.

During the winter, flocks of tame ducks, geese and mute swans can be found on many park lakes, and although present in small numbers throughout the year, numbers of coots and moorhens increase too. There is also the chance of genuinely wild ducks arriving to consort with their tamer relatives.

Harsh weather may bring some rare strangers into the park. A beautiful little diving duck called a smew may turn up on the lakes in some London parks. In spring, a migrating black-necked grebe may drop in.

Outside the breeding season, black-headed gulls are a conspicuous and noisy feature of many urban lakes. Check the flocks for more unusual species – for instance, in the south of England, you may see Mediterranean gulls. As adults, they can be distinguished by their pure white wingtips; those of the black-headed gull are black.

Where fish are stocked in urban ponds and lakes, there is a good chance of seeing grey herons stalking in the shallows and great crested grebes out on the open water. In some London parks, where trees and marginal vegetation are allowed to flourish, both species have been known to breed successfully.

▲ Mallard are among the commonest ducks to be found on urban lakes and often become tolerant of people, even approaching visitors if there appears to be food on offer.

▲ Grey herons nest in trees. There are only a small number of pairs breeding in a few parks. The largest London park colonies are in Battersea Park and Regent's Park.

◄ A flock of Canada geese swim on a park lake, safely beyond the reach of predators. They sometimes dabble for food in the water but mostly they graze on parkland grass.

A surprising diversity of birds, including geese, ducks and gulls, can be found on even the most modest of urban park lakes.

shrubs in most parks to provide ample cover for roosting and nesting along with open areas for feeding.

Woodpigeons are regularly to be found in many parks. In rural areas these portly birds are rather wary of people, but in urban settings they may become extraordinarily tame, even nesting in clear view of passers-by. Urban jays, too, are much less shy than their countryside cousins; and as long as there are a few older trees in the park, great spotted woodpeckers may feed and nest in conspicuous locations.

Despite the fact that many parks are well-lit after dark, most birds settle down for the night when the sun sets. As darkness falls, nocturnal tawny owls start hunting. In towns and cities, birds from the size of the little blue tit to the thrush make up a large part of the tawny owl's diet. They also hunt the mice and rats fattened by the food dropped by daytime visitors to the park. Although tawny owls are difficult to see when it is

INSECT LIFE

A colourful array of blooms in a park's flower borders will attract numerous insects. Hover flies and honeybees are usually present and, depending on the time of year, you may find butterflies such as small tortoiseshells, red admirals, peacocks, large whites and small whites.

Stands of mature trees and shrubberies are also features of many urban parks. Inevitably, some of the species planted are alien and therefore not of much interest to native animals. Nevertheless, many of the more exotic trees and shrubs harbour the caterpillars of moths and, along with commonly grown native species such as willow, birch and alder, create wildlife havens in miniature.

▼ Hover flies are frequent and colourful visitors to parkland flowers. Harmless to humans, many have the markings of wasps and bees, probably as a defensive strategy.

The large black and yellow buff-tip moth caterpillars feed on leaves of a remarkable variety of trees and shrubs, including two classic groups of urban park and street trees – limes and poplars. The adult moths are difficult to locate since they resemble the snapped off twigs on which they often hide during the day.

Peppered moths are equally challenging to find. A few decades ago, when city pollution turned most tree trunks black with soot, the dark peppered moth predominated because it was better camouflaged against sooty tree trunks; now the form of peppered moth with natural colouring is more common

▶ These two forms of peppered moth are often found in urban parks. One has markings that match the lichens on tree bark; the other has dark wings.

since the colour affords more effective camouflage against clean tree-bark.

The leaves of willow trees provide food for the caterpillars of two of the largest common moths. If you search carefully among the willow leaves you may find poplar hawkmoth caterpillars with diagonal yellow stripes and red spots on each of the body segments and a horn-like tail projection. The adult moths are found among the leaves in May and June.

◀ One of the most attractive of all British butterflies, the peacock is a regular visitor to any park that has a flower border. Newly emerged adults are seen in July and August. They hibernate over winter, reappearing the following spring to mate and lay eggs.

The caterpillars of the red underwing are even harder to spot as they look just like the twigs along which they lie to rest. The edges of their bodies are fringed with hairs to reduce any shadow they might cast. In late summer, the adults are not easy to see, either, superbly camouflaged as they are against bark and wooden fence panels. When they fly off, they flash their red and black hind wings, probably to startle predators.

The holly blue is surprisingly common in urban parks, as long as its two foodplants – holly and ivy – are found close together. In May, adults from the first brood lay eggs on the flower buds of holly. The resulting caterpillars, having reached full size, transform themselves into pupae. At this stage in their life cycle, although not moving about, they undergo great changes beneath their protective outer skins, and break free from the pupal cases in July and August as adult butterflies. This second brood of adults lay their eggs on ivy flowers.

Many urban parks are planted with drifts of daffodils and other bulbs which bring wonderful colour in the spring.

light because they roost in dense cover, local starlings mimicking their distinctive calls is a sign that they hunt in the area.

Changes to the birdlife present in the park over the course of the year add to the interest. Summer visitors such as willow warblers and spotted flycatchers arrive in the spring. The occasional pair may even stay in the park to breed. In winter, starlings gather in huge flocks to roost each night.

Nesting boxes

There are often numerous bats living in urban locations, but their ability to colonise parks is probably limited by the number of sites available for roosting and hibernation. Some park authorities are enlightened enough to place bat boxes on suitable trees. Similarly, bird boxes encourage species such as blue tits and great tits to nest. Any nesting boxes will be carefully placed where the chances of vandalism are minimal.

Feeding the ducks

The drawback of this popular activity is that far larger numbers of birds may be encouraged to visit the park than can be supported naturally by a pond or lake. As a result, a great deal of organic matter – from uneaten food as well as the birds' droppings – fouls the water and may encourage a population explosion of microscopic plants called algae in summer. Masses of algae, so-called algal blooms, prevent light reaching submerged plants, and may

▶ Sadly, the house sparrow is disappearing from many parks where it was once a common breeder. In November 1925, for example, a census counted 2603 in Kensington Gardens, London; a similar census in 2000 recorded only eight.

▶ Descended from wild rock doves, feral pigeons are the most familiar of urban birds. The colour variations in their plumage are truly extraordinary. Feral pigeons are usually the most fearless of the birds that visit parks in towns and cities.

even produce toxins. In severe instances, not many aquatic plants or animals survive.

The number of birds attracted by feeding can also have a destructive impact on the pondside plants and animals. All those webbed feet crushing the vegetation is bad enough but, on top of this, many of the ducks and geese harvest the plants to eat or for building their nests. So, it makes sense to consider the consequences before feeding the birds on the pond.

◀ In urban parks, robins can become extremely tame. They often come to within a few feet of a visitor, in the hope that some morsel of food will be thrown to them.

▼ The wood mouse is a highly adaptable rodent that prefers woodland, but takes advantage of the scrub in urban parks. It is mainly nocturnal, but can be seen for a few hours before dusk and after dawn in summer.

◀ Muntjac, the smallest deer found in Britain, are exceptionally shy. They prefer dense cover to open parkland, but may sometimes be seen at dusk, feeding on grass, ivy, yew and brambles. They were introduced about 1900 and are spreading in the Midlands and the south.

WILDLIFE WATCH

How can I see more wildlife in the park?

● Follow the progression of wild flowers that appear on the grass in your local park. If the authorities operate an environmentally friendly approach to park management, making minimal use of pesticides, keep an eye open for more unusual species.

● Get out early and listen to the dawn chorus of breeding birds, at its best in spring. Record how many species you can hear each season. Keep an eye out for summer visitors that arrive in spring, such as blackcaps and other warblers.

● If the pond or lake in your local park has fish in it, watch the shallows in spring for spawning shoals of roach or carp. If the water is particularly clear, you may even see the courtship behaviour of sticklebacks among the dense growth of water plants in the margins.

Wildlife of a tree hole

As a hole in a tree evolves from a small crevice into an arboreal cave, it provides accommodation and sanctuary for a great variety of wildlife, including nesting birds, hibernating dormice, roosting bats and overwintering insects.

Mature trees, whether in woodlands, parks or gardens, collect holes in their gnarled and twisted trunks like honourable war wounds. As storms rage, few trees remain unscathed – fallen branches can litter the ground as a tangled testament to the wind's fury. In the space of a few hours, a storm can create hundreds of potential nest sites for birds and refuges for small mammals, insects, woodlice and spiders. The stumps and gashes that are left after boughs and trunk part company are just the starting points for many tree holes.

Violent storms may be the most dramatic way of creating tree holes, but they are by no means the only way. All manner of nooks and crannies appear as a natural consequence of the tree's ageing process, and holes may also form as the result of damage inflicted by animals and fungal attack.

Changing space

It is easy to view natural shelters and the smaller niches within them as fixed spaces rather than the dynamic systems that they really are. In fact, the tree hole, like any other niche, is constantly and subtly changing in size and role as the tree of which it is a part grows and matures. What may start off as a small hole created by the loss of a branch or the exit hole of a wood-boring beetle will eventually be worn away over a number of decades to a much bigger hole with room for ever larger and more varied inhabitants.

◄ Larger tree holes are often taken over by nesting tawny owls. As the family grows, it may be a bit of a squeeze to fit in as many as five young owlets and one adult.

▶ Introduced from the Continent to Tring, Hertfordshire, in 1902, the edible dormouse nests and hibernates in tree holes. It is found in the Chilterns region.

◄ Among Britain's oldest trees, ancient oaks are gnarled and knotted. With time, their trunks get hollowed out and provide excellent wildlife refuges.

COMMON DORMICE

The common (or hazel) dormouse is the sleepiest mammal in Britain. It spends at least half the year hibernating in a state akin to suspended animation. Even in summer, it is torpid during the day, with a greatly reduced metabolic rate.

Although they sometimes sleep and nest in bird nest-boxes in gardens and parks, tree holes are important to dormice all year round. Different sites are occupied in summer and winter. In late spring and early summer, a dormouse often weaves its nest of shredded honeysuckle bark in a tree hole high up on the trunk or in a bush. In autumn, dormice move down to ground level and hibernate in crevices among tree roots or at the base of hedges.

In the summer, a dormouse likes to nap during daylight hours, curled up in a cosy nest which it has built in a secure tree hole.

Snug in its nest of shredded and woven honeysuckle bark, this dormouse is hibernating the winter away in a tree cavity at ground level.

Tree holes provide a refuge for many bats, including this brown (common) long-eared bat. Here they are safe from predators and harsh weather.

Britain's three resident species of woodpecker – green, great spotted and lesser spotted – may peck out new nest holes each breeding season. Although this involves considerable effort, it does mean that they are guaranteed a secure nest site every year, and the old holes are not wasted. Starlings, house sparrows and nuthatches are quick to adopt second-hand woodpecker holes to use for their own nests.

An older tree hole has generally been worn away enough for larger birds to use it as a nesting site. These attract jackdaws and stock doves in parks where there is also open ground for feeding. A spacious hole may even be commandeered by a pair of kestrels or tawny owls. The owls may use good holes year after year, as long the territory around continues to supply them with the small rodents and songbirds that they eat.

Furry occupants

Tree holes can also be home to a range of small mammals. Even seemingly unlikely candidates such as bank voles and dormice are excellent climbers and regularly visit tree holes. The yellow-necked mouse is tree-based in its habits, although it is a scarcer resident than its larger rodent cousin, the grey squirrel, which often seeks shelter in larger tree holes, especially during severe winter weather.

Hollow trees provide both insect food and shelter for a number of bats, including brown long-eareds and pipistrelles. The noctule bat readily takes over abandoned woodpecker holes for roosting during the day. If the hole is large enough, well insulated

Competition

Each year, many garden and park birds rely on finding natural tree holes in which to nest. Of these, the tits are the most familiar. Blue and great tits are common throughout the country. They both use mature tree holes or man-made substitutes in the shape of nestboxes.

Competition for nest holes is intense, so it is not surprising that each type of bird favours holes with slightly different diameters. Some hole nesters will enlarge an entrance if it doesn't suit them. The nuthatch does exactly the opposite. If the entrance to a nest hole is too large, it plasters mud around the edges until the gap is quite tight. That way it can exclude the competition and most predators, and make the nest chamber cosier.

Drilling a hole

Woodpeckers don't have to wait for tree holes to develop naturally or fight to get to the front of the queue. They are masters of the art of creating their own holes from scratch. With their powerful chisel-like bills and shock-absorbing, reinforced skulls, they are well equipped for chipping out a hole in dead or dying timber.

Starlings start to breed in April. A tree hole is ideal for their loosely constructed nests; they may take over a woodpecker's home from the year before.

The great spotted woodpecker usually chisels out its nest hole at least 3m (10ft) above the ground. It feeds mainly on wood-boring insects, seeds and nuts.

The green woodpecker pecks out its hole 2–15m (6½–50ft) above the ground. Inside, it widens and deepens the hole into a nesting chamber.

Opening up

From the moment a bough is torn from its trunk, a tree carries a raw wound in its side. The exposed timber is open to attack by a variety of fungi and wood-boring insects. Gradually the timber is nibbled or crumbles away, the hole gets bigger and deeper, and larger animals start to use it.

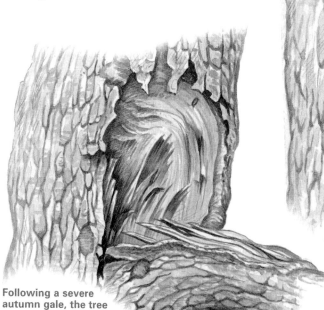

Following a severe autumn gale, the tree has lost a branch. Where the limb was ripped from the trunk there is now an open fissure.

After a few years of exposure to the elements, the torn timber has begun to rot. An inquisitive yellow-necked mouse has taken up residence in the small cavity.

and draughtproof, it may be used by several individuals, both in summer as a daytime refuge and in winter for longer-term hibernation.

Insect retreats

Birds and mammals are not the only animals in the garden or park to occupy tree holes. Woodlice, spiders, beetles and centipedes use holes in trees as temporary hideouts, mainly during the day. Other insects take up more permanent residence. In the absence of man-made hives, a swarm of honey bees will adopt an empty tree hole instead. Members of the swarm fiercely repel any attempts to oust them. Smaller holes often become the domain of bumblebees. The largest wasp species in Britain, the hornet, occupies well hollowed-out holes with a chamber large enough to house their extensive, papery nests.

Tree holes harbour more insects during summer, when there are plenty of them about. However, if you inspect a tree hole during the winter, perhaps with the aid of a torch, you are likely to find a few surprises. Hibernating insects find tree holes are the perfect frost-free venue in which to spend the cold winter months. As well as queen bumblebees and

◄ Hornets typically squeeze their nests into large tree holes. They vigorously defend the site against squatters as well as potential predators.

▲ The pale caps of the scarce *Volvariella bombycina* sprout out of the trunks and rotten stumps of deciduous trees, especially elms.

In summer, some grey squirrels use a tree hole rather than build their own nest in which to bear and raise their young.

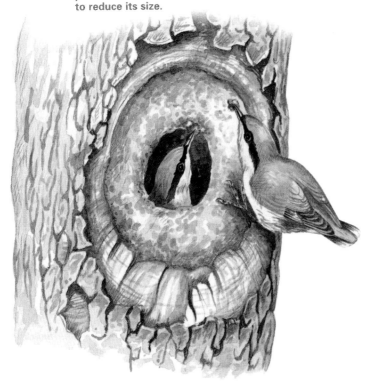

Long after the mouse has moved on, a pair of nuthatches discovers the hole. Before they begin nesting, however, they plaster the entrance with mud to reduce its size.

A decade on, the hole has been hollowed out into the trunk of the tree, creating a space large enough for a family of tawny owls.

hornets, it is possible to find clusters of small tortoiseshell and comma butterflies.

Tree-hole pools
Insects, especially those with aquatic larvae, make use of small, deep vertical holes in a tree that trap water. Depending on the time of year, recent rainfall and the age of the hole, there may be bloodworms, the larvae of chironomid midges, living at the base of the hole among the detritus, which consists of tiny fragments of dead and decaying animals and plants. Rat-tailed maggots, larvae of hoverflies, may sit on the bottom taking in air through their long breathing tubes. There are likely to be some comma-shaped mosquito larvae wriggling about in the water as well. If the hole is near the base of a trunk, a frog might take up temporary residence to feed on the insects attracted to the water to lay their eggs.

Role of fungi
As a tree hole ages, so its role in the ecology of the tree changes. Non-flowering plants such as mosses and ferns start growing around the edges of larger holes. Depending upon the hole's exposure to the weather and which animals have occupied it, the process of decay may be slow to set in.

But sooner or later, fungi start to soften up the exposed timber lining of the hole, so that it crumbles away.

Fungi play a vital role in natural recycling. Several species feed on dead tissue, others attack the living parts of trees. They are fulfilling a role that is part of the cycle of life in mature gardens and parks.

Kestrels will nest in tree holes as well as old outbuildings in parks and larger gardens, where there is the opportunity to hunt for small mammals and birds.

WILDLIFE WATCH

Where will I find tree holes?

● Almost any tree is likely to have a few holes once it has reached a sufficient height and girth. However, individual trees that are more than 50 years old are likely to have the greatest range of cavities.

● Oaks and beeches have the best tree holes. Some of the finest examples can be found on the Ashridge Estate in Hertfordshire and in Windsor Great Park. In Richmond Park, Surrey, all three species of British woodpeckers nest in the tree holes.

● The ancient woodland practice of pollarding – cutting the tree periodically at a level above the reach of grazing animals – can create hollow trunks with plenty of cavities and holes where birds nest. Willows are the most frequently pollarded trees.

Kew Gardens: a natural treasure trove

Internationally renowned for its collections of exotic plant life, the Royal Botanic Gardens at Kew are also rich in native plants and animals. They can be at their most entrancing during springtime.

Kew Gardens were never intended to be a wildlife refuge. The location was originally part of a royal hunting ground, the Old Deer Park, enclosed by James I in the early 17th century. Some of the sweet chestnut trees planted at this time still survive. In 1729 the north-eastern half of the park was turned into a royal garden, and 30 years later Augusta, Princess of Wales, established a small botanical collection near what is now the main gate. After Augusta's death in 1772, the garden was gradually expanded under the guidance of scientists Sir Joseph Banks and Sir William Hooker, who introduced plants from all around the globe. Today, Kew houses one of the most important botanical collections in the world.

Yet despite its reputation for exotic rarities, Kew has kept in touch with its roots. As long ago as 1898 the importance of local wildlife was recognised by Queen Victoria, no less, who donated Queen's Cottage and its surrounding 300-year-old oak woodland to the gardens on condition that '... this unique spot may be preserved in its present beautiful and natural condition'. The oaks are magnificent in their own right, but together with the nearby hazel coppice they also provide a habitat for a huge range of native insect life.

Much of the grassland in the gardens retains the wild character of old pasture, and includes herbaceous plants

A WORLD HERITAGE SITE

For many of the visitors who pass through the spectacular main gate, Kew Gardens are a particularly elegant city park, with ornamental flowerbeds, magnificent trees and historic hothouses. But Kew is far more than that. In July 2003, it was awarded the status of a World Heritage Site by UNESCO, the United Nations Educational, Scientific and Cultural Organisation.

The award is a recognition of Kew's unique combination of qualities. For it is not only a glorious landscape garden, but an internationally respected scientific institution. Its plant collections are unrivalled, with at least 50,000 species of living plants – including some that may be extinct in the wild – and a herbarium consisting of some 6 million preserved specimens. Its research facilities and expertise in plant diversity and conservation are used by scientists from all over the world, and Kew plays a major role in environmental education.

The presence of so many resident and visiting experts is one reason why Kew can boast such a variety of scarce native plants. Some have been introduced by enthusiasts for indigenous plant life, and have naturalised, or spread naturally. They include the martagon lily, which occurs in scattered localities in southern England. At Kew the lily now grows in the grounds of Queen's Cottage, where it unfurls its glamorous deep red flowers in late spring. Nearby there are specimens of the Plymouth pear, a very rare tree that now grows wild on just a handful of sites in Cornwall. It was planted at Kew as part of a Species Recovery Programme, coordinated by the Royal Botanic Gardens in association with English Nature.

Other plants on Kew's list of rarities originating in this country have no history of deliberate introduction, and have simply been spotted and recorded by the many botanists who visit the gardens. These plants include chamomile, wild clary, meadow saxifrage and star-of-Bethlehem.

While botanists have sharp eyes for interesting plants, they may also play an unwitting part in spreading the objects of their interest. A former director of the Royal Botanic Gardens, Sir Edward Salisbury, once raised 300 plants of 20 different species from one sample of the seeds he found in the turn-ups of his trousers. Some of Kew's rarities may have found their way into the Gardens in similar fashion, just as other plants, such as California brome grass and the well-named Kew weed, or gallant soldier, have found their way out.

◀ The martagon lily is a rare plant of chalky woodlands, closely related to cultivated lilies. It was introduced to Kew from a naturalised colony in the Lake District.

▼ Declining British grassland plants such as mouse-ear hawkweed flourish among the grass at Kew, where they are treated as valuable additions to the flora rather than weeds.

▲ In May the brilliant white flowers of star-of-Bethlehem, a rarity in London, appear among the long grass near the main gate of the Botanic Gardens.

◀ Tulips bloom in front of the Palm House, one of the finest surviving 19th-century glasshouses. First opened in 1848, it was then the largest greenhouse in the world.

that provide food for butterfly caterpillars. The ponds and the lake support thriving populations of native aquatic animals, from water fleas to fish, and while most of the plants in the gardens are alien species, their flowers provide plenty of nectar for hungry adult butterflies, moths and other insects. The extensive tree cover provides a range of habitats for a wide variety of amphibians, reptiles, birds and mammals.

Wild invaders

One reason for the diversity of wildlife at Kew is its situation. Although it is within easy reach of the city centre, it also lies next to a long stretch of the River Thames that has retained much of its natural character. Parts of the Old Deer Park to the south-west are semi-wild, with woodlands, rough grass and flooded ditches, such as the ha-ha – a wall in a ditch – that runs down the north-western boundary. These areas act as reservoirs of native plants and animals, which then spread into the gardens whenever they get the opportunity.

In the past when this happened, many of the plants were treated as weeds and destroyed but today they are recognised as botanical specimens in their own right. The ancient meadow near the Isleworth Gate, for example, is particularly rich in wild haymeadow species, including ten varieties of native grass. Now the meadow is cut just once a year, after the plants have set seed, to conserve and encourage its natural diversity.

Even regularly mown areas of grass are now dotted with plants such as sheep sorrel and cat's ear, as well as local rarities such as fiddle dock and knotted clover, thanks to a decision to abandon the use of selective herbicides on the grasslands. As part of a recent festival celebrating indigenous wildlife, a small field of wheat was deliberately sown with cornflower, common poppy, corn cockle, crimson clover and corn marigold, to show how traditional agriculture encourages biodiversity.

At Kew there is no such thing as a weed – only a fascinating native plant that might be growing in an inappropriate place.

Every year great crested grebes breed on the lake and on the Palm House Pond, following a spectacular courtship ritual in which the birds dance face to face on the water.

Residents and visitors

The wide variety of seeding plants – native and exotic – and the flourishing insect life in the Royal Botanic Gardens attract an array of wild birds, of which more than 40 species breed in the gardens every year. Many of these are garden birds, such as the blackbird, sparrow, starling, robin, dunnock, wren, blue tit and great tit, but since much of the land is planted with trees, there are also several woodland species. These include warblers, such as the blackcap and chiffchaff, which can be heard defending their breeding territories in spring when they return from their winter quarters in the tropics.

The goldcrest – Britain's smallest bird – nests up in the conifer trees, where it searches for food with restless agility, and long-tailed tits weave their wonderful purse-like nests down in the bushes.

In the wooded areas treecreepers spiral up tree trunks, probing the bark for small insects and other morsels. Nuthatches can be seen on the same quest, and occasionally heard as they stop to wedge seeds in bark crevices and hammer them open with their bills. A much louder hammering is usually the work of the great spotted woodpecker, one of three species of woodpecker that breed in the gardens.

Carrion crows, magpies and jays are all resident breeders, and the small birds, mammals and insects also support a few pairs of sparrowhawks, kestrels and tawny owls.

The most conspicuous birds at Kew are the captive waterfowl on the lake and on the Palm House Pond, which include ducks such as the shoveler, mandarin, wigeon, gadwall and pochard, and geese such as the greylag and pink-footed goose. In winter they are joined by wild birds of the same or similar species, but these visitors rarely breed at Kew. Regular wild breeders on the lakes include Canada geese, tufted ducks, coots, moorhens and great crested grebes.

All these garden, woodland and water birds are Kew residents or regular spring and summer visitors, but many other species have been noted within the grounds or over the nearby river. Between 1978 and 1992 a total of 128 species were recorded, including such unlikely ones as the oystercatcher, guillemot and curlew. Some are seen every year, particularly in winter, while others have been recorded just once, probably stopping off to feed while migrating.

QUEEN CHARLOTTE'S COTTAGE

The fabulous golden pheasant is one of three or four species of pheasant that roam free in the Gardens. Originally from the forests of Central China, these birds look at home in the Rhododendron Dell.

Songbirds nest in the wooded areas and are at their most vocal in spring. They are also much easier to see at this time, before the buds burst into full summer leaf.

▲ Bluebells carpet the ground around the cottage in May, creating an ethereal blue haze beneath the English oak trees.

◄ The sharp-clawed nuthatch displays startling agility as it searches the bark for prey, often descending tree trunks head first and even clinging to branches upside down.

► The sparrow-sized, secretive lesser spotted woodpecker forages high in the trees. It is best detected in spring by its call and its rattling territorial drumming on dead wood.

The best place to see woodland birds at Kew is the grounds of Queen's Cottage. Built for Queen Charlotte in 1761, this picturesque thatched house was used by the royal family for picnics amid private oak woods that were preserved in a semi-natural state. When Queen Victoria gave the grounds to Kew, they had not been managed for many years, and dead timber was still lying where it had fallen. The result was – and is – an ideal habitat for insects and birds, as well as wild flowers that thrive in a woodland setting such as bluebells.

Much of the dead wood has been retained because it provides food and shelter for a host of wood-boring insects such as the larvae of wood wasps and stag beetles. These are sought out by woodpeckers, which excavate their nest holes in the standing dead timber. The great spotted woodpecker is the most conspicuous of these, but in spring it is worth listening out for the *pee-pee-pee* call of the much scarcer and more elusive lesser spotted woodpecker.

One of the most rewarding aspects of watching wildlife in these grounds is the unusual tameness of many birds. Tits, robins and even nuthatches feed confidently within a few feet of you, and may even take food from your hand. This magical experience offers a chance to see the birds at much closer range than usual, giving an insight into their lives that has inspired many a budding birdwatcher.

◀ Deep blue wing spots on male banded demoiselles create a distinctive flickering effect as they fly slowly from perch to perch around the Waterlily Pond. The females are an equally striking metallic green, with no wing spots.

▶ The dappled chocolate and cream wings of the speckled wood are a common sight among the spring woodland at Kew, where the males defend sunny patches of vegetation against intruding rivals.

▼ Grass snakes, big but harmless to humans, hunt frogs and toads. You are most likely to see one around the Larch Pond, where the snake may take to the water in pursuit of its prey.

Small wonders

Some of the most dazzling wild inhabitants of Kew Gardens are insects. An amazing 28 species of butterflies have been recorded in recent years, thanks partly to the ready supply of nectar from the flowers, and partly to the presence of food plants for the caterpillars. Ten of the recorded species feed on native grasses, which are encouraged by the grassland management regimes at Kew. Others feed up in the trees; the caterpillars of the purple hairstreak, for example, feed on oak leaves in spring and when they emerge in summer,

the adults spend most of their time high among the branches. So the colourful butterflies that are common in many town gardens, such as small tortoiseshells and peacocks, are supplemented by many species typical of open grasslands and forests, such as the meadow brown and speckled wood.

Other conspicuous insects include the many species of wasp-like but harmless hover-flies that feed on flower nectar, and the dragonflies and damselflies that hatch from aquatic larvae living in the lake and ponds. Many dragonflies do not appear until the summer, but the

broad-bodied chaser and black-tailed skimmer are on the wing in May, hunting small flies over the water. Their high-speed hunting style contrasts with the delicate, fluttering flight of damselflies such as the blue-tailed and common blue damselfly, and the exquisite banded demoiselle.

Secret hunters

In spring the voracious dragonfly larvae living in the ponds enjoy a seasonal feast of tadpoles, thanks to the spawning activities of common frogs, common toads and three species of newt.

These amphibians must return to water to breed, and the Larch Pond in the grounds of Queen's Cottage is a favourite spawning site. Here they provide food for grass snakes, which were introduced to the gardens a few years ago. They are also taken by the foxes and badgers that live in the woodlands, and emerge to hunt by night when all the visitors have gone.

Badger setts spread through the woodland around Queen's Cottage. The badgers feed largely on earthworms, as well as beetles, juicy insect grubs, frogs and even young rabbits.

NOCTURNAL NEWTS

All three species of British newt – common, palmate and great crested – live in Kew Gardens, where they hunt worms, slugs and insects beneath the cover of low vegetation. Although resembling lizards, they are amphibians, like frogs, with thin, soft skins that dry out easily. So they usually hunt by night, and spend the day concealed beneath logs and stones. Each spring, newts lay their eggs in water, and

Nationally rare and strictly protected, the great crested newt is Britain's largest newt species. In 1993, 100 of them were released into the Larch Pond, where they now breed.

these hatch into tadpoles, rather like those of frogs. The tadpoles gradually turn into miniature newts over the summer and emerge from the pond to live mainly on land like their parents.

Kew Gardens

Dominated by the magnificent glasshouses, an ornamental lake and hundreds of mature trees from every continent, the Royal Botanic Gardens extend over 120 hectares (300 acres) of land to the south of the River Thames. The site is threaded with a network of paths that pass through a variety of wildlife habitats, as well as giving access to one of the finest plant collections in the world.

1 Queen's Cottage Grounds
This remote corner of the gardens is managed as a semi-wild woodland, and is the part of Kew that is richest in native wildlife.

2 The Lake
Created by Sir William Hooker in the mid-19th century, the lake was originally filled with water from the Thames, and used as a reservoir for watering the gardens. Today its four thickly wooded islands are important nature conservation areas.

3 River Thames
The riverside walk along the south bank of the Thames provides opportunities for watching birds feeding on the tidal mud, and views across the river to Syon Park.

4 The Princess of Wales Conservatory
The newest of Kew's public glasshouses, this complex of controlled environments was named after Princess Augusta, founder of the gardens.

How do I get there?

Kew Gardens are in south-west London, on the A307 (Kew Road). They are conveniently reached by public transport:
• Underground District (green) line towards Richmond – Kew Gardens station.
• Silverlink Metro train from Stratford to Richmond – Kew Gardens station.
• South West Trains from Waterloo to Brentford – Kew Bridge station.
• Bus services 65, 237, 267 and 391.
• In summer, river boats run from Westminster to Hampton Court, calling at Kew Pier.

Visitors arriving by car can reach the gardens from the M4 or the North Circular via the A205 over Kew Bridge; from the M3 via the A316 and A307 (Kew Road); or from the South Circular via Mortlake Road and Kew Green.

There is a car park near the Brentford Gate, reached via Ferry Lane off Kew Green. Parking is also available on Kew Road.

Opening times
The gardens open at 9.30am throughout the year, except for Christmas Day and New Year's Day. Last admission is at 3.45pm in the winter, 5.00pm in early spring, 6.00 on spring and summer weekdays (7.00 on weekends and bank holidays), and 5.30 in autumn. The gardens close half an hour after last admission.

Entry fees
• Adults: £7.50 (late entry £5.50)

• Accompanied children up to and including the age of 16: free

• Concessions (senior citizens, students, UB40 etc): £5.50

• Wheelchair users: £5.50 with free entrance for essential carers

• Blind or partially sighted: free

• Season tickets: standard £24; concession £15; standard couple £43; concession couple £26

The spectacular pagoda was completed in 1762 and forms the focal point of two long, open 'vistas' through the gardens. At dusk, bats flutter around its distinctive silhouette, hunting moths and small flies.

WILDLIFE WATCH

How can I see wildlife in Kew Gardens?

● Arrive early, before most of the visitors, and head straight for the remoter corners of the gardens such as the grounds around Queen's Cottage. You may have the area to yourself for an hour or two, giving you the chance to watch some of the more elusive birds and other wildlife.

● Come alone, or agree to keep quiet. Conversation may alert shy animals to your presence – it also distracts you and prevents you noticing subtle clues such as soft rustling in the undergrowth or faint twitterings up in the trees.

● Use binoculars to scan the flowers, grasses and pond margins for insects that might fly away at your approach. You can also use the binoculars to search shallow water for spawning fish and amphibians.

Animals and plants in focus

Garden watch

- The hedgehog
- The mole
- Recognising tits
- The blackbird
- Recognising garden birds' eggs
- The bumblebee
- The mating snail
- Recognising common garden bugs
- Shimmering speedwells

The hedgehog

Britain's only spiny mammal, the hedgehog is also one of the most ancient. It often takes advantage of the refuge offered by gardens, but may still forage far and wide each night, in search of food and maybe a mate.

Despite its secretive and largely nocturnal habits, the hedgehog is one of Britain's best-loved creatures. Its spiny coat makes it unmistakable. A frequent visitor to suburban gardens, the hedgehog often benefits from food put out by well-disposed wildlife watchers. In return, they get an intriguing glimpse of their visitor when it appears each evening to snuffle and snort at the food bowl. But despite their familiarity, few people ever get the chance to inspect a hedgehog closely – it is a timid creature when humans approach, and capable of unexpected turns of speed. The hedgehog's thousands of spines also make it hard to examine the details of its body, and if caught or threatened, the hedgehog rolls into a tight ball, showing few of its more vulnerable parts.

The spines are modified hairs that become sharp and rigid as the hedgehog matures. They cover the animal's back and sides, while the belly is covered by long sparse hair that offers little insulation or protection. This hair is probably better suited to the hedgehog's low-level lifestyle than soft fine fur, which would become wet and matted as it trundled around in wet grass.

Surprisingly, hedgehogs can run quite fast – at up to about 10 kilometres per hour (6mph), even more over short distances. The feet have five toes, each of which is furnished with a long, but not very sharp, claw, used mainly for scraping away soil and leaves in search of food. The hedgehog's tail is about 2cm (¾in) long, but is normally hidden by its over-hanging spiny coat.

Altogether, the hedgehog is well-adapted to sifting through dead leaves and other ground cover in search of invertebrate prey. Few of those who welcome it into their gardens realise that they are playing host to one of the most ancient types of mammal alive today. Hedgehogs evolved over 15 million years ago, and have survived, essentially unchanged, through geological changes, ice ages and the rise of Man, while more spectacular species have flourished briefly and become extinct.

Senses and salivation

Although its ears are not especially large, the hedgehog relies on them a great deal. On hearing a sudden noise, it freezes and bristles its spines. Being close to the ground, it can hear its prey – even worms and beetles sound quite noisy to sensitive ears so low down.

Smell is also important – the snout has a large moist tip, and the parts of the brain used to interpret scents are well developed, an indication of how useful this sense is to hedgehogs. They use smell to find food and can easily follow scent trails, so they probably use smell to detect and recognise each other as well.

Sight is less vital, as down in the undergrowth they cannot see very far anyway – even blind hedgehogs can survive quite well. Indeed, their night vision is probably no better than that of some humans.

In spring and summer, hedgehogs rest up by day in loose patches of vegetation, located in a suitably quiet and sheltered spot.

HEDGEHOG FACT FILE

Widespread over most of the British and Irish mainland and many islands, the hedgehog is nocturnal and most easily seen by torchlight in gardens, especially in areas of short grass where plenty of earthworms are present.

● **NAMES**
Common name: hedgehog
Scientific name: *Erinaceus europaeus*

● **HABITAT**
Farmland, short-grass areas, hedges, woodlands, town parks and gardens

● **DISTRIBUTION**
Throughout Britain and Ireland, including urban areas; absent from mountains and other very open places; introduced to most offshore islands – its liking for bird's eggs has made it unwelcome on some of these

● **STATUS**
Between 1 and 2 million individuals in UK. Nationally common although probably declining; may be more numerous in north-east England than elsewhere

Hedgehogs are partially protected through the Wildlife and Countryside Act. They may not be trapped or killed without a licence. Recent anti-cruelty legislation offers protection from ill treatment, making it an offence to tease or torture wild animals.

● **SIZE**
Length 20–30cm (8–12in); weight average 450–680g (1–1½lb), but up to 800g (2lb) before hibernation. Can reach up to 1.2kg (2½lb) in wild

● **KEY FEATURES**
Unmistakable due to brown spiny coat

● **HABITS**
Mainly nocturnal, normally solitary, does not defend territory

● **VOICE**
Various snorts and grunts; pig-like squeal if threatened

● **FOOD**
Beetles, worms, caterpillars, slugs and wide range of other small animals, including small mammals and nestling birds and eggs

● **BREEDING**
Usually 4–5 (up to 7) young born mainly June–July; late litters born September to October

● **NEST**
Constructs bed of tightly packed leaves for winter hibernation; in spring, builds similar but larger nest to give birth; in summer shelters in any long vegetation, often with no real nest, especially in warm weather

● **YOUNG**
Born after about 40 days' gestation. Spines develop rapidly – white at first, then brown; eyes open at 14 days old. Young are independent at around six weeks

Hedgehog mothers will eat their babies if they are disturbed within hours of birth. These two-day-old babies are old enough to escape that fate and will be carried to safety if their nest is disturbed.

Distribution map key

■ Present

□ Not present

Spines are modified hairs. They do not moult seasonally, but instead are lost continuously. Each of the adult hedgehog's 5000–7500 spines grows slowly and stays in place for over a year before falling out and being replaced by a new one.

The ears are small but very sensitive, especially to sudden sounds. Hedgehogs can easily detect worms and beetles by the noise these creatures make moving in the soil.

A skirt of fringing hairs along the flanks hides relatively long legs that enable the hedgehog to run quite fast when necessary.

Each foot has five long, sturdy claws. The hind feet are longer and narrower than the front feet.

In addition to being an effective smelling tool, the nose is highly mobile, enabling the hedgehog to extract food from crevices and around plant roots. The hedgehog also uses its nose to make small holes in the ground to search out prey.

One very unusual aspect of hedgehog behaviour is known as self-anointing. Sometimes after chewing a sharp-tasting or strong-smelling substance, but often with no apparent trigger, a hedgehog will start to produce copious amounts of frothy saliva. It then twists and turns frenetically to spread the foam all over its body using its tongue. This can go on for an hour or more, with the animal completely engrossed in this seemingly bizarre activity. Self-anointing occurs in both sexes and in young as well as adults. Nobody knows why hedgehogs do it, and no other animal behaves in a similar fashion.

On the scrounge

Hedgehogs find their food by foraging, and they can often travel as much as 2–3km (1–2 miles) each night. Males are especially active, scurrying here and there in search of food and mates. In the breeding season, some may clock up 4km (2½ miles) before returning to their nest at dawn. A different nest may be used each day or two, especially in summer, with sites scattered over a wide area, perhaps as much as 60 hectares (150 acres). By contrast, females often have a much smaller range, using the

Midnight feast

Out on patrol, the hedgehog is constantly sniffing out tasty morsels to eat. Almost any small living thing at ground level will be investigated and, in many cases, eaten. Hedgehogs are quite noisy eaters and sometimes may be heard even when they cannot be seen.

same nest every day for a couple of weeks before moving on. Different hedgehogs may use the same nest.

Although hedgehogs are usually active only after dark, around midsummer, when nights are short, they may come out early and will still be active after dawn. At night, they are more likely to find their favourite foods, including caterpillars, slugs, worms and beetles. The hedgehog's front teeth point forward, making a scoop to seize small prey such as spiders. Curiously, the lower front teeth bite

A liking for eggs can sometimes get hedgehogs into trouble with conservationists. Large eggs are difficult to tackle – they must first be smashed before the contents can be eaten, leaving an incriminating mess of yolk and broken shell.

into a gap between the upper ones. This reduces the power of the grip, so hedgehogs cannot deliver much of a bite and rarely manage to draw blood from humans or large animals. The teeth are quite blunt, especially in older animals that have eaten a lot of gritty earthworms.

Hedgehogs will frequently come to the edge of a puddle or pond to drink, especially in dry weather. They may even hunt for food such as pond snails.

Apart from invertebrates, hedgehogs also eat carrion, including dead mammals and birds. Occasionally they will even attack live mice and the chicks of ground-nesting game birds. This habit, combined with a predilection for birds' eggs, makes them unpopular with gamekeepers, who kill several thousand hedgehogs each year as a consequence. Predation on eggs and chicks is now recognised to have had a serious effect on seabird and wader populations where hedgehogs have been introduced close to nest sites on islands naturally free of such predators.

Coat of spines

One of the main reasons for the hedgehog's success is its most distinctive characteristic – its spines, which bristle aggressively in all directions when the animal is threatened or attacked. A hedgehog's coat typically shelters a population of hundreds of specialised fleas, adapted to the conditions of the hedgehog's skin. These parasites rarely invade other hosts such as pets or humans, and if they do, they soon leave.

Rolled up and encased in its spiny skin, the hedgehog is so well protected that few predators will touch it. Foxes, polecats, owls and eagles may take the occasional one, especially very young babies whose spines are not fully developed and who lack the ability to roll up properly, but generally hedgehogs have little to fear except badgers and cars. Badgers kill quite a few hedgehogs and, as their populations increase, it is possible that hedgehog numbers will decline in some places.

MYTH AND FOLKLORE

Hedgehogs are reputed to attack and eat snakes, and have indeed occasionally been seen eating adders. But it is unlikely that hedgehogs are the aggressors – in reality the snake may end up with self-inflicted wounds from attacking such a well-armoured target, leaving the hedgehog simply to finish it off.

Other tales suggest that hedgehogs suckle milk from cows, even though they are too short to reach the udder. If a cow is lying down, however, milk often seeps from the teats and could conceivably attract a passing hedgehog to latch on. They might even come specially as hedgehogs are very fond of milk and may be attracted by its smell. However, cow's milk can upset a hedgehog's digestion. For this reason, hedgehogs should never be given large amounts of milk in the garden – in the wild, if a hedgehog did manage to find some cow's milk, the effect would be diluted by other elements of its diet.

Another widespread folk tale is that hedgehogs collect fallen apples on their spines by rolling on them, then carrying the fruit off to their nests. Although hedgehogs will eat squashy fruits, and occasionally one may have accidentally impaled its spines on a fallen apple, this story is hard to believe. Food is not normally carried away, nor is it stored in the nest. Nevertheless, the story has persisted for centuries and turns up in the folklore of many different countries.

The tradition linking hedgehogs with fruit was probably encouraged by the fact that they are often seen near fallen fruit. They like to eat the soft parts, and any slugs and insects that are present.

The hedgehog's snout is very mobile and is used to winkle out food from crevices and plant roots.

▲ With its nose tucked up close to its tail, and completely surrounded by a spiny coat, this hedgehog is safe from most threats. Its mottled colouring also acts as good camouflage.

◄ The hedgehog's attention is normally concentrated on the ground immediately in front of its nose as it seeks out food. The head is raised periodically to sniff the air and listen for more distant movements.

Road traffic kills many more hedgehogs than any natural enemy. Nobody knows how many die on the roads each year, but it may be as many as 100,000. The animals are also at risk from careless gardeners – falling victim to lawnmowers and bonfires or succumbing to pesticides scattered around the garden or accumulated in slugs and other prey. As their habitat becomes more developed, hedgehogs increasingly meet their end in swimming pools and on building sites.

Provided they escape all these hazards, hedgehogs can live for up to seven years, and exceptionally to ten. However, the majority probably survive for about three years and many die young. Females are able to breed in the year following their own birth, and usually produce about four young in a litter. These are usually born in June and July, but there are some late births in September or even October. Late-born young will be lucky to survive because they need a couple of months to fatten up before hibernating. This may be possible when there is a mild autumn, but if cold weather comes early, unprepared youngsters will probably die.

Hibernation habits

The hedgehog is one of Britain's few true hibernators. Its body shuts down for the winter to save energy while food is in short supply. Apart from a few brief periods of arousal, it usually sleeps from November to March, although younger animals may still be active as late as Christmas, especially in mild weather, as they try to fatten up.

Winter is spent in a nest made of leaves. The hedgehog gathers them in small bundles in its mouth and pushes them into a heap below a bush or garden shed. Then it burrows inside and shuffles about to arrange the leaves as a thick covering all round its body. Young hedgehogs are inexperienced at making nests, and often need several attempts – it is important to get it right as the nest is the hibernating animal's only protection from cold and

Families normally consist of mother plus four or five babies, but sometimes there may be as many as seven. They stay together for about six weeks, before dispersing to live on their own.

bad weather, and must remain intact and waterproof for at least five months.

The availability of suitable nest-building materials is vital, and this is probably why hedgehogs are rarely found in places where naturally fallen leaves are scarce, such as moorland and dense pine woods. For the same reason, hedgehogs suffer when leaves are cleared away and suitable nest sites in towns and gardens are tidied up. Although hibernation usually ends around March, earlier in some years, if a cold snap occurs the animals may go back to sleep and wait for better weather.

Population changes

There are probably between one and two million hedgehogs in Britain, but researchers have no really accurate way to estimate their numbers. Moreover, they do not know for certain if the species is holding its own or declining. Hedgehogs are still widespread and fairly common, yet the majority of experts suspect they are less numerous than they were.

This possible decline in the hedgehog population is chiefly due to loss of habitat. A century ago, the British landscape was dotted with paddocks and small fields bounded by hedgerows. Short grazed turf with nearby dense cover was ideal for the hedgehog. Today, intensive farming means that much of this habitat has been replaced by arable crops, and hedgerows have been removed in order to provide access for large agricultural machines. The new landscape offers far less hedgehog food and fewer refuges.

Many find useful retreats in towns and gardens, but these are often too small and too tidy to provide food and nest sites. Urban developments leave hedgehogs isolated in small pockets that cannot be renewed from outside. However, thanks to humans, hedgehogs that do survive in urban areas often find more food than in many parts of the countryside.

NATURAL BLOND

Hedgehog spines are usually banded in brown and cream, giving the animal a grizzled appearance. However, in some animals the dark pigments fail to develop, leaving the spines a pale cream or white.

These are not real albinos, but 'blond' hedgehogs. They are very rare on mainland Britain, but on Alderney, in the Channel Islands, a quarter of all the hedgehogs are this attractive colour. This probably results from inbreeding among the small number of animals that were originally released there.

Blond hedgehogs have pale spines but dark eyes like this one. True albinos have pink eyes as the dark pigment fails to develop there, too. Both types are very rare in mainland Britain.

WILDLIFE WATCH

Where can I see hedgehogs?

● In the garden, hedgehogs are best seen at night using a powerful torch. Select an area of short grass, preferably on damp soil where worms are abundant. Still, warm evenings are best.

● Look for characteristic black droppings on the lawn that show that a hedgehog has visited. The droppings are about 3cm (1in) long, crinkly, and studded with the shiny black remains of beetles.

● Outside the garden, golf courses are generally good places to see hedgehogs, except for the greens where the heavy application of chemicals removes all the hedgehog's invertebrate prey.

● Playing fields are also worth investigating. Cemeteries and places with longer grass are even more likely to have hedgehogs, but they are difficult to spot among tall vegetation.

▲ **Pet food will regularly attract hedgehogs to the garden. This extra source of food may be one of the reasons why hedgehogs manage to survive better in towns and gardens than in parts of the countryside.**

▶ **Hedgehogs can swim, but sadly often drown in even quite small ponds because the smooth sides of plastic pond liners offer no chance of escape. An escape ramp or some chicken wire dangling into the water allows the animals to climb out of a pond before they tire and drown.**

The mole

Easily located thanks to its molehills, the ever-active mole burrows night and day to excavate an often extensive network of underground tunnels in which to trap its prey.

Most people are familiar with the work of moles from seeing the characteristic heaps of soil that they throw to the surface as they dig their underground tunnels. Molehills are among the most distinctive sights on British grasslands and grassy spaces, and are so easy to recognise that the mole's distribution is better known than that of any other native mammal – it is found almost everywhere except Ireland and some smaller islands.

Yet despite the familiarity of molehills, few people have ever seen one of the animals themselves. This is because moles spend nearly all of their time underground and out of sight in a damp, dark environment. Here, they burrow through the earth, unseen and undetected, until they eject a pile of soil above ground, often to the fury of the lawn-lover and gardener.

Born to burrow

The mole is a squat creature, supremely adapted to its burrowing lifestyle. It has short, usually dark fur, a cylindrical body and a tapering head that appears to join directly to the body without a neck. Broad front paws stick out from the front of the body, with no apparent sign of arms.

This unusual design has evolved to ensure that moles can exert very powerful leverage with their forelimbs. The upper arm bone is short, almost rectangular and hidden from sight within the creature's fur. This shape creates a relatively enormous area for the attachment of digging muscles, and makes the mole amazingly strong for its size. Anyone who picks up a live mole is immediately astonished by how powerful this small animal is. Moles are easily able to burst a firm human grip, forcing the fingers apart as though thrusting aside heavy soil.

In contrast to the forelimbs, the mole's hind legs are slender and are used to propel the animal along its tunnels. They are also jammed into the burrow wall for stability while the mole uses its front feet to dig, and to kick the earth backwards out of the way during tunnelling. As the mole's limbs are so well adapted for other tasks, they are rarely used to support its body. Instead, its weight rests on its belly, and the mole has thick, tough skin on its underside to cope with this – in most mammals the skin on the stomach is usually the thinnest.

Moles spend most of their time underground, but they surface to catch food and collect nest material, and when they move from the tunnel where they were born to dig a burrow of their own. It is at this time that they fall prey to owls and other predators.

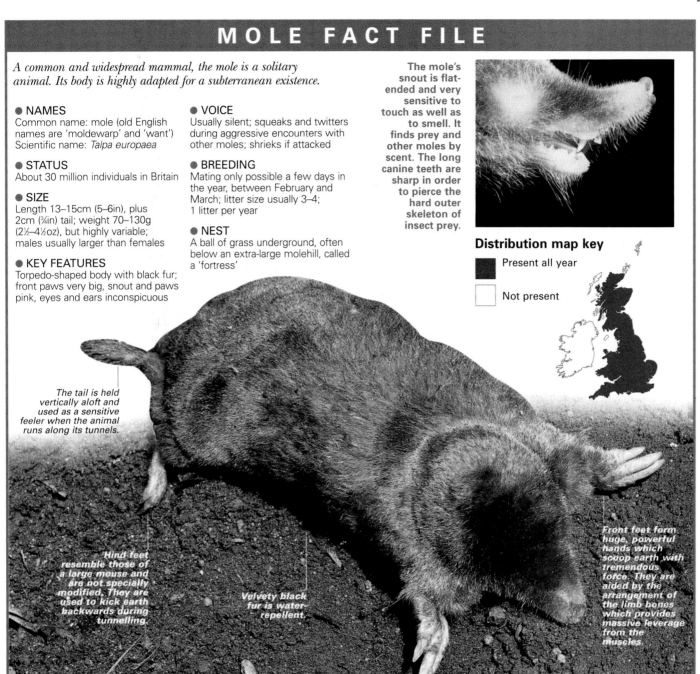

MOLE FACT FILE

A common and widespread mammal, the mole is a solitary animal. Its body is highly adapted for a subterranean existence.

● **NAMES**
Common name: mole (old English names are 'moldewarp' and 'want')
Scientific name: *Talpa europaea*

● **STATUS**
About 30 million individuals in Britain

● **SIZE**
Length 13–15cm (5–6in), plus 2cm (¾in) tail; weight 70–130g (2½–4½oz), but highly variable; males usually larger than females

● **KEY FEATURES**
Torpedo-shaped body with black fur; front paws very big, snout and paws pink, eyes and ears inconspicuous

● **VOICE**
Usually silent; squeaks and twitters during aggressive encounters with other moles; shrieks if attacked

● **BREEDING**
Mating only possible a few days in the year, between February and March; litter size usually 3–4; 1 litter per year

● **NEST**
A ball of grass underground, often below an extra-large molehill, called a 'fortress'

The mole's snout is flat-ended and very sensitive to touch as well as to smell. It finds prey and other moles by scent. The long canine teeth are sharp in order to pierce the hard outer skeleton of insect prey.

Distribution map key

■ Present all year

□ Not present

The tail is held vertically aloft and used as a sensitive feeler when the animal runs along its tunnels.

Hind feet resemble those of a large mouse and are not specially modified. They are used to kick earth backwards during tunnelling.

Velvety black fur is water-repellent.

Front feet form huge, powerful hands which scoop earth with tremendous force. They are aided by the arrangement of the limb bones which provides massive leverage from the muscles.

Telling tails

At the end of its body, the mole has a small tail, about 2cm (¾in) long. Despite its size, the tail is very important to the mole's underground lifestyle. It is carried pointing upwards, like a flagpole, constantly feeling the way along tunnels. This is especially useful when the mole needs to travel backwards – although the mole can twist itself around within the tight confines of its burrow, it usually finds it easier to reverse. Stiff tail hairs are linked to sense organs in the tail itself, allowing the mole to identify and interpret obstacles in its path. The tail is so effective that moles can run backwards almost as fast as they can move forwards.

To assist in reversing, the mole's fur is also specially adapted. Any other mammal would be slowed down by the lie of its fur,

which normally points backwards and would be forced in the wrong direction by tight-fitting burrow walls, jamming the animal in the tunnel. A mole's coat has hairs that can lie either forwards or backwards with equal ease. This, and the very fine, silky texture of the hairs, gives the fur a velvety feel, and it was once much prized for use in waistcoats and coat collars.

Multicoloured moles

Mole fur is longer in winter than in summer, growing to 9mm (⅜in) as opposed to 6mm (¼in). Unusually, the hairs are of almost uniform length over the whole body – most mammals have longer hair on some parts of the body than on others. The fur is almost always black, but ash-grey varieties occasionally occur, as do orange, cream and piebald

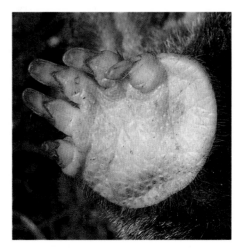

In relative terms, the mole's broad flat hands are among the most powerful in the animal kingdom, but they cannot bend to grip, nor do the fingers move separately.

ones. White moles include true albinos. These colour varieties appear in about 1 per cent of the population, which makes them extremely common compared to variations in other small mammals. One explanation may be that even pale moles are relatively safe from predators because they are underground. By contrast, a very pale mouse would be quickly seen and eaten by an owl or other predator, so its peculiar colour could not be passed on to the next generation. Moles can survive whatever their colour, so perhaps the surprise is that so many are simply black.

Sight, sound and scent

At first glance, a mole's head appears to be completely lacking ears and eyes, and folklore often has it that moles are blind. In fact, both sets of sensory organs are present, but apparent only on close examination. The ears are about 5mm (⅕in) long and hidden in the mole's fur. The eyes are the size of pin heads and are normally closed. A mole's sight is not as good as our's, but it can see movement

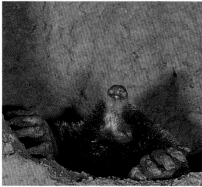

▲ **When a mole catches an earthworm, it pulls the animal between its hands to scrape off most of the gritty soil stuck to the worm's surface. This action also squeezes unwanted soil out of the worm's intestine.**

▶ **Powerful legs allow a mole to bury itself completely within a few seconds. In loose soil, the mole almost 'swims' into the ground.**

ALL IN A DAY'S WORK

Moles can be active both by day and night. A typical day consists of three periods of activity – spent digging, feeding and patrolling their network of tunnels – and in between, the animal returns to its nest to rest and sleep.

Curiously, moles usually start work at the same time each day, regardless of the season, even though they can have little knowledge of whether it is day or night outside their underground burrow. Perhaps enough light filters down through loose soil to provide clues, or maybe the activity of birds and other animals above can be heard by the mole.

Males are generally more active than females, and in the breeding season they may stay away from their nest for several days at a time, sleeping in odd corners of their seasonally enlarged burrow system.

▼ **Moles feed on a wide variety of soil animals, but especially favour earthworms, which are easy to catch although a poor source of nutrition. Beetles, caterpillars and other insect larvae are also eaten.**

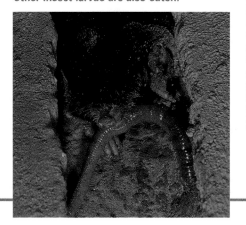

▲ **The mole relies on patrolling its tunnel system to pick up whatever prey animals have dropped in. When it can't find enough underground, it must come to the surface to forage.**

and tell light from dark, although it cannot distinguish colours. Large eyes would fill with earth during digging, so the mole has evolved to live with tiny ones.

To compensate for its poor eyesight, the mole has a highly developed sense of smell – its most important sense apart from touch, and the one it mostly uses in hunting its invertebrate prey. The mole's snout ends in a flat plate, like a pig's nose. This area of bare pink skin is incredibly sensitive to touch. Pimple-like growths called Eimer's organs cover the surface and detect tiny movements, as well as temperature and humidity changes.

Scent is enormously important to moles as a means of communicating, since vision is almost useless underground. They leave scent marks on the walls of the tunnels, which are renewed every time the animal brushes by. These pungent signs act as a warning to others to stay away and appear to be very effective, as moles are almost never found occupying each other's tunnels.

Breeding and young

In moles, it is very difficult to tell the sexes apart because they are so well protected by fur, and there is very little external difference between males and females. Moles distinguish each other by scent. Their belly fur is often discoloured by brownish yellow secretions from scent glands beneath the skin called preputial glands. These secretions are particularly noticeable in the breeding season.

Moles live solitary lives, belligerently expelling intruders, except for just a few hours each year when the female is on heat and will tolerate the presence of a male. A receptive female leaves a scent

▲ The mole's eyes are very tiny and not much used underground. However, at the surface, moles sometimes survey their surroundings in a rather short-sighted manner.

message to indicate to a potential mate that it is safe to approach.

Moles can breed when they are one year old. The female gives birth to three or four young, occasionally more, usually around April or May (later in Scotland). The young are tiny, naked, and blind at birth. Their fur begins to grow at two weeks old

▲ Baby moles are born pink and hairless, but already have characteristically large hands. They grow quickly and are expelled from their mother's burrow system as soon as they are able to fend for themselves.

Busy life

The mole is a very active creature both above and below the surface. It scurries about, pushing its sensitive nose into any place that might harbour food. Digging is often done in the morning, resulting in fresh molehills appearing at the surface.

Moles often get wet and dirty in the mud. They keep their fur clean and in good condition by squeezing through their tight-fitting tunnels or among grass roots.

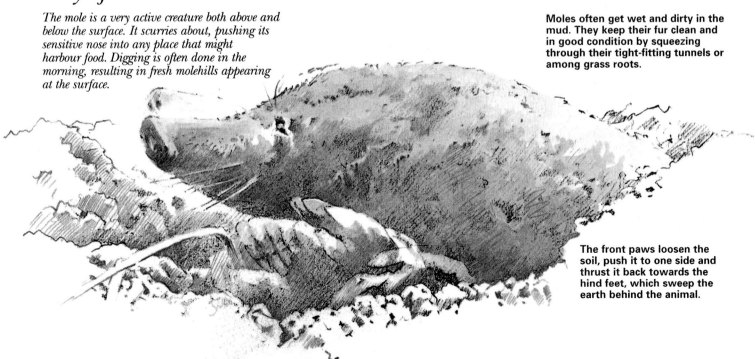

The front paws loosen the soil, push it to one side and thrust it back towards the hind feet, which sweep the earth behind the animal.

Dropping in for dinner

The earthworms, insects and centipedes that fall through the roof of the mole's tunnel try to dig their way back out, so potential prey is continuously entering and leaving the burrow. The mole moves through its tunnels, catching and eating as many of its unwitting guests as possible.

Earthworms may form more than 90 per cent of a mole's diet in winter and about 50 per cent in summer.

high proportion of moles in their diet in early summer, when many juvenile moles are moving from their maternal homes. Many others are the victims of cars.

Tunnel vision

It is a popular misconception that moles dig through the soil to catch worms. This would be totally impractical because the mole would expend far more energy moving soil than it would recoup eating the prey it came across. In fact, the mole excavates a series of burrows that form a permanent tunnel system. This serves as a giant pit trap for any worms, beetles and other invertebrates that happen to be wriggling their way through the soil. If they break into the mole's tunnel, they will be exposed and vulnerable to attack. The mole constantly patrols its tunnels on the lookout for such creatures.

Where large numbers of prey animals are present, the mole can survive with a relatively small burrow system and high densities of moles can occur. Conversely, in poor sandy soils, worms and other soil animals are less frequent, so each mole needs a larger tunnel system. The number of moles per hectare is consequently lower in such places. The number of molehills is never a true indication of the size of a population. Sandy soils are light and easy to dig, and extending the tunnel system and creating more molehills is not difficult. Accordingly, some sandy areas have huge numbers of molehills, caused by maybe just two or three moles.

and they start to leave the nest and become independent between 35 and 40 days after birth. Juvenile moles leave their mother's tunnel system as soon as they are weaned, otherwise she will drive them away. Moles will not tolerate lodgers competing for food, even their own offspring. The numbers born seem to be just enough to maintain the population. Unlike the populations of many small mammals, which vary greatly from year to year, mole numbers appear to be remarkably stable.

Young moles must find an unoccupied area in which to set up home. This is not easy, especially where population densities are high. Young moles can travel farther and faster on the surface than by burrowing. Some probably make quite long journeys, and may cross inhospitable ground. They mostly travel in darkness, but are then vulnerable to attack by owls and other predators, including badgers, foxes, cats and dogs. Tawny owls take a

Moles are supremely adapted to tunnelling underground, but are not much good at moving about on the surface. They propel themselves in a rather ungainly way, with their hands held vertically because they are unable to place them flat on the ground as other animals do.

DIETARY HABITS

● The mole attacks its prey ferociously with 44 sharp teeth, but gritty food, such as worms, inevitably causes the teeth to become worn down. Despite this, some moles manage to live for up to six years. This is a long time for a small mammal, but blunted teeth could be a major cause of their demise at a younger age.

● Worms form a major part of a mole's diet. In good times, such as when it is raining, there may be a surplus of them falling into the mole's tunnels – too many to eat at once. However, the opportunity is not wasted, as the mole reacts by collecting the worms and biting each one's head off: the worms remain alive, but are unable to burrow to safety. These paralysed prey are stashed away in a small chamber off to

the side of the main burrow, ready for future use. Some of these larders may contain over 1000 worms, weighing up to 2kg (4½lb).

● A mole needs to eat about 50g (1¾oz) of worms per day, equivalent to about half its own body weight. Its diet is supplemented by other morsels, including caterpillars and other insect larvae that live in the soil. These are especially abundant in summer. Cockchafer larvae and other significant garden pests are also eaten, so, although most people want to be rid of moles, the harm they do is at least partly offset by good deeds. However, these benefits go unseen and are poor consolation to the gardener confronted with a new crop of molehills on a freshly mown lawn.

Although moles spend most of their lives in their burrows, it is wrong to imagine that they are never active at the surface. Apart from the need to disperse, shortage of food may also drive them above ground. This happens commonly during hot dry summers, when a long period of drought will cause earthworms to burrow deep in the soil and become inactive. The mole's normal supply of worms dwindles dangerously and finding food can be very difficult. Faced with this problem, many moles will emerge at night or around dawn to seek other food in the dew-dampened grass.

Excavated soil has to be ejected after every few metres of tunnelling. The resulting molehills are not burrow entrances, but do indicate the mole's route underground.

Densely populated

Moles occur in a variety of habitats, even where there is only a thin layer of soil on top of solid rock. They are common in deciduous woodland, though their presence often goes unnoticed because the molehills are hidden by fallen leaves. Here, they may live at a density of four or five per hectare (2½ acres). They are more obvious in farmland, especially pasture, where the habitat is rich in food. There may be up to 16 moles living in a hectare of good pastureland in the summer months. They also invade arable fields, where the molehills are obvious

soon after ploughing, but are soon obscured by the growing crops.

Deep ploughing and heavy rolling of the soil makes life difficult for moles. They are often driven out of crop fields and have to recolonise from nearby woods and hedgerows, moving into parks and gardens. Similarly, winter floods can force moles to retreat from low-lying areas – but they usually return, lines of their molehills spreading outwards from hedge banks and higher ground.

Moles can also be found in upland areas, up to 1000m (3300ft) above sea level in Scotland, but tend to be scarcer at high altitudes. This is partly because the soil is difficult to tunnel but also because worms and other prey are in shorter supply. Moles are infrequent in conifer plantations and heathlands for similar reasons.

Disappearing act

Moles are very vulnerable on the surface and remain exposed for as short a time as possible. If it is surprised, the mole will scrabble vigorously with its hind feet in order to get back down into its burrow system.

A mole's tail is very sensitive and is the only means by which the mole can tell what is happening behind it. The tail is often wagged vigorously, seeking out obstacles or detecting the approach of a predator.

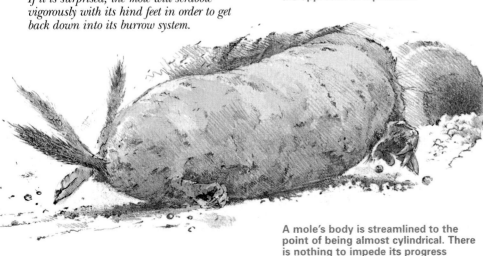

A mole's body is streamlined to the point of being almost cylindrical. There is nothing to impede its progress through the soil and the result is an animal that resembles a furry torpedo.

WILDLIFE WATCH

Where can I see moles?

● In long periods of hot dry weather, moles find it difficult to obtain sufficient food underground, and they spend a lot more time at the surface. Go out very early in the morning after a few weeks without rain and you may hear a mole as it tears at clumps of grass in search of food. You might also be able to see one scurrying from one feeding place to another.

● If you are lucky, you might glimpse a mole as it swims across a small stream or crosses a road.

● If you watch a fresh molehill quietly, you may see it begin to move as the mole pushes up more soil from below. Your patience may be rewarded as the mole emerges onto the surface and you can get a good look at it.

Recognising tits

Acrobatic and agile in the air, tits are among the most popular of British birds. Whether you encourage them to nest in your garden or observe them in the countryside, you are sure to enjoy watching these lively creatures.

Stand for a few minutes in almost any garden, park or woodland in spring and you are certain to hear the calls of blue tits or great tits, the two most common species of their kind in Britain. Once you have followed the sounds and spotted the birds, their bold and often inquisitive behaviour immediately commands attention. Their seeming indifference to human observers allows prolonged and close-up views of their antics, which, in addition, makes it relatively easy to identify the different types of tit.

Nesting habits

All the true tits found in Britain – the six species that belong to a family called the Paridae – are essentially hole nesters. Blue tits, great tits, coal and marsh tits will make use of naturally accessible sites such as abandoned woodpecker holes and cracks formed where branches have fallen off the main trunk of a tree. Not surprisingly, they also use nestboxes if available.

Willow tits and crested tits excavate a new nest hole each year, usually favouring the softer, decaying wood of standing dead trees.

In contrast to the hole-nesting habits of the true tits, the long-tailed tit builds one of the most intricate and extraordinary nests of any British bird. The bearded tit's nest is also quite unlike that of the true tits. It builds a woven cup-shaped nest among the tall stems of its specialised reedbed habitat.

Winter survival

During the breeding season in spring and summer, tits claim and aggressively defend territories against intruders of the same species. During the winter, however, they are more sociable and their main aim is to find enough food to survive. Blue tits, great tits, coal tits and marsh tits in particular often form mixed-species flocks. Sometimes, such flocks also contain other species, such as nuthatches, lesser spotted woodpeckers, treecreepers and goldcrests, all of which roam the woods together in search of insects and seeds. Parties of long-tailed tits tend to keep their own company.

Thanks to their inquisitive and adventurous natures, several of the tits – notably blue tits and great tits – have discovered the advantages of man-made birdfeeders in winter. They are especially fond of peanuts and sunflower seeds, and in harsh weather, up to a dozen birds can be found in the vicinity of a single feeder, often noisily competing for space.

Long-tailed, marsh and willow tits may also visit feeders, but as a rule do so much less frequently than other tit species.

Unlike true tits, the long-tailed tit builds a nest in the open. A purse-shaped construction of moss and animal hair, bound together with spider silk, camouflaged with lichen and lined with feathers, it is sited in a dense, often thorny, bush or tree. The parents enter the nest via a small, round opening, where the young birds wait.

EASY GUIDE TO SPOTTING TITS

Blue tit

Great tit

Coal tit

Marsh tit

Willow tit

Crested tit

Long-tailed tit

Bearded tit

WHAT ARE TITS?

The odd name 'tit' dates from Middle English via the Icelandic word 'tittr' (meaning small) and was originally applied to many kinds of small birds. It is used nowadays to describe just eight species found in Britain.

● All the true tits belong to the same subgroup or genus, *Parus*, which forms the first word of their scientific (Latin) name.

● The long-tailed tit is quite closely related to the true tits and to the babblers, a group of mainly tropical songbirds.

● Despite its common name, the bearded tit is not closely related to the true tits and is sometimes called the bearded reedling.

Nestboxes provide an ideal way of attracting tits into your garden. Tit nestlings grow fast; their parents return every few minutes with a supply of caterpillars and other insects.

HOW CAN I IDENTIFY TITS?

Most of the tit species are quite distinct, which makes it relatively easy to identify individual species. Listen carefully to the distinctive calls made by the different species. These can provide valuable clues to identification.

● The blue and great tit are quite easily distinguishable – the great tit is considerably larger than the blue. It also has a different, bolder head pattern, a broad black band running down its underside, and lacks the bright sky blue patches of feathers of the blue tit.

● The coal tit, which is the smallest of the true tits, can be recognised by the bold white patch extending from the rear of its crown to the nape of the neck. It also has two white wingbars.

● The marsh and willow tit are extremely similar to one another. Differences in their shape and plumage are very subtle, so it may be advantageous to learn and listen for each species' distinctive calls and song. Note that the willow tit has a dull cap and a thicker neck.

WILDLIFE WATCH

Where can I see tits?

● Blue tits are abundant and widespread. They are found in most gardens – city or country – and in broad-leaved woodlands.

● Great tits are also common in gardens, parks and broad-leaved woodlands. Like blue tits, they visit birdfeeders regularly, all year round, and often rear their chicks in suitable nestboxes.

● Marsh and willow tits both live in broad-leaved woodland. Despite its name, the willow tit is more likely to be found in damper areas than the marsh tit and it does not favour willow trees. It is also found in coniferous and mixed woodlands. Both species are more likely to visit larger, rural gardens than those sited in urban areas.

● Coal tits are found in both broad-leaved and coniferous woodlands, tending to favour the latter and mixed woodland. They also visit gardens, especially those with coniferous trees.

● Crested tits are found exclusively in conifer woodland, but they are restricted to the Scottish Highlands.

● Long-tailed tits are found in broad-leaved woodland, and they nest mainly in thick scrub and hedgerow bushes. They visit gardens less often than the true tits, but once one has eaten at a birdfeeder, others are likely to follow.

● Bearded tits live in extensive reedbeds and are seldom seen elsewhere.

BLUE TIT *Parus caeruleus*

Distinguished immediately from other true tits by a bright blue crown, this bird's white face is defined by blackish blue lines. Its wings and tail are blue; its back greenish and the underparts bright yellow (sometimes showing a thin, diffuse dark line). The blue tit frequently visits gardens, giving a harsh warning call when other birds arrive at a feeder.

● SIZE
Length 11.5cm (4½in)

● NEST
In existing hole in tree or in nestbox; nest of moss and grass, lined with hair and feathers

● BREEDING
Lays 6–15 eggs, mainly late April–June; incubation takes 13–16 days

● FOOD
Mainly insects and spiders, but also seeds, especially during winter months

● HABITAT
Almost any habitat with trees (especially broadleaved), including gardens, parks and woods

● VOICE
Harsh '*tsee-tsee-tsee*' and churring alarm calls; song contains elements of both these calls

● DISTRIBUTION
Common and widespread

Distribution map key

■ Present

□ Not present

▲ Unlike any other British tit, this bird has a blue cap.

▼ This young blue tit, peering from a nestbox, is almost ready to fly the nest.

Thin black line on white cheeks

Blue cap

Single, small white wingbar

Combination of blue, green and yellow plumage is unique among small British birds

▲ A blue tit will often grip a sunflower seed with its feet so that it can chisel away at the hard case with its bill.

GREAT TIT *Parus major*

Largest of the true tits, the great tit may be recognised by the bold black-and-white markings on its head. The thick black line running down the centre of its underparts is broader in males than in females. Its wings are mainly blue-grey with a white bar, and its back is green.

● SIZE
Length 14cm (5½in)

● NEST
Built in existing hole in tree or in nestbox; nest of moss, lined with hair and often feathers

● BREEDING
Lays 5–12 eggs, mainly April–June; incubation takes 13–14 days

● FOOD
Mainly insects and spiders, but also seeds, especially during winter

● HABITAT
Almost any habitat with trees (especially broadleaved) including gardens and woods

● VOICE
Has a large number of calls, commonly a harsh, ringing '*tink-tink*'; song is loud, typically '*teacher-teacher-teacher*'

● DISTRIBUTION
Common and widespread resident

▶ Like the blue tit, the great tit pecks at milk bottle tops to reach the cream.

Conspicuous, unmarked white cheeks

Bold black crown, collar and bib

Bright yellow underparts

Broad black stripe

▲ The great tit has a distinctive broad black stripe running down its front.

▶ Short, rounded wings are characteristic of tits. They allow the birds to manoeuvre easily among trees.

COAL TIT *Parus ater*

The smallest of the true tits, this bird's black head shows white cheeks, while a white stripe stretches from the rear of the crown down to the nape. Its upperparts are olive-grey, while its pale underparts show a pinkish buff hue on the flanks. Two white wingbars are clearly visible. Regularly visits birdfeeders in wooded areas.

● **SIZE**
Length 11.5cm (4½in)

● **NEST**
In hole in tree stump or other crevice; nest of moss and roots, lined with hair

● **BREEDING**
Lays 7–11 eggs, mainly April–June; incubation takes 14–16 days

● **FOOD**
Mainly insects and spiders in summer, but mainly seeds in winter

The coal tit has a big head, small body and short tail. Very active, it often feeds high in the tree canopy and also searches tree trunks for insects and spiders.

● **HABITAT**
Wooded areas, mainly coniferous but also mixed and broadleaved

● **VOICE**
Call a sad piping '*tseu*'; song a loud '*peechoo-peechoo-peechoo*'

● **DISTRIBUTION**
Common throughout Britain and Ireland

White nape stripe

Two pale wingbars

MARSH TIT *Parus palustris*

Much scarcer than the blue, great and coal tits, this bird is recognised by its black cap, white cheeks, grey-brown upperparts and pale grey-buff underparts. It looks very similar to the willow tit, but its black cap often appears glossier, it has a smaller, neater black bib, and it lacks a pale wing panel.

The marsh tit's crown looks glossy only in bright sunlight and from certain angles.

● **SIZE**
Length 11.5cm (4½in)

● **NEST**
In natural tree hole; nest of moss, lined with hair and feathers

● **BREEDING**
Lays 7–9 eggs, mainly April–June; incubation takes 13–15 days

● **FOOD**
Mainly insects and spiders in summer but mainly seeds and nuts in winter

● **HABITAT**
Broadleaved woodland (especially oak or beech); also visits larger gardens especially in winter;

despite common name, does not favour damp ground

● **VOICE**
Calls include distinctive nasal '*ptchoo*'; usual song a series of '*schip*' notes running into a trill

● **DISTRIBUTION**
Resident in much of England and Wales, and parts of southern Scotland

Glossy black cap

Buffish brown plumage

WILLOW TIT *Parus montanus*

This bird is extremely similar to the marsh tit, with a black cap and bib, white cheeks, grey-brown upperparts and pale greyish buff underparts. Useful features distinguishing it from the marsh tit include a dull cap, a 'bull' neck, a larger, more diffuse bib and a pale wing panel (on some birds), and a harsh, nasal call. Sadly, like the marsh tit, this is a declining species.

● **SIZE**
Length 11.5cm (4½in)

● **NEST**
Excavated in tree stump; nest of plant fibres and lined with hair

● **BREEDING**
Lays 6–9 eggs, mainly April–June; incubation takes 13–15 days

● **FOOD**
Mainly insects and spiders in summer, but seeds and berries in winter

● **HABITAT**
Mixed or broadleaved woodland on damp ground; visits larger gardens

This willow tit has excavated its own nest hole in the stump of a rotting tree.

● **VOICE**
Calls include a nasal, buzzing '*eez-eez-eez*'; short, sweet warbling song is not often heard

● **DISTRIBUTION**
Resident in much of England and Wales, scarce in Scotland

Black bib

Thick neck

Pale panel visible on wings in most individuals

CRESTED TIT *Parus cristatus*

The variegated black-and-white crest distinguishes this species from all other small British birds. Its face is marked with black and white, while its upperparts are grey-brown and underparts buffish white. The crested tit is almost entirely restricted to forests of Scots pine in the Scottish Highlands, but is not uncommon there.

● **SIZE**
Length 11.5cm (4½in)

● **NEST**
Hole excavated in tree stump; nest of moss, lined with hair

● **BREEDING**
Lays 4–7 eggs, mainly April and May; incubation takes 13–16 days

● **FOOD**
Mainly insects and spiders in summer, but mainly seeds in winter

● **HABITAT**
Scots pine forests, especially ancient native ones

● **VOICE**
Calls include a distinctive purring trill and the tit's usual '*tsee-tsee-tsee*'; song comprises a combination of these calls

● **DISTRIBUTION**
Restricted to part of the Scottish Highlands between the Spey Valley and Moray Firth

Conspicuous crest

Black-and-white facial markings

Crested tits favour natural pine forests because the trees are ancient with many rotting stumps suitable for nesting.

LONG-TAILED TIT *Aegithalos caudatus*

This round-bodied, long-tailed bird resembles an animated feather duster. The adult has mainly black upperparts, a pink rump and 'shoulders', and white underparts and crown. Roving flocks are often seen in woods and hedgerows outside the breeding season.

The nest of the long-tailed tit is lined with up to 3000 feathers, all of which are collected from the surrounding area.

● **SIZE**
Length 14cm (5½in), over half of which is tail

● **NEST**
Expandable nest of moss, lichen and feathers

● **BREEDING**
Lays 8–12 eggs, mainly April–June; incubation takes 13–14 days

● **FOOD**
Mainly insects and spiders

● **HABITAT**
Broad-leaved woodland, scrub and heaths

● **VOICE**
Calls a trilling '*tsirrup*', abrupt soft '*trpp*' and

high nasal '*tsee*'; song a rapid series of call phrases

● **DISTRIBUTION**
Common and generally widespread

Stubby bill

Plumage pinkish buff, black and white

Disproportionately long tail

BEARDED TIT *Panurus biarmicus*

Highly distinctive, the bearded tit has bright orange-buff plumage and a long tail. The adult male has a blue-grey head and its undertail is black. The female is similar in colouring, but lacks the distinctive head pattern. It is restricted to reedbeds, though may also feed in vegetation nearby.

● **SIZE**
Length 12.5cm (4⅞in); tail 7cm (2¾in) of total

● **NEST**
Low among reeds; nest of dead reed leaves, lined with reed flowers and feathers

● **BREEDING**
Lays 4–8 eggs, mainly April and May; incubation 10–14 days

● **FOOD**
Mainly insects in summer, but reed seeds in winter

● **HABITAT**
Extensive reedbeds

● **VOICE**
Call an explosive '*ping*'; song a subdued twittering

● **DISTRIBUTION**
Mainly in parts of coastal southern England and East Anglia

Orange-buff plumage

Male has dark 'moustache'

Long tail, sometimes cocked upwards

Bearded tits usually forage within the cover of the reedbed but do occasionally perch prominently for brief periods.

The blackbird

Highly vocal, the blackbird is at its most noticeable in spring and early summer, when both male and female birds patrol the territory surrounding their chosen nesting site.

One of the most familiar British birds, the blackbird is a distinctive sight in gardens, parks and woods throughout the year. It may often be heard rustling in the undergrowth before being seen.

Blackbirds are fiercely territorial – each pair protects the area in which they live and raise their young. Males conduct regular bowing and running displays to warn intruders. Blackbird territories are densely clustered in many parts of the country as a result of their success as a species. In one study, a density of 7 pairs per hectare (2½ acres) was recorded. In open woodland and large, mature gardens, one pair's territory may be as large as a single hectare. The constant territorial behaviour is very obvious for four or five months over the spring and summer, especially in areas with well-mown lawns on which the blackbirds can display and feed.

Songs and calls

The other manifestation of the birds' territorial struggles is their loud, varied and persistent song. The full song, used during the breeding season and for a few weeks before (from January to June or July) is an outpouring of sweet whistles and other melodious notes. These calls can be immensely varied, but they are all immediately identifiable as the blackbird. This variety enables individuals to recognise their close rivals, and confuses newcomers – they may be deterred from trying to snatch a territory in an area where they think there are more birds than actually are present. One study of blackbird song recorded over several years revealed that some birds increased their repertoire each season, and sometimes learnt or imitated distinctive song-phrases from their neighbours.

The other sounds that blackbirds make are the distinctive alarm calls. The '*tchook, tchook, tchook*' winter roosting calls are a sure sign of a guarded communal roost in the vicinity, and a repeated '*mik, mik, mik*' alarm call is used to alert other birds to the presence of a ground predator, such

The bright orange-yellow bill and eye ring show that this male blackbird is ready to breed – these signals will be very apparent to the females of the species.

BUILDING A NEST

The blackbird's distinctive song is the first sign that the breeding season has arrived. Once paired, the birds begin nesting as early as February in mild weather, and their efforts can be easily spotted. Nests are built in bushes, shrubs or trees, usually from near ground level to 4m (13ft) up, or sometimes in crumbling brickwork. Sheds and outhouses are other frequent nesting sites, and gardeners should be careful not to disturb any nests that they come across.

The male blackbird will search for suitable materials and bring them back to his mate. The female does most of the construction work, and a mud strengthening layer helps to produce a strong, spacious construction, with enough room for the female and her clutch of four or five eggs.

Nest-building is a cooperative effort, but the female does most of the actual construction.

▶ An indication of the blackbird's tolerance of humans is their choice of nesting sites. A shed offers protection from the elements and makes an ideal place to hatch their young.

woods where they evolved, blackbirds were probably found on the woodland edge and in clearings where trees had fallen. The nest would have been built in similar locations to those favoured today – generally against a large branch or other structure to ensure that ground predators cannot easily see it. Coating the nest with a layer of mud makes it less likely to be damaged or displaced by wind or rain.

Changing feathers
The blackbird has several distinct plumages, allowing an observant person to assess the age of individual birds. All blackbirds emerge from the egg without any feathers, but these grow from the fourth day onward.

By the time the nestlings are nine days old, the tips of the main wing and tail feathers have emerged from the growing quills, and a careful look at these will reveal the sex of the bird – dark and glossy black for males and sooty brown for the females.

The next stage is streaked and mottled reddish brown juvenile plumage – this is shed in the autumn to be replaced by the distinctive black feathers of the adult male or brown ones of the female.

Some juvenile feathers are retained until the next autumn, and this also allows the birds to be aged. The easiest juvenile feathers to spot are those that overlay the secondary (inner) wing feathers. Generally, three to six of these feathers form a pale panel that identifies birds as youngsters. The main wing and tail feathers are retained for so long – up to 17 or 18 months in some birds – that they can become very worn and bleached, almost beige in some of the females.

There are also differences between the look of the birds in summer and winter – both in their plumage and in the colour of the bill. Some blackbirds, particularly

as a cat. In summer, a thin '*seep*' call, evolved to be very difficult to locate, alerts a mate or chicks to the presence of danger. This is also similar to the alarm call that warns of avian predators such as sparrowhawks. A very different, rattling alarm call is used to warn of nearby humans. Generations of gamekeepers have kept an ear open for these alarms to alert them to intruders on their land.

Breeding colours
The rich egg-yolk-yellow bill and eye ring of the breeding male lose their colour in autumn, and return to the older birds in midwinter. First year birds may not develop really bright yellow bills at all in their first breeding season, and females always have a lot of brown on their paler bills. These bright signals show that the male is coming into breeding condition and ready to find a mate.

Sometimes adult males still have dull beaks in late February and March, and there are two possible explanations for this. The first is that the bird is in poor physical condition and not up to competing for females. The second and more likely reason, however, is that it is part of a migrant population overwintering in Britain. These males have to fly back home, possibly over 2000km (1250 miles) away, and therefore must wait two or three more months before competing for a mate.

After blackbirds have paired, they begin to build their nest. In the ancient wild

Hop, skip and a jump

Blackbirds may find prey using both sight and hearing – a combination that gives rise to a distinctive gait as they comb a lawn looking for food.

The blackbird's 'hunting' technique on mown grass is a series of bounds, the bird listening intently for the slightest sound.

The bird stops abruptly on hearing movement under the grass, and identifies the precise location of a potential meal by cocking its head to one side and watching the ground intently.

Blackbirds and their young are fairly flexible about what they eat, adapting to whatever is available. Earthworms are a favourite, but they will eat spiders, snails, slugs and even wasps. They have also been known to catch small fish and newts from garden ponds. The blackbird is also partial to fruit and vegetables.

When taking off, the blackbird flexes its legs and leaps into the air, often travelling its own length before spreading its wings, extending its tail and pointing its beak skywards.

The blackbird is not always successful in finding a worm, and it may have to make do with a slug or small insect.

Blackbirds scare easily, and will take flight at the slightest sound, although they are now a familiar sight in our towns and cities. When alarmed, they will fly off in a flurry of activity, usually staying near the ground. They remain close to cover, and can often be seen skulking under bushes.

WILDLIFE WATCH

Where can I see blackbirds?

● Blackbirds are easy to observe since they can be found wherever there is cover. Outside the breeding season, they can be seen in the open, far from trees and bushes. Only high mountain areas completely lack breeding blackbirds.

A hardy creature, the blackbird does not suffer the effects of winter as badly as some birds do. It is not uncommon for them to dig through 6–7cm (2½–3in) of snow to find food.

males, gradually develop patches of white feathers as they grow older, which can help distinguish between generations.

Hazards of life

Blackbirds thrive in the conditions of the modern world, and are one of the most successful generalist species. Disease and starvation are responsible for most blackbird deaths, but human activity also takes a large toll. Britain's eight million pet cats, for example, may catch about 60 million birds each year – including millions of blackbirds. The bodies of blackbirds tagged with identification rings have shown that three females are killed by cats for every two males. This is because the females are lower in the pecking order and therefore likely to be at the edge of feeding flocks. Females are also vulnerable to cat attacks while they are incubating their eggs in the nest.

Cars are an even bigger killer. They travel faster than any natural predator, and birds are slow to realise that an approaching hazard could be moving at

The early bird catches the worm...

The blackbird is often one of the earliest birds to start feeding in the morning. Earthworms, which form an important part of the bird's diet, are most active when the moisture from the early morning dew is on the ground, and blackbirds tend to forage for a meal.

Momentarily still and silent the blackbird listens for any sound.

Then it violently throws twigs and leaves into the air in the hope of uncovering a worm or small insect.

This method of finding prey can be extremely effective. On a good day, a blackbird can find more than enough food to feed itself and its young family.

BLACKBIRD FACT FILE

A member of the thrush family, blackbirds are easily identified. Young birds are sometimes mistaken for the smaller song or larger mistle thrushes, although both these are always much paler below than any blackbird.

● NAMES
Common name: Blackbird
Scientific name: *Turdus merula*

● DISTRIBUTION
Familiar and abundant all over Britain, except in high hills lacking cover

● STATUS
About 6 million pairs

● SIZE
Length 24–25cm (10in); weight 80–135g (3–4½oz)

● KEY FEATURES
Males matt black, females and young brown and spotted; male beak bright yellow, brightest in older birds; males quarrel over breeding territory, singing loudly and indulging in persistent chases

● VOICE
Varied but easily recognisable song used by males for many months; specific alarm calls warn other birds of humans, cats or birds of prey

● FOOD
Insects, worms and other invertebrates, taken on ground; fruit in autumn and early winter, both on ground and from trees

● BREEDING
March to July, later if summer is damp; if dry, August nests very rare; often 2 or 3 broods per season (occasionally 4 or even 5), with a new nest usually built for each attempt

● NEST
Neat structure of grass, small twigs, and fine roots, plastered on the inside with mud, which is covered with a layer of soft, fine grass; built between ground level and 15m (50ft) in bushes, shrubs or hedges, in climbing shrubs on a wall, or in buildings on a shelf or ledge

● EGGS
Pale blue-green with brick red mottling; half of British clutches have 4 eggs, a quarter 3 eggs, less than a fifth 5 eggs; eggs hatch after 2 weeks, fledge 2 weeks later

● YOUNG
Look similar to female, but with reddish tone, streaked paler above and mottled below; generally tended by both parents (mainly male, if female sitting on the next clutch) for up to 3 weeks

▲ The female incubates the eggs relying on the male to bring her food.

◄ Juvenile blackbirds are a mottled red-brown colour. They are similar to adult females but have distinctive small pale markings on the head and upperparts. The adult characteristics appear after about a year.

Distribution map key

■ Present all year round

■ Present during summer months

□ Not present

The black feathers of the male are a striking contrast to the orange beak and eye ring.

A bright orange beak indicates that the male is sexually mature.

The long, broad fan-like tail is raised in a highly distinctive manner when the bird lands after flying.

The blackbird has a hopping, bouncing gait and is very agile on the ground.

THE BLACKBIRD CALENDAR

JANUARY • FEBRUARY

Cold weather and snow forces blackbirds, like other species, to congregate wherever food is available. Windfall apples remaining in orchards and gardens are an important resource, but gardeners can also put out foodscraps for them.

MARCH • APRIL

The blackbird's dawn chorus can be heard all over Britain. In many gardens, up to half a dozen or so birds may be audible. The birds are looking for mates at this time, building up to the important business of making nests and laying eggs.

MAY • JUNE

Mottled baby blackbirds that have recently left the nest conceal themselves in hedges or shrubs, and make a '*chuck-uk*' contact call at regular intervals. This ensures that the parent responsible for feeding each chick knows where it is.

JULY • AUGUST

A time of change for all blackbirds – the juveniles moult out of their spotty plumage into the first winter feathers, which are very like the adults. The adult birds become very shy and reclusive during their moult, when they replace all their feathers.

SEPTEMBER • OCTOBER

During the autumn, huge numbers of migrant blackbirds flock to winter in Britain from Scandinavia, Finland and even as far east as Russia. The weather conditions in their home regions are much too harsh for them to survive at this time of year.

NOVEMBER • DECEMBER

Berries on bushes, such as haws and holly in hedges, and cotoneaster and pyracantha in gardens, attract flocks of blackbirds. They prefer to feed on invertebrates in the soil, but these are difficult to reach if the ground is frosty.

such high speed. Males are more likely to be killed than females since they are often distracted by territorial chases, and both males may die if they are close together. Such deaths early in the breeding season are particularly serious as they can affect breeding patterns. Other hazards range from entanglement in fruit nets to collision with windows, buildings or wires.

Despite all these obstacles, blackbirds are prolific breeders. Although recent years have seen a population decline, especially over farmland, this now seems to have stopped, and the birds are still plentiful. It is possible for a pair to raise three or even four or five families in one season. This ensures that their distinctive looks and familiar song will continue to welcome us in the spring for years to come.

THE RING OUZEL

The scarce and elusive ring ouzel looks very similar to a male blackbird, but has a distinctive crescent on its lower breast, which is white in males and duller in females. Both sexes also have pale fringes on the main wing feathers.

In the uplands of Scotland or northern England, a simple, halting song of flutey notes from a wooded gully may come from a ring ouzel. The birds are migrants that winter in North Africa and southern Europe. They are sometimes seen in scrubby and open areas, especially with short grass, in southern and eastern England as they fly out from

The ring ouzel is much rarer than the blackbird and has a completely different song.

late September to early November. Many of the sites where they rest during migration are used year after year. These frequently have good cover to hide the birds.

Breeding ring ouzels are found in much of the Scottish Highlands, Lake District and Pennines. Populations in the southern uplands of Scotland, in Wales and in south-west England have declined recently, and there are probably fewer than 10,000 pairs left in Britain. The migrants return from early April onwards, and some raise two broods. In certain areas, these birds nest below ground level in the entrances to pot-holes and old mine shafts.

At first sight the dipper – always associated with water and sometimes called the water ouzel – looks similar, but this is a dumpy rounded bird, whereas the ring ouzel is clearly first cousin to the blackbird.

Recognising garden birds' eggs

Fragments of eggshell are sometimes found scattered on the ground on paths and lawns after chicks have hatched. They can provide useful clues to the identity of birds that may be nesting nearby.

All bird species, be they large or small, produce eggs. This method of reproduction has several advantages for birds. For one thing, laying eggs keeps their weight down, very useful for a creature that flies. Also, the young develop inside a protected environment that contains all the nutrients they need, while the hen remains free to search for food and divert predators away from the nest.

In essence, eggs are incubators in which chicks grow. Without their own internal source of heat, however, they have to be kept warm by the parent birds.

Sometimes the parents share this task, but in many cases the hen takes sole charge.

When the female is ready to breed, microscopic eggs, called ova, form yolks in the ovaries. After mating, as each egg ripens it is shed from the ovaries, in a process known as ovulation. The egg is then fertilised as it passes down the hen's reproductive tract, where the male's sperm has been stored in a special tube since mating.

A layer of albumen then forms around the yolk and its outer layer calcifies in a part of the reproductive tract called the shell gland. This can take from 24 hours to a week,

depending on the species. Once the egg is fully formed all that remains is for it to be laid, which usually occurs at a rate of one every 24 hours.

The production of eggs is an extremely tiring process for the hen. During the laying of the eggs, her intake of food invariably increases and usually includes a higher proportion of calcium than normal, as may be found in snail shells. This mineral helps to form the eggshell.

Size and shape

Although as a general rule big birds lay larger eggs than small birds, there are many variations in terms of size.

Younger birds of a species, for instance, tend to lay smaller eggs than the older birds. Another factor is the number of eggs in a clutch, that is, the total number of eggs laid by one bird during one nesting. For example, some birds, such as the gannet, lay a single egg because its often cramped, cliff-ledge nest site prevents a larger clutch being raised successfully, whereas many small songbirds lay ten or more eggs per clutch, their nests being more safely positioned in a tree or shrub.

Generally, clutch size is more or less fixed for each species. The number of

The rounded eggs of the blue tit are laid in a deep, cup-shaped nest lined with down feathers.

WILDLIFE WATCH

How can I identify birds' eggs?

● If you find a fragment of shell on your lawn or garden path, pay particular attention to the colour and any pattern you may be able to distinguish. In many species, the parent birds remove the fragments of eggshell from the nest after the chicks have hatched, so as to make the nest less conspicuous to predators. This is why you may find fragments of egg in unexpected places.

● It is illegal to remove eggs from birds' nests. Even searching for nests can cause distress to the parent birds.

clutches laid per year is influenced by food availability. Some species, such as the blue tit, feed their young almost exclusively on insect larvae, which are most abundant in early summer, and lay a single, large clutch of eggs in late spring. The blackbird, by contrast, which has a steady food supply, will lay two, three, four or even more clutches of several eggs over the course of the spring and summer.

Variations on shape
The popular image of a bird's egg is roughly oval in outline, rounded at one end and more pointed at the other, but many subtle variations exist.

The internal anatomy of the individual bird species inevitably has a bearing on the shape of the egg it produces, but other factors also play a part. For instance, birds that nest in holes or tunnels usually lay eggs that are nearly spherical, while in some ground-nesting species, the eggs are pear-shaped, so that

The chaffinch's nest is a work of art, incorporating grasses, moss and feathers, all bound together with spiders' silk. The majority of eggs are laid in late April or May.

they fit neatly together, points inward, enabling the incubating bird to cover them easily.

Colour and pattern
The most striking feature of eggs is their coloration. Although many eggs are white, they may display a wide range of background colouring and intricate markings. Both these are derived from pigments obtained as breakdown products of the blood: reds, browns and blacks come from haemoglobin, and blues and greens from bile.

Usually, egg colouring is the same for a species. All robins, for example, normally lay whitish brown eggs with reddish spots. There may, however, be some variation in the background colouring and markings in the eggs laid by

individuals of the same species. Most importantly, studies have shown that variations in the eggs laid by individual birds may result in them being able to distinguish their own eggs from a mass of others of the same species.

Just as vital as recognition, is the part colour and pattern play in camouflage. The eggs of birds such as the blackbird and chaffinch are speckled

and spotted, helping to camouflage them in their nests among the dappled light and shade of the trees and shrubs that are their preferred nesting sites.

Birds that nest in dark recesses – holes or tunnels, for instance – tend to lay white eggs. Here the white shells enable the parent bird to distinguish the eggs and thus avoid trampling them.

WHAT IS AN EGG?

THE STRUCTURE OF AN EGG

● At the centre of the egg is the bright yellow yolk. Rich in fat and protein, this provides food for the embryo, which develops at the top of the yolk surface. The yolk is surrounded by a tough membrane that extends to the shell at each end in a twisted strand called the chalaza. This ensures the embryo remains in position when the yolk rotates.

● Surrounding the yolk is the albumen – often referred to as the egg white. This is mainly composed of protein and water. Its primary role is to cushion the embryo, but it also serves as insulation and helps to prevent the developing chick from drying out. It has anti-bacterial properties that protect the embryo from infection.

● The albumen is surrounded by fine membranes and a hard shell. The calcareous portion of the shell is known as the 'testa' and it, in turn, is covered by an outer cuticle layer. Taken as a whole, the shell protects the embryo, regulates gas exchange and combats water loss and bacterial attack.

DID YOU KNOW?
The formation of eggshell requires a huge investment from the female bird. The calcium carbonate required to produce the shells of a pair of pigeon or dove eggs is equivalent to approximately one third of that present in the bird's entire skeleton.

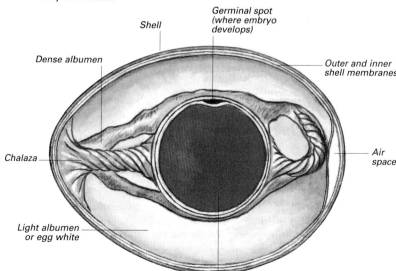

Shell

Germinal spot (where embryo develops)

Dense albumen

Outer and inner shell membranes

Chalaza

Air space

Light albumen or egg white

Yolk

Chicks draw their first breath from the air space in the egg. They escape from the shell by chipping out a small hole or line of weakness in it with an egg tooth on the tip of the bill, which soon disappears.

COLLARED DOVE *Streptopelia decaocto*

This bird's eggs – usually two of them – are glossy white at first, but they may become slightly grubby towards the end of incubation. This takes 14 days and is undertaken by both male and female.

The collared dove's nest is typically a flimsy structure, comprising a rough platform of twigs and roots, sited well up a tree on a level branch, or sometimes on the ledge of a building.

● **SIZE**
Length 32mm (1¼in)

● **SHAPE**
Rounded to broadly elliptical

● **PATTERN**
Unmarked

● **SEASON**
Eggs laid February–October; 3–6, or even more, broods per year (rarely, up to 9)

Pure white colour

Glossy texture

HOUSE MARTIN *Delichon urbica*

The usual clutch size of the house martin is three to five eggs. These are incubated by both parents over 14 to 15 days. Several nests may be found together, usually under the eaves of a building or some other man-made structure such as a bridge.

Made of mud and straw, the deep, cup-shaped nest is well lined with feathers.

● **SIZE**
Length 19mm (¾in)

● **SHAPE**
Sub-elliptical, with obvious blunt and pointed ends

● **PATTERN**
Generally unmarked, but sometimes with faint red spotting

● **SEASON**
Eggs laid May–August; 2, sometimes 3, broods per year

Pure white colour

Glossy texture

DUNNOCK *Prunella modularis*

Also known as hedge sparrows, dunnocks lay four to six eggs, which are incubated by the female for about 13 days. The deep, bulky nest is built from twigs and lined with hair and wool. It is sited low down in tangled bushes and brambles.

Despite their colour, the dunnock's eggs are not easy to find because the nest is located in dense cover.

● **SIZE**
Length 19mm (¾in)

● **SHAPE**
Sub-elliptical and fairly rounded

● **PATTERN**
Generally unmarked, but sometimes with faint red spotting

● **SEASON**
Eggs laid April–July; 2 broods, occasionally 3 per year

Bright blue colour

Generally unmarked

ROBIN *Erithacus rubecula*

Four to six eggs is the usual clutch size of this garden bird. The female incubates them for 13 to 14 days. She also builds the nest, usually in dense undergrowth, occasionally in a tree hole, bank or even in a shed, a wall crevice or on a ledge.

The domed nest is a woven cup of moss, grass, dead leaves and other plant fibres, lined with hair.

● **SIZE**
Length 20mm (¾in)

● **SHAPE**
Sub-elliptical and broadly rounded

● **PATTERN**
Variably marked with reddish brown spots

● **SEASON**
Eggs laid April–June; 2 broods, rarely 3 per year

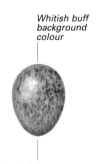

Whitish buff background colour

Marked with reddish flecks and spots

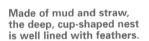

BLACKBIRD *Turdus merula*

The female blackbird generally lays three to five eggs, which she incubates for 13 to 14 days. The nest is made from grass, moss and mud, and is usually sited in a bush or shrub.

The mud layer inside the blackbird's nest is lined with leaves and plant debris. This provides an insulating cushion during incubation.

- **SIZE**
  Length 30mm (1¼in)
- **SHAPE**
  Sub-elliptical
- **PATTERN**
  Marked with reddish brown mottling and speckles
- **SEASON**
  Eggs laid March–August; usually 2 or 3 broods per year

Greenish blue background colour

Reddish markings

SONG THRUSH *Turdus philomelos*

The clutch usually comprises three to five eggs and incubation, which typically lasts 13 to 14 days, is undertaken mainly by the female. The song thrush is a fairly common garden bird, although it has recently suffered a major decline.

The song thrush's nest can be distinguished from a blackbird's because its smooth mud lining is not covered with grasses.

- **SIZE**
  Length 25mm (1in)
- **SHAPE**
  Sub-elliptical and fairly rounded
- **PATTERN**
  Variably marked with black spots, often concentrated towards blunt end
- **SEASON**
  Eggs laid April–July, sometimes earlier; usually 2 or 3 broods per year

Blue background colour

Variable black spotting

GREAT TIT *Parus major*

The great tit, like other true tits, takes readily to nestboxes. Otherwise, its nest is often sited in a hole in a tree or wall. The usual clutch size is five to 12 eggs, which are incubated by the female.

Made from moss, and thickly lined with hair and wool, the great tit's nest is small, considering the size of the clutch.

- **SIZE**
  Length 17mm (¾in)
- **SHAPE**
  Sub-elliptical and broadly rounded
- **PATTERN**
  Variably speckled and spotted with reddish brown
- **SEASON**
  Eggs laid May–June; usually 1 brood per year

Pale background colour

Variable reddish marks and flecks

BLUE TIT *Parus caeruleus*

The nest of this garden bird is made from feathers, hair and wool on a base of compacted moss, usually sited in a hole in a tree. The clutch size is between six and 15 eggs, which are incubated by the female for 13 to 16 days.

In many cases, it is a struggle for the female blue tit to fit all her eggs into one nest. They are often piled high.

- **SIZE**
  Length 15mm (⅝in)
- **SHAPE**
  Sub-elliptical, but fairly rounded
- **PATTERN**
  Marked with reddish freckles and spots; occasionally unmarked
- **SEASON**
  Most eggs laid April–May; second broods rare

Whitish background colour

Reddish markings and smooth, glossy texture

HOUSE SPARROW *Passer domesticus*

Crevices in walls and roofs provide this declining bird's usual nesting places, but old house martins' nests, bushes or trees may also be chosen. The nest is made of straw and grass, lined with feathers. Usually a clutch is four or five eggs, but may be up to seven. Incubation, mainly by the female, takes 12 to 14 days.

Differences in egg markings are apparent even in a single clutch.

- **SIZE**
Length 22mm (⅞in)
- **SHAPE**
Broadly sub-elliptical
- **PATTERN**
Variably marked with brown and grey flecks and spots
- **SEASON**
Eggs laid April–August; often 2 or 3 broods, rarely 4, per year

Whitish or pale greenish background colour

Brown and grey markings and smooth texture, but not glossy

STARLING *Sturnus vulgaris*

Starlings tend to nest in groups, in the eaves of houses or in holes in trees. The usual clutch size is five to seven. Fragments of shell are often deposited far away from the nest site after the chicks have hatched. Numbers have declined rapidly in recent years.

A starling's nest is an untidy affair made of dry grass, straw, feathers and even man-made objects.

- **SIZE**
Length 28mm (1⅛in)
- **SHAPE**
Ovoid
- **PATTERN**
Generally unmarked but sometimes spotted red with specks of blood
- **SEASON**
Eggs laid April–June; sometimes 2 broods per year

Pale blue colour

Usually unmarked, but sometimes flecked with red

CHAFFINCH *Fringilla coelebs*

The usual clutch size of the chaffinch is three to four eggs and these are incubated for about 12 days, mostly by the female. The neatly woven nest is a deep, cup shape and usually built in a hedge, bush or tree, often close to the trunk.

The irregular dark markings on a chaffinch's egg are sometimes bordered by a paler wash of colour.

- **SIZE**
Length 19mm (¾in)
- **SHAPE**
Sub-elliptical, but broadly rounded
- **PATTERN**
Variably marked with brownish streaks and spots
- **SEASON**
Eggs laid mainly late April–May; sometimes 2 broods per year

Background colour variable, from pale blue to pale buff

Marked with brown spots

SPOTTED FLYCATCHER *Muscicapa striata*

A summer visitor, the spotted flycatcher favours mature gardens. Nests are often sited on a level branch or a ledge and are built from a mixture of moss, wool and spiders' silk. The usual clutch size is four to six eggs, which tend to be darkest at the blunt end.

Spotted flycatchers take readily to open-fronted nestboxes placed in suitable shady places in the garden.

- **SIZE**
Length 18mm (¾in)
- **SHAPE**
Sub-elliptical but rounded
- **PATTERN**
Variably marked with reddish brown
- **SEASON**
Eggs laid mainly May–July; sometimes 2 broods per year, especially in south

Background colour variable, from pale blue to pale buff

Markings reddish brown

The bumblebee

Despite having a bulky body compared to a honeybee, the bumblebee is a strong flier, capable of carrying half its bodyweight in pollen as it buzzes around spring gardens in search of pollen and nectar.

In early spring, large, furry bumblebees are a common sight in parks and gardens. These are mostly queen bees that, after mating the previous year, have slept peacefully through the cold of winter. On waking, they refuel their bodies with nectar from pussy willows, deadnettles and other spring flowers, and then settle down to start new colonies.

Nest sites vary slightly from species to species, as does the detailed structure of the brood chamber, but the annual cycle of events is much the same for all bumblebee species. Some bumblebees colonise old birds' nests well above ground, others occupy nest boxes or niches in garden sheds and garages, and some nest on the ground if there is a good supply of dry grass and moss.

Nests can also be constructed underground, sometimes in the abandoned hole of a mouse, vole or other small mammal, where any existing bedding material can be reworked to form the bee's nest. Extra grass or moss, shredded up in the bee's jaws, is added if necessary until the nest is about as big as a tennis ball. In the centre of the ball, where the finest material has been concentrated, the queen hollows out a chamber up to 30mm (1¼in) across. She may bind the lining material together with nectar and she constructs a narrow entrance tunnel.

Having built her nest, the queen goes off to collect pollen, which she carries in basket-like structures on her hind legs.

In spring and early summer, buff-tailed bumblebees are a familiar sight. They are collecting pollen as food for the grubs developing in the nest.

BUMBLEBEE WHO'S WHO

There are about 25 species of bumblebee (*Bombus*) in Britain, and they can be distinguished from honeybees by their thicker, more rounded and hairier bodies. Most species of bumblebee are rare or found in specific areas, but six are common everywhere. The following descriptions apply only to queens and workers because males often have different patterns.

● The buff-tailed bumblebee (*Bombus terrestris*) has a golden-yellow collar and is unusual in that the queen has a yellowish buff tail, while the worker's tail is much paler and often white.

● The white-tailed bumblebee (*Bombus lucorum*) has a lemon-yellow collar and a white tail.
● The garden bumblebee (*Bombus hortorum*) is similar, but has a yellow band at the rear of the hind body as well.
● The common carder bee (*Bombus pascuorum*) is the only common species with an orange-brown hind body.
● The red-tailed bumblebee (*Bombus lapidarius*) is jet black with a deep red tail and black pollen baskets.
● The meadow bumblebee (*Bombus pratorum*) is a relatively small bumblebee with a golden collar and an orange tail.

Like all bumblebees, these white-tailed workers make excellent carers and tend the eggs and subsequent grubs diligently, protecting them from would-be predators.

The queen lays her eggs in batches within carefully constructed chambers. Each egg pack is well stocked with clumps of pollen to feed the grubs as soon as they hatch.

She moistens the pollen with nectar and moulds it into a cushion on the floor of the nest chamber. Then she lays up to 16 eggs in or around the pollen mass, and covers them with a mixture of pollen and wax from her own body. The queen also makes a wax pot for storing nectar – in case bad weather stops her from flying.

Pockets of pollen
The eggs hatch in about five days and the grubs feed on the pollen mass. Meanwhile, the queen continues to forage for pollen and nectar. This may be stored in wax cells and fed to the grubs on demand or, in other species known as pocket-makers, stored in wax pockets attached to the original brood clump, so the bee grubs can feed themselves.

The queen raises the first workers herself. The grubs take about 14 days to reach full size, depending on the temperature and the quantity and quality of the food they receive. The mature grubs spin spherical silken cocoons around themselves. The silk is yellowish, but is soon stained with faeces, quickly becoming rust-coloured.

After a further 14 days, the new bees bite their way out of their cocoons, on top of which the queen has already constructed more egg clumps. The young bees are all female workers, very much smaller than the queen, especially if the weather has not been good and the queen has not been able to forage regularly. After an energy-giving drink from the nectar pot, they begin their working life, taking over all foraging duties. They feed the new grubs while the queen continues to construct the egg cells and to lay further batches of eggs.

Establishing a colony

The notion of bees as busy and tireless workers applies to bumblebees as well as it does to honeybees. Throughout the spring and summer months, bumblebees spend all the hours of daylight working for the good of the colony.

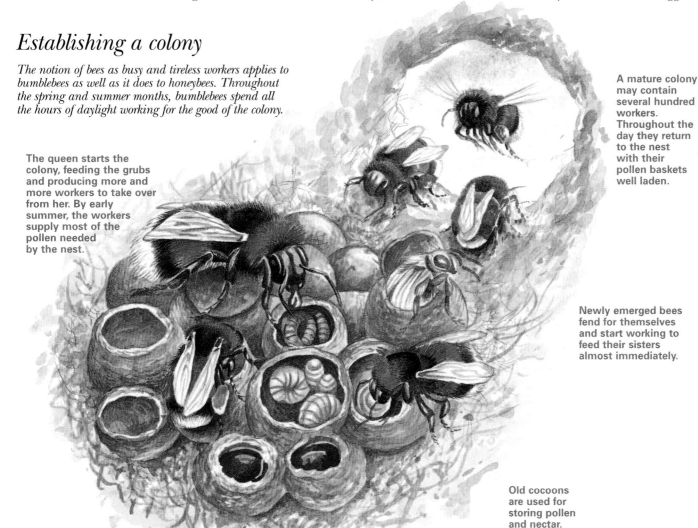

The queen starts the colony, feeding the grubs and producing more and more workers to take over from her. By early summer, the workers supply most of the pollen needed by the nest.

A mature colony may contain several hundred workers. Throughout the day they return to the nest with their pollen baskets well laden.

Newly emerged bees fend for themselves and start working to feed their sisters almost immediately.

Old cocoons are used for storing pollen and nectar.

In early spring, queen garden bumblebees are a familiar sight in both garden and hedgerow where they visit the blooms of early flowering species such as primroses.

The next generation

After rearing several batches of worker bees – the number depends on the species and the weather – the colony begins to prepare for the next generation by producing males and new queens. This may be as early as June for the meadow bee, but as late as August for the common carder bee. Males are reared from special eggs, but the queens develop from eggs identical to those that give rise to workers. The amount of food given to the grubs is the major factor determining whether they grow up to become workers or queens.

The males usually mature and leave their nests a few days before the queens, spreading out around the area so that when the queens emerge there is less chance of inbreeding. The males all die soon after mating, but the queens feed up and prepare for hibernation, usually in some cool but well-drained site in the soil. After the males and queens have been reared, the bumblebee colonies break down and the workers soon die. Most of them have disappeared by September, although common carder bees can often be seen in October.

In general, bumblebees go through only one nesting cycle in a year, but the garden bumblebee and the meadow bumblebee sometimes produce two colonies in a single season. Both of these species tend to have rather small colonies that mature fairly early in the summer, and some of the mated queens are

Many of the amazingly diverse forms of flowers are designed to ensure that as much pollen as possible is deposited onto the backs of visiting insects.

known to initiate new colonies straight away instead of going into hibernation. They sometimes restart the cycle by taking over existing nests from their mothers.

Feeding on nectar

Bumblebees exhibit none of the elaborate dances by which honeybees communicate with each other – they all have to search for food by themselves. They feed their grubs with both pollen and nectar, but the adult bees feed mainly on energy-rich nectar which they suck from flowers with their tubular tongues. The nectar is carried back to the nest in the honey stomach, a pouch near the front of the digestive tract.

The bees need a lot of energy to fly and it is obviously inefficient to waste time and energy investigating flowers if nectar has already been taken from them. Recent research suggests that these insects leave scent on every flower they visit, and that other bees detect this scent and ignore these flowers. The scent lingers for about 20 minutes, which is time enough for the flowers to secrete more nectar. The tongues of some bees

COLLECTING POLLEN

Pollen is collected on the bees' bodies where the hairs are long and branched – ideal for picking up sticky pollen grains. The pollen is periodically brushed from the body and packed into the pollen baskets, which are formed by stout hairs on the hind legs.

Foraging bees can often be seen with their pollen baskets bulging. The colour of the pollen, often yellow, orange or red, varies according to which flowers have been visited.

The bees can bear pollen loads of up to half their own body weight. Although they carry most of it away, plenty remains on their bodies to pollinate other flowers, and bumblebees are valuable pollinators of many crops, including beans, clovers and numerous fruit crops.

▲ The stiff curved hairs of the back legs act as baskets to hold accumulated pollen. The bees use their other legs to pack the grains in tight.

The pollen baskets on this garden bumblebee are evenly loaded with densely packed grains, enabling it to maintain balanced flight.

During bouts of hot, dry weather in the summer, bumblebees frequently visit the margins of pools, streams and garden ponds to drink water.

are very long – the garden bumblebee, for example, has an average tongue length of about 13.5mm (½in), and it can reach nectar deep inside tubular flowers such as red clover and even honeysuckle.

Most other bumblebees have shorter tongues, averaging some 7–8mm (⅜in), and generally feed from flowers with more accessible nectar. However, they can sometimes plunder nectar from deep-throated flowers, such as honeysuckle, by biting holes in the base. This means they avoid contact with the pollen and is often known as nectar stealing.

Cuckoo in the nest

In addition to 19 species of true bumble-bees, Britain is home to six species of cuckoo bees (genus *Psithyrus*). These bees look very much like bumblebees, but they are less hairy, have no pollen baskets and produce no workers. Female cuckoo bees wake from hibernation somewhat later than the bumblebee queens and, after a

period of refuelling on nectar, they search for the nests of their bumblebee hosts, which are already well established. Each species of cuckoo bee generally sticks to one host species, to which it usually bears a strong resemblance.

Cuckoo bees have particularly tough bodies and seem immune to the stings of the host bees, determinedly laying their own eggs, even if they have to kill the rightful queens in order to do so. The bumblebee workers feed the cuckoo bees' grubs in the usual way, but only new queens and males develop from these grubs. They leave the nest during the summer and spend several weeks feeding on nectar. The males are especially fond of thistles and knapweeds and several individuals can often be found on a single flowerhead, from which they are reluctant to move even when touched. After mating, the queens hibernate in much the same way as bumblebees.

Enemies and pests

Protected by their stings, bumblebees have relatively few enemies. Mice and other small mammals cause the greatest damage by attacking the nests in the early stages and eating the grubs and pollen stores. Badgers also enjoy the bumblebee grubs and are not deterred by the workers' stings. Spotted flycatchers and rare migrant red-backed shrikes regularly catch adult bumblebees, but the bees' most important enemies are the numerous flies and other parasites that attack them.

Superbly adapted mouthparts, including a long tongue, enable bumblebees – along with butterflies and certain hoverflies – to gain access to sources of pollen and nectar that many other insects cannot reach.

Bumblebees may spend a long time gathering food on plants with complex flowers, but the pollen and nectar rewards more than compensate for the energy expended.

The mating snail

Spring nights are the best time to watch out for snails engaged in their slow-moving, but fascinating, breeding rituals. Often, the pair will have just met by chance.

Some 80 different species of land snail are native to or naturalised in the British countryside. Most feed on living plants and decaying vegetation, but a few prey on small invertebrates. All snails continuously secrete a calcium-rich substance that forms a more-or-less spiral shell to protect their soft, moist bodies. The most common British snail species is the garden snail, with a flecked, light-brown shell up to 36mm (1⅜in) across. It is found throughout the country in suitable habitats, though in Scotland it is most common around the coasts.

Gardens on the chalk and limestone soils of southern England may well harbour Britain's largest land snail. This is the Roman snail, also known as the edible snail – although it is not the only edible species. It is widely distributed south of a line from the Severn to the Wash, but it is confined to lime-rich soils. The Roman snail's largest populations are found on the North Downs and the Chilterns.

The Roman snail is more susceptible to cold than other British snails, and it hibernates for up to six months of the year. It is a secretive creature, preferring long grass and scrubby areas, and its empty shells – creamy white or pale brown and up to 5cm (2in) across – are more often seen than the actual living animals. They are easiest to observe after an April shower.

Mating snails adopt a 'top-to-tail' position to bring their right sides as close together as possible. The shells are a potential hindrance throughout the process.

Both male and female

Snails are hermaphrodites, which means that individual adult snails produce both eggs and sperm. Every snail is thus male and female at the same time. However, they cannot usually fertilise themselves – they have to pair up and mate just like other animals. For slow-moving creatures such as snails, the main benefit of being a hermaphrodite is that they do not have to waste time searching for a partner of the opposite sex – any adult of the same species is a potential partner, so the chances of bumping into a mate are greatly increased.

Having come together by accident, or possibly by having followed each other's slime trails, two snails embark on a complex courtship dance, crawling around and over each other and caressing each other with their tentacles. They secrete large amounts of mucus and the

Seemingly locked in an embrace, Roman snails may spend more than an hour engaged in their slow, slimy courtship dance before actually mating.

ground beneath them may become quite sticky. The pair may even rear up and press the soles of their bodies together.

Getting to the point

The caressing can go on for an hour or more, but the snails eventually settle down with their sides in close contact. The tentacles droop at this stage, for the blood that kept them turgid during the earlier stages of courtship is now needed elsewhere. A swelling appears on the right side of each snail, just behind the head, as the genitals are prepared for action, and each snail then fires a dart like a harpoon into its partner's flank. The sharply pointed dart is made of chalky material and is up to a centimetre (½in)long. The arrival of the dart stimulates the final act of mating, possibly by raising the blood pressure. The genital apparatus erupts from each snail like a white blister. While locked together, each animal transfers a packet of sperm to its partner.

Eggs and young

The snails separate after a few hours, and each then goes off to lay its eggs. The darts may stay in place for a while, but often fall out as soon as the snails start to crawl away. Eggs are usually laid in the soil or in rotting wood within a few weeks of mating. Each snail excavates a hole and lays a batch of 30 or more pearly white eggs, each with a fairly hard, but brittle, chalky shell. The eggs are released through the same opening, just behind the head, through which the genitalia appeared during mating. At other times, this opening is closed and nearly invisible.

The baby snails emerge from the eggs within a month or so. They take up to four years to reach maturity and start the cycle again, although some of the smaller species mature in a single year. The rate of growth depends very much on the temperature and the abundance of food.

▲ Snails provide no parental care. Young snails fend for themselves and most hibernate over two or three winters before reaching full size.

◀ Eggs are laid in a damp hole. The shells are not waterproof, so they need to be kept moist to avoid drying out.

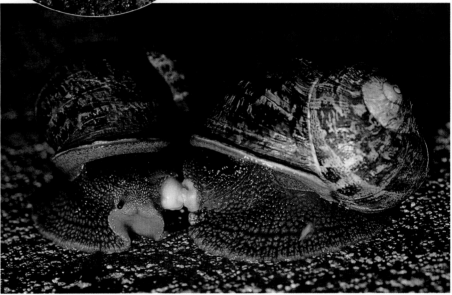

▲ The snails' genital apparatus bursts open and each pushes out a small packet of sperm called a 'spermatophore'. Mating ends when these have been exchanged.

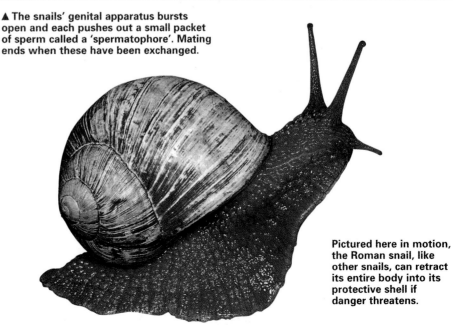

Pictured here in motion, the Roman snail, like other snails, can retract its entire body into its protective shell if danger threatens.

Recognising common garden bugs

Found on a wide variety of plantlife, these 15 common bugs can be identified by their distinctive colours and decorative markings – and in some cases by the vegetation they feed on.

Many people think of 'creepy crawlies' when the word 'bug' is mentioned. In fact, bugs are a specific group of insects which have specially modified mouthparts designed to pierce and suck liquid food from plants or other animals. Their feeding habits sometimes bring them into conflict with gardeners, but not all species damage the plantlife they feed on. The common green shield bug, for instance, leaves a small mark where it feeds on leaves, but is otherwise harmless. Some bugs can be beneficial in the garden, such as the common damsel bug, which feeds on aphids.

Colour and size

Bugs are a wonderfully assorted group. Some blend in with the background while others, such as the red and black common froghopper, advertise their presence with flashes of colour, warning would-be predators that they taste nasty. They come in a range of sizes, from the tiny, but conspicuously active rose aphid to sizeable aquatic bugs, such as the greater water boatman.

Such is the variety of form that it can be difficult to identify an insect as a bug at all. For example, some bugs resemble beetles, aphids are often misleadingly referred to as flies and some aquatic bugs appear to have nothing in common with other members of the group.

The common green capsid bug sucks the sap from garden plants, but often finds itself in competition with other smaller, more numerous bugs, such as the rose aphid.

WILDLIFE WATCH

Where can I find garden bugs?

● Many bugs live on just one type of foodplant, or on a very restricted range. Rose aphids, for example, spend the spring and early summer on roses only. Likewise, if you keep a nettle patch for small tortoiseshell, peacock and red admiral butterflies, it may well harbour a colony of nettle ground bugs.

● Some bugs, however, feed on a wide range of garden plants and weeds. Examples are the sloe bug and the common green shield bug.

● Predatory bugs, such as the common damsel bug or the red-spotted plant bug, may be found on almost any kind of vegetation in the garden.

● Various families of bugs have adapted to living in or on water, and a garden pond may support several different species. Some make little attempt to conceal themselves, such as the predatory pond skater, which scoots around in the surface film, feeding on tadpoles and any insects that fall in.

● Look just beneath the surface of the pond, and you may see a greater water boatman hanging there. These powerful predators feed on tadpoles, dead or dying small fish and water insects. Do not pick one up – it is quite likely to plunge its stabbing mouthparts into your finger, which can be painful.

WHAT ARE BUGS?

● Bugs belong to the order Hemiptera and are divided into two groups, Heteroptera (meaning 'different wings') and Homoptera (meaning 'same wings'). Heteroptera have forewings that are tough and horny at the base, thin and membranous at their tips. In Homoptera, the forewings are of a uniform texture, either horny or membranous. Most bugs have two pairs of wings, although in some species these may be absent or very much reduced in size. All predatory bugs are Heteropteran.

● All bugs have piercing and sucking mouthparts in the form of a tube, called the rostrum or beak, which is pushed into a plant to suck sap, or into another creature to suck its blood.

● The eggs hatch into nymphs (larvae), which mature into adults by casting off, or moulting, outgrown outer layers, often several times.

HOW CAN I IDENTIFY BUGS?

● In Heteropteran bugs, such as capsid bugs, both pairs of wings are held flat against the body at rest. Unlike beetles, with which bugs may be confused, there is no straight line down the top of the abdomen showing the separation between the front pair of wings.

● In Homopteran bugs, such as aphids, both pairs of wings are held like a roof above the body when at rest.
   In aphids, both pairs of wings are colourless, but in other groups of plant bug they may have colours and patterns on them.

Distribution map key

■ Present   □ Not present

In April and May, frothy balls of 'cuckoo-spit' are a familiar sight on plant stems all over the garden. Inside each one, a tiny froghopper larva is growing, safe from predators.

GREEN SHIELD BUG *Palomena prasina*

Despite being numerous and brightly coloured, the green shield bug can be difficult to spot since it blends in so well with the leaves on which it usually rests. It hibernates through the winter, turning a dark, reddish bronze colour and becoming green again in the spring.

The nymph on the right is almost ready to undergo its final moult, when it will lose its juvenile markings and emerge looking like the adult on its left.

● SIZE
Length 12–13.5mm (½–⅝in)

● HABITAT
Range of plants

● SEASON
Adults appear from late August, may survive until following July

● DISTRIBUTION
Common and widespread in England, Wales and Ireland; scarcer in north

SLOE BUG *Dolycoris baccarum*

An attractive shield bug – so called because the flat, broad body is shaped like an heraldic shield – the sloe bug's decorative forewings often include purple or red tones, and have strikingly patterned margins.

Seen here on a spear thistle, the sloe bug may be found in mature gardens with plenty of shrubs, feeding on fruits such as damsons, flowers and even aphids and other insect's eggs.

● SIZE
Length 11–12 mm (½in)

● HABITAT
Wide variety of shrubs and plants

● SEASON
Overwintered adults appear April or earlier, survive until July; new adults appear late August

● DISTRIBUTION
Common and widespread throughout Britain and Ireland; scarcer in north

COMMON DAMSEL BUG *Nabis rugosus*

Fully winged individuals may be encountered occasionally, but the common damsel bug is more often seen at a stage when its wings reach scarcely halfway along its abdomen. This bug may be small but it is fiercely predatory, seizing its prey with its front legs and stabbing with its beak.

The common damsel bug feeds on larvae and insects, including other bugs such as this sycamore aphid.

● SIZE
Length 6.5–7.5mm (¼in)

● HABITAT
Long grass, herbs and low shrubs

● SEASON
Overwintered adults survive until early July; new generation appears early August onwards

● DISTRIBUTION
Throughout Britain and Ireland

COMMON FLOWER BUG *Anthocoris nemorum*

Noticeably shiny, this little bug may be found on almost any plant in the garden, especially those in flower. Spider mites, aphids and other harmful garden insects provide its food. It also sucks plant sap, and will suck human blood, leaving an itchy spot resembling a mosquito bite.

This species relies on stealth to creep up on and subdue surprisingly large prey such as this hoverfly.

● SIZE
Length 3.5–4mm (³⁄₁₆in)

● HABITAT
Wide range of plants and flowers

● SEASON
Adults emerge in spring; new adults appear late June–July; sometimes second generation appears early September

● DISTRIBUTION
Common and widespread

COMMON GREEN CAPSID *Lygocoris pabulinus*

Of all the species of green plant bugs to be found in the garden, this is perhaps the most common and may sometimes occur in large numbers. It feeds on a wide variety of plants including potatoes, apples, pears and roses, as well as soft fruits.

The common green capsid bug may cause damage to plant leaves and stems by probing them to feed on the sap.

● SIZE
Length 5–6.5mm (¼in)

● HABITAT
Wide range of garden plants, including fruit trees and bushes

● SEASON
Overwinter as eggs in twigs of fruit trees; second generation adults appear late autumn

● DISTRIBUTION
Common and widespread

BIRCH PSALLID BUG *Psallus betuleti*

The birch psallid bug is usually found on leaves or catkins of birch trees. Apart from birch seeds, adults and nymphs feed on tiny insects. Also quite commonly found on garden birches is the larger and sturdier birch shield bug.

Colouring and patterns of the birch psallid bug closely resemble the ripening birch seeds on which it feeds. It is easiest to see on leaves.

● SIZE
Length 4.5–5.5mm (³⁄₁₆in)

● HABITAT
Birch trees

● SEASON
Overwinter as eggs in young wood; adults active May–September, lay eggs and die

● DISTRIBUTION
Common and widespread

RED-SPOTTED PLANT BUG *Deraeocoris ruber*

The two most common forms of this capsid bug are predominantly either brown or black, with a red mark towards the end of each wing, hence the name. The nymphs are dark reddish purple, with a bump on the end of the abdomen. They feed on aphids and other small insects.

The mostly black individuals of this species are more likely to be males than females, which tend to be brown.

● SIZE
Length 6.5–7.5mm (¼in)

● HABITAT
Wide range of garden plants

● SEASON
Overwinter as eggs; adults active July–September

● DISTRIBUTION
A southern species; absent from Scotland, Ireland and northern England

STRAWBERRY BUG *Scolopostethus affinis*

Although the adults feed mainly on strawberries, and overwinter in the leaf litter on the ground, female strawberry bugs often lay their eggs in nettle patches, and the larvae feed on these weeds. Strawberry bugs have tough, slightly flattened bodies and spiny legs, while the antennae are low down on the head.

Dull-coloured strawberry bugs congregate in large numbers and may cause considerable damage to ripening fruit.

● SIZE
Length 3.5–4.5mm (³⁄₁₆in)

● HABITAT
Strawberry plants

● SEASON
Overwinter as adults and nymphs; adults of both old and new generations are found from spring–autumn

● DISTRIBUTION
Widespread; scarcer in north

NETTLE GROUND BUG *Heterogaster urticae*

Black or dark brown in colour, the nettle ground bug may be found in large numbers on its stinging nettle foodplant – the adult feeds mainly on the seeds – although it will drop to the ground to escape if disturbed. It hibernates under bark or in the hollow stems of dead plants.

Mating is a prolonged affair for nettle ground bugs and the couple may remain together for several days, attracting the attention of other bugs.

● SIZE
Length 6–7mm (¼in)

● HABITAT
Stinging nettles

● SEASON
Overwintered adults survive until early July; new adults appear in September

● DISTRIBUTION
Lowland England and Wales; absent north of Yorkshire

COMMON POND SKATER *Gerris lacustris*

Among the most widely distributed of all British bugs, the common pond skater characteristically darts across the water's surface on spindly legs. It has large eyes and is very sensitive to vibrations in the surface film, so it easily detects prey such as tadpoles and insects in distress.

Pond skaters are voracious predators. They will even attack dying fish.

● SIZE
Length 8–10mm (⁵⁄₁₆–³⁄₈in)

● HABITAT
Ponds

● SEASON
Overwinter as adults; different generations live together; hibernate in autumn

● DISTRIBUTION
Common and widespread

WATER MEASURER *Hydrometra stagnorum*

A predator feeding mainly on small insects and water-fleas, which it spears through the water's surface, the water measurer may be found among surface and marginal plants in stagnant or sluggish water. It resembles a miniature stick insect.

A water measurer moves stealthily among the fairy moss on the surface of a garden pond in search of small insects that have fallen in.

● SIZE
Length 9–11.5mm (³⁄₈–½in)

● HABITAT
Stagnant and slow-moving water

● SEASON
Overwintered adults, emerge to mate in spring; new adults appear from June onwards

● DISTRIBUTION
Common

COMMON WATER BOATMAN — *Notonecta glauca*

Also known as a backswimmer because it swims on its back, the common water boatman dives rapidly if disturbed. The two hind legs are long, flattened into paddles at the tip and fringed with hairs. It feeds on almost any pond animal up to tadpole size.

A common water boatman hangs beneath the surface as it replenishes the air supply carried as a film over its body.

- **SIZE**
Length 14.5mm (⅝in)

- **HABITAT**
Ponds

- **SEASON**
Found in any month of the year, but less active when water very cold

- **DISTRIBUTION**
Widespread and common

ROSE APHID — *Macrosiphum rosae*

Commonly known as the greenfly, the rose aphid may be either pink or green. It is distinguished from other aphids by two backward-pointing black projections on its back. Rose aphids suck the sap from rose stems early in the season, then vast armies of them gather before moving on to another foodplant, such as scabious.

Rose aphids may be observed *en masse* in both winged and unwinged stages.

- **SIZE**
Length 2–3mm (⅛in)

- **HABITAT**
Roses, scabious, teasel and other garden plants

- **SEASON**
Adults found on roses in spring, spreading to other plants for summer generations

- **DISTRIBUTION**
Widespread

COMMON FROGHOPPER — *Philaenus spumarius*

Adults of this species leap from stem to stem of grasses and other plants. The nymphs of the common froghopper are the cuckoo-spit insects that live in the centre of a ball of froth on various garden plants and weeds. The nymphs secrete the froth after sucking sap.

Adult common froghoppers are mottled brown. When disturbed, they can jump a considerable distance.

- **SIZE**
Length 6mm (¼in)

- **HABITAT**
Wide range of cultivated and wild plants

- **SEASON**
Adults found late May–September

- **DISTRIBUTION**
Common and widespread

RED AND BLACK FROGHOPPER — *Cercopis vulnerata*

The nymphs of the red and black froghopper live communally in masses of froth underground, among the roots of grasses, bracken and dock. When they are mature, they emerge to climb up the plant stalks. This species tends to frequent gardens with trees or those close to wooded areas.

The red and black froghopper, the largest British froghopper, is a vividly marked bug that will fly away when disturbed.

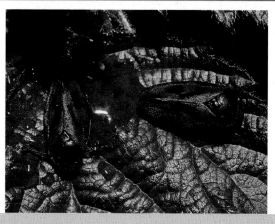

- **SIZE**
Length 8–12mm (⁵⁄₁₆–½in)

- **HABITAT**
Wide range of herbaceous plants and garden shrubs

- **SEASON**
Adults found April–August

- **DISTRIBUTION**
Widespread

Shimmering speedwells

Whether growing as wild flowers or garden weeds, speedwells are an enchanting sight in spring and early summer, when their deep blue flowers are often seen scattered across cultivated ground and waysides.

The blue-flowered speedwells (of the genus *Veronica*) are easily recognised members of the figwort and foxglove family, known scientifically as Scrophulariaceae. The 25 British species fall into two broad groups: perennial plants found in woods, grasslands, wet locations and on mountain ledges, and annual weeds that grow in cultivated ground. Along with the perennial thyme-leaved and slender speedwells, it is these annuals that are most often found in gardens and parks.

Laying down roots

Records have it that the slender speedwell was introduced to British gardens from its native Caucasus in the 1830s, as a decorative alpine plant for rockeries. Nearly a century later, in 1927, this elegant plant was reported to have escaped, and it has now spread widely through these islands. It rarely sets seed here, but rooting fragments are spread by disturbances such as mowing.

Leaves and blossoms

Speedwells all look similar, whether annual or perennial. Their stems are slender, with the leaves usually falling in opposite pairs. These are mostly small and often deeply toothed, but rarely lobed or deeply divided. Single flowers are arranged alternately along the stem or in spikes or elongated clusters. The speedwell flower's outer whorl

(or calyx) consists of four leaf-like sepals, fused at the base. The inner whorl (the corolla) is made up of four petals. The lowest of these is often smaller and narrower than the other three. The petals are fused like those of foxgloves, but instead of forming a long tube, they radiate from the mouth of an extremely short tube into a cup-shaped or almost flat structure. The two stalked male stamens are attached to the base of the petals. The whole delicate flower is shed as a single unit after pollination.

Usually coloured blue, often of a very intense dark shade, the flowers may also be lilac, pink or whitish. The fruit capsule splits lengthways when mature, exposing a few seeds inside each one.

Of the 11 annual speedwells, seven are native, although one of these, the Breckland speedwell, is suspect, as it was only discovered in Britain in

Dense mats of slender speedwell make a pretty sight from a distance, and the delicate flowers are equally beautiful seen close-up.

The common field-speedwell is an Asian species that has found a niche in this country. It now flowers all year round, particularly in the south.

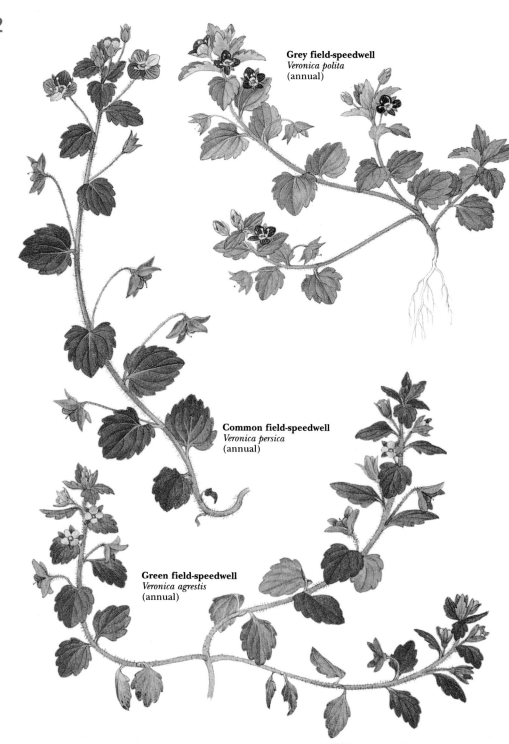

Grey field-speedwell
Veronica polita
(annual)

Common field-speedwell
Veronica persica
(annual)

Green field-speedwell
Veronica agrestis
(annual)

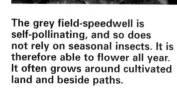

The grey field-speedwell is self-pollinating, and so does not rely on seasonal insects. It is therefore able to flower all year. It often grows around cultivated land and beside paths.

Green field-speedwells like dry soils and will spring up among arable crops and in other cultivated areas. Usually, the flowers are mainly blue, with white at least on the lower petal, but they may be all-white, as seen here.

SPEEDWELL FACT FILE

● Common field-speedwell
Veronica persica
Habitat and distribution
Introduced in early 19th century; now the common speedwell of cultivated ground, sometimes forming dense mats; less widespread in Wales and the north
Size 60cm (2ft) tall
Key features
Leaves broadly oval, conspicuously toothed; flowers solitary, 8–12mm (⁵⁄₁₆–½in) across, blue with dark veins, lower lobe paler; fruit capsules flattish, with two widely diverging lobes
Flowering time
February–November, sometimes all through winter

● Green field-speedwell
Veronica agrestis
Habitat and distribution
Cultivated light soils, especially in south-east, Midlands and north-west England. Decreasing as a result of intensive farming
Size 30cm (12in) tall
Key features
Neater plant than common field-speedwell; leaves oval, with irregular, rounded teeth; flowers 3–6mm (⅛–¼in) across, typically blue with whitish lower petal and white on lower part of lateral petals; fruit capsules deeply notched, with sparse straight hairs
Flowering time
March–November

● Grey field-speedwell
Veronica polita
Habitat and distribution
Cultivated ground on light soils, commoner in the south than the north; appears to be decreasing
Size 30cm (12in) tall
Key features
Similar to green field-speedwell, but lower leaves slightly wider than long, and greyish green colour, with regular, rounded teeth; flowers 3–6mm (⅛–¼in) across, blue; fruit capsules notched, with short curled hairs
Flowering time
March–November

1933. The others are truly naturalised and here to stay. Indeed, two – the common field-speedwell and slender speedwell – are important members of Britain's flora.

Annual varieties

The common field-speedwell, sometimes called Buxbaum's speedwell, arrived from south-west Asia and was first recorded in Berkshire in 1825, from where it has spread throughout Britain and Ireland. It is a pest of allotments and gardens, but a cheering sight in early spring as the flowers brighten cultivated ground.

Most of the other annual speedwells are decreasing due to intensive agriculture, although two close relatives of the common field-speedwell, the green and grey field-speedwells, may still be seen.

Three others are great rarities, restricted to the sandy Breckland region of East Anglia, where they survive precariously at the fringes of arable fields and among rabbit scrapes. These are plants of southern and eastern Europe at the very edge of their range.

The introduced Breckland speedwell is found very rarely in a few warm, sandy spots in East Anglia and Oxfordshire.

Ivy-leaved speedwell
Veronica hederifolia subsp.lucorum
(annual)

Wall speedwell
Veronica arvensis
(annual)

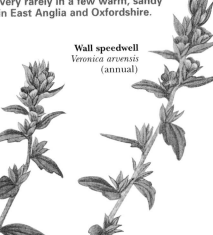

Spring speedwell
Veronica verna
(annual)

SPEEDWELL FACT FILE

● **Ivy-leaved speedwell**
Veronica hederifolia
Habitat and distribution
Cultivated ground, especially in gardens in spring; scarcer in much of Wales, northern England, Scotland and Ireland
Size Usually prostrate with stems up to 50cm (20in) long
Key features
Leaves hairy, with 3–5 lobes, like tiny ivy-leaves, the central lobe is usually wider than long; flowers solitary, 6–9mm (¼–⅜in) across, pale blue; fruit capsules stout, wider than long, hairless
Flowering time
March–August

Subsp. *lucorum*
Found on open ground in woods, hedgerows and gardens; 5–7 leaf-lobes, central one longer than wide; whitish to pale lilac flowers 4–6mm (⅛–¼in) across

● **Wall speedwell**
Veronica arvensis
Habitat and distribution
Dry, open places on cultivated ground, paths and pavements, walls, heaths and sand-dunes; common across much of Britain
Size 30cm (12in) plus tall
Key features
Leaves oval, coarse-toothed and hairy; stem hairy; tiny flowers in erect, leafy spikes, 2–3mm (⅛in) across, blue; heart-shaped fruit capsules about as long as wide, hairy
Flowering time
Late March–October, but often over by July

● **Spring speedwell**
Veronica verna
Habitat and distribution
Rare in sparse grassland, bare sandy ground and fields in the Brecklands of East Anglia
Size Up to 15cm (6in) tall, often much smaller
Key features
Similar to wall speedwell, but upper leaves shallowly lobed rather than toothed; fruit capsules kidney-shaped, wider than long
Flowering time
April–June

Breckland speedwell
Veronica praecox
(annual)

SPEEDWELL FACT FILE

● **Fingered speedwell**
Veronica triphyllos
Habitat and distribution
A few sandy field margins in the Brecklands of Norfolk and Suffolk, now virtually extinct; once scattered from Surrey to Yorkshire
Size 20cm (8in) tall
Key features
Similar to spring speedwell but upper leaves divided almost to base; flowers 3–4mm (⅛in) across, deep blue, on longer stalks; fruit capsules about as long as wide
Flowering time
April–June

● **Breckland speedwell**
Veronica praecox
Habitat and distribution
Perhaps introduced; discovered in Britain in 1933; found in a few sandy fields in the Brecklands of Norfolk, Suffolk and also in Oxfordshire
Size 20cm (8in) tall
Key features
Leaves oval, more rounded than fingered and spring speedwells, toothed, not deeply lobed; flowers stalked, 2.5–4mm (⅛in) across, deep blue; fruit capsules longer than wide, notched
Flowering time
March–June

● **American Speedwell**
Veronica peregrina
Habitat and distribution
Introduced from temperate America; damp, broken ground of gardens and nurseries, northwards to central Scotland; in Ireland mainly in the north
Size 25cm (10in) tall
Key features
Hairless, with erect stems; leaves elliptical, indistinctly toothed or untoothed; flowers in loose spikes, 2–3mm (⅛in) across, lilac; fruit broader than long, slightly notched, hairless
Flowering time
April–August

Fingered speedwell
Veronica triphyllos
(annual)

American speedwell
Veronica peregrina
(annual)

The rare fingered speedwell flowers from April to June. It benefits from the open space on arable land before the crop grows each spring.

SPEEDWELL FACT FILE

● **Thyme-leaved speedwell**
Veronica serpyllifolia
Habitat and distribution
Sparse, short, often damp grassland, waste ground, lawns, paths and flower-beds, especially on lime-poor soils
Size 30cm (12in) tall
Key features
Elegant perennial with creeping, rooting stems; leaves oval, almost untoothed, stalkless, shiny; flowers 6–8mm (¼–⁵⁄₁₆in) across, whitish to pale blue with dark veins, up to 40 in erect, loose, leafy spikes; fruit capsules slightly wider than long, hairy
Flowering time
April–October
Subsp. humifusa
Found on rock ledges and gravel in mountains of the Scottish Highlands, northern England and North Wales; downy, with almost circular leaves, and spikes of up to 12 bright blue flowers, 7–10mm (¼–⅜in) across

● **Slender speedwell**
Veronica filiformis
Habitat and distribution
Lawns, churchyards and other mown, grassy places, flower-beds and river banks; introduced from gardens and spreading over last 75 years
Size 50cm (20in) tall, but usually shorter
Key features
Downy perennial, rooting at the base of each pair of leaves and forming a mat of leafy stems; leaves kidney-shaped, with rounded teeth; flowers solitary on thread-like stalks, 8–15mm (⁵⁄₁₆–⅝in) across, pale mauve-blue; fruit capsules rare
Flowering time
March–June, with a few flowers until August

Thyme-leaved speedwell has creeping stems that take root readily. It flowers throughout the summer in gardens, heaths and damp grassy areas, especially in areas of acidic soil. A separate subspecies grows in the uplands of Scotland and Wales.

Slender speedwell
Veronica filiformis
(perennial)

Since its escape from cultivation, the slender speedwell has become a frequent, tenacious but attractive weed. Its spread is all the more impressive because the flowers rarely set seed in this country.

Thyme-leaved speedwell
Veronica serpyllifolia
(perennial)

Park watch

- The fallow deer
- The pipistrelle
- Recognising pigeons
- The mute swan
- Recognising aristocrat butterflies
- The earwig
- Recognising deciduous parkland trees
- Daffodils and snowdrops
- Miniature wild pansies

The fallow deer

Despite being shy and easily startled, the fallow deer often ventures out of its woodland shelter into parks, fields and other grassy spaces to graze in large herds, the fawns trotting after their mothers.

The Normans introduced fallow deer to this country nearly a thousand years ago, specifically so that they could be hunted. The medium-sized deer were imported from mainland Europe, and strict laws to protect them from being poached by the peasantry were enforced. Coupled with the establishment of deer parks where these animals were encouraged to breed, such laws helped the newcomers to flourish.

The deer parks lasted throughout the Middle Ages and were later augmented by the gardens of stately homes where fallow deer were preserved as an ornament to the landscape and a useful source of venison for banquets. Occasionally, animals were released deliberately into natural forests, and many others escaped. As a result, the fallow deer has now become the most widespread deer in the British Isles, and is common in many areas, though found in only a few parts of Scotland.

Coat of many colours

Typically, fallow deer are a rich brown with a black stripe down the middle of the back and large white spots on the body – the pattern of spots is unique to each animal. In winter, however, the general coat colour turns a paler, duller greyish brown, and the spots become less distinct. This winter colour may be the origin of the deer's name – 'fealou' was an old English word for pale brown.

The most common variation on this basic colour scheme is called 'menil'. Menil deer are very pale – the general coat colour is a light fawn and the black line down the back and the black horseshoe around the animal's tail are replaced by brown markings. The white spots are large and conspicuous, and are more noticeable in winter than on a typical fallow deer. Not surprisingly, the overall result closely resembles the classic Disney cartoon image of 'Bambi'.

In some parts of the country, fallow deer are often very dark brown, almost black, with no white spots, although paler patches are visible on close inspection. The belly may be a deep mushroom colour, but any black markings are practically invisible.

In wild herds, all colour varieties can be found, although one usually predominates in a particular locality. Park herds may be of just one type, established by selective culling. There is also a curious long-haired version of the fallow deer found only in Shropshire, which has fur twice the normal length and even longer curly hairs on the forehead and tail.

Most fawns are born in June, although some may arrive a little later. Their mothers may continue to provide them with milk for up to nine months, by which time the young deer will be almost fully mature.

TURNING TAIL

During spring or early summer, male fallow deer shed their distinctive antlers, which can make identification more difficult. The females – known as does – do not have antlers at all. This is why deer are often best recognised from behind, especially as their back view is frequently all that is seen as the animal flees from would-be observers.

The rear of the fallow deer is white with black edges like an upside-down horseshoe. The tail has a black top, which appears as a vertical stripe down the centre of the backside. Only the sika deer has a similar pattern.

THE WHITE HART

The word 'hart' is an old hunters' term for a mature male red deer, six or more years old. White specimens of red deer are unusual, and in the late 14th century one was adopted by King Richard II as his personal emblem. It soon caught on among patriotic innkeepers, explaining the popularity of the name 'The White Hart' among pubs and inns. But over the years, zoological accuracy has declined, and pub signs today often show a white fallow buck, complete with distinctive palmate antlers.

Unlike other British species, fallow deer are very variable in colour. Although in some herds the animals are all of one colour (especially in privately owned deer parks where 'deviants' are culled by the keeper), in other herds several different coats may be seen, varying from very light to almost black. Pure white individuals are more common in fallow deer than in perhaps any other British mammal. White fallow deer are born a sandy colour and get steadily paler with each successive seasonal moult, until after a couple of years they are pure white.

In natural circumstances, such conspicuous creatures would be weeded out by predators and few of them would survive. However, just as the fallow deer population became established in Britain, predators such as wolves became scarce or extinct, so the white deer were no longer at a particular disadvantage. Indeed, the white coat became an advantage, as locals often thought the deer had magical properties, a little like mascots, and protected them from harm.

White fallow deer are not true albinos (which are very rare), since they do not have the albino's pink eyes. Their white coats are merely one extreme of the natural colour variation shown in this species – at the other extreme are very dark individuals.

Flat antlers

Male fallow deer, called bucks, are easy to recognise through most of the year because they are the only deer in Britain with flattened antlers. The shape of the antlers is usually described as 'palmate', because it resembles the palm of a hand – flat with short finger-like prongs at the edges. A buck's antlers first begin to form at about six to ten months old. They are shed between April and June and regrow over the summer in preparation for the rut, or breeding season. During the regrowth, antlers are covered in 'velvet', a soft furry covering of skin that makes the antler look thick and blunt. This is scraped off on tree trunks and branches in late summer, leaving the bony interiors exposed. Each year, the new set of antlers grows bigger than the last – in mature bucks they can be up to 70cm (28in) long.

Herd instinct

A sociable species, fallow deer are usually found in herds of up to 50 or more. They share this tendency to form large groups with red and sika deer, whereas roe deer live in smaller family groups and muntjac are solitary. One unusual trait in fallow deer herds, though, is that the groups typically comprise all males or all females. Bucks form bachelor herds, often inhabiting areas well away from the does and their young for much of the time. The sexes only come together in the autumn for the rut.

Bucks move into areas occupied by females in about September. Older bucks may return to the same place they rutted

Challenging males

During the autumn rut bucks, resplendent in new antlers, compete for mating rights over does. These encounters do not always end in a fight and body language plays a major part in settling many disputes.

A bold challenger crosses behind the posturing dominant buck ...

... and then moves alongside, matching the dominant male stride for stride.

▲ Although rival males will usually attempt to solve disputes by display, fights are not uncommon in the rut. The antagonists lock antlers and wrestle, but these contests are usually more a test of strength than a genuine attempt to do each other harm.

▶ Social groups outside the breeding season usually comprise females with their young or groups of older males. Larger mixed groups such as this one will occur only in a good quality habitat.

in previous years, and mature does also frequently revisit familiar areas to breed. Sometimes the does are accompanied by their daughters and granddaughters, and this can result in bucks interbreeding with their own offspring.

Although young males are capable of breeding at about 7–14 months old, the vigilance of older bucks usually means they are chased away and kept from

Strutting in parallel, both bucks have the opportunity to size up their opponent.

Usually the weaker male will recognise his own deficiencies and retire from the contest.

The majority of encounters end with one male the clear winner. He will have to face more challengers before the end of the rutting season, and if he meets an evenly matched or bold opponent, he may have to fight with clashing antlers.

FALLOW DEER FACT FILE

The fallow deer is usually rich brown with white spots, but looks paler and duller in the winter. It is most frequently to be seen in deer parks where it lives in large herds, although wild herds are also commonly found throughout southern and central England.

● NAMES
Common name: fallow deer
Scientific name: *Dama dama*

● HABITAT
Woodland, farmland and deer parks, with dense undergrowth in places; often semi-domesticated

● DISTRIBUTION
Most of southern and central England; parts of Wales, northern England and Ireland, and a few scattered localities in Scotland

● STATUS
Around 100,000 individuals at start of breeding season. Common within its range, absent in other areas except for the occasonal stray or escaped animal

● SIZE
Length 160cm (5ft 3in); tail 20cm (8in); height about 85cm (33½in) at the shoulder; male weight about 70kg (155lb), female weight just over half this total

● KEY FEATURES
Flat antlers unique among British deer; colour varies from white to almost black, but typically rich brown with white spots, brightest and most boldly spotted in summer and autumn; tail usually black on top, surrounded by white patch edged with black

● HABITS
Feed by grazing grass or browsing trees and bushes; often active mainly at night, especially on farmland; may spend the day hidden among trees or shrubs

● VOICE
Usually silent, but young sometimes bleat and does may bark if threatened; rutting bucks make deep groaning noises

● BREEDING
Bucks gather harems of does in autumn, mate in October; fawns born singly in June – twins rare

● NEST
Deer make no nest, but hide young among long grass, bracken or weeds

● YOUNG
Usually pale brown, spotted with white; lie hidden for a few days before following at mother's heels

Distribution map key

■ Present all year round

□ Not present

PROTECTED!

Fallow deer are protected by legislation that controls hunting: they may not be killed at certain times of the year. Various laws regulate methods of capture, types of weapons that can be used to cull them, and how they may be moved around.

Only males have antlers, which grow during the summer. The size and number of tines increases with age until the buck is past his prime. Old antlers are shed in between spring and early summer.

The tail is relatively long, and in most colour varieties the white tail patch is ringed with black.

A prominent tuft of hairs, called a brush, is clearly visible on the penis sheath. This is a useful identifying feature in young males without antlers.

Males in rut give belching groans, the volume and duration of which are a good indication of their strength and condition.

mating with any does during their first rut. Does breed for the first time aged about 16 months, in the autumn of the year after they were born. After that, most breed every year. However, when the population density is especially high, there is often insufficient food to support the whole herd. Many animals are less well fed and, as a result, a high proportion of females may fail to breed. In this way, a natural form of population control operates among the deer.

Typically, each buck will vigorously defend his own patch and attempt to keep a harem of females to himself, although sometimes two bucks may work

▲ This new-born fawn will spend the first week of its life lying quietly in hiding, until it is strong enough to follow the herd. Its mother will return regularly to suckle it.

◄ Not surprisingly for an animal that was long hunted, fallow deer are nervous animals. They have excellent eyesight and hearing, and an acute sense of smell. Their large ears, which measure more than half the length of the head, are mobile and turn quickly towards any small sound.

together to defend a harem. During the rut, the bucks are very active and noisy – they will strut about and perhaps clash antlers with a persistent rival. The does may ignore these displaying males altogether, but the bucks still nuzzle them frequently and make characteristic groaning noises.

Rutting deer usually form groups well distanced from each other, but on occasion herds may be quite close together – much depends on the type of habitat and the relative numbers of males and females capable of breeding in a particular year.

All of this behaviour may be seen in deer parks, where the animals are familiar with people, but is harder to observe in the countryside. After the rut, the bucks often disperse to live separately from the does once again, although in some areas mixed-sex herds can be found throughout much of the year.

Wobbly start

A fallow doe usually gives birth to just one fawn in a given year; very occasionally there may be twins. Fawns are generally born in June but sometimes may appear a

A DISTINCTIVE VOICE

Throughout the rut, fallow deer bucks make short, low-pitched groans while following the does or herding them together into groups. By recording the groans from known individual bucks and analysing them electronically, researchers have shown that each male has his own distinctive voice and pattern of groans. This helps the study of their social behaviour, as it is possible to recognise individual males, at least during the rutting season, and potentially from one year to the next. Scientists have also learned that the does favour mating with bucks that have been around since the beginning of the mating season and are familiar to them, as well those that groan most frequently. The fact that individuals make recognisably different patterns of sound may help females to recognise the males with which they mate.

Bucks repeatedly groan during the rut to challenge other males and to advertise themselves to females, both before and after mating. Groaning and other rutting behaviour uses a lot of energy, and males are often exhausted by the time the breeding season ends in November.

Deer with menil colouring, like this one, are lighter than most of their herd companions. Each fallow deer has a pattern of spots as unique as a human fingerprint.

little later in the summer. On average, a fawn weighs about 4½kg (10lb) at birth.

Fawns are born among clumps of bracken, long grass or other cover. As soon as possible, the mother moves some distance away in order to avoid drawing attention to her fawn, although she returns at intervals to suckle it. The fawn lies quietly with its neck stretched out along the ground or folded back against the flank.

For the first few hours, sometimes days, the fawn reacts to danger by 'freezing' – keeping motionless and relying on its spotted camouflage to avoid detection. But fawns are surprisingly agile, even when only a few hours old, and their response to danger soon becomes a swift retreat. After about a week, the fawn joins

its mother and becomes part of a social group, following the herd and learning to feed itself.

Grass eaters

Fallow deer are creatures of habit and will use the same tracks and paths repeatedly to get from place to place. Each animal is probably familiar with an area of about 20 hectares (50 acres) or more. They are woodland animals, preferring deciduous trees to conifers and plantations, but this environment is used mainly for shelter, so they can live happily in quite small copses.

Unlike other deer, they prefer to feed by grazing grass rather than browsing leaves off trees. About 60 per cent of their summer diet is grass. In the autumn, they eat acorns if these are available, together

with fallen fruits. Over winter they turn to heather, conifer needles, brambles, ivy and other such vegetation, but they prefer grass whenever they can find it. Even at this time, when the grass is not growing, it still forms about a fifth of their food intake. In order to graze, deer often leave the cover of the woods and venture into the open. They can become a nuisance when they stray onto farmland and raid crops, usually under cover of darkness.

In large areas of forest, herds may migrate seasonally, seeking new feeding areas as different food resources are exhausted. Where large deer herds occur, especially in smaller patches of woodland, they can cause a lot of damage to young trees and smaller plants, creating an open forest floor devoid of undergrowth. This is not good for other species such as dormice and shrub-dwelling birds.

Deer also eat woodland flowers, including rare species, and have become a serious conservation problem in some areas. However, because fallow deer are particularly attractive, most people do not like the idea of controlling them through culling and so the problem worsens. Nevertheless, many deer populations are managed by shooting, to keep the average density below about one animal per five hectares (12½ acres). In parks, of course, much higher densities can be reached – but then the deer often need to be fed over winter or many of them will starve.

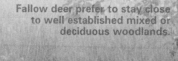

Fallow deer prefer to stay close to well established mixed or deciduous woodlands.

WILDLIFE WATCH

Where can I see fallow deer?

There are many deer parks all over the country where fallow deer (and in some cases other species as well) can be seen. Good examples are:

● Richmond Park, Surrey

● Charlecote Park, Stratford-upon-Avon, Warwickshire

● Powderham Park, near Exeter, Devon

● Studley Royal Park, near Ripon, Yorkshire

● The Scottish Deer Park, Cupar, Fife

● For more information about deer, and to find out about deer in your area, contact the British Deer Society, Fordingbridge, Hampshire SP6 1EF. Telephone 01425 653553 www.bds.org.uk

The pipistrelle

This tiny bat is mostly seen at dusk when it begins to feed. Fantastically manoeuvrable, it is able to snatch its insect prey out of the air while flying at high speed.

With a wingspan of around 20cm (8in) and a typical weight of less than 8g (¼oz) – barely more than a lump of sugar – the pipistrelle is Britain's smallest bat. Contrary to popular belief, not all small bats are pipistrelles, although it may be impossible to distinguish them as they flit by in the gathering dark.

Until very recently, most pipistrelles in Britain were thought to be one species, the so-called common pipistrelle. But new technology, in the form of ultrasound

Flying requires massive amounts of energy, especially for a mammal lacking the lightweight hollow bones of birds. To get that energy, bats are voracious feeders, each one catching perhaps 200 insects in a night. They also need a great deal of fluid and usually roost close to water.

recorders, has revealed that there are in fact two different species co-existing throughout Britain and Ireland. First identified by a difference in frequency of their echo-location calls, they are now known as the 45 pipistrelle (*Pipistrellus pipistrellus*, calling at 45 kilohertz), and the 55 pipistrelle (*Pipistrellus pygmaeus*, calling at 55 kHz). Researchers soon found tiny physical differences between the two species – 55 pipistrelles are slightly smaller and paler, while 45 pipistrelles have a dark 'mask' around their eyes.

Small spaces

Of all bats, pipistrelles are the ones most often associated with buildings, entering them in search of suitable temperature conditions. The females need warm places to rear their young and frequently invade buildings in considerable numbers

in May or June. The males need cooler places and usually remain alone or in small groups. While bats are usually associated with deserted places such as derelict buildings, pipistrelles are just as likely to be found in modern bungalows. They can get into very small crevices, through gaps less than 1cm (½in) across, and they especially like to squeeze up behind the weather boarding and hanging tiles that clad the walls of many cottages and houses, particularly in the south-east of England. They are common in old churches, but are more likely to be found behind noticeboards or in gaps between beams and walls than flying around the belfry. The church bells would cause great distress to creatures with such sensitive hearing.

Pipistrelles are at home flying over gardens and parks, including those in towns and large cities. They also occur in other habitats, such as farmland and open woodland, and are most abundant near water, where insects are plentiful. They like to fly along linear features such as rivers, tree lines and hedges, which are easy to follow in the dark, and help the bats to orientate themselves. This is important because they may forage an area up to 3km (1¾ miles) from their roosts – a long way for a creature that is only 4cm (1½in) or so long.

HOW MANY ARE THERE?

By mapping the distribution of nursery roosts over a wide area, it is possible roughly to estimate the population density of bats. In the case of pipistrelles, researchers in Scotland have found an average density of about five breeding females per square kilometre (13 per square mile). Assuming that there are equal numbers of males and females in the population, this would add up to about two million pipistrelles in Britain.

However, it is hard to find all the roosts in a given area, and some areas may provide much better habitat than others. Densities may be higher than estimated and the total population could be somewhat larger. Conversely, counts during the 1970s and 1980s suggest that this species has declined in numbers, perhaps by more than half in places. In the 1960s, it was not unusual to find colonies of more than 1000 pipistrelles, but by 1987 there were very few such colonies left.

Night hunter

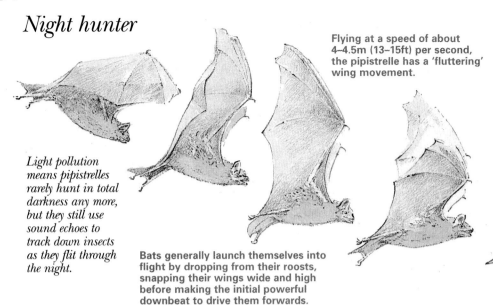

Flying at a speed of about 4–4.5m (13–15ft) per second, the pipistrelle has a 'fluttering' wing movement.

The powerful wing downbeat imparts a very fast forward motion. Small bats such as the pipistrelle flap their wings very rapidly. The distinctive whirring sound gave rise to the common country name of 'flittermouse'.

Light pollution means pipistrelles rarely hunt in total darkness any more, but they still use sound echoes to track down insects as they flit through the night.

Bats generally launch themselves into flight by dropping from their roosts, snapping their wings wide and high before making the initial powerful downbeat to drive them forwards.

To hunt their prey, pipistrelles rely entirely on echo-location – a natural form of radar based on high-frequency sound inaudible to humans.

▲ Baby pipistrelles are born hairless. This is why it is so important for the females to find a warm roost in which to give birth, especially as they do not make nests or insulate the roost in any way.

Predators on patrol

Pipistrelles emerge from their daytime roosts soon after sunset, earlier on warm nights. They feed at night by flying fast, between 2 and 20 metres (7–70ft) above the ground, in search of small flying insects. They patrol one 'beat' for a few minutes, then zoom off to another, perhaps returning to the first area later. If there are few insects to be found they are likely to give up on the area quickly and try somewhere else, but when there is plenty of food they may continue to fly around the same patch for two hours or more.

Their main prey are midges and slow-flying insects such as caddis flies, but their diet varies according to what is most abundant on the night. Warm, still nights are best and feeding intensity is greatest at dusk when the bats are hungry after their day's rest. They can catch up to 20 insects per minute and may consume several hundred in a night.

Mating and breeding

Pipistrelles live in colonial groups throughout the year and it is very rare for them to leave their home colony to go to live with another group. During the winter, mixed-sex groups are formed and the bats mate – then around Easter, the females fly off to form nursery roosts in warm places. These maternity groups average about 40 to 60 bats, but there may occasionally be several hundred present.

Females can breed in their first year, and usually produce just one baby a year. A baby bat is nearly one-third the size of its mother, equivalent to a human baby weighing about 18kg (40lb), so twins are rare. The foetus develops over a period of about six weeks, and birth usually takes place in late June or early July. Babies grow quickly, nourished by their mother's milk; she returns to the roost in the night to provide additional feeds.

By about three weeks, the babies are furry, their eyes are open, and they begin

to fly. Most of the females will have offspring by then, and adults and young all flit around the roost entrance in the evening. July is when householders are most likely to notice a nursery roost, but soon after the babies can fly, the whole group leaves of its own accord, and will not return until the following summer.

In periods of cold weather, when the mother bats have not fed well, their hungry babies may crawl out of the roost before they can fly properly. Even in good years, when the young first leave the roost they cannot fly well and often fall to the ground. Here they may be caught by cats or found by people. They can be rescued, fed, and released, but caring for bats is a painstaking job and they do not respond well to extended captivity. Sometimes bad weather coincides with the main period for raising young, and mortality rates can be very high. This is serious because the single offspring cannot be replaced for a full year. However, if the babies make it

When searching for food, pipistrelles often fly in more or less complete circles. Each bat emits more and more echo-location sounds as it closes in on its prey.

At around 75cm (30in) from its target, while still flying at high speed, the bat begins its capture tactic by tilting its tail membrane forward into a position perpendicular to its body. It is now ready to catch the prey in its mouth.

Due to their small size, pipistrelles manoeuvre extremely well in flight. However, unlike small birds of a similar size, they do not hover. This is thought to be either because they are unwilling or cannot afford to expend the energy it requires.

Bats locate insects in flight, snatch them from the air and consume them on the wing. The process takes a matter of seconds, and is completed while flying at high speed, often in pitch darkness.

RARE SPECIES

A third pipistrelle bat, previously thought to be a mere visitor from the Continent, is now known to be resident in Britain. This is Nathusius' pipistrelle (*Pipistrellus nathusii*), first recorded here in 1969. It has been found all around the country, from Kent to Shetland, and even on North Sea oil rigs. Larger than the common pipistrelle it is otherwise similar, except for small differences in its teeth. Kuhl's pipistrelle (*Pipistrellus kuhli*) has also been recorded in Britain, but only once.

Occasionally pipistrelles may catch larger insects such as moths. These cannot be dealt with in mid-air, and are usually carried to a perch to be dismembered and eaten.

WILDLIFE WATCH

Where can I see bats?

● Often the first signs of pipistrelles are their tiny droppings, around 5mm (¼in) long and scarcely thicker than a piece of black thread. Slightly crinkly and irregular in shape, unlike the oval pellets of mice, they are sometimes seen sticking to walls and windows, ejected by the bats in flight or as they leave the roost. Bats eat insects, so if the droppings are crumbled and inspected with a magnifying glass, tiny bits of insect may be seen.

● Bats are harmless, but you may not like them living at close quarters. This is not, however, an excuse for killing them or blocking the roost entrance, leaving the young inside to starve to death. All bats are legally protected, even when they are living in your own house. If they cause genuine problems, you can get advice from the Bat Conservation Trust, 15 Cloisters House, 8 Battersea Park Road, London SW8 4BG (020) 7627 2629 www.bats.org.uk

Unlike birds' sturdy feathered wings, bats' wings are almost translucent. They are made from modified hand bones, with a thin membrane of skin stretched between each 'finger'.

through the first few months, pipistrelles enjoy a fairly high survival rate, with almost two-thirds living from one year to the next.

Benefits

With large colonies that return to the same place year after year, the accumulated droppings may become a little smelly if they get damp, and in churches there may be a few droppings on the pews, but that is the worst that they do. Bats do not attack masonry or damage houses and only very rarely spread disease – in this country at least.

Such problems as they cause are trivial compared to the benefits that bats provide. Many of the insects they eat are a nuisance, such as midges and mosquitoes, or damaging to houses, such as woodworm beetles.

PROTECTED!

Like all other bats in the UK, pipistrelles are fully protected under the Wildlife and Countryside Act, 1981; roosts are also protected.

PIPISTRELLE FACT FILE

The pipistrelle bat is found throughout Great Britain. It has a tendency to congregate in colonies that take refuge in buildings such as churches, but it may also roost in residential properties.

● **NAMES**
Common name: Pipistrelle
Latin names: *Pipistrellus pipistrellus; pipistrellus pygmaeus; pipistrellus nathusii*

● **HABITAT**
Various, including parks, gardens, farmland and open woodland; prefers areas near water

● **DISTRIBUTION**
All of mainland Britain and Ireland, and some islands

● **STATUS**
Most numerous British bat – perhaps about 2 million individuals, but probably declining in numbers overall

● **SIZE**
Length, head and body, 35–45mm (1⅜–1¾in); wingspan 18–25cm (7–10in); weight 3.5–8.5g (⅛–¼oz)

● **KEY FEATURES**
Postcalcarial lobe – small bulge, about 3x2mm (⅛x¹⁄₁₆in), on outer edge of the calcar, a tiny spur that projects from the heel of the hind foot, stiffening the edge of the tail membrane

● **HABITS**
Flies at dusk until shortly before dawn, depending on weather

● **VOICE**
Main sounds are very high-pitched squeaks; used for echo-location of prey

● **FOOD**
Small insects, especially midges

● **BREEDING**
Mates in autumn, birth of single young in June–mid-July

● **NEST**
None; roosts in crevices, especially in buildings, under tiles and behind wooden cladding

● **YOUNG**
Resembles adult, capable of first flight at 3 weeks but remains in the nursery roost until 5 weeks old; can catch food for itself at 6 weeks, but mothers and young stay in contact for much longer

Curved, slightly blunt tragus (small spike of skin) pokes up from the base of the ear, about half the height of the ear itself.

Pipistrelles cling together in tight masses within their daytime roost to conserve body heat.

Fur has uniform colour from dark to orange-brown above, and usually paler colour from grey-brown to yellowish fawn below.

Recognising pigeons

From the common feral pigeon to the scarce turtle dove, as a group these birds are among the most instantly noticeable. They can be distinguished from each other by their plumage and also by their distinctive cooing.

The ubiquitous feral pigeon is descended from rock doves that became accustomed to humans through generations of selective breeding for racing, ornament and even for the table. As these birds found their way back into the wild, they adapted so successfully that interbreeding now threatens the genetic identity of the surviving wild rock dove populations. While some feral pigeons retain typical rock dove markings, others have developed a wide range of colour varieties. Apart from the rock dove and its feral cousin, there are four other native or naturalised species: the woodpigeon, stock dove, collared dove and turtle dove.

Pigeon or dove?

Despite the different names, there is no real scientific distinction between pigeons and doves, though in most cases larger birds are called pigeons. The woodpigeon and stock dove are both grey birds with similar markings but there is a difference in size – the woodpigeon is the largest pigeon in Britain. The turtle dove is a small, boldly patterned migrant and the least common native dove. It has declined due to modern agricultural methods as well as damage to its wintering grounds in Africa, and it is threatened by hunting as it flies back and forth across Europe. The collared dove, in contrast, is a successful and unmistakable buff-coloured newcomer that originated in Asia. It reached Britain in 1955 and is now common throughout the country.

Large flocks of feral pigeons are often seen in urban parks because food is plentiful.

EASY GUIDE TO SPOTTING PIGEONS AND DOVES

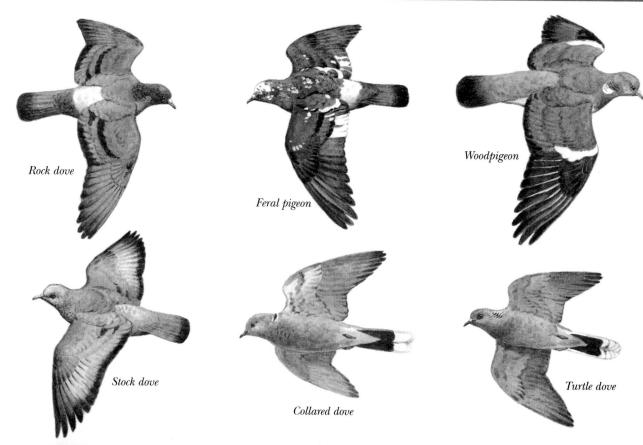

Rock dove

Feral pigeon

Woodpigeon

Stock dove

Collared dove

Turtle dove

Adult collared doves, such as this courting pair, are easy to recognise from the white-edged black neck stripe.

WHAT ARE PIGEONS AND DOVES?

● All pigeons and doves belong to a family of birds called the Columbidae. Within this family, two genera are found in Britain, *Columba* and *Streptopelia*. One or other forms the first part of their scientific names.

● Recent studies of pigeon DNA show that they are not closely related to any other bird group, despite suggestions that they may be allied to gamebirds, waders or parrots.

● Two of the best-known extinct birds were pigeons. Two centuries ago, passenger pigeons flew across North America in their tens of millions, before they were systematically destroyed – the last one died in Cincinnati Zoo in 1914. The dodo was also related to pigeons and doves – it was wiped out by human hunting in the 17th century.

HOW CAN I IDENTIFY PIGEONS AND DOVES?

● Outside the breeding season, woodpigeons and stock doves often occur in mixed flocks. To distinguish them at rest, look for the white patch on the neck of woodpigeons, but note that this is absent in immature birds. In flight, the white crescent on the woodpigeon's wings is a giveaway.

● Experienced birdwatchers identify pigeons and doves simply by their calls and songs – although the birds are often quite easy to see.

● Rock doves and feral pigeons are superficially similar to stock doves, but in flight are easily distinguished by the whitish patch on their lower backs.

● Collared doves are slightly smaller, more elongated and longer-tailed than the larger pigeons. The broad white tip to the tail is most noticeable from below.

● The turtle dove has a strong chequered pattern of black feathers on its rich orange-brown back. The white tip to its black tail is narrower but whiter than the collared dove's. It is a summer visitor, making a long journey to spend the winter in sub-Saharan Africa, and it occurs in Ireland only as a scarce passage migrant in coastal counties.

Distribution map key

 Present all year round

 Present during summer months

Not present

ROCK DOVE/FERAL PIGEON *Columba livia*

The rock dove and the familiar feral pigeon are in fact members of the same species, although they can have dramatically different markings. The wild rock dove has essentially blue-grey plumage with two conspicuous black bars across the rear half of each innerwing. The head and upper breast have a greenish purple sheen. In flight, the white rump and underwings are striking; note also the black terminal band to the tail. Some feral pigeons are indistinguishable from rock doves in appearance, but many show a range of colours from white with darker markings and pale buff to brown, reddish and almost all-black. White fantail doves are a variation on the rock dove that have been bred for their pure white plumage.

Bill narrower than feral pigeon's, with smaller white fleshy base

Two black bars across rear half of innerwing

Glossy green and purple sheen on sides of neck

Black bars on wings more extensive than on stock dove

ROCK DOVE

Tail feathers elongated compared to those of ancestors

Bold white rump and black terminal band of grey tail

Pure white plumage

WHITE FANTAIL DOVE

- ● **SIZE**
  Length 30–35cm (12–14in)
- ● **NEST**
  On ledge or in crevice; rock dove on natural sites, feral pigeon on man-made structures
- ● **BREEDING**
  2 eggs laid any time of year but mainly in spring and autumn; incubation 16–19 days

- ● **FOOD**
  Rock dove eats mainly seeds of cereal crops and wild plants; feral pigeons also eat grain and a wide range of other food
- ● **HABITAT**
  Rock dove favours wild, rocky cliffs and coasts; feral pigeon occurs mainly in urban locations

- ● **VOICE**
  Various cooing calls include distinctive crooning '*cooo-roo-cooo*' during courtship display
- ● **DISTRIBUTION**
  Rock dove restricted to remote rocky coasts of north-west Scotland and Ireland; feral pigeon wide-spread and common

General colour not dissimilar to rock dove's

Bill dark with white fleshy base

Dark band at tip of tail

FERAL PIGEON

Young pigeons, known as 'squabs', are cared for by both parents.

All traces of ancestral colours absent

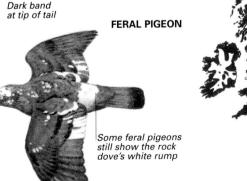

Some feral pigeons still show the rock dove's white rump

Pale wings and tail common in feral pigeon

EXTREME COLOUR VARIETY OF FERAL PIGEON

WOODPIGEON *Columba palumbus*

The largest pigeon in the British Isles, the woodpigeon's song is a familiar sound from the countryside to towns and city centres, as is the clattering sound made by its wings on takeoff, landing and in display. It gathers in large flocks outside the breeding season. The sexes are similar in appearance. Adult birds have largely blue-grey plumage, pinkish on the breast and a conspicuous white neck patch. In flight, the white crescents on the wings are striking. The bill is reddish with a yellow tip and a white fleshy base, and the legs are pink. Juvenile birds are duller than adults and lack the white neck patch and iridescent neck feathers.

Bold white crescent on each wing

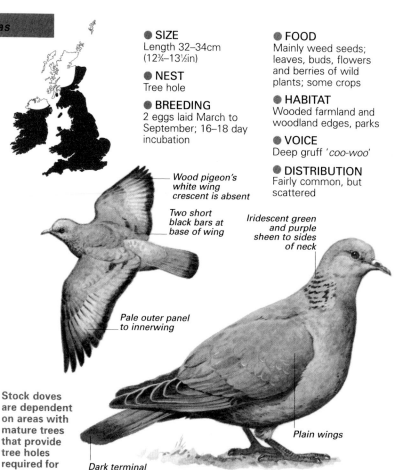

Distinctive white patch on neck between iridescent green and purple feathers

White band on wing

While preening, this woodpigeon reveals the black terminal band across its tail feathers.

● **SIZE**
Length 40–42cm (16–16½in)

● **NEST**
Flimsy collection of twigs arranged on branch or in tree fork

● **BREEDING**
1–2 eggs laid between March and October; 17-day incubation

● **FOOD**
Mainly plant roots, leaves, shoots and seeds; eats many crops

● **HABITAT**
Open farmland and edges of woodland; increasingly seen in urban habitats

● **VOICE**
Soft, husky cooing '*coo-cooo coo, coo-coo cook*'

● **DISTRIBUTION**
Widespread and generally common

STOCK DOVE *Columba oenas*

Although it often associates with woodpigeons outside the breeding season, the stock dove is noticeably smaller. Adult birds have largely blue-grey plumage with a pinkish flush to the upper breast and a green sheen to the sides of the neck. In flight, the innerwing has a pale outer panel and shows two truncated dark bars at the base. The tail has a dark terminal band. The bill is dull yellow with a narrow fleshy patch at the base, and the legs are pinkish. Juveniles are duller and browner than adults and have no iridescent neck feathers.

● **SIZE**
Length 32–34cm (12¾–13½in)

● **NEST**
Tree hole

● **BREEDING**
2 eggs laid March to September; 16–18 day incubation

● **FOOD**
Mainly weed seeds; leaves, buds, flowers and berries of wild plants; some crops

● **HABITAT**
Wooded farmland and woodland edges, parks

● **VOICE**
Deep gruff '*coo-woo*'

● **DISTRIBUTION**
Fairly common, but scattered

Stock doves are dependent on areas with mature trees that provide tree holes required for nesting.

Wood pigeon's white wing crescent is absent

Two short black bars at base of wing

Pale outer panel to innerwing

Dark terminal band to tail

Iridescent green and purple sheen to sides of neck

Plain wings

COLLARED DOVE *Streptopelia decaocto*

The small and slender collared dove is a familiar sight in most villages, towns and cities. The sexes appear similar, although males often have greyer heads than females. Adults have warm pinkish buff plumage on head, neck and underparts, with a conspicuous half-collar. The back and inner upperwings are sandy brown; in flight, they show dark wingtips separated from the innerwing by a pale grey panel. The bill is dark, the eyes ruby red and legs deep pinkish red. Juvenile birds are duller than adults with no black half-collar.

Distinctive black half-collar, edged in white

Red eyes

Plumage overall sandy-buff

Prominent pale-tipped undertail, dark at base

Uppertail dark brown with pale tips to feathers

Young collared doves are fed with 'crop milk', as are all pigeons and doves. This is a curd-like substance delivered from a storage pouch leading off the bird's gullet.

● SIZE
Length 31–33cm (12–13in)

● NEST
Flimsy platform of twigs in tree

● BREEDING
1–2 eggs laid any time from February to October; 16–19 day incubation

● FOOD
Mainly cereal grains and other seeds; berries in autumn

● HABITAT
Gardens, town parks, farmland

● VOICE
Repetitive cooing 'coo-cooo cu'

● DISTRIBUTION
Widespread

TURTLE DOVE *Streptopelia turtur*

Attractive and well-marked, the turtle dove is the smallest of the family to be found in the British Isles. Adult birds have blue-grey on the head, a warm pinkish breast and neck with a distinctive patch of black and white stripes on the side, and a pale belly. At rest, the back and upperwings are attractively marked with dark-centred bright orange-brown feathers. In flight, this feather area is bordered by blue-grey. The flight feathers are dark grey and the dark tail feathers are boldly tipped with white. The orange eye is surrounded by a red ring, the bill is dark and the legs are pinkish. Juvenile birds are duller than adults and lack the neck patch.

● SIZE
Length 26–28cm (10–11in)

● NEST
Flimsy construction of twigs in a hedge

● BREEDING
1–2 eggs laid mainly June and July; incubation up to 14 days

● FOOD
Mainly seeds of arable and grassland weeds

● HABITAT
Lowland farmland with tall, dense hedgerows

● VOICE
Soft, purring 'cooor', often repeated

● DISTRIBUTION
Increasingly scarce summer visitor

Newly arrived from their African wintering grounds, turtle doves start to engage in courtship rituals.

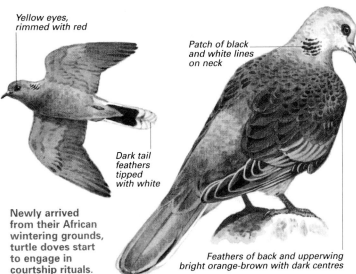

Yellow eyes, rimmed with red

Patch of black and white lines on neck

Dark tail feathers tipped with white

Feathers of back and upperwing bright orange-brown with dark centres

The mute swan

The swan most often seen in towns and cities, the graceful mute swan is easily recognised by its striking orange and black bill. Its name is deceptive, since it hisses and snorts loudly when angry.

The majestic mute swan is a common sight all year round on urban rivers and park ponds and lakes. Swans have lived alongside humans for many centuries – although they were not classified scientifically until naturalist Thomas Pennant did so in 1768 – and their lifestyle and behaviour have been well-studied. Many swans in Britain today are fitted with plastic identification rings for research purposes and relevant information is routinely collected.

In medieval times, swans were prized for their meat and, while not strictly farmed, their wings were clipped to stop them flying away, a practice known as

Mute swans are attentive parents and vigorously defend the cygnets against any intruder that ventures close to the nest.

pinioning, long since abandoned. Today, most mute swans are wild, with a few exceptions such as those on the Thames, which are royal property and are famously rounded up and inspected in the annual ceremony of 'swan-upping'.

Facts of life

Mute swans are well known for being highly territorial and mating for life, but in fact, juvenile swans that have left their parents, as well as unpaired adults, form

GREY CYGNETS

The stately, gleaming white parent swan, with its long neck and massive wings, seems to be far removed from the fluffy, grey cygnet – it is hardly surprising that the story of the ugly duckling should ring so true. The transition from juvenile grey-brown plumage to the white of the adult begins at around six or seven months and marks an important stage in the young bird's development. At this point, the father may become aggressive towards his still-not-entirely white offspring, forcing them to leave the territory and fend for themselves. In other cases, however, cygnets remain with their parents throughout the winter.

MUTE SWAN FACT FILE

The largest and heaviest British bird, the mute swan has a powerful body concealed beneath its thick feathers. Its size prevents it flying away without warning, so it is often easy to observe at close quarters.

● NAMES
Common name: mute swan
Scientific name: *Cygnus olor*

● HABITAT
Reasonably sized and fairly sheltered bodies of slow-moving fresh or brackish water, except very steep-sided reservoirs and highland lakes

● DISTRIBUTION
All over Britain and Ireland except far north

● STATUS
Around 47,000 in Britain and Ireland

● SIZE
Length from bill tip to tail tip 125–160cm (49–63in); weight, females average 10kg (22lb), males 12kg (26½lb)

● KEY FEATURES
Long curving neck; orange bill – whooper and Bewick's swans have yellow patches on bills

● HABITS
Grazes on banks, grassland or marshes

● VOICE
Various grunting and snorting sounds; loud hissing when angry; young have a high-pitched whistle; wings make a loud, throbbing noise in flight

● FOOD
Aquatic vegetation while on water; grass if feeding on dry land; also some small animals such as snails and insects

● BREEDING
Strong pair-bond formed, usually for life if breeding is successful

● NEST
Huge pile of vegetation often collected by the male but constructed by the female; usually at least two metres (6ft 8in) across and may be considerably bigger; up to 4m (13ft) if built in water

● EGGS
Round, pale, dull greenish and chalky; clutch may be as small as 3 or 4 or as many as 8; usually laid between late March and early May

● YOUNG
Cygnets remain in nest for a day or so and then take to the water; they fly at 4 or 5 months

Although not under any immediate threat, mute swans are legally protected under the Wildlife and Countryside Act, 1981.

A female mute swan carries her young cygnets on her back between slightly raised wings. The young climb up by scrambling on to their mother's lowered tail. In this illustration, the female has raised her tail high like a drawbridge to signal that, for the time being, passengers are not welcome.

Adults have an orange bill with a black base and tip. The black knob at the base is larger in the male.

Distribution map key

◼ Present all year round

☐ Not present

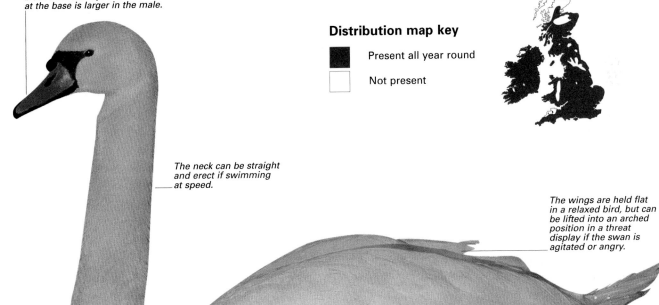

The neck can be straight and erect if swimming at speed.

The wings are held flat in a relaxed bird, but can be lifted into an arched position in a threat display if the swan is agitated or angry.

large flocks. The young usually do not mate until their third or fourth year, at which point they leave the flock.

Most successful swan pairings do continue until one partner dies, when the remaining swan, especially if it is a female, returns to the flock to find a new partner. This may also happen if a pair fail to raise young.

Mute swans in Britain rarely stray far from where they were born, even when they leave their parents to fend for themselves. In some cases, males grow up to 14 or 15kg (31–33lb) and are too heavy to fly. A handful of swans, however, travel farther afield, and a few are found as far away as France each year. Elsewhere, migrations are triggered by food shortages – continental mute swans, far shyer than their cousins, are frequent visitors to Britain – but for native mute swans, this is rarely an issue, especially in urban parks where the swans' diet of weeds and grasses is supplemented with bread and other food items left by visitors to the park. Sometimes pairs will rejoin the flock to feed over the winter months, but usually they remain in their territory.

Territorial habits

A pair of swans establishes a territory in order to raise young and its size tends to depend on the availability of food. At the Abbotsbury swannery in Dorset, for example, some nine centuries of plentiful food, coupled with selective weeding out of aggressive birds, have created a colony of swans happy to nest within a few metres of each other. The situation is similar at nearby Radipole

▼ Mute swans often form flocks during the winter months. By early spring, the birds can sometimes be seen displaying to one another in the run-up to courtship proper.

Mother and young

Young cygnets remain in the company of their parents throughout the spring and summer after hatching.

Large shallow lakes with a plentiful supply of pondweed, the staple diet of swans, are an ideal breeding territory.

Swans do not feed their young directly, but for their first few weeks, cygnets rely on their parents to pull up weeds for them from below the water, since their necks are not long enough to reach many of the submerged plants.

The 'S' shape in which the neck is held is characteristic of the mute swan and allows certain identification even at a distance.

WILD SWANS

Two other species of swan can be seen in Britain during the winter, usually in sizeable flocks. The smaller of the two – Bewick's swan – comes from the Arctic tundra of Russia. It is rather goose-like and is famously present in very large numbers on the Ouse in the Fens, and at Slimbridge. The birds can be individually identified by the shape of the yellow on their bills, as well as by ringing, and the family relationships of the flock at Slimbridge have been traced over about 30 years.

The bigger and longer-necked species is the whooper. Most of these come from breeding areas in Iceland but a few of the birds in south-east England come from northern Scandinavia, Finland and Russia.

Both species are vocal and can be identified from a long way away by their calls. A passing Bewick's flock sounds like a pack of hounds but the whooper whoops and trumpets. These sounds reflect the different anatomies of the birds' windpipes, and it was through anatomical study of these that the two species were differentiated about 170 years ago. The 18th century naturalist and artist Thomas Bewick is commemorated in the smaller bird's name.

The pulled weed is untangled in front of the young cygnets to entice them to feed.

Once one cygnet gets the idea and dips its head under the surface to catch the loose weed, the others usually follow suit.

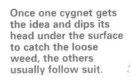

The nutritional value of pondweed is not great, so cygnets must eat large quantities in order to grow.

As time goes on and the cygnets' necks grow, they gradually learn how to fend for themselves.

Few sights are more adorable than a family of young cygnets in the first week after hatching. They retain their greyish downy plumage for several weeks.

Cygnets seldom stray far from their parents, both of whom help them to feed and guard them from potential predators.

DANGER!

Although the ban on lead fishing weights has alleviated the danger of poisoning for mute swans, old weights still remain trapped in the sediment on the bottom of ponds and lakes. Another hazard is discarded nylon fishing line – tough and non-biodegradable, it can easily become caught around the bird's head, neck or body, often with fatal results.

NESTING SWANS

Swans often build their nests on the same site every year and are loathe to move from it. In some instances footpaths or even minor roads have been closed to allow the birds to nest undisturbed.

The sites are often cunningly placed in areas that are protected from floods, but sometimes nests may be washed out by heavy rain or even high tides. If this does happen, it is worth collecting the eggs and gently putting them back in the remains of the nest if they have been out of it for an hour or two only. Heavy eggs that do not float have not been incubated for long and are most likely to hatch. Eggs that float are close to hatching, and it is likely that the chicks inside will have died as a result of being exposed to the cold temperatures.

While incubating eggs, the female swan (called a pen) is most reluctant to leave the nest. If danger threatens, the vigilant male, or cob, will see off any intruder.

The flight of the mute swan is both powerful and graceful; the wingbeats produce a loud throbbing sound.

Lake, Loch of Harray in Orkney, and in Donegal and Wexford in Ireland.

In other areas, however, single pairs of mute swans occupy small or medium-sized bodies of water. In most parts of the British Isles, a pair will need several hectares (acres) of their own, including a good stretch of shoreline if the main water areas are too deep for the birds to reach submerged vegetation. On relatively small rivers and streams, a nest may be built every 2–3km (1¼–1¾ miles).

The boundaries of the territory are well known to neighbouring swans, and the males, called cobs, guard them by posturing aggressively towards each other for long periods without coming to blows. The pair may also be aggressive towards other large water birds – particularly if they have white or pale plumage.

Under threat

Adult swans are formidable birds, able to defend themselves from nearly all predators and parents keep a careful watch over their cygnets. However, females can be vulnerable if weakened – they rarely eat while incubating their eggs, and often lose a substantial amount of their body weight. Males can occasionally injure and even kill each other in territorial fights, but most disputes are settled through posturing rather than direct attack. The major

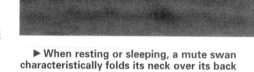

▶ When resting or sleeping, a mute swan characteristically folds its neck over its back and tucks its head and bill under its wings.

threats to swans come directly or indirectly from humans.

Theft of eggs or mindless attacks on the birds themselves are a serious problem, while other dangers are to be found in the swan's environment. Between the 1950s and 1970s, lead poisoning from discarded or lost fishing weights was a major problem, but fortunately a non-toxic material was eventually found to replace the lead. It is to be hoped that lead shot for guns will soon be phased out for the same reason.

Another problem occurs in flight. Due to their weight, swans tend to fly at full speed rather than slowly, but this means they have difficulty seeing and avoiding

approaching obstacles, especially power lines. As more and more electricity and communication cables are erected, so collisions have become more frequent although high-visibility marker balls are now often strung onto power lines where they cross known swan flight paths.

Putting on a show

Mute swans are very territorial, and defend their lake against intruders. Small waterfowl such as tufted duck and mallard may be ignored, but other swans and geese are not tolerated.

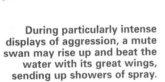

When displaying to potential mates or rivals, the male mute swan arches its neck in a swept-back 'S', fluffs out its neck feathers, and raises its wings to enhance its size and stature. This intimidating display is known as 'busking'.

During particularly intense displays of aggression, a mute swan may rise up and beat the water with its great wings, sending up showers of spray.

WILDLIFE WATCH

Where can I see swans?

● Lakes and ponds in urban parks often support swans and these city birds are frequently quite tame. Individual swans have distinct personalities, and the boldest ones often push their way to the front and may take bread from the hand. Some may get to know regular visitors who feed them, but will remain wary of new people who approach them.

● In rural areas, swans often live on small bodies of water, including village and farm ponds.

● On many sites, where food is plentiful, swans remain all year round, but in other areas that are not very productive in winter, the swans forsake their breeding territories to join the non-breeding flocks. In Scotland, swans avoid harsh winter weather by moving to the milder conditions of the coast.

Recognising aristocrat butterflies

What could be more spectacular than a profusion of brightly coloured butterflies, fluttering among nettle patches or through a woodland glade? The chances are they will be boldly marked aristocrats.

Chief among the butterflies to be found in parks and gardens in spring and summer are members of a select band referred to as the aristocrat butterflies. There are 11 species and those most often seen are the small tortoiseshell, peacock, red admiral and comma. Of the remaining seven species, the white admiral is common in specific locations in the southern half of England.

The swallowtail and the purple emperor, although resident, are both rare. The swallowtail can be found in a few fens on the Norfolk Broads, while the purple emperor is restricted to ancient woodlands in south-central England, where sallow and oak thrive side by side.

Migrant beauties

The other four species are all visitors and their numbers vary from year to year. The large tortoiseshell, which occurs mostly in south-eastern England and East Anglia, used to breed extensively in Britain, but no longer does so. Any occurrence that may be recorded is presumed to be either a migrant from northern Europe or an individual released or escaped from a butterfly farm or zoo.

The same is true of the Camberwell beauty, although there is no evidence that it has ever bred in Britain. This butterfly was first discovered in this country in 1748 in Camberwell, then a small village just outside London.

Painted ladies arrive in late spring, occasionally in large numbers, and sometimes they do breed here, but most are unlikely to survive the winter.

The ragged outline of the comma's wings provides it with superb camouflage. This insect spends much of its time sunbathing.

The monarch is a most impressive migrant but it doesn't appear every year. A few of these fabulous butterflies wander off course en route from their native North America to Mexico, and are blown across the Atlantic, some 3500 miles, by westerly gales. They arrive in the south-west in the autumn.

EASY GUIDE TO ARISTOCRAT BUTTERFLIES

WHAT ARE ARISTOCRAT BUTTERFLIES?

● The aristocrat butterflies are a group of varied species that all have medium to large wings and bold or colourful markings, or sometimes both.

● Nine species of aristocrat butterfly belong to the family Nymphalidae. These are the small and large tortoiseshells, painted lady, red admiral, peacock, comma, white admiral, purple emperor and Camberwell beauty. In comparison with their upper-wings, the underwings are mostly drab. All nymphalids have small front legs that are not used for walking.

● All aristocrat butterflies are powerful fliers. However, the purple emperor, swallowtail and white admiral seldom stray far from their chosen habitats. The comma is more of a wanderer, but does not travel very far. All the remaining species are long-distance migrants, some travelling hundreds or, in the case of the Monarch, even thousands of miles.

● The swallowtail is the only British member of the family Papilionidae. Most of its relatives are also extremely large and colourful, and many share the tail streamers that give the insect its name.

Distribution map key

 Present all year round　■ **Present during summer months**　□ **Not present**

SMALL TORTOISESHELL *Aglais urticae*

One of our most common garden butterflies, the small tortoiseshell is a widespread and attractive species with upperwings marked in orange, yellow, blue, black and white. The underwings are marbled brown, black and buff.

● **SIZE**
Wingspan about 50mm (2in)

● **FOODPLANT FOR LARVAE**
Stinging nettles

● **CHRYSALIS**
Suspended from foodplant, eaves of garden sheds, or windowsills

● **ADULT SEASON**
March–October or later; 1–2 broods

● **HABITAT**
Gardens, parks and waysides

● **DISTRIBUTION**
Widespread and fairly common throughout lowland Britain

Small tortoiseshells thrive on nectar-rich plants in gardens. The species is seen almost everywhere in Britain.

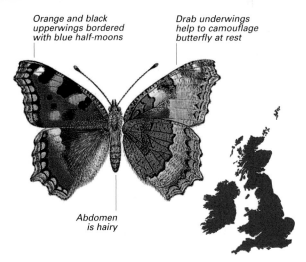

Orange and black upperwings bordered with blue half-moons

Drab underwings help to camouflage butterfly at rest

Abdomen is hairy

LARGE TORTOISESHELL *Nymphalis polychloros*

This relatively large species has orange buff upperwings, marked with black. The underwings are marbled brown. It probably no longer breeds in Britain, but migrants and escapees from captivity may be seen in southern England and East Anglia.

● **SIZE**
Wingspan about 62mm (2½in)

● **FOODPLANT FOR LARVAE**
Mainly elms

● **CHRYSALIS**
Suspended from foodplant

● **ADULT SEASON**
March–September

● **HABITAT**
Woodlands and hedgerows, parkland

● **DISTRIBUTION**
Formerly quite widespread in southern England and midlands; now probably extinct as a breeder

The demise of elm trees, the main foodplant of large tortoiseshell larvae, is partly responsible for this species' disappearance from Britain.

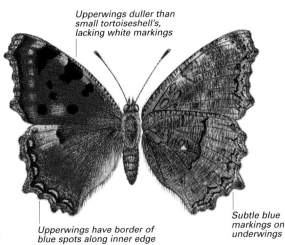

Upperwings duller than small tortoiseshell's, lacking white markings

Upperwings have border of blue spots along inner edge

Subtle blue markings on underwings

PAINTED LADY *Vanessa cardui*

Pale salmon-pink to dull orange upperwings are strikingly marked with black and white. The underside of the forewing is similar to the upperwing, but the hind wings are marbled greyish brown underneath. The painted lady is an abundant summer visitor to Britain, although numbers vary.

● **SIZE**
Wingspan about 57mm (2¼in)

● **FOODPLANT FOR LARVAE**
Mainly thistles

● **CHRYSALIS**
Suspended from foodplant

● **ADULT SEASON**
April–October

● **HABITAT**
Grassy open areas; often in gardens and parks in summer

● **DISTRIBUTION**
Most common in southern Britain; seen in smaller numbers throughout much of the British Isles in good years

Strong southerly winds in May or June often bring in large numbers of painted ladies.

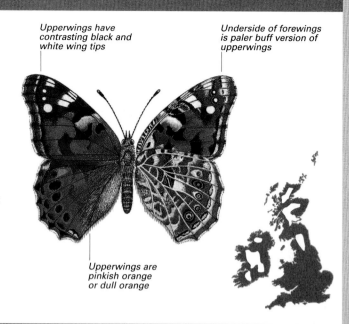

Upperwings have contrasting black and white wing tips

Underside of forewings is paler buff version of upperwings

Upperwings are pinkish orange or dull orange

RED ADMIRAL *Vanessa atalanta*

The upperwings are mainly black with bands of red, and the forewings have white patches. The pattern on the underwings is a subdued version of the upperwings. Adults feed on rotting fruit and tree sap. They also relish the nectar from ivy flowers in autumn.

● **SIZE**
Wingspan about 65mm (2⅝in)

● **FOODPLANT FOR LARVAE**
Mainly stinging nettles

● **CHRYSALIS**
Suspended from foodplant

● **ADULT SEASON**
March–early November

● **HABITAT**
Gardens, parks, hedgerows and coastal scrub

● **DISTRIBUTION**
Widespread as migrant

The indigenous red admiral population is boosted by an influx of spring migrants from the continent.

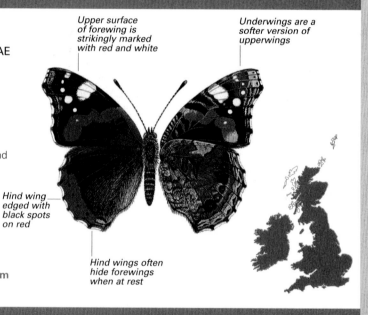

Upper surface of forewing is strikingly marked with red and white

Underwings are a softer version of upperwings

Hind wing edged with black spots on red

Hind wings often hide forewings when at rest

PEACOCK *Inachis io*

A spectacular butterfly, the peacock's wings have distinctive jagged margins. The upper surface is maroon with 'eyespots'. The underwings are marbled blackish brown and provide good camouflage when resting. The species is fond of garden flowers such as buddleia.

● **SIZE**
Wingspan about 60mm (2⅜in)

● **FOODPLANT FOR LARVAE**
Stinging nettles

● **CHRYSALIS**
Suspended from foodplant

● **ADULT SEASON**
July–September and March–May

● **HABITAT**
Gardens, parks, hedgerows and scrub

● **DISTRIBUTION**
Widespread, but absent from northern Scotland and its offshore islands

Like other aristocrat butterflies, peacocks spread their wings to bask in the sun. In late summer, in particular, they will often allow fairly close observation.

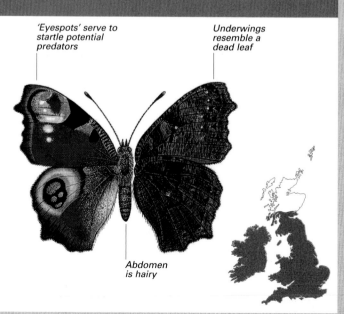

'Eyespots' serve to startle potential predators

Underwings resemble a dead leaf

Abdomen is hairy

COMMA *Polygonia c-album*

The jagged margins to the comma's wings are more pronounced than in the peacock, and may even appear tattered. The upperwings are orange-brown with brown and blackish spots. The underwings are mainly marbled blackish brown, but the hind wings show the small white comma marking that gives the species its name.

● **SIZE**
Wingspan about 48mm (2in)

● **FOODPLANT FOR LARVAE**
Mainly stinging nettles

● **CHRYSALIS**
Suspended from foodplant

● **ADULT SEASON**
First brood usually flying in July; second in late August and September, individuals of which overwinter and fly March–April

● **HABITAT**
Woodland, hedgerows, parks and mature gardens

● **DISTRIBUTION**
Most common in southern England

Commas may be mistaken for large tortoiseshells, but a close look reveals the ragged wing shape.

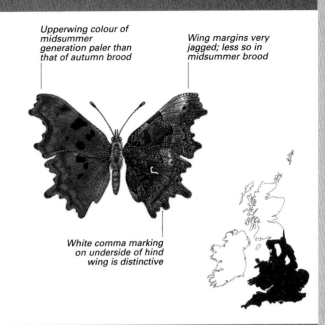

Upperwing colour of midsummer generation paler than that of autumn brood

Wing margins very jagged; less so in midsummer brood

White comma marking on underside of hind wing is distinctive

WHITE ADMIRAL *Limenitis camilla*

The white admiral is an attractive woodland butterfly with powerful and graceful flight. The upperwings are mainly black with bold white markings. The underwings are similar, but the black is replaced by orange brown.

● **SIZE**
Wingspan about 60mm (2⅜in)

● **FOODPLANT FOR LARVAE**
Honeysuckle, but usually only plants in shade

● **CHRYSALIS**
Suspended from foodplant

● **ADULT SEASON**
July–August

● **HABITAT**
Mature woodland, mainly oak, with honeysuckle and bramble

● **DISTRIBUTION**
Southern England

White admirals are on the wing for a few weeks in summer only. They have a limited habitat but are a delightful sight in the woodland clearings they favour.

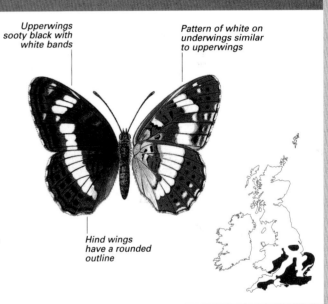

Upperwings sooty black with white bands

Pattern of white on underwings similar to upperwings

Hind wings have a rounded outline

PURPLE EMPEROR *Apatura iris*

A large butterfly with powerful flight, the purple emperor favours treetops and is therefore often difficult to see. The upperwings of the male have a purple sheen; those of the female are brown. The upperwing pattern of white markings is similar in both sexes. The underwings are duller.

● **SIZE**
Wingspan about 73mm (3in)

● **FOODPLANT FOR LARVAE**
Mainly goat willow (sallow)

● **CHRYSALIS**
Suspended from foodplant

● **ADULT SEASON**
Late June–mid-August

● **HABITAT**
Mature native deciduous woodlands, mainly oak

● **DISTRIBUTION**
Restricted to southern England where it is common in specific areas

The upperwings of the male purple emperor have a bluish purple sheen, visible at certain angles only. The female is larger than the male.

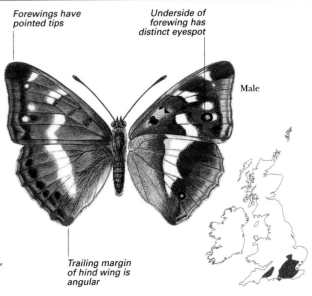

Forewings have pointed tips

Underside of forewing has distinct eyespot

Male

Trailing margin of hind wing is angular

SWALLOWTAIL *Papilio machaon*

With yellow wings that are beautifully marked with a pattern of black veins and patches, this is the largest of our native butterflies. Blue areas and a red spot adorn the hind wings, which also show a distinctive tail streamer. The species is easy to see in the right locations.

● **SIZE**
Wingspan about 95mm (3¾in)

● **FOODPLANT FOR LARVAE**
Milk-parsley

● **CHRYSALIS**
Attached to foodplant by silk girdle

● **ADULT SEASON**
Mainly May–June; second brood in summer

● **HABITAT**
Fens and marshes

● **DISTRIBUTION**
Breeding restricted to Norfolk Broads; a few migrants from Continent or released captives recorded in southern England

Nectar-rich wetland flowers, such as ragged robin, are attractive to the swallowtail.

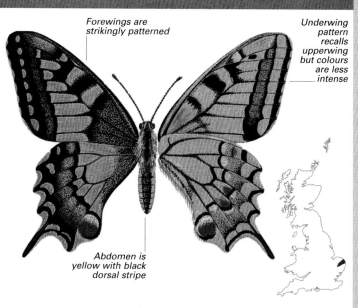

Forewings are strikingly patterned

Underwing pattern recalls upperwing but colours are less intense

Abdomen is yellow with black dorsal stripe

CAMBERWELL BEAUTY *Nymphalis antiopa*

Another butterfly with jagged-edged wings, the Camberwell beauty is a rare species. The upperwings are maroon purple with a row of blue spots behind a broad creamy white outer margin. The pattern on the underwings is similar but the maroon elements are replaced by smoky brown.

● **SIZE**
Wingspan about 64mm (2½in)

● **FOODPLANT FOR LARVAE**
Does not breed in Britain

● **ADULT SEASON**
Migrants seen July–September

● **HABITAT**
Migrants seen mainly in coastal scrub

● **DISTRIBUTION**
A rare wanderer to Britain in variable numbers, chiefly from Scandinavia; seen mainly in south-eastern England and East Anglia; not recorded every year

Camberwell beauties characteristically feed with outspread wings on ripe fruit.

Wings are broad with a jagged margin

Duller underwings afford resting insect good camouflage

Blue spots vary in size

MONARCH *Danaus plexippus*

This is the largest butterfly to be found in Britain, but it is seasonal and extremely rare. Bright orange wings with bold black veins make this species unmistakable. Its flight is powerful, but the monarch often pauses to visit flowers for nectar, folding its wings back over its body.

● **SIZE**
Wingspan about 100mm (4in)

● **FOODPLANT FOR LARVAE**
Does not breed in Britain

● **ADULT SEASON**
Mainly September

● **HABITAT**
Mainly coastal

● **DISTRIBUTION**
A rare wanderer to Britain from North America, may cross Atlantic in strong westerly winds; recorded mainly on Isles of Scilly and in western Cornwall

There is one record of a monarch butterfly breeding in Britain – at Kew Gardens in 1981 when a few individuals escaped from captivity nearby.

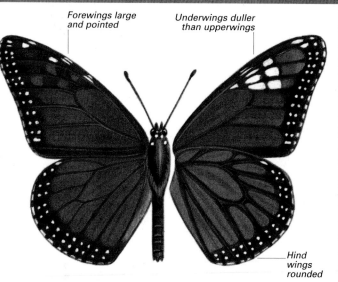

Forewings large and pointed

Underwings duller than upperwings

Hind wings rounded

The earwig

Commonly seen in parks and gardens, earwigs are to be welcomed because they feed on aphids and other pests. They may do some damage to flowers in the process, but otherwise these insects are completely harmless.

Whether strongly or gently curved, sturdy or slender, an earwig's pincers, which are situated at the rear of its body, provide useful clues to its species. Curved in males, in females they are more or less straight and may sometimes just cross at the tip.

The pincers are used for defence, and the common earwig may nip the fingers of anyone handling it, but they are not strong enough to cause any discomfort. Occasionally used for catching prey, the pincers may also be used to assist in opening and folding the wings before and after flight.

Native earwigs

Of the four British species, the most widespread is the common earwig (*Forficula auricularia*), which is around 15mm (⅝in) long and dark brown in colour, with strongly curved pincers on the male. Also widely distributed, the lesser or small earwig (*Labia minor*) is some 4–8mm (⅛–⅜in) long, with very slender pincers, and is pale brown in colour and hairy. Both these earwigs are fully winged and able to fly, although only the lesser earwig does so frequently. The forewings, often called wing cases, are tough, horny and more or less square, but the hind wings are extremely thin, with a texture similar to that of peeling skin, which gives the earwig group its Latin name of Dermaptera (skin-wings). Hind wings are normally kept elaborately folded beneath the wing cases, with just the tips protruding from the rear edge.

In the other two British earwigs – Lesne's earwig and the short-winged earwig – the hind wings are reduced to tiny flaps, incapable of generating the power needed for flight. Lesne's earwig (*Forficula lesnei*) is around 8mm (⅜in) long, is paler in colour than the common earwig, and has strongly curved pincers. The slightly larger

DID YOU KNOW?
Earwigs got their name from their disconcerting habit of occasionally crawling into human ears. In the past, when people slept on straw mattresses and even on straw-covered floors, a warm dark ear opening would have made an enticing resting place for an insect that likes narrow crevices. Fortunately, today people will rarely get so uncomfortably close to an earwig.

▲ Although essentially nocturnal, earwigs – like the common earwig above – can sometimes be found resting on flowers on sunny days.

▶ The nibbling activities of earwigs can irritate gardeners, but their role in pest control far outweighs any damage they may do.

and darker short-winged or hop-garden earwig (*Apterygida media*) has gently curved pincers about half the length of its body and slightly longer than Lesne's. The female short-winged earwig may be confused with Lesne's, but is in fact darker in colour.

Maternal care

Common earwigs mate in the autumn and overwinter in the soil, usually at the base of a plant. Soon after mating, the male may die – at best he will be banished by the female. In winter, the female lays a batch of 20–50 pearly white eggs, each just about 1mm in diameter, well hidden in her winter retreat. Larger batches containing as many as 90 eggs have occasionally been reported, but these are likely to have been supplemented with the eggs of another female. Throughout the winter, the female earwig stands guard and assiduously tends the eggs, cleaning them with her tongue and keeping them clustered together.

Early in spring, the eggs hatch to produce wingless translucent nymphs (the earwig's larval stage), all with straight, very slender pincers. The mother

▲ The female earwig keeps mould and bacteria at bay by picking up each of her eggs separately and licking it clean.

▲ Earwig young hatch early in the spring and are cared for by the female until their pincers develop to an extent where they can fend for themselves.

▼ Although the common earwig is fully winged, it is very reluctant to fly and prefers to scuttle away from danger or drop to the ground if disturbed on vegetation. The whole body is armoured by a tough and shiny outer case.

earwig regurgitates some food from her stomach for each baby, and then goes off in search of her first meal for several months. She continues to keep watch over her brood and bring them food for several weeks until they eventually wander away to fend for themselves. Meanwhile, wings and pincers are developing gradually, and the insects are mature by midsummer. If not totally exhausted by rearing so many young in one batch, the female may produce a second brood during the course of the summer.

Omnivorous scavengers

Earwigs will eat almost anything. They attack flowers and seeds, and may be found lurking in clusters of apples, chewing little holes near the stalks. Aphids and other small insects, living or dead, add animal protein to the diet. Decaying material on compost and dung heaps is a particular favourite with the lesser earwig.

Recognising deciduous parkland trees

With the advent of warmer weather, broad-leaved deciduous trees burst into life. The great majority of them are well-known native species, although several introduced and naturalised species are also often seen in parks.

Trees are usually divided into two groups: coniferous and broad leaved. Many broad-leaved species are deciduous and are abundant in woods, parklands and gardens across Britain and Ireland.

The common deciduous trees are mostly British natives.

They tend to prefer deep, rich soils, and over the years, farmers have cleared large areas in order to use this fertile ground for crops. Some woodlands are preserved for commercial reasons because deciduous trees are the timber trade's durable 'hardwoods'. But a great number of native broad-leaved trees still grow in wild or semi-natural groups and many fine examples can also be seen in parks and larger gardens.

Several species have been introduced, for their timber or ornamental value or both, and these can be found in parks, gardens and even as street plantings. Some, such as horse chestnut, have become as much a part of the British landscape as church, pub and village green.

In general, broad-leaved trees have stout trunks and broad, spreading crowns of upper branches. Apart from the holm, or evergreen, oak, they shed their leaves in the autumn, leaving resting buds protected by a tough outer layer. In the spring, the buds burst, revealing new young shoots.

Flowers and fruit

The flowers of most species are wind-pollinated catkins, produced in late winter or early spring, before the leaves appear. However, the horse chestnut and sweet chestnut (unrelated despite their names) produce conspicuous, insect-pollinated flowers after they have come into leaf. Horse chestnut flowers have distinctive whitish or pink petals; the flowers of sweet chestnut are also conspicuous but with no petals.

Male and female flowers are generally separate, whether on the same or different trees. Male flowers often take the form of elongated, hanging catkins; the female flowers may be similar or much smaller, like tiny buds.

Fertilized seeds are enclosed in an ovary that ripens to form a fruit, which is scattered in several different ways. Dry fruits are often elaborate, with adaptations in the form of broad wings to aid wind dispersal. Other trees develop larger, fleshy fruits to attract fruit or seed-eating animals to distribute them.

◀ The compound leaves of horse chestnut are among the first to appear in spring.

▼ Some broad-leaved trees, such as this ancient oak, grow to great size, their youthful height replaced by girth in old age.

EASY GUIDE TO DECIDUOUS TREES

English or pedunculate oak

Sessile or durmast oak

Turkey oak

Holm or evergreen oak

Beech

Sweet or Spanish chestnut

Horse chestnut

Ash

English or common elm

Wych elm

Hornbeam

The alder grows alongside streams and rivers. The related grey alder, introduced from Europe, is widely planted in towns.

HOW CAN I IDENTIFY BROAD-LEAVED TREES?

Common broad-leaved trees belong to just a few families, and share several important features that distinguish them from conifers.

● Generally, they have broader crowns (upper trunk and branches) than conifers.

● Leaves are mostly broad in outline, either entire, dissected (cut into) or compound (with more than one leaf attached to each stalk).

● The silhouette can be a helpful guide to identification, especially in winter.

● Shape and colour of buds is a useful way to identify trees in winter. Autumn leaf colour also varies between species.

● Study all parts of the tree – bark, leaves, flowers, catkins and fruits can all provide features for accurate identification.

● Most species can be recognised by their leaves. Only ash and sweet and horse chestnuts have compound leaves.

● Holm oak is the only evergreen broadleaf.

WILDLIFE WATCH

Where can I find broad-leaved trees?

Deciduous trees can be seen in ancient or semi-natural woodland all over the country, or in plantations, arboreta, parks, gardens and streets. You need go no further than your own street, local park or wood. Some species, however, do need special conditions:

● The best beech woods are to be seen on chalk soils in the south of England or on limestone in the Cotswolds.

● Ash often dominates woods on limestone in the north and west of Britain.

● Hornbeam occurs in well-drained woods in south-east England, especially Essex. Epping Forest is perhaps the best example.

● Sadly, large tracts of elm are a thing of the past in Britain, thanks to the ravages of Dutch Elm disease. However, fine examples are still to be found, particularly in Essex.

ENGLISH OR PEDUNCULATE OAK *Quercus robur*

The traditional native oak has a massive trunk, stout, spreading branches, a wide crown, closely fissured grey-brown bark, and egg-shaped buds.

Appropriately, the English oak's scientific name *robur* translates as 'sturdy'.

● **SIZE**
Height up to 40m (130ft)

● **LEAVES**
Shallow and blunt-lobed, with a pair of ear-like lobes at the base of the blade. Glossy and leathery on upper side, almost hairless beneath

● **FLOWERS AND FRUITS**
Male flowers in bunches of yellow-green catkins; female flowers inconspicuous; both appear with young leaves; acorns stalked

● **HABITAT AND DISTRIBUTION**
The dominant tree of parks and woodlands on deep and well-drained soils, especially limestone soils in the south and east; may hybridise with sessile oak when the two share a habitat

SESSILE OR DURMAST OAK *Quercus petraea*

Distinguished from English oak by its open crown, longer leaf stalks and lack of acorn stalks, sessile oak also prefers more acidic, wetter soils.

Britain's second native oak is also widespread in Europe and parts of Asia.

● **SIZE**
Height up to 40m (130ft)

● **LEAVES**
Shallow- and blunt-lobed; wedge-shaped without lobes at base of blade; surface leathery, a few tufts of brown hair on underside

● **FLOWERS AND FRUITS**
Male flowers in bunches of yellow-green catkins; female flowers inconspicuous; acorns more or less stalkless

● **HABITAT AND DISTRIBUTION**
Native across Britain but mainly in west, north and much of Ireland; sometimes planted for timber and ornament; related North American oaks are common introductions to parks and gardens

TURKEY OAK *Quercus cerris*

Ascending branches are characteristic of this quick-growing oak, as are long, narrow scales around the buds. Its bark is more fissured than that of native oaks.

Acorns of the Turkey oak grow inside mossy cups.

● **SIZE**
Height up to 38m (125ft)

● **LEAVES**
Quite deep, rather pointed lobes; blade runs into stalk without a pair of lobes at base. Leathery, rough on upper surface, hairy beneath

● **FLOWERS AND FRUITS**
Male flowers in bunches of yellow-green catkins; the female flowers are inconspicuous; acorns on very short stalks; cups densely covered with long, soft, bristle-like scales

● **HABITAT AND DISTRIBUTION**
A native of southern Europe planted for timber and ornament, especially in southern and eastern England and on acid soils

HOLM OR EVERGREEN OAK *Quercus ilex*

This large non-coniferous evergreen has an oak tree's typical massive trunk and branches. Its scaly grey bark flakes readily, but the wood is very hard.

Salt tolerance makes this oak a popular choice for parks and gardens near the sea.

● **SIZE**
Height up to 28m (92ft)

● **LEAVES**
Spear-shaped to elliptical, or holly-like with shallow spines; very leathery, dark green above, greyish and hairy beneath; soft and reddish when young in late spring

● **FLOWERS AND FRUITS**
Bunches of pale yellow male flowers; female flowers inconspicuous, appearing with young leaves in May; acorns tapered, pale brown, on short stalks; cups with overlapping, greyish haired scales

● **HABITAT AND DISTRIBUTION**
Native to Mediterranean countries; planted mostly in southern and central England and eastern Ireland, often near the sea for ornament or shelter; naturalised here and there in the south

BEECH *Fagus sylvatica*

A slender tree, the young beech has smooth grey bark, a loose crown, long twigs and narrow-pointed brown buds. Older trees have a huge, many-branched dome.

Beeches growing together tend to shade out other trees and shrubs.

● **SIZE**
Height up to 40m (130ft)

● **LEAVES**
Oval, untoothed, with prominent veins, glossy when mature, pale green with silky-haired margins in spring; bright orange-brown in autumn

● **FLOWERS AND FRUITS**
Male catkins tassel-shaped on long, hanging stalks; females inconspicuous; both appear with young leaves; nuts ('mast') triangular

● **HABITAT AND DISTRIBUTION**
Native to chalk and well-drained sand and gravel soils in parts of southern England; widely planted elsewhere for timber, shelter and hedging. Related southern beeches planted for ornament and timber

SWEET OR SPANISH CHESTNUT *Castanea sativa*

Scaly, brown with deep, spiral fissures distinguish the sweet chestnut's broad trunk from that of the horse chestnut.

Summers must be hot for the nuts to ripen to full size. Most are imported from Europe.

● **SIZE**
Height up to 35m (115ft)

● **LEAVES**
Up to 20cm (8in) long, spear-shaped, saw-toothed, dark green and glossy with conspicuous veins and a pointed tip

● **FLOWERS AND FRUITS**
Flowers have a sickly scent; male flowers pale cream-yellow in a long erect spike; a few green female flowers

at base; produces 1–3 glossy brown, edible nuts in a spiny case

● **HABITAT AND DISTRIBUTION**
Native to mountains of southern Europe; few genuinely wild; planted for timber and ornament on sandy or lime-poor soils, often several together; once extensively coppiced

HORSE CHESTNUT *Aesculus hippocastanum*

An unmistakable, stately tree, the horse chestnut has greyish or brown unfissured, flaky bark. The buds are sticky, unlike those of the sweet chestnut.

Horse chestnuts are popular for their decorative properties. The wood is of limited economic value.

● **SIZE**
Height up to 40m (130ft)

● **LEAVES**
Compound with 5–7 large, shallow-toothed leaflets on a long stalk that falls in autumn to leave a horseshoe-shaped scar

● **FLOWERS AND FRUITS**
Flowers pyramid-shaped, candle-like clusters; 5 petals, white with yellow-to-pink central blotch; one or more fruits (conkers) form in a spiny case

● **HABITAT AND DISTRIBUTION**
Introduced to Britain from mountainous regions of the Balkans in the 17th century, now widespread in parks and gardens, and sometimes also woodland. A pink-flowered species can be found in parks and gardens

ASH *Fraxinus excelsior*

The common ash is a tall tree with a broad crown and widely spaced branches. Its silvery-grey bark tends to fissure.

Grown mainly for its pale, tough timber, the ash has seeds that support small mammals and birds such as the bullfinch.

● **SIZE**
Height up to 37m (121ft)

● **LEAVES**
Compound; 7–15 toothed, pointed leaflets, hairless except on mid vein beneath; little autumn colour

● **FLOWERS AND FRUITS**
Flowers tiny, lacking petals; forming small, purplish clusters that appear before leaves. Fruit ('keys') have a paddle-like wing; often clustered like a bunch of keys

● **HABITAT AND DISTRIBUTION**
Widespread in woods, parks and hedgerows; less frequent in north; often found in mixed woodland with oak; may be dominant on wet, lime-rich soils; invades gaps in other types of woodland

ENGLISH OR COMMON ELM *Ulmus procera*

Devastated by the arrival of Dutch elm disease in the 1960s, which destroyed around 25 million English elms, the sight of an adult tree has become a rare one in all but a few areas of East Sussex.

● **SIZE**
Height up to 38m (125ft); often much smaller

● **LEAVES**
5–9cm (2–3½in) long, oval, double-toothed; surface rough above, paler beneath, with tufts of hairs in angles of veins; one lobe at base larger, not quite hiding short stalk

Elms are usually sown or planted although they may reproduce naturally by putting out sucker shoots.

● **FLOWERS AND FRUITS**
Small clusters of reddish flowers appear before leaves; fruit oval, reddish, with broad pale green wing

● **HABITAT AND DISTRIBUTION**
Once widespread in hedgerows, parks, gardens and woods; now survives here and there, mainly in pockets of south-east England

WYCH ELM *Ulmus glabra*

A hedgerow or woodland tree with a spreading crown and arching branches, the wych elm's smooth, grey bark becomes greyish brown and deeply furrowed with age. Unlike other elms, it does not form suckers.

● **SIZE**
Height up to 38m (125ft)

● **LEAVES**
8–16cm (3–6¼in) long, oval, double-toothed, rough on upper surface, paler and hairy beneath, with large lobe almost concealing short stalk

● **FLOWERS AND FRUITS**
Flowers reddish, in small clusters, appearing before the leaves; fruit oval with a broad pale green wing

● **HABITAT AND DISTRIBUTION**
Widespread in woodland and hedgerows, especially in north and west and in parts of Ireland; has suffered less from Dutch elm disease than other elms

Sheep and cattle are partial to all elm leaves, so where parks are used as grazing pastures, the elms often have a neatly trimmed 'browse line'.

HORNBEAM *Carpinus betulus*

A smallish tree with a rounded crown, fluted and buttressed trunk and smooth, grey bark, the hornbeam is superficially similar to beech, but with egg-shaped buds pressed close to the twigs.

● **SIZE**
Height up to 30m (98ft); often smaller

● **LEAVES**
Oval to broadly spear-shaped, superficially similar to beech but narrower and double-toothed

● **FLOWERS AND FRUITS**
Male and female flowers form hanging greenish catkins, appearing with the young leaves; fruits in hanging clusters, each tiny nut forming at base of a leafy 3-lobed bract

● **HABITAT AND DISTRIBUTION**
A tree of woodland and hedgerow growing on well-drained soils; native in south-eastern England, where it was traditionally pollarded; also planted in parks and gardens and used for ornamental hedging

The Old English name 'hornbeam' refers to the exceptionally hard wood yielded by this handsome native tree.

Daffodils and snowdrops

The appearance of a carpet of wild daffodils and snowdrops, and sometimes the closely related spring and summer snowflakes, is one of the most delightful indications that spring is in the air.

Among the most instantly recognisable of all wild flowers, daffodils and snowdrops are perennial bulbs. Together with spring and summer snowflakes, they are classified with the family Amaryllidaceae, which is itself sometimes included with the lilies and their allies in the Liliaceae. The Amaryllidaceae group is mostly found growing in warm-temperate or tropical regions, but the natural range of a few species extends northwards to Britain. Here, they are counted among the earliest and most showy of spring flowers, both in the wild and cultivated in gardens. Wild plants prefer moisture-retaining, humus-rich soils

that do not dry out too much in summer. Summer snowflake is, in fact, a native of swamp woodland, found beside rivers and flooded for much of the winter.

Daffodil lore
The Latin name for the daffodil, *Narcissus*, goes back at least to ancient Greece, where Narcissus was a legendary youth condemned by the gods to fall in love with his own reflection. The word daffodil itself may be a corruption of the ancient Greek *Asphodelus*, a wild lily.

In folklore, daffodils have often been linked with death, and with good reason since they and all their close relatives are harmful to humans. Daffodils are poisonous – especially the bulbs, which contain toxic substances called alkaloids.

Although the wild daffodil is native to this country, it has been joined in the wild by many other varieties that have strayed from parks and gardens all over the country.

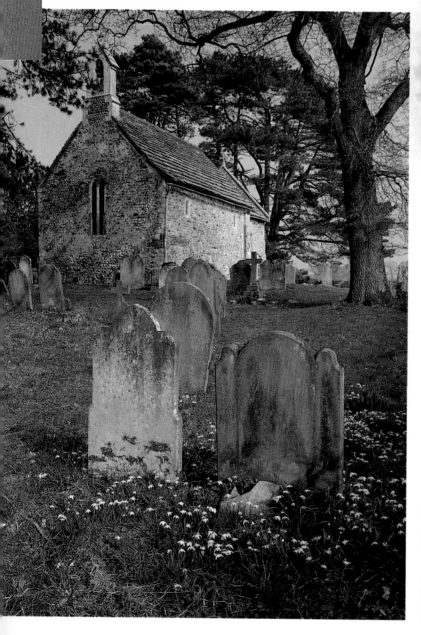

Snowdrops are frequently found in churchyards. With immaculate white flowers, they are a Christian symbol of purity.

Spring snowflake
Leucojum vernum

Snowdrop
Galanthus nivalis

**Summer snowflake
or loddon lily**
Leucojum aestivum

**Wild daffodil or
lent lily**
Narcissus pseudonarcissus
subsp. *pseudonarcissus*

DANGER!

It is not wise to pick or touch wild snowdrops, snowflakes or daffodils. These attractive flowers have poisonous sap, and the bulbs are potentially lethal if eaten. Some people may be allergic to the pollen.

People have sometimes mistaken them for onions, with unpleasant and even fatal consequences. An extract from the bulbs has been used in medicine as an emetic, and in homoeopathic treatments for respiratory illness. Juice from daffodil stems and leaves gives some people dermatitis, while others are allergic to the pollen. Farm animals avoid eating the plants.

Seeds and offsets
Daffodils and snowdrops reproduce by seed dispersal and by offsets, which simply means that the bulb produces a cluster of new bulbs.

Wild daffodils have become much less common in the last century or so, probably due to the destruction of their habitat. Human interference does not seem to have been a factor, although they were once picked in huge numbers by gypsies and others, even as recently as the 1980s. Snowdrops, in contrast, appear to be spreading.

Native or not?
The wild daffodil is almost certainly a native, but the status of the snowdrop is doubtful. Nevertheless, some botanists suspect this exotic-looking plant may indeed be a true native of south-west England.

At the same time, it is probably no coincidence that snowdrops are frequently found in association with old churches and even pre-Christian sites of pagan worship – suggesting they may have been deliberately introduced in the distant past for religious reasons. Indeed, snowdrops have become a symbol of the Christian celebration of Candlemas, the Purification of the Virgin Mary, on 2 February.

SNOWDROP AND DAFFODIL FACT FILE

● **Spring snowflake**
Leucojum vernum
Habitat and distribution
Possibly introduced – known from just two sites, in Somerset and Dorset, apart from isolated garden escapees
Size Slightly larger than snowdrop; length 15–40cm (6–15¾in)
Key features
Perennial; green leaves 1–2cm (½in) wide; bell-shaped, usually solitary flowers
Flowering time
February–March

● **Summer snowflake or loddon lily**
Leucojum aestivum
Habitat and distribution
Wet woods and marshy fields in southern England, especially the Thames and Loddon valleys, and more rarely in other parts of England, South Wales and Ireland; also sometimes elsewhere as an established garden escapee
Size 20–60cm (8–23½in) tall.
Key features
Perennial; green leaves 1–2cm (½in) wide; bell-shaped flowers in clusters of 2–5
Flowering time
April–May

● **Snowdrop**
Galanthus nivalis
Habitat and distribution
Damp woodland, beside streams, hedgerows and churchyards throughout Britain; deliberately planted or an escapee from gardens, but perhaps native to a few places in south-west England
Size 10–25cm (4–10in) tall
Key features
Perennial; narrow, grey-green leaves and solitary flowers distinguish it from summer snowflake
Flowering time
January–March

● **Wild daffodil or lent lily**
Narcissus pseudonarcissus
subsp. *pseudonarcissus*
Habitat and distribution
Widespread, in specific areas of damp but well-drained woodland, grassy fields, hedgerows and churchyards; most common in west of England and the Welsh borders; not native in Scotland
Size 15–35cm (6–13¾in) tall
Key features
Perennial; flowers solitary, the central trumpet a deeper yellow than the six surrounding petals; Spanish daffodil and other garden daffodils established in the wild are usually more robust, with uniformly yellow flowers
Flowering time
March–April

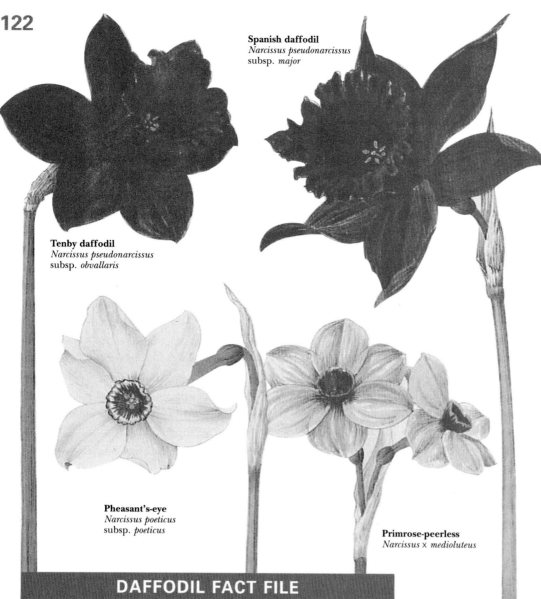

Spanish daffodil
Narcissus pseudonarcissus
subsp. *major*

Tenby daffodil
Narcissus pseudonarcissus
subsp. *obvallaris*

Pheasant's-eye
Narcissus poeticus
subsp. *poeticus*

Primrose-peerless
Narcissus x *medioluteus*

DAFFODIL FACT FILE

● **Tenby daffodil**
Narcissus pseudonarcissus
subsp. *obvallaris*
Habitat and distribution
Churchyards and roadside banks in Pembrokeshire, Carmarthenshire and Cardiganshire, probably deliberately planted or escaped from gardens; known mainly in Britain, but similar plants have recently been found in southern Spain
Size Up to 30cm (12in) tall
Key features
Perennial; similar to Spanish daffodil but generally smaller, with shorter, narrower and greyer leaves and neat flowers with flat, untwisted petals of uniform colour, unlike the wild daffodil
Flowering time
March–April

● **Spanish daffodil**
Narcissus pseudonarcissus
subsp. *major*
Habitat and distribution
Widespread; deliberately planted or an established garden escapee; a native of south-west Europe
Size 30–60cm (12–23½in) tall
Key features
Perennial; robust; uniform yellow flowers distinguish it from wild daffodil, of which it is probably a subspecies
Flowering time
February–April

● **Pheasant's-eye**
Narcissus poeticus
subsp. *poeticus*
Habitat and distribution
Established here and there where it has escaped from gardens; a native of the mountains of southern Europe
Size 20–50cm (8–20in) tall
Key features
Perennial; flowers scented, 5–7cm (2–3in) across, the six outer petals white, the very short trumpet yellow, edged with red or crimson; the latest-flowering British daffodil
Flowering time
April–May

● **Primrose-peerless**
Narcissus x *medioluteus*
Habitat and distribution
Hedgerows and waysides as an established garden escapee; perhaps a natural hybrid from southern France, but this species has long been widely grown in gardens
Size 30–60cm (12–23½in) tall
Key features
Perennial; flowers in pairs, each 3–4cm (1½in) across; the six outer petals are pale primrose-yellow or white; central yellow trumpet is short
Flowering time
March–April

Although often confused with snowdrops, summer snowflakes can be distinguished by their wider flowers and leaves. Each plant grows clusters of two to five flowers, unlike the solitary snowdrop.

Miniature wild pansies

Pansies are popular cultivated garden plants, but most varieties derive from native wild species. Search open parkland to find clusters of these beautiful flowers in colours ranging from pale cream to deep purple.

Together with violets, pansies are members of the Violaceae family – scientifically, they are all species of *Viola*. However, pansies are easily distinguished from violets by two large, lobed, leaf-like structures at the base of the leaf stalks, called stipules. Those of violets are simpler in outline, and are toothed rather than lobed. All native British violets have purple, bluish or white flowers, whereas pansy flowers can be various combinations of purple, yellow and cream.

The pansies are annuals or perennials, with compound, bluntly toothed leaves. Their showy flowers are solitary, and are carried on erect, slender stalks. Each has five petals in a regular pattern resembling a face. The two side petals point upwards in pansies, whereas in violets they radiate outwards. The central and largest petal extends into a hollow, blunt spur, and is filled with nectar to attract pollinating insects.

Pansy flowers actually hang upside down, since the flower stalk bends sharply just below the flower head. Five stamens (male, pollen-producing reproductive parts) are grouped around the ovary (female part) at the centre of the flower. Once it has been pollinated, the ovary develops into a seed capsule, which, when ripe, splits into three segments to release its seeds.

Pansies show great variation in growing habits, leaf shape, flower size and colour. They also readily cross pollinate, producing hybrid plants, so it is often difficult to tell species apart. Heartsease–mountain pansy hybrids are frequently found in Derbyshire and central Wales, where these two species co-exist.

Cultivated varieties

Gardeners have long made use of the pansy family's tendency to cross breed in order to grow a whole range of artificial varieties, known as cultivars. The colour variants of heartsease, for example, have been selected to produce a wide variety of cottage garden plants. Once introduced, these can become persistent plants of borders

Heartsease comes in a wide variety of rich colours. From spring to autumn, it swathes sandy grassland with sheets of violet and yellow.

and vegetable patches. Commercial violas, violettas and pansies derive from crosses between variants of mountain and wild pansy, together with the Asian *Viola altaica* and other species. Some cultivars can have petals up to 10cm (4in) across.

The field pansy also crosses with heartsease and with the familiar small garden pansies. The result of all this inter-breeding is an astonishing array of flower colours, including reddish purple, blue, lilac, blue and black.

WILD PANSY FACT FILE

● **Wild pansy or heartsease**
Viola tricolor
Habitat and distribution Sandy grassland and fields, especially in northern regions
Size Up to 45cm (17¾in) tall
Key features
A more or less hairless annual or short-lived perennial with a short rhizome (underground root stem) and branched stems; leaves oval to broadly spear-shaped, bluntly toothed; stipules deeply lobed, end lobe larger and slightly leaf-like; flowers violet, yellow or a mixture of both, 15–25mm (⅝–1in) across; petals longer than sepals
Flowering time April–November

● **Seaside pansy**
(*Viola tricolor* subsp. *curtisii)*
Habitat and distribution
Coastal sand dunes and inland on dry grassy heaths in East Anglia, as well as beside lakes in Northern Ireland
Size Up to 15cm (6in) tall
Key features
A short, tufted perennial, with narrower, fleshy leaves and numerous, mostly yellow flowers
Flowering time
April–September

● **Field pansy**
Viola arvensis
Habitat and distribution
The commonest British wild pansy, found on cultivated and disturbed ground, especially on light or lime-rich soils
Size Up to 40cm (15¾in) tall
Key features
Similar to heartsease but always annual; end lobe of stipules more leaf-like; flowers very variable, cream, often marked with yellow and violet, 8–20mm (⅜–¾in) across, petals slightly shorter than sepals
Flowering time March–November

● **Dwarf pansy**
Viola kitaibeliana
Habitat and distribution
Rare; sand-dune grassland in Isles of Scilly and Channel Islands
Size Up to 10cm (4in) tall
Key features
Similar to field pansy but tiny, grey-downy leaves, and stipule lobes more rounded; flowers 4–6mm (⅛–¼in), distinctly concave
Flowering time
March–June

Wild pansy or Heartsease
Viola tricolor

Dwarf pansy
Viola kitaibeliana

Field pansy
Viola arvensis

Seaside pansy
Viola tricolor
subsp. *curtisii*

Found on sand dunes around rabbit warrens, and in short dune turf, the dwarf pansy is very rare and confined to the Channel Islands and the Isles of Scilly.

Increasingly common on arable ground, the pale yellow flowers of the delightful field pansy can be seen in almost any month.

The large-flowered and long-stalked horned pansy is grown in many gardens and escapees have become naturalised in the countryside.

WILD PANSY FACT FILE

● **Mountain pansy**
Viola lutea
Habitat and distribution
Mountain grassland, especially on lime-rich soils, often where lead or other minerals are present, coastal cliffs and sand dunes; from Wales to northern Scotland, also south-western Ireland and Wicklow Mountains
Size Up to 20cm (8in) tall
Key features
Perennial; long, slender, creeping rhizome (underground root stem); stems unbranched; leaves oval to spear-shaped, hairless or sparsely downy; stipules 3 to 5-lobed, end lobe no larger than others; flowers yellow, violet, or both, lower petal darker, 20–35mm (¾–1⅜in) across, petals longer than sepals
Flowering time
April–August

● **Horned pansy**
Viola cornuta
Habitat and distribution
A native of the Pyrenees, sometimes escapes from gardens
Size Up to 30cm (12in) tall
Key features
A hairless annual or short-lived perennial; stipules deeply lobed, end lobe small, triangular; flowers violet or lilac, 20–40mm (¾–1½in) across, spur 10–15mm (½in) long, about twice as long as in other pansies
Flowering time
June–August

● Self-sown garden pansies – the complex hybrid *Viola x wittrockiana* – have a short spur and flowers with large, much-overlapped petals in a wide variety of colours

Mountain pansy
Viola lutea

Horned pansy
Viola cornuta

WILDLIFE WATCH

Where do wild pansies grow?

● Pansies are plants of open and disturbed ground, including gardens, parks, cultivated land, mountain grasslands and coastal sand dunes.

● Some, especially mountain pansy and related species, flourish on soils that have a high mineral content, even those contaminated by heavy metals.

Colourful blooms of mountain pansies speckle the short turf of hills in Scotland, Wales and northern England from April to August.

Index

Acknowledgments

Photographs: Front cover Britain On View/Stockwave, inset BC (Kim Taylor); Back cover BC (G McCarthy); 1 BC; 2-3 Woodfall Wild Images; 4(c) Ardea (J Mason), (b) BC (Kim Taylor); 5 Ardea; 6(bl) NP, (bc) NP, (br) NP (Geoff du Feu); 7(bl,bc,br) NP; 8(bl) NP (EA Janes), (bc,br) NP; 9(bl,bc,br) NP; 10-11 Mike Lane/NHPA; 12(tr) NP (Geoff du Feu), (bl) FLPA (J Tinning), 13(tl) FLPA (S Maslowski), (cr) BC (Kim Taylor), (b) NP (Paul Sterry); 14(tr) FLPA, (cl) NP (Paul Sterry), (br) BC; 15(tr) FLPA, (cl) NP (O Newman), (br) BC (Hans Reinhard); 16(all photos) BC; 17(tr) FLPA (W.Wisniewski), (c) NV (Heather Angel); 18(l) NV (Heather Angel), (br) NP (Paul Sterry); 19(tr) NP (B Burbridge), (cl) NV (Heather Angel), (br) Andrew Gagg; 20(tr) NP (Paul Sterry), (cl,br) NV (Heather Angel); 21(tr,cl) NV (Heather Angel), (b) Andrew Gagg; 22(tr) NPL, (bl) NV (Heather Angel); 23(tl) NV (Jeremy Thomas), (tr) NV, (c) NV (Heather Angel), (bc) NV (Jeremy Thomas); 24(all photos) NV (Heather Angel); 25(t,cl,cru,br) NV (Heather Angel), (cr) NV (Jeremy Thomas), (bl) BC (Hans Reinhard); 26(cr) Ardea (Stefan Maiers), (br) NP (Hugh Clark); 26-27(b) Ardea; 27(tc) Ardea (Ian Beames), (tr) NP (Robin Bush), (c) NP (WS Paton); 28(tr,cl,c) NP, (b) Ardea (JP Ferrero); 29(tr) NP (Rick Strange), (cl) OSF, (cru) NP (NA Callow), (cr) FLPA, (bl) NPL (David Kjaer); 30(l) FLPA (W.Rohdich), (c) Woodfall Wild (M.Hamblin), (br) NP (EA Janes); 31(tl) NP (Paul Sterry), (tr) NP (M Grey), (bl) NPL, (br) BC (G.McCarthy); 32(tl) NV (P Ormerod), (bl) NP (SC Bisserot), (bc) NV, (br) NV (Jason Venus); 33 NP (R Tidman); 34 GPL (JS Sira); 35(cl) Andrew Lawson, (c) GPL (Geoff Dann), (cr) Harpur Garden Library (Marcus Harpur); 36(tl) NP (TD Bonsall); 36-37(b) GPL (John Glover); 37(tl) NV (Heather Angel), (tr) Garden World Images, (cl) FLPA (W Wisniewski), (cr) BC (Colin Varnell); 38(tl) FLPA (Jeremy Early), (tr) FLPA (Robin Chittenden), (cr) FLPA (Hugh Clark), (bl) NPL (Paul Hobson) (br) NPL (Kevin Keatley); 39(br) GPL (Ellen Rooney); 40-41 BC (Kim Taylor); 42 Ardea (JP Ferrero); 43(tr) BC (Jane Burton), (b) Summertime Books; 44(t) BC (Jane Burton), 45(c) BC (R Maier); 46(tl) FLPA (D Middleton), (tr) Laurie Campbell, (cr) FLPA (Silvestris); 47(tr) NV (Jason Venus), (cl) NP (Geoff du Feu), (br) BC (R Maier); 48 Ardea (J Mason); 49(tr) FLPA (Panda/V Gianotti), (c) Ardea (Ake Lindau), (br) Aquila (M Lane); 50(tl) Aquila (M&V Lane), (cr) Aquila (M Birkenhead), (b) FLPA; 51(tr) BC (AJ Purcell), (cr) Pat Morris; 52(br) FLPA (E&D Hosking); 53(tl) BC; 54(l) Mike Read; 55(c) NP (EA Janes); 56(tl) NP (Paul Sterry), (tc) Mike Read, (c) BC (G Langsbury), (bl) NP (EA Janes), (bc) NHPA (Stephen Dalton), (bcu) BC (Kim Taylor); 57(tl, cl) NP (Paul Sterry), (bl) NP (EA Janes); 58(tl) NP (Colin Carver), (cl) NP (Paul Sterry), (bl) NP (Geoff du Feu); 59(l) BC; 60(tc & inset) FLPA (Roger Wilmhurst); 61(t) FLPA (Roger Wilmhurst); 62(tc) FLPA (David Hosking), (cr) FLPA (Roger Wilmhurst); 63(all photos) FLPA; 64(tl) Mike Read, (tc,tr,cl,c) FLPA, (cr) FLPA (Roger Wilmhurst), (bc) BC (Allan G Potts); 65(b) BC (P Hinchcliffe); 66(tr) FLPA (M Jones), (br) NPL (R Ruiz); 67(t,cu) Aquila (P Castell), (c) FLPA (M Jones), (bc) OSF (D Green); 68(tc) BC (Kim Taylor), (cu,c) FLPA (M Jones), (bc) BC (Kim Taylor); 69(tc,bc) FLPA (M Jones), (cu) Aquila (P Castell), (c) BC (Kim Taylor); 70(l) OSF (J Cheverton); 71(tl) OSF (P O'Toole), (tc) OSF (D Shale); 72(t) PW (KG Preston-Mafham), (c,br,cr) OSF; 73(t,tr) PW (KG Preston-Mafham), (bl) BC (Kim Taylor); 74(cl) NV, (b) OSF; 75(tc) Natural Image, (tr,b) NP (Paul Sterry), (c) Michael Chinery; 76(b) OSF (H Taylor); 77(tr) OSF, (cu,c,b) PW (KG Preston-Mafham); 78-80 (all photos) PW (KG Preston-Mafham); 81-85 Andrew Gagg; 86 John Cancalosi/naturepl.com; 87 NPL (A Cooper); 88(tc) FLPA (RP Lawrence); 89 FLPA (E&D Hosking); 90(b) NPL (John Cancalosi); 91(tr) FLPA (R Tidman), (cl) BC (G McCarthy), (br) FLPA (Silvestris); 92(tc) NP (R Tidman), (b) FLPA (OT Grewcock); 93 BC (Kim Taylor); 94(cl) BC (Kim Taylor), (cr) BC (Antonio Manzanares); 94(b) BC (Jane Burton); 95(t,bl) BC (Kim Taylor), (bc) Ardea (Denis Avon); 97 OSF (David Boag); 98(cl) NP; 99(cr) NP (Roger Tidman); 100(tl,bl) NP; 101(tl,bl) NP; 102 BC (John Cancalosi); 103(b) BC (John Cancalosi); 102(c) Mike Read, (bl) BC (G Gore); 105(l,r) BC; 106(all photos) BC; 107(b) BC (P van Gaalen); 108 BC (Kim Taylor); 109(cl) D. Bevan, (bl) NP (Geoff du Feu); 110(tl) NV, (cl) NP (Geoff du Feu), (bl) NP (R Bush); 111(tl) D Bevan, (cl) NP (R Bush), (bl) NP (Paul Sterry); 112(tl) NP (R Bush), (cl) NP (Geoff du Feu), (bl) NP (Roger Tidman); 113(b,r) PW (KG Preston-Mafham); 114(t) OSF (Tim Shepherd), (c) PW (KG Preston-Mafham), (b) Aquila (Abraham Cardwell); 115(b) NV (Heather Angel); 116(bl) NV (Heather Angel); 117(tl,clu) FLPA (MJ Thomas), (cl,bl) NV (Heather Angel); 118(tl,clu) NV (Heather Angel), (cl) FLPA (W Wisniewski), (bl) FLPA (J Watkins); 119(tl) NV (Heather Angel), (cl) FLPA (MJ Thomas), (bl) OSF (Geoff Kidd); 120(l) FLPA (Roger Wilmhurst), (r) FLPA (W Wisniewski); 122(br) FLPA (A Wharton); 123 FLPA (A Wharton); 124(bc,br) Andrew Gagg; 124(tl) Natural Image (Bob Gibbons), (br) Andrew Gagg.

Illustrations: 32-33 Clive Pritchard; 39 Kevin Jones Assoc; 44-62 John Ridyard; 71 Clive Pritchard; 82-85 Ian Garrard; 88-95 John Ridyard; 98-101 Robert Moreton; 103-105 John Ridyard; 109-112 Gordon Riley; 116-119 Summertime Books; 121-125 Ian Garrard.

Key to Photo Library Abbreviations: BC = Bruce Coleman Ltd, FLPA = Frank Lane Photo Agency, GPL = Garden Picture Library; NHPA = Natural History Photo Agency, NP = Nature Photographers, NPL = Nature Picture Library, NS = Natural Science Photos, NV = Heather Angel/Natural Visions, OSF = Oxford Scientific Films, PW = Premaphotos Wildlife.

Key to position abbreviations: b = bottom, bl = bottom left, blu = bottom left upper, br = bottom right, bru = bottom right upper, c = centre, cl = centre left, clu = centre left upper, cr = centre right, cru = centre right upper, l = left, r = right, sp = spread, t = top, tl = top left, tlu = top left upper, tr = top right, tru = top right upper.

Wildlife Watch
Gardens & Parks in Spring

Published by the Reader's Digest Association Limited, 2003

The Reader's Digest Association Limited
11 Westferry Circus, Canary Wharf
London E14 4HE
www.readersdigest.co.uk

Reprinted 2004

We are committed to both the quality of our products and the service we provide to our customers, so please feel free to contact us on 08705 113366, or by email at: cust_service@readersdigest.co.uk

If you have any comments about the content of our books you can contact us at: gbeditorial@readersdigest.co.uk

® Reader's Digest, The Digest and the Pegasus logo are registered trademarks of The Reader's Digest Association, Inc., of Pleasantville, New York, USA

For Reader's Digest:
Series Editor Christine Noble
Project Art Editor Jane McKenna
Editorial Assistant Katharine Swire

Reader's Digest General Books:
Editorial Director Cortina Butler
Art Director Nick Clark

This book was designed, edited and produced by Eaglemoss Publications Ltd, based on material first published as the partwork *Wildlife of Britain*

For Eaglemoss:
Editors Marion Paull, Debbie Robertson, Giles Sparrow
Art Editor Phil Gibbs
Consultant Jonathan Elphick
Publishing Manager Nina Hathway

Copyright © Eaglemoss Publications Ltd/Midsummer Books Ltd 2003

Printed and bound in Europe by Arvato Iberia

CONCEPT CODE: UK 0133/G/S
BOOK CODE: 630-002-2
ISBN: 0 276 42882 X
ORACLE CODE: 356200002H

The Illustrated Book of CAR CARE

TIGER BOOKS INTERNATIONAL
LONDON

This edition published in 1997 by
Tiger Books International PLC, London

Produced by Marshall Cavendish Books
(a division of Marshall Cavendish Partworks, Ltd)

ISBN 1–85501–589–7

British Library Cataloguing in Publication Data:
A catalogue record for this book is available from the
British Library

Printed in China

Some of this material has previously appeared in the
Marshall Cavendish Partwork Car Fix It

INTRODUCTION **6**

CONTENTS

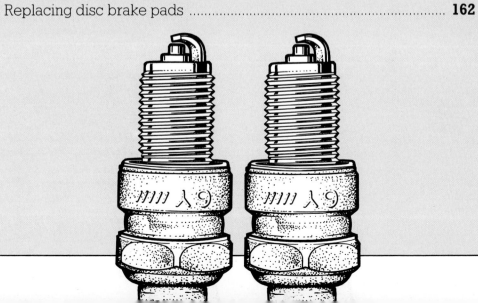

INTRODUCTION

The car is a passport to many freedoms and a very real necessity for many people. It may be the second most expensive purchase, after the home, that an individual will make, both in terms of its initial price and the continuing commitments it brings — maintenance and repair, tax and insurance cover. So, it does pay to understand your car well enough to keep it in good and safe condition at all times.

There are not many short cuts you can take in running a car. For safety and reliability, it must be serviced regularly, according to the manufacturer s standards, which state mileage and time intervals. During the first year or two, while the car is under warranty cover, it must be serviced at the manufacturer s appointed dealer to maintain the validity of the guarantee. But, after this period, you do have a choice between regular garage check-ups and taking care of the car yourself. There is the

same choice when one of the car s many parts becomes worn or eventually breaks, and it is your choice, too, whether to leave the fitting of the accessories in the hands of a specialist or to fix them yourself.

Motoring D-I-Y has many rewards. A lot of jobs can be completed very quickly and conveniently, without booking appointments and coping without the car while it is standing in the garage. Many tasks require only the minimum of basic tools and materials, and more complex jobs can easily be undertaken with readily hired tools and a trip to a parts and accessory shop. Few tasks take longer than a morning or an afternoon, but all yield the enormous satisfaction of a job well done. Most important of all, motoring D-I-Y saves money.

For nearly every car, parts are relatively cheap and widely available. At discount centres and specialist accessory shops, good

quality branded parts can be far cheaper than the prices you would pay at an appointed service garage. There are big discounts on regularly replaced items such as filters and spark plugs, and real savings to be made on materials such as oil and anti-freeze additive. And running a well-maintained car in itself saves money. An engine in tip-top tune uses less fuel, and caring for the tyres can stave off the need for replacements for thousands of miles.

Looking after your car and the safety of your family, enjoying motoring D-I-Y, and saving money is what this book is all about. *The Illustrated Book of Car Care* explains, in clear, straightforward terms, how to keep your car in good condition and how to put it right when something goes wrong. Every job is illustrated with colour photographs and diagrams to enable you to identify parts,

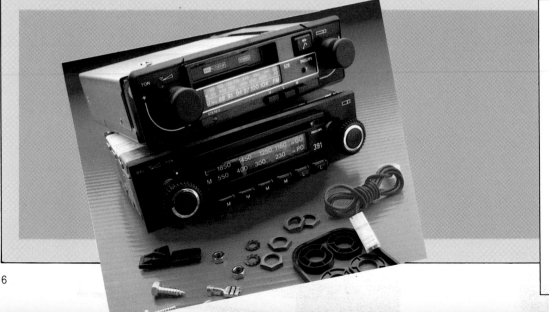

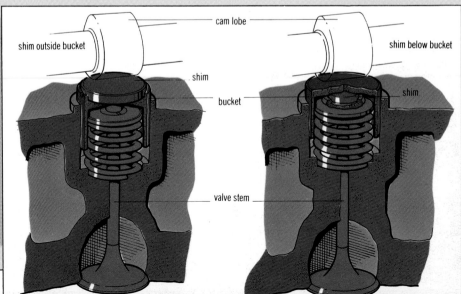

understand how they work and carry out the task safely and efficiently.

Before you begin each task, there is a summary of the work involved, a comprehensive list of the tools and materials required, and an assessment of the difficulty of the job. The instructions follow a step-by-step approach, which is logically arranged to lead you through the work in simple stages, so that you complete each job with confidence.

Throughout the text, you will find Fact Files which explain the operation of the car s various systems, both electrical and mechanical. Tip boxes help you to diagnose faults faster, give quick solutions to common problems with cars and provide handy hints on using tools. If you do not have the right tool to hand, a Tip box will often suggest a practical alternative to specialist equipment.

The book is arranged in four chapters. The first, CAR CARE, shows you how to maintain and repair bodywork, gives advice on looking after tyres, and explains how to fit useful accessories such as fog lamps, radios and child seats. Sooner or later, your car will be put through its paces by an MoT examiner. The checks you should make to ensure a pass are covered in detail. *The Illustrated Book of Car Care* provides plenty of tips and a thorough guide to buying a second-hand car.

SIMPLE SERVICING covers all the routine tasks that make up regular maintenance. From lubrication and brake adjustment to ignition and renewing oil and air filters, the basic tasks and checks are dealt with in depth. There are some taboo areas. Without complex and expensive equipment, and considerable skill, tuning carburettors and injection systems should not be tackled. But, this is a job that a tuning specialist can perform quickly and economically.

The third section, RUNNING REPAIRS, guides you through fifteen of the most common electrical and mechanical problems, giving numerous cost-saving hints, to help you keep your car on the road with the minimum of inconvenience.

WHAT S WRONG?, the final section of the book, is a storehouse of information on the irritating and elusive problems that may suddenly prevent the car starting, play havoc with the electrical system or lead to long-term faults such as uneven tyre wear. At the end of this chapter, there are tricks of the trade , which will help you shift the stubborn nuts and bolts that could otherwise thwart you in any one of the more than fifty tasks that are comprehensively covered in *The Illustrated Book of Car Care.*

Chapter ONE

CAR CARE

Fitting rear seat belts

Seat belts save lives — and not just when they are fitted in the front of the car. Take a tip from the makers and fit them to the rear too

There is very little point in having the front seat passengers of a car safely belted in if the rear seat passengers do not wear belts too. This is because if there is an accident, any unrestrained rear seat passenger is likely to be thrown forwards to hit and badly hurt anyone in the front seat.

You can transfer the belts when you change cars, or if you wish, leave them in the car when you get rid of it--rear belts may even be a selling point.

A few rear seat belt kits provide protection for every member of the family. These restraints can be suited to match most age's needs.

What this job involves
Choosing rear seat belts
Removing the rear seat cushion and backrest
Finding the mounting points
Marking and drilling new mounting points
Fitting reinforcing plates
Bolting in the belts

Related jobs in this handbook
Fitting a child's safety seat
Please see Index for page numbers

To do this job
Tools: Screwdrivers; spanner; tape measure; felt-tip pen; hammer; centre punch; utility knife; junior hacksaw; electric drill and HSS bits; round file; right-angle drill attachment
Materials: Seatbelts; mounting bracket adapters (maybe); reinforcing plates (maybe)
Time: About 3 hours if mounts provided by manufacturer; allow 1 to 2 hours extra if drilling your own mounts
Degree of difficulty: Easy, but ready-made mounts can be difficult to find

If you have the job professionally done . . .
Are the belt mountings secure? Do inertia reel belts retract smoothly and completely? Do they lock up when you brake sharply? Have the seat and trim panels been replaced properly?

Before you go straight out and buy a pair of rear seat belts, it makes sense to see exactly what is on the market to fit your car. You can do this by checking the application lists of the various seat belt manufacturers.

There are two types of belt commonly offered as after-market fittings: the static belt and the inertia reel belt (**fig 1**). The static belt is the cheaper of the two to buy, but it has the disadvantage of needing to be adjusted for each passenger. The inertia reel belt adjusts automatically to fit each person, but it is more expensive and shorter people may find them uncomfortable (they tend to rub across the neck). It is not always possible to fit inertia belts in some cars as the mounting positions are unsuitable.

Saloon cars should not pose too much of a problem as the belts can be bolted to the parcel shelf, and most seat belt manufacturers supply both inertia reel and static belts to fit. However, hatchbacks and estate cars can often present problems as neither has a parcel shelf on which to mount the reel end of an inertia belt. In these cases, check the maker's list. If inertia reel belts are not listed, they probably cannot be fitted so you will have to go for static ones. However, it is possible to buy adapter kits for some cars which allow inertia belts to be fitted. For instance, to fit inertia belts to a Ford Cortina Mk3/4 estate car, you can buy special adapter brackets from Ford which bolt between the roof and rear side panel. So, if you are in any doubt, it is best to contact the individual seat belt manufacturer who will be able to tell you what belts will fit your car, and also if you will need an adapter kit.

The final problem arises if you carry more than four passengers in the car. The only sort of belt which is available for the centre rear seat passenger is a static one—it is impractical to make the belt fasten at three points (and virtually impossible

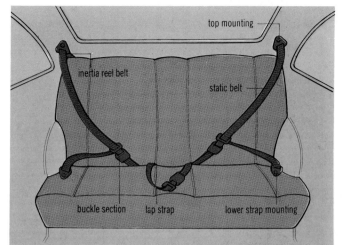

1. **Inertia reel belt, centre lap belt and static belt**

in an estate car or hatchback) so your only option here is to fit a two-point mounting lap belt.

Even here there are difficulties. If your car is rated as a four-seater by the manufacturer, even though it will take five people, there is a possibility that any built-in rear seat belt mountings will not be strong enough to take more than one seat belt each.

The lower mountings of five-seater cars are specially reinforced to cope with the load that an extra person would cause in an accident—in a four seater, the lower mountings might pull free. If you think that your car may be like this, check with your dealer.

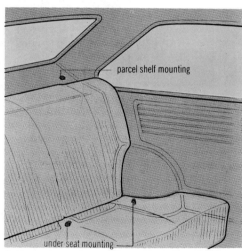

1. **Mounting points under seat and on shelf**

2. **Hatchbacks have rear pillar mounts**

Since the late 1960s, many car manufacturers have been fitting rear seat belt mounting points as standard. However, not all cars are fitted with them (and some have lower mounting points but no upper ones) as it has only been compulsory to include them since 1981 in the UK.

If you think that your car has mounting points built-in, the best way to find out where they are is to look in the handbook. If you do not have a handbook, ask your local dealer as he will know whether any mounting points are fitted.

Failing that, the best way to find any mountings is to look for them. Lower mounting points for the buckle part of the belt are nearly always under the rear seat (**fig 1**), so the first job is to remove this for clear access.

Once the seat is out, search carefully for any threaded holes (**fig 3**) which are often blanked off by plastic or rubber bungs. If you find any bungs prise them out to expose the holes and then check that they are the right ones by screwing in one of the bolts supplied with the seat belt kit. Seat belt mountings all use the same size bolts, so if your bolt fits you have

found a mounting point.

Now look for the top mounting points. In saloon cars, the upper mounting points accept the inertia reels and the best place for these is the parcel shelf. Some manufacturers provide mounting points in the rear side pillars (**fig 2**), but unless the instructions supplied with inertia seat belts say that the reels can be mounted in this position, only static belts may be attached to these points.

Hatchbacks and estate cars are even more of a problem. If your chosen belts are static ones, the upper mounting points are likely to be in the pillars behind the doors, but where inertia belts are used, you need two mounting points for each belt: one for the reel and one for the upper guide.

The reel mounting is likely to be somewhere in the load area, but often the mounting will be hidden behind a trim panel. Again, if you are in any doubt, get in touch with your dealer.

The top mounting should be on the pillar behind the door, but where there is none you will need to get an auxiliary bracket

3. **Threaded mounting hole**

4. **Marking reel position**

to take the belt guide. The seat belt manufacturer will be able to tell you if such a bracket is available.

If you find that any of the mounting points are not provided, you will have to drill holes to fit the belts. Begin by unpacking the belt, then get into the car and arrange the belt so that it fits comfortably around you without chafing on your neck; the buckle must be low

down on your thigh. Once you are happy that the belt is in the right position, get a helper to mark each mounting point using a crayon or felt-tip pen (**fig 4**).

Check that there is nothing in the way on the other side of the panel to be drilled. If there is, you must either use a different mounting point or take out the component to avoid damaging it. Then drill the holes as described in Step 3.

DRILL THE MOUNTING POINTS

When you know where you want the belts to be fixed, you can drill the bolt holes—bear in mind that you will have to fit metal reinforcing plates behind the panel, so make sure that you can put them in place.

If you are drilling through the parcel shelf of a saloon car, it is a good idea to take out the trim panel. Many cars have a foam padded panel, and if you try to drill through it, the foam could wrap itself around your drill bit and may rip a hole in the covering.

The trim panel may be held by screws or by metal or plastic clips which fit into holes in the metal parcel shelf. Alternatively, you may find that the trim is held by being sandwiched between the rear seat and the rear window panel.

If screws are used, you may need to search for them — clips are visible either from inside the car or where blind clips are used, from inside the boot.

You will usually find that the trim will not come out without removing the rear seat backrest. This is normally held at the bot-

1. Punch hole position

2. Hole after drilling

tom by screws and at the top by metal U-brackets. First find and undo the screws then pull the bottom of the backrest forward. To release it from the U-brackets simply push it upwards—it may be tight, so give it a good heave—then lift the backrest out.

Now mark the hole positions on the metal rear shelf—make sure that each hole is at least

1½in. (35mm) from the nearest cutout stamped in the metal. Stick masking tape over each of the mounting positions to prevent the drill slipping. Then use a hammer and centre punch to dent the exact drilling point in the metal (**fig 1**).

When drilling metal, it is always a good idea to drill a pilot hole which is much smaller than the final size you need. This will

3. Enlarge hole with file

4. Positioning plate

be easy to drill and will act as a guide for the much bigger drill (**fig 2**), preventing it wandering.

Using an HSS (High Speed Steel) drill bit, make a pilot hole at each mounting point. If the bit is lubricated by light oil or household detergent, a cleaner hole will result.

Now change to another HSS bit of the right size. If you do not have one big enough for the job, use the largest you have, then

ease the hole with a file (**fig 3**).

If you are drilling the parcel shelf, you may find that the rake of the rear screen prevents you from holding the drill in position. You can get round this by using a right-angle drill attachment, or by drilling from inside the boot.

The mounting points provided by car manufacturers are reinforced when the car is

made, so if you have drilled your own you cannot fix the belts in place using just the nuts and bolts provided. If you do, there is a very real chance of the bolts ripping out of the car in an accident.

Most seat belt manufacturers have kits of reinforcing plates for fitting behind the holes you have drilled (**fig 4**). Some are flat metal plates with threaded holes, while others have bolts welded to them. A few designs of plate have to be held in position by a small self-tapping screw for which you need to drill an extra hole.

When drilling the extra hole, use one of the seat belt mounting bolts to hold the plate in position, then centre punch and drill in the same way as the main hole. Fit the self-tapping screw, then take out the mounting bolt. If you have removed the parcel shelf trim, refit it and carefully cut holes in it to match the drilled holes. Use a sharp utility knife to avoid damaging the trim.

Finally, replace the seat backrest and fit the belts.

FIT A STATIC BELT

First lay out the belt and check that you have all the bolts, reinforcing plates and other parts that you need. Read the instructions to see how each mounting bolt fits through its anchor bracket. Each type of belt is slightly different, but **fig 1** shows a typical set of mountings.

Fit the buckle section of the belt first (**fig 2**), bolting it to the mounting nearest the centre of the car—if you are fitting a centre lap belt, see Step 5 as this uses the same mountings.

Now offer up the lap and diagonal section of the belt and fit its upper bracket in place first—leave the belt loose for the moment. Run the belt down to its lower mounting, making sure that it is not twisted, and bolt it

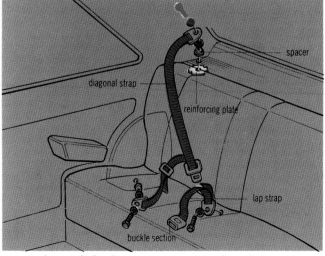

spacer

diagonal strap

reinforcing plate

lap strap

buckle section

1. Typical static belt, showing mountings and reinforcing plates

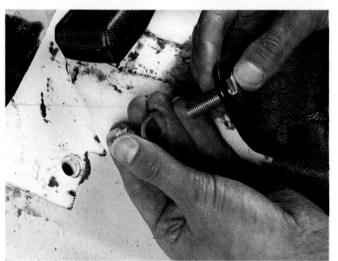

2. Fitting buckle section — get the washer and spacer in order

into position. Get a helper to check that the bolt does not foul on anything — shorten it with a hacksaw if you need to.

If the belt has reinforcing plates which are not held in place by self-tapping screws, fit them now—you will need a helper to hold the plates in place while you do up the bolts. Put the rear seat back in temporarily, then get into the car and try the seat belt—you can make small adjustments by turning the upper mounting a little until the belt is comfortable. Also check that the buckle is at the right height — adjust it as shown in the instructions.

Tighten all the bolts, then test the belt by tugging the webbing.

Inertia reel belts are more complicated to fit than static ones because the belt reels must be accurately mounted to work properly. On some cars the reel box must be mounted upright (**fig 1**), while others have the reel at an angle. Belts for parcel shelf fitting are mounted horizontally.

Bolt the buckle section into place first, using the mounting nearest the centre of the car. If you are fitting a centre belt, see Step 5 as this uses the same mounting points.

Angles

If you are having trouble setting the angle of the inertia reel or webbing, a piece of stiff card can help.

Draw a baseline on the card and use a protractor to mark off the angle you need to mount the reel at (the instructions will tell you what this angle should be). Use a rule to extend the line along the angle. Finally, complete the triangle by drawing a vertical line up from the baseline. Cut out the triangle and use it to set the reel in the right position—first time.

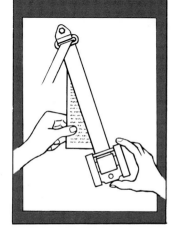

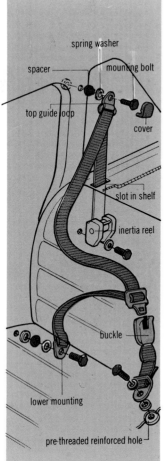

1. Typical inertia belt

2. When you have decided on reel position, bolt it in place

If you are fitting belts to a hatchback, you may find that there is a slot cut in the rear panelling to allow the belt through from a hidden reel position (**fig 3**). If you cannot find a slot, look carefully to see if it is blanked off by a plug or plastic casting. Remove the panel and take the plug out; if there is a casting instead, you must carefully cut it out. Then use a fine flat file to smooth the edges—make sure you do a good job, as any ragged edges will snag on the belt and may stop it working or even damage it. Feed the belt through the slot. Next drape the belt over the seat backrest and fit the lower bracket to the outer mounting on the car, checking that the belt is not twisted.

If your belts are the sort which mount to points on the side of the car with the inertia reels mounted low down in the boot area, the next job is to fit the upper belt guide to its mounting point. Assemble the bolt and spacer together with any washers, then screw the bolt into place. Be very careful when you do this as the bolt supplied can be quite long and there is a danger of it damaging the outer skin of the car—if you think that the bolt is too long, shorten it.

Now you can mount the reel in position. Read the instructions and make sure that you know exactly how the reel is meant to fit—you may find that you have to use an adapter kit to get the reel in the right position but the instructions should have warned you if this is so.

Fit the bolt to the reel assembly together with the spacers and washers and mount it in the car (**fig 2**). If you have to fit a mounting bracket, bolt it on to the reel first, then fit the bracket to the car, using a reinforcing plate if necessary.

Adjust the position of the reel until it is at the right angle—it may help to make up a measuring device for this (see Tip—Angles). Once you are satisfied that the belt is in the right position, do up the mounting bolt.

Remove the polystyrene packing piece from the belt and check that the webbing reels back in. Now try to pull the webbing out of the reel-pull slowly and the belt should move easily. If it does not want to come out,

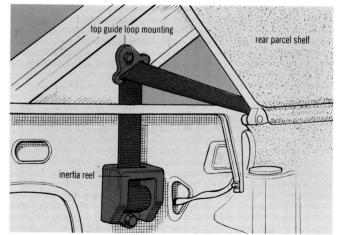

3. Some reels are in load area — belt goes through slot in shelf

the angle is wrong so check again.

To check that the belt works, pull it slowly out of the reel for about half its length and then give it a sudden jerk—the belt should lock immediately.

To test the inertia action, get a helper to sit in the back seat with the belt on. Then pick a quiet stretch of road, check that there is no-one behind you and then slam on the brakes from about 10 mph—the belt should lock instantly. If it does not, recheck the reel angle.

The centre belt uses the same two mounting points as the buckle sections of the outer two seat belts (**fig 1**), so it makes sense to fit it at the same time.

However, if your car is only a four seater and you want to fit a centre belt for an occasional fifth passenger, you are likely to run into problems because the mounting points will not have been reinforced sufficiently. If you have an accident, the extra load of the fifth passenger might pull the mountings free. If your car is like this, you need to drill two extra mounting holes as shown in Step 3 and fit reinforcing plates.

You will probably find that the standard bolts supplied with the seat belt are too short to go through both the lap belt anchor brackets and the one for the outer belts, so you may need to buy longer bolts from your dealer.

Fit each mounting bolt through the lap belt and outer belt anchor brackets, making sure that you get all the spacers and bent (wave) washers in the right place and then carefully screw the mounting bolt into place. Take care that the bolt is not too long and fouling on anything behind the panel—if it is, shorten it with a hacksaw.

Do up both mounting bolts, and when all the belts are fitted, refit the seat cushion, making sure that none of the belts are twisted. Then adjust the belts until comfortable.

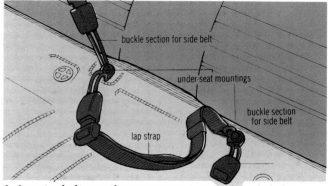

1. A centre belt uses the same mountings as the side belts

Fitting a child's safety seat

Whether you are on a family outing or just taking the kids to school, the safety of a child in a car is something you cannot afford to neglect. The answer is to fit a child's safety seat or a harness

The safest place for a child travelling by car is in the rear seat in a specially designed safety seat or harness. In this position the child is able to sit comfortably with a good view of what is going on around but without any risk of being thrown around while the car is in motion.

A restraint of this type is easy to fit — it is usually just a matter of linking the seat or harness securely to a number of anchorage points mounted on the body of the car. In many cases your car will already be provided with pre-drilled anchorage points designed specifically for this purpose.

What this job involves
Locating suitable anchorage points
Fitting a child's safety seat
Fitting a safety harness
Adjusting and testing the restraint

Related jobs in this handbook
Fitting rear seat belts
Please see Index for page numbers

To do this job
Tools: Spanners; screwdrivers; and possibly: hacksaw; tape measure; knife; paint scraper; drill; ¼ in. (6 mm) drill bit; hole saw or tank cutter
Materials: Safety seat or harness and fitting kit; straphanger (maybe)
Time: Up to two hours
Degree of difficulty: Fairly straightforward, although locating correct anchorage points may be tricky

If you have the job professionally done . . .
Does position of seat harness allow child to sit comfortably with a good view of the road? Does harness hold child securely? Are fastenings easy to operate and childproof?

The four ages of restraint

Children grow up fast and there isn't one single safety aid that can adequately restrain a child through its entire infancy. Various systems cope with the four ages of restraint; babies, toddlers, school-age and over-fives.

Latest restraints for the youngest children include rearward facing seats firmly fixed by adult front or rear safety belts. These are a more flexible alternative to a carry-cot restraint (not considered the ultimate in safety as a baby can still be thrown out of the carrycot or injure itself on parts of the cot frame).

The new recliner seats require no fixing at all in the conventional sense. They are easily removed from the car for use as a baby chair within the home or while the family is out and about.

The fitting instructions, overpage, refer to the full four-point anchorage seat for toddlers. This is still a popular choice for saloon cars. But another option is the two-point anchorage seat using only the lower adult seat belt mountings. This is a boon for estates and hatch-backs where any upper mountings might intrude on rear load space. For this type of seat follow instructions on locating lower anchorage points in Step 2.

After the age of around four (it depends on the child's physical development) there is no real need to provide a special child seat. By using a booster cushion to prevent 'submarining' of the child under the lap section of the belt, the full adult rear harnesses provide good protection (see Fitting rear seat belts — from page 39 to 42). For the final age of restraint, insist children always wear the rear seat belts.

Secondhand child restraints — take care

Because of the heavy investment by a parent in a child safety restraint system (especially if it is a Straphanger type, or a series of modular restraints that take a child up to adult belt status) some people consider buying secondhand kits. If you want a totally reliable form of protection for your child, this practice is not recommended, as it is possible that the apparatus may already have been strained in an accident.

To assess the safety system, first of all check that the restraint meets at least one of the relevant British Standards. Carrycot restraints are approved (and should have a label saying so) to BS AU186. Four-point and two-point anchorage seats should bear a label showing conformance to either BS 3254 or to the European standard ECE 44. These same standards also cover junior safety harnesses. Booster cushions are approved under BS AU185 or ECE44.

Next check whether you have a full set of instructions. Even if you don't, a reputable manufacturer should provide them for you on written request. It is also particularly important to check that you have a full set of fitting parts. The condition of the bolts should be checked for thread-stripping and all washers and spacers shown in the fitting instructions should be supplied with the seat. Every single part vitally affects seat safety.

There is an alternative to purchase of a new or secondhand child safety restraint. In many areas health groups will hire them out — check at your local ante-natal clinic.

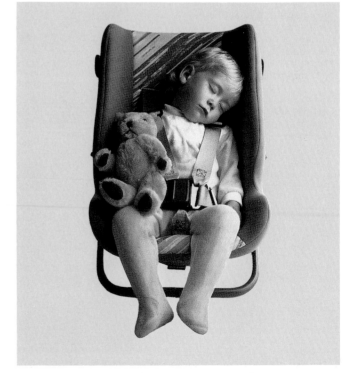

There are a variety of safety seats and harnesses on the market. The exact type you choose depends largely on personal taste but most manufacturers help by giving some indication of the age range for which each product is intended.

Safety seats (**fig 1**) are designed for children aged between six months and four years while harnesses (**fig 2**) are intended for children from four to twelve years old. But remember that children of the same age vary in size, so these figures should only be taken as a rough guide.

Also available for children in the four to twelve age group is a booster seat. This is a shaped cushion which is placed on the rear seat and raises the child to a high enough position for a conventional rear seat belt to fit.

When choosing a seat or harness make sure that it fits

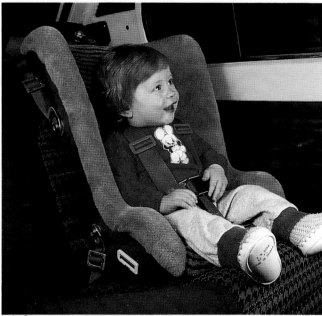

1. Safety seats are designed for smaller children

correctly so that your child will be held comfortably and securely. If possible, take the child with you when buying and try the device out by seating the child in position and fastening the belt. The buckles should fasten and release easily, but they should be completely tamperproof so that the child cannot release the catches.

If you are choosing a safety seat make sure that it has an adequate harness and check that the back and sides of the seat are well padded for comfort and protection.

The seat or harness should come complete with fixing instructions and a fitting kit. The only extra fitting you are likely to need if you have an estate or hatchback, is a straphanger — a long adjustable metal bar which fits across the car when no other anchorage points are available (see Alternative Step 3).

2. Safety harnesses are more suitable for older children

Whether you intend to fit a safety seat or harness, it must be secured firmly to the car body. The number of fixing points and their exact location vary from one model to the next, so study the manufacturer's fitting instructions carefully.

The seat or harness can be positioned either in the centre of the rear seat or slightly to one side. A central position gives the child a better view of the road and allows easier access for adults sitting in the front seats, but it can often make it difficult when you want to carry other passengers in the back of the car.

Fig 1 shows where the anchorage points are normally located — the bottom fixings in the rear of the seat pan, the top fixings in the rear parcel shelf. If you have an estate car or hatchback the top fixings are either secured to the floor of the boot or attached to a special straphanger (see Alternative Step 3).

If you are unsure of the best position for the anchorage points, place the seat or harness in position and use this as a template (see Tip — Marking guide).

To get to the bottom

anchorage points you may have to remove the rear seat. These often slide or fold forward but they may be secured by screws or press stud fixings. If so, undo these first, then lift away the seat and remove it from the car. If the back parcel shelf is covered by carpet or a piece of hardboard you will need to lift this away to expose the metal surface underneath.

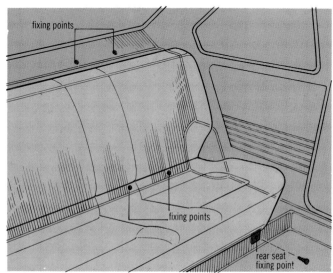

1. The usual location of the anchorage points

fixing points

fixing points

rear seat fixing point

TIP

Marking guide

It is quite possible that the location of the anchorage points will be unclear from the fitting instructions. If this happens the solution is quite straightforward. Simply place the safety seat or harness on the back seat and spread the straps out at 45°. You can then use the fixing brackets as a template to mark the position of each anchorage point accurately against a suitable point on the car body. If you do this make sure you do not position the seat too close to the door.

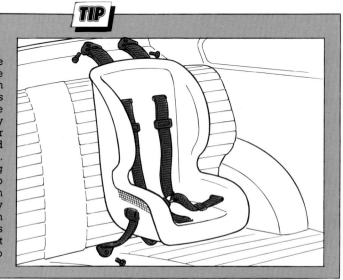

STEP 3 — DRILL ANCHORAGE POINTS

Some cars have pre-drilled anchorage points designed to fit most types of child's seat or harness. Check your car handbook if you are unsure whether these are present and where they are located. Pre-drilled anchorage points are usually sealed with protective bungs (**fig 1**), so remove these first with a screwdriver.

On the majority of cars, however, pre-drilled anchorage points are not provided, or they may be located in the wrong positions. If this is the case you will have to drill the anchorage points yourself.

Check the exact location of each anchorage point using the fitting instructions provided and

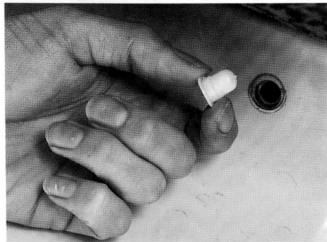

1. Removing bung from pre-drilled anchorage point

measure and mark these points in chalk on the car body.

Before you start drilling make sure that each mark is free from hidden obstructions such as electric cables or the fuel line. If any obstructions are in the way, you will need to move the mark slightly to one side. And remember that you will have to get at the back of each hole so that you can hold a reinforcing plate and bolt on the far side.

Centrepunch each mark or drill a pilot hole using a ¼ in. (6 mm) bit (**fig 2**). Then drill a hole to the correct size to take the anchorage fixings. Double thickness bodywork is common in these areas and light oiling of the drill bit is recommended.

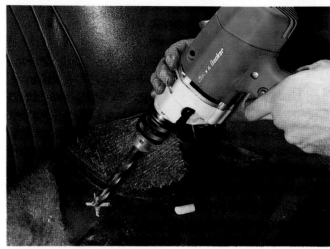

2. Drilling a new anchorage point with ¼ in. bit

ALTERNATIVE 3 — DRILL POINTS (ESTATE/HATCHBACK)

If you have an estate car or hatchback, the top anchorage points should be mounted either on the floor of the boot or attached to a special straphanger.

If you want to mount the anchorage points on the floor of the boot, remove the carpet first. This is usually held in place

by a number of press studs. Pull each stud free and remove the carpet. If the carpet is stuck to the floor you can prise it free with a broad blunt tool such as a paint scraper.

Select a suitable location for the anchorage points — the fitting instructions will tell you how far apart they should be.

The anchorage points can be located on the floor, on a wheel arch or in a wheel well but they should be arranged so that the fixing straps run at an angle of about 45° (**fig 1**). To determine this angle temporarily fix the upper straps to the mounting brackets and hang them over the back of the rear seat. Adjust

3. Securing straphanger bracket

4. Slotting the straphanger into place

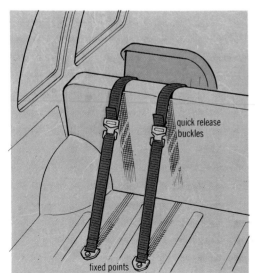

1. Fixing straps should run at 45°

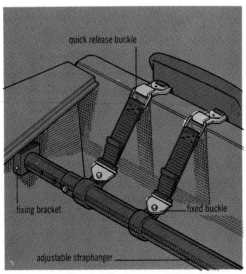

2. Use a straphanger for top mounting points

the brackets carefully until the straps form an angle of 45° with the floor, then mark the anchorage points on the floor with a piece of chalk. Drill the fixing holes as described in Step 3.

The straphanger is an adjustable metal bar which is fixed across the boot to provide a strong mounting point for the top anchorages (**fig 2**). The hanger is secured at each end by brackets which can be mounted on the side of the boot or on top of the wheel arches.

Secure the hanger according to the manufacturer's fixing instructions. Secure the brackets at either end using the

screws provided (**fig 3**). Push the bar into place so that it is held securely by the bracket at one end. Then adjust the length of the hanger by pushing the two outer sections towards the centre. Slot the other end of the hanger into place in its bracket (**fig 4**) and tighten the bar so that it sits rigidly in place.

It is difficult to adjust the fixing straps once the brackets are bolted in place so do this first. Thread the straps on to the brackets as shown in **fig 1**. Then loosen the webbing and adjust the length of each strap. The bottom fixing straps should be adjusted so that between 1 in. and 3 in. (25 mm and 75 mm) of the straps will protrude through the seat cushion. The upper fixing straps should be adjusted until the top end is about 4 in. (100 mm) behind the top edge of the seat. Once all of the straps are adjusted correctly, you can then tighten them by pulling on the free end of the webbing.

Next, bolt the brackets into position. If any of the bolts are too long they may obstruct the boot or some part of the car such as the suspension. If so, shorten the bolt by cutting it flush with the nut using a hacksaw then file off any rough edges to prevent snagging.

If your car is provided with threaded pre-drilled anchorage points simply bolt the

bracket into place as shown in **fig 2**. If you are fitting the brackets to a self-drilled anchorage point you must fit a reinforcing plate to the underside, with the right number of washers (**fig 3**). These should be supplied as part of the fitting kit; if not, they can be purchased from most car accessory shops.

Push the reinforcing plate behind the panel, insert the fixing bolt and tighten it fully with a spanner. You may need someone to help you hold the reinforcing plate in position while you insert and tighten the bolt from above.

If the upper brackets are fitted to a straphanger, simply bolt them into the holes provided in the bar.

When all of the brackets are bolted into place, replace the rear seat and make sure that all the fixing straps are in position.

Next, move the safety seat into place (**fig 4**). Attach the upper hooks to the top anchorages. Pull on the end of the strap until the seat is suspended vertically. Then attach the lower hooks to the bottom anchorage straps. Pull the free ends of the webbing and at the same time press down gently on the front edge of the seat to bring it down firmly against the car seat back.

In some cases you may have to cut slots in the boot carpet or rear parcel shelf cover to accommodate the fixing straps. If so, use a sharp knife to cut a slot at least 2 in. × 1 in. (50 mm ×

25 mm). Then thread the straps through and replace the carpet or cover (**fig 5**). If you cut a slot through a parcel shelf (**fig 6**), check that the straps are not chafing.

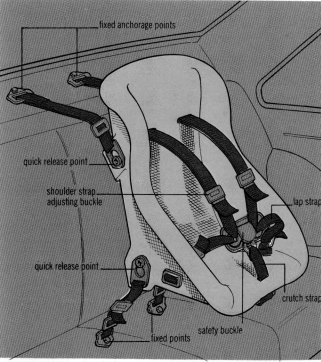

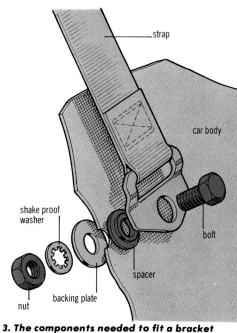

1. *Fixing straps should be adjusted with the seat in place*

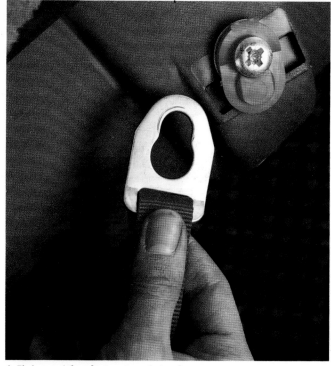

4. *Fixing quick release strap into place*

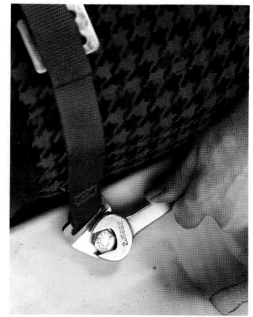

2. *Bolting the bracket into place*

3. *The components needed to fit a bracket*

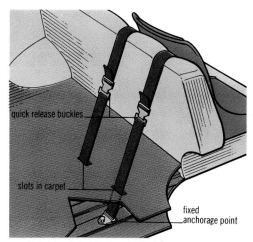

5. *You may have to cut two slots in the carpet*

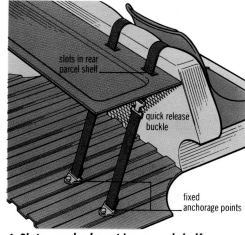

6. *Slots can also be cut in a parcel shelf*

Fitting a safety harness is done in much the same way as fitting a safety seat, although adjusting the webbing can present problems unless it is approached methodically.

Begin by bolting the bottom and lower brackets into position as described in Step 4. The straps are pre-fixed to the mounting brackets so no adjustment of length is possible. Then replace the back seat and the boot carpet or parcel shelf with the harness in position (**fig 1**).

Next hook the brackets to the top anchorage brackets. You can then set about tightening the straps by pulling on the loose ends of the webbing (**fig 2**). If you find you have long strands of excess webbing these can be secured above the parcel shelf. In hatchbacks straps must go back at 45° to the boot floor.

The hooks used to secure the harness to the top anchorage brackets can be either quick release or permanently fixed (**fig 3**). As a general rule if you are bolting direct to the boot floor you should fix the fixed variety. If you have an estate or a hatchback and are using a straphanger then the quick release type is probably best. Providing you follow the manufacturer's instructions both types are perfectly safe.

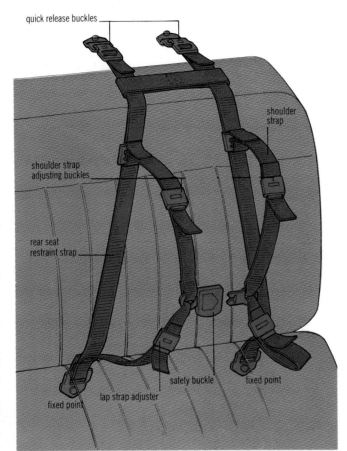

quick release buckles

shoulder strap

shoulder strap adjusting buckles

rear seat restraint strap

fixed point

lap strap adjuster

safety buckle

fixed point

1. The harness assembly installed with back seat in position

2. Tightening the straps of the harness

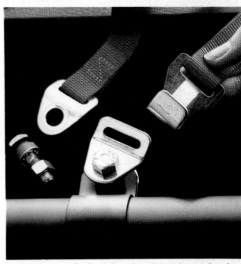

3. Permanently fixed and quick release hooks

TIP

Roll it up

Excess webbing on the parcel shelf or in the boot should be rolled up neatly and secured with a piece of plasticine, Blu-Tack or a double-sided sticky pad. Wrap a piece of tape or an elastic band around the webbing to keep it in place.

Before you take the car out on the road it is essential to test the harness. Pull on each of the fixing straps in turn. If there is any sign of movement check the anchorage points and retighten if necessary. Check also that there are no sharp obstructions which might rub on the belts. You may be able to alter the angle of the fixing brackets slightly to avoid any points of friction.

Then sit the child in position, move the straps into place and make sure that the buckle is

1. Adjusting the shoulder strap to take out any slack

fastened correctly.

Now adjust the shoulder straps at front (**fig 1**) and back so that any slack is taken up. Now tension the lap strap by pulling the loose end of the webbing on the lap adjuster (**fig 2**). The strap should be comfortably tight so that the webbing passes over the bony part of the child's hip to offer maximum support.

Many harnesses have a crutch strap. Adjust this until the lap strap is correctly positioned and held tightly so that it cannot ride up.

2. Tensioning the lap strap — it should be comfortably tight

Fitting extra driving lights

Driving lights not only make your car look better, they make night driving safer by helping you see farther

Town drivers rarely need extra lights. But in the country, additional driving lights help make those dark, dangerous roads safer. To get the best from your lights it is important to set them up correctly. For maximum performance mount them above the front bumper, and make sure they are secure and free from vibration to avoid upsetting the beam adjustment.

When to do this job
When you want more or better driving lights

What this job involves
Drilling holes in bumper or body
Fitting special brackets to mount lights on
Wiring in the lights
Aligning the lights

Related jobs in this handbook
Making electrical connections
Drilling holes in bodywork
Shifting stubborn bolts
Please see Index for page numbers

To do this job
Tools: Spanners or sockets; screwdrivers; pliers, electric drill (maybe); drill bits (maybe); rat-tail file (maybe); wire strippers
Materials: Wiring 28/.012 gauge; crimp-on connectors; insulators; Scotchloc connectors (maybe); rubber grommets; insulating tape or plastic sleeving; in-line fuse holder (maybe); 15 amp fuse; relay; switch (maybe); assorted nuts, bolts, washers and screws
Degree of difficulty: Drilling holes requires care, bumper removal often hampered by rusty nuts, but wiring not difficult with the right tools

If you have the job professionally done . . .
Do the lights work? Are the lights correctly aligned and vibration free? Do the lights go off when you dip the headlights?

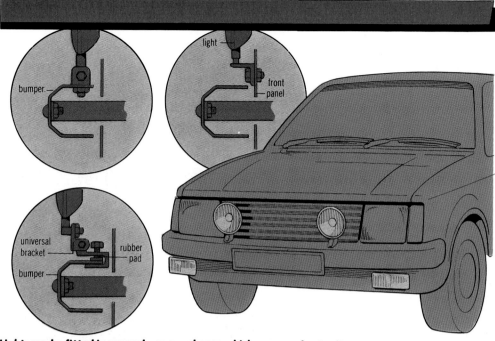

Lights can be fitted in several ways — choose whichever one best suits your car

FACT FILE

Extra lights law

Most countries have regulations covering the fitting and use of lights. Although these tend to change from time to time, any extra lights you fit must fall within the guidelines laid down by the law.

If you are in any doubt about the regulations for the type of lights you want to fit, your local authority or police force will usually help.

In the UK, for example, if you fit a pair of lights, each must be mounted at the same height and the same distance from the centreline of the car.

There are also rules covering the height at which you can fit them. If you want to use them as driving lights to supplement your headlight main beam, mount them not less than 24 in. (610 mm) and never more than 42 in. (1070 mm) from the ground. If they are set up as driving lights they must be wired so they go out when you dip the headlights.

If you fit the lights so they are permanently dipped towards the road in line with dipped beam, they can be wired independently from the headlights but must have a dashboard mounted warning light to tell you they are on. Lights wired like this can be used instead of headlights or in conjunction with them.

If you fit the lights below 24 in. (610 mm) then they can only be used in fog, falling snow or heavy rain and you need a warning light for them. Also, if your car was registered before December 1970, the distance between the inner edges of the lights must not be less than 14 in. (350 mm). Otherwise, you must fit them not more than 16 in. (400 mm) from the edge of the car, measured from the outer edge of the light.

If you fit a single light, the same fitting distances apply, and it can only be used in conjunction with the headlights — not on its own.

maximum height of light centre

42 in. (1070 mm)

24 in. (610 mm)

maximum distance 16 in. (400 mm)   minimum distance 14 in. (350 mm)

STEP 1 — DECIDE WHERE TO FIT THE LIGHTS

Before you decide where to mount your new lights, you must be aware of the regulations governing extra lights (see Fact File — Extra lights law). Some of the regulations are very specific and your choice of location is restricted.

Once you know where the law allows you to mount lights, you can look at the alternatives. To some extent your choice is influenced by the type of light and mounting bracket. But whatever type you use, the mounting points must be strong and rigid to avoid the lights vibrating.

Usually, you will have to drill holes in the bumper or a front body panel — in either case you should remove the bumper first. Alternatively, if you have 'universal' clamp mounts, you can clip the brackets directly over the bumper (see Alternative step 2). This avoids removing the bumper, but it is just as easy for thieves to take off the lights as it is to fit them.

STEP 2 — REMOVE THE BUMPER

On most cars, the front bumper is easily removed by undoing the fixing bolts and pulling it off.

Although mounting positions vary from car to car, most bumpers are bolted to the body in four places. The main bumper mounts are two thick steel brackets bolted to the inside of the bumper. They fit through two holes or slots in the front panel and bolt to the main frame of the car, usually under the wheel arches (**fig 1**) or inside the engine compartment. In some cases the fixing bolts go right through the inner wing, so you may need a helper to hold a spanner on one end of the bolt as you undo the nut.

Most bumpers are also fixed to the edge of the front panel or the wing. Sometimes this fixing is a bracket which is bolted to the bumper and the front panel (**fig 1**) — otherwise there are plastic clips which are screwed to the panel (**fig 1**) and the bumper wraparound section is a push-fit on to them. A third fixing type uses a long self-tapping screw which screws into the bumper from the inside of the front panel (**fig 1**).

Take all the bolts out — watch out as you do this as there are often earth connections attached to them (**fig 3**). Pull the bumper free — if it sticks check that it is not snagging anywhere, or that you have not missed any bolts. Now go on to Step 3 and drill holes for the lights or brackets.

When you refit the bumper make sure that you only put the bolts in finger-tight at first. Remember also to refit any earth connections. Then shift the bumper around until it is straight and tighten up all the bolts fully.

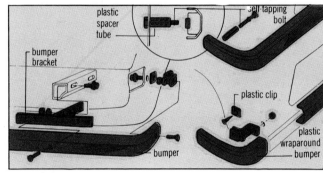
1. Bumpers are fixed to the car in several places

plastic spacer tube
self-tapping bolt
bumper bracket
plastic clip
bumper
plastic wraparound bumper

2. Undoing the mounting bolts

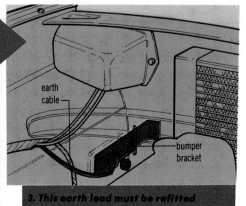
earth cable
bumper bracket
3. This earth lead must be refitted

ALTERNATIVE 2 — FIT 'UNIVERSAL' BRACKETS

The 'universal' clamp-on bracket type is designed to clip over the top or bottom lip of the bumper and is clamped in position with two bolts (**fig 1**). This type is not suitable for all bumpers — but if you sell the car and want to keep the lights you can take the brackets off without leaving ugly holes.

Use a tape measure to help you decide where to position the brackets (see Fact File — Extra lights law) — then bolt them in position. With the brackets in place all you have to do is fit the lamps (see Step 4) and wire them in (Step 6).

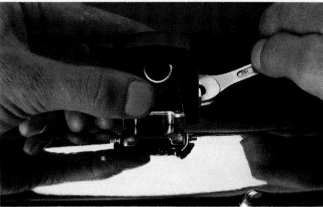
1. Bolting on the 'universal' type of bracket

STEP 3 — DRILL THE BUMPER OR BODY

With the bumper removed, you can now drill the holes for the light mounts. But you must only drill through metal sections: plastic will not be strong enough. Before you drill any car body sections, check behind them as well to make sure you will not damage anything if the drill bit goes through suddenly (see Tip — A corking tip).

The Fact File on Drilling body work (page 29) tells you all you need to know about making the holes. Once the holes are drilled fit the lights (Step 4) and then refit the bumper.

(page 29)

TIP

Cool tip

When drilling on horizontal surfaces there is an easy way to keep the drill bit fed with oil to keep it cool. Take some Plasticine and mould it into a ring around the point to be drilled. Fill it with oil and drill. The drill bit is automatically kept cool.

1. Drilling the bumper — be careful not to slip

TIP

A corking tip

All spot and driving lights are fitted with a bolt to fix them in place. Usually this is attached to some kind of movable bracket (**fig 1**) which allows you to adjust the light beam once you have done up the main fixing bolt.

In all cases, the lights simply bolt through the holes in the mounting brackets or the holes you have drilled directly in the bumper or front panel. Alignment is not critical at this stage, but at least make sure that the adjustable brackets are fitted so the lights point straight ahead.

You may find that the light mounting bolt sticks down too far and fouls something when it is in place. There are two solutions to this. You can shorten the bolt with a hacksaw, or fit spacing washers (**fig 2**) between the lamp bracket and

the bumper or panel. Do not fit too many washers — it can make the lamp unsteady, and allow it to vibrate and upset the light beam. If, when the lamp is fully tightened up, it still seems too sensitive to vibration, you can fit

a steady bar (see Step 5).

Protect the threads of the fixing bolts with a coat of zinc primer. Some lights include rubber sleeves which fit over the threads — pack these with rubber grease.

1. This bracket is adjustable

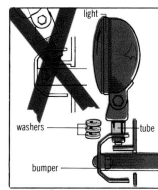

2. Use washers to raise light

To make sure the lights remain steady under all conditions and do not vibrate, you can fit them with steady bars. Some new lights have steady bars included in the kit, and to fit them you should follow the manufacturer's instructions.

However, it is easy to make your own from lengths of ¼ in. (6 mm) threaded rod (available from good ironmongers). You do not have to remove the lights to fit the bars but you must drill a hole in each casing.

First, measure the distance between the light casing and the car body or grille. Cut a piece of rod about 2 in. (50 mm) longer than your measurement. Take off the glass and reflector, then use a 5/16 in. (8 mm) drill bit to drill a hole in the back of the light casing. The position of the hole depends on where you

want to fit the other end of the bar.

Fit the rod at the other end to either the grille or the body — if you fix it to the body you must drill another hole for it. Finally, assemble the nuts and washers on the rod as shown in **fig 1** and tighten up fully after the lights have been aligned (see Step 9).

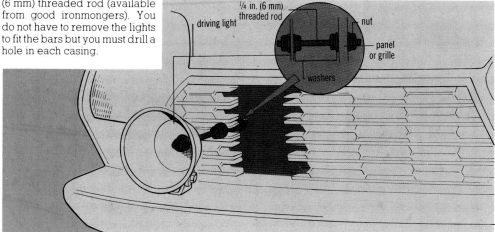

1. How to make up your own steady bar with threaded rod, washers and nuts

If your lights do not earth through the fixing bolt you will have to fit an earth wire. If you are not sure what type of lights you have take off the front and check the metal casing of the light for a terminal or wire with a spade connector on it. If there is one, the light earths through its fixing bolt. If not, the lights need a separate earth which fits to a terminal near the bulb (**fig 1**).

Take a piece of wire long enough to reach from the lamp to a nearby earth point, preferably somewhere behind the front grille, out of sight. Feed the

end of the wire through the front grille then bare about ½ in. (13 mm) of wire and twist the strands together, fold it over and twist again. Now fit a ring type terminal on to it and crimp it into place with pliers or the proper crimping tool — fit the ring terminal under the screw or bolt and tighten it up.

Push the wire through the rubber grommet on the back of the lamp (**fig 2**) and pull it into the lamp. Fit a terminal to suit the earth connection on the lamp — usually a spade connector. Crimp the coloured end of

the connector firmly and give the wire a gentle tug to check it is fixed.

Do the same with the other lamp — if the earth point is far from the lamps you may want to fit a single earth for both lamps. Fit the earth wire for one of the lamps as described above, but use heavier gauge cable. Then fit a short length of wire to the other lamp and run it through the grille. Connect the two wires together using a Scotchloc connector — both lamps now use the same earth wire and earthing point.

1. The earth wire fits to this terminal

2. Pushing the wire into the light

FACT FILE

Relays

A relay is a special type of remote control switch. It is usually fitted in the circuits of electrical accessories which draw a heavy current. This avoids running thick heavy duty cables from accessories, like lamps or the starter motor, to switches on the dashboard.

The relay is wired into the main power feed for the accessory and carries the heavy current needed while a thin wire goes from the relay to the dashboard switch.

Although relay designs differ they all work in the same way. The main difference is that some have four terminals and need

earthing when wired into circuits; others have only three terminals and earth through their metal casing. If you are in any doubt which type to choose follow the manufacturer's instructions for use and suitability.

Whatever type you fit, make sure it is up to the job — the relay rating must be higher than the current drawn by your lamps. Relays are rated in amps, so if you want to fit a pair of spotlights rated at 55 watts (4½ amps) each, then you should buy a relay capable of handling at least ten amps, preferably 12 amps to be really safe.

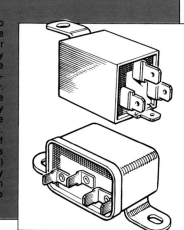

STEP 7 — FIT AND WIRE THE RELAY

Before you do any wiring to live feed wires disconnect the earth lead from the battery.

There are several types of relay you can fit — so choose one to suit your lights (see Fact File — Relays) and then find somewhere to fit it in the engine compartment. You should be able to find an existing bolt or screw — alternatively, drill holes and mount it (**fig 1**) with self tapping screws.

Now fit the wires from the relay to the lights (see **fig 3**). Feed the wires either through the grille or holes drilled in the front panel. When you have to drill, check behind the panel first and afterwards paint the bare edges of the hole with primer and topcoat to prevent rusting. Use grommets where the wires pass through the grille or holes in the body panels and make sure the connections are tightly made. Cover any joins with plastic sleeving or tape.

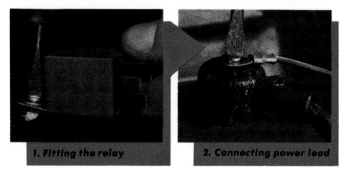

1. Fitting the relay 2. Connecting power lead

Now fit the bulbs. Take great care not to touch the glass as greasy fingermarks may cause bulb failure. If you do touch it, wipe off any marks with a rag moistened with meths.

If you have not fitted a fused relay then the live feed wire has to be fused. Fit an in-line fuseholder (**fig 3**) and secure it in the wire with crimped terminals. A 15 amp fuse should be quite adequate but check to see if the relay manufacturer

recommends a certain rating.

On many cars you can take the live feed from the accessory terminal on the fuse box. Otherwise, connect a large ring terminal to a length of wire long enough to reach the relay and fix it directly to the live terminal of the battery (**fig 2**).

Now move to the other end of the wire, fit an insulating cover and crimp on a spade terminal, and fit it to the relay.

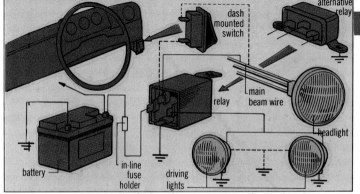

3. How to wire up the lights showing optional switch

You will now be left with one or two terminals on the relay, depending on whether your relay earths through the casing. If it does there will only be one terminal left, but if you have two terminals the relay needs to be earthed. Use a short length of wire and crimp a spade connector to one end and a ring one to the other. Earth the ring connector using the relay mounting screw if possible, and fit the other end to the relay.

You now have to decide whether you want the lights to come on with main beam all the time, or whether you want to be able to switch them off independently. If you choose the latter then you need a dashboard mounted switch (Step 8).

If you choose to have the lights on whenever you use main beam then you only need make one more connection — from the remaining relay terminal to the main beam wire. If you cannot

identify the right wire, find the wires as they come out of the back of the headlamp and follow them back into the engine compartment. Now reconnect the battery earth lead.

To find which is the main beam wire, you need a test lamp with a probe. Attach the test lamp's clip to a good earth — bare metal on the car body — then switch on main beam. Probe each of the wires in turn until the lamp lights. Now turn the headlights to dip beam — and if the lamp goes out then you are on the right wire. If not, you have found the sidelight wire — so carry on probing until you find the right one. When you are sure you have the right wire, use a Scotchloc connector to join the relay wire to the main beam wire. Turn on the headlights — the lights will come on as you select main beam. The final step is to align them (Step 9).

STEP 8 — FIT SEPARATE SWITCH

If you want the option of switching the new lights independently of your main beam headlights, you need to fit a switch in the circuit between the main beam power wire and the relay.

First choose a switch to suit your dashboard — simple two-way switches in a variety of styles are available from accessory shops (**fig 1**) — and find a convenient place for it.

If you do not have any blanked off spare switch holes in your dashboard, either drill a hole in the dash or fit the switch to a small auxiliary panel mounted below the dash (**fig 2**).

Now wire up the switch to the relay and the main beam circuit. Make sure you have enough wire, allowing for slack. The best way to get the wire into the car is to use a single piece of wire, twice as long as a single cable run, folded in two. Then you can force it through

grommets more easily.

Find a grommet near to the general area where you have mounted the switch. Push the folded end of the wire through the grommet. Get inside the car and find the cable as it emerges from the bulkhead — use a torch if necessary. Pull the cable carefully into the car while someone pushes it through from the other side.

Cut the loop of wire and bare both the ends. Fit spade connectors and insulators to the wires, then connect one end to the relay, the other to one of the switch terminals.

The terminal on the dashboard switch is wired in to the main beam wire in the same way as described in Step 7.

The lights will now light up when you turn on the headlamp main beam and go out when you go to dip beam. Now align the lights (see Step 9).

1. Switches come in all shapes

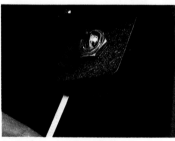

2. Fitting switch to dash

STEP 9 — ALIGN THE LIGHTS

There are several ways of aligning the lights, depending on what sort of performance you want from them.

If you want them to add extra main beam light then set them so that they illuminate the road just ahead of main beam and overlap into the main beam area.

If you want to light up the outside edges of the road, set up the lights so that they are level with the main beam and point outwards slightly.

Whatever you decide, the adjustment is done in the same way and for best results this should be done when it is dark.

Drive the car about 30 feet from a large door or a wall. Switch on main beam and mark a chalk cross at the centre of the light patch on the wall (**fig 1**). Use a coat or a piece of thick card and masking tape to cover up your headlights so that you are left with only the beams

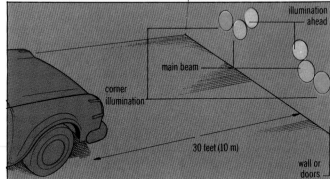

1. Use this diagram as a guide for aligning the lights

from the new lights.

See where the beam strikes. Depending on whether you have spot or driving lights, the light will either be concentrated at a point, or spread more widely but still with a distinct bright spot.

Loosen the bolt at the base of the light body and adjust the

beam until it is right. If you want the beam ahead of the headlights then aim the beam above the cross — go on adjusting until you are satisfied you have the lamps set correctly and tighten up the bolt. Make sure you do not upset the beam adjustment as you do this. Finally, tighten up the steady bar nuts (see Step 5).

Fitting towing accessories

If you want to transport a caravan or boat, or just pull a trailer, then why not fit a tow bar and increase your car's versatility?

Having a tow bar on your car opens a wide range of leisure activities; it means you can pull a caravan, a boat or a camping trailer. In addition, the availability of a wide range of trailers for hire means you can use your car to haul bulky cargoes and do away with the need to rent large vans or employ specialists.

So, fitting a tow bar to your car is a sensible move and while there are many companies who will do the job

for you, there is no reason why you should not do it yourself. The job is quite straight-forward and there are tow bar kits to cover most makes of car.

But the tow bar isn't all. To comply with the law you will have to have a lighting connec-tor (N-type) for the caravan's riding, indicator and brake lights. It's also wise to use a proper extended towing mirror and, so your car can tackle the additional suspension strain, rear suspension assisters.

What this job involves
Removing the bumper
Drilling mounting bolt holes
Assembling the tow bar
Bolting the bar into place
Fitting wing mirrors
Fitting suspension assisters

To do this job
Tools: Tape measure; centre punch; hammer; electric drill and selection of HSS bits; spanners or sockets; car ramps
Materials: Tow bar kit suitable for the car; appropriate size ball hitch
Time: Allow half a day
Degree of difficulty: Not difficult at all if manufacturer's instructions are followed and care is taken over marking bolt hole positions

If you have the job professionally done . . .
Does the ball hitch sit squarely on the car's centreline? Is the ball hitch of the right size? Is the ball hitch clear of the number plate? Are all the mounting bolts tight?

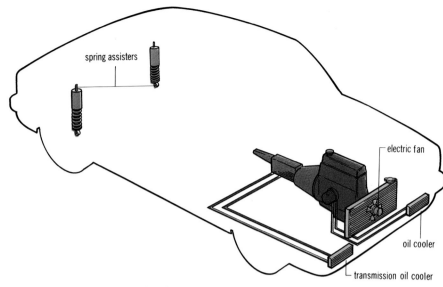

spring assisters
electric fan
oil cooler
transmission oil cooler

1. When towing you may have to fit other accessories to your car

When you first tow a trailer or caravan with your car, keep an eye on the temperature gauge, if the trailer is light and you never carry any heavy loads, you will probably not notice any difference. However, if the trailer is large and heavy, you may find that the extra load imposed on the engine will make it run hotter. If this is the case, fit a thermostatically controlled electric cooling fan

to keep the heat down. It is a good idea to fit an oil cooler as well. If your car has an automatic transmission you must fit a transmission oil cooler to prevent damage to the transmission.

When a trailer is connected to the tow bar, either pressing down or pulling upwards depending on how the trailer is loaded. If either condition is allowed to continue to

extremes it will cause severe handling difficulties and may actually make the car/trailer combination illegal.

To make sure the trailer is safe, it should be loaded so that its nose weight is within the limits specified by the car's manufacturers (check in your handbook or with the car dealer). You can measure the nose weight yourself by supporting the tow hitch at its normal towed height with a block of wood placed on a pair of bathroom scales (**fig 2**). If the nose weight is more or less than the specified limits rearrange the trailer load until it is correct.

Another point to remember is to ensure that the load is packed securely and strapped down to stop it moving around.

One final point to consider is that of insurance. It is unlikely that your existing policy will cover towing indeed it may specifically exclude it. So contact your brokers or insurers immediately and have the cover amended as necessary.

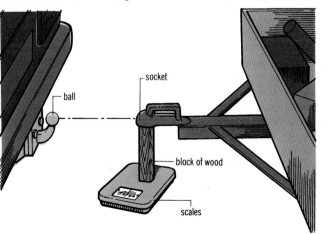

socket
ball
block of wood
scales

2. Use a block of wood and some scales to measure nose weight

One important point to consider before you buy a tow bar is whether your car is in a fit state to accept one. Early cars with their separate chassis · presented few problems in this respect, since the bar could be bolted directly to the strong chassis side members which were quite capable of taking the added load of the trailer (**fig 1**).

However, modern cars no longer have a separate chassis, relying instead for their strength on their box-like structures made up from a number of thin metal sheets welded together. This form of construction means that a tow bar must be designed with fixing points that spread the load evenly over the rear portion of the car's floorpan (**fig 2**). If there is any heavy rust across the back of the floorpan you should have this repaired before you fit the tow bar. Otherwise the added load of a trailer or caravan might well pull the bar mountings free with potentially fatal results.

You may be able to obtain a tow bar from a local accessory shop but owing to the large range of bars needed to cater for most common cars, it is more likely that you will have to go to a specialist who fits tow bars or to a trailer or caravan dealer.

Always specify the make, exact model and year of your car when you buy a tow bar, this is essential since each tow bar assembly will be designed to fit a specific car. For the same reason, do not be tempted to adapt a secondhand unit from any car other than the exact make and type of your own.

Tow bars for DIY installation usually come as a kit of bolt-together parts — **figs 3** and **4** show two typical kits, **fig 3** is for an older saloon, **fig 4** is for a large executive car. Sometimes one-piece units can be found —

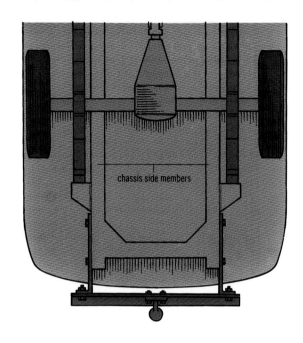

1. On older cars a tow bar is fixed to chassis side members

chassis side members

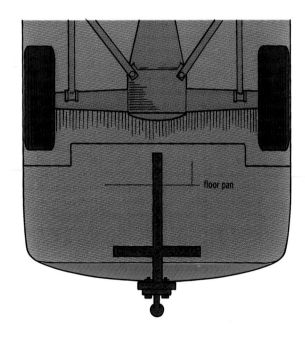

floor pan

2. On modern cars the bar is fixed to the floorpan

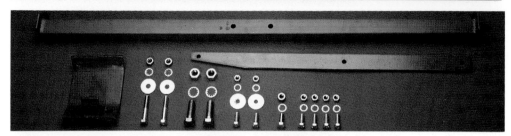

3. This tow bar kit comes complete with crossbar, support bracket and drop plate

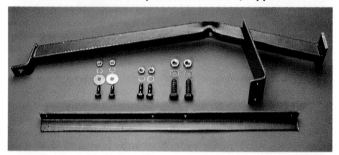

4. With this kit the support bracket and drop plate are in one piece

5. Both types of towing ball come with protective coverings

again, it depends on the car they are for. Some may simply be attached by means of the bumper iron bolts or nuts whereas others will need mounting holes drilled to the boot floor. Alternatively the method of fixing may use a combination of existing mounting points and new ones.

The kit will have the necessary multi-pin socket and wiring for connecting to the car's lighting circuit (see pages 17 to 20), but one item that is not likely to be included is the tow ball itself.

Even though the standard ball and socket size in the UK is now 50 mm, other imperial sizes have been available in the past and there are many trailers still in use with this equipment. So if you are buying a trailer or caravan (either new or secondhand) make sure that you find out the socket size before you buy the tow ball. Hired trailers invariably have 50 mm sockets, so if you only ever intend hiring trailers you would be fairly safe in fitting a 50 mm ball. Whatever you do, do not be tempted to mix old 2 in and new 50 mm fittings, the former are slightly larger than the latter and mixing them up could be dangerous.

The tow bar kit will have a pre-drilled mounting plate for the tow ball which simply bolts in place. When you buy the ball you may come across two different types (in addition to size), both are shown in **fig 5**. One is simply a ball mounted on a metal plate, the other is a ball on top of a pin which is held in a forked yoke by a spring lock. The latter, as well as being more expensive, provides two types of hitch in one: a normal ball-and-socket and a pin for trailers with towing eyes as opposed to sockets. When towing this type of trailer, the pin is pulled from the yoke after releasing the spring lock, the trailer eye inserted in the yoke and the pin pushed back through it. It provides a very secure fastening, but is considerably more expensive and is really intended for commercial towing operations.

You can get plastic protective coverings for both types of towing ball, also shown in **fig 5**.

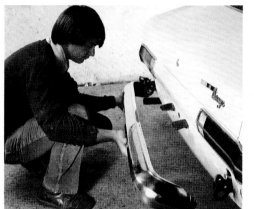

1. Removing the rear bumper from the car

2. Pointing number plate light shrouds upwards

3. Bolting crossbar to bumper mounting points

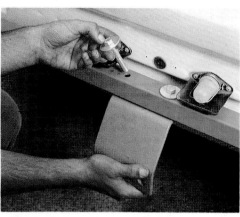

4. Fixing the drop plate to the crossbar

5. Drilling mounting hole into the floorpan

6. Fitting the support bracket into position

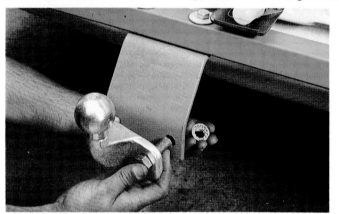

7. Fitting the tow ball on to the drop plate

Unless your new tow bar relies purely on the bumper iron mountings for support, you will need to drill some mounting holes through the boot floor and this means working beneath the car. Ideally, an inspection pit should be used but if one of these is not available, then run the back of the car up on to a pair of car ramps, or support it on a pair of axle stands. When you are working under the car wear a pair of safety goggles to protect your eyes from small bits of dirt.

First, empty the boot of the car completely, taking out any floor covering, the spare wheel and anything else that is

removeable. Check on the position of the petrol tank and be particularly careful if you have to drill any holes near it. Similarly, make a mental note of the position of any electrical wiring. If necessary, unclip it and pull it out of the way — it is a good idea to chalk the position of anything you have to remove. It is also a good idea to temporarily bolt the pieces of the kit together and then offer up the assembly to make sure there are no obvious obstructions or other problems.

The exact method of installation will vary from one car to another, so make sure you read the instructions carefully and that you

understand them fully before you begin.

It is essential that the tow hitch falls on the centreline of the car, if it is off-centre it will produce some alarming handling problems when a caravan or trailer is towed. To ensure accurate positioning of the tow bar, most manufacturers use existing mounting points — the bumper iron for example — for at least some of the brackets in the kit. This provides a known location from which the remaining mounting bolt holes can be found. In the example shown in **figs 1** to **7** part of the bar attaches to the bumper iron mounting points. The first job is

to remove the bumper (**fig 1**). Since the number plate on this car has been removed and will have to be replaced higher up, the shrouds covering the lights to illuminate the number have been fixed upside down to compensate for the new position (**fig 2**).

Next bolt the crossbar on to the bumper iron mounting points (**fig 3**) and then fix the drop plate on to the crossbar using the screws and washers provided (**fig 4**). Then all that is necessary is to drill the remaining mounting holes at points which coincide with the bolt clearance holes in the tow bar brackets

If, for some reason, no

existing mountings can be used the manufacturer will give precise instructions for the accurate positioning of the first bracket, once this is in place, the remainder can be assembled and the mounting holes drilled as before. Double check all measurements before you mark or drill any holes and centrepunch each hole centre to prevent the drill bit wandering.

The bar will be held in place by substantial bolts which will require you to drill fairly large diameter holes. To make this easier always drill a small pilot hole first and then follow up with the appropriate size bit, using masking tape

under the floorpan should prevent your drill slipping (**fig 5**). If at all possible use a multi-speed drill, and use a high speed when drilling small-diameter pilot holes and the slowest for large-diameter bits. This will prevent them snagging as they break through the metal. Lubricate the tips of the drill bits with some oil to prevent them becoming blunt.

Fit the support bracket according to the manufacturer's instructions (**fig 6**), making sure any washers or spacers are fitted the right way round and in the right sequence. Tighten the nuts and bolts fully and replace the bumper if it was removed. Then bolt the ball hitch to the bar mounting plate (**fig 7**).

Remember that the tow bar must not obscure any part of the number plate. If it does, the plate must be removed and refitted higher up or in some other position so that it can be clearly read. If you have to move it a long way from its original position, you will also have to move the number plate light ensuring the new position does not allow white light to be seen at rear.

Finally, wire up and fit the trailer socket and S-type accessory power socket.

1. Two types of replacement damper: air adjustable (top) and one with a heavy duty spring (below)

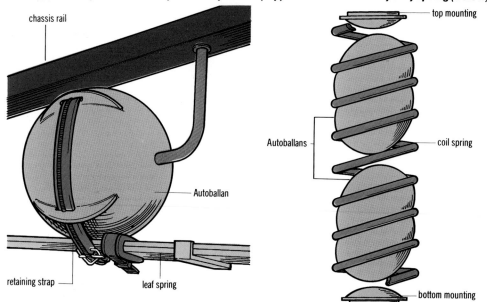

chassis rail

Autoballans

top mounting

coil spring

Autoballan

bottom mounting

retaining strap

leaf spring

2. The Autoballans is fitted between the coil springs or between the leaf spring and chassis

Just fitting the tow bar to the car and wiring in the lighting socket are not the only jobs you may have to do to make towing possible. You may have to make several other modifications to the car to make it handle properly and reduce the strain imposed by the extra load of the trailer or caravan. It is unlikely that you will have to make all the changes covered here; it will depend on the results of your first trial runs with the trailer in tow. Make

sure you test everything and get the 'feel' of towing before you go on a long journey.

The first obvious move is to check in the car handbook or with the manufacturer's dealer for any special recommendations regarding your car when used for towing. Make any changes suggested immediately. The handbook should give you figures for rear tyre pressures when towing, since they will almost certainly need to be increased to accommodate the extra load.

You may also find that the extra weight put on the back of the car by a trailer will compress the rear springs until the car is riding on the bump stops. Not only will this make the ride uncomfortable but it will seriously affect the handling by lifting the front end, making the steering light and reducing the grip of the front tyres.

In this situation the suspension can be uprated by fitting various types of spring fitted quite easily. Some take the form of replacement shock absorbers which may be adjustable for different loads or have auxiliary coil springs round them (**fig 1**). An inflatable spring assister, known as the Autoballans (**fig 2**), fits between the floorpan and leaf spring, or inside a coil spring. These are simply inflatable balls which, under load, are squeezed and act as air cushions, giving the springs a more progressive action than normal.

Aeon spring assisters are hollow rubber springs which fit in place of the car's bump stops (**fig 4**). Another Aeon kit — called the Coil Lift — consists of a set of rubber blocks which are fitted to each spring as shown in **fig 3**.

One further assister is an additional leaf that clamps to the underside of the leaf springs to stiffen them.

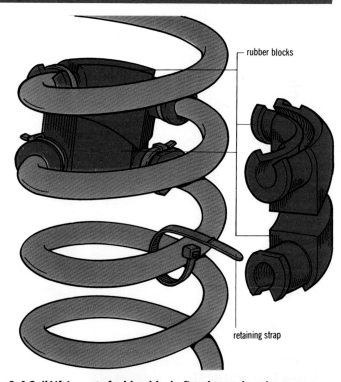

rubber blocks

retaining strap

3. A Coil Lift is a set of rubber blocks fitted to each spring

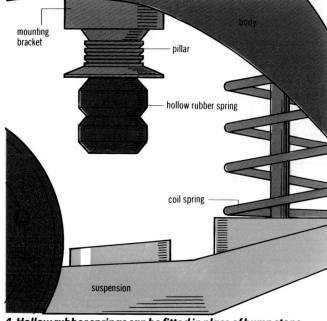

mounting bracket

body

pillar

hollow rubber spring

coil spring

suspension

4. Hollow rubber springs can be fitted in place of bump stops

1. One extension mirror clips to existing mirror

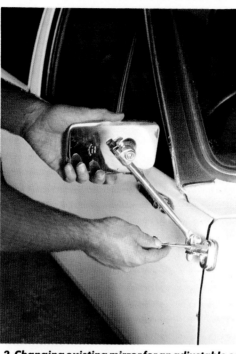

2. Changing existing mirror for an adjustable one

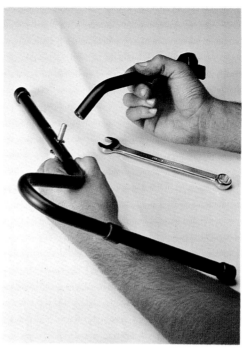

3. Assembling extended mirror kit

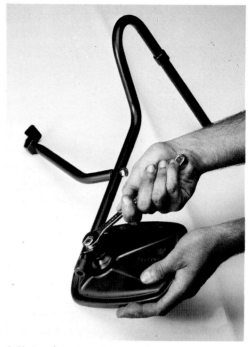

4. Fixing the mirror to the main arm

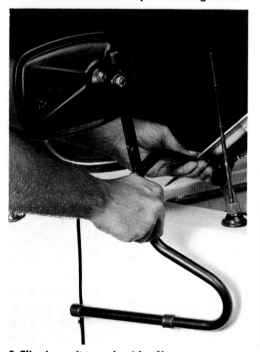

5. Clipping unit to underside of bonnet

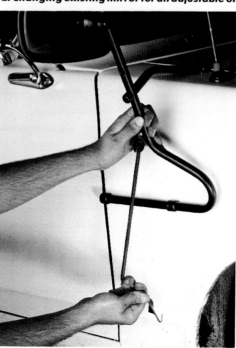

6. Fitting elasticated strap to bottom of wing

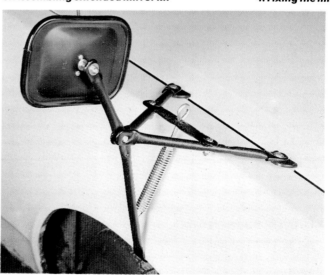

7. A similar mirror uses a spring in place of the elasticated strap

When towing it is important to fit some form of extended mirror so that you can see around the caravan or trailer. Various types are available, the simplest is merely a larger mirror head which clips over the existing wing mirror (**fig 1**). Another type is a replacement mirror which you simply bolt to the wing in place of your original mirror.

There are more elaborate versions available as well, such as the Raydyot. **Figs 3** to **6** show how to fit an extension mirror which has one arm clipping under the bonnet and an elasticated strap which fixes to the bottom of the wing.

Fitting is straightforward as the kit comes with all the parts you need. First attach the arm that goes under the bonnet to the main (mirror) arm (**fig 3**). You can then attach the mirror to the main arm (**fig 4**) and clip both arms to the underside of the bonnet and the door end of the front wing (**fig 5**). Finally, fix the elasticated strap to the underside of the wing (**fig 6**).

The spring shown in the extension mirror in **fig 7** replaces the elasticated strap and allows a slightly stronger mounting, it has two fixing points in the bonnet and one under the wheel arch.

25

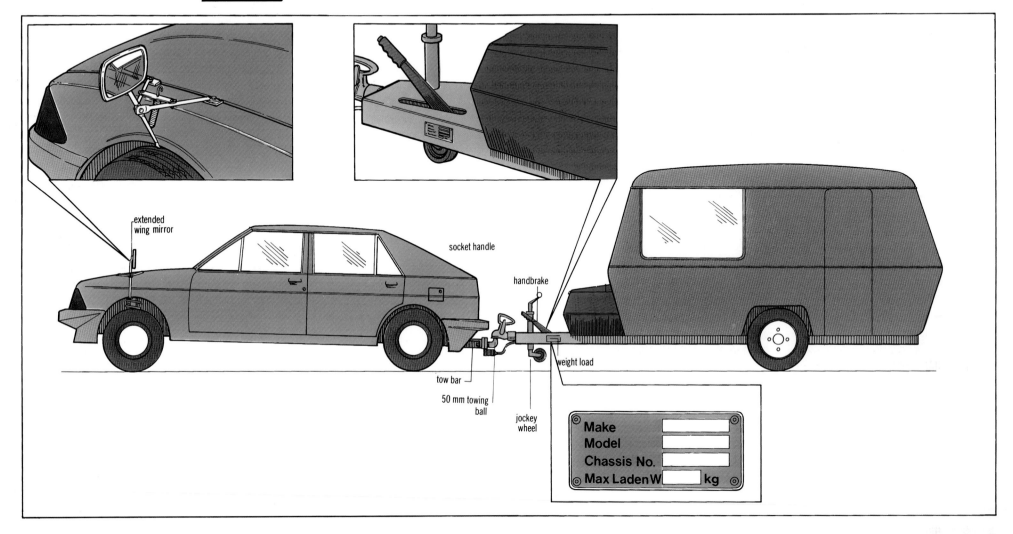

FACT FILE

extended
wing mirror

socket handle

handbrake

weight load

tow bar

50 mm towing
ball

jockey
wheel

Make	
Model	
Chassis No.	
Max Laden W	kg

Towing and the law

Both your tow car and caravan or trailer must be equipped and set up to meet certain legal requirements before you can take them on the road. Particularly important is the weight of the trailer or caravan compared to that of the car.

The first job is to find the kerb weight of the car — its weight with the oil, coolant and petrol topped up but without any passengers or luggage. In most cases, you should be able to find this figure in the car's handbook, but if not take the car to a weighbridge where you can have it checked. The maximum laden weight of the trailer must never be more than the car's kerb weight, or the weight specified by the car's manufacturer, which may be lower.

Any trailer with a laden weight of more than 102 kg (2 cwt) must be fitted with brakes on all its wheels, but these need not be operated by the car's braking system; they can be of the 'overrun' type, coming on automatically when the trailer begins to catch the car up. The trailer must also have a separate handbrake capable of holding it on a 1 in 6 slope. If the trailer is not fitted with brakes, its laden weight must be clearly displayed on its chassis or bodywork and never exceeded.

The trailer must also be equipped with a number of warning signals, lights and signs. Both a trailer and a caravan should have rear lights brake lights, reflective triangles, and an illuminated rear number plate carrying the number of the towing vehicle.

If you have a particularly wide trailer you must fit side repeater lights at the points of maximum width on either side of the trailer. They show a white light to the front and red to the rear.

Providing the trailer meets all the weight requirements described above, you can tow it at speeds of up to 50 mph on ordinary roads, 60 mph on dual carriageways and motorways where you are restricted to driving in the inside and middle lanes only.

One extended mirror must be fitted to the car for towing.

Fitting a radio cassette

If you want to listen to music on the move, a radio-cassette unit is the answer. Fitting is simple — just follow the procedure shown here

Gaining the very best of audio quality from in-car entertainment equipment is a matter of applying good standards of installation — for the set itself, the speakers and the aerial.

This step by step guide takes you through selection of a unit and the many fitting options that a modern car presents. Don't ignore the fitting instructions that come with a unit. Some modern electronic units demand that no earthing connection is made within the loudspeaker circuits.

What this job involves
Fitting the radio-cassette unit
Connecting earth and power leads
Wiring to ignition switch
Fitting door speakers
Wiring speakers

Related jobs in this handbook
Fitting an aerial/reducing interference
Fitting an electrically-operated aerial
Testing for electrical faults
Please see Index for page numbers

To do this job
Tools: Screwdriver; spanner(s); drill fitted with bit for drilling metal; hacksaw blade (maybe); felt-tip pen; wire stripper; sharp knife; pliers; hole cutter;
Materials: Radio-cassette player; speakers; in-line fuse (maybe); earthing strap (maybe); self-tapping screws; spare wire for speaker leads (maybe); block connectors (maybe); tape; spade connectors; aerial;
Time: A morning or afternoon
Degree of difficulty: Straightforward, but care needed to get a neat result

If you have the job professionally done . . .
Is the unit in a position where it can be reached easily? Are door speakers free of obstructions such as handles and winders? Are speaker leads protected by rubber grommets where necessary? Are speaker leads out of sight and taped neatly to the car body?

Two models from Phillips: DC550 (top) and DC954.

There's a bewildering choice of car audio units on today's market—around 30 makers with over 250 units pitched at prices ranging from that of a new car battery, for a humble radio, to that of a modest secondhand car for equipment that combines a radio, cassette deck and even a compact disc player. Indeed, many people are so concerned about the quality of their in-car audio that the equipment may cost more than the car itself.

Surprisingly, there are very few simple radios. Most makers concentrate on radio-cassette players (combination units), a market encouraged by the fact that the majority of cars already have at least a pushbutton radio fitted to them

as standard. Drivers are increasingly throwing away the simple units fitted as standard, on the grounds of lack of stereo FM reception. Virtually all modern combination units feature stereo cassette and FM radio.

Even if your budget is restricted it is worthwhile spending sufficient money—say about the cost of a couple of good quality tyres—for a combination unit that has a deck reliable enough not to mince cassettes and pushbutton, rather than manual, tuning for added convenience.

In the next price range—say the cost of three new tyres—you will have a choice of several budget digitally tuned units with a higher capacity for

storing favourite stations and greater tuning accuracy on the FM band.

Above this point, around the cost of a set of new quality tyres, tape decks improve from being simple autostop or autoeject models, which require turning of the tape to hear the second side, to full auto-reverse specification. An auto-reverse deck winds on and plays the second side automatically.

From this point on the features pile in. A major benefit is a high power internal amplifier —12 to 22 watts per stereo channel rather than the normal 5 watts. This facility improves the dynamic quality of the sound output and is really necessary for the clean and powerful bass notes.

Major improvements to the tape deck appearing at higher prices include the Dolby B tape noise reduction system and the facility to adjust equalization for different types of tape, such as chrome or metal, which are better than normal ferric tape.

Really expensive units may offer the new Dolby C noise reduction circuit and even the alternative dbx technology, although these functions are only useful if you have a home player able to record tapes with the coded signals for these systems. Music search systems to find the next tape track or track repeat facilities are other deck enhancements.

Tuners available on higher-priced sets may include automatic tuning to the best stations in any area (Autostore, Best Station Memory or Signal Auto Memory) or systems that change frequency to find the best reception of a national station.

Many modern units can be upgraded by the addition of a graphic equaliser or booster amplifier as well as higher power handling loudspeakers.

TIP

Buttoned up

Push button radios, standard equipment on many cars built in the last ten years, are much more convenient to use than manual tuners out on the road.

To retune a mechanical

push button radio, pull out the selected button and then manually tune to the required station. The selection is 'memorized' when the button is pushed home again.

1. Radio and radio-cassette with standard fitting kit

Fitting the set involves mounting it directly in a ready cut slot in the facia. If your car is not fitted with such a slot, mount it as described in Alternative Step 1, opposite.

Remove the blanking plate covering the slot. It is usually clipped in place and can be pulled out with your fingers. If the plate does not come out immediately it may be held by spring straps at the back. Remove these by pulling them off from behind the dashboard. Now disconnect the earth terminal from the battery to prevent possible short circuits while fitting the set.

Next, measure the dimensions of the facia slot and those of the radio-cassette set. These dimensions are standardized (a DIN standard) so most new radio-cassette units simply push fit into the slot on a modern car and clip in place with the standard fitting kit (**fig 1**) provided with most sets, or bought separately.

If you have an older set or car with non-standard dimensions you could find that the facia slot is quite a lot bigger all round than the set.

To get rid of the ugly gap and to ensure the set sits neatly and squarely in the slot, you need to fit a facia plate (**fig 2**). This sits just inside the slot and is usually held in place with self tapping screws (see Fact File — Drilling bodywork) or clips to the set. Facia plates are made in a wide range of sizes and are available from some accessory shops and most specialist car radio-cassette dealers.

To make sure you buy the correct one, note down the height and width of both radio and slot and take the dimensions along with you. If you want to give the set additional support you can buy rear or side support brackets. But check first that these can be fixed to the bulkhead or facia.

2. If the slot is larger than the set you need a facia plate

TIP

Covering up

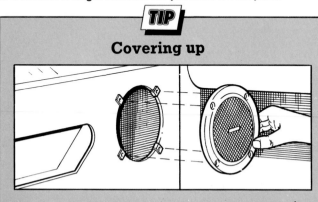

When you come to sell your car, you may wish to remove the radio. Rather than leaving an unsightly hole in the facia, keep the blanking plate somewhere safe so you can replace it. If you want to remove the speakers as well, you can cover the holes with standard speaker grilles, so it may be worth buying spares of these at the same time as you buy speakers.

1. Under dash fixing brackets

If your car facia is not fitted with a ready-cut slot you can mount the radio in a number of alternative places. Wherever you choose, try to position the set where you can reach the controls easily and safely from a normal driving position.

Some commonly chosen sites are immediately below the dashboard or parcel shelf on either the driver's side or towards the centre of the dash.

If mounting a set in this way it may be worth choosing a place where it will be out of sight. This simple precaution can be an effective anti-theft measure and may prevent your car being broken into and the set stolen — an increasingly common occurrence. A lockable glove box, for example, is a good place, as is the very rear of a parcel shelf, or under the driver's seat. However, the disadvantage is that the set may be difficult or impossible to operate while you are driving.

New sets for non-slot fitting are usually ready supplied with a suitable type of mounting bracket. If not, universal mounting bracket kits for all types of set are available from most accessory shops (**fig 1**). On the other hand you could buy an under dash cradle which looks like part of the facia once it is screwed into place (**fig 2**).

Do not fix the mounting and radio permanently in position at this stage — you may need access to the back to make electrical connections later. First adjust the mount to fit the radio, then try it for size by holding it in position. Remember that the aerial plug may protrude 2 in. (50 mm) from the back, so do not fix the set where this will be obstructed.

Line up the brackets and mark the position of screw holes. Then remove the set from the brackets and screw each bracket firmly into place.

2. Under dash cradle — supports the set and matches the facia

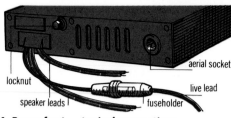

1. Rear of set — typical connections

locknut / speaker leads / fuseholder / live lead / aerial socket

2. Earthing the set to the bodywork

earthing bolt / earthing strap

Fig 1 shows the back of a typical set and various connections that have to be made. These consist of an earth, a live power feed and two sets of speaker connections. Connect the earth first. Some sets are designed to be earthed by direct contact between the set and the car body. This is not always satisfactory so it is worth connecting up a separate earth strap just to make sure.

To earth the set you will need a braided earth bonding strap at least ½ in. (13 mm) wide. A large strap like this helps cut down interference in the system. A few manufacturers supply a suitable strap as part of the fitting kit; if not, buy one from a motor accessory shop.

Connect one end of the strap to the set. Sometimes there is a locknut post on the back of the unit especially for this; otherwise you will have to loosen one of the mounting screws, wrap the end of the strap around the screw thread then fix it to the body (**fig 2**). You should be able to secure the other end of the strap to the car body using an

FACT FILE
Drilling bodywork

Drilling holes in the car's bodywork, inside or out, for attaching accessories or making electrical connections is neither as drastic nor as difficult as it may seem. It is relatively easy to drill through the thin metal panels used on most parts of the bodywork with only a hand drill and a bit for drilling steel.

In fact, it is often better to use a hand drill rather than an electric one because you do not need a long length of cable to reach the nearest power supply. Only where you cannot fit a hand drill in the space available will you need to take advantage of the more compact electric drill.

It is usual to centrepunch the centre of your mark before drilling metal, to stop the bit from slipping out of position. But on thin sheet metal or pressed steel panels tapping a punch may make a large dent. To avoid this, firmly stick down a piece of adhesive tape to the metal where you want to drill and mark it accurately with a felt-tip pen. Put your bit tip on the mark and drill — the tape will help keep the bit on the mark and stop it slipping across the metal and causing an ugly scratch.

Self-tapping screws are usually used to secure various components to the bodywork via the holes drilled in steel panels. These are sharply tapering short screws with a deep, sharp thread made especially for gripping in small holes in thin sheet metal panels.

If you have to buy a drill bit, choose one slightly smaller than the diameter of the self-tapping screw you want to use. The screw will then partly cut into the metal as it is screwed into the hole and give a good strong grip.

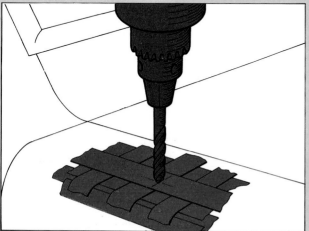

existing nut or screw which you find within easy reach. Loosen the fixing and clean the surrounding bodywork down to bare metal with a piece of wet-and-dry paper. Then push the bolt or screw through the strap and retighten it fully.

Next, find the live wire on the unit. This is usually already connected to the back of the set or emerges from it. If not, connect a length of wire to the relevant terminal on the back of the unit.

The wire should already contain a 5 amp in-line fuse. Open the plastic fuseholder and make sure — the cap is usually held by a spring-loaded bayonet clip.

If for some reason your set

does not come with a fuse-holder, you will have to buy one and fit it to the wire. Try to get the type with blade connectors which can be connected simply by crimping the ends with pliers — this saves having to do any soldering (see Fact File — Making connections).

To fit the in-line fuse, cut the live wire about 6 in. (150 mm) from the back of the set and bare the two loose ends. Push the bared end of each wire into the metal connectors of the fuse-holder and crimp them securely with pliers (**fig 3**).

Now you can connect the end of the live wire up to the car's power supply. There are three possible connections — to a spare terminal on the fuse box,

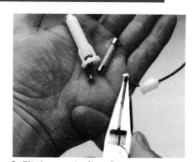

3. Fitting an in-line fuse

to an accessory terminal on the ignition switch, or to an existing live feed, like the live wire to a cigarette lighter. Which you choose depends on the precise wiring arrangements on your car, but each method has advantages and disadvantages.

Probably the best place to connect the live feed is to an accessory terminal on the ignition switch. You may be able to tell if your switch has such a terminal by looking near the key hole. If the marked key positions include a figure 2 stamped on the switch, then it is likely your switch has one. Connecting the radio-cassette set to this terminal means that it will only work with either the engine on, or, when stopped, with the switch at the '2' position. But it also means that when you leave the car and take the key with you, it ensures that the set is switched off. Leaving a set on by mistake overnight — which is quite easily done — can flatten a poorly charged battery.

To gain access to the rear of the ignition switch, to identify an accessory terminal and make a

connection, you may have to remove a section of plastic trim. This usually involves unscrewing several self-tapping screws and is normally described in detail in your manual.

The accessory terminal

should be obvious either because it is the only unused terminal on the switch and has no wire coming from it (**fig 1**) or has a very short length of wire ending in a loose, insulated female bullet connector (**fig 2**).

1. Isolating the accessory terminal on the ignition switch

FACT FILE
Making connections

There are many different types of connector made to help you make neat, insulated joints. Those shown here make good electrical connections without soldering — though solder can be added later to certain types if required.

Spade (Blade) connectors are small, flat, two-part metal connectors. One part is the 'male' and the other a 'female'. One of each is crimped with pliers (or soldered) on to the bared end of the wires to be joined. The two parts are then pushed together to make the joint, and can also be undone whenever needed. If you fit this type, use small plastic sleeves, sometimes supplied with them, to cover the joint and insulate it.

Double spade connectors are similar to those described above but one of the parts, usually the 'female' has provision for fitting two rather than just one 'male' part. This means you can take a feed wire off an existing power wire where it connects to a component.

Ring spade connectors are crimped with pliers (or soldered) to the bared ends of wires. The hole in the flat blade means it can be attached with a small nut and bolt or screw to make the connection.

Scotchloc connectors can be used to connect one wire to another directly without having to cut and join. The device is simply crimped to the bared end of a new wire, then attached to the existing power wire that you want to tap, and clipped into place with pliers over and around the wire.

Connector blocks are small plastic blocks containing individual metal tubes. They are made in large blocks for neatness and convenience — you simply cut off as many or as few as you need with a knife. Connector blocks are useful for making easy, quickly disconnectable joints in lengths of wire. A screw at either end of the connector clamps the bared ends of wires to make an insulated, secure joint.

spade connectors

double spade ('piggy back') connector

ring spade connector

Scotchloc connector

connector block

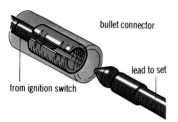

2. Insulated bullet connector

3. Using a test lamp to check that the accessory terminal is live

Some ignition switches are fitted with a multiplug connector. If you can see that there is no spare terminal yet know that your car already has electrical extras fitted that only work with the ignition in the fully on or '2' position, turn the ignition to '2' and remove and replace each switch terminal connection in turn until the particular accessory fails to work. If this

happens you can identify an already used accessory terminal — but you can still use this with a joint connector to supply the radio-cassette.

Check that you have isolated the correct terminal with a test lamp. Switch the car ignition to the '2' position. Clamp one end of the tester to a suitable earth, then touch the blade of the screwdriver to the terminal —

the test lamp bulb should immediately light up (**fig 3**).

Fit a single or double spade connector (see Fact File — Making connections) to the radio-cassette live wire depending on how many accessories the terminal serves and connect it to the terminal. Make sure the live wire is routed to the switch so that it will not hang loose below the dash.

ALTERNATIVE 3 — WIRE TO FUSE BOX OR ACCESSORY

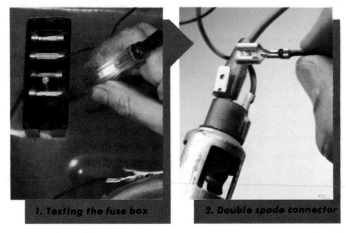

1. Testing the fuse box

2. Double spade connector

If your car has no accessory terminal on the ignition switch, it is best to wire the live feed from the set to the fuse box. This means connecting the wire to the 'out' side of a fuse circuit — one that does not demand that the ignition is fully switched on to make that circuit work. On more modern cars, this means, for example, a circuit such as

hazard warning indicators. On cars with no hazard warning you can use the sidelight circuit instead.

Find out which fuse serves either of these circuits first by switching the appropriate circuit on, then by systematically removing the fuses until you find the one which stops that circuit working. Having found

this, the next move is to find the 'out' side of the circuit. Test for this by removing the fuse, as above, and using a test lamp (**fig 1**) (see page 193). Leave the sidelight or hazard warning switch on, and clip one terminal of the tester to earth. Next, put the tester probe on one fuse terminal, then the other. One will light the tester, the other will not. The 'dead' terminal is the fused or 'out' side of the circuit, and the wire which serves this is the one to which you can connect the live feed to your radio-cassette set.

If you can neither connect the set's live feed to ignition nor to the fuse box, as described above, you can connect it direct to a permanent live feed which supplies a component which works with the ignition fully off — such as a clock or cigar lighter. All that is needed is a double connector (see Fact File — Making connections) connected to the feed supplying the unit (**fig 2**).

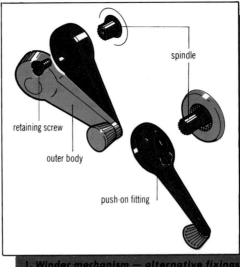

1. Winder mechanism — alternative fixings

spindle

retaining screw

outer body

push-on fitting

2. Unscrewing the handle and arm rest

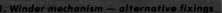

closely spaced holes drilled around outside

hacksaw blade

5. Cutting through the inner door skin

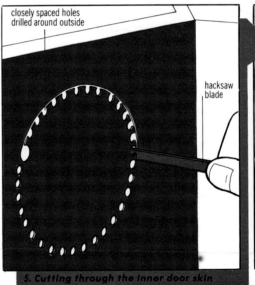

6. Fixing the speaker using spire clips

The speakers you choose may be door or parcel-shelf mounted types, or both. Door mounted types are more tricky to mount and wire up so deal with these first.

To fit door mounted speakers first remove the door trim. This is usually held by self-tapping screws which hold the door

handle, window winder and any other items such as arm rests, in place (**fig 1**).

Unscrew the handle, window winder and any other items you can see (**fig 2**). Then use your finger to ease the trim away from the press studs around the outer edge of the door.

Many modern cars have pre-

cut holes or gaps in the inner skin of the door, for mounting speakers (**fig 6**). If so, all you have to do is to cut a corresponding hole in the trim and secure the speakers.

If no pre-cut hole exists, you will have to make a careful assessment of the best place to position the speakers. Ideally,

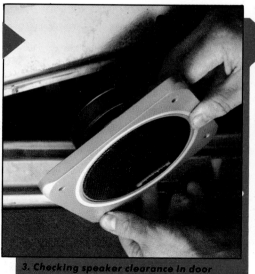

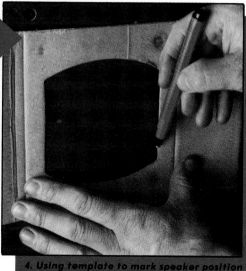

3. Checking speaker clearance in door

4. Using template to mark speaker position

they should be placed as far forward as possible, to avoid the sound being blocked out either by the car seats or by the driver's legs. At the same time, a speaker must be placed to avoid any internal obstructions in the door, such as bracing struts and the window glass or door handle mechanisms. Check this by holding the trim in position and positioning the speaker against it.

Once you have chosen the best position for the speaker, mark the cut-out on the door trim. A paper template is usually provided with the speakers to help — if not, make one yourself. Position this on the trim and mark around the edge with a felt-tip pen (**fig 4**). At the same time mark the position of the fixing screws. Then lay the trim on a flat surface and cut along the line with a sharp knife. Score around the circle a number of times until you have cut clean through the trim.

Remove the door trim and cut out the marked section. To make this easier, drill a series of closely-spaced holes around the outside of the proposed aperture, until you can break through the surface just by pressing the skin. Then insert a hacksaw blade and cut away the rest of the metal (**fig 5**).

Next mark and drill four holes in the trim for the speaker mounting screws. The speaker is normally held in place by four spire clips; push these over the edge of the trim and line them up with the holes (**fig 6**). Then screw the speaker body into position.

ALTERNATIVE 4   FIT SPEAKERS TO REAR

If you want to fit flush-mounted speakers to the rear parcel shelf, proceed as for fitting door speakers (see Step 4). When fitting pod speakers it is best not to fix any of the speakers in position until the wiring has been fed to the speakers and connected up. At this stage, mark and drill fixing holes and a hole to carry the speaker lead (**fig 1**). If you want to fix speakers to the foot wells also mark and drill fixing holes at this stage.

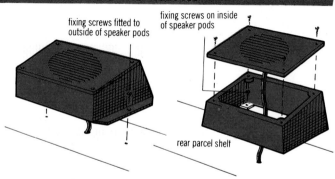

fixing screws fitted to outside of speaker pods

fixing screws on inside of speaker pods

rear parcel shelf

1. Alternative fixings for pod speakers on rear parcel shelf

Once the speakers are in position, connect the speaker leads to the back of the radio-cassette unit and sort out the wires. Normally these are colour-coded — two wires of one colour to the 'left' hand speaker(s) and two wires of another to the 'right' hand speaker(s). Sometimes, each wire is separately colour-coded to aid connecting them to the speaker terminals the right way round (see right).

If you have installed only two speakers, simply connect up the wires as above. For four speakers split the leads four ways using block connectors as shown in **fig 1**.

Leads to front door speakers should be run underneath the facia directly to the door pillars. If there are no pre-drilled holes, drill a small hole, about ¼ in. (6 mm) in the edge of the door and another in the door pillar. The holes should not exactly line up

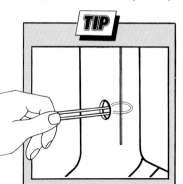

TIP

Leading question

You may find it difficult to lead the end of the wires through the holes you have drilled, especially in the door pillar. An easy way to catch hold of the end is to loop a piece of wire — an offcut of speaker wire is ideal — and push it through the hole. Once the wire is level with the hole, it will get caught in the loop and can be pulled through to the outside.

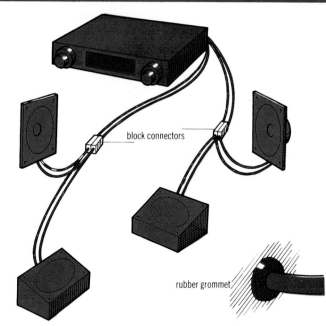

block connectors

rubber grommet

1. Connecting four speakers

2. Protective rubber grommets

with each other; drill one a little higher than the other so that the lead does not get crushed when the door is shut. Fit rubber grommets in each hole (**fig 2**) and lead the wire through to the hole cut in the inner door skin for the speaker (see Tip box).

Leads to the rear of the car should be run underneath the carpet. If you need to extend the wires use block connectors to connect one length to another. Tape the wire to the floor at about 6 in. (150 mm) intervals to stop it moving around and chafing (**fig 3**).

Lead the wire under and behind the rear seat into the boot then push it up through the hole you have drilled in the parcel shelf.

Connect the wires to each of the speaker terminals. The leads may be colour-coded so they can be connected the right way round — look at the fitting instructions supplied with your set.

Screw each of the rear shelf speakers into position. Then

3. Taping the wire to the floor

replace the door trim and door fittings (see Tip box). Door-mounted speakers usually have a front grille over each speaker which should be screwed or snapped into position.

To complete the radio-cassette fitting it remains to fit the aerial and suppress any sources of electrical interference — this is dealt with in the next eight steps of the car audio fitting process.

1. Three possible fixing positions for body-mounted aerials

Before you buy an aerial, first consider exactly where you want to mount it since this influences the type you choose.

Body-mounted types usually give better reception than temporarily mounted aerials, like those which clip to the top of the window or stick to it.

Fig 1 shows the best three places to site a body-mounted aerial — on the roof, on the front wing, or on the rear wing. The position you choose depends partly on personal preference and the amount of room there is to fit the aerial.

Roof-top aerials are normally fitted centrally on the front of the roof. In this position they are well away from potential sources of interference and are often regarded as giving best reception. However, roof-top aerials are not fully retractable and this means that even if it is possible to lay them flat, you still run the risk of getting the aerial broken off in an automatic carwash.

If you fit a roof-top aerial bear in mind that, in most cases you will have to remove part of the roof lining and thread the lead

down the inside of the door pillar (see Alternative Step 7) — so check that this is possible first. If you decide to fit the aerial to the rear wing, you may have to buy an extension lead from an accessory shop or radio dealer. If so, try to buy one with ready-fitted connectors so all you have to do is to plug the extension into the existing lead — soldered connections are difficult and not a satisfactory

way of joining the co-axial cable used for aerial leads.

If you want to fit a fully retractable aerial, check first that there is enough space behind the panel, either in the boot itself or under the front wing. In the boot check that the base section which contains the retracted aerial can be tucked away where it will not interfere with luggage. Under the front wing make sure that the base section is kept well away from tyres and suspension components. Also remember that to fit the aerial you may have to push it up from below — so you need more room underneath than just the length of the base section. With a hatchback, or in a car with a small boot, it may not always be possible to find a suitable space at the back. But if you have the choice, it is better to fit the aerial to the rear rather than to the front wing: this will keep the aerial as far away as possible from sources of interference.

At the top end of the market are electric aerials which can be operated from inside the car at the flick of a switch. Installing an electrically operated aerial is different to fitting an ordinary aerial — follow the maker's instructions closely.

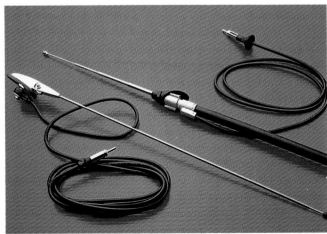

2. Typical wing-mounted aerial (top) and roof aerial

Fitting an aerial to the wing involves a slightly different procedure to fitting a roof aerial. If you want to mount an aerial on the roof, fit it as described in Alternative Step 7.

To help protect the paintwork and prevent the drill from slipping on the wing panel, cover an area about 3 in. (75 mm) square around the site with masking tape (**fig 1**). Check that there are no cables or other obstructions under this part of the panel. Mark the centre with a felt-tipped pen then lightly punch the mark with a nail or centrepunch.

Depending on the size of the aerial, you need a hole about ¾ in. (19 mm) diameter. There are two ways of cutting a large hole like this: you can either use a hole saw or drill a pilot hole with the largest bit you have and then enlarge it to size with a rat-tail file. Using a hole saw is quicker but you will have to buy one (see Fact File — Hole saws).

1. Covering up with tape

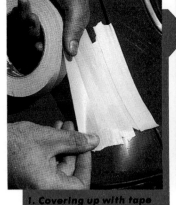

2. Using file to enlarge hole

If you use the drill and file method, first drill a pilot hole large enough to get the end of the file into it. When working with the file, hold it upright and work slowly around the outside of the circle (**fig 2**). Make sure that the file does not slip and damage the paintwork at any stage (see Tip — Protective

wrapping). Stop occasionally to try the aerial for size.

Then carefully remove the masking tape. If the area around the hole shows signs of damage or rust, rub the edges down to bare metal with a piece of wet-and-dry paper and paint with metal primer.

It is essential that the aerial makes a good connection with the bodywork. Scrape off any thick underbody sealant from around the underside of the hole with a screwdriver.

On most aerials a spiked earthing plate or serrated ring is used to maintain a good earth

Hole saws

Hole saws are ideal for cutting neat, large diameter holes in metal. The saw consists of a circular metal centrepiece — the arbor — with a length of flexible saw blade round it. At the centre of the arbor is an ordinary drill bit which helps to locate the saw accurately.

A few hole saws are pre-fixed to drill holes of one size only, but most can be adjusted so you can cut holes of different sizes.

There are two ways of adjusting the diameter of the blade according to the type of saw you buy. On some saws, the blade size is adjusted by means of a screw mounted on the side of the arbor; on others a number of separate saws of various standard diameters are supplied, and all fit the same arbor.

Tank cutters can also be used for drilling large holes. They consist of a central locating bit with an adjustable cutting arm.

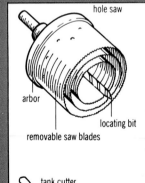

5. Mounting the aerial

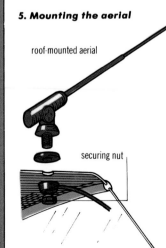

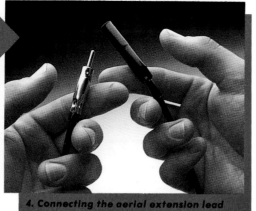

3. Hand tightening the aerial mounting nut

4. Connecting the aerial extension lead

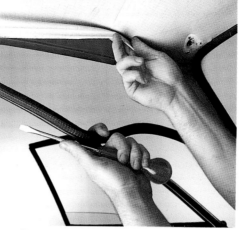

aerial lead

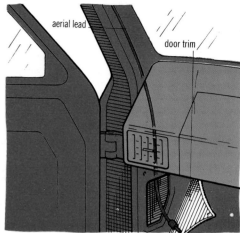

door trim

1. Pulling the lining away from the roof panel

2. Roof aerial lead channelled down door pillar

connection between the panel and aerial — when the aerial is bolted into position this plate bites into the underside of the panel (see Tip — Earthing point).

Fit the aerial through the hole you have drilled. You may have to push it into position either from above or below according to the type. Fit the ring and securing nut in position and tighten the nut by hand (**fig 3**). Swivel the aerial until you find the right angle with the aerial fully out, then tighten the nut with a spanner.

Next, decide where to run the aerial cable to reach the radio-cassette unit. If you have to lead the cable through the bulkhead or any other panels either use existing holes or drill new holes. Fit rubber grommets in new holes to stop the cable chafing.

Try to route the cable away from the engine compartment and from any components which might cause electrical interference, such as the wiper motor or electric screen-wash motor. Extend the cable, if necessary (**fig 4**).

When you reach the set, push the aerial plug in. If you have any surplus cable on a standard length lead do not cut it off — shortening it could affect reception quality. Instead, tape any surplus to the body.

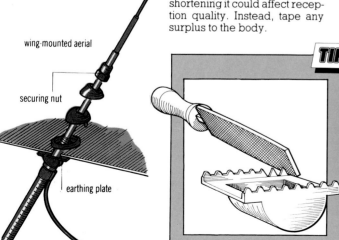

wing-mounted aerial

securing nut

earthing plate

TIP

Protective wrapping

When filing out a hole to size with a rat-tail file, wrap a few layers of masking tape around its tip. This will help to protect the paintwork if the file happens to slip out of the hole and slide across unprotected paintwork while you are working.

TIP

Earthing point

The earthing of the aerial depends to a great extent on whether the spikes or serrations on the earthing plate are sufficiently proud and make good contact with the underside of the body panel. To help the spikes take a firm hold, either bend them up with a pair of pliers and/or sharpen the points with a flat file.

First pull away part of the roof lining directly below the proposed hole. This is usually held in place by rubber seals running around the top of the windscreen and the door frames. Alternatively the strips may be secured with small screws which have to be removed first. Push the blade of a screwdriver or the handle of a metal spoon under the strips and pull the lining away from the roof panel (**fig 1**).

Drill the hole for the aerial as described in Step 7. To make sure that you get a good earth, remove the paint from the underside of the hole with wet-and-dry paper. Then push the aerial into position from above, attach the securing bolt from below and tighten it fully with a spanner.

Thread the lead down the door pillar to the near end of the dashboard then up to the back of the set. You may have to remove part of the door pillar trim to do this; it should unscrew or just snap away from the rubber mounting seal on either side (**fig 2**).

Connect the aerial to the socket mounting on the set. Then replace the roof lining and, if necessary, the door pillar trim, making sure they fit tightly into place.

1. Adjusting the aerial trimming screw

Modern electronic units require no aerial trimming (adjustment to match the capicitance of the aerial) but on most older, manual or button-tuned units you do this by altering the trimming screw with a screwdriver. The screw is usually on the front of the set — you may have to remove the front plate to get at it — but on some sets it is on the side or at the back.

Reconnect the battery and make sure that the aerial is extended fully. Tune the radio to a weak signal on the medium wave — about 200 metres or 1500 kHz. Then adjust the trimming screw until you find the spot which gives the maximum volume (**fig 1**).

Start the engine and switch the set on. Try to tune in to the strongest station that you can find. You may hear a variety of clicks and crackles over the station's signal. This is due to interference caused by various electrical impulses from the car's circuits, and these must be suppressed.

Before starting to fit suppression devices, though, make sure that the aerial and set are correctly earthed. First check that the earth strap between the set and the car body is securely fixed at each end and is making good contact.

To test whether the aerial is correctly earthed, tune in to a station and turn the volume up loud so you can hear it from outside the car. Grab hold of the aerial — if it is not earthed correctly, you should hear an immediate improvement in volume and reception. Undo the aerial and clean up the bodywork on the underside of the wing or roof to make sure that the earthing plate is making good contact. Then retighten the aerial mounting nut and try again.

If there is still interference on the radio it is most likely to be caused by the ignition system — either the LT side (the generator or coil) or the HT side (the HT leads and spark plug caps). Otherwise the trouble might be interference from one of the car's electric motors — such as the wipers, the heater fan, electric screenwash or electric clock.

The source of the interference can usually be tracked down just by listening to the exact noise coming from the speakers (see Interference checklist right). But once it has been isolated, the interference can be stopped quite easily by fitting one of the many suppression devices to the component. Suppressors are commonly available from accessory shops or specialist car radio dealers.

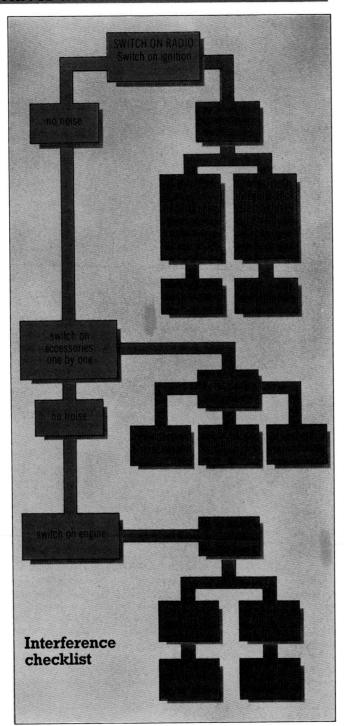

Interference checklist

To suppress the generator — the alternator or dynamo — you should fit a capacitor. Use a 1 to 3 microfarad (μF) capacitor for a dynamo or a 3 μF capacitor for an alternator.

Connect the lead of the capacitor by pushing it on to the output terminal of the dynamo or alternator (**fig 1**). With some alternators you may have to remove part of the outer casing to get at the terminal. If this is not possible connect the capacitor lead using a Scotchloc connector (**fig 1**).

The alternator output wire is usually the thickest one which comes out from the casing. If you cannot identify it, there may be a + or B+ marking on the alternator casing.

A few alternators — such as the Lucas ACR type — have a capacitor fitted as standard. This may be mounted inside or outside the casing — if it is visible, check that both body and lead are secure.

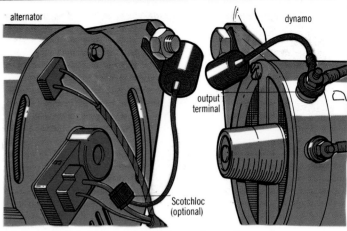

1. Suppressing the generator (alternator or dynamo)

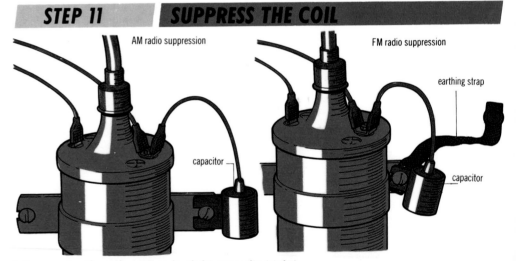

1. Suppressing the coil — AM radio (left), FM radio (right)

The equipment you need to suppress the coil depends on whether or not your radio is fitted with FM. For a radio with AM or with medium or long wave only, fit a 1 μF capacitor. For an FM radio you will need a 2.5 μF capacitor plus an earthing strap long enough to stretch from the coil to a suitable earthing point on the car.

On cars with negative earth push the capacitor lead on to the coil connection marked either positive (+) SW or BAT (**fig 1**) — on positive earth cars it goes on the negative connection (marked —). Undo one of the bolts holding the body of the coil in place and clean up the surrounding metal with a piece of wet-and-dry paper. Then push the forked end of the body connector under the bolt. With an FM set, push one end of the earthing strap under the securing bolt as well. Then retighten the bolt fully.

Lead the other end of the earthing strap to a suitable bolt or screw on the body and undo the fixing. Clean up the surrounding metal with a piece of wet-and-dry paper, fit the earthing strap in position and do it up tightly.

2. Clamp the capacitor terminal securely

3. Make sure the mounting bolt is tight

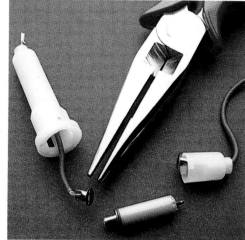

1. Fitting an earthing strap to the wiper motor

2. An in-line choke — fuseholder type

STEP 12   SUPPRESS HT CIRCUIT

All spark plugs caps are made ready suppressed. But these often fail, so if you suspect the HT system is at fault, it is well worth renewing them and at the same time fitting new carbon-cored HT leads to help cut down interference. New caps are simply pushed or screwed on to the HT leads.

To renew the leads all you have to do is to pull each of the leads free from the distributor cap one at a time and reconnect the new ones in their place (**fig 1**).

The lead between the coil and distributor should be fitted with a 5k ohm or 10k ohm resistor — the type which pushes into the centre socket on the top of the distributor (**fig 2**).

If you are still getting interference which sounds as if it is coming from the HT circuit, check the type of spark plug which is fitted to your car. (If you are unsure, simply remove one of the plugs and take a look at it.) If standard plugs are fitted, it may be possible to change to suppressed plugs instead. These are not always available as replacements for all plugs — check in your handbook or with a local dealer to make sure.

Electric motors — such as wipers, heater fan, screenwash or electric clock motors — often cause interference.

The most noticeable is usually the wiper motor since it is usually the most powerful and practically the only one which you need to leave on for any length of time (apart from the clock). To stop interference, connect an earthing strap between the body of the motor and a suitable bolt or screw on the car body (**fig 1**). Make sure that you get good metal to metal contact by cleaning both points with a piece of wet-and-dry first.

If this fails to work you should fit a 7 amp in-line choke to each lead running to the wiper motor (**fig 2**). The choke(s) should be connected by cutting each lead and crimping the chokes into position (see Fact File — Making connections, page 29).

To cure interference from other motors first connect a 1 μ f capacitor between a suitable earthing point and each of the feed lines (**fig 3**). The capacitor lead should be fixed using a Scotchloc connector (see Fact File — Making connections, page 29).

If this fails to work, fit a 7 amp choke to each live lead (**fig 3**).

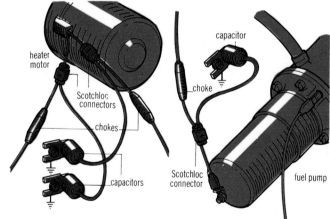

heater motor

Scotchloc connectors

chokes

capacitors

capacitor

choke

Scotchloc connector

fuel pump

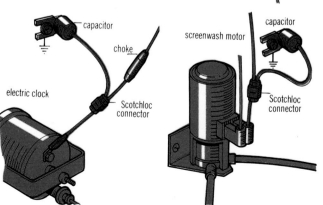

capacitor

choke

electric clock

Scotchloc connector

screenwash motor

capacitor

Scotchloc connector

3. How to suppress interference from electric motors

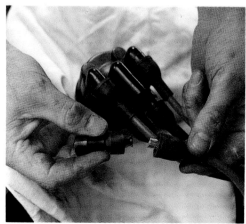

1. Renewing the HT leads and plug caps

2. Fitting a resistor to the king lead

Which tyres should you fit?

Tyres have a crucial effect on the way a car handles, and are also relatively expensive to buy. So it is doubly important that you choose carefully and fit tyres well matched to your car and style of driving

Choosing tyres for your car that will suit your style of driving and offer the best compromise between performance and value for money is, however, not so easy. The range of tyre designs, styles and sizes is so bewildering that it can be difficult to know where to begin. Furthermore it helps if you understand something of tyre design and construction as it is impossible to simply look at a particular tyre or tread pattern and tell whether it is the right one for your car.

Tyre design and construction

The tyre tread is the most visible part of a tyre and often it is the only distinguishing feature. But while the basic principles of how the grooves and sipes clear water and allow the tyre to grip the road are easy to understand even by non-professionals, the designs that work best under all different road and weather conditions require a computer to predict. And only after exten-sive computer modelling will a prototype tyre be developed.

When a tyre manufacturer develops a new tread pattern they begin by producing a completely bald tyre. On to this they stencil the new tread design. The tread is then carefully cut into the tyre by skilled technicians using a hand-held cutting tool.

The prototype produced in this way can take many forms, ranging from a totally new design concept to a simple experiment with a different tread pattern on an existing production tyre. A new tread compound may also be pro-visionally tested in this way.

The new tyre is then machine tested for slip angle, grip, durability, rolling resistance and its operating temperature is measured at different speeds to check that it does not overheat. Only when the tyre has passed all these tests will further proto-types be made and fitted to cars for track testing.

But grip and durability are not the only factors affecting tread

Tyres must offer good grip in all conditions

Typical tyres

Michelin TRX

This is a top of the range tyre, offered as an option by several manufacturers on their larger, heavier, high performance cars. The low profile gives the tyre a squat appearance, and the tyre is safe at speeds over 130 mph (210 km/h)

Michelin XDX

The XDX is a slightly less advanced tyre, intended for use on high performance sports cars and saloons. The XDX is safe over 130 mph (210 km/h), but is really only intended for use up to 140 mph (225 km/h)

Pirelli P6

The Pirelli P6 is a low profile tyre intended for lighter high performance cars such as the Ford Escort XR 3 and the Lancia HPE Volumex. It gives good handling with plenty of grip

A braking test is a good way of comparing different tyres

Tyres are tested for noise suppression on different surfaces

cornering, sharp braking and careless scraping against kerbs wears any tyre quickly. But that is only part of the story. Two tyres of the same size, type and rating may perform quite differently when subjected to different types of stress. One may perform best and last longest when used principally for motorway driving where the lateral loads on the tyre are small. But on fast country roads where the surface is uneven and there are a lot of bends, the other tyre may perform best by an equal margin.

Choosing the 'best' tyre is further complicated by the fact that tyre design is riddled with compromises. The classic example, which still largely holds true, is the trade-off between grip and durability. This is due to the fact that the softer, sticky 'high hysteresis' compounds which grip the road best also wear fastest. But as with tread patterns, it is virtually impossible to assess a tyre's potential grip or durability just by looking at it — or even by poking it with a fingernail!

There is also very little good, consumer orientated, objective information on tyres with which to weigh up the bewildering claims made by the manufacturers for their many and various products. This is largely due to the fact that testing tyres is both time consuming and costly. So much so that the only people who really know the qualities of a wide range of tyres are the manufacturers themselves who not only exhaustively test their own products but those of their rivals too. And while in private the leading tyre makers such as Dunlop, Michelin, Pirelli, Goodyear, Firestone and Uniroyal might admit that in each class their tyres are roughly comparable, it is not so easy to find someone who will be so candid in public. As many of the large tyre retailers are owned

or franchised by one of the big tyre manufacturers unbiased advice cannot be sought there either. And while the smaller independent firms have nothing to gain in the long run by selling you inferior goods, their advice may be influenced more by their need to meet sales quotas or by the difference in profit margins between brands than by any inside information they may have on how particular tyres perform.

Original equipment tyres

A good starting point when considering which tyres to fit to your car is to look at the tyres

your car's manufacturer fitted when the car was new.

This is worth doing because tyres are no longer an afterthought but a part of a car's original design and carefully matched to its suspension. The car manufacturer will have looked for tyres that give good handling, traction, comfort and low noise. From the shortlist of tyres which met these criteria, the manufacturer will then probably fit the cheapest. Durability, a factor important to many motorists may, however, not have been given much weight.

The car manufacturer will carry out tests quite similar to those done by the tyre manufacturer, except that the car maker

design. As stricter controls have made cars increasingly quiet, the reduction of tyre noise has increasingly preoccupied the tyre designer.

Tyre noise occurs at frequencies which are particularly annoying so attempts have been made to isolate these frequencies and eliminate them.

Tyre noise is caused principally by the shoulder of the tread drumming on the road surface. Oscilloscope tests showed that the problem was largely caused by harmonics produced as each block of tread hit the road in rapid succession. By designing a

tread with blocks of different sizes arranged in an assymetric pattern it was found that the noisome harmonics could be avoided and a much quieter tyre could be produced.

Because of all these complex variables, predicting a tyre's performance can only be done through such exhaustive testing. Even the tyre designers themselves are sometimes surprised by some of the results of the computer modelling!

However, while a tyre must perform up to certain objective standards, at some stage a subjective evaluation of the tread pattern will also be made.

For despite there being no practical value in such an assessment, the tyre manufacturers are keenly aware that tyres also have a cosmetic role to play and that few motorists would choose a patently unattractive design, however good its performance on the road.

But apart from not being able to judge a tyre purely on its tread pattern, there are other reasons why choosing tyres is so difficult. First, the life expectancy of a tyre depends as much on the way it is used as on the way it was built. Severe handling, especially fierce

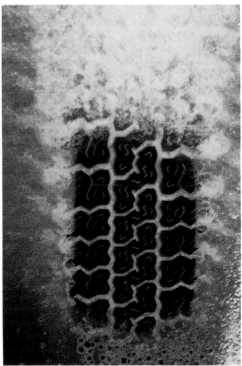

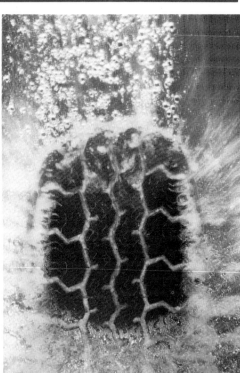

Tyre footprint shows its ability to clear water

Footprint of Dunlop SP4 at 60 mph on wet road

High performance tyres all show similar design criteria

Mud and Snow tyre has deep block tread and square shoulders

test them on specific models of car. Starting with a shortlist of tyres whose specifications match the car's requirements of size, construction, speed and load ratings, each tyre will be tested first on a rig designed to measure grip and wear qualities. The tyres are tried out on a wide range of road surfaces and are also tested for noise. Only when a tyre has passed these simulated driving tests is it fitted to a car and tried out on the test track, where experienced drivers assess its performance for real.

So replacing your car's tyres with those recommended by the manufacturer assures you a high standard of performance and safety. You should never fit a tyre of a lower specification than that recommended by the manufacturer. This could negate your insurance claim if an accident happened and may also be an illegal modification of the car.

On the other hand, if you exploit your car's performance to the full or cover a very high annual mileage then you may decide to fit tyres of a higher specification.

But whether you fit lower, higher, or equivalent specification tyres or those from another manufacturer, it is vital that you weigh up the pros and cons and choose the right tyre for your needs.

Changing tyre size

Changing from your car manufacturer's recommended tyre size is, in most cases, not a good idea. There is always a temptation to fit wider tyres than those fitted as standard in the hope that better handling and even

better looks will be the result. Cosmetically, wider wheels may be an improvement but their effect on your car's handling is less likely to be beneficial. While the extra tread might result in a marginal increase in dry weather grip, wet weather traction would be reduced.

The amount of contact between the tyre and the road is a crucial part of the handling equation when the car designer is calculating the performance characteristics of the car. Often the spread of weight achieved by widening the tyres is unfavourable and in wet weather water can build up under the tyre as there is insufficient weight on the tyre's contact patch to pump it away. At high speed in very wet conditions the car may even aquaplane

with possibly disastrous consequences.

Changing from a regular tyre profile to a low profile tyre is also a way of changing tyre size. Although if you simply fit a tyre with a lower profile to your car's standard wheel rims your tyres will have a smaller diameter. At the very least this will render your speedometer inaccurate and in some cases may also throw unwanted strain on the engine as you will have to use higher engine speeds to achieve a given road speed.

There are benefits to be gained from fitting low aspect ratio tyres, however. The somewhat stiffer sidewalls of these low profile tyres give more precise steering and handling. And in some cases the lower rolling resistance of these tyres can also benefit fuel consumption. Against this low aspect ratio tyres do tend to give a somewhat harsh and noisy ride. But to really benefit from this type of tyre you need to change your wheels as well so that you can can maintain the same overall wheel diameter as the standard fitting.

Choosing replacement tyres

If you are only replacing one or two tyres your choice of tyre type may be limited. If your car has cross plies fitted and you only want to fit one new tyre then it will have to be a cross ply. This is because the only permissable mix of cross ply and radial tyres is cross plies on both front wheels and radials on both rear wheels.

If your car already has good quality radials and you are just replacing a single tyre then there is a case for fitting another tyre of the same make and type. But any equivalent tyre from another manufacturer could be fitted instead.

These tyres are: 165 mm wide, 70% aspect ratio, radials, safe to 113 mph; and fit 13 in. rims

wheel cross section

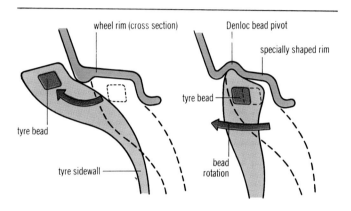

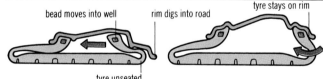

Effect of a blowout on a conventional and Denloc beaded tyre

When changing all your tyres your choice is wider. Fitting the tyres chosen as original equipment by your car's manufacturer guarantees a minimum standard of safety and performance. But there are reasons why you may wish to consider alternatives. For example, if your car was originally fitted with cross ply tyres then a switch to radials would save you money both in the short and long term. This is because cross ply tyres are now often dearer than radials due to the diminishing demand. Radial tyres also last longer and have a lower rolling resistance and so can cut your fuel bills.

But even if your car already has radials the ongoing developments in tyre compounds, tread design and bracing materials could mean that the tyres originally specified for your car have been superseded. A newer model of tyre could well substantially enhance the performance of your car. Although care must be taken to still choose a tyre that will compliment the car's suspension design, otherwise the gains in handling may be at the expense of ride comfort.

Another reason to change your brand of tyre may be take advantage of a cheaper tyre from another manufacture. For as new profiles and compounds become available the maker's original fitment may become less economic than one of the discounted newcomers. So if, for example, your car had Goodyear G800s, then there is no reason why you should not replace them with Goodyear Grand Prix S, Avon Turbo-steels, Firestone S-211 or Michelin MX should you find them at a lower price.

To find out whether one tyre is compatible with another you need only decipher the writing on the sidewall. All tyres are marked with a code which is almost universal. If, for instance, your tyres are marked 175/70 HR 14 then you know that they are 175 mm wide across the tread, have an aspect ratio of 70%, are safe up to 130 mph, are radials and fit 14 in rims.

The way in which speed ratings are applied to tyres is under revision but you will still commonly find tyres marked either R,S,T,U,H, or V which indicate that the tyres are safe at sustained speeds of up to 105, 113, 118, 124, 130 and over 130 mph respectively. Newer tyres also carry an index number which indicates the load capacity of the tyre.

If you intend to stick with the standard size of tyre all you have to do is try all the local suppliers and compare their prices for your particular size and make of tyre. If you plan to try a different make or a slightly different size of tyre (see page 38) then it is a good idea to call the local main agent for your make of car who should be able to tell you if there are any serious objections to your choice.

Bargain hunting

When shopping around for tyres never sacrifice safety for a bargain. Assess your driving style and the requirements of your car, choose a tyre or range of tyres which are suitable, then go in search of the lowest price.

There are, in fact, several ways that you can obtain tyres at bargain prices. A manufacturer may be clearing old stock to make way for a new model. You may then be able to find the older tyre offered at a discount.

Tyres from little-know foreign manufacturers are often the cheapest tyres advertised, and are worth investigating. Try asking the dealer which manufacturers fit them as standard. If the distributor cannot tell you then it is probably best to steer clear of them unless they met all the relevant DIN and BS specifications regarding your needs.

Another way to save money is to ask the dealer if he has any tyres with cosmetic defects. These can be minor in nature, such as the manufacturer's name failing to appear in detail, but often these tyres are sold extremely cheaply. In no way will such tyres be inferior in performance to perfect ones.

If you are really not worried about the appearance of the tyres and never drive faster than the legal limit a set of remoulds from a reputable manufacturer could save you money but be careful that they meet all the specifications required by the law.

Many reputable car breakers supply second hand tyres. If you are tempted to follow this path make sure that you examine any tyres which you buy very carefully.

Look after your tyres

A car's only contact with the road is through its tyres — through them a car is accelerated, steered and stopped. It is vital, therefore, that you keep the tyres in good condition

It takes only a small flaw in a car's tyres for the safety of the occupants to be threatened. If the tyres are damaged or worn, or if they are under or overinflated then the car's handling may become unpredictable — even dangerous. So to steer clear of trouble and to keep your car safe and roadworthy thorough checks on the condition of the tyres and wheels are essential and should be made at regular intervals.

When to do these jobs
Check tyre pressures and tyre condition every week
Inspect tread and sidewalls closely every month

What this job involves
Removing wheels for thorough inspection
Checking tyre pressures
Checking tread depth
Replacing a valve core
Tyre and wheel care

Related jobs in this handbook
Tyres wear unevenly
Please see Index for page numbers

To do this job
Tools: Tyre pressure gauge; tyre tread depth gauge; wheel wrench or appropriate socket spanner; torque wrench for alloy wheels; valve core removing tool; tyre inflator; small flat-bladed screwdriver; file; hammers; brushes; torch or inspection light
Materials: Tyre-cleaning solvent; new valve core; tyre paint
Time: Inspection 20 minutes; repairs 30 minutes to 1 hour
Degree of difficulty: Very easy

If you have the job professionally done . . .
Are the tyre pressures correct? Have the wheel trims been replaced? Has the spare been taken out and checked too?

Tyre pressure gauges

Garage gauges
A garage is likely to have one of three different types of pressure gauge. The most common type incorporates the dial in the air line nose. Another common type has the dial mounted on a stand somewhere at the side of the forecourt. This dial swivels so that you can see the reading on the dial from any position. The third type — and now rarely seen — is also swivel mounted but is pre-calibrated — that is, you set the pressure you want on the dial then push the button to pump air into the tyre. As it does this it pings. Once the pressure you want is reached, it stops pinging.

Connecting the air line to the valve can be tricky. There are basically two types of connector; one type has a long rod and angled head, which you hold in place over the valve. The other has a catch that locks the connector in place over the valve. Pull back the knob that releases the catch, push the head over the valve and release the knob; the catch then locks securely on to the valve.

To pump up the tyre, you simply push a button or lever, whichever is provided. Some air lines also have a button or lever to let air out.

DIY gauges
Two types of tyre pressure gauge are available at accessory shops. The more common design has a calibrated plunger inside a barrel fitted with a connector which you hold firmly against the tyre valve. As the pin inside the valve is pressed the air pressure pushes up the plunger and you can read the pressure against the engraved calibration marks on the plunger itself.

A second design, not usually quite as accurate as the plunger type, is a dial gauge. With this type of gauge, the air pressure operates a needle which you then read off against a calibrated scale on the dial.

Both types of gauge are usually calibrated in the Imperial measure of pounds per square inch (psi) and the metric measure bars or kg/cm^2.

But if you find that your handbook or the gauge you are using has only one scale then you can convert psi into bar by multiplying by 0.069. To convert bars to psi simply divide by the same factor. Easier still, charts showing both figures are displayed in most garages.

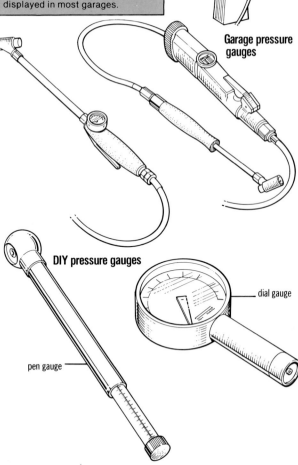

Garage pressure gauges

DIY pressure gauges

dial gauge

pen gauge

Most tyre problems can be spotted by carefully inspecting the tyres while they are on the car. Use a torch or inspection light to see the inside tyre walls and roll the car forward so that you can check the full circumference. For a closer inspection jack up the car and turn the wheels by hand. Always support the car on axle stands if you are going to work under it. To make full checks on the wheels they must be removed — it makes sense to do either the front or the rear pair or one side of the car at a time.

Park the car on level ground, put the handbrake on and chock the wheels that are to remain on the ground. Loosen the wheelnuts on the two wheels to be removed — about a turn is enough. Jack up the car so the wheels are well off the ground and put axle stands in place, then lower the car on to them. Scratch or paint corresponding marks on the hub or studs and wheel so you can replace the wheel in the same position and not upset their balance. Undo the wheelnuts and take off the wheels.

Now inspect the tread for wear or damage. The wear on the tread should be evenly spread across the whole width of the tyre. If the tyre has plenty of tread left, use a depth gauge for this (see Step 2). You will not otherwise be able to spot anything but the most severe unevenness. But it is well worth the effort — even a small amount of uneven wear is a sign of trouble, and if left uncorrected will shorten the life of a tyre by months.

If one part of the tread is wearing more than another there can be a number of causes. Undue wear in the centre of the tread is due to persistent overinflation (**fig 1**). Check that the tyre pressures are within the manufacturer's recommended range. If they are not, adjust them accordingly.

1. Wear due to overinflation   **2. Wear due to underinflation**

3. Feathering caused by suspension or steering faults

As a general rule it is best to always check tyre pressure with a good quality tyre pressure gauge — do not rely on the accuracy of the gauge on the garage air line or your foot pump.

Excessive wear on both the inside and outside tyre edge points to regular underinflation (**fig 2**). It takes about 5000 miles for such a pattern to appear and normally results in a smooth rubber surface. Again, check the pressures and make any adjustments necessary.

A pattern of baldness on just one side of the tread accompanied by a visible roughness, or 'feathering', of the rubber surface indicates a problem of wheel alignment (**fig 3**). The wheel may either have been knocked out of alignment by

violent kerbing or there may be damage to or wear in parts of the steering or suspension mechanism. (See page 231 for details on how to check steering geometry).

It is quite common for just one wheel of the front pair to show this type of wear. Although both wheels may be out of alignment the geometry of the car's steering tends to make one of them run true while the other suffers all the wear. But if a tracking check shows that the alignment is correct, the fault must be somewhere in the suspension — such as a bent or damaged MacPherson strut.

Next, turn your attention to the sidewalls. Watch out for splits and cuts (**fig 5**). In the UK if they are greater than one inch long

4. Badly damaged wheel rim caused by kerbing

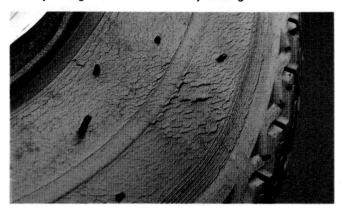

5. Splits in tyre wall caused by the rubber perishing

or if they are deep enough to expose, or even cut through the tyre reinforcement belting, you must replace the tyre as it is illegal. A surface texture of minute cracks is caused by the effect of atmospheric ozone and other oxidizing agents acting on

Skinny spares

Some European makers supply cars with a narrow width spare tyre that is designed to take up less boot space. The use of these so-called 'skinny' spares has been controversial although they are now cleared for emergency use only.

The tyres have the full circumference of the car's normal tyre and wheel combination and bolt on in the normal way. To support the car's weight across a narrower tread they must be inflated to a much higher pressure than normal tyres. As they have much poorer heat dispersal and other properties they must be used strictly in accordance with the maker's maximum speed and mileage instructions.

the rubber. This is not usually a safety problem but it would be wise to consider replacing the tyres on a little-used car after about five years.

Missing tread blocks or bulges in any part of the rubber are signs of very serious tyre structure damage. Sometimes resulting from a fault in manufacture (especially on retreads), a bulge or loss of tread may be a symptom of a problem with the rubber composition or the bonding of the various layers of the tyre's construction. Occasionally bulges on the sidewall may result from pinching the tyre against a kerb; tread loss can be accidental, too, but in either case it is worth reporting the fault to the tyre retailer, or direct to the manufacturer quoting all the code numbering you will find on the tyre side wall. The problem may affect all the other tyres in the same batch.

Kerbing is the most common cause of wheel damage (**fig 4**). Violent knocks dent the wheel rim, sometimes seriously enough to upset the seating of the tyre bead and cause a slow loss of air. While the edge of the rim can be repaired (see Step 4), it is not advisable to try to repair dented or buckled seating areas. While the wheel is off the car carefully examine the wheelnut seats for any signs of cracking that may have resulted from overtightening or accident damage. If you do find cracks, get a new wheel.

You can now refit the wheels. Put the wheel on the hub in the same position as it was before removal. Replace the wheelnuts or bolts and do them up handtight into the seatings. Remove the axle stands and lower the car to the ground. Firmly tighten the wheelnuts using only the hand force you can exert on the car's standard wheel wrench — even better use a torque wrench at the handbook's recommended setting.

In the UK the law demands that there is a continuous band of tread pattern at least 1 mm (.04 in.) deep around the whole tyre and that the pattern should be visible over the complete width of the tyre tread area But this is the minimum required for safety. Some experts say that when the tread wears below 2 mm (.08 in.) there is a serious deterioration in road-holding and the ability to stop, especially on wet or greasy roads.

So it makes good sense to ensure that there is at least 2 mm of tread depth all round the tyre. The best way to measure tread is with a special depth gauge which consists of a probe attached to a scale which slides inside a barrel. Put the probe on

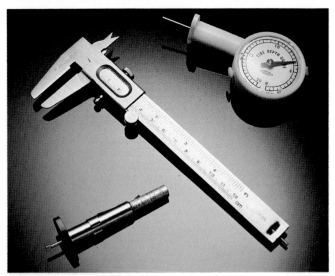

1. Alternative tools for measuring tread depth

2. Using dial gauge

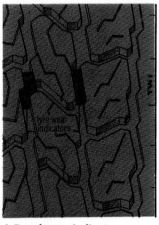

3. Using 10p coin

4. Tread wear indicator

the bottom of the tread groove and hold the barrel, which has a flattened base, touching the top of the tread block. Now read the depth off on the scale. Repeat the measurements several times around the tyre's circumference.

Even though most of the tread is over 2 mm (.08 in) you may find a flat spot, perhaps caused by heavy braking, where the tread is substantially lower. It is best to replace tyres early – for safety's sake and to avoid prosecution.

There are two more quick checks you can make on the legality of a tyre. A handy tread depth gauge is the dotted line inside the raised rim of a British 10p coin which is almost exactly 1 mm from the coin edge. Insert the coin edge-on into the tread groove and the dotted line should not be visible from the side (**fig 3**). Repeat the check in several parts of the tyre.

The other clue to tyre legality is the tread depth indicator bars often called the tread wear indi-

cator (TWI) found on most tyre designs. Running across the tread pattern, the markers are raised ribs of rubber 1.6 mm (0.6 in) higher than the bottom of the tread groove (**fig 4**). The position of each indicator bar is marked on the tyre's sidewall, by the letters TWI or the manufacturers trade symbol, sometimes accompanied by a small triangle. When these bars appear level with the surrounding tread blocks the tyre is nearing the minimum tread depth.

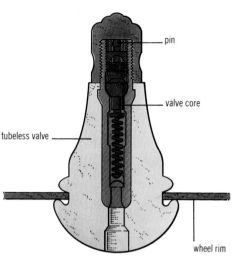

pin

valve core

tubeless valve

wheel rim

1. Cross-section of a tubeless tyre valve

2. Checking for air leaks

Valves can occasionally leak through wear or, more usually, through minute dirt particles sticking in the seat of the valve. To check for a leak put a blob of spit or washing-up liquid on the valve tip — any loss of air will be betrayed by bubbles forming within a couple of seconds (see **fig 2**).

On the majority of valves of the Schrader type it is possible to replace the valve core (**fig 1**). The valve core is removed using a special tool available from garages and accessory shops. To replace the core jack up the car and let the tyre down by pressing on the valve centre pin. Insert the valve tool and unscrew the valve core (**fig 3**). Screw in the new core and reinflate the tyre. Note that if the bead seal has broken on a tubeless tyre you will probably have to take the wheel to a high pressure air line at a garage — this is because a foot pump will not give enough pressure to force the bead against the rim. But if you only have a foot pump, try the Tip — Rope trick.

Although valve core removing tools can be purchased at accessory shops many motorists

3. Removing valve core

will already have one lying around unrecognized. The most common type is incorporated into a tyre valve cap, the kind that has a pointed shape with a broad groove across the tip. This tip can be inserted into the valve and engaged with the core to unscrew it. Another place you might find a valve tool is screwed into the top of the barrel of your tyre pressure gauge. You should be able to recognize this by the groove, which engages the valve core.

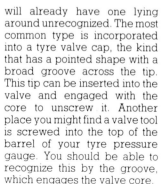

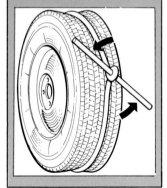

At monthly inspections use a small screwdriver to lever out any stones, glass or other road debris that has found its way into the tread grooves or has punctured the tread blocks (**fig 1**). Take tacks and nails out carefully, using pliers, as they may be bent inside the tyre and you may cause damage to the reinforcing belts if you pull them out violently. If you hear the hiss of a puncture when you pull a nail out get the tyre repaired by a specialist.

At one time car handbooks used to recommend swapping the tyres around the car to even up wear. There are several reasons why this is no longer considered a good idea. First, it means all the tyres wear out at once so you have to replace all four in one go. Second, front wheels usually need to be balanced, which is an additional expense once you have swapped them. And finally, tyre technologists have discovered that the constant rotation of a tyre in one direction 'sets' the rubber and the reinforcing belts in a pattern of internal tensions. Changing the direction of rotation, either on purpose or by chance, will change this pattern and shorten tyre life. If you feel you must rotate tyres to even up the wear the only allowable way is to swap wheels front to rear *on the same side of the car.*

For the sake of appearance and especially when you sell your car it is very pleasing to clean up the car's tyres and wheels.

Proprietary cleaners are available to dissolve away the persistent dust that results from the wear of disc pads and mars the appearance of wheels, particularly alloy wheels. Brush the cleaner on, leave it for a while and then rinse it off.

To repair minor denting on the lip of a steel wheel let the tyre down and break the seal between the bead and the rim. Hold the bead away from the damaged section using a suitable G-clamp to squeeze the

tyre between two pads of wood. Using a hammer on one side of the dent and a heavy mallet on the other, the dent can be flattened out. Use a file to smooth off any rough spots. Apply a rust treatment to any bared metal according to the product instructions and then mask the wheel before using an aerosol wheel paint to finish the cosmetic treatment. Release the

G-clamp and use an air line to reseat the bead and inflate the tyre to the correct pressure.

The paintwork on a steel wheel can also be thoroughly cleaned by using a wire brush attachment to an electric drill. Mask off the tyre and then apply three or four coats of wheel paint.

Tyre rubber can either be restored to a new appearance by using a proprietary solvent treatment or tyre paint. Follow the directions for the solvent treatment very carefully as the liquids used are highly flammable, may damage paintwork and can weaken the tyre wall.

Tyre paint can be used on the sidewalls at any time and this is a very quick way of sprucing up the whole car's general appearance. Wash the tyre thoroughly with detergent and water and allow it to dry before lightly buffing the surface with sandpaper (**fig 3**). Apply the paint with a brush or painting pad using two coats, if necessary, to get an even colour. Allow the paint to dry before taking the car out. A cheap alternative to tyre paint is shoe polish. Apply the polish with a brush or cloth then buff to a shine.

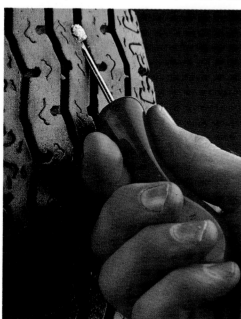

1. Removing stones from tyre tread

2. Old tyre ready for dressing

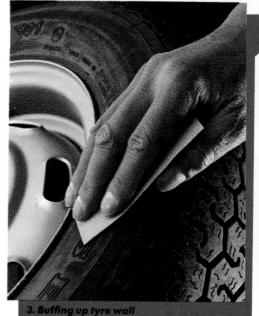

3. Buffing up tyre wall

4. Freshly painted tyre and wheel

Replacing old carpets

A new carpet brightens up the interior of the car and helps to make it more comfortable and soundproof. The job is made easy if you use a ready-cut carpet tailored to fit your car

If the floor coverings in your car are tatty or worn, it is quite a simple matter to replace them with new pre-cut carpets. Old and worn carpets detract from the appearance and value of a car just as poor bodywork does. New carpets, ready cut and shaped for virtually every model of car, are not expensive and are widely available. It should take only a couple of hours to fit new carpets but they will transform the interior of your car making it more comfortable and soundproof.

Alternatively, you can repair small areas of damage in your existing carpet if you just want to spruce up the interior, perhaps to sell the car. To create small patches of carpet, look under the front seats where there is often enough extra material.

What this job involves
Removing seats
Removing seat belt anchorages
Removing handbrake and gear lever gaiters
Pulling up old carpet
Fitting new carpet

Related jobs in this handbook
Fitting rear seat belts
Please see Index for page numbers

To do this job
Tools: Spanner to fit seat mountings (maybe); cross-head screwdriver; large scissors (maybe); utility knife (maybe); wide chisel or paint scraper (maybe)
Materials: Carpet kit; spare piece of matching carpet (maybe); rubber based adhesive (maybe)
Time: An afternoon
Degree of difficulty: Very straightforward, although removing old carpet which has been stuck down can be difficult

If you have the job professionally done...
Have all the fittings been properly replaced? Are the new carpets fixed down firmly? Has all the trim been fixed without any gaps? Are the seats secure? Can you operate the pedals properly?

When buying carpet kits, make sure that you buy the right one for your car. Also check the quality — most suppliers offer two grades, polypropylene or viscose yarn. You may feel it is worth investing in a set made from the more hard-wearing viscose yarn. If you want exactly the same carpet as the original one, you can order it from your local franchised dealer, but it is likely to be much less expensive if you buy from a general kit supplier.

If your car is quite an old model, you may find that the dealer can only supply carpets in a very limited range of colours. Look in car magazine advertisement sections for the names and addresses of kit suppliers. The range of colours may be wider than from the main dealer, but you may find that the fit and edging is not as good, particularly in the case of the cheaper kits — as with many car accessories you usually only get what you pay for.

1. Pre-cut carpets are available for most models

2. Part of the colour range

4. Look for protective edgings

3. Best quality carpets are latex backed

Before you can take out the old carpets you will have to remove some of the interior fittings. Very often the front seats will have to be removed and, in addition, you may have to take out the seat belt mountings, the sill trims and the central console, if one is fitted.

The front seats may be secured in a number of different ways, but you should be able to see how to take them out by looking underneath.

On many models, the runners on which the seat slides are secured to the floorpan. In this case slide the seat as far forward as it will go and remove the two rear retaining bolts. Then slide the seat right back and undo the front bolts (**fig 1**). You can then lift out the whole assembly.

Some types of seat, where the whole unit tips forward to allow passengers to get into the back of the car, are secured to the floor by one or two brackets at the front of the seat. When you unbolt these note the position of any spacers or bushes; these must be replaced in their original positions.

If your seats are hinged at the front you might also have to remove a locking bar from the rear of the seat assembly. This will probably be bolted through the floorpan of the car and the bolts are very likely to be rusted in place. Soak the bolts thoroughly with penetrating oil or releasing fluid before you attempt to undo them.

If you are very lucky you may find that there is no need to unbolt any part of the seat. On certain cars it is possible to lift the retaining catch and move the seat forward until it is fully clear of its runners.

With the seats out of the car, you will be able to see clearly whether any further dismantling is necessary. Quite possibly you will find that the runners, if they have not already been removed, will have to come out before you can free the carpet.

Seat belt mountings should be no problem — they are simply bolted to the floorpan, transmission tunnel or a bracket between the seats (**fig 3**). It is very important to make sure that if the securing bolts are fitted with any washers or locking devices you refit these correctly later.

Now look along the door sills. On most cars, the plastic, or metal sill trim is secured over the carpet and will have to be removed. The trim is held in place by a number of self-tapping screws, but you may also find a small bolt at each end. Simply remove the bolts or screws and free the trim (**fig 4**).

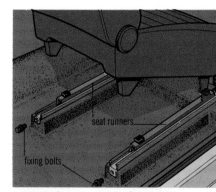

1. Unbolting a sliding seat

3. Removing the seat belt mountings

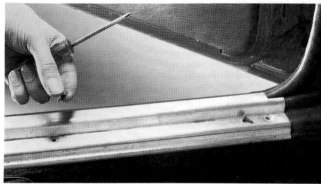

4. Unscrewing the sill trim to free the carpet

seat runners

fixing bolts

2. Hinged seat — typical assembly

ALTERNATIVE 2 — REMOVE CENTRE CONSOLE AND GAITERS

If your car is fitted with a central console (**fig 1**), you have to remove it to get at the transmission tunnel carpet. The console will be held in place by screws or bolts, which might be concealed under covers. Prise out the covers, if fitted, and remove the bolts or screws (**fig 2**). Now lift the console up over the handbrake lever.

If the console is still attached to the handbrake by the rubber gaiter, simply pull the gaiter's base from the console and leave it attached to the lever. Before pulling the console right away from the transmission tunnel check to make sure you will not damage or strain any electrical wiring. Disconnect any wires, which could be damaged, first labelling them with masking tape tabs so that you reconnect them correctly later.

The gear lever knob may need to be unscrewed to allow you to lift the console gaiter over the top.

On many cars, the carpet is also secured to the transmission tunnel by the gear lever gaiter. If this is the case, simply unscrew the bolts or screws at the plastic or metal base of the gaiter. If the gaiter is made completely of rubber, simply pull it out of the floor. There is no need to take the gaiter from the car — just slide it up the gear lever until it is out of the way of the floor pan (**fig 3**).

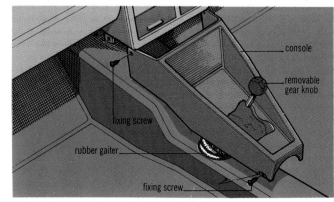

console

removable gear knob

fixing screw

rubber gaiter

fixing screw

1. How the central console is fixed in place

2. Some screws may be awkward to find

3. Pulling back the rubber gaiter

The old carpet will be held in place either by a number of press studs or screws around the edges or by an adhesive. In some cases you will find a combination of the two.

Studded or screwed carpets are simple to remove — simply work around the edges, pulling each stud free (**fig 1**) or un-screwing each screw. Once the studs or screws have been released the whole carpet can be lifted clear. On most cars the carpet comes in two pieces — one at the front and one at the rear. But if a central console is fitted, each front seat footwell may have separate carpets.

If the carpet is glued, start by releasing one corner and pull gently to see if the rest of the carpet will come free. There is no point in using too much brute force. All you will achieve is a ripped carpet, with most of it still stuck to the floor.

TIP

Removing stubborn adhesive

If you find it difficult to free the carpets because of the bonding adhesive, use acetone or a similar solvent to soften the adhesive and break the bond. Then use a broad tool such as a paint scraper to prise the carpet free. If you do have to resort to using any type of solvent, remember they are highly flammable. Many solvents also give off fumes which can be harmful in a confined space — so open the car doors and windows.

Try prising it free with a paint scraper (**fig 2**) or a mason's chisel. A screwdriver might do the job, but could well just make holes in the carpet or even the floor pan if it is rusty.

When the carpet is free you will have to manoeuvre it past the gear lever and handbrake. Make a mental note of how the old carpet pieces come free, because although fitting new carpets looks simple, position-ing fitted carpets can some-times be quite tricky.

1. Removing stud fixings on old carpet

2. Prising off a carpet secured with glue

Before putting down the new carpet, scrape clean and sweep the floor of the car. This is particularly important if you are going to use an adhesive to keep the new carpet in place.

The majority of carpet kits come in two pieces, manufac-tured to fit a specific car. However, it is important to check what you are getting in your kit — some contain only carpet cut to fit the floor area. A full kit includes carpeting for the sills, wheel arches and transmission tunnel. It should also have a sewn-in heel pad, usually of plastic, for the driver's side (**fig 1**).

Pre-cut holes should already be made in the carpet for the gear lever, pedals and, in some cases, seat runners. Work the carpet into position and, if studs are fitted, simply go around the outside of the carpet pressing them into place.

If you intend to use adhesive this may be supplied with your kit; if not, use a rubber-based adhesive and apply a thick film to the floorpan (**fig 2**) and to the back of the carpet. It is not necessary to cover the whole of the carpet area with adhesive — do the footwells, sills and trans-mission tunnel thoroughly, then a couple of blobs on the floor-pan will be sufficient.

The procedure is exactly the same for the rear section of carpet — positioning this will be much easier than the front part, but you may find that you need to lift out the rear seat squab to do the job properly (**fig 4**). This will be held only by a couple of screws or spring clips at each side. If you cannot find any screws, simply pull it — it should lift away.

Finally, replace the interior trim — gear lever gaiter, console, seats and sill trims.

2. Applying the rubber-based adhesive

3. The front carpet in position

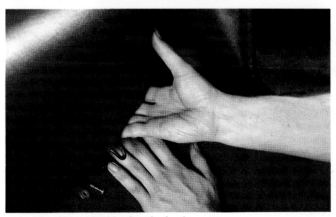

4. Tucking the carpet under the back seat

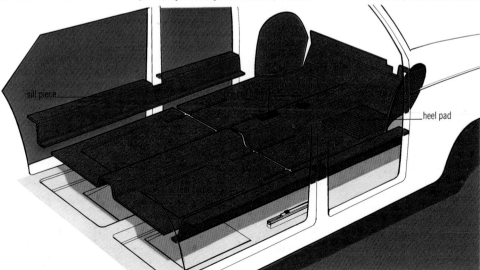

sill piece

heel pad

1. The contents of a typical carpet kit (in red) and how it fits in place

The procedure for replacing a worn or damaged boot or hatchback carpet is exactly the same as for interior carpeting and many proprietary kits will include these extra pieces.

But even if boot carpet is not included in a kit, it is a simple matter to buy a matching piece of carpet, cut it to size, and fit it yourself. Fitting a carpet in the boot is a good idea as it prevents your luggage from scratching the paintwork and it also helps considerably in cutting down noise levels.

To make up your own carpets, the most important thing is to get the measurements right. Do not rely on a ruler or tape measure, but make up a template from paper or thin cardboard (**fig 1**).

Put the paper or cardboard in the boot and mark it by pushing it into the boot corners with your fingernail or a screwdriver. Take your time over this and make sure at the end that the template exactly fits the boot space. Cut it to size with a large pair of scissors. Once you have made the template, mark the side which is uppermost before you remove it from the boot. Place the template on top of the carpet. Now carefully cut around the template, using large sharp scissors or a utility knife (**fig 2**). Cut the carpet very slightly oversize at this stage — about ½ in. all round.

Put the carpet in to the boot to check its fit. You may find it necessary to trim it around the edges but if the template was made accurately there should be no problem — the slightly oversize carpet should wedge into the boot corners snugly.

Once you are satisfied that the fit is correct, glue the carpet to the boot floor with adhesive (**fig 3**). However, if your car has the spare wheel fitted into a well in the boot floor do not glue the carpet down, simply lay it in place. Because of the uneven shape of the majority of boot areas, the carpet should stay put without any further fixing. It is also handy to be able to lift the carpet occasionally to check for dampness and rust in the spare wheel well. If a bolt with its head inside the boot secures the spare wheel in a bracket which hangs underneath the car, take care not to glue the carpet down over this.

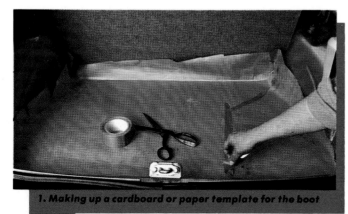
1. Making up a cardboard or paper template for the boot

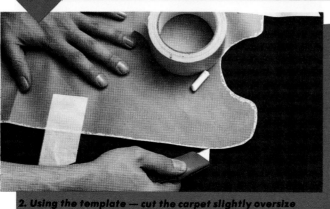
2. Using the template — cut the carpet slightly oversize

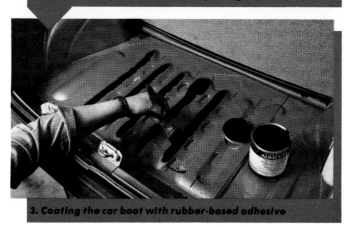
3. Coating the car boot with rubber-based adhesive

Rather than going to the expense of replacing all the carpets in the car, it may be possible to repair isolated areas of damage or wear.

The most common problem is when carpets come loose at the edges and then start to fray. If you notice any carpeting coming loose you should deal with it as soon as possible to prevent unnecessary wear.

Where the carpet has come loose, pull it back a little farther and apply a thin layer of adhesive to the back of the carpet and to the floorpan or footwell. Then press the carpet back into place. If the carpet has frayed badly, you may be able to repair it by binding the edge with heavy-duty tape (**fig 1**). For the best results, the tape should be sewn on but this can be difficult without going to all the trouble of taking the carpet out of the car. As an alternative it is possible to attach the tape to the carpet edge using a suitable fabric adhesive.

If a patch in the centre of the carpet needs a repair, it is probably best to replace the whole carpet — to repair it you will have to remove the carpet anyway. Bear in mind that unless the repair is needed because of accidental damage the chances are that other areas will be worn quite badly as well.

You can repair a small damaged area — a cigarette burn, for example — with a piece of matching carpet. A small offcut from a carpet shop is ideal for this purpose.

1. Taping the edge

First remove the piece of carpet containing the damaged area. Use a sharp knife to cut a square or oblong-shaped section out of the carpet around the damaged area (**fig 2**).

Turn the carpet over and attach four lengths of carpet tape around the outside of the hole (**fig 3**). The tape should overlap the outer edge of the hole. If the tape is not self-adhesive, apply a suitable rubber-based carpet adhesive to the underside.

Turn the carpet right side up, cut a matching piece to fit and press it into position. When the repair has been made, refit the carpet in the car.

TIP

Dyeing the worn carpet

Worn areas which look untidy can be dyed the same colour as the surrounding carpet. Find a dye the same colour as your car carpet and make up a solution of dye and water according to the instructions supplied with the dye. Rub the solution into the worn area of carpet with a clean rag.

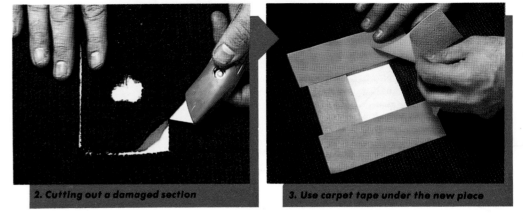
2. Cutting out a damaged section

3. Use carpet tape under the new piece

How to repair dents and chips

Don't be afraid of bodywork repairs. If you prepare well and choose the correct materials, you can achieve a great result

Careful preparation is the key to success in bodywork repairs. This includes removing all the paint and rust in the affected area, rustproofing, applying filler and primer.

That said, the faster you do the job, the better. This is because you are sure to get areas of exposed metal at some stage of the job. So cover them quickly to stop rust setting in.

The materials used can be bought in kits containing a selection of resins, fillers and reinforcing materials or the items can be bought separately. Take as much time as you can in their use — the best results are achieved by very careful work.

When to do this job
When you have chips, stone bruises and dents not more than about ½ in. (12 mm) deep and a handspan wide

What this job involves
Preparing the surface
Removing any rust
Filling chip(s) or dent(s)
Priming

Related jobs in this handbook
Simple panelbeating

To do this job
Tools: Wire brush; rasp or Surform; electric drill with grinding attachment (maybe); small artist's-type paintbrush
Materials: Wet-and-dry abrasive paper in grades 200, 400 and 600; rustproofing compound; cellulose putty; epoxy resin filler (dents only); white spirit; zinc-based primer
Time: About 2 hours, spread over two or three days
Degree of difficulty: No experience needed, but requires great care and patience

If you have this job professionally done . . .
Is the repaired area invisible against its surrounding metal? Does new colour match exactly?

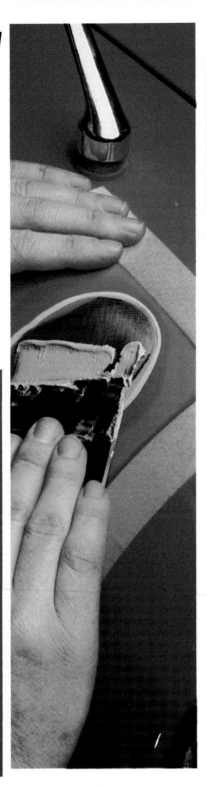

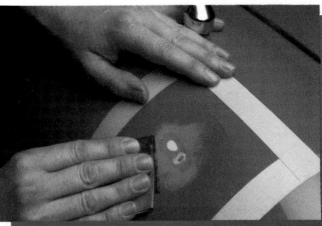

1. Rubbing away paint with wet-and-dry until metal gleams

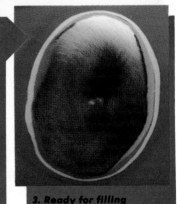

2. Scoring with wire brush

3. Ready for filling

Before you begin any repair, use a good car shampoo to make sure the area is clean.

Next, apply short strips of masking tape in a tight square around the repair area. This will protect the surrounding paintwork from accidental scratches.

What you do next depends on the type of repair needed:

Dents which have not broken the paint surface
Rub away the paint with coarse grade wet-and-dry (see Fact File box) until the metal below gleams, covering an area a little larger than the dent (**fig 1**). This step is essential — if you simply apply filler straight on to the paintwork it may lift off.

Then use a wire brush, a sharp knife or a sheet of coarse wet-and-dry to score the metal surface (**fig 2**). This will provide a good key for the filler (**fig 3**).

Now proceed to Step 2.

Chips which have not exposed bare metal
Smooth the edges of the old paintwork with 400 grade wet-and-dry, used wet. This will lightly score the bottom of the

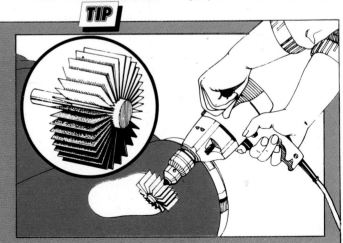

TIP

Time saver
Removing the paint from an area of bodywork can be a tedious chore — particularly with the larger dents. You can make the job easier with a flap wheel attachment on an electric drill.

Use a coarse grade of flap for this job — the finer ones are more suited to smoothing down.

A flap wheel is easier to control on paintwork than a wire brush is — but a wire brush works better on rust.

chip — enough to hold a fine layer of filler — but do not make the chip any deeper than you can help.

Now go to Alternative Step 3.

Dents or chips which have exposed bare metal

If you can see any rust, you can be almost certain that it will have taken hold not just where the chip or dent is, but also in the area immediately around it.

So use the point of a penknife to pick away the paint until all the rust is exposed and you reach clean metal.

(If the rust is very even-looking, and you do not seem to reach clean metal even if you are an inch (25 mm) or so out from the dent, stop work. You may be unlucky enough to have a panel which was not painted properly in the first place, and which has a fine coating of rust all over. Short of stripping and respraying the whole panel,

about the only thing you can do is fill the immediate hole.)

Now remove all traces of paint and rust from the area to be repaired. If the rust has bitten very deep, you may find that you need a wire brush, or even an electric drill with a small conical grinding attachment. These grinders are widely available from car accessory shops or model shops, but a piece of tightly-folded 200 grade wet-and-dry will do almost as good a job.

FACT FILE

Using wet-and-dry

The best type of abrasive paper for car bodywork repairs is wet-and-dry — so called because it can be used either wet or dry. Used dry, it is more abrasive at first but rapidly clogs with particles of paint. Used wet, it is initially less abrasive but clogs far less rapidly and can be rinsed clean when it does. It is best used with cold water — though reasonably waterproof, warm or soapy water will shorten its life.

Wet-and-dry is available in a

wide variety of grades. These are numbered according to their roughness — the lower the number the coarser the paper. For car repairs you will find the most useful grades are 200, 400 and 600. Lower, rougher grades might appear to do the job faster but they will often remove too much material or badly scratch the surrounding paintwork.

It is a good idea to keep well-used sheets for the later stages of a repair.

STEP 2 — REMOVE ANY RUST

1. Applying a coat of rustproofer with small paintbrush

Once you have the metal clean and bright, rust will start to form immediately, though it does not become obvious at first. So brush on a coat of chemical rust remover as directed by the maker's instructions (**fig 1**).

This will effectively neutralize any surface corrosion (though not rust that has penetrated right through) and inhibit further rusting.

Take great care not to spill the rustproofer on your skin or on the car's paintwork.

Most rust removers are acid based and are simply brushed on, left to react and then washed off with clean water. As soon as the area is dry start filling the dent or chip.

STEP 3 — FILL THE DENT

1. Mix filler and hardener in correct proportions

2. Use a spatula to mix thoroughly

3. Final colour must be even, not streaked

For repairing dents, use a one or two part epoxy resin or polyester based filler. A two-pack filler comprises a paste and a hardener that have to be mixed, which sets hard and can be sanded to a smooth surface.

Once mixed, two part resin filler hardens in about 20 minutes. This time can be increased or decreased by varying the amount of hardener you use. For most applications a 1:10 hardener-to-paste mixture is about right, but the exact proportions are not critical. Make sure the filler is thoroughly mixed to a consistent colour.

It is impossible to get body filler to follow exactly the original contours of the car. However careful you are, you will always have to overfill and then sand back. But the more you overfill, the more sanding you will have to do.

So build up the filler layer by layer, about ¼ in. (6 mm) at a time. Do this by using a flexible spatula to press the filler firmly

into the dent (**figs 4 & 5**). Leave the top surface of each layer rough to provide a 'key' for the next layer.

Wait until each layer has stopped being sticky — but not until it is rock-hard — before applying the next layer.

Once your top layer is standing slightly proud of the surface, wait for it to set. Then start sanding down. First, remove any obvious ridges or high spots with a file, rasp or, a Surform. This is better than coarse sandpaper, which might slip and score the surrounding paintwork.

As the filler gets closer to its final shape, swap first to 400 grade wet-and-dry (used wet) and then to 600 grade (also used wet) (**fig 6**). It is best to wrap the sandpaper around a cork block or small piece of wood so you can control it better — if you use just your fingers you will probably wear hollows in the middle of the repaired area.

When you have finished

TIP

A handy way to check shape

A woodworker's profile gauge comes in handy when sanding down a filled dent. Carefully set its points to

match an undamaged area, then scrape it over the filled dent. It will score any filler standing proud.

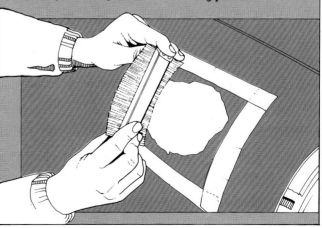

sanding, the filler should be just a coat of paint lower than the surrounding area. This is very hard to judge by eye. So — depending on which bit of the car you are working on — use a steel rule, or a bit of cardboard cut to match the curve of the car, or both, to help you.

You are almost certain to end up with a number of tiny flaws in the surface of the filler. Fill these with cellulose putty (see Alternative Step 3), applied with a fingertip (**fig 7**).

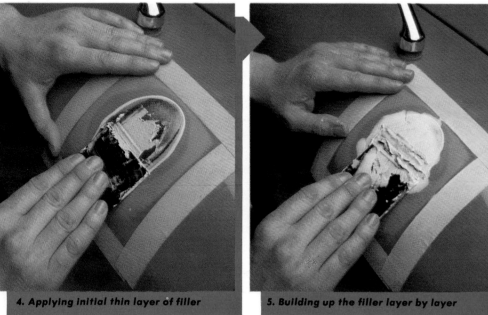
4. Applying initial thin layer of filler

5. Building up the filler layer by layer

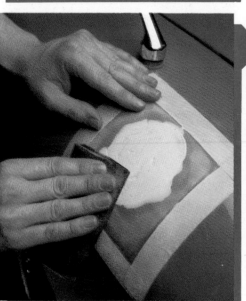
6. Sanding rough spots with wet-and-dry

7. Filling tiny flaws using a fingertip

1. Filling with cellulose putty

Even if there is no dent in the metal, as with a stone chip, you will still need to fill the repair before priming and painting. These paints do not have the bulk of the original treatment, and primer alone will not fill the gap. The best type of filler for small chips is cellulose putty. This one-pack filler — so called because it does not require a hardener — is generally sold in smaller quantities than two-pack resin fillers, is easier to work with and provides a smoother finish.

Apply the filler a little at a time, using a plastic spatula or a piece of stiff cardboard (**fig 1**). Once you have filled the depression, draw the edge of your spatula across the repair to remove any ridges standing proud of the surface. Then use a rag soaked in acetone to lift any blobs of putty from the surrounding paintwork.

The filler will be touch dry in minutes, but ideally you should leave it overnight to harden fully. When it is completely dry you will find it has shrunk slightly. With luck — or practice — you will find that this shrinkage leaves just enough room to build up the new paint finish level with the old.

If the filler stands proud, use a piece of well-used 600 grade wet-and-dry to flat the surface, taking care not to damage the surrounding paintwork. If it is too low, score its surface with 400 grade and fill again.

STEP 4 — PRIME THE REPAIR

The best way to tell whether you have produced a perfect repair is to run your fingertips lightly over the area you have filled. If you can feel an imperfection, you can be sure it will show once you apply the paint. Wipe away any fingerprints using a rag or tissue moistened with thinners — do not rub hard as existing paint may be damaged. Even if the filler feels absolutely smooth, apply a coat of rust-proofing primer (**fig 2**). This is necessary because topcoat paint is slightly porous. It will also help show up any flaws on the filler, rustproof any metal-work which you have exposed around the repair, and provide an ideal key for the topcoat.

If the repair area is up to about 2 in. (50 mm) across, you can apply the primer with a fine-haired brush. If it is bigger, the primer is better sprayed on. Either way, try to confine the primer to the actual repair area — do not lap it on to the surrounding paintwork.

Wait for the primer to dry right out — about four hours — and then sand it very carefully with old 600 grade paper before you apply the finish coat using a matching aerosol paint.

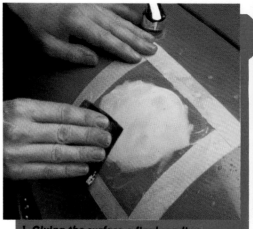
1. Giving the surface a final sanding

2. Applying rust-inhibiting primer

Knocking out dents

If your car collects a knock during parking or town driving, you can usually straighten it out — all you need is common sense and a little practice

Modern car design often makes it more efficient to replace damaged panels complete rather than repairing them. This still costs money, though — a cost which you can avoid by repairing the panel yourself.

If your car has been in a serious crash, on no account try to carry out the repairs yourself. There is always the possibility that some of the chassis and suspension components have become invisibly distorted, and this type of damage can only be checked in a professional body shop using special equipment. If the car is not correctly straightened and aligned the chances are that it will never handle properly again.

However, minor dents and bodywork damage can be dealt with very successfully using similar techniques to the professionals. There is a wide range of bodywork repair materials on the market.

What this job involves
Assessing the type and area of damage
Removing any trim fitted on the panel
Treating rust damage
Knocking out the dent

Related jobs in this handbook
How to repair dents and chips
When the bolt won't budge
Please see Index for page numbers

To do this job
Tools: General purpose panel beating hammer, dolly or wood block; dent-puller (if applicable); screwdriver; electric drill and sanding discs
Materials: Aerosol can of primer; masking tape; rust killer; new trim and fastenings (if required)
Time: A day or so, depending on the dent and allowing for dealing with rust and repainting
Degree of difficulty: Needs patience and care

If you have the job professionally done...
Does the dented area look well-finished? Is the body filler rubbed down properly? Has the rear of the panel been undersealed?

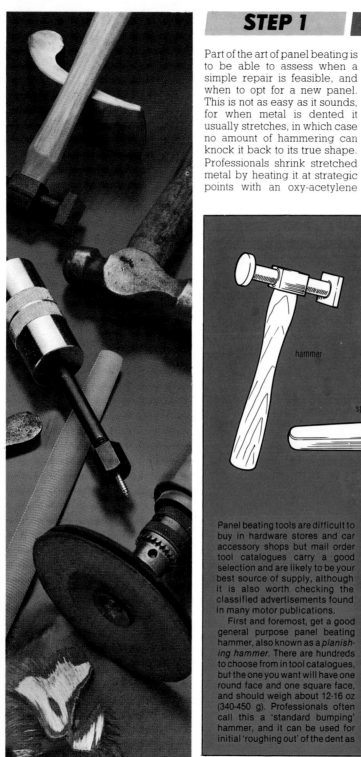

Part of the art of panel beating is to be able to assess when a simple repair is feasible, and when to opt for a new panel. This is not as easy as it sounds, for when metal is dented it usually stretches, in which case no amount of hammering can knock it back to its true shape. Professionals shrink stretched metal by heating it at strategic points with an oxy-acetylene torch, but this is outside the scope of the home mechanic, since you also require several other special tools. Instead you have two choices: either reduce the size of the dent as well as you can and then fill it with body filler, or replace the panel.

Generally, small dents, (**fig 1**) and light scratches hardly stretch the metal at all. On the other hand heavy impacts and collisions with sharp objects are likely to stretch it a great deal (**fig 2** and **3**) making a pure panel beating repair almost impossible.

Having assessed the nature of the dent, next consider the overall condition of the panel. If there is anything more than surface rust to be found you should replace the panel instead of repairing it.

FACT FILE

dolly

dolly

hammer

body file

spoon

Tools for panel beating

Panel beating tools are difficult to buy in hardware stores and car accessory shops but mail order tool catalogues carry a good selection and are likely to be your best source of supply, although it is also worth checking the classified advertisements found in many motor publications.

First and foremost, get a good general purpose panel beating hammer, also known as a *planishing hammer*. There are hundreds to choose from in tool catalogues, but the one you want will have one round face and one square face, and should weigh about 12-16 oz (340-450 g). Professionals often call this a 'standard bumping' hammer, and it can be used for initial 'roughing out' of the dent as

well as finishing work.

The other important tool is a dolly — a shaped piece of wood or metal against which the dented panel is beaten. Again, there are lots to choose from and professional body workers have sets to cope with a range of panel profiles, but to begin with a general purpose dolly made of drop forged steel and weighing about 45 oz (1275 g) should be suitable. A dolly is a precision tool and should be treated well: keep it clean and free from rust and underseal.

The spoon (a flat lever with a finely ground surface) is a very useful tool for levelling and flattening slightly curved surfaces, but you can get away by

using a small flat tyre lever.

The same applies to the panel beater's body file: it makes the job much easier but you can make do with a large metalworking file providing this has a flat and a round face. Flexible files into which you fit your own abrasive faces, are cheap to buy and are handy for smoothing down body filler. A coarse grit sanding disc attachment for an electric drill makes short work of removing old paintwork.

For pulling dents out as shown in Step 2, you need a slide hammer with a dent-pulling attachment. You will probably be able to hire this kind of tool for the weekend from your local tool hire shop at very little cost.

1. This dent will probably pop out

2. The metal here has been badly stretched

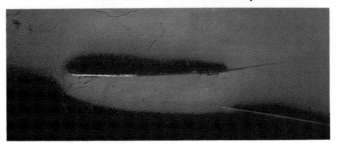

3. Creased dents often happen on doors and are difficult to reach

If the panel is hinged or bolt-on, you should be able to do this yourself, although the work involved in preparing and painting it must be taken into account. Often you can pick up perfectly serviceable replacements from a scrap yard at rock-bottom prices — simply make sure there is no structural rust. Another low-cost alternative is to ask at your local dealer for panels that were damaged in transit — again the price is low, and you can usually make good the damage using the techniques described in this article.

Even if you come to the conclusion that a repair is worth doing, you still have to decide how to tackle it. The best panel beating technique — see Step 4 — is to knock out the dent from behind using a hammer and dolly, and for this you require plenty of access. The alternative is to pull out the dent with a slide hammer, but in this case success cannot always be guaranteed.

The problems escalate when the panel concerned is double-skinned. Most rear wings use this construction as do doors, bonnets and boot lids. In the case of doors it is sometimes possible to gain access by removing the interior trim and window, but generally it is less trouble to replace the entire door with a secondhand one.

For a beginner, the easiest repairs are to small dents on the valances and front wings.

Damage to other parts of the car is best left until you have had some practice.

 TIP

Spot the damage

If there is any doubt about how far the dent extends, spray a light covering of primer over the damaged area. When this has dried (aerosol paint takes only a few minutes), wrap a piece of sandpaper around a wooden dowel or ruler and rub over the painted area. Where the panel is dented the primer will remain untouched, while the correctly contoured parts should start to shine as the primer comes off to leave you with a clearly outlined area of damage.

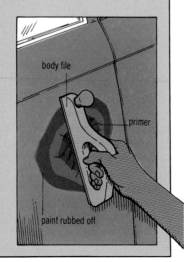

body file

primer

paint rubbed off

However, if you plan to tackle the dent, the next step is always to remove everything from the panel that is likely to get in the way, and then to prepare the surrounding surface for repair and refinishing.

Trim strips usually unclip — use a small screwdriver to prise the strips away (**fig 1**). Other types of trim such as badges are usually bolted or screwed on from behind, in which case you may have to chip away the underseal to uncover the fixings. If you cannot find any bolts or screws, prise off the badge with a screwdriver.

Next remove any components which are likely to be disturbed or damaged during the hammering process. These include the headlamp and sidelight units (**fig 2**) and grilles (see relevant project pages for details of how to remove them). Sealed beam headlamp filaments, in particular, are liable to break if you try to cut corners by leaving them in place.

Remove the paintwork around the area of the dent using a body file, metalwork file or (best) an electric sanding disc (**fig 3**). Do this gradually, feathering off the edges of the patch at least 2-3 in. (50-75mm) past the area of visible damage. Be sure to wear safety goggles or glasses to protect your eyes.

If the inside of the panel has been undersealed, this too must be removed along with any dirt so that you do not spoil the dolly later. Chip the underseal away with an old paint scraper or a cold chisel, then remove the last traces by sanding lightly. Do not try to burn the underseal off or it will melt and spread all over the place.

Finally, clean off the last traces of debris from both sides of the panel with a wire brush. If there are any traces of rust present, apply a rust killing compound and leave this to penetrate for the recommended time before washing it off.

1. Prise off the trim near the dent — do not worry about paint

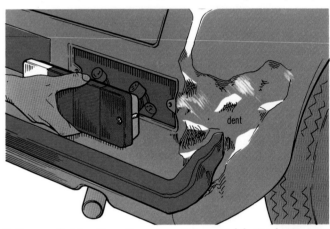

dent

2. Remove light units as they can get damaged during hammering

3. Remove the paint and underseal if the dent is severe

If your assessment of the damage leads you to decide that the dent must be pulled out rather than knocked out, obtain a dent puller together with a high speed steel (HSS) drill bit to match the self tapping screw on the puller's shaft. You will need a hole just large enough to allow you to screw the tool in — normally 1/8 in. (3 mm).

Inspect the dent or scratch carefully and you should find stress marks running outwards from a central point.

Drill the first pulling hole at this central point (**fig 1**), which represents the main point of impact. Drill any subsequent holes at intervals along the stress lines.

Fit the puller by screwing the screw tip of the shaft into the pulling hole (**fig 2**), then grip it firmly with your hand well out of the way of the sliding weight.

You exert the pulling force by sliding the weight against the end stop (**fig 3**), but it is easy to overdo it when you begin so go gently at first.

Do not try to pull out the whole dent from a single point unless it pops out almost immediately. Instead, pull on the central point until the effort required to move it becomes appreciably greater, then drill another hole on a nearby stress line and try from there instead.

Eventually, the panel should start to resume more or less its normal shape. At this stage you have to be careful not to pull it too far, or you risk stretching the metal even more than it has been already - a common mistake made by beginners. Avoid creating high spots by checking the profile regularly with the flat of your hand (not your fingertips): after a while you will be able to feel for the correct shape with uncanny accuracy. Alternatively, check the profile by laying a long flexible ruler against the surrounding surface and looking for gaps along the edge.

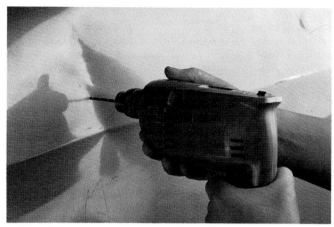

1. Begin by drilling a hole at the centre point of the dent

2. Screw in the dent puller — use a spanner if it is stiff

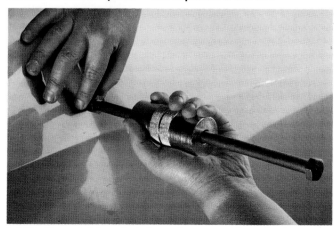

3. Slide the weight against the end stop to pull out the dent

Before starting to 'bump out' the dent with your hammer and dolly, it is a good idea to strike the dent from behind with only the dolly or a hammer (**fig 1**) in the hope of 'roughing out' the damage: if this is successful, most of the dent may spring back into place leaving less work to do with the hammer to finish the job.

There are two golden rules in panel beating. The first is to reverse exactly the cause of the damage: the deepest part of the dent will have received the greatest impact, so this is the place to start hammering.

The second golden rule is not to hammer so hard that you overstretch the metal. Beginners often make this mistake and then find themselves left with a hump of metal that has to be hammered in again and filled. In many cases overhammering makes a satisfactory repair impossible, so take great care to avoid it by checking the profile of the panel at regular intervals with the flat of your hands.

In some cases you might find it easier to rough out the dent by levering against the adjacent bodywork with your spoon or tyre lever (**fig 2**). It is also possible to ease out larger dents by applying gentle pressure with a hydraulic bottle jack and blocks of wood.

When you have roughed out the damaged area, take the hammer and dolly and begin gently to bump out the remains of the dent (**fig 3**).

It is important to use a dolly which matches the undamaged contour of the metal. If your steel dolly bears no resemblance to the shape of the panel, it might be worth making up another one from a shaped block of wood. Other household objects and tools — such as a bricklayer's club hammer — can make useful dollies at a pinch.

The easiest method of bump-

1. Knock out the dent roughly with a suitable heavy object

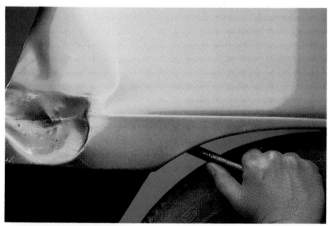

2. If you have limited space, try to lever the dent out

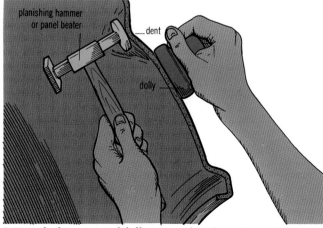

planishing hammer or panel beater — dent

dolly

3. How the hammer and dolly are used to shape the metal

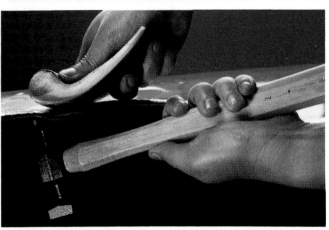

4. Using a hammer and dolly on the edge of a wheelarch

practice so do not be too ambitious at first. Use the circular face of the hammer as this will minimize the chance of your creasing the metal or forming pips in the surface. Remember that as long as the head strikes the metal flat, you are unlikely to go far wrong. When you become more proficient, you will find that the square face of the hammer is more useful for forming perfectly flat surfaces, edges for finishing off folds.

Gently tap the hammer against the dent and try to make the face of the hammer land flat on the metal. If one edge of the hammer strikes the metal, the metal could stretch or gain an extra ripple which will be difficult to remove.

If the dent is a deep one, the metal will have stretched too far for you to bring it back to its original shape. The decision then has to be made when to stop bumping and start filling. The course of action is to beat out the damage until it becomes noticeably harder to move any more metal.

ing out dents for beginners to learn is known as direct hammering. This means hammering directly on to the face of the metal — the dolly then spreads the force of the hammer blows, which stops the metal creasing and encourages it to resume its former shape.

Use gentle blows at first, until you get some idea of how the metal will behave. In the end you might find you have to hit the panel quite hard, but avoid driving the dent proud of the surrounding surface.

The correct action is to hold the hammer loosely and flick it towards the dent with your wrist: do not swing the hammer from the elbow as this can cause the head to land on its edge and cause deep scars. Without doubt, this can only be learnt by

STEP 5   FINISHING THE SURFACE

Using the body file, work it over the damaged area (**fig 1**) high spots — the metal will get shiny at these points. Tap down any you find using the hammer and dolly again (**fig 2**). You must finish with all the metal at or just below the correct contour.

Always use the body file in one direction, then at right angles to it. This gives you a clearer picture of how the metal is lying.

If the high spots are very slight, try pushing them in with the spoon or tyre lever rather than the hammer so that you spread the area of impact. This time support the metal underneath with the dolly or block of wood.

When you are satisfied that you have done as much as you

can to shape the dent, clean up the area again with a sanding disc.

You can now fill and refinish the panel as described on pages 48 to 53.

1. Rub over dent with file

2. Tap down any high spots

Adjusting hinges and catches

Sagging doors, gaping boots and bonnets can be infuriating. But often the cure is easy

Sticking doors, or boots and bonnets that are difficult to operate, are usually a result of dropped hinges or faulty catches — the sort of thing that goes wrong on every car occasionally.

Sorting out the problem is normally just a question of making a few minor adjustments — but tackle the problem early before the fault gets worse or any of the components become worn.

One of the major problems with doors is the hardening of, or damage to, seals. If the seals are showing the noisy signs of air leaks or have become cracked or perished, repair them first before beginning door adjustment. After new seals have settled in, it may become necessary to readjust the doors for a perfect air-tight fit. Small air leaks around seals can often be cured by packing them with foam draught-stopping strip.

When to do this job
When doors, boot or bonnet stick, admit water or are draughty

What this job involves
Refixing loose hinges
Adjusting door striker plate
Repairing bonnet catch
Renewing bonnet cable
Adjusting boot catches

To do this job
Tools: Screwdriver(s); spanner(s); felt-tipped pen; pliers (maybe); electric drill (maybe)
Materials: Aerosol lubricant such as WD-40; new bonnet cable (maybe); gravity toggles (maybe)
Time: Not more than 1 hour
Degree of difficulty: Easy

If you have the job professionally done . . .
Doors: Is door panel in line with the rest of the body? Is there a decrease in road noise and draughts?
Boot: Is there movement once boot is shut? Does boot lid foul bodywork when closed?
Bonnet: Does the bonnet open smoothly as you pull the release handle? Are there no gaps around the outside? Does the safety catch stop the bonnet springing up unexpectedly?

STEP 1   ADJUST FAULTY DOOR HINGES

Most hinges are secured to the door pillar with machine screws or bolts. As **fig 1** shows, screws are fixed into a thread cut in the door pillar itself or into a strengthened metal plate behind the pillar. Bolts are usually screwed into a nut welded to the inside of the door pillar.

A common problem, particularly on older cars, is that these mounting screws or bolts have come loose, so that the door drops and will not fit.

To test for loose mountings, open the door about half way, grip it under the bottom edge and try to lift it. If it is possible to move the door, even a little, you will need to check the hinges and tighten the screws or bolts.

To do this, open the door fully so that the hinges are exposed and you can work on them comfortably. On some cars you may have to disconnect the door stop (**fig 2**). This has a central pin held in place by a split pin; pull out the split pin and the central pin to free the stop. With the door open, prop it with a short length of timber so that it will not shut unexpectedly and trap your fingers.

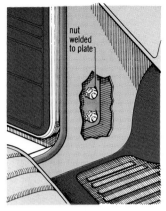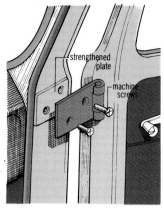

1. How the hinges are bolted or screwed to the door pillar

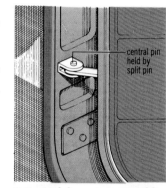

2. Typical door stop assembly

Now examine the screws or bolts which hold the hinge in place. The fault may be quite simply that they have worked their way loose, and just need to be retightened. So try this first to see if it makes any difference.

Another common fault is that the whole body of the hinge itself has dropped — a fact you can usually detect straight away if you spot an area of different coloured paint where the hinge was originally attached. If so, you will need to slacken off the hinges and move them back into place — or into a position where the door will open and close more easily.

To do this, have a helper support the far end of the door, or prop it up with a box or axle support. If you use your car jack (**fig 3**), put a cloth pad between the jack and the door to avoid damaging the paint.

Undo the bolts or screws gradually until each hinge is loose enough to move. Never fully loosen the bolts or screws in case the metal plate holding the hinge in place becomes detached and falls down inside the door pillar. Ease the door up into its new position and retighten the bolts or screws. Try the door for fit — you may have to repeat this procedure a number of times until you are satisfied.

3. Supporting the door with a car jack while working on the hinges

 TIP

'Quickie' hinge repair

The fixing screws which hold door hinges in place sometimes cannot be tightened successfully — either a screw thread has worn out or a welded-on nut has dropped off inside the door pillar.

In such cases tapping a new bolt hole is time-consuming and fiddly, while welding a new nut inside the door frame can be impossible.

But there is a 'quickie' alternative. You refix the door with a gravity toggle — a device used by builders for attaching fixtures to cavity walls.

Each toggle has a swivelling metal bar which folds neatly against a bolt so you can push it in the hole. Once there, it opens out at right angles to the thread so that the bolt can be tightened and the load spread over a large area.

Try to select a toggle whose head will fit into the recess in the door hinge; otherwise you will have to grind down the head after you have tightened it.

If you need to widen the screw hole to take the toggle, use a variable-speed drill running at its slowest speed.

Always fit a spring-loaded washer to the toggle bolt before you insert it. This will help prevent vibration from making the toggle work loose.

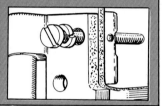

STEP 2   ADJUST THE DOOR STRIKER PLATE

Another common fault is that the catch on the door does not line up with the striker plate on the door pillar. To correct this fault, first check that the hinges are correctly aligned (see Step 1). Then adjust the position of the striker plate so that the latch slides smoothly into position and is held firmly.

If the door lifts slightly when you close it, the striker plate should be lowered slightly. Start by opening the door and examining the latch and striker plate. The points of contact — where you see clean pieces of metal — will tell you by how much you have to raise the plate. It is often difficult to judge how much you have moved the striker plate so, before you make any adjustments, mark around the outside with a felt-tipped pen or pencil on the door pillar (**fig 1**).

Next, undo the screws which hold the plate in position. The screws are likely to be tight, so use the largest available screwdriver for maximum leverage. Move the plate a bit (**fig 2**), making sure that its top is level so that the catch can engage correctly. Then re-tighten the screws and try the door for fit. You may have to repeat this procedure a number of times before you find the correct alignment.

If the door closes, but not tightly, the solution is to move the striker plate inwards. Start by measuring the amount by which the door stands proud of the bodywork (or adjoining door) beside it. This will tell you how far to move the plate.

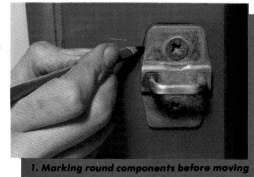

1. Marking round components before moving

2. Moving striker plate to adjust door

Making sure that the boot closes tightly may seem unnecessary but, particularly on a hatchback or estate, a tight boot or tailgate cuts down road noise and draughts and makes sure that fumes from the exhaust are kept out of the car. And in any car a secure boot is necessary to protect your belongings.

Boots differ from car to car, but all have roughly the same closing mechanism. In some, as **fig 1** shows, the 'striker plate' (usually a U-shaped stirrup) is bolted to the inside panel of the boot and closes against a catch fitted to the boot lid. In others, the striker plate is screwed to the boot lid and engages against the latch which is fixed to the inside of the boot. Either way, opening your boot and checking the mechanism carefully will show which of the two parts can be adjusted to tighten the boot lid.

With the relevant bolts or screws loosened, make the adjustment by moving the components as required (**fig 2**).

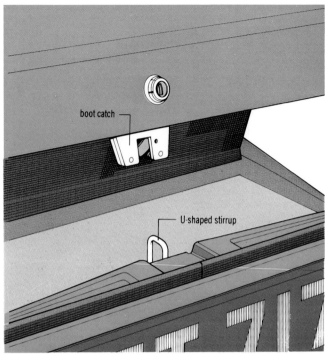

1. Boot mechanism, showing U-shaped 'striker plate' and catch

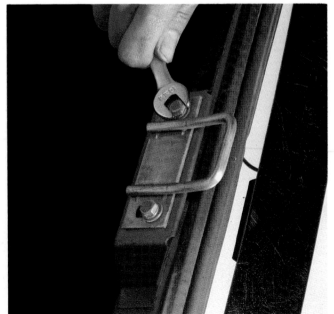

2. Loosening the bolts and making adjustments to the striker plate

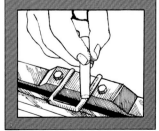

TIP

Line it up correctly

On concealed components such as door strikers, it is often impossible to see exactly where adjustments need to be made. So cover the two meeting parts with chalk or crayon. When you close the door, bonnet or boot the scrape marks on the chalk will show clearly where the mechanism is sticking.

Most car bonnets are held in place by a central spigot fixed to the front of the bonnet lid which engages in a catch mounted on the body just above the grille (**fig 1**). A common problem is that the bonnet refuses to open and close properly because the spigot and catch are not aligned correctly. The simple solution is to adjust the position of the spigot or catch so that the two line up.

Start by opening the bonnet and checking the mechanism. On some cars minor adjustments can be made by altering the position of the spigot; on others you will have to move the catch.

First close the bonnet slowly and look at the spigot as it engages the catch. You will be able to see clearly in which direction to move which part. Undo the machine screws or bolts holding the adjustable part of the mechanism (**fig 2**) and alter its position slightly. Retighten the screws and close the bonnet slowly. Continue to make slight adjustments until the bonnet closes properly.

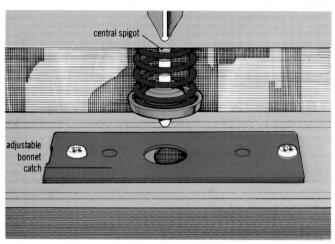

1. Bonnet closing mechanism, showing central spigot and catch

If the spigot and catch are correctly aligned but the bonnet will still not close correctly or seems a little loose, check whether the spigot itself is adjusted correctly. On most cars you can alter the length of the spigot by slackening the lock nut mounted at the top and then adjusting the length of the spigot with a suitable screwdriver (**fig 3**).

First loosen off the lock nut with a suitable spanner. If the bonnet does not close properly, slacken the spigot; if the bonnet is loose, screw the spigot up. Make sure you do not overtighten the spigot, or the bonnet may jam. Once you have found the correct adjustment, retighten the lock nut. Then close the bonnet, try it for fit and make adjustments as necessary.

2. Making adjustments to the position of the catch

3. Altering the spigot length with a screwdriver

If the spigot is so far out of line with the catch that minor adjustments do not work, you should alter the position of the whole bonnet (and with it the spigot) by adjusting the position of the hinges holding the bonnet to the body of the car (**fig 1**).

Open the bonnet lid and, with a felt-tipped pen, draw around the hinge plates on the bonnet lid to give yourself a known starting point. Then loosen the bolts or screws holding the bonnet in place. This will allow you to adjust the position of the bonnet backwards and forwards and from side to side until you reach the required position. Then retighten the bolts or screws and close the bonnet slowly, checking for fit as you go. Continue to make minor adjustments if necessary until the spigot aligns correctly with the catch.

At the side of the spigot there is usually a safety catch (**fig 2**). This is designed to prevent the bonnet lifting if the main catch fails as you are going along.

Altering the alignment of the spigot and main catch may move the safety catch out of position. So check this and alter its position, if necessary. The catch is held in place by bolts or screws fixed inside the bonnet.

TIP

Avoiding oily streaks

Oiling hinges and catches is a good way to keep them working well but, unless you are careful, will cause oil streaks to run down your paintwork. A better way is to use an aerosol lubricant such as WD-40.

First wipe off any dirt or grime with a clean cloth moistened with white spirit. Then hold the aerosol nozzle hard against the component concerned while you give it a good squirt.

A good aerosol lubricant will repel water, minimizing the chances of rust taking hold, as well as lubricating the moving parts.

1. Loosening the bolts holding bonnet in place   **2. Checking that the safety catch engages**

Most bonnets are opened using a cable release system operated by hand from inside the car (**fig 1**). Occasionally, faults can develop when the cable snaps or comes loose.

The first sign of trouble is usually that the bonnet fails to open when you operate the release handle. If this happens, do not pull repeatedly on the handle or try to open the bonnet

1. Bonnet cable release mechanism — how it works

release handle

cable operating bonnet catch

forcibly. You could easily break a stiff cable or do other damage.

Try first to operate the mechanism by pulling normally on the release handle while a helper leans on the bonnet directly above the catch.

If this does not work, or the release handle feels loose, the cable has probably snapped or

2. Releasing bonnet by pushing a screwdriver through the grille

worked its way free of its fixing brackets. Either way, you will have to operate the catch manually.

On a rear-hinged bonnet, push a long screwdriver or length of wood through the radiator grille (**fig 2**) and try to push the cable attachment arm to one side so that the bonnet springs open. If you cannot reach the arm directly, you may be able to hook a length of wire around the lever. Or you could unscrew the grille, if its retaining screws are on the outside, and reach the catch through the hole.

Another alternative, particularly if you have a front-hinged bonnet, is to work from underneath to see if you can reach the catch through the engine compartment. To do this, drive the front of the car on to ramps or jack up the car and put it on axle stands. Make sure that the handbrake is fully on and that both back wheels are chocked with two bricks or blocks of wood.

Once the bonnet is open, check the cable along its length. If it has come loose from its fixing brackets or from the cable attachment arm, screw or bolt it firmly back into position. Before you close the bonnet, check that the mechanism is working smoothly by pulling the release handle.

If the cable has snapped, remove it and replace it with a new one. Pull gently on the release cable inside the car until the loose end of the old cable comes through the bulkhead. Replacement release cables usually come with a new handle.

Install the new cable by pushing it through the bulkhead from the interior of the car. Normally a rubber grommet is fitted to the bulkhead to prevent water leaks, so renew this if it is not in sound condition.

At the bonnet catch, remove any loose ends of old cable and then attach the new one (**fig 3**). Tighten the cable and test the mechanism before you shut the bonnet.

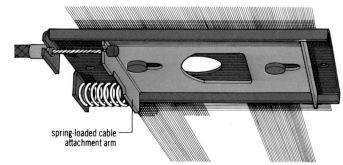

spring-loaded cable attachment arm

3. Bonnet catch, showing cable nipple fitted to the release arm

Buying a secondhand car

Checking a secondhand car before you buy it requires close attention — and a methodical approach

Start by deciding how much you are going to spend and then look around to see what is on offer at that price so you have a clear idea of the sort of quality you can expect to get. By following the steps given in this and the subsequent chapter you can get a very clear picture of the overall condition of the car you are looking at and an idea of what you would have to spend on it to put right any faults or damage. You should allow 5 to 10% of your budget for putting right faults and servicing after buying the car.

As you check the car over use the checklist opposite to make a summary of your findings so that you can take everything into consideration.

What this job involves
Checking the service history
Checking the bodywork
Inspecting the interior
Checking the suspension and brakes
Looking for signs of poor maintainance
Judging the overall condition in relation to the price

Related jobs in this handbook
Check your car's roadworthiness
Buying new or secondhand
Choosing your next car
Please see Index for page numbers

To do this job
Tools: Old screwdriver; torch; magnet; axle stands; jack
Time: Allow at least one hour, preferably two for a thorough inspection
Degree of difficulty: Assessing a car is easy if you are familiar with the model in question

If you have the job professionally done . . .
Does the report cover all the items in this article? Are the faults described in relation to the age of the car? Does the report give a judgement of overall condition and value for money? Are details given of any repairs that are needed?

BUYING A SECONDHAND CAR — CHECKLIST

INSPECTION	COMMENTS
Service history: documentation	
Body: condition; trim; paintwork	
Interior: seats; trim; carpets; boot; tools; underbonnet	
Underbody: condition; oil leaks; brake pipes; exhaust	
Running gear: tyres; suspension; driveshafts; brakes	
Engine: oil leaks; hoses; general appearance; damage	
Fluids: oil; coolant; brake fluid	

ROAD TEST	COMMENTS
Cold start: ease of start; cold running; first noises	
Engine noise: knocking or tapping; exhaust blow	
Gears: clutch action; noise; operation	
Performance: smooth running; smoke; acceleration	
Steering: Straight running; feel; drive shaft noise	
Brakes and suspension: balanced action; noises; bumps	
Hot engine: starting; tickover; noise; fumes	

CONCLUSIONS	COMMENTS
Overall condition considering age and mileage	
Estimated cost of any repairs needed	
Assessment of realistic price	

As you work through your series of checks on the car make a note of what you find so that you can take everything into account when making your final judgement

STEP 1   CHECK THE SERVICE HISTORY

To avoid wasting a lot of time you should make a check of the registration particulars before looking at the car. Check the roadworthiness certificate and year of registration, and make sure that the person selling the car is the registered owner. If this is not the case, find out why. A lot of the cars advertised 'privately' in local papers are really being sold by spare-time traders.

Then ask what there is in the way of a service record. With an older car that has had several owners, this is not likely to be much, but the more you can find out the better. A fully stamped-up service book means that the owner has been prepared to spend money to look after the car and the general condition is likely to reflect this.

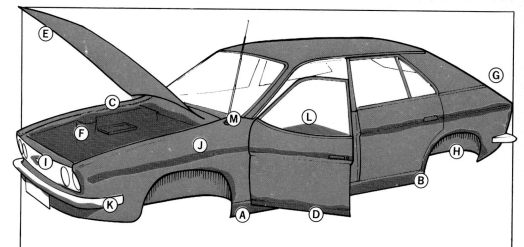

Start by taking a very careful look at the exterior bodywork and try to decide if the condition of the paint and panelwork is all right considering the age and price of the car. It helps if you can get a bit of practice in, looking at various cars until you can spot the difference between factory paint and respray, and between respray over metal panels and respray over plastic filler. If you think a car has had damage repaired with filler use a magnet to test. The magnet will stick to steel panels but not to thick layers of filler.

Serious rust damage will be obvious once it has broken through the paintwork (**fig 2**) but you should also look for the less obvious signs of rust damage. See if there are any bubbles or blisters in the paint as these are a sign of rust developing underneath. Pay particular attention to the bottoms of the doors, the sills and the wings (**fig 3**).

Once a car is a few years old the chances are that it will have needed some paintwork to repair a parking scrape, for example, and some touching up of rust spots is inevitable. You just have to make up your mind if the bodywork has lasted well for its age and has been properly repaired where necessary. A recent respray should make you doubly careful. If it has been expertly done then it may maintain a good appearance for years and save you the cost of doing it. A good place to check if the car has been resprayed is on the closing edges of the doors. Normally these are not painted on a respray and so provide an example of the original finish. If the car has been resprayed in a different colour it will be immediately clear, but if the respray was in the original colour it may not be so easy to see.

Remember that the body paintwork will probably have faded in the sunlight while the paint on the door edges will be closer to the original colour and

so should look brighter. But the biggest danger sign of all is a recent bad respray with an uneven finish (**fig 1**) and traces of over spray on the trim or inside the wheel arches. It means that the car has been quickly done over to help sell it, so take care. You need to make sure that the fresh paint is not covering any serious damage. Only buy such a car if you are really confident about its overall condition.

While looking over the exterior, check for damaged or missing bits of trim. They may seem relatively unimportant, but they do help show if the owner has looked after the car, and they are often astonishingly expensive to replace. Similarly check that the chrome work is in good condition with no pitting or damage. Make a note of any lights with cracked lenses or corroded reflectors — especially the big, shaped headlights. These units can be very expensive to replace.

Do not forget to check the bonnet for rust, then open it and

check the inner wings — particularly MacPherson strut top mountings (**fig 4**) — and the battery tray.

Under the bonnet is one of the most important places to check for signs of repairs to accident damage. Many cars have had replacement wings fitted and are none the worse for it — in

fact the new wings may be the best part of the car. But you must take a good look to see if any repair work that has been done has been carried out properly. If you can see obvious signs of repair with badly fitting joints and lumpy welds the chances are that the car has just been patched up for sale.

A. Sills and jacking points
B. Underbody panels
C. Wing at joint to body
D. Bottom edge of door
E. Bonnet edge and hinges

F. Engine compartment, battery tray, strut mounting points, also welded seams
G. Boot lid or tailgate edges
H. Spring and damper mountings

I. Headlights and mountings
J. Mounting holes behind trim
K. Pitting in bumper chrome
L. Floor panels under carpets
M. Accessory mounting holes

3. Make a special check of the bodywork rust danger points

1. A poor respray, like this orange-peel effect, is a bad sign

2. Rusting is not always as obvious as this

4. Checking strut mountings in the engine compartment

STEP 3 — CHECK THE INTERIOR AND BOOT

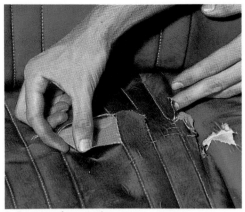

1. Damaged seats show poor car care

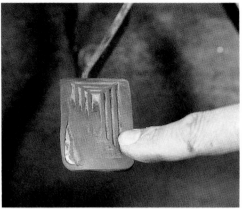

2. Heavy wear on the pedals indicates a lot of use

Check the doors for twisted or worn hinges and try all the window winders. Check that the seat belts are undamaged and that inertia reel types move freely — they are expensive to replace. Is the seat wear about right for the age and recorded mileage of the car? Badly sagging and damaged seats (**fig 1**) show heavy wear and so should go with high mileages.

Then look at the pedal rubbers (**fig 2**), steering wheel and door aperture scuff plates. Again, the wear should correspond with the car's mileage.

Lift the carpets to check any underfelt for signs of water leaking in (**fig 3**) and the floor for any rusting or repairs. If it has been dry, a musty smell of the carpets or underfelt shows that leaks are a problem.

A similar check in the boot for signs of heavy use such as badly worn carpets and damaged trim, together with dampness can be very revealing. See if there is any smell of petrol indicating a leak in the tank — tanks can develop rust holes surprisingly quickly. While in the boot you can also check the tools (if any) and the condition of the spare tyre.

3. Checking under the carpets

STEP 4 — CHECK THE UNDERBODY

1. Inspecting the underbody for signs of rust damage

You need to inspect the underside of the car (**fig 1**) both for signs of accident damage and for rusting. The older the car the greater the risk of serious corrosion, and although some models are much better than others, there are always some bad examples. So do not skimp on your inspection just because the car has galvanised body parts.

You need to take some suitable clothing such as overalls, something to lie on in case the ground is wet, an old screwdriver for probing the body with (**fig 2**) and a torch for peering into the dark areas.

If at all possible take a look at some badly rusted examples of the car you are going to inspect. This will let you know where to look first but make a full check anyway. Even if the car has had a full rustproofing process, make a full check (**fig 5**). Rustproofing treatments may be very good, but can be very disappointing.

An older car may already have had some chassis welding done. Check carefully around any patches to see if the repair has been carried through to sound metal. Complete repair patches have been known to fall off when badly fitted.

Be especially suspicious of any new-looking underseal — it is probably there to hide defects. If it covers a repair, you will want to check that it has been properly done.

Check the brake pipes (**fig 4**) brake cables and exhaust mountings for corrosion and other damage, and look out for tell-tale patches of oil spread along the underside betraying a serious oil leak from the engine or gearbox (**fig 3**). While you are under the car see if there is any evidence of a towbar having been fitted. Towing puts extra loads on the car's transmission.

2. Probing suspect areas

3. Checking for oil leaks

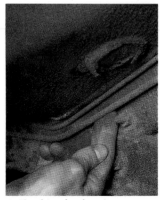

4. Checking brake pipes

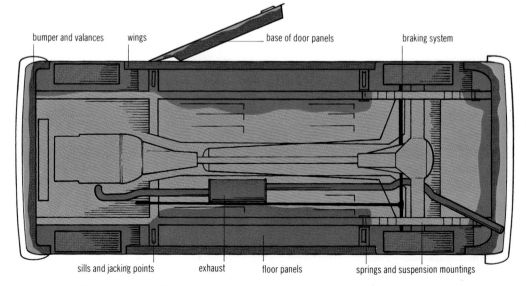

bumper and valances   wings   base of door panels   braking system

sills and jacking points   exhaust   floor panels   springs and suspension mountings

5. Rusting of structural members underneath the car is a major fault so check the problem areas

1. Lift car and support on axle stands to check the suspension and steering

2. Tyres should be in good condition and, ideally, a matched set

do — jacking up each corner to remove the wheels in turn can take a lot of time. See page 65 for details of how to go about testing the suspension and at least do enough to let you get a good idea if any repairs are needed (**fig 3**). If the suspension is fitted with grease nipples you will be able to judge whether servicing has been thorough by seeing if the nipples are clean and if there are signs of fresh grease round the joints. Worn rubber bushes are often easy to spot with clear cracks in the rubber or even bits missing.

Remember that lever-type shock absorbers, such as those forming part of the Marina front suspension, are expensive to replace so give them special attention, checking the bearings of the lever arm on the damper body.

If the car has disc brakes check the disc surfaces for any wear grooves. If the car has been left standing for a while there may be a thin film of surface rust on the discs but this is nothing to worry about. Take a good look at the brake pipes and components for signs of fluid leaks.

Similarly, with front wheel drive cars take a good look at the protective gaiters (**fig 4**) on the constant velocity joints — damage here can quickly result in dirt getting into the joint, leading to rapid wear and failure of the joint — and they can be very expensive to repair. With front wheel drive cars also check that the oil seals where the drive shafts come out of the gearbox do not show any signs of leakage. Although the seals are not particulary expensive replacing them often involves a lot of work.

To check the dampers push a corner of the car down on its springs and release it. The car should quickly return to the level position without any bouncing. If it does bounce, the dampers are worn out.

The condition of all the tyres is important as the cost of replacement if they are worn (**fig 2**) or damaged can be high — do not forget to check for cuts and scrapes on the inside faces — and they can also give a pointer to the standards of the car's previous owners. A matched set of top-name tyres is a good sign, even if they are worn. A mixed set of tyres suggest low-budget maintenance which is likely to have extended to the rest of the car.

Wear patterns on the tyres can also give a lot of information about the suspension and steering gear. Uneven wear patterns on the front tyres with a feathered pattern of the tread may just be due to the tracking being out, but can also be the result of more serious damage to the suspension or steering — see page 64 for more details.

You will have to decide just how much testing of the suspension and brakes it is practical to

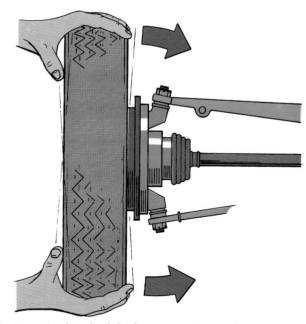

3. Rocking wheel to check for bearing and suspension wear

4. Making sure that the driveshaft gaiters are in good condition

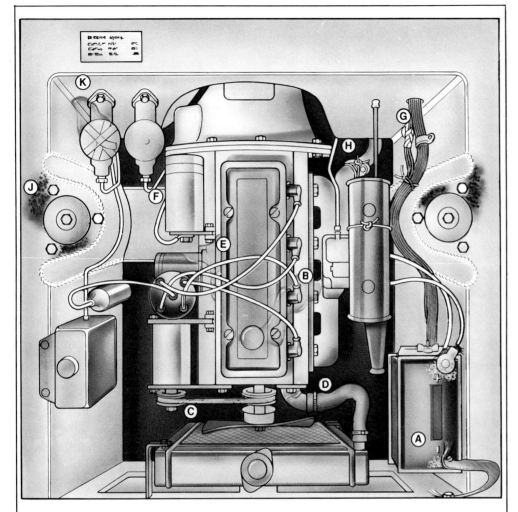

A thorough check of the engine compartment can tell you a lot about the car and how well it has been looked after. Pay particular attention to the following:

A. Battery terminals free from corrosion with well-clamped connectors. Battery tray free from corrosion.

B. Engine block reasonably clean with no signs of rust streaks due to water leaks from gaskets or core plugs

C. Fan belt tight with no serious wear

D. Water hoses in good condition with no sign of perishing; hose clips tight and no traces of coolant leakage

E. Gasket edges clean with no signs of oil or water leaks. Traces of jointing compound along the gasket line show where repairs have been carried out

F. Engine mounting blocks sound with no signs of the rubber perishing

G. Wiring clipped properly in place with no fraying or damaged insulation or repairs

H. Exhaust system free from serious rust (some surface rust is inevitable on mild-steel systems) with joints well clamped. All fixing bolts and nuts in place with no broken studs or missing nuts

J. Suspension strut mountings — where appropriate — free from rust. If repairs have been made check the welds carefully

K. Brake and clutch cylinders topped up with no signs of leakage — look for paintwork damaged by brake fluid

1. The engine should be clean but it need not be spotless

2. Checking drive belt is tight and in good condition

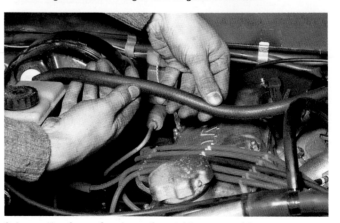

3. Inspecting hoses for signs of perishing or cracking

Moving under the bonnet, before taking a detailed look at the engine make a note of the overall appearance of the engine compartment. If it has just been steam cleaned it may be the sign of a keen seller wanting the car to look good — and there is nothing wrong with that. But it may be a sign that various engine leaks were obvious and so were cleaned away to give a better impression.

On the other hand, if the engine compartment is covered in settled grime it is clear that the car cannot have been serviced or the levels checked for ages. Similarly, any clear signs of repairs like jointing compound oozing out round gaskets may indicate a keen owner, but can also act as a warning that the car has been giving trouble.

The very best under-bonnet appearance is the in-use look, which you get with regular servicing but not too much attention in between (**fig 1**). Make a check for any signs of damage to the water hoses, frayed wires and loose fan belts (**fig 2**) since these also give a good idea if the engine has been well looked after.

While you are looking make a special check of all the fixing nuts and bolts. See if any of them have rounded edges where they have been done up or undone with the wrong size spanner or with self locking grips. This is a clear sign of someone doing their own maintenance and repairs — and possibly not doing it too well. If any of the nuts have fresh and bright marks on them it is possible that repairs have been made to get the car ready for sale.

At the same time check if there are any nuts or bolts missing: it is impossible to check them all but pay particular attention to the rocker cover and the inlet and exhaust mountings.

1. Checking engine oil for level and colour. Emulsified oil shows head gasket leak

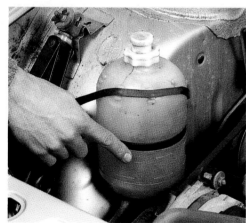

2. Coolant should have no sludgy deposits

3. Checking that the brake fluid is clean

Your impressions of the engine condition can be reinforced by a check of the oil and coolant. Take out the dipstick (**fig 1**) if the oil is black and smelly and down to the minimum mark on the dipstick, it is clear that servicing has been neglected. Drops of water on the dipstick point to the possibility of a blown head gasket. But if the oil is absolutely new, ask the owner why. Not many people choose to spend money on servicing a

car they are selling unless they have to. What you want to see is a normal brown oil colour with the level above the minimum.

Also take a look inside the oil filler cap — if there are any traces of a thick creamy deposit the chances are that the engine is in poor condition. The colour of the coolant is also important (**fig 2**). A strong clear green or blue anti-freeze colour is very reassuring, though older cars tend to have a rusty colour to the

coolant. But a thick brown sludge shows up problems in the cooling system quite often caused by a faulty head gasket.

The brake fluid should also look clean and be up to the mark (**fig 3**), as should the transmission fluid on an automatic. The battery electrolyte levels should be right — over the cell separators — and the terminals clean and free from corrosion. A good sign is a coating of fresh grease on the posts.

If you really want to get as much information as possible about the car you are looking at, you should start the engine from cold. The ease with which the engine starts will tell you a lot about its general condition.

Open the bonnet so you can watch and listen to the engine while a friend, or the seller, starts the car. As the starter is operated check how well it spins the engine over. If it seems sluggish, the battery, the battery leads, or the starter motor are suspect. As the engine catches note how the engine fires. All of the cylinders should come in together, even on cars which need a couple of seconds spinning on the starter

before firing. If the engine splutters along on a couple of cylinders before the remainder fire, it may be due to fouled spark plugs (**fig 1**). Fouling, however can occur if a car is started and just allowed to idle without going for a run — and this is often the case when a car is for sale. Unfortunately you cannot be sure if the car has a serious cold-starting problem unless you can return the next day to try again after your test run.

Listen carefully during the first moments the engine is running. It takes several seconds for the oil to circulate from a cold start and in the meanwhile any bad wear should be clearly audible, quietening down once

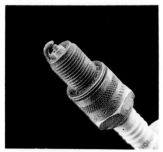

1. Check plugs for fouling

the oil pressure has built up. Worn timing chains are often detectable on starting, and although a rattle lasting less than a second may not be serious, any rattle that lasts any longer is a cause for concern.

Once the engine is running, push the choke as far in as you can without stalling the engine. If the car has an automatic choke, blipping the throttle will set it part way in. Then get hold of the throttle cable or linkage and pull it to make the revs rapidly rise and fall between tickover and a good speed (about 2500 rpm if there is a tachometer). Listen carefully for any unusual sounds as you do this noting whether or not they occur at engine speed. A heavy knocking sound at engine speed could be worn big ends, while a light tapping sound also at engine speed could indicate worn little ends. Piston slap may

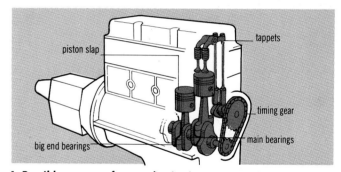

1. Possible sources of unusual noise in a worn engine

also be detectable if there is excessive bore wear, but it does take experience to recognize. Wear in the geartrain can usually be detected as a rattle occuring at half engine speed.

But noises are very hard to describe in words, and can still be difficult to pick out even if you know exactly what you are listening for. If the engine makes a really alarming noise, however, which you cannot identify, go no further.

As the car warms up check the exhaust for smoke. Do not be misled by drops of water splattering out of the exhaust tailpipe after a cold start. Water

2. Check exhaust for water

is produced as the petrol burns and normally it comes out of the exhaust as very hot, clear steam. If the exhaust system is cold, however, it cools the water vapour to give white steam and some drops of water. Similarly while the choke is out a smokey smell in the exhaust is normal. Once you have given the car a run, the smoke and smell should disappear completely. If water still drips, the head gasket has probably blown. While you are checking the exhaust, hold a gloved hand over the end of the tailpipe to check for leaks in the exhaust system. If the system is sound the engine should stall.

1. Checking for free selection of the gears

When you have finished the listening tests, close the bonnet and take the car for a drive — make sure you are insured first. Use the first part of your test drive to get used to the general feel of the car.

The clutch take-up should feel the same, hot or cold, Most cars should have a smooth action and juddering often indicates an oil leak onto the clutch. On the other hand, some models never have a really smooth clutch action, a point about which it would be worth consulting secondhand car reviews or library road test reports.

Automatic cars should take up promptly and smoothly. Low fluid level will cause a delay after you press the accelerator, but you should have already checked the fluid level — if this was correct, any delayed take-up signals more serious prob-

lems. Check for smooth gear changes (**fig 1**) — both when accelerating and when slowing down — and try the kickdown for rapid response. Also use the manual selector to see if all the gears lock-in.

On a manual box the gears may be stiff to engage when cold, and a slight crunch if you engage second too quickly is only to be expected if the car has covered a high mileage. Any tendency to baulk or crunch should vanish when the car has warmed up. Worn synchromesh can be accepted on a high-mileage car as one of those faults you learn to live with. Transmission noise should be normal for the model — but any bad whines or rumbles mean there could be problems. The feel of the gearchange also varies from model to model. A sloppy gearchange action is usually due to wear in the external linkage and so not too serious.

While driving, accelerate and lift off sharply in each gear. If the gear jumps out of engagement, there is probably internal wear in the gearbox. This will take a lot of work to repair.

As the engine warms up it should pull smoothly without any disturbing noises or obvious flat spots. More information can be gained if you have a friend follow you in another car and watch as you accelerate hard and long in top gear — make sure the road is

clear. Smoke from the exhaust during acceleration (**fig 1**) indicates wear in the pistons, rings and cylinder bores.

Lift your foot right off the accelerator for about five seconds and then accelerate hard again. This causes oil to be sucked down the valve guides on the

overrun and burnt off as visible smoke on acceleration. A little puff of smoke from the tailpipe is quite normal, and on a high-mileage car a fairly big puff must be expected, but a great cloud of smoke means that the valve guides are worn and in need of replacement.

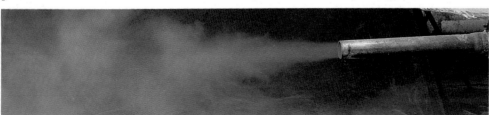

1. Exhaust smoke may be a danger sign

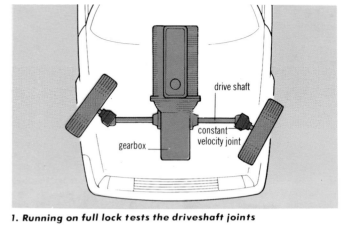

drive shaft

constant
velocity joint

gearbox

1. Running on full lock tests the driveshaft joints

If you release the steering wheel while travelling on a straight and level stretch of road, the car should continue to run straight (**fig 2**). A very slight tendency to run towards one side may not be serious — this can be due to slight errors in the wheel alignment and can even be caused by the front wheels having perfectly good tyres of different makes. Any strong tendency to pull to one side, however, could indicate damaged suspension or steering and requires thorough investigation.

Steering feel is hard to judge as it varies a lot from model to model and with the tyres fitted. Basically the car should feel the same when steering to the right as to the left. Find an empty car park and turn the steering from lock to lock while driving at a slow walking pace. Any stiffness or free play felt while turning the wheel indicates wear or poor adjustment in the rack or steering box, or possibly a tight steering idler or

faulty suspension bearings.

If you are carrying out these tests on a front wheel drive car listen out for any odd noises while turning on full lock. A regular hard clicking while driving slowly round on full lock means there are worn constant velocity joints on the drive shafts, while any juddering can mean wear on the inner universal joints (**fig 1**). The cost of

renewing these parts varies enormously so if there are any signs of wear you should check the costs before you make any decision.

While you are in the car park, you can also check reverse gear for noise and for jumping out on the overrun. Also use this (same) opportunity to test the efficiency of the brakes when the car is running backwards.

2. On a flat, clear, road the car should run straight without any steering action

STEP 13   TEST BRAKES AND SUSPENSION

Test the brakes on a clear, straight and dry stretch of road, but before applying the brakes make sure that there is nothing following you. Then relax your grip on the steering wheel so that you are only just holding it as you gently apply the foot brake. The car should slow down without any signs of pulling to one side or the other. If the car behaves properly you can repeat the test, but this time really stamp on the brake pedal as for an emergency stop, again the car should pull up straight. Repeat the tests using the handbrake.

When making these tests you must be prepared to tighten your grip on the steering wheel and correct your course should the car veer to one side. Any tendency to swerve or pull to one side shows that something is wrong; either the brakes are unbalanced or the suspension is misaligned and you will have to investigate further, see pages 70 and 72.

The brakes should have a smooth and progressive action, and should feel the same at the start of the test when they are cold as at the end of the test when they will have warmed up. Do not be too worried by a little squealing from the brakes when cold, this is a problem that often occurs but if the noise con-

tinues — or if there are other grating noises — you should look for damage or excessive wear in the brake system.

Many brake faults, such as those due to worn linings or leaky brake cylinders, are relatively easy and inexpensive to cure and so should not put you off the car if everything else is acceptable. But some brake faults like seized disc brake calipers or badly grooved brake discs (**fig 1**) and drums may mean the renewal of expensive components.

All the time you are driving the car you should listen for any suspension noises, knocks or thuds as the wheels go over

1. Badly scored brake discs can cause uneven braking

bumps. Try and find a suitable bump, such as a manhole cover or a shallow pothole and drive to hit it deliberately with each wheel in turn. Any severe knocks, thuds or rattles from the suspension mean that there could be wear and you should investigate further. Similarly make sure that the bumps do not push the car off its line as this is another sign of suspension wear or damage.

While driving the car you should also be forming a general impression of how it handles and of the ride quality. A gentle rolling and swaying motion could be a sign of worn dampers.

STEP 14   CHECK THE HOT ENGINE

While driving check that any instruments fitted are giving the right readings (**fig 2**). Few cars have an oil pressure gauge, but if there is one check that the reading is in line with the pressures given in the manufacturer's handbook. Contrary to popular belief, the 'higher the better' idea does not apply to the oil pressure on modern engines — a high pressure reading may just mean that the owner has put some additives in the oil to thicken it up and so try to conceal engine wear. You should not be alarmed at the oil pressure dropping at tickover, as long as the warning light does not come on. Also watch out for sudden variations in the water temperature — this can indicate a faulty head gasket.

At the end of your test drive, switch the engine off and then start it up again to check how readily it starts when hot. Then see if the engine maintains a slow, even tickover. Some cars, notably front wheel drive models, emit rattles from the transmission if the tickover is too slow but if increasing the tickover slightly gets rid of the noise

1. Removing crankcase breather pipe to check for blowing

there is probably nothing to worry about.

Now open the bonnet and remove the crankcase breather pipe (**fig 1**) to check if there is a definite 'blow' effect from the pipe. If there is it may mean there is piston ring and bore

wear, but this depends on the type of engine you are working on, and whether it can be said to be a 'heavy breather' or not. At this stage, while you are looking under the bonnet see if there are any signs of oil or coolant leaks on the hot engine.

2. All instruments should show normal readings when the engine has warmed up

STEP 15   SUMMARIZE YOUR FINDINGS

Having completed your examination it is time for careful consideration of your findings before deciding if you should buy. A really thorough checkover will inevitably result in a list of faults — even brand new cars are rarely faultless — so the

crucial factor is whether the overall condition of the car represents the best buy you are likely to get for the price in question.

Above all you should budget to buy a car and have some money — 10% of the purchase

price is a good allowance — over for the repairs which may be necessary. Your thorough test should make sure you know what needs to be done, how much of the work you can do yourself and how much all the repairs will cost.

Check your car's road worthiness

Many cars fail their annual test because they are not checked over fully first. Don't take your car in until you know it will pass

In the UK it is illegal to use a car which is over three years old on the roads unless it has a valid test certificate. The annual Road-worthiness test (still called the MOT test after the now defunct Ministry of Transport) is designed to ensure that unroad-worthy cars are kept off the road. After three years you will have to get a new certificate every year. If the car has been well maintained, passing should present no problems.

When to do this job
When the car is due for its roadworthiness test. In the UK, this is when it is three years old and every year thereafter

What this job involves
Checking the various components that are covered by the test
Adjusting and repairing where necessary to meet the required standards

Related jobs in this handbook
Checking and servicing the brakes
Adjusting the headlamps
When indicators fail to flash
Checking the suspension
Rustproofing your car
Rear wheelbearing service
Front wheelbearing service
Checking the tyres
Please see Index for page numbers

To do this job
Tools: Spanners; pliers; hammer; screwdrivers; self-locking wrench (depending on the work that is required)
Materials: Possibly lamps, bearings, tyres, exhaust, suspension and steering components as required
Time: Two hours to conduct the checks. More if repairs are necessary

First check the lights on your car, which must conform to the following requirements. They must function correctly and be even in their illumination. The lenses must be intact and each lamp should be securely mounted. It is not allowed for any white light to be shown at the rear of a vehicle, except for the reversing lights.

The law also states exactly where each light should be positioned, but so long as no changes to the design of the car have been made since the car left the factory, this is not likely to be a problem. However, you do have to ensure that all lights are working and are reasonably efficient.

Examine all the lights for damaged lenses and make sure they are secure, then check that each one works and is properly visible.

Get an assistant to turn on the ignition and put his foot on the brake. Check that the rear stop lamps are working. Then get him to turn on the indicators and check that the lights flash both at the front and the rear of the car. If your car is fitted with further indicator lamps on the front wings, they too should be in good working order. It is a good idea to test all the lights simultaneously, to show up any earthing faults which only occur when a heavy current passes, and to check the lights with the engine running as well as switched off.

Any damaged lenses must be replaced as must corroded reflectors or coloured lenses that have faded. Change any burned or blackened bulbs — make sure you change them for bulbs of the correct design and wattage. If the lights appear dim check their earth connections – see pages 143 to 148. If the lights do not work first check that the fuses are intact (see page 194) before you change the bulbs.

If the indicators do not work, the fault may lie with the flasher unit, rather than the individual

1. Check that headlight mountings are secure and undamaged

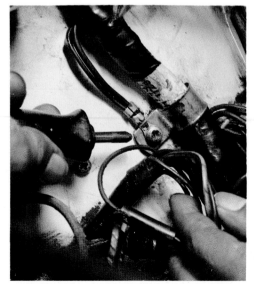

2. Faulty earths could give electrical problems

3. Check that the wipers are sound

4. Clearing clogged jets

5. Adjust horn like this

alternate in pitch. Generally, there are not many repairs that can be done if it does not work. However, before replacing it check that it is mounted securely as if it is loose it may not be earthing properly enough to sound. Check also the fuse, wiring and relay (if fitted). If all appears to be in good order, look on the rear of the horn. Most have a small adjusting screw that acts upon the armature. Undoing the locknut and turning the screw one way or the other (**fig 5**) may do the trick.

The MOT test regulations state that windscreen wipers (**fig 3**) must operate efficiently and that windscreen washers must be fitted and working.

Washers must provide an adequate flow of water to each blade and on normal systems the water should flow after no more than two pushes of the pump. If nothing happens check the washer bottle and, if full, use a pin to clear any blockage from the the jets (**fig 4**). Overhauling wipers is covered on pages 134 to 138.

bulbs — see pages 143 to 148. Should the indicator flash rate be outside the limits specified after you have checked through the system you have no alternative but to change the flasher unit (see page 128). In the UK the indicators must flash at least 60 but not more than 120 times a minute.

As the headlight beam settings will also be checked during the test, make sure these are correct by following the procedure on pages 112 to 117. Also check that the headlight mountings are secure and rust-free.

Next, check that the horn is in good working order; it must give an instant response, and if there is more than one horn control, all must work. Furthermore, cars registered after 1973 must have a horn that does not

wear in centre of tread — overinflation | wear at sides of tread — underinflation

1. Effects of overinflation (left) and underinflation

Tyres on the same axle of the car must be the same size and must be the same construction. So both must be the same sized radials or the same sized cross plies. Additionally, if you have a mix of tyres, the radials must be at the back and cross plies must be at the front. However, mixing tyres is not a good idea, it is better to have all the same kind.

You should check each tyre for cuts, bumps, bulges or any other signs of damage. Remember to look on the inward facing wall of the tyre as well as the side facing outwards. If you can see any damage buy a new tyre. You should also examine the tread depth, using a tread depth gauge if there is any doubt. If you do not have a depth gauge, a rough and ready tread check is to use a 10p coin. The edge of the coin should disappear fully into the tread. The law says that the tyre must have a minimum of 1 mm of tread in a continuous pattern that covers at least three quarters of the original tyre

tread. The rest of the tread should be visible, with no bald patches (**fig 3**).

This legal minimum is enough to keep you on the right side of

the law. But if the tread is so worn that you need to use a gauge to measure it, you should buy new tyres.

The spare tyre is not included in the test, but common sense dictates that its condition should be checked and that it should be replaced if necessary. All tyres — including the spare — should be maintained at the correct pressure.

The MOT regulations say that each wheel should be inspected but without removing hub caps or wheel trims; but this is only because the mechanic's time has to be limited if the test fee is not to be excessive. From a safety point of view, you should remove any trim so that you can make a thorough check.

Each road wheel must be securely fixed and there should be no loose or missing hub nuts or broken studs. Look for any signs of damage and distortion on the wheels and check the rims carefully. Any damage that is likely to cause the wheel to leak air (**fig 2**) will result in failure, as will bent or loose spokes in a wire wheel.

2. Damaged rims can cause tyre sealing and balance problems

1. Belts damaged like this should be renewed

2. Change any buckles which do not work

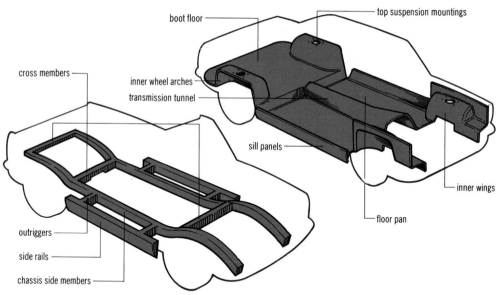

1. Main structural areas that will be checked. Many test failures are due to rust

boot floor

top suspension mountings

cross members

inner wheel arches

transmission tunnel

sill panels

inner wings

outriggers

floor pan

side rails

chassis side members

Before taking any car on a road test, the examiner will make sure that the driver's seat is secure. If the seat is loose or broken the car will fail.

All cars first registered after 1 January 1965 must be fitted with seat belts for the driver's and passenger's seats in front.

Check that the belts are in good condition, if there are any cuts or other visible signs of damage (**fig 1**), the belts should be replaced. Then make sure that the locking mechanism is in

good order (**fig 2**). It should securely lock the belt and should release the belt properly.

You should also carefully check the conditions of the seat belt anchorages (**fig 3**). The regulations state that a failure certificate should be issued if there is any excessive corrosion within 30 cm (12 in) of the seat belt anchorages.

If your car is fitted with inertia-reel seat belts, the retracting mechanism should be in good

order. Pull out the belt and then release it to see that the webbing is automatically wound back into the unit.

Some types of inertia reel belt can be fully tested by braking sharply from 20 mph and checking that the belt locks as you lurch forward. Once the deceleration is over the belt should reel out normally when you lean forward. A different design can be tested by a sharp pull on the webbing to check that it locks.

2. Rust holes in cross members will fail the car

3. This damper could pop through

3. Give anchorages a tug

4. Make sure that the belt locks and returns

4. The door doesn't matter but the sill does

5. This worn rubber is more serious than the rust

The basic structure of the car has to be in good condition if the vehicle is to be safe on the road. Assuming there is no un-repaired crash damage, the single major cause of MOT failure in this respect is corrosion.

How much corrosion is acceptable depends very much on the nature of the component or panel; any corrosion on a structural member would be unacceptable, but rust bubbling through a wing or boot lid is unlikely to result in failure.

Fig 1 shows the important load bearing parts of different types of typical vehicle construction. In general, important areas are those near suspension mounting points, steering components, sub-frame mountings and other major chassis

areas. These areas should all be checked by pressing them with — for example — an old screwdriver. (Test inspectors are not allowed to jab at suspect areas in this way, but they will certainly lever and push the structure as well as carry out visual checks.)

If the areas you are checking give or distintegrate, serious corrosion has set in and welding will be required. You should not hammer under the car, or use a sharp implement to dig at the structure. However, tapping can reveal where metal is corroded or where corrosion has been hidden by filler.

How much corrosion is acceptable depends very much on the individual tester, using his experience and judgment to assess the extent of any weakening. The Depart-

the rear wheels.

Check any points where the suspension is anchored to the body, as well as damper body mounts (**fig 3**). Boot pans must be sound and rear bulkheads on vehicles with subframes should be carefully inspected. Note that old underseal often hides chronic rust patches. No corrosion that has holed bodywork, or accident damaged panels are allowed within 12 in (300 mm) of suspension mountings.

Next inspect the sill area closely. On some cars the whole sill structure constitutes a load-bearing part of the chassis while, on others, it is only the inner part of the sill that must be free from corrosion damage. Seek expert advice on the structure of your car's body. On many cars some rust holes in the outer sill may be allowable provided the inner sill member is intact. Any repairs made to load-bearing sill members must be correctly welded — a job best left to a specialist.

Central floor pans should be rust-free and again any repair will involve welding in new metal. Also check chassis cross-members and outriggers.

Now move to the front of the car and examine the front suspension mounts and the anti-roll bar mounts (**fig 5**). Inspect any subframe or chassis members and the steering system mounts. Corrosion is not the only point to look for — you should also check for wear and also distortion caused by accident damage.

If the car has MacPherson struts as its front suspension, look inside the bonnet and check that the inner wing metal around the top suspension mount has not corroded (**fig 6**).

The same rule about damage or rusting through within 12 in (300 mm) of a front suspension mounting point applies as at the rear. Any other bodywork rusting of a superficial nature will not normally be taken into account by the tester.

At the test, the examiner will look carefully at all the brake components to ensure that there are no obvious signs of damage, corrosion or wear. Assuming all appears to be well, the brakes will be tested on a rolling road to ensure that they are reasonably efficient. stopping the car.

Start by checking the handbrake. It should not be difficult to apply and the travel distance to pull the brakes hard on should not be excessive. The normal amount of travel allowed is between three and five clicks on the ratchet, although different design toler-ances are taken into account.

Next check the handbrake mountings on the floor (**fig 2**) or under the facia. Lever types have been known to pull out of

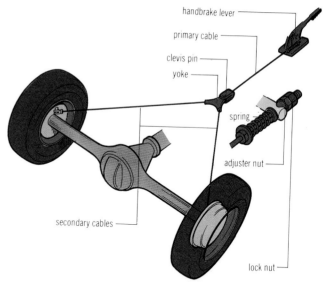

1. Wear points to look for on a typical handbrake layout

the floor, so look for cracks around the mounting brackets.

Most car manufacturers seem to have different ways of connecting brakes at the wheels to the handbrake, but regardless of the system it must be regularly lubricated.

With the car on axle stands or ramps let the handbrake off and follow the route of the linkage, cleaning off any dirt with a wire brush, and dosing stiff joints with penetrating oil. On cable systems look for signs of fraying — more than two

strands or signs of fatigue will cause a failure (**fig 3**).

The lever pivot and its bear-ings should be in good condi-tion. Grasp the handbrake and test for any sideways play (**fig 4**). If there is more than ½ in. (12 mm) travel go back under the car and check the pivot bearing and the lever attach-ment to ensure there are no signs of corrosion and no other damage within 12 in. (30 cm) of the lever attachment pivot. Handbrake adjustment and service is on pages 109-111.

6. Rust is too near strut

7. This rust is not serious

ment of Transport manual suggests that the tester should consider whether he personally would feel safe riding at speed in the vehicle with the possi-bility of an emergency stop taking place. It is a good idea to think about corrosion in the same way when you make your checks.

Start at the rear and look for any heavy rust or holes in the chassis or subframe members (**fig 2**). Pay particular attention to any box members or out-riggers, especially in front of

8. Candidate for failure

2. Checking the handbrake mountings

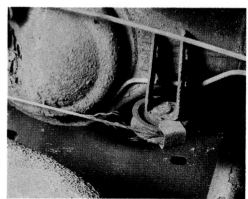

3. Finding a frayed handbrake cable

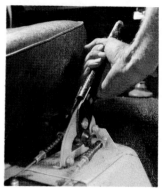

4. Testing for sideways play

69

Much of the MOT brake test is carried out on a rolling road providing a very accurate check on performance which it is difficult to reproduce even on a road test. However, the tester will also make a close visual inspection of parts of the system to ensure there are no fluid leaks and other damage that could lead to brake failure.

First check that the brake pedal is not fractured or twisted. Press it down, first slowly, then more rapidly, each time pressing down to the point at which pressure can be felt.

1. Finding leaking fluid from marker cylinder under brake pedal

2. Checking level

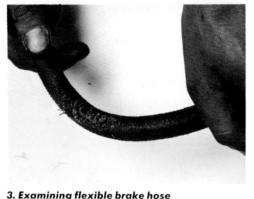

3. Examining flexible brake hose

The pedal action should be firm before it has travelled half way to the floor. If it feels spongy, there is probably air in the system which means that you will have to bleed the brakes — see pages 101 to 104. If the pedal keeps creeping down when you are applying sustained pressure, the chances are that there is a leak in the system. Finally, stamp with full force on the pedal as in an emergency stop. If the pedal hits the floor a cylinder seal or brake pipe has failed.

Next, check the fluid level in the brake master cylinder reservoir and top it up if necessary (**fig 2**). If there are leaks (or if the system has failed) there are three main points to check for signs of

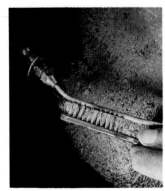

4. Wirebrushing brake pipe

fluid.

First examine the lever entry point of the master cylinder or the area around the point at which it is bolted to the bulkhead. Fluid sometimes leaks

into the car interior (**fig 1**). Then look at the flexible hose connections in the system. There can be up to four of these — one at each wheel — that allow for steering and suspension movement. Even if there are no signs of leaks these pipes must display no signs of chafing. Any other than minor surface cracks or splits (**fig 3**) will mean the pipes need to be replaced.

Finally, check around the brake back plates and calipers or drums (**fig 5**). Any sign of fluid here will mean that there is a seal failure inside the cylinder. Although replacement seal kits are available for both slave and master cylinders it is wise to replace the whole unit if a leak is found because a common cause of seal failure is

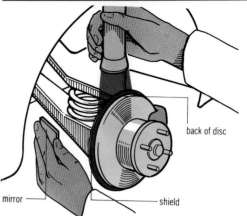

mirror — shield — back of disc

5. Use a mirror to check for leaks on the back-plate   *6. Checking the brake caliper*

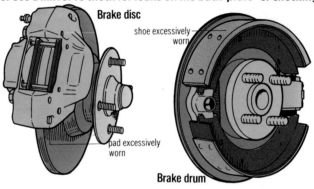

Brake disc

shoe excessively worn

pad excessively worn

Brake drum

7. Missing springs or retaining pins will fail test

pitting corrosion of the cylinder wall.

Next, look at the steel brake pipes which should be clipped firmly to the underside of the body. If the pipes are hanging loose, renew all clips. Use a wire brush to remove surface rust from the pipes (**fig 4**). If the pipe is smooth underneath it will pass the test. If there is severe pitting it is likely to be failed and pipe replacement would be a wise measure.

Checks will also be made to ensure no pad retaining springs, securing pins, or split pins are damaged, missing or broken (**figs 6-7**).

A road test will tell you whether or not the brakes are functioning as they should — a

replacement for the rolling road the tester will use (**fig 8**). Drive slowly (20 mph is adequate) on a quiet road. Check there is no other traffic about and apply the brakes fairly sharply while

holding the steering wheel gently. The car should stop in the straight ahead position without having pulled to either side. While applying the brakes gently check for any grabbing or judder. For full brake checks and overhaul see pages 101 to 108.

To pass the test the car's handbrake must also operate efficiently. Very little play is allowed — the brake must be applied within about one third of the lever's travel. If adjustment is required refer to pages 109 to 111. During your road test perform a stop with the handbrake from 20 mph while holding the steering wheel gently. Again the car should not pull to one side.

8. Testing the brakes on a rolling road

1. Testing the front wheel bearings

2. Checking security of U-clamps on drive shaft

The tester examines your bearings audibly and by touch. To check the front bearings — rear wheel bearings are not part of the test — jack up the front of the car. While the car is being jacked up, look for movement in the inner wishbone bearings.

When the car is fully jacked up spin each wheel in turn, listening for sounds that might indicate roughness or wear in the bearings. Next, grip the wheel top and bottom and rock it. see if this reveals any play (**fig 1**). There is bound to be a small amount but if it is excessive, or no play at all, this indicates that the bearings need to be overhauled — see pages 119 to 123.

Front wheel driveshafts are part of the test as well. On continental cars with exposed driveshaft couplings look for signs of rusting in the bearings. On early Austin Rover front wheel drive cars look for oil soaking the cross shaped rubber and metal couplings, and check the nuts for tightness.

Engage first gear and rock the car backwards and forwards. Rubber couplings should flex a little but there should not be movement of the rubber.

You can test front driveshaft constant velocity joints on the road. Find an open space and reverse the car in a tight circle, then repeat on the opposite lock. If you hear any knocking sounds from the outer ends of the drive shafts, the joints will probably need replacing. To check, jack up the car, grip the drive shaft and rotate the wheel back and forth. If there is much free movement the joint needs to be replaced.

The steering mechanism should not be worn, neither should it suffer from excessive wear if it is to pass the roadworthiness test (**fig 1**).

Start your checks on the steering from the driver's seat. Rock the steering wheel from side to side testing for any movement between the steering wheel and the column shaft; only a small amount of play is acceptable.

Again rock the steering wheel from side to side. If there appears to be movement in the steering column universal joints or couplings open the bonnet and grip the joint while an assistant holds the steering wheel. You will be able to feel any slackness in a universal joint and you can generally see when a flexible joint has excessive movement. Even if there is only a small amount of play in the column joint the car may fail.

Any excess play at the steering wheel must now be checked against the steering linkage.

With a steering box, there must be no more than 3 in. (75 mm) play before the drop arm moves. The car will fail if the arm works up and down or the selector moves in and out of the box.

If you have rack and pinion steering get your assistant to rock the wheel fairly vigorously while you check for any up and down play inside the gaiter between the rack and its housing (**fig 2**). Any excessive. play will cause the car to fail. At this point check the rubber gaiters for splits and cracks.

The rack must be securely mounted, so check the U bolts are securely fastened. Use a tyre lever or metal bar between the rack and car body and look for any signs of movement (**fig 3**).

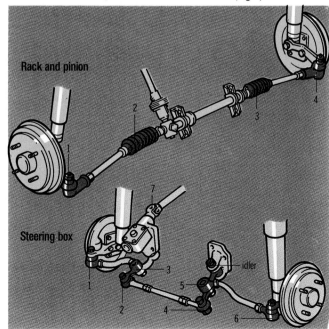

Rack and pinion

Steering box

idler

1. Points to check for wear on two types of steering system

Next test the track rod ends. Place your hand firmly over each joint and feel for play as the steering wheel is turned from side to side (**fig 4**).

Finally, check the upper and lower swivel joints for play (**fig 5**). Jack up the car and support it on axle stands. Ask a helper to turn the steering wheel back and forth quickly — watch for movement. If you have wishbone type suspension put a jack under the lower wishbone and raise it until the suspension is compressed. Use a tyre lever and try to push upwards — any play in either swivel should be apparent.

2. Checking the rubber gaiter

3. Testing rack mountings

If you have MacPherson struts you can only check the lower joint for wear. Place your tyre lever on the inner rim of

your front wheel and push underneath the track control arm. The car will fail if you feel any play in any direction.

4. Checking track rod ends

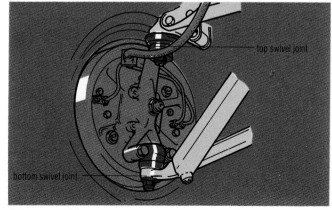

top swivel joint

bottom swivel joint

5. Upper and lower swivel joints must be checked as well

STEP 9 — CHECK SHOCK ABSORBERS/DAMPERS

Each shock absorber will be given a bounce test to see that it works properly. The examiner will press down on each wing of the car in turn, then releasing the pressure on the downstroke. The body of the car must come to rest after one and a half strokes, otherwise the car will fail.

You need to check each damper in turn to see whether it is badly damaged or corroded, whether there are any perished rubbers or whether it leaks (**fig 1**). The top and bottom mountings must be secure.

If you have lever arm dampers fitted to your car, the lever linkage will be checked to make sure it is not loose. Use a tyre lever or something similar to check as shown in **fig 2**.

On cars with MacPherson strut front suspension the struts will be examined for leaks and to see that they work properly; fluid stains on the damper body spell failure. The damper rod in the top mount will be checked to see that it fits properly.

In all cases you will need to replace defective dampers before your car will pass.

1. Leaking shock absorbers must be replaced

2. Using metal bar to check lever arm damper

STEP 10 — CHECK THE SUSPENSION

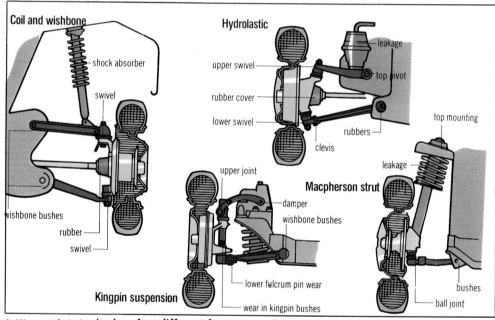

1. Wear points to check on four different front suspension systems

Coil and wishbone — shock absorber, swivel, wishbone bushes, rubber, swivel

Hydrolastic — upper swivel, rubber cover, lower swivel, clevis, rubbers, leakage, top pivot

Macpherson strut — damper, wishbone bushes, leakage, top mounting, bushes, ball joint

Kingpin suspension — upper joint, lower fulcrum pin wear, wear in kingpin bushes

2. Testing the kingpins for wear

3. Checking MacPherson strut mountings

4. Testing security of leaf spring clamps

A full check of the suspension system varies according to the car, but on all vehicles the objective is the same — to find any looseness or wear in joints and pivots. **Fig 1** shows some common wear points to look for on a number of systems.

Raise the front of the car and support it on axle stands with the tyres about 2in off the ground. Ask a helper to move the wheels up and down using a long lever while you watch for any free movement at pivots or mountings. Another check is to ask the helper to apply the foot-brake (this eliminates bearing play) while you grip the tyre top and bottom and rock the wheel while feeling and watching for play in joints. With the wheels off, use a tyre lever test for kingpin or joint wear (**fig 2**) and for looseness of lower MacPherson strut mountings (**fig 3**).

Joint wear may also be discovered by lowering the wheels onto a smooth surface (two glossy magazines allow easy wheel movement) and, while a helper turns the steering, watching carefully for signs of free play.

Examine the condition of all parts of the suspension, especially the upper and lower plates where the coils are mounted, the wish-bones and radius arms. There should be no distortion or fractures visible. Any rusting should be of the surface type only.

At the rear of the car, check coil springs and their displacers, making sure they are in good condition and properly seated. Leaf springs should not cause problems but you should check that all the leaves are intact and all the clamps are in good order (**fig 4**).

Also carefully examine all locating links and radius arms making sure that there are no distortions or fractures. Check the anti-roll bars for signs of distortion or fractures (**fig 5**).

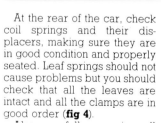

5. Anti-roll bar rubbers must not be perished

The remainder of the checks are under the car. At the MOT test station, the car will be put up on a ramp or driven over a pit, at home, ramps or axle stands will do just as well.

Start the checks under the car with the exhaust system — it should be in good condition, securely mounted, with no leaks and have an effective silencer.

Examine the complete system for corrosion or other damage and tap any suspect areas lightly with a screwdriver (**fig 1**). Very small holes can be repaired using proprietary pastes and bandages (**fig 2**) but any major corrosion means you will have to replace all, or part, of the system.

1. See if the exhaust is about to fall apart by tapping it

2. Exhaust patch-ups are frowned upon but this might pass if gas-tight

Check the mountings to ensure they are all present and are in good condition and that they are securely fixed to the underbody (**fig 3**). Replace any damaged or missing parts.

Get an assistant to start the engine and check for leaks with your hand (do not touch the hot pipework). Small leaks in pipes or boxes that are well sealed with exhaust paste and bandaged will usually pass. Badly sealed leaks will fail.

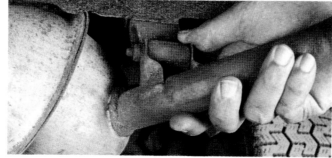

3. Exhaust hangers should all be present and in sound condition

Drive shafts on front-wheel drive cars have already been covered in Step 7 above. If your car has independent rear suspension, check the rear half-shafts in the same manner, looking for wear in the universal joints and splits or perishing of the rubber boots.

On rear-wheel drive cars, check the prop-shaft for wear in the universal joints. You can do this by grasping the joint and seeing if there is any movement (**fig 1**). You should be able to tell from driving the car if there are any problems; listen for whining, clonking or rattling sounds.

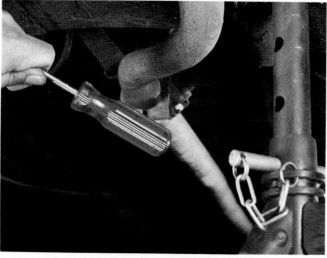

1. Checking the universal joint on the prop shaft

Front lamps	☐	Condition of underbody	☐
Rear lamps	☐	Efficiency of handbrake	☐
Headlamps	☐	Condition of brake hydraulics	☐
Headlight aim	☐	Condition of brake hoses pipes	☐
Stop lights	☐	Condition of calipers	☐
Rear reflectors	☐	Condition of discs and/drums	☐
Indicators	☐	Effectiveness of braking system	☐
Windscreen wipers	☐	Steering controls	☐
Windscreen washers	☐	Steering mechanism	☐
Horn	☐	Power steering (if fitted)	☐
Security of seat belt mountings	☐	Wheel bearings	☐
Condition of belts	☐	Drive shafts (fwd only)	☐
Operation of seat belts	☐	Check shock absorbers	☐
Tyre condition	☐	Check suspension	☐
Road wheels	☐		
Condition of exhaust system	☐		
Effective of silencer	☐		

Chapter TWO

SIMPLE SERVICING

All-round lubrication

Regular lubrication of all components is the key to miles of trouble free motoring. We show you how and when to lubricate your car

Many components on modern cars are 'sealed for life' and never need lubrication, but there are still many vital lubrication jobs which should be done regularly to prevent premature wear.

Do-it-yourself lubrication is not a difficult or long job — it can even be done in stages, when you have the time, provided it is done regularly.

To ensure that each component gets lubricated

When to do this job
As recommended by the car manufacturer, as part of routine maintenance or if a particular component becomes stiff to operate

What this job involves
Lubricating moving parts
Checking and topping up oil levels
Using a grease gun

Related jobs in this handbook
Lubricating wheel bearings
Renewing oil filters
Please see Index for page numbers

To do this job
Tools: Jack; axle stands; spanners; screwdriver; grease gun (maybe); medium size pump oil can; small funnel; wire brush; universal drain plug spanner (maybe)
Materials: Aerosol lubricant; light machine oil; high melting point grease; special oils for transmission parts (maybe); shock absorber fluid (maybe)
Time: Depends how many lubrication points your car has but about 2 hours overall
Degree of difficulty?: No strength or skill needed, but filler holes may be awkward to reach

If you have the job professionally done . . .
Do hinges, linkages and controls operate smoothly? Can new grease be seen near grease nipples? Have filler plugs been wiped clean?

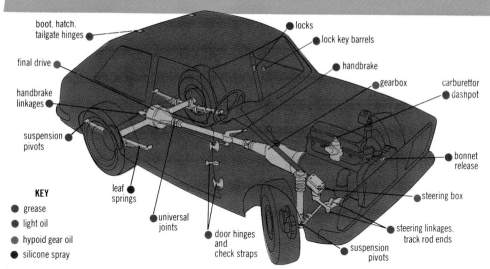

boot. hatch. tailgate hinges
locks
lock key barrels
final drive
handbrake
handbrake linkages
gearbox
carburettor dashpot
suspension pivots
bonnet release
KEY
leaf springs
● grease
● light oil
● hypoid gear oil
● silicone spray
steering box
universal joints
door hinges and check straps
suspension pivots
steering linkages, track rod ends

1. The key components which need regular lubricating — although not all cars have grease points

regularly, make yourself a checklist with the aid of your manual — 'sealed for life' components should also be checked at regular intervals. Then refer to the appropriate section in this chapter, make the check and mark the date or mileage on your checklist.

Apart from spanners, few tools are needed for carrying out general lubrication on your car, but if your car has grease nipples fitted you need to buy a grease gun.

It is important to use the correct lubricant on your car. Using the incorrect grease, oil

or fluid could cause premature wear or expensive damage. It is particularly important to use the correct fluid in automatic transmissions and power steering systems — putting in the wrong fluid (or even the wrong make of fluid) could ruin all the fluid seals.

CHECK OIL LEVELS

Although the oil in such components as differentials does not get burned away as engine oil sometimes does, you should still check that the oil levels remain topped up in case oil has leaked out of a loose drain plug or faulty oil seal. If you come across a very low level yet know that it was recently filled up, make sure you find the cause before adding further.

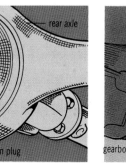

rear axle
filler-level plug
drain plug
filler-level plug
gearbox
drain plug

2. Drain and filler plugs on rear axle and gearbox

rear axle/final drive	lock key barrels	air cleaner
manual gearbox	bonnet release	water pump
power steering	leaf springs	clutch cable
auto transmission	carburettor damper	handbrake cable
steering box	throttle control	propshaft joints
shock absorbers	choke control	suspension ball joints
hinges	dynamo bearing	steering ball joints
door striker plates	distributor	gearchange linkage

Your checklist will include many of these items

Rear axle

The oil level in the rear axle on conventional rear wheel drive cars should be checked and topped up if necessary, usually every 6000 miles (10,000 km). The car should be on level ground when the check is made. If it is difficult to reach the rear axle, the car should be raised and supported on axle stands at the rear to the minimum height for access.

The combined filler-level plug is normally situated at the rear or side of the differential casing at the middle of the axle (**fig 2**). If the plug head has a hexagon you can use a spanner to undo it, but if it is a square recessed socket you will need a universal drain plug socket. Wipe the area around the plug before unscrewing it.

The oil level inside the axle is correct when it is level with the bottom of the filler plug hole. The level can be checked by inserting your finger into the hole and using it as a dipstick.

If you need a top up, use an Extreme Pressure (EP) hypoid gear oil. This is normally available in a plastic 'squeezy' bottle with a long flexible spout to make filling easier. Top up (**fig 3**) until the oil just trickles from the filler plug hole. Check the condition of the filler plug washer (if fitted) before refitting the plug.

Manual gearbox oil level

The gearbox oil should be checked as detailed in the car manufacturer's service schedule — normally every 6000 miles (10,000 km).

Raise the car and support it on axle stands at the rear for safety making sure that the car is on level ground.

On cars with an in-line engine and gearbox arrangement, the filler-level plug is usually

situated about halfway up the side of the gearbox (**fig 2**).

On some transverse engine cars, there may be several drain plugs and filler plugs close together, so check in your manual to find which plug is which before unscrewing any of them.

Some transverse engined cars also have a separate filler-level plug for the final drive differential unit if it has its own separate oil supply.

The oil level is correct when it

is level with the bottom of the filler plug hole. A hypoid gear oil should normally be used in the gearbox and final drive (if separate). The oil can be obtained in a plastic squeezy bottle with a flexible spout to make filling easier. Top up the oil until it just starts to trickle out of the filler plug hole. Check the condition of the sealing washer (if fitted) before refitting the plug. Do not overtighten the plug on aluminium casings as this may strip the threads.

3. Topping up the rear axle — a squeezy bottle makes it easier

Power steering reservoir

The fluid reservoir for a power steering system is normally located at the front of the engine compartment (**fig 4**). The fluid level should be checked periodically but rarely needs topping up. The fluid level is checked using the dipstick on the underside of the filler cap.

Unscrew the cap and clean the dipstick with a clean non-fluffy cloth or tissue paper. Refit the cap and then remove it again. Note the fluid level on the side of the dipstick in relation to the full or fill marks. Some dipsticks have marks on both sides to indicate a hot or cold fluid level in the reservoir.

If the fluid level is at or below the fill mark, add fluid to bring the level up to the full mark.

Make sure the fluid is the correct type for your car — most power steering systems use automatic transmission fluid — but check in your handbook to be sure.

If the fluid reservoir needs frequent topping up, there must be a leak and you should check the system thoroughly.

cap
power steering reservoir

4. Power steering reservoir

Automatic transmission fluid

The automatic transmission fluid level should be checked from time to time at the combined dipstick/filler tube on the side of the transmission housing (**fig 5**). The fluid should be checked while at its normal operating temperature — take the car for a short run first.

Absolute cleanliness is essential when checking or topping up the fluid in an automatic transmission, as the slightest trace of dirt or incorrect fluid may cause transmission damage. Carefully clean all oil or dirt from the dipstick handle and the top of the filler tube before removing the dipstick.

The hydraulic circuits in the transmission must be primed before the fluid check is made. Make sure the car is on level ground with the handbrake fully applied, then, with the engine idling, move the lever through all the positions at least three times before returning it to the 'P' (Park) position.

With the engine idling, pull out the dipstick and wipe the marked end clean with tissue or a clean non-fluffy cloth. Refit the dipstick fully and then pull it out again immediately.

Check the fluid level against the two marks on the dipstick end. If the level is near or below the lower mark, it should be topped up to the upper mark with the correct Automatic Transmission Fluid (ATF).

Automatic transmission fluid is normally obtainable in a plastic squeezy bottle with a flexible spout. Alternatively, a small plastic funnel can be used to pour the fresh fluid into the filler tube. Only add small amounts of fluid at a time, and recheck the level frequently until it is correct. Note that the transmission must never be overfilled as this may lead to overheating.

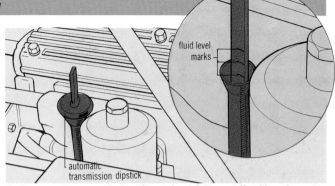

fluid level marks

automatic transmission dipstick

5. Automatic transmission dipstick with (inset) fluid level marks

Steering box lubrication

Only steering systems with a steering box need to be lubricated regularly. Rack and pinion type systems are usually sealed and do not need lubricating.

The steering box is located at the bottom of the steering column in the engine compartment. Always clean all dirt and oil from the top of the steering box first to expose the filler-level plug. Remove the plug (**fig 6**), either by unscrewing it, or by levering it out carefully with a screwdriver.

With the car on level ground, the oil in the steering box should be level with the bottom of the filler plug hole. Extreme Pressure (EP) gear oil is normally used in steering

boxes, and can be obtained in a plastic squeezy bottle with a flexible spout. Alternatively, a small plastic funnel can be used to pour fresh oil into the box until the level is correct.

Shock absorber fluid

Cars with lever type shock absorbers should have the damper fluid level checked at least once a year. The car should be raised and supported clear of the ground and the wheels removed to check the fluid level.

The combined filler-level plug is situated on the top cover of the shock absorber unit. Brush away all the road dirt from the top cover and wipe it clean before unscrewing the filler plug.

You may need to use a small mirror or your finger to check the fluid level as the filler holes are sometimes almost inaccessible.

Special hydraulic shock absorber fluid must be used for topping up, and this should be applied using a pump-type oil can which has been thoroughly cleaned of any traces of other oil. When the fluid level is correct, refit the filler plug. A very low fluid level can only result from leakage, and you may need to renew the shock absorber or the sealing washer (see pages 170 to 173).

6. Steering box level plug

GENERAL LUBRICATION

There are a lot of items on the car which need only the simplest kind of routine maintenance. A little time spent on general lubrication will greatly help keep everything running smoothly.

Lubricating hinges

Periodic lubrication of all hinges on the car is a simple and straightforward job which only takes a few minutes, and will prevent wear and premature seizure. Thin or light machine oil, preferably in a pump-type oil can (**fig 7**), should be used as it has good penetrating properties. However, on hinges where access is difficult an aerosol lubricant such as WD-40 can be used instead.

Start with the door hinges and door check straps. Wipe or brush away any oil or road dirt

7. Oiling the door hinge

from around the hinges and straps. On some cars, there is a plastic cap pushed into the top of a hollow hinge pin. Prise the cap out first with a screwdriver so that you can oil the hinge. Put a few drops of oil on to the top and sides of each hinge and check the strap, then open and close the door fully a few times to help the oil to find its way around. If necessary, apply a few more drops of oil until the door opens and closes freely. Refit the plastic caps (if fitted) to

the hinges, then wipe off any surplus oil to prevent dripping and staining afterwards.

Next, lubricate the boot, tailgate or rear hatch hinges, the bonnet hinges and, if fitted, the petrol filler cover hinge, using the same method as for the doors. On some estate and hatchback models, the hinge is hidden behind the roof trim panel. You need to unscrew or unclip the trim panel to get at the hinge. Use an aerosol lubricant and give two or three short bursts of spray to each hinge. Wipe off any excess oil drips afterwards to avoid staining the roof lining.

Door, boot and tailgate locks

Locks are best lubricated with petroleum jelly (Vaseline) or general purpose grease (**fig 8**). Clean off any grease and road dirt from the exposed parts of the lock mechanism, and from the lock striker plate on the car body. Smear a little fresh grease over the lock and striker plate parts, then wipe off any excess grease to avoid soiling your clothes.

Some older cars have a small hole in the exposed part of the door lock. In this case, squeeze in a few drops of thin oil and wipe off any drips afterwards.

Lock key barrels

Lock barrels should be checked fairly regularly, particularly during cold weather, to prevent the tumblers inside the barrel from freezing. Special lock oil or graphite powder (from a ground-up soft pencil lead) could be used on key barrels. The best way of getting the lubricant into the barrel is to dip the key into the oil or graphite powder (**fig 9**), then insert the key into the barrel and with-

9. Lubricating the door lock

draw it again. This process can work, but is not strictly recommended by experts.

Ignition and steering column lock barrels should only be lubricated very sparingly when they become stiff as there is a risk of oil finding its way on to the electrical contacts of the lock.

8. Make sure the door lock striker plate is well greased

Bonnet release mechanism

Lubricating the bonnet release mechanism is one of the most frequently neglected jobs on a car. Lack of attention can lead to cable breakage or seizure, so that you cannot open the bonnet. The inner cable should be lubricated at both the release lever or handle end, inside the car, and the bonnet lock end.

Pull the lever or handle as far as it will go then apply a smear of general purpose grease to the exposed inner cable and lever or handle pivot. At the bonnet lock end, apply high melting point grease to the exposed part of the inner cable and cable nipple attached to the lock latch plate. This is usually located underneath the bonnet lock panel.

On the rod operated type of bonnet release, apply silicon lubricant or general purpose grease to the brackets which support the rods and the lever pivot points. Operate the linkage several times to check that it is working smoothly.

The bonnet release lock should be smeared with high melting point or general purpose grease (**fig 10**). Work it well into the sliding parts of the lock from above and below. Apply a smear of grease to the lock striker post on the underside of the bonnet as well.

Finally, close the bonnet and operate the release mechanism. The release lever should operate smoothly and the bonnet should spring up freely.

Lubricating leaf springs

On cars with leaf spring rear suspension the springs should be cleaned and lubricated at least once a year.

The car must be raised and supported on axle stands under

10. Lubricating the bonnet lock — use plenty of grease

the body so that there is no load on the suspension when you service the springs.

Use a wire brush to clean all the road dirt from the springs, particularly between the gaps.

The springs should be lubricated with a water repellent silicone aerosol spray. Cover the springs in the fluid (**fig 11**), particularly the gaps between the spring leaves.

Carburettor damper oil

On SU and Zenith Stromberg type carburettors, the piston damper oil level should be checked every 1000 miles (1600

11. Spraying the leaf springs

km) and topped-up if necessary.

SU type: unscrew the cap and pull up the piston damper rod so that you can check the oil level in the reservoir. If the damper oil is low, top up the level (**fig 12**)

12. Topping up the carburettor with oil

with multigrade engine oil until it is between ¼ in. and ½ in. (6 mm and 13 mm) from the top, then refit the damper.

Zenith Stromberg type: unscrew the damper rod cap and withdraw the damper rod and piston. The oil level should be about ¼ in. (6 mm) below the top of the hollow damper rod tube. If the level is low add multigrade engine oil until the level is correct, then refit the damper piston and rod.

Throttle and choke controls

Apply a few drops of general purpose lubricating oil to the throttle cable or linkage, and the manual choke cable (if fitted) at the carburettor. Smear high melting point grease over the contact areas of all cams and levers. On many cars you need to remove the air cleaner body from the carburettor (see page 81) so you can get to the control cable or linkage at the carburettor end. Watch out for any pipes and wires under the air cleaner body.

Remember that to operate smoothly, the throttle and choke cables should not be kinked or sharply bent.

Dynamo rear bearing

Modern alternators do not require any lubrication, but dynamos fitted to older cars have a rear bearing which must be lubricated with engine oil at least once a year.

Thoroughly clean all dirt and grease from the rear end bearing plate. Squeeze two or three drops of engine oil into the bearing through the central hole in the rear end bearing plate (**fig 13**). Do not over-oil the bearing, otherwise the brushes and commutator may become contaminated.

Air cleaner

Some cars — mainly older models — may be fitted with a wire gauze mesh filter which requires periodic servicing and cleaning.

Wire gauze type air filters are usually fitted to a slightly deeper type of air cleaner body. Unscrew the bolt or wing nut and remove the top cover from the air cleaner body. Lift out the circular filter gauze and thoroughly wash it in a solvent such as petrol or paraffin. Blow the filter gauze dry with compressed air — a tyre foot pump is ideal for this.

Finally, cover or soak the filter gauze in fresh engine oil and shake off the surplus drips before refitting it to the filter body.

Distributor lubrication

The internal parts of the distributor should be lubricated occasionally with multigrade engine oil or thin machine oil.

Remove the distributor cap and pull off the rotor arm (see page 208) to expose the distributor shaft and contact breaker plate (or trigger plate on electronic 'breakerless' distributors). Dab one or two drops of oil on the felt wick at the top of the distributor cam shaft and on the moving contact pivot post on conventional distributors. On some types of distributor, there is an additional hole in the contact plate for lubricating the mechanical advance weights inside the distributor body, so apply two or three drops of oil.

The distributor cam should always be lubricated with high melting point grease whenever the contacts are adjusted or replaced. With the rotor arm removed, apply a thin smear of grease around the cam using a thin bladed screwdriver to spread the grease uniformly. Take great care not to get any grease over the contact points.

Avoid overlubricating the cam and carefully wipe off any surplus grease, making sure the contacts are clean and dry, then refit the rotor arm and distributor cap.

13. Oiling the dynamo rear bearing — do not over oil

LUBRICATE WITH GREASE

Not all cars have grease nipples fitted — many parts are factory-packed with grease and sealed for life. But where you find grease nipples you should regularly lubricate the parts with a grease gun. Also, most cars benefit from the occasional application of grease in certain areas, like linkages.

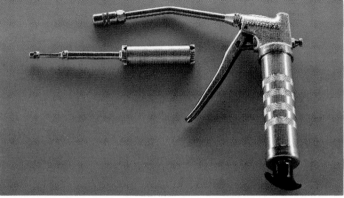

14. Two typical grease guns — a small one is useful in cramped areas

Water pump lubrication

Water pumps on older cars may have a grease nipple or a blanking plug fitted for lubricating the impeller shaft bearings.

Clean the area around the nipple or plug to remove all dirt then remove the plug, if fitted, and screw in a standard grease nipple. Apply a grease gun filled with high melting point multi-purpose grease, and give five strokes only to the nipple. Do not overfill the bearing because it can damage the rubber seals and cause coolant leakage.

Clutch cable lubrication

Where a cable operated clutch is fitted, the cable attachment points at the clutch pedal and at the operating arm end should be greased regularly to avoid premature wear and possible cable breakage.

At the pedal end inside the car, apply a generous blob of general purpose grease to the exposed part of the inner cable and its attachment to the pedal under the facia on most cars.

On cars where the lower end of the cable can be reached from inside the engine compartment, lubricate the cable and operating lever attachment in the same way as the pedal end.

The inner cable is normally plastic sheathed and should not need lubricating. However, if the pedal action is stiff check the route of the cable. It should follow a gentle curve without any sharp bends.

Handbrake cable lubrication

To ensure correct and trouble-free operation of the handbrake, the linkage or cable should be regularly cleaned and lubricated at least every six months.

The rear of the car will have to be raised and supported on axle stands to allow access to the linkage or cable from the underside. Remember to chock both front wheels and release the handbrake lever first.

Brush or clean off all road dirt from the exposed parts of the handbrake mechanism using a wire brush, paying particular attention to any places where the cable runs inside a channel. Check any linkage pivots for free movement and apply penetrating oil to free them if they are stiff. Then work them backwards and forwards until they are properly freed off.

Apply high melting point or general purpose grease to all sliding or pivoting parts of the mechanism. Where a cable passes through a channel or guide tube, apply the grease generously, working it as far

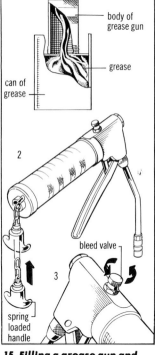

15. Filling a grease gun and bleeding off any air

into the channel or tube as possible.

On some cars, a grease nipple is fitted to the outer cable sleeve so you can lubricate the inner cable. Make sure the nipple is clean. Then use a grease gun filled with multi-purpose lithium based grease. Give about five strokes of the grease gun to lubricate the inner cable adequately.

Propshaft / drive shaft joints

The propshaft and driveshaft universal joints (**fig 16**) — mainly on older cars — should be lubricated with fresh grease every 6000 miles (10,000 km). Use a grease gun filled with high melting point lithium based grease.

As the job can only be done from under the car, the car should be raised at the rear and supported on axle stands first. Chock both front wheels and release the handbrake.

Find and clean the grease nipples on the propshaft and driveshafts (if applicable). There may be an additional nipple fitted to the sliding yoke sleeve on the driveshafts or front part of the propshaft.

Turn the propshaft or driveshaft as necessary to align each nipple with the grease gun, then pump the gun until you can see the old grease coming out from the joint seals or yoke sleeve.

16. Grease nipple on propshaft

TIP

Block of ages

If the grease is difficult to get into the nipple, the nipple could have been blocked for years with hard grease. The best way to unblock the nipple is to unscrew it and then pump grease though to unblock it. Refit the nipple and tighten it securely, but do not overtighten.

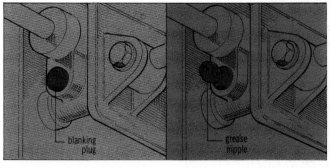

17. Where a blanking plug is fitted (left) screw in a grease nipple

Ball joints & pivots

Because they are vital to the safety of the car, all front and rear suspension joints, and pivots which have a grease nipple or blanking plugs (**fig 17**), must be lubricated at least every 6000 miles (10,000 km).

To lubricate each joint fully, it is important that the suspension should be relieved of all load.

Raise the car and support it on axle stands then take off the front wheels. Brush and clean the area around each grease nipple to remove all road dirt first. Some cars are fitted with a blanking plug at the grease point. This should be unscrewed and a grease nipple fitted in its place. Substitute nipples are normally available from your local dealer.

Using a grease gun filled with multi-purpose lithium based grease, apply several strokes of the gun to each nipple until old grease emerges from the seals.

Steering ball joints

The steering linkage and/or track rod end ball joints on some cars have a grease nipple fitted (**fig 18**).

The front of the car should be raised and supported on axle stands, and both front wheels removed first. Locate and clean the grease nipple on each joint, noting that there may be up to four joints in the linkage.

Using a grease gun filled with

multi-purpose lithium based grease, apply two full strokes of the gun to each nipple. Rotate the steering from lock to lock and apply two further strokes of the grease gun. Do not overfill the joints as the grease pressure may split or dislodge the rubber dust boot.

18. Greasing a ball joint

Gearchange linkages

Many cars have an external gearchange linkage which needs periodic lubrication of the linkage pivots to avoid undue wear on the pivot pins and lever holes.

Raise the front of the car and support it on axle stands so that you can get to the linkage alongside the gearbox or transmission.

Clean all oil and road grit from the pivot ends of the linkage, then apply a generous coating of high melting point grease to the pivot points. Make sure the grease is worked well in.

Renewing oil and air filters

Renewing oil and air filters is an 'easy way in' to car repairs. You can learn in half an hour

When to do this job
As recommended by your handbook or:
Engine oil: Town driving — at recommended intervals or every six months, whichever is first
Long distance driving — every 6000 miles (10,000 km) or every six months
Oil filter: Town driving — every 6000 miles (10,000 km) or every twelve months
Long distance driving — every 12,000 miles (20,000 km) or every twelve months
Air filter: Normal conditions — every 12,000 miles (20,000 km) or every twelve months
Dusty conditions — every 6000 miles (10,000 km) or every six months

What this job involves
Draining engine oil
Changing engine oil
Changing oil filter
Changing air filter

Related jobs in this handbook
All round lubrication
Curing fuel flow problems
Please see Index for page numbers

To do this job
Tools: Spanner or socket to fit sump drain plug; filter wrench or large screwdriver and hammer (maybe); container to drain oil into(maybe); spanner or screwdriver for air filter box (maybe)
Materials: New oil (see text); new oil filter or filter element; new air filter element
Time: Not more than an hour
Degree of difficulty: Easy, though sump nut and filter may be hard to undo

If you have the job professionally done...
Is oil on dipstick clean and to full mark? Is oil filter body clean? Is air filter element inside filter box clean? Are oil filter seal and sump plug free of leaks?

Changing your car's oil and filters is one of the easiest routine jobs which will make your car go better and help the engine to last longer.

Your handbook will tell you how much and what grade of oil you need. Most manufacturers recommend a multigrade oil, so called because it behaves as a thin oil when cold and as a thick oil when hot. A variety of multigrades are available, such as 20W/50 and 15W/40 — they are all general purpose oils and are suited to most cars.

However, 10W/30 oil used in an engine in good condition may aid starting and improve fuel economy, while an older engine may burn less oil if you use a 20W/50 multigrade.

Flushing oil always used to be recommended for getting the sludge out of engines. It is a kind of light, thin oil which flows easily and carries away impurities from the engine when it is drained out. Nowadays flushing oil is regarded as unnecessary, because modern good quality oil contains additives which clean the engine.

STEP 1   ASSEMBLE TOOLS AND COMPONENTS

First check that you can find your sump drain plug. As **fig 1** shows, this is usually a large nut located at the lowest point of the engine nearer the front. Some cars, for example the Renault 12, have a recessed square-shaped socket in the drain plug. Other cars, like the Talbot Horizon, have a recessed six-sided socket. You will need a special tool — from any good accessory shop — to undo any recessed-socket type of drain plug.

Check also that you can find the oil filter. This is a cylindrical device about the same size as a toilet roll, usually located low down on the main part of the engine. Note that some Renault 4s have no oil filter and only the oil needs to be changed.

Cleaning the oil filter on VW Beetles and on cars which have centrifugal oil filters — like the Fiat 500, 600, 850 and 126 and the Simca 1000 — is covered in a later article.

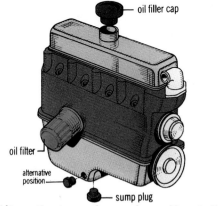

1. Alternative types of sump plug and how to find them

Check that you have a spanner or socket spanner large enough for the sump plug and that your drain tray will both fit under the car and contain the contents of the sump. Your car's oil capacity will be given in your owner's handbook or manual.

On a few cars — notably some Austin Rover front wheel drive models such as Minis — the engine and gearbox use the same oil, so the capacities are combined. In most other cases the gearbox oil is completely separate and is not drained with the engine oil, or not drained at all.

Once you know the engine's oil capacity you can choose a suitable container for draining the old oil into, and go and buy the right amount of new oil. It is no disadvantage to have to buy ten litres when you only need six, since the rest will be useful for routine topping up.

There are two basic types of oil filter (**fig 2**) — the screw-in type and the replaceable cartridge type. Most cars now have the screw-in type which screws directly into the engine. They are generally brightly coloured and bear their maker's name. But if you have an older car you may have the cartridge type of filter. This comprises a metal casing containing a replaceable filter and is attached to the engine by a central bolt.

Both types of filter perform exactly the same task of straining the oil, and both need changing at the same intervals.

Oil filters are widely available from motor factors and accessory shops but when buying a replacement be sure to quote your car's make, model and year of manufacture.

2. The two types of oil filter

Before draining the oil you must first warm the engine up thoroughly — for example, by driving round to buy the new oil. The oil will drain from the car much more quickly when it is hot and any sludge will be drained away with the oil rather than lingering in the nooks and crannies of the engine.

Once the engine is hot, park the car on level ground and position your drain tray under the sump. Take off the oil filler cap to help the flow of oil. Loosen the sump plug with a spanner (**fig 1**) or socket and then unscrew it with your fingers. Hold it tightly so that you do not drop it when the oil gushes out (**fig 2**). The oil will be hot and dirty — so be prepared.

If you are changing the filter, now is the time to remove it (see Step 3). Allow at least 15 minutes for all the oil to drain out. Then refit the sump plug and the new filter.

To refill, pour the new oil in through the filler, using a funnel if necessary. The oil will take a little time to reach the sump so be sure to allow about a minute for it to pass through the engine before checking the dipstick or you may overfill the engine. If you do significantly overfill the sump you must remove the sump plug and drain away the excess.

When the dipstick reading is correct, run the engine at idle for a few minutes. Switch off and allow about five minutes for the oil to drain down into the sump. Then recheck the level and top up if necessary.

1. Loosening the sump plug

2. Draining the sump

██TIP██

Filling up with oil

When you use a five litre can to pour oil into the filler, hold the spout uppermost. This will let air flow into the can so that the oil will run out smoothly.

To make sure you read the dipstick correctly, pull it out of its hole and wipe the oil off the end with an old rag. Then push the dipstick fully back and pull it out again. The dipstick will now show an accurate reading.

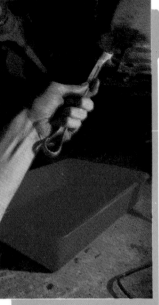

██FACT FILE██

Buy the right part!

When buying components, you usually need to quote only the make, model and year of your car. But car manufacturers sometimes swap, partway through a model year, from one type or make of component to another. So you can easily make a mistake and buy the wrong replacement.

To avoid this, take a note of the engine number and chassis number of your car — both are given on your car registration papers — and keep the numbers handy, in your glovebox or diary, when you go shopping.

Main dealers and good accessory stores have reference books (or computerized records) which match engine and chassis numbers to the components the manufacturer actually used, and from which replacements can be bought accurately.

It often helps to take the old component along with you to make sure the one you buy is the same. If you can park near the spares shop, you can usually persuade someone from the shop to look at your car and tell you what you need.

Screw-in oil filters screw straight into the engine block. You may be able to remove this type of filter simply by gripping it with both hands and turning it anticlockwise. Cleaning the filter first and wearing rubber gloves (**fig 1**) may increase your chances of success. But if the filter simply will not budge the best way to remove it is to use a filter wrench (**fig 2**), which uses a chain or a strap to grip the filter body. The filter will be full of hot oil, so handle it gingerly if you want to avoid a sleeve full.

If you do not have a filter wrench you may be able to improvise with a piece of rope and a length of pipe. Tie the rope around the filter and use the pipe to twist the rope up tight. Then lever the pipe against the filter. If the rope is gripping it tightly enough the filter should unscrew.

Another, more drastic, method is to hammer a screwdriver right through the filter (**fig 3**). You will then be able to grip the screwdriver handle and unscrew the filter.

There is very little risk that the metal of the filter body will tear. It is tough enough that you will need to use force to hammer the screwdriver through the metal casing of the filter.

When fitting the new filter, take care to position its sealing ring in the groove on the filter correctly and only tighten it hand tight.

Smear a little grease on to the sealing ring to hold it in place.

1. Gloves give a firmer grip **2. Using a filter wrench** **3. Screwdriver as filter lever**

██ALTERNATIVE 3██ — RENEW OIL FILTER (CARTRIDGE TYPE)

Cartridge type oil filters (**fig 1**) are secured by a bolt running right through the casing into the engine block. Unscrew the bolt with a spanner and withdraw the whole assembly. The casing is usually full of hot oil, so have the drain tray handy to avoid a mess. Have some newspaper handy on which to lay out the cylinder and its components in order. These filters usually comprise the through bolt and washer, the cylinder, filter cartridge, spring and sealing ring.

Take out the old sealing ring — it is usually in a groove on the engine block, and you may need to prise it out with a pin. Throw away the old filter cartridge and clean all the other components thoroughly in paraffin (kerosene), keeping them in the same order. If you mix them up the filter might not work.

Reassemble the casing with a new filter element and refit it to the engine. If the sealing ring does not fit securely in its groove, use a little grease to hold it in place.

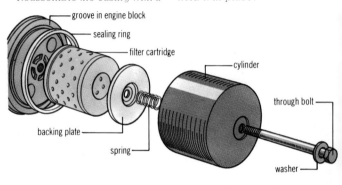

groove in engine block
sealing ring
filter cartridge
cylinder
backing plate
spring
through bolt
washer

1. Exploded view showing how a cartridge filter comes apart

The oil filter fitted to air-cooled Fiat models is a centrifugal type and is built in to the crankshaft fan belt pulley (**fig 1**). To change the oil and clean the filter start by running the engine to heat it up to normal working temperature. Drain the oil in the normal way by undoing the drain plug in the bottom of the engine. Access to the filter unit is gained by unbolting the rear valance from the car (support the engine on a jack).

The filter front plate on the pulley is held in place by six bolts and you should undo these bolts evenly, half a turn at a time to start with, working your way round the set of bolts. When the bolts are all loose remove them and pull off the cover plate. Some oil will drain out from the pump when you do this so have a rag ready to catch it. Then wipe all the remaining oil out of the pulley body and off the cover plate.

The centrifugal action of the filter deposits dirt from the oil as a layer on the outside faces of the pulley body and the cover and you should scrape the dirt out (**fig 2**). When you have got the dirt out clean the inside of the pulley and the cover plate thoroughly with a cloth dipped in paraffin.

A rubber seal is used between the pulley body and the cover plate and you should fit a new seal on the cap before

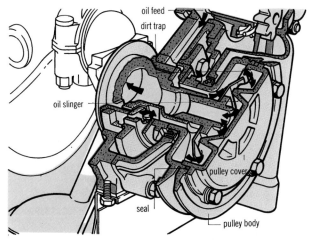

1. Centrifugal Fiat oil filter is in the crankshaft pulley body

2. Cleaning dirt deposits out of filter

you position it on the pulley body. Refit the bolts, tightening them home in turn, taking care not to overtighten as this could

crack the cover. Finally refit the engine drain plug and fill the engine with normal multigrade engine oil.

The most common type of air filter is the disposable paper element, two types of which are in **fig 1**. You will find this inside the large metal or plastic box which either sits on top of the carburettor or is connected to it by a large diameter pipe.

To take out the old filter you should undo the nuts, screws or clips which hold the cover of the filter box in place and then lift off the cover (**fig 2**).

Normally an air filter element is good for around a year, or 12,000 miles (20,000 km). But if you cannot see the original colour of the element in the folds of the paper you should renew the element (**fig 3**). If only one area of the element is clogged, try rotating it so that the dirty part is moved to a different position.

Wipe away any loose dust inside the filter box, using a rag

'plug' to make sure that none falls into the carburettor.

If your car handbook mentions that the air intake to the filter box has 'summer' and 'winter' positions, make sure that the setting is correct. Refit the cover of the filter box and tighten it down evenly.

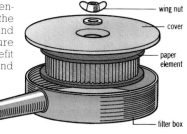

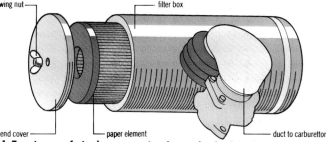

1. Two types of air cleaner — circular and cylindrical

2. Removing the air cleaner cover

3. Putting in a new filter element

ALTERNATIVE 4 — CLEAN AIR FILTER (WIRE MESH TYPE)

Some cars have filter elements made of wire mesh. Open the filter box as described in Step 4. Take the filter elements out and wash them in paraffin (kerosene) (**fig 1**). Then they can be lightly oiled with engine oil and reused. In rare cases where the wire mesh cannot be removed

from its housing, the whole air cleaner has to be washed in paraffin and then a little oil poured into the mesh.

When you have fitted the clean filter, check that the cover of the filter box is fitted correctly. Tighten it evenly, turning each nut a little at a time.

1. Wash mesh type in paraffin

Simple spark plug service

Keeping your spark plugs in peak condition will help your car to start more easily, run better and use less fuel

Spark plugs are among the most vital parts of the ignition system. Their condition and adjustment affect both performance and economy. Although they look simple in construction they are designed to work in direct contact with the extreme temperatures and pressures inside the engine's combustion chambers.

The constant passage of electrical energy across the gap between the two electrodes gradually erodes away the metal. You should check and adjust your spark plugs about every 6000 miles (10,000 km). Spark plugs need to be renewed about every 12,000 miles (20,000 km).

When to do this job
Check and adjust plugs every 6000 miles (10,000 km)
Renew plugs every 12,000 miles (20,000 km)

What this job involves
Removing spark plugs
Cleaning spark plugs
Adjusting spark gaps
Replacing spark plugs

Related jobs in this handbook
Overhauling the distributor
Curing starting problems
Getting your timing right
Please see Index for page numbers

To do this job
Tools: Plug spanner; plug gapping tool; feeler gauges; contact file (maybe); long bristled paint-brush
Materials: New set of spark plugs (maybe)
Time: Half an hour to one hour
Degree of difficulty: Easy, unless plugs are inaccessible or overtightened

If you have the job professionally done ...
Does engine idle smoothly and fire on all cylinders?
Do the plugs have clean insulators?

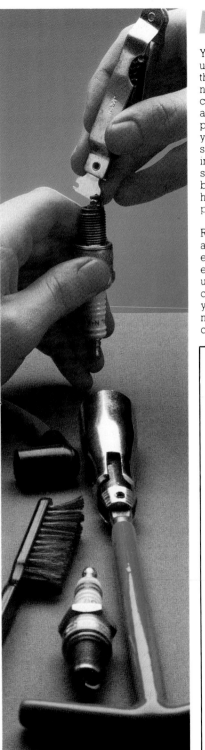

You must have a plug spanner to unscrew the spark plugs from the cylinder head. Most plugs need a 14 mm spanner but a few cars, such as some Vauxhalls and Peugeots, need a 10 mm plug spanner — check what size you have before buying a plug spanner. Most car makers include one in the tool kit but special plug spanners can be bought (**fig 1**) — the best ones have a rubber insert to grip and protect the ceramic plug body

On some small cars — the Renault 5 is an example — access to one spark plug is extremely difficult because one end of the engine is buried under a bulkhead or some other components. To reach this plug you will need a plug spanner made specifically for your own car, unless you have a compre-

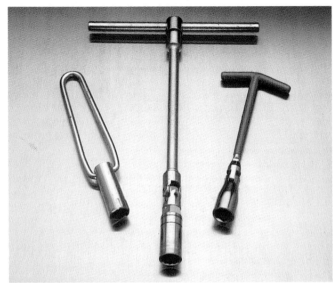

1. You need a long spanner to reach hard to get at plugs

HOW IT WORKS

Spark plugs: features and types

The main feature of a spark plug is a ceramic insulator inside a threaded metal shank. Through the middle of the ceramic body runs a conductor which links the outer terminal of the plug (on to which the plug lead and cap are clipped) and the centre electrode, visible inside the hollow shank. Reaching out towards the centre electrode from the rim of the plug tip is the side electrode. The spark plug gap is the space between the tips of the two electrodes.

There are two main types of spark plug. The most common type has a small metal compression washer or gasket to seal the plug tightly to the cylinder head. The other type has a taper seat machined on it which mates with a seat around the spark plug hole in the cylinder head.

Each of these two basic types of plug can have up to four further design variations.

The *reach* of a plug refers to the length of the threaded shank and determines the position of the plug tip inside the combustion chamber. It is vital to have plugs of the correct reach — too long a shank might allow the piston to

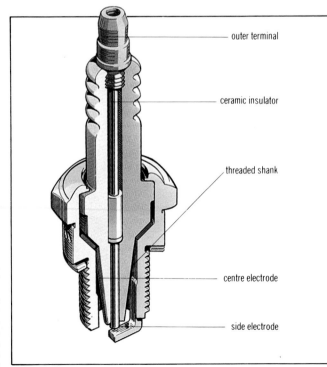

outer terminal

ceramic insulator

threaded shank

centre electrode

side electrode

hensive socket set. These include plug sockets, a universal joint and an extension bar, which should allow you to cope with anything.

You can buy a combined set of feeler gauges with a gapping tool cheaply from most accessory shops (**fig 2**). You may have a set of long feeler gauges (**fig 3**) but these do not have a lever

3. Typical set of feeler gauges — marked in thousandths of an inch

2. A plug gapping tool can be used to clean and adjust the plugs

notch for adjusting the plug gap. Each feeler gauge has its thickness marked on it (see Fact File — Using a feeler gauge, page 204). If the gapping tool and gauge set does not include a contact file (a very thin file used on electrical contacts) you should buy one. A long-bristled paint brush is also useful to clean away loose dirt around the plug seat.

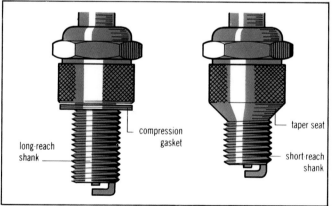

Champion's RN9Y type of plug is identical in operation to the N9Y type but the R in the code denotes that it has a resistor.

Finally, there can be some variation in plug tip design. A few models have up to four side electrodes for better sparking.

The type of plug that a car needs will normally be given in the owner's handbook or workshop manual. Always use that type or the exact equivalent from another plug maker's range.

long-reach shank

compression gasket

taper seat

short-reach shank

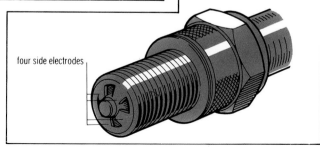

four side electrodes

touch the plug tip, and too short a shank will result in poor ignition.

A plug's temperature range denotes the ability of the plug's centre electrode to conduct away heat. A cold plug cools faster than a hot plug as it has a shorter heat path between the centre electrode and metal body.

To provide radio interference suppression, some plugs have an electrical resistor inside the ceramic body. For example,

1. Loosen the spark plugs and then brush out any dirt

Before pulling off the plug connector caps, label each plug's high tension lead with its cylinder number so that it can be replaced correctly. Then pull off the plug caps — always pull the cap itself, not the plug leads.

Push the plug spanner firmly on to the first plug and unscrew it about four turns (**fig 1**). Use the paint brush to clean out any dirt or flakes of corrosion from around the plug hole to prevent them from falling inside the cylinder when the plug is out. Some cars have a particularly deep plug recess where a brush will not go — either blow out the dirt or use a vacuum cleaner to remove it. Unscrew the plug completely and repeat

STEP 3   CLEAN UP PLUGS

Badly blackened spark plugs or those with hard deposits can be cleaned by grit blasting — never use a wire brush on the tip of the plug because the bristles can leave conductive tracks of metal across the centre electrode insulator. Some garages will grit blast plugs for a small charge — but compare their charge with the cost of new plugs before you go ahead,

because the saving may be insignificant. There is also a DIY plug cleaner (**fig 1**) that works in the same way as the professional machine.

You can clean off any soft, dusty deposits with a toothbrush. A wire brush can be used to remove any dirt from the screw threads of the plug (**fig 2**). Wipe off any dust or oil on the ceramic insulator body.

Next, use the contact file to clean the tip of the central electrode and the inside face of the side electrode. If the file will not fit between the electrodes, use the lever notch on the gapping tool to bend back the side electrode slightly (see Step 4). File the surfaces of the electrodes until they are clean and flat — be careful to keep the file level while you are using it.

1. A DIY grit blaster for cleaning plug tips

2. Using a wire brush to clean the threads

the procedure for all the other plugs. Bear in mind that if the engine is still hot, the plugs will be too.

Do not use too much force if you have a stubborn spark plug. Try sliding an extension steel pipe over the handle of the plug spanner to get more leverage. If this does not work, take the car to a service garage which will have the tools and experience to do the job. Garages can repair damaged plug hole threads with a spring-like steel thread insert — essential if the plug has been cross-threaded into the cylinder head.

Look at the colour and condition of the tip of each spark plug. If the engine is well tuned all the plugs should be the same

2. Plug in serviceable condition

3. Plug with worn electrodes

light biscuity brown colour (**fig 2**). Plugs of a significantly different appearance are a sign of a problem needing further investigation, dealt with in another article. Worn plug tips, however, are quite normal.

Marked rounding of the centre electrode together with pitting of the side electrode (**fig 3**) means that the plug should be discarded. It is not a good idea to renew just one plug — always fit a whole new set.

A very light smear of engine oil on the plug threads (**fig 2**) will make them easier to screw in and help to prevent them seizing up. However, plugs which are too greasy can cause bad running so give the insulators a final wipe before you screw them in (**fig 3**). Screw the plug into the hole by hand for at least the first four turns so that there can be no possibility of cross-threading.

Plugs should never be over-tightened — they must only be screwed down hard enough to make a good gas seal. Screw in each plug until you feel it meet the seal. Then, if the plug has a metal compression gasket, screw it down by a further quarter of a turn. If the plug has a taper seat, screw it down by only one sixteenth of a turn.

Before you reconnect the plug leads, note the type of terminal connection on the top of the plug. There are two types. Some plug caps push home directly on to the thin screw thread which protrudes from the ceramic insulator, while others fit over a much thicker

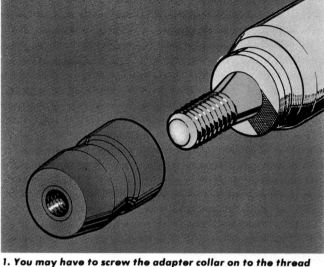

1. You may have to screw the adapter collar on to the thread

adapter collar which screws on to the plug terminal (**fig 1**). Depending on which type of lead connector you have, you may have either to remove or to screw on this collar.

Push the plug caps firmly home over the plug-top terminals. Make sure you have

the plug leads on the right plugs by checking that the labels on the leads are in order.

Finally, check your work by running the engine and making sure that it idles smoothly without any of the lumpiness that would suggest that one cylinder is not firing.

STEP 4   ADJUST PLUG GAP

1. The feeler gauge should just slide in the gap

Most cars have a plug gap of about 0.025 in. (0.6-0.7 mm), but the gap recommended for your car should be given in your manual. Pick the feeler gauge of the correct thickness and use it to measure the gap between the electrodes. The feeler gauge (see Fact File — Using a feeler gauge, page 205) should be a tight sliding fit (**fig 1**).

You can adjust the gap by bending the side electrode (**fig 2**). If the gap is too narrow, bend back the side electrode with the lever notch on the gapping tool. If the gap is too wide, tap the side electrode gently with a spanner so that it moves closer to the central electrode. Always check that new spark plugs have the right gap.

1. Adjusting the plug gap

2. Smearing a little oil on the plug threads

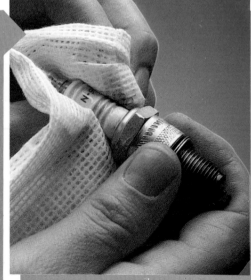

3. Cleaning plugs before replacing them

Adjusting the engine's timing

Bad timing can waste fuel, contribute to poor starting and running and may even damage the engine — so it's essential to get it right

---

When to do this job

Regular checks: As recommended by your handbook or every 12,000 miles (20,000 km)

Running repairs: When you experience bad running, poor starting or the car is using too much petrol (and you have already checked the car's electrical and petrol systems as well as points and plugs)

When you remove the distributor

When you renew the contact breaker points

What this job involves

Finding the timing marks

Static timing: Lining up the marks
            Setting the timing

Dynamic timing: Connecting the strobe
               Setting the timing

Related jobs in this handbook

Curing starting problems

Spark plug service

Please see Index for page numbers

To do this job

Tools: Spanner to fit bolts holding distributor in place; 12 volt test lamp (static method); strobe light (dynamic method); hand mirror (maybe)

Materials: Chalk/white paint

Time: Not more than one hour

Degree of difficulty: Easy — biggest problem is often getting information on the correct setting for your car

If you have the job professionally done . . .

Is the car running smoothly without pinking or running on? Is petrol consumption normal?

There are two ways of checking the timing of the engine — *static timing,* which is carried out while the engine is switched off; and *dynamic timing,* which is done while the engine is actually running.

Either method can usually be used successfully, but check your handbook first: some cars can be adjusted only by the dynamic method, others only by the static method. If you have the choice, dynamic timing is easier and quicker and gives more accurate results.

Static timing requires no expensive equipment — just a simple 12 volt test lamp. You can either buy a ready-made kit from a motor accessory shop or make up your own (see Fact File — Cheap test equipment, page 193). It is even possible to do the job with no equipment at all (see Tip — Timing the easy way, page 87).

For dynamic timing you need a strobe (stroboscopic) light — a small gun-shaped instrument which flashes in time with the sparks at one of the plugs, illuminating the timing marks so that, if the flashes occur at the same time in each cycle, the marks appear to stand still. Any adjustments can then be made while the engine is running and their effects instantly seen.

Strobe lights are relatively cheap and they can be bought from most motor accessory shops. Some shops will even hire them for a small charge. But a word of warning — to use a strobe accurately you need to know the precise speed at which the engine is running. So, in most cases, they should be used only if the car is fitted with a rev counter (tachometer).

HOW IT WORKS

Marks and sparks

When you set the ignition timing, you actually change the exact moment at which the spark occurs in each cylinder to ignite the petrol. This is done by altering the position of the distributor (which controls the flow of sparks).

To simplify the operation, only one cylinder — your handbook or main dealer will tell you which — is used for timing purposes. All the pistons move in relation to one another in a predetermined order, so when this cylinder is timed correctly, the others automatically follow suit.

The spark should occur when the piston in the timing cylinder is at or near the top of its stroke. This means that there must be some way of finding out the exact position of the piston in relation to the spark being produced. To help you, there are a number of *timing marks* on the engine usually near or on the flywheel or pulley.

All the basic movements of the engine are linked, with no risk of slippage. As the crankshaft (to which the pistons are connected) turns, so does the pulley at one end and the flywheel at the other. So, either of these can be marked at manufacture to show the exact stage the engine rotation has reached. Once the moving timing mark is lined up correctly with the fixed marker, the piston is in the right position to adjust the spark.

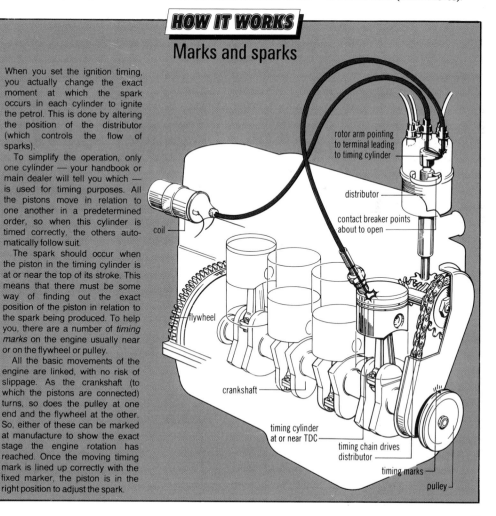

rotor arm pointing to terminal leading to timing cylinder

distributor

contact breaker points about to open

coil

flywheel

crankshaft

timing cylinder at or near TDC

timing chain drives distributor

timing marks

pulley

STEP 1 — FIND THE TIMING MARKS

The location of the timing marks varies from one car to another, so consult your handbook or manual. As **fig 1** shows they usually consist of a number of closely spaced lines or notches on or near the flywheel or drive belt pulley. If the timing marks are on the flywheel, you may have to remove a small plate bolted to the engine housing so you can see the marks. You may even have to use a mirror to help you (**fig 2**).

The timing marks have to be lined up with a pointer or notch. In some cases the timing marks are on the moving part of the engine — the flywheel or pulley — with the stationary marker on the engine housing. In others, the marker is on the flywheel or pulley while the timing marks are on the engine housing.

You are likely to find a number of timing marks. The largest mark indicates the

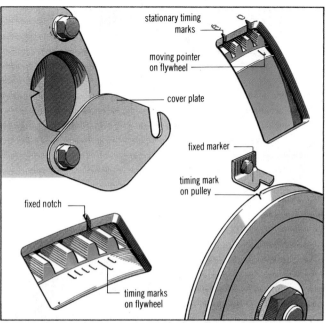

stationary timing marks

moving pointer on flywheel

cover plate

fixed marker

timing mark on pulley

fixed notch

timing marks on flywheel

1. Typical timing marks on crankshaft pulley and flywheel

position of the crankshaft when the piston used for setting the ignition timing is at the top of its stroke — a position known as *Top Dead Centre (TDC)*. The other marks just before TDC are the *advance marks*. Ignition is rarely set at TDC but usually a number of degrees in advance. This gives the spark the vital split second it needs to fully ignite the petrol just as the piston in the timing cylinder is approaching the top of its compression stroke.

Sometimes there is just one advance mark which refers to the correct timing position. But many cars have a calibrated scale marking off the number of degrees the crankshaft turns before TDC (**fig 3**). In this case you will have to refer to a workshop manual which should tell you the exact number of degrees Before Top Dead Centre (BTDC) the ignition

3. Timing marks: close-up view

timing should be set to. Mark this point in chalk on the calibrated scale so you can refer to it later. If you are not sure exactly which engine you have, check with a main dealer, quoting the engine number (see Fact File — Buy the right part, page 80).

What you do next depends on whether you intend to time the ignition using the static method (see Steps 2 and 3) or the dynamic method (see Alternative Steps 2 and 3).

2. Using a mirror to see marks

STEP 2 — LINE UP THE TIMING MARKS (STATIC)

First look in your manual to see which of the cylinders is used for setting the ignition timing. Usually this is the Number 1 cylinder — often the one nearest the fan. In some cases, however, it is not obvious which is Number 1, so to be certain you

should ask a main dealer.

You can then start the job by removing the distributor cap so you can see the rotor arm and contact points clearly. Next connect up the test lamp. Remove the two LT leads from the coil and clamp one clip to

each of the connectors on the leads (**figs 1 & 2**). It does not matter which way round the two leads go.

Now slowly turn the engine by hand (see Fact File — Turning the engine over by hand, page 203) until the stationary marker on

the engine lines up with the correct advance mark.

If you can find somebody to help, get them to turn the engine over while you keep an eye on the timing marks. Never turn the engine backwards — you will get a false reading. (If you are not sure which way the engine turns normally, put the car into a high gear, push it forwards and look at any moving part of the engine.)

While the engine is turning, make a note of the direction of travel of the rotor arm in the distributor — you will need this information later when you adjust the timing.

Once the stationary marker on or near the flywheel is aligned with the appropriate advance mark, follow the HT lead from the timing cylinder spark plug to the distributor. The rotor arm should be pointing directly towards the terminal leading towards that

cylinder (**fig 3**). If it is pointing in the opposite direction it is because the engine turns twice in each cycle and you are 180° out. If so, rotate the engine another turn until the rotor arm lines up with the terminal leading to the timing cylinder.

1. Removing the two LT leads from the coil

2. Connecting the test lamp to the LT leads

3. Checking that the rotor arm lines up with the timing cylinder

1. Making fine adjustments to timing using the Vernier gauge

distributor one way and the other slowly — you should see the test lamp go off and on as the points open and close. Turn the distributor the other way to the rotor arm's rotation until the test lamp goes off. Then move it slowly in the same direction as the rotor arm until the light just comes on (**fig 3**). Now the ignition is correctly adjusted.

Check the adjustment by turning the engine over once or twice by hand to make sure that the light comes on once the advance timing mark is exactly in line with the stationary marker. Then retighten the bolts holding the distributor in place. They do not need to be very tight — just enough so that there is no chance of the distributor moving. Take care not to move the body of the distributor otherwise the adjustment you have just made will be altered.

Then make fine adjustments using the Vernier gauge, if one

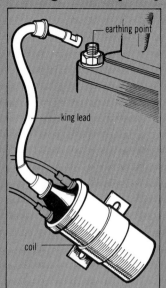

Timing the easy way

It is often possible to set the ignition timing statically with no equipment at all — just by removing the central (king) lead from the distributor. This method works when only a small adjustment is needed — when the car has been running fairly well and the distributor has not been disturbed.

Find out which way the engine normally turns — operate the starter briefly, for example. Then switch off the ignition and turn it by hand till you reach a point just before the timing marks start to line up.

Detach the king lead and let its end rest within a few millimetres of a good earth point — virtually any clean part of the engine will do,

but keep it well away from the carburettor and from its normal socket. Also make sure there are no petrol fumes which could ignite. Turn on the ignition.

Continue to turn the engine by hand in the direction of rotation. At the instant when the points separate you will see and hear a spark jumping from the king lead to the engine.

Adjust the distributor until the spark occurs when the timing marks are exactly aligned. Alternatively, align the marks to the correct setting and turn the distributor body against the direction of the rotor until the spark occurs. The exact point of sparking is the correct setting.

First switch on the ignition. If your distributor is fitted with a Vernier screw gauge (**fig 1**) you may be able to use this to set the timing — providing not too large an adjustment needs to be made.

Turn the screw in one direction and then in the other and look at the test lamp — you should be able to find the exact spot where the test lamp lights up. At this point the timing is set correctly. If turning the screw has no effect on the lamp, you set the timing by hand and use the Vernier to make fine adjustments at the end (see below). But before you start, move the screw gauge to its midway position, so you have plenty of adjustment in either direction.

To adjust the timing manually loosen the pinch bolts holding the distributor in place (**fig 2**). You need not slacken them any more than is just enough to allow the distributor body to move freely. Turn the body of the

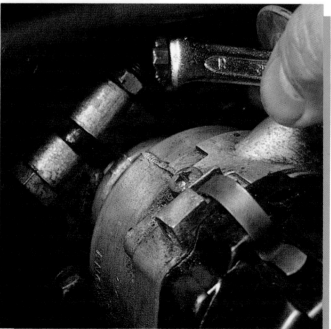

2. Loosening the pinch bolts holding the distributor body

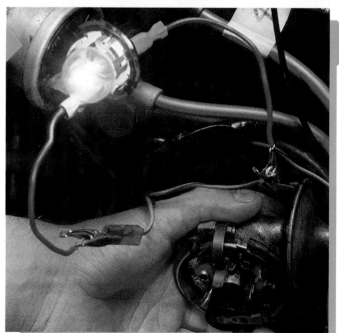

3. Once the bulb just lights up the timing is set correctly

4. Final tuning using the Vernier

is fitted. Turn the screw slowly backwards and forwards looking at the test lamp all the time until you find the precise spot where the lamp lights up (**fig 4**).

Unclip the test lamp, replace the distributor cap, reconnect the LT leads to the coil and switch off the ignition.

Before you start, read the instructions supplied with the strobe light and also find out which cylinder is used for timing by looking in the car's manual.

Xenon strobes have three leads — two power leads which are connected to the battery terminals (or one lead that plugs into the mains) and a sensor which is attached to the timing cylinder spark plug or to the HT lead running from it. Some sensors have an inductive trigger that just needs to be clipped around the lead which runs from the plug. More usual is the type which fits between the spark plug and the plug cap (**fig 1**). To fit this type, pull the cap off the plug. Then push the sensor on to the plug terminal and the cap on top of the sensor.

Neon strobes have two leads so they can be connected in line between the spark plug and the HT lead. Pull off the cap and push one lead on to the top of the exposed spark plug terminal and the other lead into the plug cap (**fig 2**).

Check also in your manual whether or not the vacuum advance pipe should be disconnected during timing. The vacuum advance pipe is a flexible tube running from a bell-shaped housing on the side of the distributor to some point below the carburettor. You can disconnect it from either the distributor end or from the carburettor.

On some models, the manufacturers specify that the vacuum advance should be blocked off during timing. You can do this by leaving the pipe in place and clamping a G-clamp to it. Or you can remove the pipe from the distributor and then block up the vacuum advance pipe with a suitable screw or bolt.

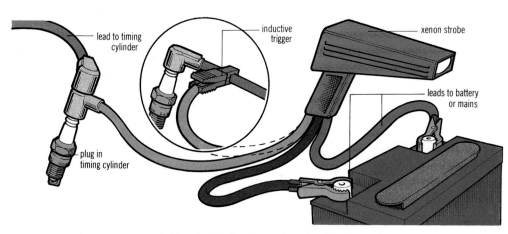

1. Xenon strobes are powered either by the battery or by a lead to the mains

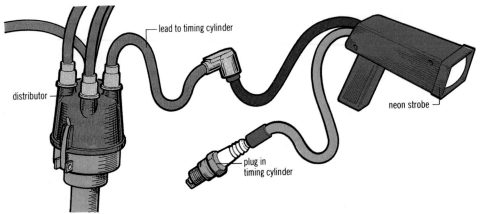

2. Connecting a neon strobe between the timing plug and the plug cap

Strobe timing usually has to be carried out while the engine is running at a certain speed, usually tickover speed. This varies from car to car, so check the manual. Turn on the engine and look at the rev counter (tachometer) to make sure that the engine speed is correct. If the speed needs to be altered you can do this by adjusting the idling screw on the carburettor (see Fact File — Altering engine speed).

Aim the strobe light at the timing marks (**fig 1**). The light flashes very briefly every time a spark voltage flows to the chosen cylinder, so in that instant everything seems to be stationary. This is because each time it flashes the moving mark has rotated by two turns, but since the spark comes at exactly the same instant in the cycle, the mark appears not to have moved at all.

The other moving parts of the engine have an odd appearance. The fan and generator pulley may seem to be moving quite slowly — often backwards. If the flashes are bright or the surroundings are dark this can be very misleading — and though you know the fan is really moving quickly you can

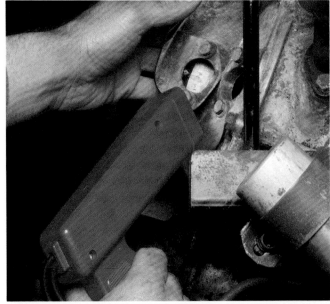

1. Timing marks appear to stand still under the strobe

be fooled in an unguarded moment into thinking that it is almost stationary — so take care. Any onlookers may be caught out, so keep children in particular away from the engine when using a strobe light.

If the timing is correct, the flashes will illuminate the moving marker at the correct timing position. If the timing is set wrongly, loosen the pinch bolt holding the distributor in place (see Step 3, **fig 2**) and turn the body in the opposite direction to that of the rotor until the correct timing mark lines up with the marker. Then retighten the pinch bolt just enough to make sure that there is no chance of the distributor moving.

The ignition timing should now be correctly adjusted. Continue to run the engine for a short while and check with the strobe light that the marks still coincide.

If a Vernier gauge is fitted you can use it to make adjustments finer than those you can make manually, with the distributor body clamp. Point the strobe at the timing marks and turn the screw gauge slowly backwards and forwards until you find the precise spot where the stationary marker lines up with the correct advance mark.

Turn off the engine and unclip the strobe light. Finally, replace the vacuum advance pipe.

FACT FILE

Altering engine speed

Engine speed (rpm) is critical when setting the ignition timing with a strobe. You can alter this if it is wrong by adjusting the idling screw. This is fixed to the side of the carburettor close to the point where the accelerator cable or rod is attached. To help you locate the idling screw, have someone press down on the accelerator pedal while you look carefully at the carburettor. Turn the screw clockwise to speed up the engine, anticlockwise to slow it down. Always return the engine to its normal tickover speed setting when you have finished.

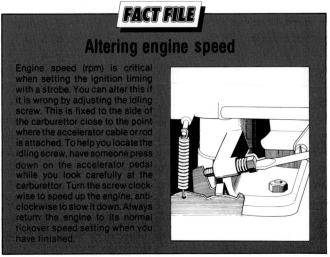

Adjusting valve clearances (OHV)

Adjusting the valve clearances — setting the tappets — will keep your car's performance and economy at a peak

Regular adjustment of the valve clearances is an important part of the maintenance of an engine. Only with these clearances set correctly will you be able to benefit from your engine's full performance and economy. Incorrectly set clearances will cause excessive heat and wear and will shorten your engine's life. This article deals with valve clearance adjustment on overhead valve (OHV) engines and those overhead cam (OHC) engines which use rocker arms fitted with adjusters. This design makes setting the valve clearance an easy job — the sort that any DIY mechanic can tackle.

When to do this job
Every 6000 - 12,000 miles (10,000 - 20,000 km) or as recommended by the car manufacturer. If cylinder head or rocker assembly has been disturbed or if the engine sounds 'tappety'

What this job involves
Removing rocker cover or cam box
Checking valve clearances
Adjusting valve clearances
Fitting new rocker cover or cam box gasket

Related jobs in this handbook
Adjusting valve clearances OHC shim type
Replacing air filter
Checking engine compression
Please see Index for page numbers

To do this job
Tools: Spanners; screwdriver; feeler gauges
Materials: Rocker cover or cam box gasket; gasket cement
Time: About an hour
Degree of difficulty: Getting adjustment exactly right can be tricky

If you have the job professionally done . . .
Does engine idle smoothly without ticking noises?
Is the rocker or cam box oiltight?

The first step before you can adjust your valve clearances is to check your manual. You need to know the type of valve gear your car has; the valve clearance settings; the order for checking them and whether they should be checked with the engine hot or cold. This last point is very important. If your manual specifies a hot clearance, take the car out for a run of at least five miles (eight kilometres) and then do the job straight after you turn the engine off. This will ensure that it reaches normal running temperature — it is not enough for the engine to be merely warm, it must be thoroughly heated through.

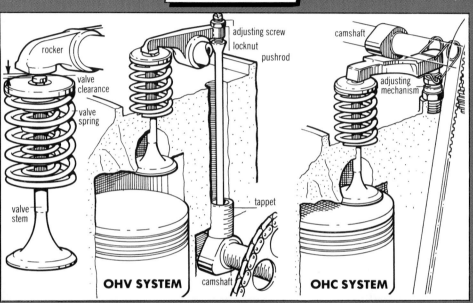

HOW IT WORKS

adjusting screw
locknut
pushrod
rocker
camshaft
adjusting mechanism
valve clearance
valve spring
valve stem
tappet
OHV SYSTEM   camshaft   **OHC SYSTEM**

The operation of the valves

The job of the valves is to control the flow of gases through the cylinder head. Inlet valves open at precisely timed intervals to let the air-fuel mixture into the combustion chambers while the exhaust valves open to let the spent gases escape. To do this work efficiently the mechanism which operates the valves in time with the rest of the engine must have a small amount of free play between the moving parts. This allows for heat expansion and makes sure that there is no pressure against the stem when its spring is holding it closed. Only when this small gap is set correctly will the valves be able to operate efficiently. If the gap is insufficient the valves may not close fully resulting in low compression, overheating and damaged valve seats. If the gap is too large the engine will lose power and the valve gear will rattle and wear out relatively quickly.

The mechanism which actually operates the valves can be one of two main types; overhead valve (OHV) or overhead cam (OHC). As the name suggests, one main difference is in the location of the camshaft. This is always driven by the crankshaft but in the popular OHV design the camshaft is inside the cylinder block and operates the valves indirectly by a system of tappets, pushrods and rockers. Increasingly, manufacturers are now opting for the OHC arrangement where the camshaft is fitted to the cylinder head so that it operates the valves directly.

The method of valve clearance adjustment usually differs between OHV and OHC engines, although a few OHC designs employ the same method as OHV engines — so check your handbook to see which type your car is. All OHV and some OHC engines employ short metal arms, called rockers, to operate the valves. The rockers have a screw and locknut at one end to allow for adjustment. Most OHC designs have the camshaft operating the valves directly — simply with a bucket-shaped buffer fitted over the valve. Adjustment here is provided by removable *shims* — discs of steel rather like circular feeler gauges — fitted above or below the bucket.

On most cars the rocker cover sits on the top part of the engine and is one of the first things you see when looking under the bonnet. Engines which do not follow the in-line four or six cylinder configuration — such as the Citroën or Volkswagen flat four or the Ford V4 — are fitted with two rocker covers, one either side of the engine. In the case of the Volkswagen you can only see the rocker covers by looking underneath the car.

With many in-line engines access to the rocker cover is restricted by the air cleaner so this may have to be removed first (see page 81). Begin by undoing the nuts, bolts or screws which secure the air cleaner cover and then lift away the cover together with the filter element. To remove the filter housing, undo any nuts which attach the housing to the carburettor (**fig 1**) and take off any support brackets, pipes or hoses which are fastened to the filter housing. Finally, lift the housing away.

Some cars have vacuum or water pipes attached to the rocker cover so remove any nuts or bolts which hold these in place — often they secure the rocker cover as well. Push the pipe or pipes to one side making a note of how they should be refitted later. You may also find that part of the accelerator linkage is attached to the rocker cover. If necessary, undo the nuts holding the linkage and operating cable and lift these components to one side. Try to disturb as few pipes and linkages as possible — you may be able to leave flexible connections in place and wriggle the rocker cover off.

To remove the cover itself, simply undo the bolts, nuts or screws holding it in place. These are either fitted right on top of the cover or around the flange (**fig 2**) Finally, lift the cover away with its gasket. If the cover sticks to the engine and

1. Removing the bolts from the air cleaner housing

you are sure that you have removed everything which holds it in place, it is likely that it is held by gasket cement — a light tap with the handle of a hammer should help free it.

In the case of flat four engines there is usually nothing to restrict access to the rocker covers, although to get at the rocker covers on a VW Beetle you need to take off the rear wheels so you will have to support the car on axle stands. You may lose a small quantity of oil when removing the covers so try to work from one side and place a container underneath the engine to collect the oil. Then simply undo the nuts or, in the case of VW Beetles, release the spring clips, which hold the covers in place and lift them away.

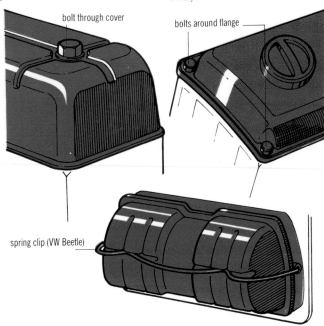
2. Alternative methods of fastening rocker/cam covers

bolt through cover

bolts around flange

spring clip (VW Beetle)

With the rocker cover removed you will now be able to see the valves and rockers. The valve must be in a fully closed position before that valve's clearance can be checked. This involves turning the engine over by hand (see Fact File — Turning the engine over by hand, page 203) until the valve you want to check is in the right position. Consult your manual for the order in which the valves should be checked. You may, for instance, find that the number one valve — usually the one closest to the front of the engine — should be adjusted when the number eight valve — usually the rearmost one — is pushed right down to its fullest open position. In this case you should rotate the engine until you see the rearmost valve move downwards so that its spring becomes compressed. Make sure that you have turned the engine over far enough to make the valve open as far as it will go. It is a good idea to turn the engine over several times before starting work just to get the feel of how the valves operate and how far down they go before starting to come back up (**figs 1 & 2**).

On conventional in-line engines which have the inlet and exhaust manifolds on the same side of the cylinder head there is a way of telling what the valve adjustment order is without consulting the manual every time. On four cylinder engines this is called the 'rule of nine' while for six cylinder engines it is called the 'rule of 13'. Both rules operate in the same way. To use the rule of nine on a four cylinder engine, you simply subtract the number of the valve you wish to adjust from nine to get the number of the valve which should be open when you measure the clearance. If, for instance you want to check the number three valve (**fig 3**) subtract three from nine and you will find that the number six

1. The valve (centre) in its fully open position

2. The same valve, now fully closed

valve must be open. The rule cannot, however be used for any other type of engine. Crossflow engines — where the inlet and exhaust manifolds are on opposite sides of the cylinder head — V engines and flat engines all differ so for these designs it is essential that you consult your manual to find out the correct order.

Your manual may specify that the clearances should be adjusted with the valves of one cylinder 'on the rock' (**fig 4**). This means that one valve has just closed and the other is just starting to open. With the engine in this position, you check the rockers on the opposite cylinder in the engine's firing order. Your manual will give full details about how this should be done.

On other engines — such as the Chrysler Avenger — the valves should be adjusted when the relevant piston is at TDC — which you check using the car's timing marks (see page 85). With the number one piston at TDC on its compression stroke, both the valve clearances for that cylinder can be checked and, if necessary, adjusted. You then turn the engine over by 180° and adjust the valve clearances on the next cylinder in the firing order, repeating this until all the rockers have been checked and set to their correct clearances.

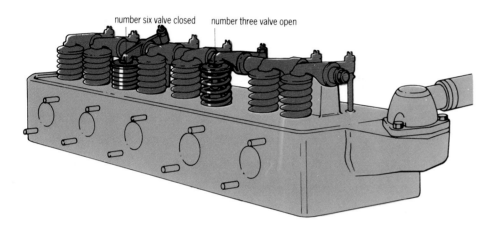
number six valve closed · number three valve open

3. The rule of nine: no. 6 valve is fully open when no. 3 valve (9—3=6) is fully closed

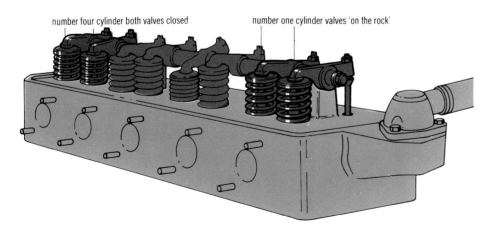
number four cylinder both valves closed · number one cylinder valves 'on the rock'

4. When both no. 1 cylinder valves are on the rock, set both no. 4 cylinder valves

Having turned the engine to the right position you are ready to measure the clearance of the first valve. With some engines the clearance is the same for the inlet valves and exhaust valves, but more often there is a separate measurement for each. Usually it is easy to tell whether a valve is an inlet or exhaust valve simply by looking to see whether it is closer to the inlet manifold flange or the exhaust manifold. But you can consult your manual if you are in any doubt.

Select a feeler gauge which corresponds to the clearance specified for the valve you are about to adjust and insert the blade of the gauge between the rocker arm and the valve stem (**fig 1**) — or in the case of some OHC engines fitted with rocker arms, between the rocker pad and the cam lobe. The gauge should be a tight but smooth sliding fit (see photo) but if you find that it is difficult or impossible to squeeze the blade into the gap, or if you find that it is a very loose fit, you will have to adjust the clearance.

1. Checking the clearance with a feeler gauge

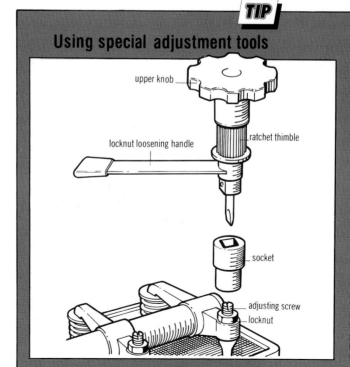

TIP

Using special adjustment tools

upper knob

locknut loosening handle

ratchet thimble

socket

adjusting screw

locknut

To make the job of adjusting the valve clearances even easier a variety of special tools are available — but these only work on conventional OHV engines using an adjuster screw and locknut system on the rockers. One such tool is the SPQR which is widely available from car accessory shops. The tool is supplied with special instructions as well as the data needed for different engines, but you will require a socket to fit the rocker adjuster locknut. These tools all work in basically the same way. With the engine correctly set up you position the socket over the locknut and adjuster of the valve to be adjusted and loosen the locknut by turning the handle. You then turn the upper knob on the tool to screw the adjuster inwards until all the clearance has been taken up. The actual adjustment is made by turning the ratchet thimble back the number of increments, or clicks, the instructions specify for your particular engine. Finally, you hold the thimble steady and tighten the locknut.

The most common way of making the adjustment involves loosening a locknut with a spanner and turning an adjuster screw until the clearance is correct.

Some manufacturers use different ways of making the adjustments, but in almost every case the valve mechanism includes a means of varying the clearance at the end of the valve stem. The only exceptions are a few cars which have self-adjusting tappets. Your handbook will tell you if your car has this feature, in which case you need not make any adjustment.

If your car is fitted with this type of rocker mechanism, begin by loosening the locknut with a ring spanner and then with the spanner still in place, turn the adjuster screw with a screwdriver until the feeler gauge is a tight sliding fit between the rocker arm and the valve stem (**fig 1**). Do not press downwards on the screwdriver as this will give a false measurement. Once the adjustment seems satisfactory, keep holding the screwdriver on the adjuster screw while you tighten the locknut (**fig 2**). Check the gap again to make sure that you did not move the adjuster while tightening the locknut with the spanner.

Once you are satisfied that the gap is set correctly it is a good idea to make a chalk mark on the rocker — it is quite easy to forget which rockers have been checked. Repeat this procedure for all the other valves making sure that each one is adjusted in the correct sequence.

Once you have checked all the valves, turn the engine over a few times and then quickly recheck the clearances — mistakes are easily made, especially where inlet and exhaust valves have different clearances and a quick check now could save a lot of time.

1. *Turning the adjuster screw to alter the clearance*

2. *Tightening the locknut when the adjustment is correct*

Although the locknut and screw method of adjustment applies to the majority of cars with OHV engines, there are some engines which differ. One of these variations is found in cars such as some Vauxhall Cavaliers and some Ford engines where the adjustment is made by simply turning a self-locking nut using a socket spanner (below left **fig 1**).

Another system, found on OHC Ford and Datsun engines, requires the clearance to be checked with the lobe of the cam facing away from the rocker and the adjustment is made by using one spanner to loosen the locknut and a second spanner to rotate the hexagonal adjuster (below, **fig 2**).

A more unusual method of adjusting the valve clearances is found on a range of Vauxhall OHC engines. Here the adjuster takes the form of a tapered screw in the tappet on the top of the valve stem (below, **fig 3**). The tappet has a slot in the side and can be turned round so that you can see the end of the screw. Then you use a hexagonal key to turn the tapered screw until the clearance is correct.

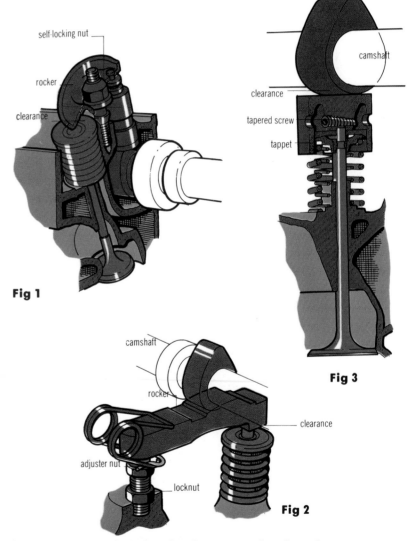

Fig 1

Fig 3

Fig 2

1. *Some alternative ways in which the valve clearance can be adjusted*

Once you are satisfied that each valve clearance is correct, you can refit the rocker cover and any other components you had to remove to gain access to the rockers.

It is always a good idea to fit a new rocker cover gasket to be sure of an oil-tight seal. To fit a new gasket, first use a blunt knife to scrape away all traces of the old gasket from the inner flange of the cover (**fig 1**) and the corresponding surface on the cylinder head. Avoid allowing any old pieces of gasket to fall down through the cylinder head into the oilways. Check that you have the correct replacement gasket and then apply a thin coat of gasket cement to the flange of the rocker cover and press the gasket into place in the flange (**fig 2**). If there are bolt holes around the rocker cover flange, make sure that the corresponding holes in the gasket are properly aligned. If you do not have any gasket cement a little grease will help hold the gasket in place while you refit the cover and align the bolts.

Place the rocker cover in position on the engine. Look all round the rim of the rocker cover to make sure that the gasket has not slipped and that nothing has got trapped.

Finally tighten down the rocker cover not forgetting to refit any other components which share the same bolts as the cover or attach to it. If the cover is secured by several flange bolts or screws, tighten them a little at a time and work from front to back alternately so that the cover seals evenly.

When you start the engine, check that there is no oil escaping around the rocker cover. Also, once the engine is warm make sure that the valves are not rattling excessively, as this would indicate that you made a mistake on one or more of the adjustments and will have to go back and do the job again.

1. Scraping the old gasket from the rocker cover

2. Pressing the new gasket into place

Adjusting valve clearances (OHC)

You should check the clearances on an OHC engine regularly, even if you do not carry out the actual adjustment yourself

One of the advantages of overhead camshaft engines is that they have fewer moving parts in their valve gear and so they often need less maintenance than overhead valve engines. However, the valve clearances of OHC engines still have to be checked at the manufacturer's recommended intervals and, if necessary, adjusted.

On some OHC engines the shims are fitted on the inside of the tappet bucket which means that you have to take off the camshaft. Seek expert advice before starting to do this. However, if you do not want to make the adjustment yourself, you can still check the clearances as described here. If you find the clearances need adjusting you can then have the rest of the job done at your local garage. Other types of OHC engines have shims fitted to the outside of the tappet bucket, so you can fit replacement shims without taking off the camshaft.

Whatever the system, all OHC designs are adjusted on the same basic principles.

When to do this job
As recommended by the manufacturer or when engine sounds 'tappety'

What this job involves
Removing the cam cover
Measuring the valve clearances
Removing the old shims
Measuring the shims
Fitting the new shims

Related jobs in this handbook
Adjusting valve clearances OHV
Please see Index for page numbers

To do this job
Tools: Feeler gauges; spanners; special tools (maybe); needle-nosed pliers; micrometer (maybe)
Materials: New shims; cam cover gasket(s)
Time: Up to two hours
Degree of difficulty: Removing shims can be fiddly

If you have the job professionally done...
Does engine run smoothly without 'tappety' sounds?

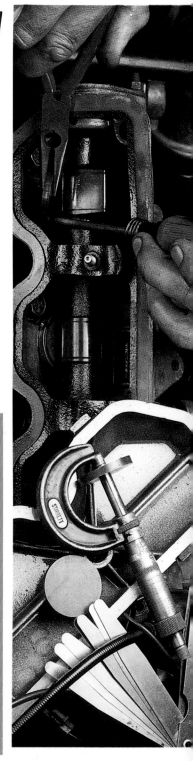

1. An old shim, shiny with wear (above) and two new ones

Before you begin work you will need to look at your manual to find out what tools are needed to remove the shims from your particular engine. Often a special tool is needed to compress the tappet bucket as well as another tool to remove the shim from the recess in which it sits.

These are available from your dealer and make the job easier to do with less risk of damaging anything. However, in most cases you can improvise by using an old screwdriver with its blade end bent over at 90 degrees. Special tools are also available for taking the shims out but you can usually manage with a thin screwdriver and a pair of needle-nosed pliers.

A selection of shims is also needed. These are available in a range of thicknesses and are available from your dealer. Do not buy any shims until you have worked out the size you need. Make sure also that you buy shims which are made specifically for your car and never try to grind down a shim to make it thinner. Also buy a new cam cover gasket as the old one will probably be damaged or unsuitable for reuse.

If you intend to continue servicing the same car it will be worthwhile buying a micrometer. However, you may be able to hire one or buy one more cheaply secondhand. Before buying, be sure to check whether your clearances are given in metric or imperial figures and choose a corresponding micrometer. This precision measuring instrument makes the job of setting the valve clearances much more straightforward. You can manage without one but only by using a trial and error process.

HOW IT WORKS

There are two types of overhead cam valve gear — the type employing rockers, where the valve clearances are adjusted in the same way as overhead valve engines (see page 89) — and the type using shims, as described in this article.

These steel shims fit between the camshaft lobe and the valve stem and the clearance is adjusted by fitting either a thicker or thinner shim, depending on whether the clearance needs to be reduced or increased.

The clearance is worked out by comparing the existing clearance with that recommended by the manufacturer and involves accurate measurements of shim thicknesses.

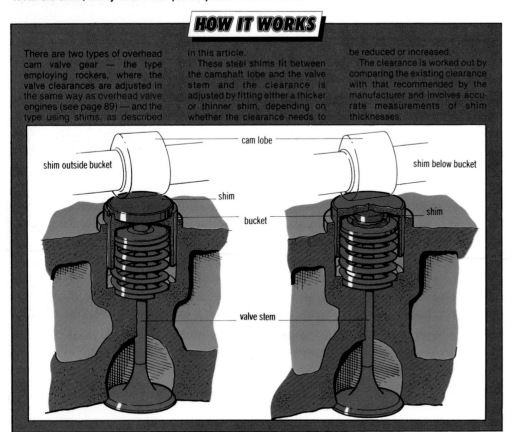

2. A micrometer and two types of angled screwdriver for compressing the valve bucket

STEP 2   REMOVE THE CAM COVER

The procedure for removing the cam cover is very similar to the job of removing the rocker cover of an OHV engine (see page 90). After removing the air cleaner assembly and any hoses or cables in the way, undo the screws or bolts holding the cam cover in place and lift away the cover. Do not be tempted to prise the cover away with a screwdriver if it sticks to the camshaft housing. Simply tap the cover with a hammer handle or something similar to free it.

1. Removing the cam cover

The exhaust and inlet valves are usually set to different clearances so you should check the specifications in your handbook or manual. This may also show that the clearances are correct if they fall within certain limits, such as between 0.006 to 0.010 in., or must conform to a certain single figure measurement such as 0.006 in.

In the case of twin cam models, the exhaust cams are the ones closer to the exhaust manifold. In other cases, such as the Audi 80 and VW Golf 1500, the valves are arranged in the sequence exhaust—inlet starting at the timing cover end of the engine.

Begin by turning the engine over by hand (see Fact File, page 203), until the camshaft lobe is pointing directly away from the tappet of the first valve you want to work on. This will make sure that the valve is fully closed. You will find that more than one valve will be closed at the same time, so you can work on these valves without turning the engine further.

Insert a feeler gauge which corresponds to the recommended clearance or to about the midway figure for your engine's clearance limits — for instance, 0.008 in. if the range specified is between 0.006 and 0.010 in.

If you find that the clearance is within the limits or is dead on, no adjustment needs to be made and you go on to the next valve, but it is a good idea to write down all the clearances as you go along.

If the valve clearance is outside the figure specified and you want to make the adjustment yourself, try other feeler gauges until you find the one which shows the actual clearance. Make a note of this figure and then move on to check all the other valves in the same way, turning the engine over so that you can check the valves of each cylinder in turn. If you are not going to adjust the clearances yourself you should take the car to a garage with your list of what needs doing.

When you have finished measuring, you should have a list of all the valve clearances — it is a good idea to mark the ones which are not correct as these are the ones which concern you now.

1. Camshaft lobes in the position where both valves are closed

2. Measuring the valve clearance with a feeler gauge

1. How to press down the tappet bucket

2. Prise out the old shim with a screwdriver

Before you can work out what size of shim you need to make up the correct clearance you will need to remove the shim which is already in place in the top of the bucket. The procedure for removing the shim varies from car to car but the general approach is to use a special tool to compress the tappet bucket enough to allow the shim to be extracted from its recess.

Make sure that the cams are in the right position, pointing away from the valves, and use the special tool or screwdriver to compress the tappet (**fig 1**). You should try to press down the edge of the tappet so that you can take out the shim from the middle of the tappet.

When the tool is in position, holding down the tappet, you can let go of it and then use a screwdriver to prise the shim out of its recess (**fig 2**). Some tappets have narrow slots in their sides so that you can get a thin screwdriver under the shim to help it out. When the shim starts to come out, catch hold of it with a pair of needle-nosed pliers and lift it out completely.

3. Removing the shim with the camshaft still in place

If the shim appears firmly lodged in place, be careful not to snap the end off the tool you are using to prise it out.

If you are not going to use a micrometer to make measurements, make a note of which shim has come from which valve as you may be able to use some of the old shims again to set some of the clearances correctly.

STEP 5 — MEASURE THE OLD SHIM

Once you have taken out the old shim, you can measure its thickness and, by comparing this measurement with the clearance that you measured earlier, work out the size of the new shim that you need.

Although shims are marked with their thicknesses, these marks often wear off and the shim itself also wears down from its original thickness. As you cannot rely on any marks on the shim, you have to use a micrometer to measure the thickness. If you have not got a micrometer, see Alternative Step 5 for another method of working out the size of shim you need.

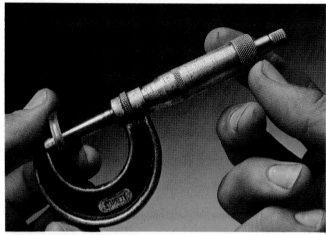
1. Measuring shim thickness with a micrometer

FACT FILE

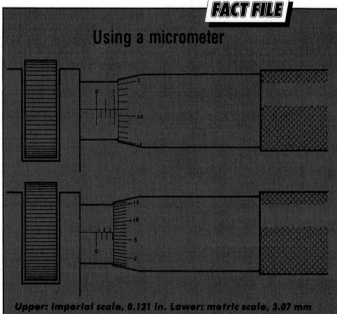

Using a micrometer

First, check that the micrometer is adjusted properly so that when the spindle and the anvil are just making contact, the '0' mark on the datum line coincides exactly with the '0' mark on the thimble. Always use the ratchet to do this to avoid putting too much pressure on the thimble. If the two '0' marks do not line up, consult the tool's instruction manual to find out how to make the adjustment.

Once you have checked that the micrometer is adjusted correctly, clean the shim with a dry cloth and place it between the spindle and the anvil, turning the thimble slowly until the ratchet starts to click. Now you can read off the figure on the sleeve. Add this to the figure on the datum line to find out the shim's thickness. The measurement may be shown in metric or imperial figures depending on which type you have.

Upper: imperial scale, 0.121 in. Lower: metric scale, 3.07 mm

ALTERNATIVE 5 — USE SUBSTITUTE SHIM

If you have not got a micrometer to measure the old shim you can use the following method which involves trial and error and may involve buying new shims only to find that they need to be changed.

First take out the old shim. Then you must put in its place a new shim which is the original thickness as recommended by the car maker. Measure the valve clearance again following Step 3. If you are lucky the new measurement will be exact or will fall within your clearance limits. If not you must buy another new shim or fit one that you have measured to bring the clearance to the correct figure (see Step 6).

STEP 6 — CALCULATE SIZE OF SHIM NEEDED

If you have used a micrometer, the calculation shown will give you the size of the shim you need. If you have not used a micrometer, base your calculation on the size of the substitute shim used in Alternative Step 5 and the clearances you found then.

First, add the thickness of the old or substitute shim to the valve clearance you measured with the feeler gauge. From this total, take away the specified clearance to give the size of shim you need. Use the midway figure if a tolerance range is specified.

Whether or not you have used a micrometer, you can easily work out the correct size for the new shim.

Take the thickness of the old shim, say	3.80 mm (0.15 in)
Add the clearance measured	+ 0.53 mm (0.02 in)
Total	= 4.33 mm (0.17 in)
Take away specified clearance	− 0.43 mm (0.017 in)
Shim required	= 3.90 mm (0.153 in)

ALTERNATIVE 6 — CALCULATE SIZE OF OLD SHIM

If you have not used a micrometer, you will now have three figures: the original valve clearance when the old shim was in place, the size of the new shim and the clearance with the new shim in place. By comparing the two clearances, you can work out the thickness of the old shim.

If, for instance, the two clearances are the same, then the shims must also be the same thickness. If the clearance with the new shim in place was 0.005 in. greater than the clearance with the old shim in place, then the old shim must be 0.005 in. thicker than the new one.

In this way you can work out the thickness of the old shims. Make a note of these figures in case any of the shims are the right size to use on any of the valves.

Mark the thickness on each shim with a felt pen so that you do not confuse them.

STEP 7 — FIT THE NEW SHIM

1. Inserting a new shim

2. Check the new shim is fitted properly

Make sure that the recess in the top of the tappet and the surfaces of the shim are clean. Coat the new shim in clean engine oil and take care to position it squarely in its recess, with the numbered side of the shim facing downwards. Use the feeler gauge to check that the clearance is now correct.

When you are satisfied that all the valve clearances are correctly set, fit a new cam cover gasket and refit the cam cover to the engine. Tighten each of the fixing bolts or screws a little at a time until they are all tight. Start the engine and look at the cam cover to make sure than no oil is leaking out around the edges.

OHC drive belt service

Overhead camshaft drive belts are generally reliable and long lived. But to get the best out of them without risking engine damage they should be inspected periodically

Overhead camshaft drive belts are very hard-wearing and hardly stretch at all in service. However, manufacturers do recommend that the belt should be checked at regular intervals and adjusted if necessary. If the drive belt has reached the end of its useful life or is badly damaged it should be renewed at once, as it could slip or break causing serious and expensive engine damage.

When you are inspecting the belt you should look for signs of wear or damage. Belts are not expensive and should be renewed if they are wearing out or can no longer be tensioned correctly. When doing the job, take care to keep the belt clean and, once you have set the engine position, do not turn any of the sprockets.

When to do this job
At intervals recommended by the manufacturer — usually about every 40,000 miles or 60,000 km — or if a whining noise comes from front of engine

What this job involves
Lining up timing marks
Removing drive belt cover
Setting tension of drive belt
Fitting new drive belt

Related jobs in this handbook
Adjusting valve clearances (OHC)
Tensioning generator belts
Please see Index for page numbers

To do this job
Tools: Spanners; screwdrivers; spring balance (maybe); splined tool (maybe)
Materials: New belt (maybe)
Time: Up to two hours
Degree of difficulty: Requires care and cleanliness

If you have the job professionally done . . .
Does engine run quietly? Is generator drive belt correctly tensioned?

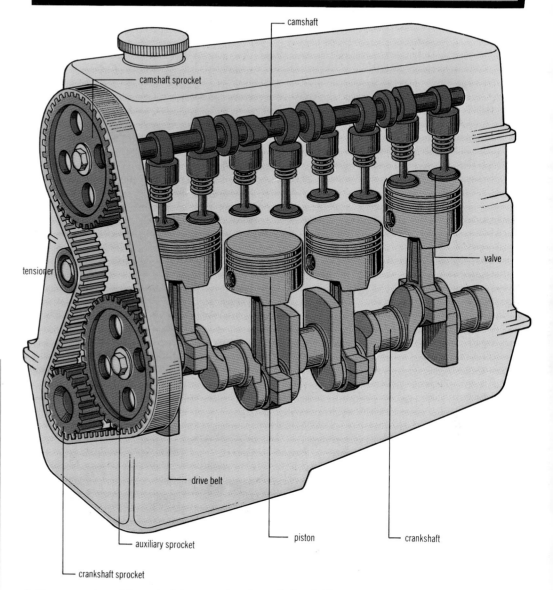

1. How an engine with a belt-driven overhead camshaft is laid out

Most modern OHC engines use a flexible toothed belt to drive the camshaft. The first types of OHC drive belt were made of rubber braced with steel cords but nowadays glassfibre is more commonly used as a bracing material.

The camshaft goes around at half the speed of the crankshaft. For this reason, the cogged sprocket wheel on the crankshaft is smaller in diameter than the one on the camshaft.

The camshaft drive belt needs to be kept taut or else it will be noisy and might fall out of engagement with its drive wheels. To keep the belt taut and to make it easier to change the belt, there is a belt tensioner. Often, the tensioner is spring-loaded so that it pushes against the smooth side of the belt and stops the belt from getting slack and possibly slipping which could damage the engine.

STEP 1 — LINE UP TIMING MARKS

Before removing and replacing the timing belt it is very important that the engine should be turned to the correct position. The crankshaft and camshaft must always be lined up in the right way or else the engine will not run and a lot of damage may be caused. The manufacturer of the car provides marks on the crankshaft pulley for lining up the crankshaft (**fig 1**) and marks on the camshaft sprocket for lining up the camshaft.

Your manual will show you where these marks are and how they should look when the engine is in the correct position. You can now line up the crank-

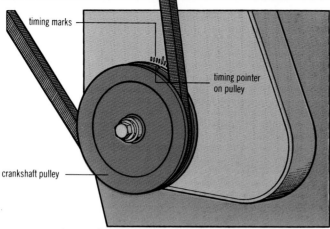

1. **Line up the notch on the pulley with the static timing marks**

timing marks
timing pointer on pulley
crankshaft pulley

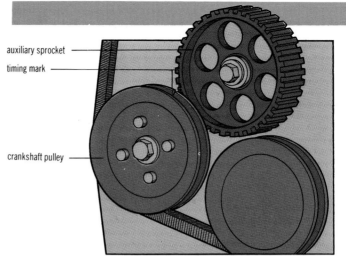

auxiliary sprocket
timing mark
crankshaft pulley

2. **On some cars the pulley notch has to be aligned with sprocket**

shaft but you will not see the camshaft marks until you have removed the drive belt cover. Before doing this it is a good idea to disconnect the battery not only for electrical safety but also to make sure that the starter is not accidentally operated.

You now have to turn the engine over by hand (see Fact File, page 203) to line up the timing marks on the crankshaft pulley. When the marks are exactly aligned put the car in first gear and pull the handbrake on hard. This should prevent the engine from turning at all while you are doing the job — if it does, you must line up the marks again.

STEP 2 — REMOVE BELT COVER

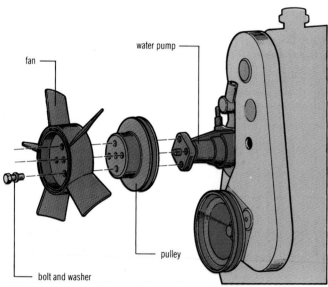

fan
water pump
pulley
bolt and washer

1. **The fan is bolted through the pulley to the water pump**

2. **Pulling hose off radiator**

On in-line engines the camshaft drive belt cover is mounted on the front of the engine. If your car has a transverse engine, you will see the belt cover on one end of the engine. Check to see that you can find the bolts which hold the cover in place. Your manual will tell you whether you need to take off any other components before

you can get the belt cover off, but you will almost certainly need to take off the belt which drives the alternator. See Fact File — Generator drive belt adjustment, page 217. Slip the belt off the alternator pulley and then off the crankshaft pulley.

Another component which may well need to come off is the fan. The fan is usually bolted to

its pulley (**fig 1**). Loosen each bolt in turn, moving the fan round so that you can reach the next bolt in the sequence. When you have taken out all the bolts, lift the fan away. If the fan pulley needs to come off to make way for the camshaft drive belt, it should now be easy to pull it away from the engine.

Some cars, notably Honda

models, have an engine compartment layout which makes it necessary to move an engine mounting in order to get the camshaft drive belt off. Properly support the engine before removing the mounting.

You may need to take off the crankshaft pulley so that the belt will slide off the toothed sprocket which is behind the crankshaft pulley. Crankshaft pulley removal may require hiring special tools.

The only other part which may stand in your way before you can take off the drive belt cover is the top hose of the cooling system (**fig 2**). On some cars this hose needs to be moved out of the way before the belt cover can be removed. You should not need to drain the whole cooling system, but the job will be less messy if you drain a few pints of coolant into a bowl so that the level in the system falls below the level of the top hose. See

your manual for details of how to find the drain plug and how to remove radiator hoses.

You should now be able to take off the camshaft drive belt cover. Undo the bolts which hold the cover to the engine (**fig 3**). You may have to jar it free using a mallet (**fig 4**), but if the cover will not move easily, check that you have not missed one of the securing bolts. The cover should now slide away from the engine (**fig 5**).

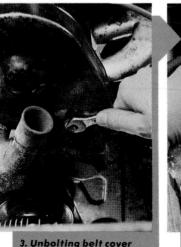

3. **Unbolting belt cover**

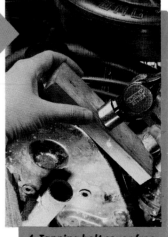

4. **Tapping belt cover free**

5. **Removing belt cover**

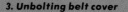

Check first that the camshaft timing marks are correctly lined up (**fig 1**). If you find that they are out of line, check to see whether the engine has been turned. If this is the case, turn the engine by hand until they are again lined up.

Now look at the condition of the drive belt. It should not be oily or greasy. If you find that the belt is oily, find out where the oil is coming from and fix the leak before you fit a new drive belt. If leakage is heavy, take professional advice.

See whether the teeth of the belt have started to wear. Normally, drive belts are very long-lasting, but if the belt has been tensioned too tightly, it may now be wearing out. The teeth on the belt should be smooth and have sharply defined shoulders. If you are in any doubt about how long the belt has been in use or whether it is still fit for service, now is the time to fit a new one.

If the belt is in good condition, check the tension of the belt. Some cars have automatic tensioners which do not need to be

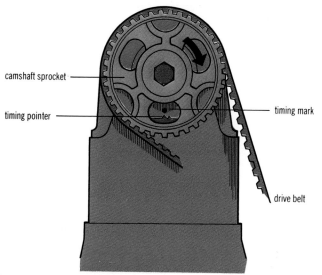
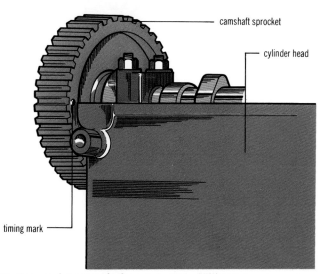

1. Timing mark on camshaft sprocket lines up with head or points to a mark cast into the cylinder head

adjusted, but you should still check that the tensioner is doing its job. Your car's manual will tell you the correct tension for your belt and how you should measure it.

Some tensioners set themselves automatically when you loosen the bolts which hold

them in position. First loosen the locking bolt with a socket or spanner and then loosen the pivot bolt. You may need to buy or borrow a special splined tool to loosen the pivot bolt (**fig 2**). This allows the spring in the tensioner to adjust the tensioner assembly to the right setting. The tension of the belt may need to even itself out before you tighten the tensioner bolt again. If this is the case, your manual will tell you to turn the engine over — either turn the nut on the crankshaft pulley or else put the car into top gear and push it forwards. If you had to take off the crankshaft pulley to make room for the drive belt cover, bolt the pulley back on so that you can use it to turn the engine. You should not try to drag the engine round by pulling on the camshaft drive belt as this may well damage the belt.

Another method of setting the tension involves slackening off the tensioner bolts and then turning the engine anticlockwise by a quarter of a turn. Again, do not use the starter to turn the engine as it will operate much too quickly.

Some engines have their belts

adjusted according to how far the belt can be moved from side to side in much the same way as you would adjust the fan belt. This movement may either be measured when you push the belt with your finger or when you pull the belt using a spring balance to measure how hard

you are pulling.

If your manual describes the spring balance method, find a nail or bolt which will sit between the teeth of the belt. Then loop a length of string around the ends of the bolt and around the hook of the spring balance so that you are pulling

between the teeth of the belt with the length of the bolt (**fig 3**). Follow the directions in your manual about how hard you should pull and how far the belt should move.

Another way of checking belt tension is to try to twist the belt through 90 degrees. Twist the belt at a point halfway along the longest run between two sprockets. Just use firm pressure with your thum and forefinger. You should be able to turn the belt through a right angle and no further if the tension is correct (**fig 4**).

If you find that the tension needs to be adjusted, loosen the bolt which locks the tensioner in place and turn the tensioner, then tighten the bolt and make the check again.

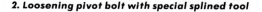

2. Loosening pivot bolt with special splined tool

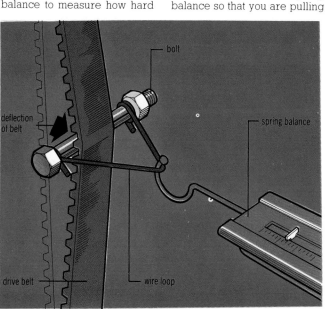

3. Using a spring balance to measure the belt tension

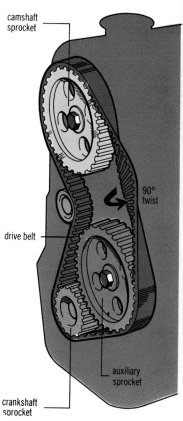

4. Twisting belt through 90°

STEP 4   REMOVE DRIVE BELT

To remove the drive belt, first slacken off the tensioner as far as possible. Loosen the tensioner adjustment bolts and lever the tensioner away until the belt is as slack as possible (**fig 1**). Then tighten the bolts to hold the tensioner off the belt.

Make sure that your hands are not oily when you take the belt off as the new belt will be damaged if oil gets on to the sprockets. Do not turn any of the sprockets as you take the belt off as this will affect the timing of the engine. Ease the belt gently forward on the camshaft sprocket until it slips off the teeth (**fig 2**). There should now be enough slack in the belt for you to slip it over the crankshaft pulley and lift it away. Turn the belt so that its edge will slip past the pulley. If there is not enough space for the belt, you will have to take off the crankshaft pulley.

If you accidentally turn the crankshaft sprocket or camshaft by more than a degree or two when the timing belt is off, you may do a lot of damage to the engine. Setting the sprockets correctly when they are out of line needs expert assistance.

1. Levering the tensioner away from the drive belt

2. Pulling the belt off the camshaft sprocket

3. Removing crankshaft pulley - note keyway

STEP 5   FIT NEW BELT

Before you fit a new belt, check once again that both the crankshaft pulley and camshaft sprocket are aligned with their timing marks. If either of them has gone slightly out of line, turn them carefully back to the right position.

Now slip the belt over the crankshaft sprocket. Try not to twist the belt unless you have to and do not let the belt get kinked as this may damage the reinforcing strands in the belt. Feed the belt around the other sprockets and tensioners, working from the bottom of the engine towards the top. Then fit the belt on to the camshaft sprocket. Make sure that the teeth of

the belt are midway on the teeth of the sprockets.

When you are sure that the belt is correctly in place, set the tension as described in Step 3.

Now refit the drive belt cover and any other components, such as the generator drive belt. If you have to refill the cooling system and the coolant is more than two years old, use new antifreeze.

When you start the engine with the new belt in place, listen for any unusual whining noises from the front of the engine. Such noises might indicate that the tension of the belt is wrong and you would need to readjust it before anything wears out.

1. Fitting new belt around the crankshaft sprocket first

2. Slipping the new belt over the camshaft sprocket

When the brakes feel spongy

Brakes which are spongy mean the car is not as safe as it should be. Bleeding them will restore full braking power

Air in the braking system will give you a lack of braking efficiency and a spongy, dead-feeling brake pedal. If the situation is really bad then you might find yourself having to pump the brake pedal to stop at all — obviously a very dangerous situation.

There are many ways that air can get into the braking system. You may, for example, have been careless when renewing brake pads, or there may be a leak in the system. For this reason you should make a periodic check for leaks throughout the system and, if necessary, bleed the brakes to remove all air from the hydraulic system. If the system is faulty, though, there is no point bleeding it until the cause of the problem has been found so you must check all brake parts for signs of fluid leakage.

When to do this job
If the brake pedal feels spongy and the brakes do not feel very efficient
If the pedal travel before the brake operates is unusually long

What this job involves
Finding the nipples and the fluid reservoir
Bleeding the brakes

Related jobs in this handbook
Replacing disc brake pads
Replacing drum brake shoes
Please see Index for page numbers

To do this job
Tools: Jar; flexible tube; spanner for bleed nipples, one man bleeding kit (maybe)
Materials: New brake fluid
Time: About an hour
Degree of difficulty: Really needs two people. Can be time consuming if the air in the system is hard to find

If you have the job professionally done...
Does the brake pedal feel firm? Can you find any fluid leaks? Does the car stop any better? Does it pull up without veering to one side?

STEP 1   FIND THE RESERVOIR

The fluid reservoir can be either cylindrical or flat — older types are metal with a small steel or plastic screw-top, while more modern ones are made of translucent plastic so you can see the fluid level without having to remove the cap.

The reservoir is normally attached to the master cylinder which is almost always mounted on the front bulkhead inside the engine compartment, just above the driver's feet, as the piston operated by the brake pedal is connected to it. However, some types of car may have the reservoir remotely mounted somewhere else in the engine compartment and attached to the master cylinder by a piece of flexible or metal pipe.

Cars with hydraulic clutches will have two master cylinders, one for the clutch and one for the brake, normally each with its own reservoir. Older cars might only have one reservoir, shared between the two.

If the car has two or more reservoirs, one may be for the power steering (if fitted) and one for the clutch. To find out which is which, you could begin bleeding the brakes (Step 4) and then see in which reservoir the fluid level drops. However, if you want to make absolutely sure which is which before you start the job, the only way is to follow the pipes down from the reservoirs and see where they go.

Pipes from clutch reservoirs will end up at the gearbox, while power steering ones will finish at the steering rack.

It is just possible that, having identified all the other systems, you find you still have two reservoirs left over — do not worry as this may be part of a dual circuit braking system.

However, whatever type or however many reservoirs you have, the same rules apply. That is, you should keep an eye on the fluid level during bleeding and top it up.

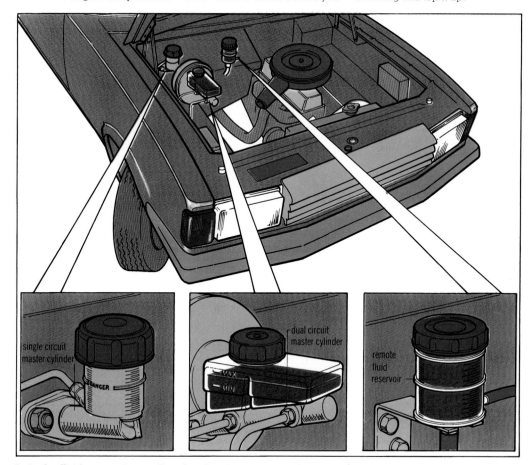

1. Brake fluid reservoirs are fitted under the bonnet — these are the most common types

Most cars now have the plastic type of reservoir so you can check the fluid level easily. There should be 'max' and 'min' markings on the side of the reservoir, or simply a line marked 'danger' below which you must not let the fluid drop. If the reservoir has no markings or is of the metal type then the correct fluid level will be half an inch or so (10-15mm) from the top of the reservoir. With the metal ones you have to take off the cap to check the level; you might find that you need a torch as very little light gets into the reservoir, making it difficult to check the level accurately.

Clean the reservoir cap with a rag before you remove it to top up the fluid — even the tiniest speck of dirt in the hydraulic

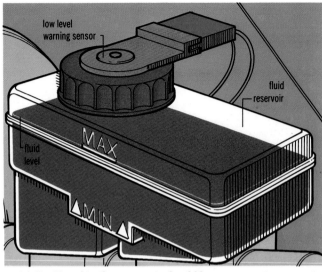

1. The fluid level in the reservoir should be up to maximum mark

system can damage the various rubber seals and cause leaks. Use only proper brake fluid from a new can. The colour may vary from that already in the sytem, but this does not matter. Only a few cars — such as Citroens — do not use the now standard universal hydraulic fluid. Do not shake the tin — this will produce air bubbles in the new fluid. If you see that the fluid does contain tiny bubbles, stand it overnight in a dry place.

Brake fluid is very corrosive so take care not to spill any on the paintwork when topping up the reservoir. If you do spill any, wipe it away promptly.

Should you get any fluid in your eyes, bathe them in running water as soon as possible and see your doctor.

2. Wipe the top of the reservoir before you remove it

To allow you to remove air from the system, bleed nipples are fitted at the end of each brake line, normally at the brake unit itself, on the back of the brake backplate. When you loosen the nipple slightly it allows brake fluid to pass out of the system, through the central hole, taking any air bubbles with it.

The nipples should have small rubber dust caps fitted but these may have been lost.

The nipple is small, with a tiny nozzle at its end and a hexagon locknut fitting just behind.

Sometimes you might confuse a bleed nipple with a drum brake adjuster but, whereas the adjuster is normally mounted at the bottom of the brake unit, the nipple is almost always at the top. Bleed nipples are very easy to spot on disc brake calipers as, apart from the brake hose, they will be the only things sticking out from the calipers.

Some cars with a solid rear axle may have only one bleed nipple at one side to bleed both rear brakes at once, so do not worry if you only find one nipple at the back of the car. Check to see if your car has a brake servo. This will be a black or silver drum-shaped unit about the size of a medium saucepan normally mounted behind the master cylinder. You may, however, find the servo remotely mounted elsewhere in the engine compartment with brake pipes running to it. Larger brake servos, espec-

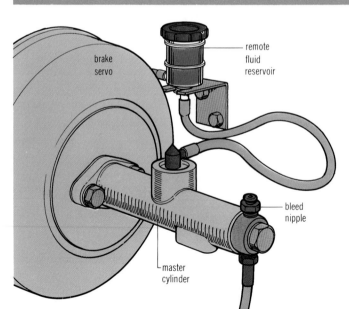

2. Some cars have a bleed nipple on the brake servo unit

ially remotely mounted ones, might have a bleed nipple fitted though this is rare — and if there is one fitted it will be easy to spot on the servo body (**fig 2**).

Once you know where all the nipples are, it is worth checking that they are all free to move. Clean the area around the nipple with a wire brush then give the area a good squirt of penetrating oil. Leave the oil to soak in for a while, then try to move each nipple using a good fitting ring spanner.

Once the nipple is free, do not open it more than a fraction or more air will get into the braking system. Now go to Step 4 for the procedure for bleeding the brakes.

TIP — Watch it

If you have to bleed the system yourself, you will find it very difficult to pump the pedal, open and close the bleed nipples, and watch the fluid level at the same time.

However, you can make the job slightly easier by propping a mirror in the engine compartment so that you can keep an eye on the fluid level from the driving seat, while you bleed the brakes.

1. Bleed nipple looks like this — do not confuse it with adjuster

1. The bleed tube in place

For convenience and speed, at least two people will be needed for best results — one to pump the brake pedal, the other to open and close the bleed nipples. A third person would come in handy to check and top up the fluid level in the reservoir, (see Tip — Watch it), otherwise one person should check the level every few pumps. You can do the job yourself if you use an 'automatic' bleed tube. But this means getting from under the car to pump the brakes and top up the cylinder. (see Alternative Step 4).

You should bleed each of the brakes in turn; if you have to bleed the servo, do this first. There are arguments as to whether you should start from the front or the back but which end you start from first does not really matter. The thing to remember is to do both brakes at one end before moving to the other two, instead of doing one side at a time. If you are in any doubt, check in your manual to see if a particular sequence is recommended.

You will probably be able to reach the bleed nipples from under the car, but if not, jack the car up and support it on ramps or axle stands one corner at a

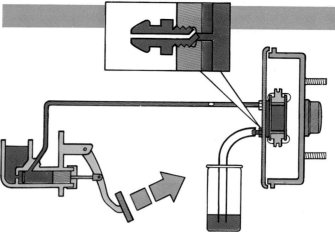

3. With the pedal up and bleed nipple shut no fluid flows

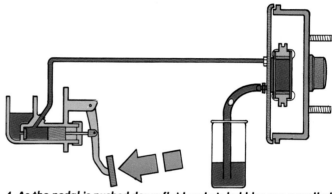

4. As the pedal is pushed down fluid and air bubbles are expelled

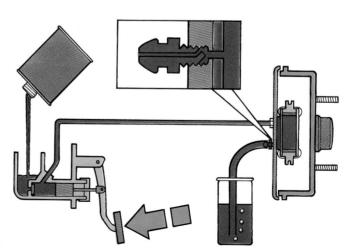

5. Air bubbles are released into jar — keep reservoir topped up

Slacken the bleed nipple about half a turn with the correct size of spanner. It is best to use a ring spanner as the flats on the nipple are quite delicate and easy to burr. If the nipple proves difficult to shift, see the tips on dismantling, page 234. Be careful not to use too much force on the nipple. It is made of relatively soft steel and can shear off unexpectedly.

With the bleed nipple slackened, shout to your helper to push the brake pedal to the floor slowly, hold it there for a couple of seconds, then release it. The first shot of fluid from the tube will be full of air which you will see bubbling through the fluid in the jar. After a couple more seconds have the pedal pressed again. Keep an eye on the fluid level in the reservoir about every half-dozen pumps and keep it fully topped up.

Repeat this until no more bubbles come out of the tube, just clean brake fluid. Finally, get your helper to push the

2. How the tube should look

time, as described on page 162.

Remove the rubber dust cap, if fitted, and slide the tube on to the nipple. The other end of the tube must be submerged in at least an inch (25 mm) of brake fluid in a clean jar. The end of the tube must not be allowed to come out of the fluid while the bleed nipple is open, otherwise air will be sucked back into the system. You can use old fluid in the jar if you have any, but you must not pour old fluid back into the reservoir.

TIP

Ups and downs

If you have problems getting the air out of the system, or if the pipes have just been renewed or replaced and you cannot get the fluid started, you can use this method each time you pump the brakes.

With the tube fitted to the nipple in the normal way, the person at the nipple slackens it off half a turn and shouts 'Down'.

Press the pedal down and hold it there until the nipple is done up and the helper shouts 'Up'. Release the pedal and repeat this process until you have bled the system. This way there is no chance that air bled from the system will be sucked back during pumping.

pedal slowly to the floor once more and tighten the nipple while the pedal is down. Do not overtighten the nipple or you may never get it undone again — it is sufficient to tighten it without force using a short spanner. Remove the tube, refit the dust cap and move on to the next brake and so on until you have bled every one.

If the brake pedal still feels very spongy after you have tightened up the last nipple then you have probably got air in the system by using the wrong technique, (see Tip — Ups and downs).

If the car has dual circuit brakes there may be more parts to bleed, depending on the system; but as long as you have bled clear fluid from each nipple the system should be free from air.

Your car may have a warning switch in the master cylinder to illuminate a dashboard light if there is a pressure drop in one part of a dual system. This switch may need to be held in a centralized position during bleeding for it to function properly. If in doubt, check your handbook for details or seek expert advice.

TIP

High rise

Sometimes despite all your efforts air remains somewhere deep in the system. If this happens, try parking the car overnight with one end higher than the other. The air will tend to rise and collect at the highest point in the system, usually near to one of the bleed nipples. All you have to do the next day is bleed the brakes at whichever end of the car is uppermost, before you move it.

There are several alternative kits for 'one man' bleeding, but they all work in a similar way, by providing a non-return valve at the bleed nipple so that fluid cannot re-enter the system once it is expelled. The valve is usually in a tube which you attach to each nipple in turn, but you can also buy nipples with built-in valves which you fit in place of the normal ones supplied on the car by the manufacturers.

The advantage of these kits is that you can pump the brake pedal yourself, release it, then go round to see whether there was any air expelled which is still in the tube. You do not need a helper, but the job is still time consuming and is easier with two people.

If you are using non-return nipples, you will still need a plastic tube, and with either kit you will need a jar, though it does not need to contain fluid when you begin.

With either system, connect the tube to a nipple, and slacken the nipple by half a turn, ideally using a ring spanner. Pump the brake pedal as described in Step 4, keeping an eye on the fluid level in the reservoir as you do so. When air bubbles no longer emerge with the fluid expelled you can tighten up the bleed nipple, being careful not to overtighten it.

Do not be misled by tiny bubbles coming from the joint between the nipple and the tube. If you have a helper it is easy to distinguish between these and air genuinely being bled from the system.

This difficulty is overcome by the third type of system, in which the job of pumping the fluid through the brake pipes and keeping the reservoir topped up is done automatically. This system uses a second reservoir of brake fluid which is pressurized by air from a car tyre. This pressure forces fluid from the second reservoir into the main reservoir through a

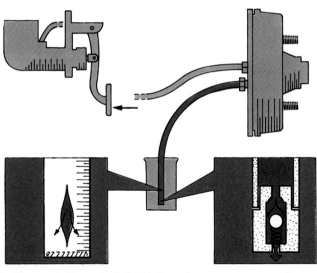

1. When pedal is pushed fluid is forced past non-return valve

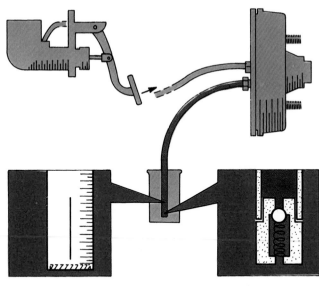

2. As pedal is released non-return valve closes automatically

tightly fitting screw cap, and keeps the whole system under pressure. A tube with non-return valve is supplied, as in the simpler kit, but you will still need a jar to catch the old fluid.

To use the kit, you must first let your spare tyre down to a pressure of 10 psi, measured with a tyre gauge. Then connect the second reservoir, which should be full of brake fluid, to the main reservoir, using one of the various caps supplied. Connect the partially deflated tyre to the second reservoir — the appropriate connector is supplied. The system is now under

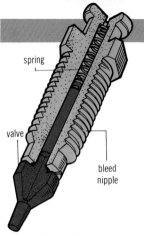

3. Non-return bleed nipple

spring
valve
bleed nipple

4. Pressurized automatic bleeding kit set up

pressure, and any leaks at the connectors should be attended to if necessary.

Now go round to each wheel in turn, connect the non-return tube and slacken off the nipple as usual. The pressure will force fluid through the tube and into the jar, and you can watch for bubbles as this happens. Go round each nipple in turn repeating the procedure. There is no need to touch the brake pedal at all.

This method has its advantages, and some manufacturers recommend the pressure method for their cars. But unless the connections are good you may be plagued with bursts which let air in at the main reservoir. The only way to avoid this is to deflate your spare tyre further, reducing the operating pressure.

This method of bleeding also leaves you without an effective spare tyre until you pump it up

again and is the most expensive of all the automatic bleeding kits on the market.

5. Non-return bleeder (left) and pressurized bleeding kit (right)

STEP 5 | CHECK THE RESULTS

When you have completely bled the system press the brake pedal. It should feel firm and solid with no sponginess, even when you leave it for a while. There may be a little free play in the mechanical linkage, but after this the pedal should not move noticeably, no matter how hard you press.

If you have to pump up the brake pedal to make the brakes work better then this clearly

confirms that there is still air in the system and it will have to be bled again. If the pedal feels firm but goes spongy again a few days later there must actually be a leak in the system.

If your car has a brake servo check the results of bleeding it by pressing on the brake pedal and starting the engine. The pedal should sink by about an inch (25mm) as soon as the engine fires.

Wipe all the brake fluid away from the bleed nipples and get someone else to press hard on the brake pedal. Check all the nipples, pipes and unions for seepage. If they are leaking only slightly, tighten them up a bit and see if this cures the problem. If the leak continues you will have to recheck the system before you bleed it again or air will get in once more.

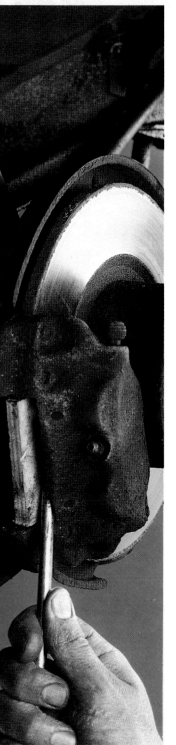

Inefficient brakes improved

Not all braking problems show up under normal driving conditions. Some only come to light when you need good brakes most

The first indication that you have faulty brakes is usually felt through the brake pedal. Leaking hydraulic fluid causes the pedal to sink to the floor, while air in the braking system shows up as sponginess and increased pedal travel. And occasionally, a pedal that feels hard simply refuses to work effectively no matter how hard you push.

When to do this job
When the brake pedal seems to need a lot more pressure than usual
If the brakes do not seem to be operating efficiently

What this job involves
Locating the inefficient parts of the system
Servicing the brake servo if it is faulty
Fitting new pads and deglazing the discs
Freeing the pistons in the calipers

Other possible causes and related jobs
Curing spongy brakes
Replacing disc brake pads
Replacing drum brake shoes
Please see Index for page numbers

To do this job
Tools: Jack and axle stands; wheel brace; spanners; pliers; light hammer; hub puller on some cars; screwdriver; knife; wooden wedge; wire brush; G-clamp
Materials: Copaslip; emery cloth; new pads or shoes (maybe); service kits (maybe); new caliper (maybe); WD 40
Time: An afternoon
Degree of difficulty: Straightforward but great care and cleanliness needed as always when dealing with the braking system

If you have the job professionally done. . .
Is there good response to the brake pedal without too much effort? Does the car stop evenly and smoothly without the brakes squealing?

If the brakes feel generally rather weak, and require a lot of foot pressure to pull the car up, the fault could lie either in the brake servo mechanism, if one is fitted, or in the individual pads and linings which may have become ineffective through misuse. However, poor front brakes can make it appear as if the whole braking system works badly. This is because the front brakes do more work — when you brake, the car's weight is thrown forward. The rear brakes are generally drum brakes rather than discs, and are designed to be less effective otherwise they would be continually locking up as the weight of the car shifts forward.

So even if the rear brakes are working well, you may notice a sharp reduction in braking performance if only the front

1. You should not be able to turn the wheel, with the brakes on

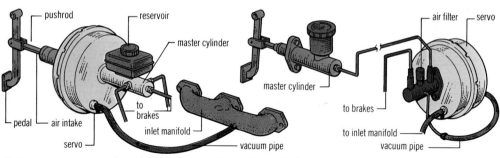

2. Servo can operate directly or via separate master cylinder

brakes have deteriorated.

A road test may help you decide where the problems lie — if the rear brakes lock up easily, then the front brakes are almost certainly poor. And if the car pulls to one side it is likely that the front brake opposite the direction of swerve is at fault.

Poor rear brakes are not easy to distinguish by road testing, so the most effective way of checking them, and indeed the brakes on the other wheels, is to jack up the car at each corner in turn and try to turn the wheel by hand while someone puts their foot on the brake pedal **(fig 1)**. Chock the other wheels to hold

the car still. You can exert considerable turning force on a wheel by hand, but if a brake is working properly you should be unable to turn it at all. If you cannot turn any wheel with the brakes held full on, get your helper to use less pressure on the pedal so that you can discover the weakest brake. Try to turn the wheel with no braking, too. If a brake is seized on or binding, you will find it very hard indeed to turn.

If just one brake is weak, check the condition of the braking parts on that wheel as outlined in Step 3 and 4. But if you find an overall loss in per-

formance and your car is fitted with a servo unit, it is likely that the servo mechanism itself needs attention as described in Step 2. The servo unit takes the form of a large diameter drum often fitted directly in front of the brake pedal so that the rod from the brake pedal passes directly into it **(fig 2)**. The servo may also be fitted remotely **(fig 2)** so look around the rest of the engine compartment as well.

If your car does not have a servo, general poor performance can only be checked by examining the brake on each wheel in turn, as described in Steps 3 and 4.

Although most brake servos use the vacuum produced by the engine for their assistance (apart from the rather special types found in Citroens and turbocharged models) they can be used and mounted in two quite different ways. The common variety is the mechanically connected servo fitted directly in front of the brake pedal, with the push rod from the pedal entering the servo from underneath the dashboard.

To check this 'mechanical' type, sit in the driver's seat with the engine off and operate the brake pedal half a dozen times. Press the pedal as hard as you can. When the servo is operating properly, the pedal should feel soft for the first application and get noticeably harder by the fourth or fifth application. By the sixth application of the brakes, the pedal should feel quite wooden and there should only be a very short travel on the brake pedal between the rest and fully on.

Now start the engine with your

1. Feeling for vacuum

foot on the pedal. The pedal should sink a little, and feel slightly more pliant. If you can feel the difference with and without the engine running, the servo is probably working well.

If you suspect that the servo is not working, find the hose that runs between the inlet manifold and the servo vacuum chamber. Check that the hose is not kinked or wrapped around

Under pressure

To confirm that the servo is working, ask an assistant to start the engine and apply the brakes a few times. You should be able to hear the hiss of air in and out of the servo as the brakes are applied and released.

If you hear a continual slight hiss from the servo when the engine is running, this indicates that the diaphragm is holed.

other components so that there is no clear passage through it. Then disconnect the end that fits on to the servo — it is held by clips — and start the engine.

When you put your hand over the end of the pipe **(fig 1)**, you should feel the vacuum very clearly. If the vacuum is poor or non-existent the pipe must be blocked or cracked and is admitting air. Look inside for

2. Removing gaiter

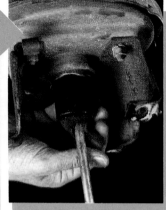

3. Taking out filter

signs of cracks or perishing, especially at the engine end. If the hose is damaged or blocked at one end you can salvage it by cutting off the damaged portion and reconnecting the hose.

While you have got the hose off, make sure that the hole in the inlet manifold is clear before reconnecting the hose and testing the servo again. If the whole hose needs renewing,

use the proper metal reinforced vacuum hose as ordinary heater hose is unsuitable and will soon collapse.

If the servo still appears to be sluggish or ineffective, check the air filter fitted to the rear chamber of the servo. The makers specify that this should be replaced every 40,000 miles or every three years but this is seldom done and the filter may

very well be blocked.

Sometimes the filter is in a separate housing but on a directly connected mechanical servo the filter is usually fitted around the pushrod from the brake pedal. Remove the clevis pin that holds the pushrod on to the pedal and pull the concertina gaiter off **(fig 2)**. You may need to undo the bolts or nuts holding the servo to the bulkhead and move the servo slightly to give yourself enough space to work. The filter is just a thick felt washer, though there is usually a retainer that you must prise off before you can remove the filter and its retainer **(fig 3)**. Reconnect the pushrod and bolt the servo back in place, then test the servo once more by pumping the brake pedal after running the engine.

If the servo works properly now, the car should stop quickly without much effort from the driver but you should not drive with an unfiltered servo. You can obtain a new filter in a servo overhaul kit but seek expert advice to carry out an overhaul.

ALTERNATIVE 2 — SERVICE THE SERVO (REMOTE TYPE)

The other variety of servo is the remotely mounted hydraulic servo, usually fitted some way from the master cylinder and the brake pedal. This is operated by vacuum from the inlet manifold in the same way as the directly connected type but it gives a different feel at the pedal. However, you can still test it in the same way as the directly connected type (see Step 2).

You can check and service the vacuum hose in exactly the same way as the hose on the mechanical servo. Also check the operation of the non-return valve often fitted to the vacuum chamber of the servo where the hose fits on, or at the other end where the hose joins the inlet manifold. Remove the non-

return valve **(fig 3)** and suck through it in both directions. Air should only go through it in the direction of the arrow stamped on the side.

The filter on a hydraulic servo is in a separate housing either on the servo body or underneath the cast hydraulic cylinder **(fig 1)**. You can remove the filter by undoing the screw in the centre or prising out the circlip and lifting out the filter and its perforated retainer **(fig 2)**. If you are sure that the servo is not operating and the checks already detailed in this step do not solve the problem, you can overhaul both types of servo with repair kits. Both Lockheed and Girling supply kits for their own products and some foreign makes as well.

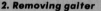

hydraulic cylinder — servo

vacuum hose

from master cylinder

to brakes

air filter

filter retainer

spring clip

filter housing

vacuum pipe

1. Location of filter

2. Removing air filter and retainers

3. Removing non-return valve to check it

If your car's braking is just generally poor, jack up the front of the car and remove both wheels.

On cars equipped with disc brakes, examine the inside and the outside face of each disc. If any of the surfaces are covered in rust across their full width (fig 1), or the metal is less polished on one face, suspect a seized caliper (see Step 5).

Now take out the brake pads (see pages 162 to 165) and examine them in comparison with the disc surface. Though the face of the pad and the disc should be polished and smooth, you may find that these surfaces appear to be super-polished to a very high shine (fig 3). This condition is known as glaze and can be caused by a number of different things.

Occasionally, oil or grease can get on to the face of the pad — it can then get heated by the application of the brakes. This is not a very common problem but someone might have been careless sometime when servicing a suspension joint or wheel bearing and held the disc with greasy hands. Try removing the glaze on the pads and disc with a piece of emery paper (fig 4). If the friction material is dark and discoloured all the way through, the only solution is to fit new pads as well.

Pads can also become glazed if you have overheated the brakes severely. If you began to suspect that your brakes were not up to scratch after charging down a steep hill or following several really hard applications of the brakes this could be your problem. This sort of use can cause your brakes to 'fade' — to lose their effect — due to overheating.

If you get out of the car immediately this happens and bend down close to the front wheels, you will smell the overheated friction material and feel the heat. If melted wheel bearing grease is oozing out of the hub bearing caps you can be sure that the brakes have overheated.

Fade can occur with any friction material that has been overheated, but the high quality branded varieties are much less likely to suffer from it and they usually recover better when they cool down. If your car is suffering from brake fade and the pads are glazed as well, there is no alternative but to fit a new set of pads. Fit either the manufacturer's replacements sold by your main dealer or the alternatives supplied by specialist manufacturers.

Many unknown varieties of pads are on the market now and if you drive fast enough to experience brake fade, you should spend the extra money on a good set of pads to ensure your brakes can stand up to heavy use. The well known makers of pads and brake shoes will also supply special high grade items for heavy use that resist fade even better than their standard products. Though they are a little more expensive and they need a harder push at the brake pedal, the extra safety margin is well worthwhile if you use your car's performance to the full.

If you have had pad problems, the discs will probably be glazed as well. Remove any heavy rust around the outside of the disc with a wire brush and then find some fine emery cloth or wet and dry paper. Use the emery cloth or wet and dry paper to remove the glaze from both faces of the disc — this can be quite a long process. You must hold the emery tight up against the disc and continue the process until all the excess shine has been removed. This will improve your brake's stopping power and their feel.

1. Rusty discs point to sticking pistons

2. Clean up rusty discs with emery paper

3. Glazed pads will reduce braking efficiency

4. Try removing the glaze with emery paper

1. A scored drum will affect braking efficiency

2. Check that the pistons move in and out

Cars equipped with drum brakes can suffer from similar faults to disc brakes. Pull or tap off the drums and check the surface of the shoes for glazing, and also for grease, oil or hydraulic fluid that has soaked into the friction material. As drum brakes are fully enclosed and are often exposed to the oil in the back axle, this is the most likely cause of poor braking at the back of a car fitted with rear drums.

Try to salvage the shoes by sanding off the oil-soaked surface with emery paper or a file. If the contamination is light, this might work but you might find the oil soaking back through — the best solution is to first cure the leak and then to fit new shoes if you find any of these conditions. This job is described on pages 166 to 169.

The brake drums suffer from the same kind of faults as the discs, so examine them carefully. If a drum gets glazed or scored inside where the shoes rub (fig 1), it is worth having it skimmed if a replacement is expensive or difficult to find. Many light engineering firms will carry out this service for a reasonable price but there is a limit to how much metal can safely be removed.

When you have got the shoes off, ask the assistant to press the brake pedal down very slowly while you hold the pistons in the hydraulic cylinders with your fingers and thumbs (fig 2) — stop as soon as the pistons begin to move very far or they could pop out. As the brake pedal goes down all the pistons should move outwards, indicating that they are free in their bores and not seized. If a piston does not move even if you help it along, and looks corroded, then it is definitely seized and you will need a new cylinder. Seek professional advice on the way to fit new cylinders.

1. Forcing the pistons back

2. With a single piston caliper you can use a clamp

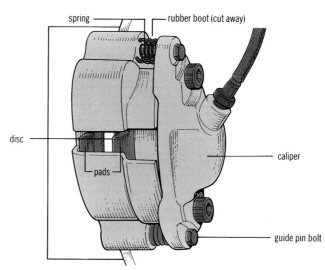

3. Some single piston calipers slide on pins — they can seize

The more conventional design of disc brake uses a fixed caliper bolted to the back of the stub axle, with a piston in each side to push each brake pad up against the disc. This type of caliper suffers from reduced efficiency if the pistons have seized.

Remove the brake pads (see pages 162 to 165) and try to push the pistons back into the cylinder with a stout lever (**fig 1**). You may be able to free the seized piston this way and then work it backwards and forwards with alternate pushes on the brake pedal and use the lever to try to overcome the stickiness in the bore that has caused the seizure. If you try this method leave a well-worn pad or a thin piece of wood between the piston and disc to stop the piston popping right out. If it does pop out, push it back in and then bleed the brakes.

If this method works, fit new seals from a caliper repair kit to lessen the chance of the problem happening again. However, in the long run, once a caliper has seized it is likely to seize again. Many modern

calipers have only one hydraulic cylinder that presses one pad up against the disc. Once the inboard pad is in contact with the disc, further pressure on the brake pedal moves the whole caliper across and this forces the other pad up against

the disc as well.

So if your car is fitted with a swinging or sliding caliper (**fig 4**), it may fail either because the piston seizes in the cylinder or because the other moving parts get dirty and prevent the caliper moving

enough.

Dampen down the outside of the caliper with water to prevent the dust from the pads floating around, then clean up the caliper with a wire brush.

Next, take off the caliper and the pads and check to see if the hydraulic piston is seized in the cylinder. You should be able to press the piston back into the bore with your thumbs without too much effort, though the piston is not intended to move too easily. When it will not move, try again with a large

G-clamp if you have one. Fit one of the G-clamp jaws over the back of the hydraulic cylinder and the other on the piston (**fig 2**). You might have to use pieces of packing to bring the pressure to bear on the piston.

Do up the clamp — if it moves easily you probably do not have to worry about seizure. If it takes a lot of force to move the piston — or it refuses to move at all — then the piston is badly seized and you will probably have to fit a new caliper.

When there is no sign of

seizure to the piston, you should be able to improve the braking performance by cleaning and lubricating the moving parts.

The open slide type of caliper (**fig 5**) is fitted to many British cars and to foreign ones like the Golf. Clean up the large yoke, using a solvent such as WD40 for the old grease and dirt. Pay particular attention to the slots in the body of the hydraulic cylinder that the yoke slides in. Tap the yoke backwards and forwards along the slots to make sure that it is free, then grease the slots lightly with Copaslip or brake grease.

Where the yoke is firmly bolted to the stub axle and the caliper is retained in the yoke with wedges at the top and bottom — as on some Girling and Bendix designs and on all Fiats — clean up the wedges with emery paper and examine them. If they are worn or ridged, fit new ones. Polish the ridges on the caliper with fine emery paper and clean the yoke carefully where it contacts the caliper and where the pads slide in. Coat all the moving parts, especially the wedges, with Copaslip.

Many other designs use a spring loaded pin to hold the caliper to the yoke (**fig 3**). You can identify this type by the concertina-style rubber boot fitted around the pin at the top and the bottom of the caliper. Undo the guide pin bolt on the inside face of the caliper, clean up the pins and the springs and lubricate them with Copaslip. Make sure that the springs have not lost their tension and fit new ones if you are in any doubt. Replace the rubber boots if they are torn or damaged.

Refit the calipers and the pads, then bolt the wheels back on. Road test the car to check that the full braking efficiency has been restored and that the car pulls up evenly with the front and the back brakes operating together.

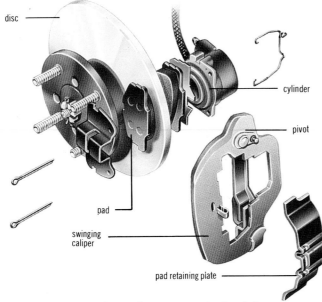

4. On a swinging caliper, the pivot or cylinder slide can jam

5. On sliding calipers, check the caliper slides smoothly

Adjusting the handbrake

If your handbrake is losing its grip you should adjust it. If it is stiff or difficult to operate you should check the cable. Both jobs can be easily done in less than a morning

The handbrake is a mechanical linkage which operates the brakes on one axle, independently of the main hydraulic braking system.

It must be capable of holding the car on hills and of stopping the car if the foot brake fails. By checking, lubricating and adjusting your car's handbrake linkage you will ensure that this vital component works effectively and will pass the annual roadworthiness test.

When to do this job
When the handbrake does not hold the car or becomes difficult to operate

What this job involves
Checking the handbrake linkage for damage or seizure
Adjusting the handbrake cable

Related jobs in this handbook
Bleeding the brakes
Replacing drum brake shoes
Adjusting drum brakes
Replacing disc brake pads
Please see Index for page numbers

To do this job
Tools: Spanners; pliers; hammer (maybe); screwdrivers (maybe)
Materials: Grease; WD-40; split and clevis pins (maybe)
Time: Up to two hours depending on the type fitted to your car
Degree of difficulty: As long as nothing is seized the job should be straightforward

If you have the job professionally done . . .
Does the handbrake hold the car on steep hills?
Does the handbrake release fully so that the brakes do not bind? Does the handbrake hold firm on about six clicks?

STEP 1 — CHECK THE HANDBRAKE

Although the handbrake is best checked on a brake tester there are a couple of tests you can carry out yourself quite simply.

The best test of a handbrake's efficiency is to find a steep hill and stop the car halfway up it. After making sure you are not causing an obstruction to anyone, pull on the handbrake and release the footbrake. The rear of the car should rise slightly, and by the same amount on both sides.

Another test you can carry out makes use of a loose gravel drive. Drive along slowly, then suddenly pull the handbrake full on to lock the wheels. The locked wheels should slide on the gravel. Check that both wheels slide, by looking at the marks in the gravel.

If either test shows that one of the brakes is working less than the other, either the brake needs adjusting, or the handbrake linkage has seized.

If you find that the handbrake does not hold the car at all, first check that the brakes are adjusted correctly (see pages 166 to 167) — they may have become badly worn.

If the adjustment appears correct the handbrake may need adjusting or part of the linkage may have seized. If this is the case, the next step is to identify the type of handbrake your car is fitted with (see Step 2), and adjust it accordingly.

STEP 2 — IDENTIFY THE LINKAGE AND ADJUSTER

There are five basic types of handbrake linkage but they all work in the same way. If you are not sure what type your car is fitted with, first check **fig 1** (below) and **figs 2-5** (overpage). A quick look underneath the car should then enable you to identify the type.

The most common type of linkage has a floor-mounted handbrake which operates a short primary rod or cable. This, in turn, tensions a short primary rod or cable. This, in turn, tensions a secondary cable attached to levers on the brake backplates.

Adjusters may be found at several points. The most common place is at the base of the handbrake lever itself where there may be one or a pair of locknuts to adjust rod or cable length. However, adjustment can be provided at the point where the lever's rod or cable pulls on a secondary cable (this type is usually found under the car) or on the backplate of the drum itself.

A few cars, notably Saab, have handbrakes which act on the calipers of the front brakes. Before starting work on the handbrake, it is best to check that the brakes themselves are in proper adjustment and that the pads or drum brake shoes have sufficient friction material to warrant handbrake adjustment.

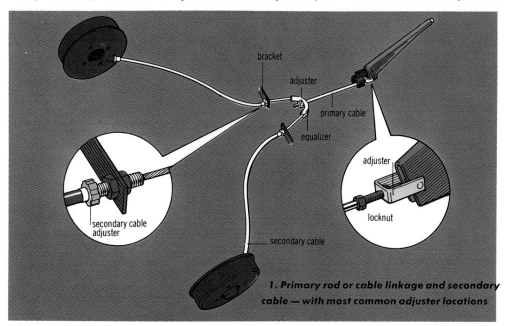

1. Primary rod or cable linkage and secondary cable — with most common adjuster locations

Labels: bracket; adjuster; primary cable; equalizer; adjuster; locknut; secondary cable; secondary cable adjuster

2. Twin cable system with alternative adjuster

adjusters

cable

adjuster

cables

adjuster

Bowden cable

adjuster

3. Transverse rod or cable handbrake

adjuster

adjusters

transverse rod

adjuster

relay lever

equalizer

calipers

4. Rod type handbrake found on Japanese cars

5. Disc type of handbrake

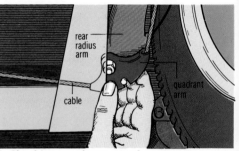

1. Greasing the equalizer assembly

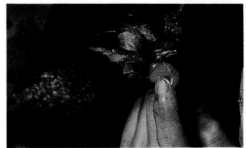

rear radius arm

cable

quadrant arm

2. Checking quadrant arms for seizure

If the handbrake does not hold the car and the brake shoes and brake adjustment (pages 166 to 167) are correct, then the handbrake linkage should be thoroughly checked for signs of wear or seizure. You will find this task much easier if the car is supported securely on axle stands as high up as possible.

The first check to make is for frayed or damaged cables or bent rods. Check all the joints in the linkage and then check the places the cables feed through a guide channel. Any evidence of fraying means that the cable must be replaced — this is covered on pages 174 to 176. Any joints which seem slack probably have worn clevis pins. These are very cheap so renew any which are grooved or worn.

Also check the cables and the equalizer for signs of seizure. Give the equalizer assembly a good spray with a lubricant such as WD-40 while a helper works the handbrake to loosen up the assembly. If your handbrake cable has a grease nipple on it, apply a little grease with a grease gun (page 78). WD-40 or grease should also be used to lubricate a cable or rod wherever it bears on a guide point — again, get someone to work the handbrake as you lubricate it.

The brake levers can also seize where they fit through the brake backplates so check that they move when the handbrake is applied. On Austin Rover front wheel drive cars, check the cable where it goes through the quadrant arm attached to the rear suspension arm (**fig 2**). Give these a good squirt with WD-40 as they are prone to seizure. If the arm does not move when the handbrake is applied you must slacken off the adjuster to release the cable tension (Step 5), then try gently tapping it from side to side with a small hammer until it frees. Finally, smother it with grease to keep it moving freely.

You should also lubricate the cable or rod where the handbrake linkage emerges from the floor. Check the condition of any rubber boot which may be fitted for cracks or splits and repair any you find using a suitable rubber adhesive.

Finally look at the return springs while your helper applies the handbrake. Check them for wear or damage where they are attached to the handbrake linkage and the car body. Any which seem slack must be changed.

If the handbrake linkage now appears to work properly but the car is still not held, then the cable needs adjusting.

STEP 4   **ADJUST PRIMARY CABLE OR ROD**

Raise the rear of the car off the ground, support it on axle stands and chock the front wheels. Release the handbrake fully and check that both the rear wheels turn freely. If not, check the brake adjustment (pages 166 to 167). If your adjuster is inside the car, remove the carpets to expose the adjusters.

Pull the handbrake lever on by three clicks to partially apply the rear brakes, and check that it is just possible to turn each wheel with both hands. Now slacken the locknut on the adjuster (**fig 1**) and use the adjuster nut to tighten up the cable until it is only just possible to turn the wheel by hand. It should need about the same force to turn each wheel.

Fully release the handbrake and check that the wheels turn without binding. If necessary, readjust the cable then tighten up the locknut.

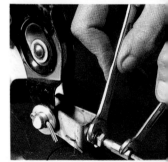

1. Adjusting a primary cable

Get the rear of the car as high off the ground as possible, support it securely on axle stands and chock the front wheels. Let the handbrake off and check that the wheels turn without binding. Check the brake adjustment (pages 166 to 167) if either brake drags at all.

Remove the carpet and the handbrake gaiter to expose the adjusters. Pull the handbrake on by two clicks from the fully off position and then turn each rear wheel by hand. Each should turn quite easily, with only a slight and equal drag from the brake shoes.

If one wheel is more difficult to turn than the other you should adjust both cables until the drag is the same. Adjust the cable by slackening the locknut on each cable and then turning the adjusting sleeve or locknut clockwise to tighten the cable. Check the drag on the wheels until both are the same — the wheels should only just drag and not be too tight.

Release the handbrake lever then pull it on by three to five clicks. Both rear wheels should be impossible to turn. Let the handbrake off again and check that the wheels turn easily without binding, then tighten up the locknut.

On a few cars the cable adjustment point is at the clevis pin end of the cable where it is connected to the brake levers. To adjust this type, first release the handbrake. Check that the brake is fully released against its end stop then go under the car and find the clevis pins. Using pliers, pull the split pin out then pull out the clevis pin (**fig 1**). If it is tight, use a hammer and punch to drift it out.

Release the cable from the brake levers and work each lever backwards and forwards by hand to take up any slack. Make sure the cable equalizer is in the central position then adjust the position of the end fork of each cable until the clevis pin can be inserted without straining the cable or leaving a lot of slack. Renew the clevis pins if they are a loose fit or have grooves worn in them and refit them to the car with new split pins.

Check that both wheels turn easily then pull on the handbrake by three to five clicks — the wheels should now be locked solid.

1. Removing the clevis pin from the brake lever

STEP 6 — ADJUST TRANSVERSE ROD OR CABLE

Jack up the rear of the car and support it on axle stands, then chock the front wheels. Let the handbrake off and make sure that both rear wheels turn easily — ignore any drag from the rear axle. Check the brake adjustment (pages 166 to 167), if the wheels are difficult to turn.

With the handbrake off and the rear axle relay lever fully against its stop bracket, check for play in the cable from the handbrake and in the transverse cable or rod. If play is present, adjust the cable from the handbrake lever as follows. Slacken the locknut at the relay lever, then turn the adjuster nut until all slack has gone and the relay lever is just clear of its bracket. Now retighten the locknut.

Some cars have a Bowden cable from the handbrake to the relay lever or equalizer, instead of an exposed cable running on rollers. In this case you adjust the cable using the adjuster at the equalizer or where the cable attaches to the brake lever. As you make the adjustment check the wheels do not bind.

To adjust the transverse cable find the adjuster on the cable where it attaches to the right-hand brake lever. Loosen the locknut then adjust the position of the cable end fork until the cable is taut. Tighten up the locknut when you have finished the work.

Where a transverse rod is fitted the adjuster is at the equalizer lever or bracket. Slacken the locknuts and adjust the rod until, with the handbrake released, the lever or bracket is in the central position. When you are satisfied with the adjustment retighten the locknut.

Test the handbrake by pulling the lever up three or four clicks if you have a floor mounted handbrake, or five or six clicks on a dash-mounted handbrake. In this position the wheels should be locked.

First raise the front or rear of the car, depending on which wheels the handbrake operates on. Chock the other two wheels for safety.

With the handbrake off, the wheels should revolve easily but if they drag check the brake adjustment.

Now pull the handbrake on by three clicks to partially apply the brakes. You should just be able to turn the wheels and each wheel should take the same amount of effort to turn it. If both wheels turn freely or only one is braked, you must adjust the handbrake.

Begin by finding the locknuts on the end of the cable where it fits to the brackets on the body. Using two open-ended spanners loosen the locknuts then screw the adjuster nut in or out until you can turn both wheels with the same amount of effort.

Release the handbrake to

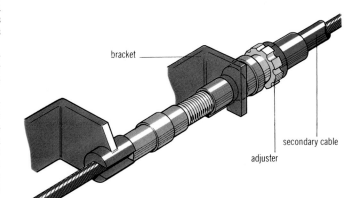

1. A secondary cable adjuster — some are turned by hand

check that the wheels turn without dragging, then tighten up the locknuts. Finally, check that the wheels are locked solid when the handbrake is pulled on by three to five clicks, and rotate freely when the brake is released.

STEP 8 — ADJUST A DISC HANDBRAKE

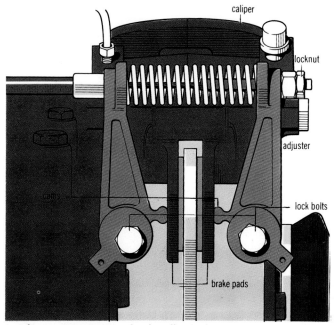

1. Adjustment points on disc handbrake levers

Try to raise the car as high as possible on axle stands to make the job easier and chock the wheels still on the ground. Let the handbrake off and make sure the brakes are not binding. If they are, check the brake pads (pages 162 to 165) and check the cable for seizure (Step 3).

On this type of handbrake the cable usually operates on levers attached to cams, which press the handbrake pads against the disc.

Using an open ended spanner, slacken off the large locknut next to the handbrake pad. To adjust the brake, turn the small adjusting bolt until the cam lever is just in contact with the handbrake pad. Holding the adjuster with one spanner, tighten up the locknut.

When you pull the handbrake on, it should only need three to five clicks to lock the wheels.

Headlight beam adjustment

Headlights which are set too high are both a nuisance and illegal. So it is well worth adjusting them yourself — even if you have them checked by a professional later

Most car headlights are only just adequate for the purpose intended — if they are in any way misaligned this will reduce their effectiveness and your ability to drive safely at night.

If the lights are set too low you will see almost nothing on dipped beam, too high and you will only light up the trees and annoy other road users. If oncoming motorists keep flashing you then probably something is wrong.

You can adjust the lights yourself but if you do you should still have them checked accurately on a garage beamsetter.

When to do this job
When your lights do not dip properly
When your main beams do not light up the road ahead or dazzle oncoming motorists

What this job involves
Checking the headlight alignment
Removing the grille or headlight trim
Adjusting the lights

Related jobs in this handbook
Renewing headlight bulbs
When the bolt won't budge
Please see Index for page numbers

To do this job
Tools: Screwdrivers; spanners; pliers (maybe)
Materials: Chalk; masking tape; WD-40; string
Time: One or two hours depending on how easy the adjusters are to operate
Degree of difficulty: Care needed to get alignment right

If you have the job professionally done...
Do the lights illuminate the road ahead properly?
Are the dip beams set so that the lights do not dazzle oncoming drivers?

Checking the headlight alignment is best done at night and to do it properly you need quite a large area. A flat piece of ground about 30 feet (10 metres) long with a wall or a large pair of doors at one end should do — you may be able to do the job in your local car park as long as you are careful.

First make sure the car is loaded normally — if you generally drive the car lightly loaded adjust the lights to suit, but if you regularly carry heavy loads in the back you may want to adjust the lights slightly lower to allow for this.

Drive the car up close to the wall and square on to it. Bounce each front wing to settle the suspension then mark the position of the light centres on the wall as follows.

Hold one end of a length of string on to the centre of the lamp glass and the other end against the wall. Keeping the string tight and parallel to the ground, chalk a small cross on the wall at the point indicated by the string. Do the same for the other headlight. If your car has four headlights mark the centre of each one.

Now move the car back from

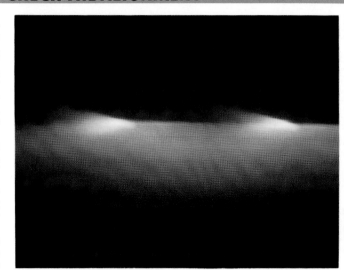

1. A typical asymmetric beam pattern with marked 'kick up' to left

the wall about 30 feet (10 metres) in a straight line.

Stop the car and apply the handbrake. Using 6 in. lengths of masking tape, highlight the chalk marks on the wall so that you can see them clearly from the car.

Switch on dipped beam and examine the pattern of light. If your headlights give a pattern like **fig 1**, your car has asymmetric headlights. This type gives a light beam with a flat cut-off at the top, and a marked 'kick up' of light to the left which lights up the kerb. These lights should be checked and adjusted on a dipped beam.

A beam pattern like **fig 2** shows that your car is fitted with elliptical headlights usually found on older British-made cars. These have a noticeable bright centre spot and lack the sharp cut-off of the asymmetric lights. This type should be checked on main beam.

If you find that your headlights are incorrected adjusted, find the adjusters (Step 2) and realign the lights (Step 3).

Cars with four headlights have to be checked on both dipped and main beam. The inner pair of lights will only work when main beam is selected so check them as for elliptical lights, described above.

The outer lights work on dipped or dipped and main beam and are usually checked on dipped beam. However, with some older four headlamp cars you might need to check them on main beam. Details of where to find the adjusters, and how to use them are covered in Step 2 and Step 3.

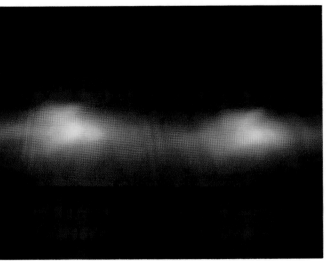

2. Older elliptical type pattern with bright centre spot

Modern asymmetric headlights usually have the adjusters fitted behind the lights (**fig 2** and **4**) This means they are reached from inside the engine compartment, although some cars have the lights boxed in by a cross-member which runs across the front of the car. In this case the screws have extension rods permanently fixed to them. A screwdriver is not usually needed to turn them as the plastic or metal ends are meant to be turned by hand — if they feel stiff a squirt of WD-40 will help to loosen them up.

Two adjusters will be fitted but their positions can vary (**fig 2**). They may be at the top and side of the light in which case the upper one adjusts the beam up and down and the other adjusts it from side to side.

Some cars have both screws fitted at the top of the light. Here they are used together for up and down adjustments and independently to adjust the beam from side to side. This is done by loosening one adjuster at the same time as you tighten up the other.

Check that the adjusters move freely before you try to adjust the lights — if they are tight use pliers to free them. Be careful, because the adjuster fits into a bush in the headlight shell and you may break it, or strip the threads in the bush.

Some French and Italian cars have load compensators fitted to the headlights (**fig 3**) (for quick adjustment when carrying heavy loads) and these can be confused with the main adjusters. In fact, in some cars the load compensator is part of the headlight adjuster, so check in your manual if you are at all unsure. Make sure before you adjust the lights that the compensators are set at their highest position. Once you are sure how they work go on to Step 3 to adjust the lights.

On older British cars and on some cars fitted with four headlights

1. On some cars you need to prise off the headlight rim

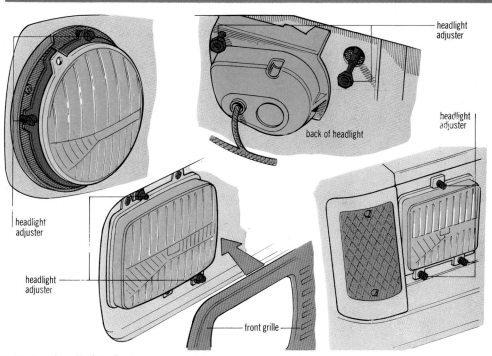

2. Various headlight adjusters — to reach some types you need to remove the grille

headlight adjuster

back of headlight

headlight adjuster

headlight adjuster

headlight adjuster

front grille

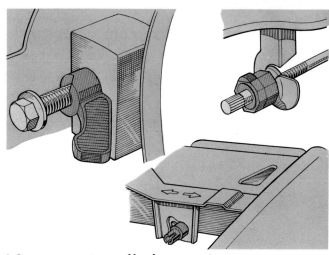

3. Some common types of load compensator

4. The small white plastic knob is the adjuster — turn by hand

the adjusters are usually hidden behind the light rim or the front grille.

The light rim is usually held by a screw at its top or bottom edge — failing that it is a press fit and can be carefully prised off with a screwdriver. Use rags to protect the paint while you lever the rim (**fig 1**).

Before you take out the screw fixing, clean out the slot of all dirt, then use a good snug fitting screwdriver to undo it. The rim should now pull off — if it sticks, lever it with a screwdriver. If your headlights are set into the grille or plastic trim, this will have to be removed first to gain access.

Once the trim is off you should

Two adjuster screws are usually fitted although older lights could have three. If yours are this type, the screw at the centre is for up and down adjustment and side to side adjustments are made with the two side screws. To move the beam you loosen one screw while tightening up the other.

Adjuster screws are usually of the plain slotted type. Again, an application of WD-40 will help free screws which have seized solid. If this has no effect, use pliers on the exposed part of the screw — this may shift it.

If any of the adjusters break off or strip their threads you can get new ones from your dealer. Prices vary but in general they should not cost more than a halogen headlight bulb. If you have some time to spend, though, you could always get the parts from a breaker's yard provided that they are in better condition than the ones you have taken off.

be able to find the adjusters — the most common ones are shown in **fig 2**. In some cases the adjusters may be behind the light itself and there should be slots or holes in the light retaining rim for a screwdriver.

Once you know where the adjusters are on your car, you can adjust the lights. Obviously, this is best done at night. Refer to Step 1 and set up the car about 30 feet (10 metres) from the wall.

Cars with asymmetric lights are adjusted as follows. Use a torch to help you locate the adjusters and check that any load compensators (see Step 2) are set to the normal load (usually the highest) position, then cover up one of the lights with a blanket or black dustbin liner taped in place. Check this cover from time to time as it may cause the light to overheat. If so, switch off every few minutes.

Turn on the dip beams and look for the brightest area of light (**fig 1**). Using the vertical adjuster (see Step 2), bring the bright spot up until it is about 8 in. (200 mm) below the horizontal arm of the cross. Depending on the adjuster design turning it clockwise can either raise or lower it so check this first. Once the beam is correctly set for height, go on to adjust the horizontal setting.

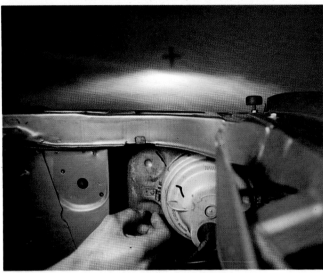
1. Turn the adjuster until the beam is under the cross

The beam has to be set so that the bright spot is to the left of the cross. Use the horizontal adjuster (see Step 2) to move the beam — the cut-off top edge of the beam should end up in line with the cross and at least 4 in. (100 mm) below it. This should leave the whole of the 'kick up' part further to the left (**fig 1**).

Once you have adjusted the first light, cover it up and adjust the other one. Finally remove the cover from the light and check that the beams look like the diagram in Step 1.

On the older British type of headlight, first remove any trim to expose the adjusters (see Step 2). Cover up one light with a blanket or dustbin liner then switch on the headlights on main beam. Using the vertical adjuster screws (**fig 1**), move the centre of the bright area of light until it is ½ in. (13 mm) below the centre of the cross. Turn the screw clockwise to raise the beam, anticlockwise to lower it.

Once you are satisfied with the beam's position, use the horizontal adjuster to bring the centre of the bright spot into line with the cross. Once you have done this recheck the vertical adjustment and make any readjustments that are necessary. Then adjust the other headlight

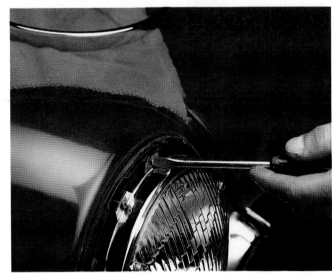
1. On this car the adjuster is at the front of the light

HOW IT WORKS

How a beamsetter works

If you have your headlights adjusted professionally at a garage the mechanic is sure to use a proprietary beam setting device.

Although there are various types of beamsetter in use they are all basically similar in design and are basically quite simple in construction.

A typical beamsetter is, in effect, just a box with a lens at the front and a calibrated screen at the rear. The device is carefully positioned in front of the headlight so that it is perfectly aligned with the centre of the beam. This operation calls for some care — the machine must be set up precisely so that the headlights can be adjusted correctly.

Once the beamsetter is in position the mechanic switches the car's lights on so that the beam is focused on the rear screen of the machine. The screen can be viewed through a

tinted viewing screen
lens
calibrated screen
parallel light from headlight

small window and calibrations on the screen allow the beam's position to be checked and adjusted precisely.

As the mechanic is working right next to the headlight, adjustments can be made and checked very quickly. Each light is set in turn in exactly the same way.

in exactly the same way.

Finally, remove the covering and check the main and dipped beam positions of both lights together (see Step 1). If all is well, refit the headlight trim or grille fittings.

If your car has four headlights first adjust the inner ones individually, masking off the other three lights as you do. The inner lights are adjusted on main beam in the same way as the older British type lights and the outer ones usually on dipped beam like the newer asymmetric lights. When adjusting the outer lights only the other outer light needs to be masked. The adjusters are all on the front of the lights so the trim or grille must be removed first to gain access.

TIP

Beam me down

If when switched to dipped beam your lights illuminate any of the back window or the interior mirror of the car in front when you are a reasonable distance behind then your beams are too high and should be adjusted.

Rear wheel bearing service

The rear wheel bearings in a live-axled car should last the lifetime of the car. Renewing them is really a garage job but you can do the preparatory work at home

All cars have bearings which allow the rear wheels to spin, but the way the bearings do their job varies from car to car. This project deals with live axle rear wheel bearings fitted to rear wheel drive cars.

Rear wheel bearings are generally reliable components but if they do give trouble you should get them seen to or do the job yourself. With the types of live axle most commonly found on modern cars, the actual job of getting the old bearings off and the new bearings on is usually best left to a garage with specialist equipment, but you can still significantly reduce the bill by doing the preparatory and reassembling work yourself.

When to do this job
As recommended by the manufacturer or if you hear rumbling noises from rear wheels

What this job involves
Checking the source of the noise
Removing the halfshaft and bearing
Reassembling rear axle

Related jobs in this handbook
All round lubrication
Renewing front wheel bearings
Please see Index for page numbers

To do this job
Tools: Spanners; hammer; pullers (maybe); slide hammer (maybe); jack; axle stands
Materials; New bearings; axle oil
Time: Depends on difficulties but allow a whole day
Degree of difficulty: Removing halfshaft is straightforward but fitting new bearings is usually a garage job

If you have the job professionally done . . .
Does car run without undue noise from rear axle?
Does any oil leak from rear axle?

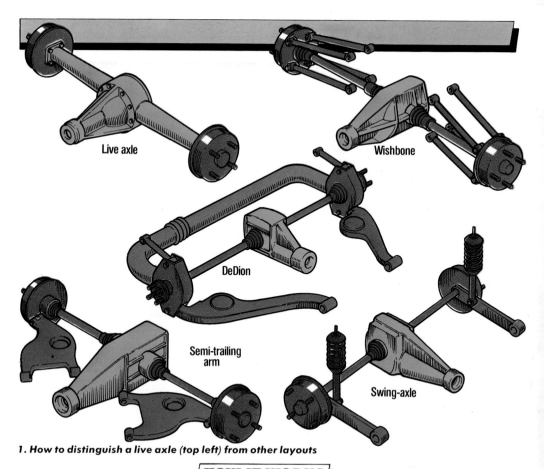

1. *How to distinguish a live axle (top left) from other layouts*

HOW IT WORKS

Types of live axle

Live axles fall into two main groups — those with *semi-floating* wheel bearings and those with *three-quarter-floating* wheel bearings. You will find that the procedures for working on the two types are rather different. Check with your manual or dealer to find our which type you have as they look similar from the outside.

The main difference between the two is the way in which the halfshafts are supported at the wheel ends of the axle. In the more common semi-floating type the bearing fits around the outer end of the halfshaft inside the axle casing. With this arrangement the bearing and the halfshaft support the entire weight of the rear of the car.

Three-quarter-floating axles are less common but are still found on many cars, especially older designs. With this type of axle the bearing does not actually touch the halfshaft itself, but instead is fitted around the outside of the axle casing inside a hub, so the halfshaft does not support the weight of the car.

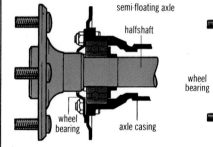
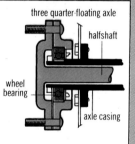

115

STEP 1 — FIND THE FAULT

Unlike the front wheel bearings which are lubricated by grease, bearings fitted to most rear wheel drive cars are lubricated by the oil inside the axle casing — usually a thick SAE 90 hypoid oil. Problems often arise with the bearings when this oil level is allowed to run low for a period — perhaps because of a leaking pinion seal in the differential casing. The result is that the bearings are starved of oil and

quickly wear out. It is usually fairly easy to tell when this has happened because there will be an obvious grinding or rumbling sound coming from the back axle.

However, before you decide to replace the wheel bearings it is worth checking that the noise is not coming from the differential gears or bearings, or even the tyres. Jack up the rear of the car so that the wheels

clear the ground and support it securely with axle stands — make sure that the front wheels are chocked (see page 162). Make absolutely certain that the car is solidly supported then release the handbrake and check that the gearbox is in neutral.

Begin by making a visual inspection of the wheels and tyres, spinning them by hand to see whether they turn smoothly

1. Listening for wear using a wooden rod as a stethoscope

and do not wobble as they spin. Check the tyre treads and sidewalls carefully for signs of damage. Make sure the tyres are the right size and type for the car — worn, damaged or incorrect tyres can make excessive noise at times and it is possible that you have mistaken this for bearing noise. Bear in mind that if you fit extra-wide tyres on the back of the car you will put more load on the rear wheel bearings possibly

causing them to wear out prematurely.

Next, ask someone to sit in the car, start the engine and engage first gear while you listen for noises around the rear wheels. Take care not to get too close to the wheels as they spin round. Sometimes the bearings will only make noises at higher speeds so your assistant may have to change to a higher gear. Usually it will be clear whether or not the noise is coming from

the outer ends of the axle close to the wheels, or from the middle close to the differential.

If you are still not certain about the precise source of the noise you can use a long wood or metal rod as a stethoscope to pinpoint the sound. Touch one end against the axle casing, first in the middle and then at the two ends, while you hold the other end of the rod to your ear. This should amplify the sound enough for you to tell where the noise is coming from.

If you are absolutely sure that the noise is from one or both of the wheel bearings you can go ahead and start work on the axle. If the sound seems to be coming from the differential you should go to a dealer or a specialist to have your diagnosis confirmed. You may end up having to fit an entire reconditioned axle assembly, although a noisy differential will often carry on for years without giving further trouble.

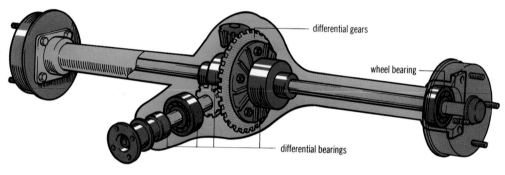

2. The parts of a live axle that may become noisy

differential gears

wheel bearing

differential bearings

STEP 2 — PREPARE FOR THE JOB

Once you are certain that it is the wheel bearings that are at fault you will have to find replacements as well as any new gaskets and oil seals which may be needed. However, before buying the parts you should check with your dealer or your manual to find out if

there are any special tools needed for the job and how much you will have to pay for them. You may need a torque wrench and you are also likely to find the job much easier if you have a special slide hammer for pulling out the halfshaft or hub — in some cases this tool is

essential. In the case of three quarter-floating types you may need a variety of pullers to do the job. Usually these tools can be hired but you may find the cost of hire plus the new parts almost equals the amount a garage would charge.

The next point to check concerns the removal of the bearings. With some types a large hydraulic press has to be used to remove the old bearing from the halfshaft and to refit the new one. Sometimes this job has to be done after the bearing has been heated up. With other types special bearing pullers are needed to pull off the bearings or to extract them from their housings. This stage of the work is best left to your dealer, local garage or even a specialist so you will have to make arrangements beforehand to have the job done on the day

you plan to do the repair. You may find that the garage is more willing to do the work if you buy

the parts from them as well. Even through you will have to pay for this service you could

still save money by doing the rest of the work yourself but the saving may not be worthwhile.

When you are ready to begin, bear in mind that if you do not jack up both sides of the car evenly you will have to drain the differential oil to stop it running out of the end of the axle when you remove the halfshaft and bearing. Use a spanner or a drain plug tool to loosen and remove the filler plug and then the drain plug at the base of the differential casing (**fig 1**).

The bearings should be removed from both sides, but if you do not want to drain the oil from the axle you can jack up one side of the car higher than the other so the oil runs away from the higher side.

Now loosen the nuts or bolts holding the road wheels in place and jack up the car and support it securely.

1. Loosening the differential drain plug

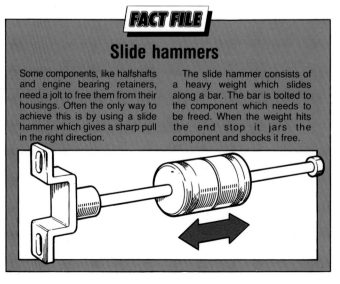

FACT FILE

Slide hammers

Some components, like halfshafts and engine bearing retainers, need a jolt to free them from their housings. Often the only way to achieve this is by using a slide hammer which gives a sharp pull in the right direction.

The slide hammer consists of a heavy weight which slides along a bar. The bar is bolted to the component which needs to be freed. When the weight hits the end stop it jars the component and shocks it free.

REMOVE BRAKE ASSEMBLY

If your axle is a semi-floating type, you may first have to take off the entire brake assembly to gain access to the bearing assembly.

First disconnect the handbrake cable from behind the brake backing plate. Usually the cable is attached to the handbrake lever by a clevis pin — this is locked in place by a split pin so use a pair of pliers or a small screwdriver to remove it before sliding out the clevis pin (**fig 1**).

No matter which type of axle you have the next step is to

1. Disconnecting handbrake cable from brake backplate

2. Bearing retainer plate bolted through backplate

remove the brake drum. Sometimes this is held in place by one or two countersunk screws, sometimes by bolts or nuts and sometimes just by the wheel nuts or bolts — see page 167.

Once the drum is off you will be able to see the flange of the halfshaft or the hub. With three quarter-floating axles, the rest of the brake components can be left in place, while with semi-floating types you may have to remove the brake shoes and springs (see page 168) if they are in the way of the bearing retainer plate (see Step 4).

DISMANTLE SEMI-FLOATING AXLE

1. Using socket to unbolt retainer plate

2. Retainer plate unbolted from axle flange

On semi-floating axles the bearing is fitted around the halfshaft so these two components have to be removed together. If you look behind the halfshaft flange towards the end of the axle casing you will probably be able to see four nuts or bolts which hold the bearing retainer plate to the axle casing. Sometimes these nuts or bolts are on the other side of the flange so that they are facing you once the brake linings have been removed — they often hold the brake backing plate in place as well. Undo the bolts a little at a time with a spanner, working diagonally from one bolt to the one opposite to avoid distorting

the bearing cover. Sometimes, when the bolts are threaded in from the front, there will be an access hole cut in the halfshaft flange so that you can use a socket spanner (**fig 1**).

At this point, in many cases you will have to disconnect the hydraulic brake pipe from the back of the wheel cylinder and plug it to minimize the loss of brake fluid. Sometimes the back plate can be left hanging on the end of the axle casing and the hydraulic connection does not have to be disturbed. The backing plate and bearing retainer plate should now be free from the flange (**fig 2**) — make a note of the shims and gaskets behind it.

A few cars do not have bolts which hold the bearing in the axle casing. Instead a large internal circlip is fitted. Use a pair of circlip pliers to release it from its groove in the casing.

Next the halfshaft and the wheel bearing have to be pulled out of the axle casing. This is where you will probably need the slide hammer. After a few fairly sharp blows with the hammer, the bearing should start to leave the casing so that the shaft and bearing can be slid out of the casing (**fig 4**).

In many cases it is possible to do this without a slide hammer although the job is more difficult this way. Begin by refitting the road wheel to the flange and

3. Fastening slide hammer in place on halfshaft flange

4. Drawing bearing out of axle casing with slide hammer

tighten the nuts or bolts enough to hold the wheel firmly in place. Now get under the car, behind the wheel, and hold a stout block of wood against the inside edge of the rim.

Hit the block of wood with a heavy hammer and then turn the wheel rim 180° and repeat the process. Several blows should push the bearing out of the casing — never hammer directly on to the wheel rim otherwise you will damage the wheel.

Handle the halfshaft with care as you slide it out of the casing and take it to a garage to have the bearing removed — dropping it on a hard surface is likely to damage the splined tip or even distort the whole shaft.

If you examine the shaft you may notice that the bearing is held in place by a strong circlip. However, it is also pressed into place with great force and can only be removed properly by using a heavy-duty hydraulic press — do not try chiselling the bearing off the shaft. Remove the other shaft in the same way and take them to your local garage or machine shop — they will also be able to install the new bearing correctly as they have the machinery needed to do the job.

REASSEMBLE THE AXLE

Once you have had the new bearings pressed into place on the halfshafts lubricate them with the same type of oil used in the axle — usually hypoid SAE 90. Do not try to prise away any oil seals from the bearing. Make sure that the splines and the rest of the shaft are spotlessly clean before sliding the assembly back into the casing. You may have to twist or rock the shaft a little as you insert it to make sure that the splines engage with the differential unit in the middle of the axle — you should never have to force the

1. Easing halfshaft into place so that splines engage

halfshaft into place except when the bearings is starting to enter the casing. Once this has started to happen you should be able to tap the end of the halfshaft all the way home using a hammer and a piece of wood (**fig 2**) — do not strike the shaft directly with the hammer, or you may damage it. Check that the bearing is going into the casing squarely as you are tapping it home. Finally, tighten the flange bolts according to the recommendations in your manual or fit the circlip back into its groove in the axle casing.

2. Tapping halfshaft home with hammer and block of wood

DISMANTLE 3/4 FLOATING AXLE

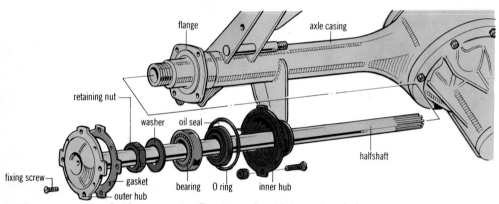

flange
axle casing
retaining nut
washer
oil seal
halfshaft
fixing screw
gasket
bearing
O ring
inner hub
outer hub

1. The components of a three-quarter-floating axle with two-piece hub

The procedure for removing the bearing from a three-quarter-floating axle is rather different. Once you have taken off the brake drum the rest of the brake assembly can be left intact. First undo the screw or screws which hold the halfshaft flange to the bearing hub — since there is no bearing holding the shaft in the axle casing the shaft can be pulled out and placed to one side. Note that there is usually a paper gasket and a rubber O-ring fitted between the inside of the halfshaft flange and the bearing

hub. A new gasket and O-ring should be fitted on reassembly.

Now you will be able to see the large nut which holds the bearing hub to the axle. Use a screwdriver or a small chisel to bend back any tabs which lock the nut in place and then use a large spanner to undo the nut. You may have to borrow a spanner large enough for the job or tap the nut round with a screwdriver (**fig 3**). With the nut removed, the hub can be pulled away using a slide hammer.

You do not need a hydraulic press to remove the bearing (**fig**

4). When the hub assembly is removed, place it with its outer face downwards on a piece of wood and use a hammer and a soft metal drift to tap the bearing out of the hub (**fig 5**). Work your way around the edge of the bearing so that it is forced out evenly. Use a screwdriver to prise out the oil seal, making a note of the way the new one should be fitted. Reassembly is a straightforward reversal of the dismantling procedure, but make sure the new bearing is well coated with oil before tapping it back into the hub.

2. Unbolting halfshaft flange from hub

3. Loosening central nut with screwdriver

4. Removing outer bearing from hub

5. Drifting out inner bearing assembly

With some three-quarter-floating axles the flange and the halfshaft are separate components and there is a completely self-contained bearing hub (**fig 1**). This type is now uncommon but you can identify it quite easily — once you have removed the wheel trim from one of the rear wheels you can see a domed cap in the middle which covers a large castellated nut.

Begin the dismantling procedure by loosening the wheel nut or bolts a half turn. Now prise away the domed cap with a screwdriver or a pair of slip joint pliers. Straighten and remove the split pin which locks the castellated nut and then use a large socket spanner to loosen the nut itself.

Support the rear of the car on axle stands. Take off the road wheel and undo the castellated nut completely. Drain the differential oil and remove the brake drum (see Step 3). The hub can now be removed but to draw it off the shaft you will have to hire a puller. Then you will be able to see the bearing housing bolted to the flange of the axle casing. Loosen these bolts with a socket spanner.

The bearings are not caged so they are likely to scatter as you pull away the housing. The inner race will remain on the halfshaft while the outer race will still stay in the housing.

If you have the right tools to do the job yourself, pull the shaft out of the axle casing and clamp it in a soft-jawed vice. Use a bearing puller to draw the inner race off the shaft — a new one

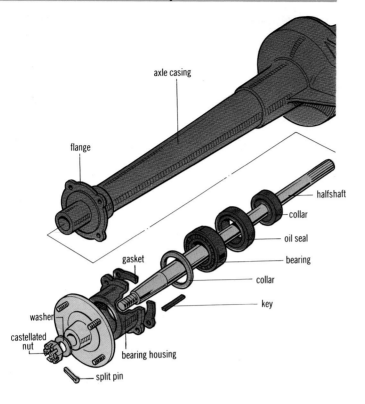

1. Three quarter-floating axle with separate hub

can be drifted back on to the shaft using a hammer and a piece of hollow metal tubing that will fit against the race. Make sure the race is fitted the right way round — usually with the smaller diameter of the taper facing the road wheel end of the shaft.

The outer race has to be extracted from the housing using another puller — it is probably best to take both the

housing and the halfshaft to your local garage and have them change the races for you.

Replace all seals and gaskets when you are reassembling the axle. Coat the bearing rollers with hypoid oil to hold them in the outer race as you slide the assembly back into the casing. The hub will be pushed home as you retighten the castellated nut to the specified torque. Be sure to fit a new split pin.

When you have put the half-shafts back into place and reassembled the brakes, fill the differential with the right quantity of oil as specified in your manual. Bleed the brakes (see pages 101-104) if you had to

unfasten the brake line.

Make sure that the brakes are working properly and then take the car for a test drive. You should not hear any rumbling noises from the rear wheels or from the differential. After you

have stopped the car, look for any oil leaks coming from the ends of the rear axle or from the differential. If you find a leak from the differential, check that the drain and filler plugs are in place and tight.

Front wheel bearing service

When the front wheel bearings rumble it means that they need attention. This may just be lubrication but new bearings may be required. Both jobs are straightforward

Faulty front wheel bearings can affect the safety and handling of your car as well as causing the front tyres to wear unevenly. In extreme cases, a wheel bearing fault can cause the entire wheel to lock up — or even fall off — while the car is in motion. For these reasons, the wheel bearings should be carefully checked as part of your car's routine servicing.

When to do this job
As recommended by the manufacturer or if you hear rumbling noises from front wheels and can feel excess play in the bearings

What this job involves
Checking wheel bearings
Adjusting wheel bearings
Removing wheel bearings
Lubricating wheel bearings

Related jobs in this handbook
Replacing drum brake shoes
Replacing disc brake pads
Please see Index for page numbers

To do this job
Tools: Jack; axle stands; wheelbrace; screwdriver; pliers; hammer; hub puller (maybe); bearing puller (maybe)
Materials: New bearings (maybe); HMP (high melting point) grease
Time: Up to two hours per wheel
Degree of difficulty: Hub may be difficult to remove; bearings may be so tightly embedded that you will need to hire a bearing puller

If you have the job professionally done . . .
Do wheels turn smoothly and quietly? Has free play disappeared when you try to rock the wheels?

You can tell when the front wheel bearings are loose or worn by checking the hub, with the wheel attached to it, for free play. Some people try to do this with the road wheel still resting on the ground, but it is far better to make the check after the front of the car has been jacked up and supported with axle stands. With the wheel off the ground, grasp the top and bottom of the wheel and try to rock it back and forth (**fig 1**). If you can feel the wheel rock, check that this play is in the hub assembly and not looseness in the suspension or steering. To do this ask a friend to rock the wheel while you check underneath the car for any signs of movement in the

1. Checking for play in the wheel bearings

suspension and steering (**fig 2**). If the play is not in the wheel bearing but is in another component, you must attend to that item first. There should only be a very small amount of play in the bearings — some manuals give a figure of about 1/16 in. or 2 mm at the wheel rim. Although adjustment can take up some of the movement, a really sloppy wheel bearing will probably need replacing.

While the front wheels are off the ground, spin them by hand and listen for any noises which could be caused by a faulty bearing. Very slight noise may be cured by packing the bearings with fresh grease. If the wheel does not spin freely, this may be because the brakes are holding it. On drum brake models the wheel can be freed by loosening the adjuster (see pages 166 to 169) but with disc brake models you may need to lever the pads away from the disc slightly or even to remove the pads from the caliper (see pages 162 to 165). Remember to check the brakes thoroughly after you have finished working on the wheel bearings.

If you find that the bearings are making excessive noise or seem to have far too much play, it is unlikely that adjustment or cleaning and greasing are going to offer anything more than a temporary cure. In these cases it is better to fit new bearings (see Step 3).

Some cars, such as the Fiat 127 and 128, have front wheel bearings which come off as a complete unit. Getting these bearings off the hub can be tricky so you may choose to save on dismantling charges by taking the hub off yourself and then getting your dealer to press out the old bearings.

If you have bearings that cannot be adjusted, such as those fitted to some Austin Rover front wheel drive cars, you should not try to take out any play in the bearings by over tightening the hub nut. This may make the bearings overheat. If the bearings are worn, the only solution is to renew them.

HOW IT WORKS

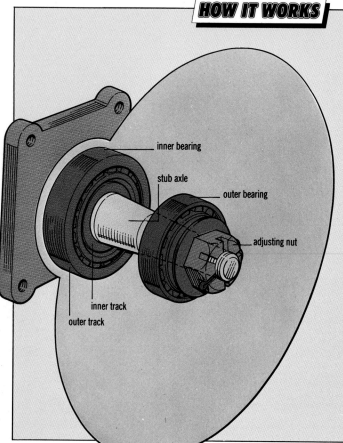

Wheel bearings

On most cars — whether front or rear wheel drive — the hub to which the front wheel is bolted spins on a stub axle. The wheel can turn because the hub is mounted on inner and outer bearings.

Depending on the type and make of car, these bearings may either be caged ball bearings or, more commonly, roller bearings which move against inner and outer races fitted to each side of the hub. Usually these roller bearings are tapered so that adjustment is possible. The bearings are packed with grease to keep them constantly lubricated.

The correct adjustment of tapered bearings is very important and, in most cases, this is a job which can be done by a DIY mechanic. Bearings that have either too little or too much clearance will rapidly wear out and will often start to make a rumbling or clicking noise which may be particularly noticeable when the car is cornering. Bearing noise is usually a sign that the bearing is badly worn and in need of renewal.

Labels: inner bearing, stub axle, outer bearing, adjusting nut, inner track, outer track

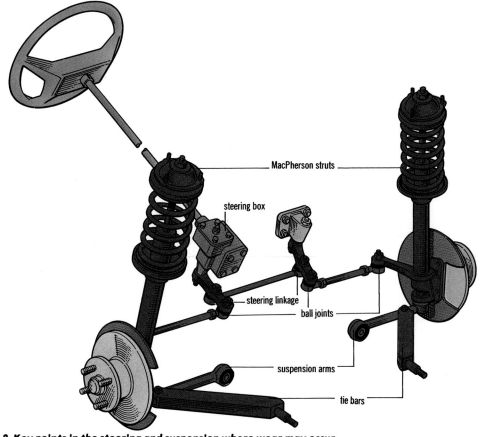

Labels: MacPherson struts, steering box, steering linkage, ball joints, suspension arms, tie bars

2. Key points in the steering and suspension where wear may occur

Small amounts of play in wheel bearings can sometimes be taken up by adjustment. The bearings and the hub assembly are usually held in place on the stub axle by a large nut or pair of nuts (**fig 1**). On some cars a single castellated nut is used together with a split pin which locks it in place. Other models use a second nut to lock the whole assembly in place.

Begin by consulting your manual to find out if your car is fitted with adjustable wheel bearings. Some are fitted with non-adjustable ball bearing assemblies which should give the right clearance as long as the hub nut is tightened to the correct torque figure.

If you find any play in this type of bearing you will have to fit a new one.

Once you are sure that you have bearings which can be adjusted, begin by loosening the nuts or bolts holding the road wheel in place. Slacken them only a little so that they can be undone easily once the car has been raised from the ground. Now jack up the front of the car and support it with axle stands so that the nuts or bolts can be removed completely and the wheel lifted away.

In the middle of the brake drum or disc you will see a domed metal cap. This holds the grease around the stub axle and prevents dirt and grit from getting inside the bearing assembly. Usually it can be removed by carefully levering it away with a large screwdriver or a pair of slip-joint pliers (**fig 2**). On some models the cap is threaded in place and can only be removed by turning it with slip-joint pliers — usually in a direction opposite to the rotation of the wheel — that is, clockwise on the left hand wheel. A few cars — notably the Volkswagen Beetle — have the speedometer drive attached to the grease cap on one wheel and the clip which holds it in place has to be

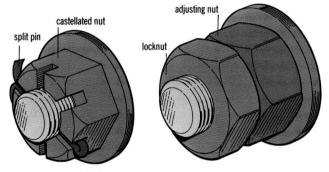

1. Alternative ways of locking the adjuster nut

castellated nut

split pin

adjusting nut

locknut

2. Levering away the grease cap with a screwdriver

3. Loosening the central retaining nut

removed before the grease cap can be levered away. When you have taken off the grease cap, you should be able to see the large retaining nut together with its locking device. If this consists of a split pin and a castellated nut, first straighten out the split pin with a pair of pliers and then gently withdraw the pin from its hole. If the split pin has broken off inside the hole and you cannot grasp it with pliers, use a hammer and a fine drift to tap the broken pin out.

On some cars the hub is held on the axle by two large nuts with a locking plate between them. Bearing adjustment is made by turning the inner nut, but before you can move it the locking tab which is hammered over the outer nut has to be straightened out using a hammer and a small cold chisel. Only then can you remove the outer nut and locking plate.

Another design, found on many Ford models, also uses two nuts which lock against one another. However a split pin is used instead of a locking plate to secure the nuts. Once you have pulled out the split pin you will need two similar spanners so that the inner nut can be held stationary while the outer nut is loosened. This done, the inner nut can be turned to make the adjustment.

Whatever system you come across, once you have freed the adjustment nut, it can be turned

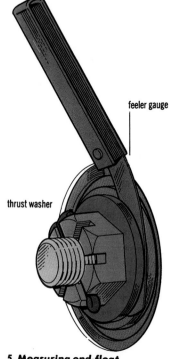

feeler gauge

thrust washer

5. Measuring end-float

inwards to take up the bearing free play. But before you make the adjustment, take off the thrust washer and the outer bearing so that you can inspect them — they should just slide off the end of the stub axle. Check that the bearing looks intact and is well coated with grease — this should not be crumbly or waxy. If you find that the grease is not in good condition, you will have to dismantle the hub and bearing assembly so that you can clean the whole assembly and pack it with fresh grease (see Step 3).

If the bearing appears to be well lubricated, slide it back in place together with the washer and carry on with the adjustment. This procedure varies from car to car. Many DIY mechanics simply turn the large nut until most of the play has been taken up, but the hub still spins freely. This approach is rather crude, but it can give fairly satisfactory results with some cars. However, this should be regarded only as a temporary solution — it is far more sensible to follow the manufacturer's recommendations. Check your manual for the procedure. You may have to tighten the central nut to a certain torque figure and to turn the hub at the same time so that the bearing beds in evenly, and then slacken the nut by part of a turn.

However, a more common instruction is for the manufacturer to give an *end-float* figure. The end-float is usually measured by sliding a feeler gauge between the outer bearing and the washer. Slide a feeler gauge of the recommended thickness between the bearing and the washer (**fig 5**) — it should be a smooth sliding fit. If the feeler is a loose fit, or is very tight, use a spanner to turn the adjuster nut until the gap is about right. You may then have to turn the nut slightly one way or the other to enable you to refit the split pin.

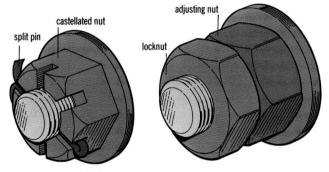

4. Removing the outer bearing from the hub

If the bearings have worn too much for adjustment to cure the problem then they will have to be replaced. Begin by following the procedure in Step 2 for removing the grease cap and the large central nut. On disc brake models, before you can slide the hub and disc assembly off the stub axle you will have to unbolt the disc brake caliper and hang it out of the way. Often it is easiest to tie it to a nearby steering or suspension component with some strong wire. This will take the strain off the flexible brake pipe which can be left undisturbed. It is also a good idea to wedge a piece of wood between the pads to ensure that the brake pistons do not come out of position. Clamp and disconnect the brake hose if a rigid pipe stops you from lifting the caliper away.

As you dismantle the wheel bearing lay out the parts in the

1. Two bolts hold caliper

2. Disconnecting brake hose

order you remove them on a clean sheet of paper. You may also find it helpful to make drawings as you go along to help you remember how everything fits together (**fig 3**).

Slide the outer bearing and thrust washer off the axle and then slide the entire brake disc and hub assembly away. In some cases a degree of force is needed to do this because the seal inside the hub will hold the assembly on to the axle. If you

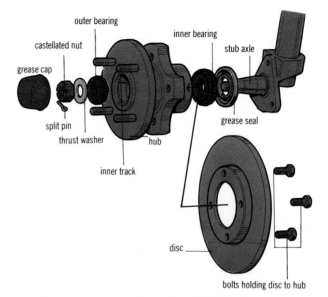

3. How the components on the stub axle fit together

fasten the road wheel back on with the nuts or bolts only finger tight you will probably get enough leverage to remove the hub from the axle.

If you have drum brakes you may need to slacken the adjusters first, but the pro-

cedure should otherwise be the same and the drum and hub assembly should slide away fairly easily. If you have a problem getting the hub off the stub axle — whether with disc brake or drum brake cars — you may have to hire an adjust-

able puller. Position the legs of the puller to grasp the back of the hub while the central column rests squarely on the tip of the stub axle. As the puller is tightened up the legs will draw the hub off.

Once you have got the hub off, use a screwdriver to prise the grease seal out of the back of the hub. This seal should always be replaced by a new one when you are ready to reassemble the bearings. If you are just going to pack the bearings with grease do not worry about removing the tracks from the stub axle. Just clean the old bearings with paraffin or petrol and dry them so that you can check them for worn rollers or general looseness. Check for signs of pitting or other damage on the rollers.

Now oil the bearings and see if they spin freely without any roughness. If you are satisfied that the bearings are still serviceable, work a quantity of high melting point (HMP) grease in between all the rollers making sure that the grease penetrates the whole bearing (**fig 4**). Also pack the hub with grease but leave room for some air. The bearings and hub can now be reassembled.

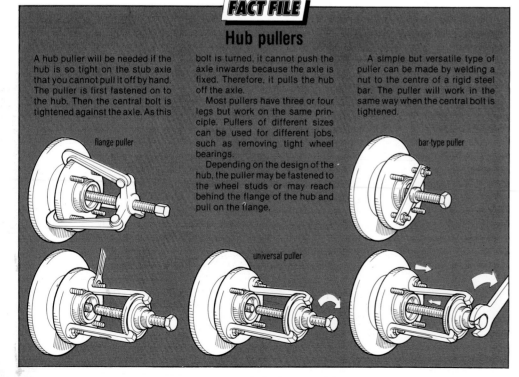

4. Packing new bearing with grease

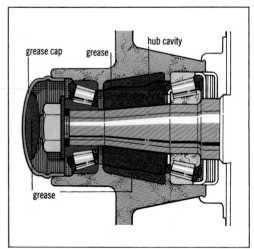

grease cap grease hub cavity

grease

5. Where to apply new grease

1. Removing inner track from hub

3. Fitting new oil seal into place on the stub axle

2. Using old track as drift

If you are fitting new bearings you will have to remove the tracks from the hub. These have to be tapped out using a hammer and a drift. To remove the inner one, carefully tap it out from the opposite side of the hub using the two slots which are usually cut into the hub for this purpose. Work from side to side until the track falls out and then repeat the job on the other track. You may need considerable effort and a heavy hammer to do this. Try not to get the track twisted in the hub or it may jam. If this happens the only solution is to try and crack the bearing using a cold chisel.

In most cases the inner track of the bearing will come away with the outer. But in a few cases the inner track will stay firmly in place on the stub axle. You may be able to get it off using a hammer and drift, in the same way that you removed the bearings from the hub. But on some cars you may end up having to hire a bearing puller.

Your manual may tell you if this is likely. In these cases you will have to consider the cost of hiring tools compared with having the job done professionally — though a bearing puller can come in handy for making a number of repairs easier and may pay for itself in the course of a few jobs.

It is not a good idea to leave old bearing parts in place simply because they are hard to get off. The tracks may be imperceptibly worn or oval, in which case the new parts will have only a very limited lifetime and you will end up having to do the whole job properly anyway.

Once you have cleaned all the parts thoroughly in paraffin you can compare the new tracks and bearings with the old parts to make sure they are the same. Save the old tracks because they are very useful for driving in the new ones (**fig 2**) — never hammer directly on to the new bearing tracks.

Pack the hub containing the new tracks with a generous amount of HMP grease and pack the new bearings thoroughly as well. Install a new seal by tapping it home with a hammer and a block of wood (**fig 3**). The assembly can now be refitted to the stub axle. Tighten the large central nut to the recommended torque setting to make sure that the tracks are pushed all the way on to the stub axle and that the bearings are firmly bedded. Now loosen the nut and adjust the bearings as described in Step 2.

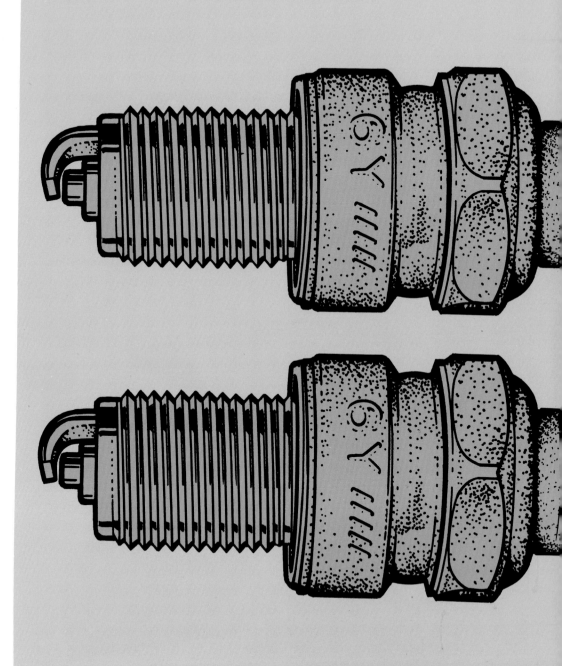

Chapter THREE

RUNNING REPAIRS

When indicators fail to flash

Have your indicator lights stopped flashing or do they flash at the wrong speed? If so, a few simple checks using the minimum of tools will soon pinpoint the fault

Indicator lights which fail to work properly are annoying as well as being illegal and potentially dangerous.

Solving indicator faults is, however, one of the easiest electrical jobs you can do on the car, so do not be afraid to tackle the repair yourself — even if you have little or no experience of this kind of work — you only need patience.

When to do this job
When the indicators do not flash properly
When the indicators do not work at all

What this job involves
Checking the bulbs
Making sure the lamps are earthing properly
Checking the wiring
Testing the flasher unit
Testing the fuse
Testing the switch

Other possible causes and related jobs
Diagnosing electrical faults
Faulty hazard warning lights
Please see Index for page numbers

To do this job
Tools: Flat and crosshead screwdrivers; spanner for lamp unit (maybe); circuit tester; test lamp; sandpaper; thin-nosed pliers
Materials: Plastic electrician's tape (maybe); bulb(s) (maybe); flasher unit (maybe), fuse (maybe); new length of wire (maybe)
Time: 10 minutes to 2 hours
Degree of difficulty: Needs patience and systematic approach

If you have the job professionally done. . .
Do all the lamps now work? Do both sides flash at the same speed?

STEP 1 — MAKE A VISUAL CHECK

You can save yourself a lot of time and effort when you are faultfinding simply by making a careful visual check first and identifying the fault accurately.

If only one indicator bulb is not working, you know that the fuse, the switch and the flasher unit are all sound. The fault must, therefore, lie between the switch and bulb and is most likely to be a blown bulb (see Step 3). But you should check all of the wiring (see Steps 6 & 7) and the bulb-holder (see Step 5) as well.

If the indicators on only one side of the car work then the fault is most likely to be in the switch (see Step 8) or the wiring (see Step 6) where both bulbs share a single wire at some point. It is much less likely that two bulbs or two separate wires would fail simultaneously.

If none of the indicators are working the most likely cause is a blown fuse (see Step 2), but a faulty flasher (see Step 9) or

switch (see Step 8) are other possible causes of the fault.

If another electrical accessory has failed as well as the indicators, suspect the fuse. If the indicators come on but do not flash, suspect the flasher unit (see Step 9). If all the lights work but do not flash, or flash much faster than normal again, suspect the flasher unit or one of the indicator bulbs (see Step 3) — this latter fault is particularly common on cars with additional repeater indicators

fitted to the side of the car.

If the indicators on one side work normally while the other ones light up but do not flash suspect a faulty earth connection (see Step 6).

So, exactly how you approach the job will depend on the symptoms of the fault. But if you feel unable to interpret the clues your car is giving, simply work through the steps one by one and you will be sure to identify and fix the fault.

1. If indicator lights stay on suspect the flasher unit

STEP 2 — CHECK THE FUSE

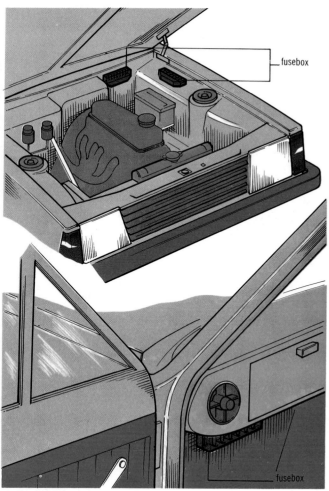

1. Common locations for the fusebox

Your car's handbook will show you the exact location of the fusebox holder. This is a small box usually protected by an easily detachable cover, with the fuses mounted side by side inside. You will usually find it fairly close to the battery, either on the engine or passenger side of the bulkhead, or inside the passenger compartment.

Your manual should also tell you which fuse protects the indicators and which other components are on the same circuit. Often the stoplights, wipers or instruments are on the same fuse — so if any of these are not working as well, the fuse is sure to be at fault.

If there is another fuse in the holder marked with the same rating as the indicator fuse, do a quick test by changing the two fuses over. If the new fuse makes the indicators work again, you will know that either the old fuse needs to be changed, or it was making a bad connection in the holder.

You can test a fuse in its holder with a test lamp. Fasten the test lamp's clip to earth and switch on the ignition. Then touch the test lamp probe in turn to both of the clips which hold the fuse (**fig 2**). If the test lamp lights in both positions the fuse works and is making good contact with the fuseholder. If it lights when touched to one end

only check that the fuse is making a good contact with the fuseholder.

Alternatively, you can test the fuse out of its holder with a circuit tester. Clip one end of the circuit tester to one end of the fuse and touch the tester's probe to the other end. If the fuse is good the circuit tester will light.

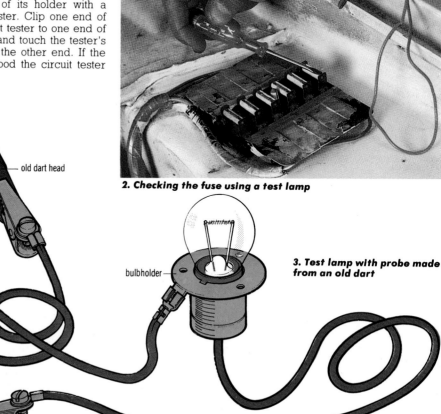

2. Checking the fuse using a test lamp

3. Test lamp with probe made from an old dart

If one indicator has failed, then a blown bulb is the most likely cause — but even if more than one indicator bulb is not working this quick and simple step is a vital part of your checking procedure.

To check a bulb, first undo the screws holding the plastic lens cover and remove the cover. Push the bulb gently inwards and turn it from the socket. If the bulb is stuck in place, spray the socket with penetrating oil and try to move it from side to side to loosen it. If only the glass comes away when you twist the bulb, you will have to remove the metal part with a pair of long-nosed pliers (**figs 2 & 3**).

You can usually check a bulb visually — hold it against the sky and look for a break in the coiled filament. But if you are unsure whether the bulb has blown or not, test it with the test lamp. Clip the lamp to the live terminal of the battery, press the base terminal of the bulb to the earth terminal of the battery, then touch the probe of the test lamp to the metal body of the bulb. If the bulb does not light, renew it.

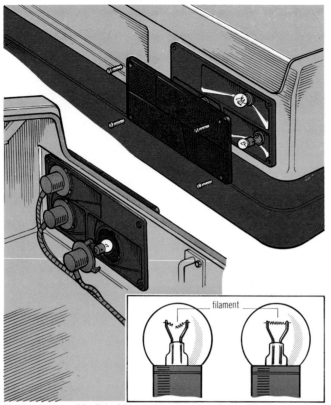

filament

1. Two types of bulbholder (top). Blown and good bulbs (inset)

2. Removing metal part of bulb with pliers

3. Another way of removing a broken bulb

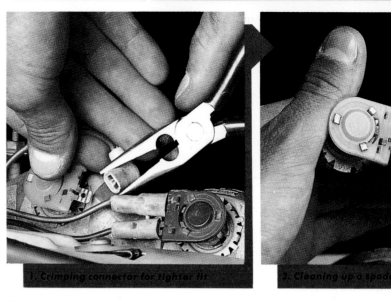

1. Crimping connector for tighter fit

2. Cleaning up a spade terminal

The indicator may have stopped working because the wires to it have worked loose. To test for this, switch on the indicators and check that the wires to the bulbholder are tight and their connections clean. Do this by pulling the connectors apart and, if necessary, cleaning them with emery paper. If poor contact was the problem then the indicator should start working when you connect the wires back together again.

Because indicator bulbs are located low down in the front and rear wings they are often exposed to the elements. So even if the bulbs appear to be tight in their holders electrical contact may not be made. To check this, switch the indicators on and try moving the bulb in its holder — removing and replacing it a couple of times may also do the trick. If the bulb flickers or suddenly lights up, the fault lies in the holder.

If the bulb does not light up the fault may still be in the bulbholder. To make sure, you will need to check whether power is reaching it (see Step 7) and whether it is properly earthed (see Step 6). If these connections both prove sound the holder must be at fault. If cleaning it with emery paper fails to have any effect you will have to renew it.

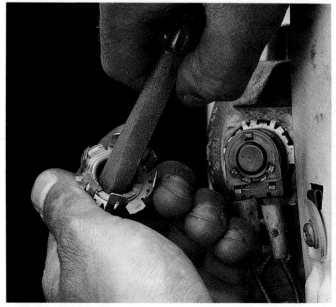

1. Cleaning bulbholder with emery paper

To check the earth connection, remove the indicator bulb and attach one end of the test lamp to the live terminal of the battery. Then touch the probe of the lamp to the inside of the bulbholder. If the lamp lights, the bulbholder is properly earthed. If the tester does not light check the earth connection. Metal bulbholders are usually earthed through their mounting bolts — check they are clean and bright and that they are secured to clean bodywork. If the indicator light unit is made from plastic or if it is insulated from the car's body there will be a separate earth wire or metal strip running from the holder into the main wiring loom or, more likely, to a nearby bolt on the car's body. Make sure that this lead is intact and that the connections are clean and bright.

If the earth connections are corroded, clean them with a file or emery paper and then coat them in petroleum jelly.

If the bulbholder is properly earthed but the indicator still fails to light, the fault may lie in the power supply wire to the bulbholder (see Step 7).

1. Checking bulbholder earth

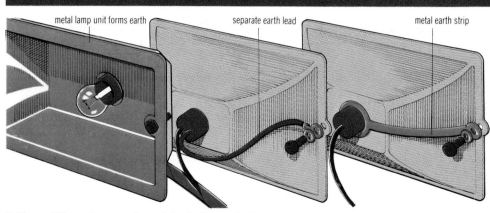

2. Three different types of earth for indicator bulbholder

metal lamp unit forms earth   separate earth lead   metal earth strip

When you have made sure that the fuse and bulb are intact and that the bulbholder is correctly earthed you should check that power is reaching the bulb.

Power is supplied to the indicators by what will probably be the only wire running to the lamp unit from the main wiring harness. If there are several wires, the power supply is the one which connects to the centre of the bulbholder. Check that it has not broken away from the socket.

Turn the indicators on and connect the clip of your test lamp to a good earth and then touch the tester's probe to the live feed. If the test lamp lights, current is reaching the bulbholder and you should check again that the bulb is firmly held and that the wiring connections are tight, since there is no other reason it should not light. If it lights but does not flash — even when the engine is running — the fault must lie in the flasher unit (see Step 9).

If the test lamp does not light, current is not reaching the bulbholder so check the power supply wire (see Step 10).

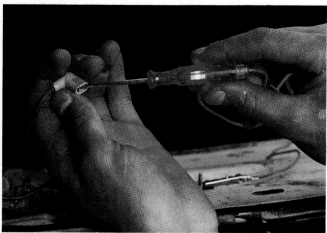

1. Checking that bulbholder feed wire is live

There are two basic circuits used for the indicator lights. Although each individual car may be slightly different, the basic parts are the same. The indicator switch — usually mounted on the steering column — directs the flow of electricity to either the left or right pair of lights. The switch receives its power from the flasher unit which is a small square or round component located either close to the indicator switch or inside the engine compartment.

As the indicator switch is moved in one direction or the other, the circuit to one side or other is completed and power is sent to the lights on one side. The flasher unit repeatedly interrupts the current as a thin strip of steel inside the unit heats up, bends away from an electrical contact, cools down and returns to its former position.

The main difference between indicator circuits is in the way that the warning light is wired into the system. On some modern cars and most older models the flasher unit has three terminals — one for the input, one for the output and the third for the warning light mounted on the dashboard.

Most modern cars, however, do not have the third terminal on the flasher but have the indicator warning light wired across the input and output of the indicator switch.

HOW IT WORKS
The indicator circuit

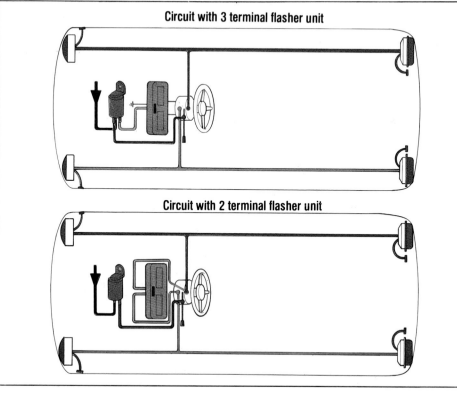

Circuit with 3 terminal flasher unit

Circuit with 2 terminal flasher unit

The indicator switch on most cars is located within a cowling on the steering column. This normally splits into two after the removal of a couple of screws. Do not try to force the cowling apart if it appears stuck. It is easy to overlook one of the fixing screws as they are often deeply recessed.

With the cowling apart you should be able to see the switch — it is usually clamped to the steering column or a stalk from it by two screws and a bracket. If you can see the switch terminals without removing the whole assembly, carry out the checks following with it in place.

If you have to remove it, first make a note of the switch position in relation to the steering column, so that you can refit it in the right place (see Tip — On your marks). Now take out the screws and lift out the complete switch assembly. Pay close attention to the three wires for the indicator lights — the input in the centre and the two outputs, one for each side of the car. Make sure they are firmly fixed to their terminals — as they sometimes move with the lever, a wire can occasionally break away from its terminal. In most cases a broken connection can be soldered back into place, but if you cannot do this yourself, disconnect the plug connecting the switch's wires to the loom and take the whole switch unit to an electrical

2. Checking switch operation

specialist for resoldering.

Another thing which can go wrong with the switch is that the contacts can become burnt or the moving contact can distort so that it no longer makes a connection. If the contacts are accessible try cleaning the contacts with emery paper and bend the moving contact so that when you operate the switch the moving contact once again reaches the static contact.

To check the electrical operation of the switch, use the test lamp to make sure that there is power going into the centre terminal. Clip the lamp's crocodile clip on an earth point, switch the ignition on and touch the terminal with the test lamp probe. The tester should light if the switch is live. If no current is reaching the switch, check the flasher unit and the supply wire that comes from it.

After you have made sure that the switch is live, turn the switch in both directions and check that power is being switched to each of the output wires serving the indicators. Do this by simply touching the tester's probe to the switch's output terminals (**fig 2**). If the power is not getting across there must be a fault inside the switch. These can rarely be repaired so you will have to fit a replacement switch. New ones are quite expensive so you may find it worthwhile buying a secondhand one from a breaker's yard. Check it before you pay for it as described above but you must use a circuit tester, with its built-in power supply, instead of a test lamp.

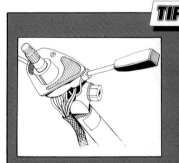

TIP

On your marks
Before removing the indicator switch from the steering column mark its position with a felt-tipped pen or paint. This will help you replace the switch correctly so that the indicators will still cancel properly when the wheel self-centres.

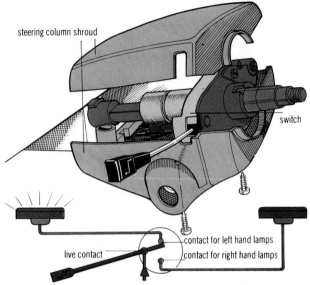

steering column shroud

switch

contact for left hand lamps

contact for right hand lamps

live contact

1. Getting to indicator switch (top). How a typical switch works

1. Checking the flasher unit

2. Checking power is reaching flasher unit

Your car's manual should tell you where the flasher unit is positioned — but the most common locations are the bulkhead and inner wings in the engine compartment, or under the dashboard near the steering column.

To test the flasher unit first disconnect the input and output wires and attach them to each end of the test lamp. If the flasher has three leads ignore the central one as this is for the warning light on the dash. Now turn on the ignition and operate the indicator switch. If the faulty indicators now come on it shows that the flasher unit is faulty and should be replaced.

If the indicators do not light check that power is reaching the flasher unit by attaching the test lamp to the power feed wire and a good earth — if the test lamp fails to light there is a power supply wire fault.

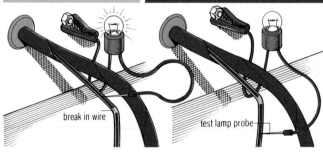

break in wire

test lamp probe

1. Locating a break in the power feed wire

If you know that the switch, flasher unit and fuse are working and live but no current is reaching the bulbholder, the fault must be a break or short-circuit somewhere along the power feed wire to the indicator bulbholder. But the same checking procedure also applies to faultfinding along wires between any two components.

The car's wiring is nearly always colour coded so this will help you to trace wires. Often a wire will disappear through a bulkhead or into a large cluster of wires which are bundled together, but generally a wire stays the same colour along its whole length. A few cars do, however, have numbered wires — each wire having a number at either end. These are harder to trace and may have to be replaced in lengths.

Test any connectors in the line either by peeling back the insulation and using the test lamp probe to the connector terminal, or by pulling the connector apart and touching the probe to the connector terminal on the live side. You can test a wire simply by pushing the point of the probe through the insulation at various points along the wire's length (**fig 1**).

As you work along you should be able to track down the exact location of the fault. If the problem is damaged insulation causing a short circuit, you can patch the wire with insulating tape. If a wire has broken, simply cut out or disconnect the damaged section and renew it.

Overhauling the heater system

In cold weather the car heater is a vital part of your car — and if it packs up you will want to fix it quickly

Although the heater is difficult to remove and expensive to replace if it springs a leak, most problems are not so serious.

Normally, checking the ducting and controls or flushing the system will solve most of your heater problems.

When to do this job
When the heater does not produce any hot air
When you are unable to shut the heater off

What this job involves
Disconnecting heater hoses
Disconnecting and readjusting flap cables
Flushing heater and complete cooling system
Checking and repairing ducting
Removing and checking the water valve

Other possible causes and related jobs
Faulty thermostat
When the engine overheats
Overhauling/replacing heater fan
Leaking heater radiator
Replacing heater unit
Please see Index for page numbers

To do this job
Tools: Spanners; screwdrivers; garden hose or funnel
Materials: Plastic electrician's tape (maybe); small Jubilee clips (maybe); self adhesive sealing strip (maybe); water valve gasket (maybe); water supply
Time: About three hours to overhaul the whole system
Degree of difficulty: Main problems arise from undoing hose clips and removing hoses

If you have the job professionally done . . .
Does the heater produce hot air when required?
Can you get fresh air when you want it? Does the coolant level remain constant over a period of time?
Are there any signs of leaks?

Before you start to check the heater, check the coolant level. Remember that if the engine is hot you must let it cool down before you take the cap off. If the level is low check for leaks (see Step 2).

It is also possible that though the heater itself is getting hot, the hot air is being obstructed for some reason. So check by feeling the flow of air out of each side of the demister slots or heater outlets (**fig 1**). If it is difficult to check, lay tissue paper over the slots, holding one side down with masking tape. The air flow should blow the tissue paper up almost equally on both sides. If it does not then part of the heater system or the ducting must be at fault, see Steps 3 and 4.

With the engine hot and running, put the blower on full and check that the air is unheated with the temperature control set in the cold position but that it is heated with the control in the hot position. If it is

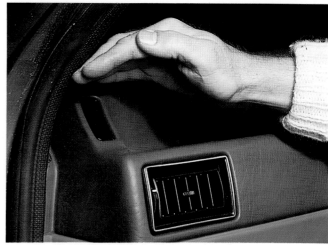

1. Feeling for airflow from the heater outlets

not operating correctly then either the control valves are at fault or the water is not flowing through the heater radiator — see Steps 4, 5 and 6. Remember not to run the engine in a confined space as exhaust gases are dangerous.

If the heater becomes more effective when the engine is revved up this is unlikely to be a heater problem but is more likely to be related to the operation of the fan belt or water pump. Checking the fan belt is covered on page 217.

HOW IT WORKS

How the heater works

When travelling at speed, the pressure build-up in front of the car forces air into a box, called the plenum chamber, which is located in front of the windscreen under the bonnet. The air is then forced into the heater where some of it is directed past the heater core, which is just a small radiator. The air is warmed by the heater and passed to the demister or the passenger compartment.

The rest of the air is directed to the fresh air vents, normally mounted on the dash panel. Slots at the rear of the passenger compartment allow the air to escape and thus stop a build-up of pressure inside the car.

The blower motor simply speeds up the flow of air for increased heating or ventilation.

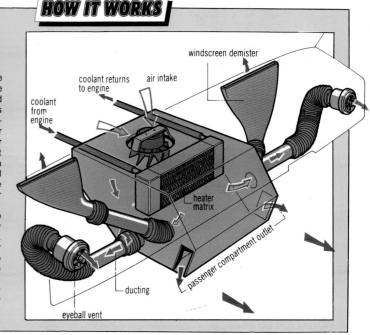

If there is a drop in the coolant level and you have already checked the cooling system then the problem could be caused by a leak from either the heater core, the water valve or the hoses connecting the heater core to the engine (**fig 3**).

The water in the cooling system usually has antifreeze mixed with it. Take care with this because it is poisonous and will quickly strip the paint from the car's bodywork if you spill it. If you do accidentally spill some on the bodywork, wash it off immediately with lots of water. When you are looking for coolant leaks, check the carpets, as you might be able to detect a smell of antifreeze if they are wet from coolant. Even if there are no tell-tale white stains, use tissues to wipe around the heater. A small amount of water will show up well on a tissue, especially if you use a coloured one.

When you are working under the dashboard, take care not to disturb any wiring and if any trim has to be unscrewed check the length of the screws to make sure they go back in the correct holes. Draw a sketch if the arrangement is complicated.

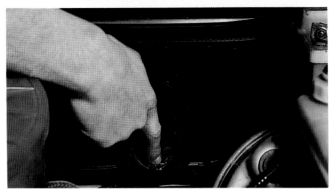
1. Unblock the plenum chamber drain hole or tube

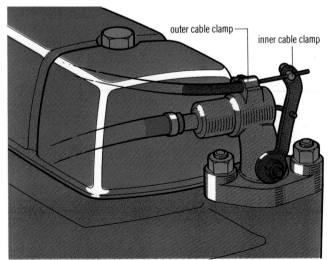

outer cable clamp

inner cable clamp

2. Some cars have a cylinder head mounted water valve

If you can see from inside the car where the pipes or hoses pass through the bulkhead behind the heater, then check for leaks here. However, if you find that the heater is mounted tight up against the bulkhead you will have to check from the engine compartment side. Open the bonnet and look for where the pipes emerge at one side of the plenum chamber. The joint here between the metal pipes and the heater hoses is a likely place for leaks, so it might be worth your while replacing the old hose clips with new worm drive (Jubilee) ones. On some cars, however, you may have to remove a plastic cowling which covers the plenum chamber before you

3. Check for leaks where the hose joins the heater

can get to the pipes and hoses.

If you cannot find any faults in the system but water still comes from the heater unit, then the heater core must be leaking.

The core is expensive and to replace it will almost certainly mean that the heater has to come out, so try a radiator sealant first. Follow the instructions carefully, but remember to turn the heater to the hottest setting or else the water and sealant will not go through the core.

The heater valve is another area where the water may be leaking, so again check this using tissues if the leak is not easily detectable. Not all heater valves are near the heater — some may be hidden in different places behind the dashboard, especially if they are thermostatically controlled, as the heat from the heater would upset their operation. Some heater valves are mounted on the top of the engine block as is the case with some early Austin and Morris models.

If the heater hose is leaking at the point where it joins the heater valve then the hoses can be removed after you have drained the cooling system. Further details on draining the system are given in Step 6.

Remove any scale from the outside of the heater valve pipes before refitting the hoses.

4. Plenum chamber leak test

If you replace any hose clips use new worm drive (Jubilee) clips which will give a better seal than the wire type which may originally have been fitted.

If water is leaking into the car but there are no problems with the heater and no fluid loss from the cooling system then rainwater could be coming through the heater itself. Check for water collecting in the plenum chamber and leaking into the heater through the passages that the fresh air normally takes. This chamber usually has drainpipes or simply a hole at the bottom (**fig 1**) which can easily be blocked by debris such as leaves. Check this by pulling off the drain pipe or duct, or lifting the covering flap.

The success of this cleaning operation can be checked by pouring water into the plenum chamber (**fig 4**) and checking that it does not enter the heater and therefore the car. Do not be overenthusiastic with this test as the chamber is not designed to withstand buckets of water, but just heavy rain. Place a bowl under the drain outlet if you are doing this test in a garage.

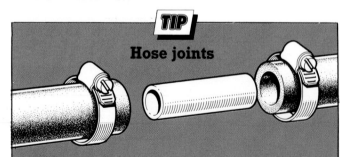

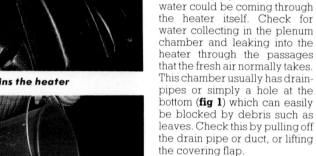

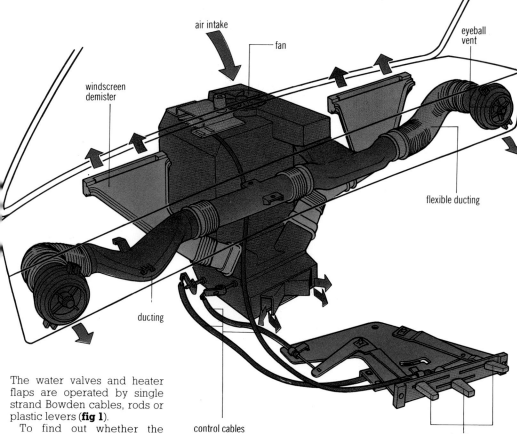

1. *The layout of the heater, vents and controls*

The water valves and heater flaps are operated by single strand Bowden cables, rods or plastic levers (**fig 1**).

To find out whether the controls work properly, operate each lever in turn and check that the flap it operates opens and closes fully. If it sticks or does not work properly, use a spray lubricant such as WD-40. If this does not free it then you will have to find out where in the control system the fault lies.

First disconnect the cable from the water valve or flap. If the lever now operates freely then the trouble lies in the water valve or flap. The flap could be blocked by debris or just in need of lubrication. For details of how to free the water valve, see Step 5. If the lever is stiff, this may be because it is rubbing on the top or bottom of the dashboard slot from which it protrudes. If so, pull off the

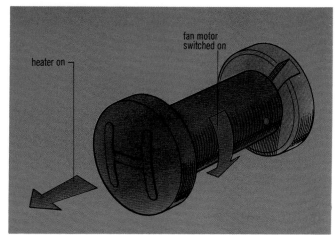

2. *Some cars have a multipurpose heater control*

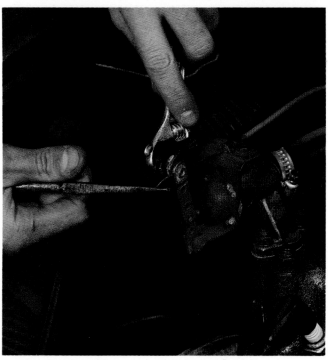

3. *Adjusting the cable on an engine mounted valve*

plastic knob and carefully bend the lever until it clears both the slot and any other control levers before refitting the knob.

If the cable is stiff it could simply need lubrication. You can do this by spraying down the side of the inner cable where it enters the outer one while operating the lever. This draws the lubricant along the total length of the cable. The routing of the cable may be causing its stiffness, in which case moving the cable slightly into a new position may free it, but you might also have to tie or tape it in place. If the lever on the dashboard itself is causing the problem then it is probably just in need of a good clean from all the fluff and dirt that collects around it. After cleaning spray it with lubricant.

If the lever operates two flaps and it is difficult to tell which one is causing the problem then check to see which flap is

moving the least and which cable is bowing or flexing — this one will be causing the problem.

If you find that cleaning and lubricating the heater controls does not make a significant improvement, or if the control lever or slider will not go to each

extent of its movement, then the problem could just be one of adjustment. Check first, though, that your car's heater is not designed to give a continual slight air bleed.

You can adjust most cables from inside the car at either the lever end or the heater end. However, with certain cars which have the heater valve fitted to the engine block or cylinder head you will have to make the adjustment under the bonnet.

The inner cable normally has coiled ends which snap over stubs on the control and flap levers and the outer cable is usually held by a spring clip. It is here that any adjustment can be made.

To adjust the cable, first check in your handbook to see whether you adjust the cables with the controls fully on or fully off, then disconnect or unclamp the cable. Set both the heater control and the valve lever to fully on or off, then pull the cable almost tight. Clamp the outer cable to its bracket with the metal clip or the clamp screw.

If you have a car with an engine mounted water valve and are adjusting the cable under the bonnet, you will usually have to adjust the inner cable instead. This is secured by a small bolt or screw.

4. *Another type of adjuster — normally inside the car*

There are three different types of ducting commonly used in car heating systems: rubber, plastic and papier mache. These can be reinforced by a wire spiral or, in the case of papier mache, tin foil. The plastic and papier mache types of ducting are very fragile and must be treated carefully.

Check the ducting by switching the blower on and feeling along the tubing for any leaks, starting at the heater and working your way along the duct. Take care not to disturb any electrical wiring when you do this.

The most common causes of an air leak are split or disconnected ducting. Before pushing the ducting back on, check if it was secured by a clip. If it was, loosen off the clip, refit the ducting and then carefully tighten the clip. If the clip will not secure it, then try using plastic tape.

Make sure that the ducting does not foul the steering column or the pedals when they are operated. You can use cable ties or plastic tape to secure it in the best position.

If the ducting is split it can be glued together or bound with tape. However, masking tape will stick better to papier mache ducting. Test the system again before refitting any trim that you had to remove and make sure that no electrical connections have been disturbed.

Check that the heater flaps are sealing properly when closed, but bear in mind that some heater flaps are not meant

1. Feel along all the ducting for air leaks

to close fully. It should be easy enough to see which type you have, as you will be able to see if the seals on the flaps are compressed or not.

If the foam or felt sealing strip around the edge of the flap is damaged and there is enough working space around it, you can replace it with domestic draught excluder which you can buy pre-glued in a number of sizes from any good DIY or hardware shop. Before you apply it, make sure that the surface of the flap is completely clean and dry.

If the heater is only working on one side of the car but there are no leaks then the ducting may have collapsed internally or become blocked. Remove the ducting completely and check the inside for debris and blockages. When you refit it make sure that it does not collapse or bend.

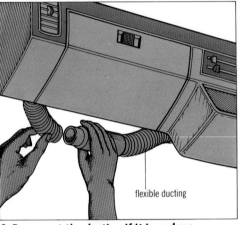

2. Reconnect the ducting if it is undone

flexible ducting

3. Tape up any splits in the ducting

First of all make sure that you do have a water valve in the system. On some heaters the temperature control depends upon the blending of the air and there is no water valve. It used to be common practice to have a water valve on the engine which you would turn on in the autumn and off in the summer. On certain Austin Rover cars the water valve remains on the engine (fig 2) but is operated by a lever from inside the car by a flexible cable.

There are two basic types of water valve — one with a moving plunger and the other with a rotating cylinder (fig 1). Before removing the water valve, drain the cooling system (see Step 6) and check that you have the necessary gasket for the water valve if one is required. A gasket is usually only fitted when the water valve

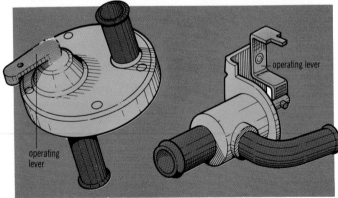

operating lever

operating lever

1. Water valves come in two basic types

is a bolt-on type, fitted to the engine or side of the heater. If you do not have a gasket or you are not sure if one is required then have a tube of instant gasket sealant handy.

Even with the system fully drained disconnecting the hoses may allow a small quantity of coolant to leak out, so have a bowl under the heater ready to collect any remaining fluid. Remove the clips and ease off these hoses. A twist of the hose may help break the seal to the water valve and

make it easier to pull off. Take care as some types of water valve are fragile and could break. Disconnect the operating cables or levers, remove the securing bolts (if any) and remove the water valve. Make a sketch of the levers and positions to make sure there is no delay during refitting when you try and remember their original positions.

Once you have taken off the water valve operate it by hand and check that it opens and closes fully. If it is blocked by rust, debris or scale carefully scrape away the blocking particles and spray with a lubricant such as WD-40, operating the lever as you do so until the valve operates fully and freely.

If the valve does not respond to cleaning and lubrication it will

2. Renew the water valve gasket if it is leaking

have to be replaced. These valves are sealed for life and it is not possible to dismantle and repair them.

After fitting, adjust the cable and controls (see Step 6) so that the water valve is fully closed when the controls are set to the cold position and fully open when set to the hot position. Refill the cooling system, checking for leaks. Run the engine for a while, allow it to cool and then recheck the coolant level. Oil the valve occasionally to keep it reliable.

Over a period of years the cooling system and heater core will become contaminated and eventually blocked, especially if you have used an antifreeze which does not contain anti-corrosion additives. The complete cooling system should then be flushed. If you only flush the heater core you run the risk of the blockage recurring once the engine is restarted and debris in the engine and radiator circulate through the narrow channels of the heater.

Check the pipes first by pulling them off their stubs at either end. Scale normally builds up in the ends of pipes because of the step down to the reduced diameter of the stub. You will be able to clear the ends of the pipe quite easily with a screwdriver then flush out the debris with a hose.

To flush the heater core, proceed as if you were flushing the whole cooling system (see page 218). Drain the radiator by the drain plug or tap (if neither is fitted simply remove the bottom hose). If the heater is mounted low down, you will also have to drain the engine by undoing the plug or tap in the side of the

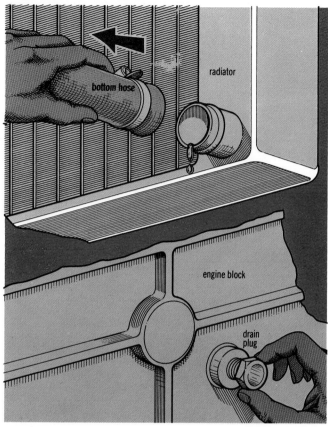

1. Drain coolant by removing the bottom hose and drain plug

2. Disconnecting the hose at the engine end

Reverse flushing

If the heater is really badly blocked and resists all attempts to clear it, try reverse flushing with a helper turning the tap on and off to interrupt the water flow. Meanwhile, poke a piece of flexible wire (such as a pipe cleaner) or even a thin plastic tube or rod through the heater inlet and attempt to clear the obstruction with that. Do not poke too hard or you may damage the heater core.

TIP

Bleeding valves

It is difficult to completely bleed all the air from some cooling systems and a heater may stop working because of an airlock. This will usually happen in the highest pipe leading to the heater and can be cured by removing the pipe from its connection with the engine running and letting the air bubble out.

But this will also mean a loss of coolant (which may contain expensive anti-freeze). So if you prefer, you can buy a cooling system bleed valve (as used on, for example, a Renault 5) or use a bicycle inner tube valve body with a metal cap and rubber seal. Drill a hole in the top of the heater hose as near as possible to the heater end of the offending pipe, allowing for connection to the heater pipe and fit the valve in, screwing down the nut and washer to secure it. You can now slacken the

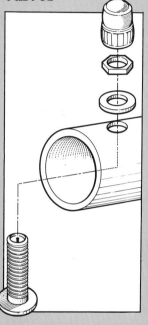

valve to release any air, without losing much coolant. The valve can then be screwed down.

engine block, if fitted (**fig 1**). To drain the heater, turn it to the hot setting and allow the coolant to pour out. Because the heater core is often lower than the point where the hoses pass through the bulkhead the coolant will not drain out by itself. It will therefore need to be flushed. Disconnect the two heater hoses from the engine (these are the hoses that pass through the bulkhead or attach to the heater pipes which pass through the bulkhead) at the engine end (**fig 2**), leaving the two lengths of hose hanging free.

Place one end of one hose into a bucket or allow it to drain directly on to the ground and connect a garden hose to the

other one (**fig 3**) (if you don't have a garden hose, pour water into a funnel pushed into the end of the heater hose) and flush through gently until clear water comes out. Repeat in the opposite direction to make absolutely sure the core is clear. The channels of the core are not very robust, particularly if they have suffered corrosion, so do not use much water pressure.

When the heater core and engine are clear, close the drain tap and refit the plugs on the engine and radiator. Connect the free end of the heater hose on to the engine with the water still slowly passing through as this will help to prevent an airlock. Then disconnect the garden hose from the other heater hose and fit the heater hose to its stub, taking care not to let too much water escape as you do. Refill the cooling system with the correct mixture of water and antifreeze. Run the engine until the radiator gets hot, then stop the engine and let things cool down for a while. When the engine is cool, check the coolant level and top it up if necessary.

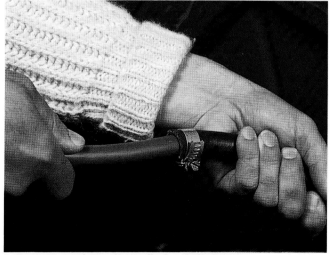

3. Connect up a hose pipe to flush out the system

When wipers won't wipe

Wipers which do not clear the screen properly are not just annoying — they are dangerous too. So if your wipers are giving problems, don't delay — fix them now

Windscreen wipers are very important for safe driving in bad weather. Worn wipers can make a car very unpleasant and difficult to drive in heavy rain. Furthermore, worn or faulty wipers will also mean the car will fail the MOT road-worthiness test. Wiper parts are not expensive and by checking them yourself you can save a lot of unnecessary expense and make sure your car is safe to drive in all weathers.

When to do this job
When the wipers stop working or work badly

What this job involves
Renewing wiper blades and arms
Removing the wiper motor
Removing the wiper linkage
Renewing wiper motor brushes
Overhauling the wiper linkage

Other possible causes and related jobs
Checking for electrical faults
Please see Index for page numbers

To do this job
Tools: Spanners or sockets; screwdrivers; pliers; crimping tool (maybe); test lamp or circuit tester (maybe); soldering iron (maybe)
Materials: Possibly: wiper blades; wiper arms; wiper motor brushes; wiper rack; wheel boxes; wire; crimping connectors; solder
Time: Varies depending on what sort of wiper linkage your car has. Wiper blades and arms only: less than an hour
Degree of difficulty: Changing blades and arms not difficult, other repairs time consuming rather than difficult

If you have the job professionally done . . .
Do the wipers work smoothly and clear the screen?
Does the motor work quietly and at the right speed?

1. A blade like this needs renewing

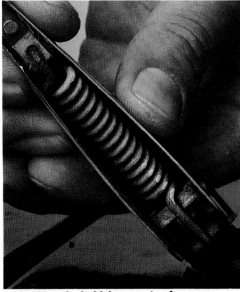

2. Checking the hold down spring for wear

First check that the windscreen is clean and clear of all squashed insects and dirt. No matter how good your wipers are, they will not be able to clear baked on filth from the screen.

3. Twisting the wiper arm

Wet the screen and turn the wipers on — watch them as they go across the screen. They should travel smoothly and should clear the screen without smearing or juddering. Make sure you keep the screen wet while the wipers are on to avoid straining the wiper motor or wearing the blades. Also make sure that the screenwashers have an additive in the water, either one of the proprietary brands available from accessory shops, or meths which acts as antifreeze as well as a screen cleaner.

If the wipers leave streaks or do not clear the screen, check the wiper rubbers — if they are cracked or frayed (**fig 1**), they must be renewed (see Step 2).

When the wipers judder across the screen or fail to clear the edges, the problem may be faulty wiper arms or an invisible film of grease on the screen. Try cleaning the screen with methy-lated spirit and a cloth or follow the Tip box. If this does not work then the arms are faulty — either the hold down spring (**fig 2**) is weak or broken, or the arm is not lying parallel to the screen. Springs are not available as spares and the only option is to buy a new arm, but you may be able to adjust the arm in relation to the windscreen.

To do this take the wiper blade off the arm (Step 2) and rest the arm on the glass. If it is not parallel with the surface of the screen twist it carefully with pliers (**fig 3**) until it is.

Try the wipers again. If there is no improvement you must change the wiper arm for a new one (see Step 3).

TIP

Screen clean
A good (if unlikely) way of cleaning your windscreen is to use toothpaste. Rub it on to a lightly dampened screen, spreading it all over, and then wash it off with clean water.

The toothpaste acts like a mild abrasive cleaner and takes off the film of dirt and grease on the screen.

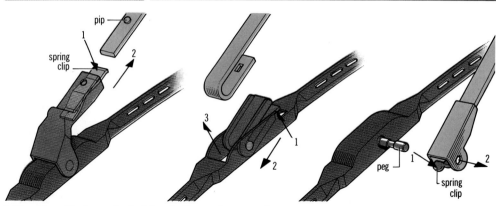

1. The wiper blade can be held on to its arm in several ways

Wiper blades come in many designs and sizes, so it is important that you get the right ones for your car. You also have the choice of buying a complete new blade or a cheaper rubber insert which fits into the blade.

With either a new blade or a refill you must detach the wiper blade from its arm. Most wiper blades are fixed to their arms in one of three ways (**fig 1**).

The most common type is a blade with a straight bayonet that push-fits on to the end of the arm. To release the blade simply insert a small screwdriver between the arm and the spring clip and pull the blade off the arm.

The second type of blade has a pivot pin that locates in a U-shaped arm. Use a small screwdriver to relieve the tension of the spring clip that holds the pin in place and pull the blade off.

The third type of blade has a pin that is locked by a spring into a hole on the arm. Push down the small clip with a screwdriver and pull the blade away — if it is tight turn the blade to break the rust seal.

If you are just changing the old blade for a new one all you need to do is fit the new one to the arm. To do this, push the blade back on to the arm until the spring clip engages and give it a gentle tug to make sure it is fully home.

If you are fitting new rubbers you must remove the old rubbers from the blade. The rubbers can be held to the blade in several ways (**fig 3**) — all of them are fiddly to remove. If you are in doubt, the refill packet should have full instructions.

Now fit the new rubber to the blade, making sure the backing strip locates through all the retaining arms, and refit the blade back on to the arm.

2. Levering the spring clip

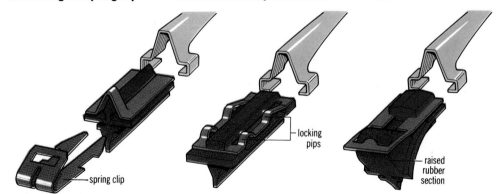

3. The rubber is fixed into the blade by a clip or by a raised section in the rubber

Wiper arms are quite simple to change. Before you take the arm off, park the wipers and mark the position of the blade on the screen with a wash-off felt tip pen or chalk. This will help with aligning the new arm later.

Some arms are held by a simple spring clip (**fig 2**) while others have a fixing nut which is sometimes hidden under a hinged cover or push-fit cap (**fig 1**). To protect the paintwork from damage as you remove the wiper arm, use a rag around the wiper spindle.

The spring type is removed by carefully levering the edge of the clip away from the wiper spindle with a small screwdriver and then prising the arm off the spindle with a large screwdriver or spanner (**fig 3**). The pressure of the hold down spring will make this difficult — try to keep the arm straight as you lift it off.

If your car has bolt-on arms, first prise up the cover (if fitted) and then undo the nut. Lever the arm off the spindle taking care not to damage the paintwork. If you are not renewing the blade take it off the arm (Step 2).

Fitting the new arms is easy, but ensure that the arm is in the same position as the old one.

Fit the blade to the arm (Step 2) and then position the arm so that the blade lines up with the mark made with the felt pen. Once you are satisfied the alignment is correct fit the arm to the spindle. Check that the spring clip is engaged or the nut is tightened, and then test the wipers. If they still judder then the wiper linkage itself may be sticking and it will have to be removed and checked (see Step 8 or Alternative step 8).

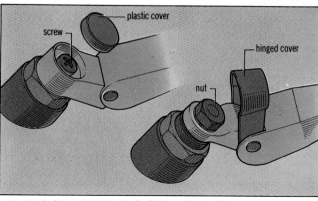

1. Fixing bolts or screws are hidden under a cap

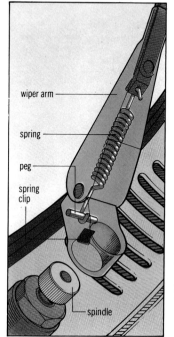

2. This arm is fixed by a clip

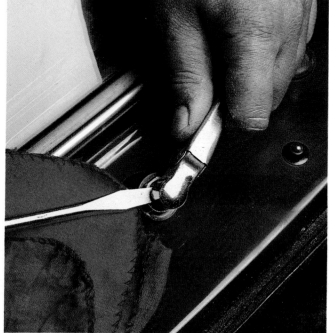

3. Using a screwdriver to prise up the fixing clip

STEP 4 — CHECK THE MOTOR SPEED

If your car's wipers operate slowly across a wet screen, you should check the speed at which the electric motor operates. To do this first remove the wiper blades and arms complete (Step 3). Now make a mark on the wiper spindle with a felt tip pen. Then, while an assistant operates the wiper switch, check the speed at which the spindles move using a watch.

If your car has single speed

1. Marking the spindle

wipers they should move from left to right and back again between 35 and 40 times per minute. Two speed motors operate at a similar speed on the low setting, but at the higher rate should move between 55 and 60 times per minute. If your check reveals sluggish performance, check the drive mechanism (Step 6). Otherwise the fault lies in the motor (Step 9) or its power supply or earth (Step 5).

STEP 5 — CHECK THE ELECTRICAL SYSTEM

If your car's wipers fail to operate, the first step is to check the system's electrical circuit.

The most common fault is that a fuse will blow. Simply replacing the fuse is not the answer, however — you should find out why it failed. The fault may lie in the wiring of the wipers, or in a seized motor, but it may also lie in the circuit of another component which shares the same fuse as the wipers.

Faults in the wiring can often

be identified by their nature, especially on modern wipers with several modes of operation, such as fast, slow and intermittent. The switch has one position for each mode, so if only one of the systems has failed it is possible that the fault lies in that part of the switch or its wiring. If nothing works, however, check that power is reaching the wiper switch and that the motor is earthed. Step 6 shows possible locations for the

motor. Pages 192-196 show you how to carry out these tests. Remember that new sections of wire should be soldered or crimped to existing sections if the job is to be permanent.

Make sure you check the motor's earth lead, as a faulty earth can make the motor run badly. If you find no fault in the wiring then you must remove the motor and possibly its linkage (Step 7 or Alternative 7) to check the brushes.

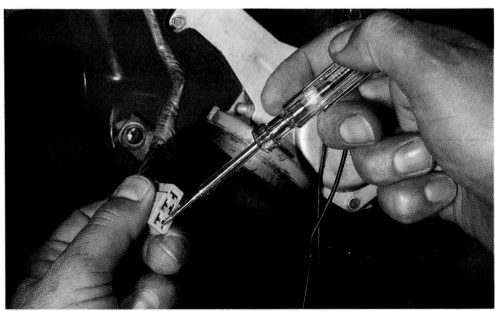

1. Checking the multi-connector plug for power with a pointed test lamp

STEP 6 — CHECK THE DRIVE MECHANISM

If the wipers judder across the screen and operate slowly, or only one works, you should check the drive mechanism.

The easiest part of the drive mechanism to check is the splines — the vertical grooves on each wheel box spindle. Remove the wiper arms (see Step 3) and inspect the condition of the splines (**fig 4**). If they are worn so badly that the end of the shaft is virtually smooth, it may be possible for the spindle to rotate inside the arm. If this is the case the wheelbox must be replaced (see Step 8 or Alternative step 8).

Wiper drive mechanisms and motors are usually located in one of three positions: immediately behind the dashboard or beneath the scuttle as shown in **fig 1**; or inside the engine compartment (**fig 2**). The biggest problem in carrying out any checks will be getting at the mechanism.

With rack and wheelbox systems, you can check that the drive from the motor is being transmitted to the rack before taking out the mechanism.

First, find the motor, which is usually situated in the engine bay. Then unscrew the union nut on the motor (**fig 3**). Get someone to operate the wipers for a moment as you watch the action of the rack. If you can see the rack moving, the fault is in

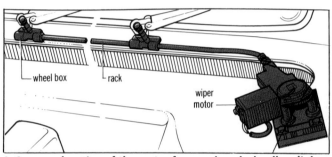

1. Pushrod linkages are mounted under the dash or scuttle

2. Common location of the motor for a rack and wheelbox linkage

the wheelboxes or further up the rack. If the motor works but the rack does not then a connecting rod may have broken inside the motor or the rack may be broken. To fit a new rack see Alternative 7.

As they are more compact, pushrod systems are normally mounted behind the dashboard, but are sometimes mounted under the rear edge of the engine compartment —

often known as the scuttle. This means they are often difficult to get at but you should be able to make enough of an inspection to find out whether any of the rods are broken or have fallen off. If they are, and the unit is under the dash, you will have to remove the whole assembly (see Step 7). If it is under the front scuttle the job is easier but you may have to remove a cover before you can get to it.

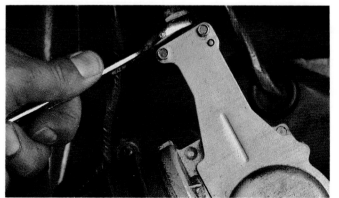

3. Undoing the union nut from the motor

4. Badly worn wiper spindle

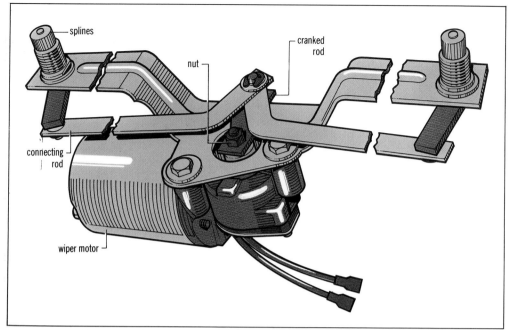

- splines
- nut
- cranked rod
- connecting rod
- wiper motor

1. A typical pushrod wiper linkage looks like this one

Before you remove the wiper mechanism, disconnect the battery earth lead for safety. Then remove the wiper arms and blades (Step 3) and store them carefully.

If the mechanism is behind the dashboard, you will have to remove the dash with great care in order to gain access. If it is

2. Undoing the spindle nut

inside the engine compartment, you will have to take off a plastic cover or air intake before you can remove it.

With the dash or intake off you can see the wiper assembly. First remove the electrical connection, usually just a multi-connector plug, which pulls out. Otherwise there are separate connectors — mark each one as you remove it so you can refit it correctly.

Some pushrod systems are held in place by nuts or bolts on the motor bracket but, in many cases, the nuts holding the wheelboxes to the body act as the securing nuts for the complete system. First slacken off the large nuts around the wheelbox spindles at the base of the windscreen (**fig 2**). Some cars do not have these nuts — the securing bolts are on the wiper motor bracket alone. Get someone to support the assembly as you remove all the bolts or screws, then gently pull the assembly free.

Once all the fixings are removed carefully withdraw the assembly. In most cases it will come straight out through a cut-out in the dashboard (**fig 3**); otherwise you will have to manoeuvre it out taking care not to catch it on any wires.

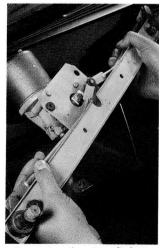

3. Removing the wiper linkage

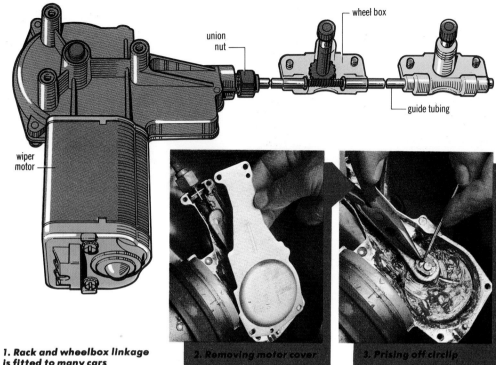

- wheel box
- union nut
- guide tubing
- wiper motor

1. Rack and wheelbox linkage is fitted to many cars

2. Removing motor cover

3. Prising off circlip

To remove a rack and wheelbox wiper linkage, first disconnect the battery earth lead to avoid a short circuit.

Now find the motor. First undo the electrical connector and then undo the nut where the rack fits into the motor casing. Undo the small bolts which hold the motor cover plate on (**fig 2**) then remove it.

Take off the connecting rod

from the motor drive cog to the rack — it may be secured by a circlip. If it is, prise it off with a small screwdriver and pliers (**fig 3**). Now remove the bolts or screws holding the motor.

The next step is to remove the rack. This just pulls out of its guide tubing. Grasp the end firmly and slowly pull the rack out. If you are renewing the rack, all you need to do is push

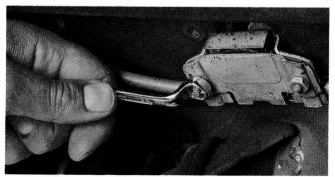

4. Undoing the wheelbox fixing nuts

the new one into the guide tubing and refit the motor. Otherwise store it carefully.

The only parts left to remove are the wheelboxes. Getting to these is often tricky or time consuming as you may have to remove the dashboard to get at them.

When you have gained access to the wheelboxes, slacken off the nuts or bolts which hold the wheelboxes together (**fig 4**).

Once the bolts are slackened, you can withdraw the guide tube and take it out of the car.

Next, get someone to hold the wheelbox from inside the car while you slacken the nuts around the spindles at the base of the windscreen. As each nut is removed withdraw the wheelbox making a note of where any washers, spacers or seals fit. You can now check the condition of the wheelbox gears (Alternative step 8).

1. Unbolt the arm

2. Remove linkage fixings

3. Grease linkage bushes

If the wipers judder or are slow the linkage may need lubricating. With the drive mechanism removed from the car carry out a careful inspection, looking for any signs of wear.

On a pushrod system check the rods are not cracked or sheared. If they are, it may be possible to have them welded; otherwise you will have to get a new rod from the scrapyard or buy a complete assembly. If the bearings are sloppy, the whole linkage appears slack, or the

wheelbox splines are worn, then the only remedy is to get hold of another linkage since spare parts are not available.

Check also for any stiffness in the linkage. If it is stiff then dismantle the linkage to lubricate it.

To remove the rods, first undo the cranked operating arm from the motor spindle (fig 1). This is held by a circlip or a nut. If your motor does not have a fixing on the motor shaft remove the rods from the end of the cranked arm instead.

Now undo the linkage brackets from the motor (fig 2) and remove the linkage. Take off each rod, marking it so you know which one goes where, and clean the whole lot carefully with a paraffin soaked rag.

Refit the rods one at a time, remembering to lubricate each joint with high melting point grease (fig 3). Unless you are going to fit new brushes, refit the wiper motor to the linkage and refit the whole assembly to the car, making sure you refit all the washers, pacers or seats.

With the rack and wheelboxes out of the car you can check them for wear. The teeth on the wheelbox gears should not be worn (fig 1) — if they are then you will need new wheelboxes. If the drive spindles are worn, then again you will have to fit new wheelboxes. Check the rack for signs of scuffing or wear — though even when there does not appear to be any, if the wheelboxes are worn it is likely the rack is too.

To fit the new wheelboxes slot them into place and screw up the nut handtight from the outside of the car, remembering to use all the necessary washers and spacers. Refit the guide tubes, making sure they locate

properly into the wheelboxes and then tighten up the wheelbox screws. Finally tighten up the wheelbox securing nut on the outside of the car. You can now refit the rack.

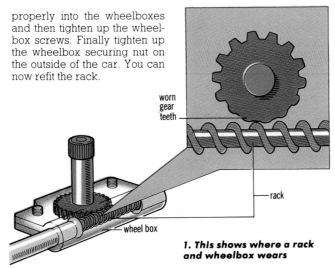

worn gear teeth

rack

wheel box

1. This shows where a rack and wheelbox wears

In many cases a motor can be rejuvenated by fitting new brushes, but first you need to know what sort of motor is fitted to your car.

There are two types of motor — the permanent magnet type which has a round body, and the field wound type which has a square body.

To change the brushes on a permanent magnet motor first check for alignment marks on the body and gearbox casing. If there are none scribe a line on both parts so you can line them up later, or the motor may operate the wrong way.

Now undo the two through bolts and pull the motor casing off the wiper gearbox. The commutator comes off with the motor casing leaving the brushes attached to the gearbox casing.

Your motor may have two or

three brushes depending on whether you have a single or two speed motor but removal is the same in both cases.

Undo the screws holding the brush pack — it comes away attached to the wires. The new brushes have to be soldered to the wires, so if you cannot solder take the motor to an auto electrician to have this done. Refit the motor to the gearbox, holding the brushes clear of the commutator (see Tip — Hold that brush). Make sure the marks line up, then refit the bolts.

To change the brushes on a field wound motor, first undo the two through screws which hold the endplate, then pull it off to expose the brushes.

Lift out the fibre locking plate and pull the brushes outwards against the spring pressure. Lift them clear of the commutator

then slowly slacken off the pressure.

Check the brushes for length — any that are less than 1/8 in. (3 mm) long need changing. Also check the surface of the commutator — remove any pitting you find with fine glasspaper then wipe it with a meths soaked rag. Refit the brushes to the motor, then fit the end plate.

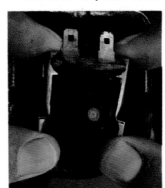

1. Field wound brushes

2. Newer type of brush pack

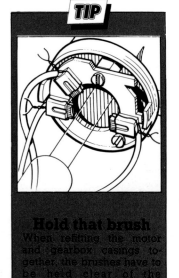

TIP

Hold that brush

When refitting the motor and gearbox casings together, the brushes have to be held clear of the armature. Wind a couple of turns of thin fuse wire around each brush.

Push the two casings together until the brushes are over the commutator, then remove the wire.

When you have reassembled and refitted the wiper motor and drive mechanism to the car, you may find it necessary to adjust the wiper's self-parking mechanism. On some older field wound motors this is done by turning the metal dome (fig 1) on the top of the motor until the wipers park in the desired place on the screen in line with the marks you made.

But on permanent magnet types the multi-connector socket incorporates the parking switch. This will be automatically set when it is fitted to the wiper motor at the factory. On this type you will have to operate the wiper switch while the wiper arms are removed. Once the wiper motor parks you can refit the arms in the correct position (see Step 3).

1. Setting the parking dome

Make yourself heard

Your car must have a device which will give 'audible warning of approach'. So make sure your horn works well

The car horn is usually one component that most people are quite unconcerned about. But on some occasions, the original fitted horn may prove unsatisfactory. If you spend a lot of time driving in the country or on motorways, a powerful horn may be essential to let others know you are coming. So if your existing horn is feeble, you may wish to either bring it back to life, or fit air horns, which will give a much more strident sound than those fitted as original equipment.

When to do this job
When you are renewing or mending existing horns or wish to replace an electric horn with more effective air horns.

What this job involves
Testing the existing horn circuit
Mounting the new horns and compressor
Tapping into existing wiring
Installing a changeover switch

Related jobs in this handbook
Fitting extra driving lights
Tracking down electrical faults
Please see Index for page numbers

To do this job
Tools: Spanners; screwdrivers; test lamp; crimping tool (maybe); drill and drill bits; emery paper (maybe)
Materials: Air horn kit; relay; changeover switch; wire connectors
Time: Usually about an hour
Degree of difficulty: Depends on how accessible existing wiring is but normally very easy

If you have the job professionally done . . .
Are all tubes and wires away from hot or moving components? Do new horns and changeover switch work reliably?

1. Testing which lead is live

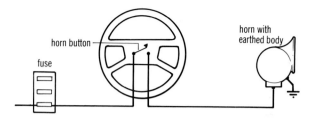

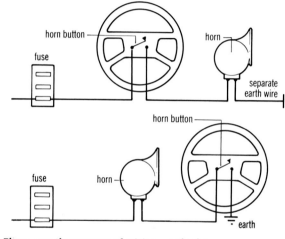

2. There are three ways of wiring up the horn

Before you can do any work on your horns, you need to find out how they are wired up. Basically, there are two wiring systems for horns: either the horn is earthed and power is supplied to it when the horn button is pressed, or the horn is live and it is earthed when the button is pressed.

To find out which kind of wiring scheme your car uses, first make a visual check. If you see that there is only one wire running to the horn, this means that the horn is of the earthed type. The single wire supplies the power from the push to the horn which is earthed to the car body through the horn's own mounting bolts.

If there are two wires running to the horn, one of these will be the power feed and the other is the earth wire. The horn may be of either the earthed or the live type. To find out which, first trace both wires as far as you can. If one wire is connected to a nearby bolt on the car's frame, this must be the earth wire and the other wire, which you will see disappearing into a bundle of wiring, is the power feed wire.

If one of the two wires leads to the fuse holder, you will know that this wire is the live feed and the other wire — running towards the horn button — is the earth wire, and the horn is the live type.

But if both wires lead into a bundle of wires so that you cannot trace their individual paths, you will need to look at the wiring diagram in your car's manual. Make sure that you can see the colour code on the wires and see which one runs to the horn button on the wiring diagram. This will almost certainly be the earth wire. Double check your findings by tracing the other wire on the diagram — it should lead to the power supply. This will confirm that it is the wire that supplies power to the horn.

If your horn does not work, go on to Step 2, but if your existing horn works, it is worth checking your findings by using a test lamp and circuit tester. Where only one wire runs to the horn, if you disconnect that wire and probe the end of the wire with your test lamp while the other end of your test lamp is connected to earth, the lamp should light when you press the horn button — this confirms that the horn is earthed.

When the horn has two wires, connect your test lamp between one wire and earth (**fig 1**). If the lamp lights permanently, you have the live wire of a live horn (**fig 2,** bottom diagram). If it only lights when you press the horn push, you have the live wire of an earthed horn (**fig 2,** middle diagram). If it does not light at all, test the other wire of the horn unit to get one of the above readings.

1. Adjuster may be behind horn

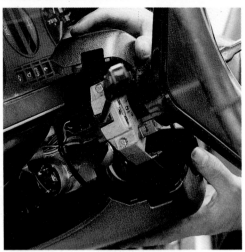

2. Removing steering column shrouds

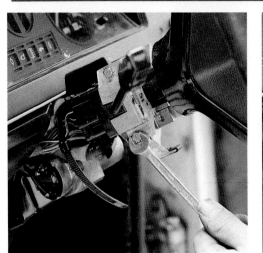

3. Undoing multi-purpose switch

4. Undoing multi-connector

5. Bypassing horn push

6. Locating horn relay

If your existing horn does not work, you will need to pinpoint the fault before you can fix it. The best place to start is with the horn itself.

Now that you know from the checks in Step 2 how the horn is wired, you can connect a wire from the live terminal of the battery to the live terminal of the horn. If necessary, run another wire from the earth terminal of the horn or from the horn's body to a good earth point. If the horn now sounds, the fault must be elsewhere in the circuit. If it does not sound, there is one

more thing you can do before blaming the horn. Most high frequency and windtone horns have an adjusting screw, often behind the horn (**fig 1**). Try turning this screw to different points of its travel and see whether the horn now sounds when it is connected to the battery and to earth. If not, the horn is faulty and cannot be repaired.

If you now wish to fit the same type of horn in place of your old one, make the checks with the test lamp and circuit tester as described in Step 1. This will let you know whether the wiring is

all working properly so that the new horn will operate when you fit it. Often the old horn will be rusted in place and you may find it easier to fit a new horn near to the old one and just switch the wires from one to the other.

High frequency horns and windtone horns are usually wired up in the same way so you can upgrade a high frequency system by fitting more powerful windtone horns in their place.

If the wiring is working properly and you want to fit air horns, go on to Step 3. That will

also show you how to add air horns to your car so that you can choose which set of horns to use.

When you tested the horn by connecting it directly to the battery, if it sounded but does not work when you use the horn button, the fault must lie somewhere in the horn's wiring circuit. Pages 192-196 describe the basic methods of electrical fault finding — you will need to check through the wiring, fuses, connectors, horn button and relay.

The horn button itself may either be a pair of sprung contacts behind a boss in the steering wheel or else it can be part of a multi-function switch.

With the first arrangement, the wheel may need to come off before you can see the contacts of the horn push. Removing a steering wheel is usually a matter of removing the centre trim and undoing the large retaining nut. When you have uncovered the contacts, disconnect the wires from the horn itself and then put a circuit tester across the contacts of the horn push. If the contacts are closing properly, the circuit tester will light when you press the horn button. If it does not light, clean the contacts with fine emery paper and try again. If

you still are not getting a good contact, see if the spring in the contacts has failed. A new spring or a little gentle bending may do the trick.

Horn buttons that are part of multi-purpose switches can also be tested. First, you will have to separate the two halves of the surround which fits round the steering column (**fig 2**). Then undo the screws which hold the multi-purpose switch to the steering column (**fig 3**). The wires from the switch run towards a multi-pin connector. Look at your car's wiring diagram to see which wires go to the horn button. Trace these wires at both sides of the connector so that you will know which pins to test when you pull apart the two halves (**fig 4**).

Use your circuit tester to test the horn button part of the multi-purpose switch. Put one end of the tester to each of the pins which serve the horn on the switch half of the connector and operate the horn push. If the horn push is making contact, the tester will light. If not, you may be able to bend the brass contacts inside the switch to make contact, but otherwise a new switch is the answer.

Test the other side of the multi-

pin connector by bridging the two terminals which serve the horn with a length of wire (**fig 5**). If the horn now sounds, either the horn button is faulty or the multi-pin connector is not making a good contact and should be cleaned with emery paper.

The tests described above can be carried out on any type of horn, but if you have air horns which are not working, there are other possible faults which can stop them from sounding.

First check all the tubing running from the compressor to the horns. Make sure that this is not kinked or perished and check that it fits tightly on to all the connections. Buy some new tubing if you are in any doubt.

When you try to work the horn, listen to the compressor. If it is spinning but no sound comes from the trumpets, the trumpets or the tubing to them will probably be at fault. If the compressor does not spin, test it by wiring it directly to the battery. If it now works, there must be a fault in the wiring between the horn button and the compressor. If wiring it to the battery does not work, the compressor itself is faulty and will need to be tested by a specialist.

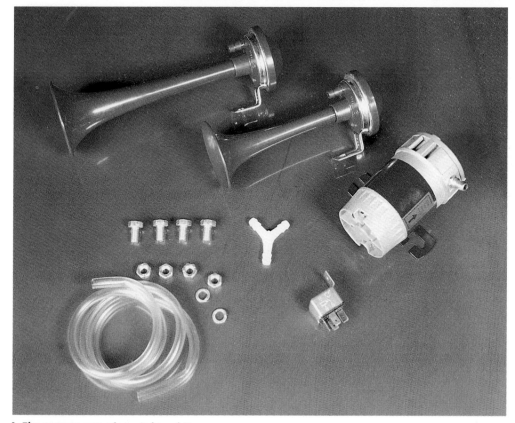

1. The components of an air horn kit

2. Marking mounting point for horn

3. Drilling hole for mounting bolt

You may wish to fit air horns to replace your old faulty horn, or you may be adding them to make your horn system louder, possibly with a changeover switch to let you choose which horns to use. In either case check that all the items listed in the kit are complete. Most kits will contain two trumpets, a compressor, fixing brackets, plastic tubing, wires and connectors and a relay.

First, carefully choose mounting sites for the horns and compressor unit so that you avoid unnecessarily long pieces of plastic tubing running between them. The trumpets need to be mounted close to the front grille to be as audible as possible but not so close that they can be easily tampered with from outside. The inner wings on most cars are usually good sites for the compressor and the horns as the brackets in the horn kit are often designed for inner wing mountings.

Clip the trumpets on to their mounting brackets before marking the bracket holes for drilling. The trumpets should point downwards slightly to stop them from collecting water in bad weather. Although nuts and bolts are usually supplied for fixing you may use self tapping screws for the trumpets since they are fairly light.

Next, choose a site for the compressor unit which does not involve running the plastic tubing around any hot parts of the engine such as the exhaust manifold. Most compressor units need to be mounted in an upright position to work properly and also to prevent any lubricating oil from the top of the unit getting into the electric motor below. If you are using nuts and bolts to mount the compressor make sure that you can get to both sides of the body panel to tighten the nuts. It may be easier to leave the tube connections until after the wiring is all in place.

4. Bolting horn in place

5. Finding place for compressor

6. Bolting compressor upright

When wiring up your air horn you may decide to fit a changeover switch, which gives you the choice of air horns for the open road or the original horns for use around town. Any single pole changeover switch with three pins is suitable (**fig 3**).

The next job is to decide where you want to place the relay. The relay is usually included in the kit. If you are fitting air horns in place of the old horns there may already be a relay in the horn circuit. If so, check that it, and the circuit fuse, are the right rating for the new horns.

The most convenient place for the relay, unless your fusebox is inside the car, is in the engine compartment. This will involve only one wire going through the bulkhead to the changeover switch. Use self-tapping screws to mount the relay in a suitable position out of the way of any hot parts of the engine. A position near to the fusebox would be ideal.

If you are using a changeover switch it may be easier to tap into the existing horn circuit near to the steering column. You will probably have to take off the steering column cowling to get at the wiring. Trace the wire from the horn button or identify it by its colour code, as it should be the same colour at the horn terminal. If possible, cut the wire close to where you have mounted the changeover switch. But if there is not enough slack in the wire, you will have to cut it at a convenient point and join an extra length of new wire to each end using wire connectors to the free ends of both new wires. Connect the wire from the horn button to the common terminal on the changeover switch and the other new wire to either of the remaining terminals. Now route a length of wire from the remaining terminal through a hole in the bulkhead and connect the wire to one of the coil terminals on the relay.

If the horn button is live, so the original horn is earthed, connect the other coil terminal on the relay to earth, using a piece of wire connected to any convenient bolt on the car body. If the horn is permanently live, tap into the existing live wire to the horn using a length of new wire and connect the other end of the new wire to one of the coil terminals on the relay. The earth connection in this case will be provided by the horn button wire. If you are not using a changeover switch you may simply tap new wires into the existing wires going to the old horn and connect the new wires to the coil terminals of the relay.

Connect the main feed of the relay directly to the live terminal of the battery with a ring connector or to the live terminal of the starter solenoid. You should always fit an in-line fuse in the wire running between the relay and the live terminal to protect the compressor motor and the rest of the circuit. The fitting instructions with the horn will give the rating of the fuse you need. Now take a wire from the switched feed of the relay to the positive terminal of the compressor unit. Check that it is the correct terminal (usually marked with +), otherwise the compressor may suck air instead of blowing it through the trumpets. Earth the other terminal on the compressor using a piece of wire to a bolt on the car body.

Test that the wiring and changeover switch are working by pressing the horn button and listening to the compressor spinning. If all is well and you are happy that all the components in the system are securely mounted, connect the trumpets up to the compressor using the plastic tubing cut to the right length. The system is now ready for use.

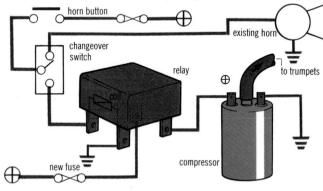

1. The wiring diagram when your horn is earthed

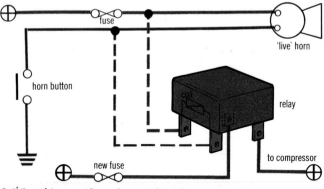

2. Wire this way if you have a 'live' horn

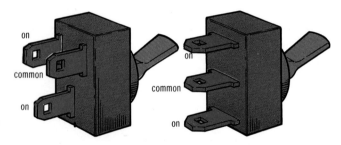

3. Two different types of changeover switch

4. Mount the relay on the bulkhead

5. Tapping into the circuit using a Scotchlok

6. Connecting changeover switch

7. Fitting tubing to horns

TIP

Use your block

When tapping into the existing wiring it is often cheaper and more reliable to use sections of plastic connecting block (5 or 10 amp). Cut through the wire to be tapped and strip about ¼in. of insulation from each end. Twist one end together with the new wire and secure into one end of the connector block. Now connect the other end of the existing wire into the block.

Fixing faulty light units

You should repair faulty light units as soon as possible to avoid falling foul of the law. Most faults are easily put right

When lights stop working it is more than just inconvenient — driving without headlights, rearlights, stoplights or indicators is illegal, even in daylight if you are stopped and asked to check them. Fitting new headlamps — bulb or sealed beam units — and replacing the lens or bulbs of other lamps does not take very long. Within an hour or so you could be back on the road and completely legal.

Headlamp bulbs, and new lens units for other lamps, can be expensive so it is worth making a few checks to ensure you know exactly what is wrong with the light before buying a new one.

There are usually clues to the problem. Dimming lamps can mean a filament is burning out or that there is an earthing fault. For headlamp problems start with Step 1. If other lamps are failing turn to page 146 and start at Step 6.

When to do this job
When a headlamp fails
When a lamp glass has broken
When a bulb has stuck in place
When a light looks dim

What this job involves
Removing damaged light unit
Cleaning light unit
Fitting new unit

Related jobs in this handbook
Finding electrical faults
Fixing faulty indicators
Please see Index for page numbers

To do this job
Tools: Screwdrivers; penetrating fluid; pliers; metal polish; cork (maybe)
Materials: New bulbs and light units
Time: Up to an hour
Degree of difficulty: Corroded bulbs may be difficult to remove

If you have the job professionally done . . .
Do lights all work? Are all lenses intact?

The first check is to open the bonnet and see whether you can see the back of the headlight with the wires protruding (**fig 1**). If so, the chances are that you can remove the bulb without disturbing the light itself. Check whether there is room to get the bulb out without it hitting the battery, radiator tank, etc. If anything is in the way shift it if possible and go to Step 3, otherwise you have to take the headlight out from the front (Step 2).

If you cannot see the rear of the light or your car has a sealed beam, then the headlight unit

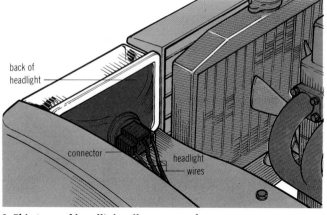

back of headlight
connector
headlight wires

1. This type of headlight allows access from rear

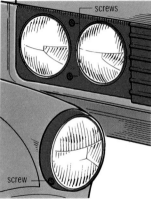

screws
screw

2. Trim fixing screws

has to be taken out from the front. Look for any securing screws around the headlight bezel rim or the plastic trim (**fig 2**). These unscrew to give access to the main light fixing screws.

If you cannot see any screws around the headlights or if the lights are set into the front grille then you have to take the grille off to get at the fixing screws. Find all the screws which hold the grille to the car and remove them one at a time. Some are held at top, bottom and sides, while others have screws at the top and lugs at the bottom which

fit into slots in the front panel. Stick each screw through a sheet of cardboard to make sure you do not lose any of them. Now carefully pull the grille off, lifting it slightly if you have to, and put it somewhere where it will not get damaged. If it will not move, check for any screws hidden in recessed holes.

Watch out for any small rubber rings which fit over the lugs if your grille has them. Put them safely away. Once you have found the headlight securing screws, go on to Step 2 to remove the light unit or sealed beam.

3. Removing a grille fixing screw

TIP

Headlight conversion
If your car has a rectangular sealed beam headlight (fitted to early Allegros and Avengers for example) you will find that these are no longer available.

The cheapest way to get round the problem is to find a bulb type headlight and its electrical connectors from a similar car in the scrapyard — failing that you will have to buy a new headlight and bulb.

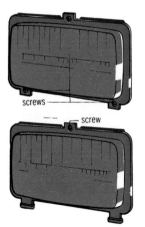

1. Headlight fixing screws

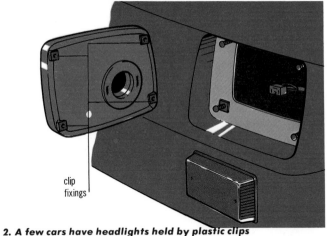

2. A few cars have headlights held by plastic clips

1. Easing the connector off the headlight

2. Peeling off the protective rubber boot

First disconnect the battery to avoid a short circuit.

With the grille off look closely at the headlight and look for any fixing screws, taking care not to confuse them with the beam adjustment screws. Rectangular lights are often held by a single screw and several lugs or by screws at the top and bottom of the headlight holding plate (**fig 1**). If there are no screws, the light is fixed by plastic lugs (**fig 2**). To remove it simply lever it forward with a thin piece of wood, and pull it out. Round units normally have three or four screws which have to be undone (**fig 3**). In some cases you will not have to take the screws out altogether. Look for keyhole slots or cut-outs around the screws — if you find them all you have to do is slacken the screws off and turn the metal ring to release the headlight unit (**fig 4**). If the screws run through a small spring you do not even have to loosen them — simply push the unit back against spring pressure and turn it.

Do not pull the unit out too far as it is still attached to the wires. Unplug the terminal block, levering it off with a screwdriver if it is tight, and release the sidelight bulbholder if it is part of the light fitting (**fig 5**).

3. Undoing the headlight securing screw

4. Lifting out the headlight

5. Pulling out sidelight

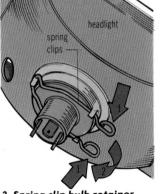

3. Spring clip bulb retainer

Once you have prised the terminal block off (**fig 1**), you can change the bulb or sealed beam.

Changing a sealed beam unit is simply a matter of putting the new one in (Step 5) but if your car uses bulbs you must remove the old one first.

First peel the rubber boot (**fig 2**) off the light — this reveals the bulb fixings. There are several ways in which the bulb can be held. There can be flat wire springs (**fig 3**) or a retaining plate which is often spring loaded (**fig 4**).

Carefully lift the springs out of their retaining grooves or, if you have a retaining plate, push it in and turn it anticlockwise. Pull the bulb free of the headlight.

While you have the bulb out look through the bulbhole and check the condition of the reflector towards the bottom of the light. Any signs of rust or lifting of the silvering (**fig 5**) mean that you should consider buying a new headlight fairly soon or the car may fail the MOT roadworthiness test. As a temporary measure, though, you can try brushing some silver paint over the damage with a small paintbrush.

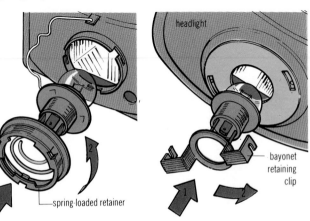

4. Both these retainers turn to release the bulb

5. Badly rusted reflector

There are several ways of checking whether or not a bulb or sealed beam has failed, and which you use depends on what equipment you have.

A burned out bulb filament is sometimes obvious because the filament is broken, but the filaments in sealed beam headlights are hard to see.

Another method is to swap the bulb or sealed beam unit for the one on the other side of the car, assuming that the other light works properly. If the apparently failed light now works, the fault is evidently in the wiring, or it may even be that one of the terminals was simply dirty, and removing it has produced a better contact. In this case just clean up the contacts

with fine emery paper.

If you have a circuit tester with its own battery (see page 193) you can check the filaments for continuity. A bulb with a metal

1. Testing headlight wiring — sidelight comes on as well

casing will have two flat contacts on its base. Test between the casing and each contact in turn. If the circuit tester lights on only one

2. Testing a halogen bulb — do not touch quartz glass

terminal then a filament has failed.

The normal bulb or sealed beam unit has three terminals — one for earth and one for each filament. You can often see which is which by looking through the glass, but if not, test between the various terminals

and find out what happens. If both filaments are working the tester should light between any pair of terminals. Only one pair of terminals will make the tester light if one filament has failed. If the bulb or sealed beam is the inner one from a four headlight system, it has two terminals.

You will have to check the wiring if your tests show nothing wrong with the bulb or sealed beam. Pages 192 to 196 describe general test procedures.

Headlight bulbs and sealed beam units are earthed by one of the three wires which lead to the connector. If you cannot identify which is the earth wire, you will have to check which two light a test lamp when the dip and main beam switches are on (**fig 1**). The other one will be the earth connection, and should make a circuit tester light when connected between the earth wire and a good earth point. If the earth wire is faulty in some way, check to see if you can find the place at which it is earthed and clean it up.

Before you fit the new bulb or sealed beam, smear a little petroleum jelly, such as Vaseline, on the bulb terminals to prevent them rusting.

If you have a halogen bulb do not touch the quartz part of it. Any finger marks will cause a hot spot which overheats when you use the light, making the bulb burn out rather quickly. If you do accidentally touch it, wipe off any marks with a rag moistened in meths and allow the bulb to dry naturally.

All double filament bulbs

have some kind of pip or ear on the mounting flange to make sure the bulb in fitted the right way up in the light. These

1. Conventional tungsten (left) and quartz-halogen bulbs

locating keys are shown in **fig 2**. Fit the bulb so that the ears or pip fit into the corresponding cut-out(s) in the headlamp. Give it a firm push to make sure it is properly seated, then refit the spring clips or the holding plate and check that the bulb is held firmly in position. Now refit the light unit (if you had to remove it) and the grille or headlight trim.

If your car has sealed beams then all you have to do is fit the new one in place of the old. Do

not worry if it is marked 'R'. This simply means it is for a right hand drive car and can be fitted to either side of the car. Make sure that any rubber pads that were fitted are put into place in the backing plate. Check to see if they are stuck to the old unit if yours are missing. The sealed beam has castings in the back which locate into the backing plate (**fig 3**) so you cannot fit it wrongly.

Refit the headlight, remem-

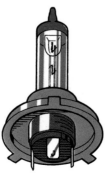

2. The three most common locating pips — make sure they align with headlight

bering to replace the sidelight bulbholder if it is fitted and then fit the retaining ring and screws, but do not tighten up the screws at once. Make sure the lights is seated properly in its mount, and only then do up the screws. Before you refit the grille or headlight trim, reconnect the battery and check that the lights work.

Finally, refit the grille or headlight trim, making sure all the screws are tight and secure.

3. The sealed beam has castings to locate it

145

Begin by making a thorough inspection of the light to assess the extent of the problem. Not only does this enable you to plan the work involved, but it is senseless to rush out and buy a selection of expensive parts if the fault can be cured relatively simply and cheaply.

If one of the headlights is not working, first refer to Steps 1 to 5 for more information on checking and renewing sealed beam units and bulbs. In the case of the separate bulb headlight, a broken lens can be renewed but in the case of a sealed beam unit, obviously this is not possible and the complete unit must be changed. Main dealers for your particular model can usually supply replacement lenses but they are generally quite expensive so it is worth visiting your local car breaker to try to obtain a secondhand lens more cheaply.

1. This lens is one continuous moulded piece of plastic

If a replacement lens is not immediately available and the cracked lens is still in place, a useful dodge to prolong its life is to cover it completely with kitchen sealing film. Clear sticky tape is not so good as it tends to shrivel up and peel off when it gets wet.

In cases of localized damage affecting multiple lens assemblies at the rear of a car, an important point is to judge exactly how much of the assembly needs to be replaced. The various lenses for the brake light, indicator, rear light and fog light, if fitted, are in some cases butted together to form one assembly and sometimes they can be removed and separated to allow broken ones to be renewed individually.

If your car has indicators that are mounted separately from the other lights, these are often supplied new as a complete assembly rather than as individual components, so renewing just a lens may not be possible unless you can find one in a breaker's yard. Likewise, a number plate lamp, repeater flasher or separately mounted foglight is usually renewed whole, unless secondhand parts can be found.

2. Whole lens needs renewing

The method of attaching a light lens varies from car to car. The simplest and commonest way is with several small screws accessible from the front of the lens. Removing these is generally easy and the only point to bear in mind is that the screwdriver you use should fit the screw head exactly. This is especially important on cross head screws since it is particularly easy to damage the head with an ill-fitting screwdriver and make it very difficult to turn.

If the light lenses on your car do not have outside fixings you will have to undo them from the rear, whether from the inside of the boot or from the hatch area.

Look behind the light unit and decide which trim parts, if any, need to be removed first. You will find that these either simply lift away, or are held by small screws or spring clips. Remove the trim, as necessary, and then study the rear of the light as you may find one of several types of fixing. A common variety uses two or more spring clips to retain a panel holding the bulbs in place behind the lens.

Alternatively, the bulb holders may be individually pressed into place in a rear panel which is sometimes integral with the bodywork. The bulb holder, complete with bulb, can be pulled out as required. Don't tug at the wire though, grasp the holder itself, or you may simply pull the wires out. If you need to detach a mounting panel, remove the fixing screws and lift the panel away.

Undoing these panel fixing screws may also release the light lens. If it does not, or if it is of the type with a clipped bulb-mounting panel, you should now be able to see the lens fixings.

These are usually threaded shanks moulded into the lens and held by small nuts or it may be that the holes in the lens are threaded and bolts inserted from behind. In either case you may find it difficult to reach the bolt head or nut with a spanner, especially if the light assembly is recessed in the wing or back panel. Sometimes the nuts or bolts can be reached with a pair of pliers but it is preferable to use a small socket and extension.

Whatever method of lens fixing your car has, it may be that the lens proves reluctant to come away even when the fixing screws have been removed. Before resorting to force, double check that you have in fact removed all the bolts or nuts, because it is surprisingly easy to overlook one.

Having made this check, place the blade of a small screwdriver under the base of the lens and gently prise it away from its seating.

The fixing methods of lenses and bases on separate indicators, repeater lights, fog lights or reversing lights are broadly similar to those outlined above. However, one common variant on some older cars is the press-fit indicator or repeater light lens. With these, a circular glass or plastic lens is pressed into a rubber seal on the light base where it is held by a tightly fitting metal trim ring.

To remove such lenses, prise the trim ring away with a small screwdriver blade and then carefully insert the blade under the rubber seal to lift the lens out. The light base is generally attached to the car by two through-bolts, or two nuts which can be undone, if necessary, and the base lifted away.

1. Removing screw which holds lens to car body

2. Sliding rubber ring from back of light

3. Separating broken lens from whole one

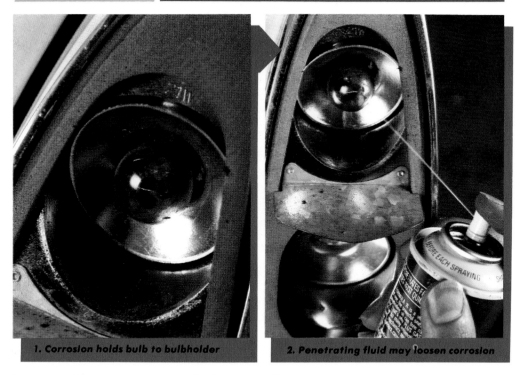

1. Corrosion holds bulb to bulbholder

2. Penetrating fluid may loosen corrosion

3. Pulling broken bulb free with pliers

4. Brushing away fragments of broken glass

Another problem that can affect lights of all types, except sealed beam headlights, is corrosion within the bulb housing. This may be so serious that the bulb cannot be removed from its housing, in which case a squirt of penetrating spray such as WD40 may loosen it (**fig 2**). Leave the spray to work for half an hour or so and then gently try to work the bulb free. If this fails to produce results, cover the bulb with a cloth, or wear a glove and twist the bulb glass firmly until it comes away from the bulb shank. Discard the glass and then use long-nosed pliers (**fig 3**) to squeeze in and distort the thin metal sides of the bulb shank sufficiently for it to come free and be lifted away. Use a small brush or a piece of wire wool wrapped round a screwdriver blade to clean the bulb housing thoroughly. If the bulb glass was broken, take care to remove all the fragments of glass (**fig 4**).

Another way of getting a broken or stuck bulb out is by using a cork. If the bulb is not already broken but merely stuck, tap it with a hammer to break the glass, then pull the central glass stalk out of the base of the bulb with pliers so that there is only the shell of the bulb left in the holder. Now push a cork firmly on to the remains of the bulb so that the sharp metal edge bites into the cork (**fig 6**). If you now push the cork in slightly and turn it anti-clockwise, it should turn the bulb with it and let you pull out the base of the bulb.

Smear the base of a new bulb with vaseline and fit it in the holder. If the bulb still fails to light, recheck the flow of electricity and the connections to the bulb holder.

While you have got the light units in pieces, you should make sure that all the lenses are clean, as sometimes dirt tends to build up on the inside and this makes the light look dim.

5. Polishing lens to remove accumulated dirt and grease

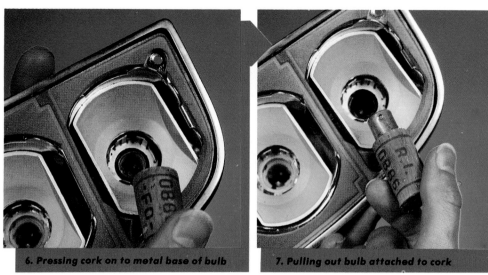

6. Pressing cork on to metal base of bulb

7. Pulling out bulb attached to cork

1. Scraping corrosion from end of terminal

2. Lubricating spring inside bulbholder

5. Peeling back rubber boot from bulbholder

6. One terminal of bulbholder has broken

A problem sometimes encountered on rear lights and indicators is that the end of the bulb does not reach the contact in the base of the holder. It may be that the spring often fitted under the contact in the bulb holder is overcompressed, or the connection to the contact could be defective or corroded.

A simple check on the spring tension with a light of this type is to see whether the bulb is held firmly in place. If it slips sloppily and can easily be moved around, the spring may not be exerting pressure on the contact. If you think this is the problem remove the bulb and feed the wire through from behind to displace the contact complete with its little coil spring. The spring can then be stretched carefully with two pairs of long-nosed pliers.

If you suspect that the power is not passing through the contact or if for some reason the wire has broken away, you may need to remake the soldered joint on the contact. This requires the use of a soldering iron which, if you do not already have one, is a relatively inexpensive and worthwhile addition to the toolbox. If the contact is still connected, feed the wire through from behind to push it out of the bulb holder. If the contact will not push out of the bulb holder to let you get at the spring, squirt a little WD40 into the back of the bulb holder and work the movable contact in and out to let the WD40 get into the spring (**fig 2**). This should help to make the spring more lively again. If the spring is weak, you can build up the central terminal with solder.

Look for any corrosion on the metal inside the light unit. Scrape away any loose corrosion with an old screwdriver and then use metal polish to brighten up the reflector as much as possible (**fig 4**). Although this will not make the reflector shine like new, it will make the light a bit more visible.

3. Cleaning corrosion from reflector

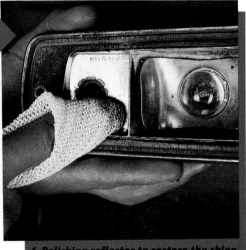

4. Polishing reflector to restore the shine

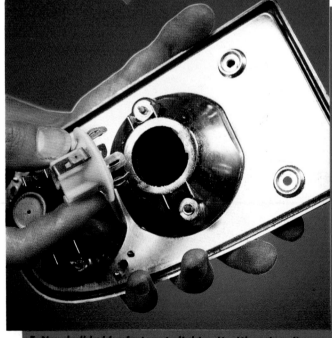

7. New bulbholder fastens to light unit with spring clips

Overhauling a distributor

Is your car starting badly and running sluggishly? To give your engine a new lease of life and restore it to peak performance, a distributor overhaul may be the answer

When to do this job

If you have recently bought a secondhand car and you want to give it a thorough tune-up
When your car is not responding to a normal service with new plugs and points
If your petrol consumption is poor and the engine idles badly but the carburettor is in good condition

What this job involves

Using a strobe light to check for wear
Removing and refitting the distributor without losing the correct timing
Stripping down and cleaning the distributor and replacing worn or broken parts

Related jobs in this handbook

Curing starting problems
Get your timing right
Please see Index for page numbers

To do this job

Tools: Strobe light; spanners; screwdriver; hammer; preferably vice and bench; plug spanner
Materials: Dismantling fluid; oil; wire; clean rags; new parts as required
Time: Half day for complete overhaul, two hours if distributor is worn out and has to be replaced
Degree of difficulty: Straightforward. Hardest part is to get the spares. Try to get new bob weight springs before you start work. Vacuum units are widely available

If you have the job professionally done . . .

Is the performance better all round with noticeably improved fuel consumption? Have they fitted a reconditioned unit or a new one?

1. The vacuum unit may be held by a spring

2. Some vacuum units are held by a circlip

The best way to confirm the ignition timing advances correctly as engine speed increases is to use a stroboscopic timing light (see pages 85 to 88). If, after contact breaker and timing adjustment, the timing marks on the pulley appear to move around there may be advance mechanism problems. On most cars advance is caused in two ways — mechanical and vacuum.

The mechanical advance alters the ignition timing according to the engine speed; the vacuum advance alters it according to the throttle opening.

To check the operation of the mechanical advance mechanisms, shine your strobe light on the timing marks and run the engine at idle. Disconnect the vacuum advance pipe which links the carburettor to the bell-shaped unit mounted on the side of the distributor. Then accelerate slowly up to full speed. The moving timing mark should move from the static mark until it reaches maximum advance. If it does not, the mechanical advance may have failed – see Step 5.

To test the vacuum advance, reconnect the vacuum tube and run the engine at around 3000 rpm. Shine your strobe on the timing marks and disconnect the vacuum advance tube.

As you pull the pipe off, the moving mark should appear to return quite close to the static timing mark. If it does, the vacuum advance and retard unit is working satisfactorily.

If the vacuum unit appears to have stopped working, it may have just become disconnected. In Lucas distributors the vacuum unit is connected to the baseplate by a spring which just slips over the top of a post (**fig 1**). Most other makes use a flat metal strap which is held on by a spring clip or circlip (**fig 2**). Check that the spring or link is in place and secure before you go out and buy a new unit.

TIP

Suck it and see

If you do not have a stroboscopic light and it is not convenient to buy or hire one, try this method to test the vacuum unit.

Pull off the vacuum pipe from the inlet manifold and wipe it with a clean cloth. Remove the distributor cap and stand so that you can see the contact breaker baseplate. Suck the end of the pipe and look to see if the baseplate moves around by about half an inch. If it does, put your tongue over the end of the pipe to seal it. The baseplate should remain in the advanced position until you remove the pipe from your mouth and let the air

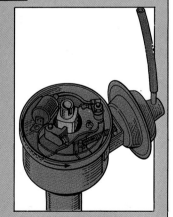

back in.

If you can suck air in through the vacuum unit or the baseplate does not move, you will need to replace the vacuum unit.

All vacuum advance and retard units look the same on the outside. It is the springs and spacers inside which tailor the unit to a particular engine. So do not be tempted to fit any old vacuum unit which happens to look like the one for your car; buy a new one. It will pay for itself very quickly in petrol saved.

Lucas distributors have a vernier adjustment which both allows you to make fine adjustments to the timing and also holds the vacuum unit in the distributor body. A small circlip fits into a groove in the end of the adjusting screw. Remove the circlip carefully with a small screwdriver or a pair of fine-nosed pliers (**fig 1**). Then lift the end of the connecting spring off its post and remove the unit by screwing the knurled adjuster right off the end of its thread. Watch for the spring plate and the spring located behind the knurled adjuster.

On most other makes of distributor the vacuum unit is secured to the side of the distributor body by a couple of short screws. Undo these and pull off the spring clip that holds the connecting link on to the baseplate. Lift the connecting link off its post if necessary and withdraw the unit from the distributor body (**fig 2**).

Fitting the new vacuum unit is a reversal of the above procedure. Make sure you check the tube connecting the vacuum advance to the carburettor for signs of wear. Particular attention should be paid to the rubber connectors at each end of the tube which should be a tight fit. Look along the length of the tube for chafing or air leaks. If you detect any signs of wear, replace the tube.

Now test the distributor with the strobe light, as described in Step 1, to make sure that the ignition timing has not been altered and that the vacuum advance works correctly.

1. Removing the vernier adjustment circlip

2. Withdrawing the vacuum unit from the distributor body

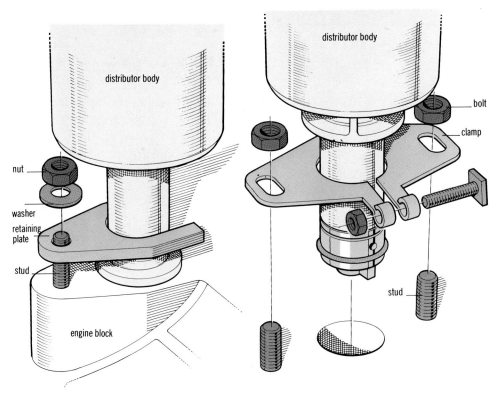

distributor body

distributor body

bolt

clamp

nut

washer

retaining plate

stud

stud

engine block

1. The distributor can be held in place by a retaining plate (left) or a clamp (right)

To overhaul the distributor, it is usually best to remove it from the engine. The only exception is if it is situated near the top of the block, in which case you can work on it in situ. The distributor is held in place either by a clamp that fits around the bottom of the unit or by a retaining plate that fits on to a stud (**fig 1**).

Remove the spark plugs and turn the engine over until the rotor arm is pointing to the contact which corresponds to cylinder number one. Remember that you usually look at the cap upside down so you must allow for this when you work out which contact is which.

Now mark the distributor body and the engine so that you can replace the distributor in exactly the same position when the overhaul is complete. Remove the nuts holding the distributor and withdraw the whole unit (**fig 2**). The body will be oily so clean it before you go any further.

2. Withdrawing the distributor from the engine

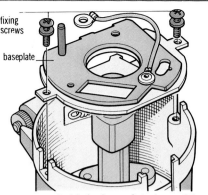

1. Comparing new and old drive gear (left) and drive dogs (right)

4. Two screws hold the baseplate in position

5. Lifting off the baseplate

You now need to examine the distributor closely to find out which individual components are worn. The test with the strobe light will have given some indication about its general condition, but there is no substitute for a proper inspection.

First examine the drive gear, or drive dog, at the bottom of the main shaft (**fig 1**). Any visible signs of wear — burred spigots on the drive dog, or a broken tooth on the drive gear — are indications that the drive gear should be replaced.

Mark the position on the distributor body so that you can replace the drive gear in exactly the same position later. Support the distributor in a vice or on blocks of wood and then tap out the pin that holds the drive gear on the main shaft. The pin is a tight fit, so use a drift or nail as a punch to drive the pin out (**fig 2**). Pull the drive gear off the shaft along with the spacer washers — there will be washers between the distributor body and the drive dog, and also on the shaft inside the body (**fig 3**). Note the order in which the washers come off so they can be replaced in the same way. Then pull the main shaft out of the body from the other end.

A further likely spot for wear is in the contact breaker plate — especially if the distributor is

2. Driving the pin out

fitted with both mechanical and vacuum advance. Lift off the rotor arm and remove the contact breaker assembly and condenser — see page 203.

Free the vacuum advance spring, undo the two securing screws (**fig 4**), lift off the earth lead and then remove the contact plate (**fig 5**).

The contact breaker baseplate in fact consists of two plates — one is held stationary in the distributor body, the other is moved by the vacuum unit. Hold the fixed plate with your finger tips and try to rock the moving plate from side to side with your thumbs. If the plate rocks it is worn. This type of wear is quite common — particularly on Lucas distributors where two nylon buttons are

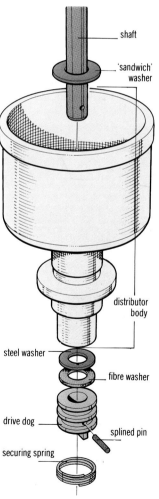

3. Spacer washers on the shaft

provided between the plates. They are intended to smooth the movement of the plates but they do in fact wear quite quickly — and sometimes disappear completely. These buttons are unavailable separately so if they have worn you will have to replace the base plate.

Some Marelli and Bosch distributors have the bob weights at the top of the main shaft immediately under the rotor arm. These types obviously do not need to be stripped down for you to inspect the mechanical advance and retard unit. But they are the exceptions and you usually have to remove the baseplate before you can inspect the bob weights and the movement of the cam.

Note carefully how the springs and bob weights fit together and interlock with the static part of the mechanism. It is a good idea to make a drawing of the different parts because it is unlikely that your handbook or workshop manual will be detailed enough to cover all the variations between the different models which you might encounter.

Remove the springs (**fig 1**) and lift the bob weights off their posts (**fig 2**). Hold the bottom of the main shaft in one hand and the contact breaker cam in the other. You should be able to turn the contact breaker cam freely and independently of the main shaft. If the movement is free and easy, just slide the cam off

the main shaft and clean off the old grease. Relubricate the shaft with engine oil and slip the cam back on.

If the main shaft and the cam are seized together, tap them apart with a mallet. Take care not to damage the bottom end of the main shaft. If one sharp tap does not dislodge the cam, spray it with dismantling fluid. Clean off any light rust on the cam or shaft with fine emery cloth, then lubricate the main shaft with engine oil.

It is usually only dirt and con-

gealed oil that prevent the bob weights from working smoothly so clean them, their posts and the cam with paraffin or methylated spirit. Then replace the weights on the posts and lightly lubricate the whole advance and retard mechanism with engine oil.

Finally fit new springs between the posts on the bob weights and their posts. These springs control the bob weight's movement so the ignition will only advance properly if they are in good condition.

1. Freeing bob weight springs

2. Lifting weights from posts

Clean the spacing washers and then slide them on to the bottom of the main shaft in the order in which they came off. Now put back the drive gear or drive dog on the bottom of the shaft and line up the marks that you made when you took the gear off (**fig 1**). If you are fitting a new gear or dog, make sure that you put them on the right way round.

Align the holes in the drive gear and the main shaft and press the pin in as far as it will go. It is important that the pin is a good fit, though a light tap should be enough to push it home. If the pin is loose, get another one from a scrap distributor — any movement between the main shaft and the drive gear will soon get very serious indeed.

Spin the main shaft with your fingers to make sure that it is not binding anywhere, and check that the bob weights and springs are still fitted correctly. Do not worry if there is some backlash as this is adjusted by the spacer washers according to the design of each particular distributor.

If you are replacing the old contact breaker baseplate, make sure that it is clean and lightly lubricated with engine oil. It can fit either way round, so make sure that the post for the vacuum unit connector is on the correct side of the distributor body. Check that the earth tag is in good condition before fitting it under one of the fixing screws. Turn the moving plate backwards and forwards a few times to make sure that the earth tag is not going to chafe.

Now fit the vacuum unit and test that it is working and the contact breaker baseplate is moving freely. All that remains to do is fit the lead from the side of the distributor to the contact breakers and condenser. The side lead should be fitted after the other small components — it must be renewed if it shows any sign of wear.

1. Putting the drive gear back on the shaft in the right position

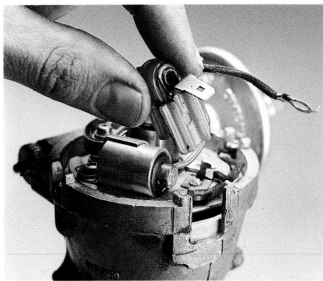
2. Fitting the plastic insert and low tension lead

Lucas supply the lead and the plastic insert as a replacement item (**fig 2**), but on other models the easiest course often is to replace the whole wire from the coil to the contact breakers. Unfortunately you will probably have to solder the end fitting from the old wire on to the new one, to be absolutely sure that it fits on to the terminal easily.

Unless you know that the condenser and rotor arm have been replaced very recently, fit new ones as you complete the final assembly (see page 203). Finally examine the contact breaker fixing screws before

you refit them. They often suffer a lot of damage over the years and this makes accurate adjustment of the gap much more difficult. Unfortunately, it is not easy to get replacements but again an auto-electrician should be able to help. Otherwise try an engineer's supplier who just might be able to find a couple of Allen screws to fit.

Lastly, if your distributor is fitted with a body clamp, loosen off the bolt and make sure that the distributor can rotate freely. If the body clamp looks bent, put it in a vice and use a pair of pliers to staighten it (**fig 3**). If there are any burrs on it remove them with a file and finish off with emery paper. Check that the distributor now rotates freely — this will make it much easier to adjust the timing — and also fit a new pinch bolt if the original one shows any signs of wear.

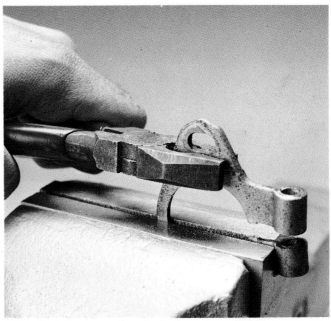
3. Using pliers to straighten body clamp in a vice

To refit the distributor set the rotor arm so that it is pointing to the contact in the distributor cap corresponding to cylinder number one and insert the base of the body into the engine so that the scribe marks you made earlier line up.

As you push the distributor home, you will feel the drive gear engage with the gear in the engine. If you do not, wiggle the rotor arm to rotate the shaft until you feel the gears engage (**fig 1**). If your distributor is fitted with an offset dog, make sure that it is the right way round before you start. Some Marelli distributors have a splined fitting at the bottom — these may also need to be rotated slightly to get them to fit.

Now time the ignition statically and then start the engine and use the strobe light to get the timing dead on (see pages 87 to 88). Turn off the engine, and refit the vacuum advance pipe.

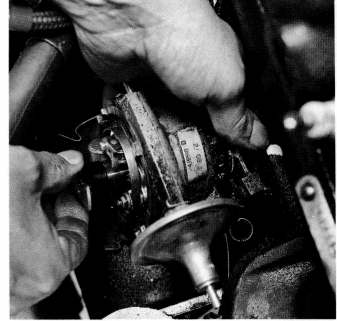
1. Ensure drive gears engage

Dynamo and alternator service

Cars have generators to power electrical systems and charge the battery. The older generator is a dynamo (servicing starts with Step 1 — this page), the modern system has an alternator (start at Step 1A — page 158)

When to do this job
If the ignition warning light stays on above idling speed
If the alternator becomes noisy

What this job involves
Dismantling and checking a dynamo
Repairing a dynamo
Dismantling and checking an alternator
Repairing an alternator

Related jobs in this handbook
Tracing electrical faults
Dealing with battery problems
Please see Index for page numbers

To do this job
Tools: Small sockets or box spanners to fit alternator bolts; spanners; screwdrivers (both flat-blade and crosshead type); puller for pulley and rear bearing (maybe); soldering iron (maybe); soft-headed mallet or a hammer and wood
Materials: New brushes; new slip ring (maybe); new regulator (maybe); new diode pack (maybe); solder (maybe)
Time: External brushes one to two hours, internal brushes about two hours, other repairs between three and five hours
Degree of difficulty: External brushes straightforward, ACR internal brushes not difficult but take some time, other repairs time consuming and need care to avoid damaging delicate electrical components

If you have the job professionally done . . .
Does the ignition warning light go out as it should? If the generator was noisy has the noise gone? Does the battery stay properly charged?

The dynamo is a cylindrical component mounted on one side of the engine (**fig 1**) and is one of two types of generator — the other is the alternator. It is usually about 8 in. (200 mm) long and 4 in. (100 mm) wide and often has a black, silver or green body.

Depending on the type, it is held to the engine block by two or three bolts and a slotted adjuster bar. The dynamo itself pivots on one or two of the bolts while the other bolt is used to adjust the drive belt tension.

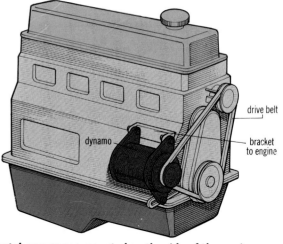

1. Most dynamos are mounted on the side of the engine

TIP

Generator test
A simple check to see whether the generator is working is to start the engine and switch on the headlights. If the lights brighten when you rev the engine the generator is working.

Dynamos are usually very reliable, so if your car has a charging system fault do not immediately assume that it is the dynamo that is faulty. First make sure the drive belt is tight and the electrical connections are clean and tight. Also check that the battery terminals are clean (see page 197) and check if the dynamo is working at all (see Tip — Generator test). If it is, check the rest of the charging circuit carefully.

HOW IT WORKS

The dynamo

The dynamo is a direct current (DC) generator driven by the engine and produces the electrical power to run the electrical system and keep the battery charged.

At idling speed the dynamo cannot provide sufficient power to run the electrical accessories so most of the electrical demand is met by the battery. To warn that the dynamo is not charging the battery the ignition warning light comes on.

When the engine speed is higher, the dynamo provides power to charge the battery and to supply the demands of the electrical system.

The electricity is generated in the *armature windings* of the dynamo. These are made up of a number of copper wires wound around the central shaft or *armature*. This armature runs in two bearings and rotates inside the *field coils* (a type of electromagnet) which are fitted inside the main casing of the dynamo.

The electrical current is fed from the armature into the *commutator* — the ring of copper segments on the end of the armature shaft. The current leaves the dynamo through two carbon brushes which are held in contact with the commutator by two springs. These brushes are connected by wires to terminals on the dynamo body.

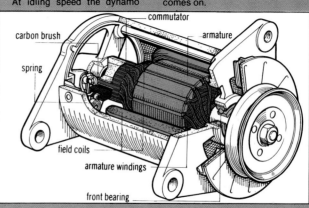

STEP 2 — REMOVE THE DYNAMO

To remove the dynamo from the car first undo the earth strap from the battery, followed by the electrical connections to the dynamo. These will be either separate push-on spade connectors (**fig 1**) or bolt-on ring connectors (**fig 2**).

Next find the bolts which secure the dynamo to the car and loosen them. Remove the drive belt (see Fact File — Generator drive belt adjustment, page 217, and then, with the generator supported, take out all the mounting bolts one by one and lift it out of position.

1. Spade connectors simply pull off their terminals

2. Ring terminals must be unbolted

3. How the dynamo bolts to the engine

STEP 3 — CHECK FOR WEAR

If the dynamo is noisy then it is very likely that the bearings are worn. A light rattle or whining noise is not serious and can be safely ignored. But a heavy rumbling, grinding or screeching means the bearings are badly worn. Do not be tempted to ignore these signs — if left the bearing will eventually seize and may wreck the dynamo.

To check the front bearing for wear hold the dynamo body and spin the pulley. If the bearing feels rough or noisy or you can rock the pulley more

than 1/16 in. (1.5 mm) from side to side (**fig 1**) it is worn and must be renewed (see Step 8).

To check the rear bearing you have to dismantle the dynamo. First take out the dynamo through bolts (see Step 4) and separate the front and rear brackets from the main body. Then put the end of the armature into its hole in the end bracket. Hold the armature body still and rock the end bracket from side to side (**fig 2**). If there is play you must renew the bearing (see Step 9).

A few types of dynamo have an inspection cover which can be removed so that you can look at the brushes without having to take the unit apart. To release the cover loosen the small screw which secures the cover and slide the cover off. Inspect the brushes and commutator for wear (see Step 5). If they are worn the dynamo will have to be dismantled so go on to Step 4.

If there is no cover you will have to take off the rear end bracket (see Step 4) to check or change the brushes.

1. How to check for wear in the front bearing

2. Checking rear bearing by rocking the bracket

STEP 4 — REMOVE THE END BRACKETS

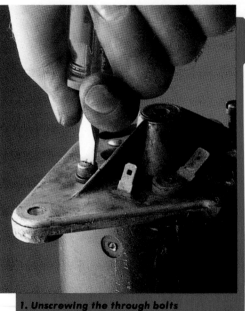

1. Unscrewing the through bolts

2. Tapping off the end bracket

Before trying to remove the end brackets, clean the outside of the dynamo with a soft brush and methylated spirit. Hold the body of the dynamo and undo the two screw-headed bolts in the rear end bracket with a large screwdriver (**fig 1**). These are often very stiff — to get extra leverage, use Mole grips on the bolt heads or use a spanner on

the flat part of the screwdriver shaft (see page 235). Do not try to undo the large screws in the main body of the dynamo — they hold the field coils, which may be damaged if you take the screws out.

Remove the bolts and separate the end bracket from the dynamo body. If it is tight, tap the bracket gently (**fig 2**),

placing a piece of wood between the hammer and bracket. There may be a washer on the armature shaft. If there is, put it safely to one side as it can easily get lost. Tap the front bracket free in the same way as the rear — hold on to it tightly as it comes free. The armature and shaft are attached to it, and it is heavy.

With the armature body held firmly, look at the surface of the commutator — the ring of narrow copper strips near the end of the dynamo shaft. Light scoring (**fig 2**) or pitting, caused by worn out brushes, is not too serious and can be removed with fine glasspaper, but if the surface is deeply scored or there is a noticeable wear ridge on it then there is no way you can repair it and you will need an exchange unit. This will have to be repolarized (see Step 10).

The surface of the commutator segments may have a glazed look to them which must be cleaned off. Wrap a strip of fine glasspaper around the commu-

1. Lightly scored commutator   **2. Commutator needs refacing**

3. Clean glaze and dirt off the commutator

4. Cutting back the commutator's insulation

tator and sand it carefully until the glaze disappears (**fig 3**).

Wipe the commutator clean and check the insulating strips between the copper segments. These should be ⅛ in (1 mm) below the level of the copper segments.

If the insulating strips are flush with the segments then cut them back with a hacksaw blade (**fig 4**).

The brushes are usually fitted into the rear end bracket. Remove the coil or 'clock' springs which hold the brushes against the commutator. They are brittle and break easily so do not lever them too hard. Check that the springs are not broken — new springs are quite cheap so buy new ones to go with new brushes.

Unscrew the brush leads from their terminals on the end bracket (**fig 1**) and remove the brushes from their holders.

Thoroughly clean the brush holders and end bracket with methylated spirit. Change the brushes if they are worn to less than ⅜ in. (10 mm).

Put the brushes into their holders (**fig 2**) followed by the springs and see that they slide freely.

Before you reassemble the dynamo, clean the main casing, field coils and armature with a soft brush or a rag moistened with methylated spirit. Fit the main casting of the dynamo on to

1. Unscrewing the brush lead

2. Putting a new brush into its holder

3. Compare old and new brushes for length

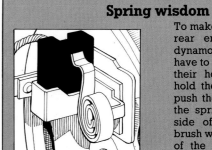

4. Make sure this pip lines up with its cut-out

the front bracket, making sure the locating pip (**fig 4**) on the bracket fits into the cut-out in the main body. Before you fit the rear end bracket check that the small washer is in place on the armature shaft. Refit the rear end brackets (see Tip — Spring wisdom) again making sure that the locating pip lines up. Replace the through bolts in position and tighten them up. Finally, use a small screwdriver to reach through the holes in the end bracket and lift the springs on to the ends of the brushes.

Before you can change the dynamo front bearing the armature has to be separated from the front bracket.

1. Undoing the pulley nut — use rags if you need extra grip

First hold the armature tightly — wrap it in rags if you need extra grip — and then undo the pulley nut (**fig 1**). If there is a spring washer behind it, take it off. Then lever the pulley off the shaft with two screwdrivers, one on each side of the pulley — it may be a tight fit on the shaft so take care not to bend the pulley flanges. Remove the cooling fan and take out the *Woodruff key* from its slot in the shaft. If it sticks, lever it out with a screwdriver (**fig 2**) taking care not to damage it. Also take off the spacer ring behind the Woodruff key, using pliers if necessary.

Put the pulley nut back on the end of the shaft and place the front bracket on the edge of a table top or workbench with the armature hanging down. Hold the front bracket firmly and then tap the end of the shaft with a soft-headed hammer to drive it out of the front bracket. It is a tight fit so you may need to hit it quite hard.

A less brutal method is to use a two — or three — legged

2. Lever out the Woodruff key

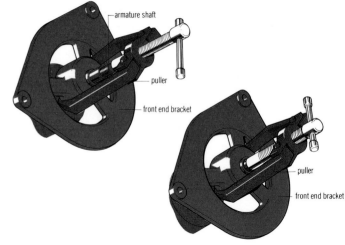

3. Using a puller to remove the armature

puller to pull the bracket off the armature (**fig 3**). Locate the legs of the puller under the lip on the front bracket making sure it is under the central lip (**fig 3**). Do not fit the puller legs over the outer edge of the bracket. The strain may break it and you will have to buy another dynamo. Then slowly tighten the central bolt or crossbar on the puller. The bracket will be slowly pulled off the shaft, complete with the bearing. Hold on to the armature as you pull the bracket off — it is heavy and it may suddenly loosen and drop out on to the floor.

The front bearing in a dynamo is a sealed ball bearing race. If it is worn it must be replaced — it cannot be greased.

The front bearing wears more than the rear one because it has to cope with the load from the drive belt. The most common cause of front bearing failure is an overtightened drive belt.

Before you can get at the front bearing the armature has to be removed from the front bracket to see Step 7.

With the front bracket face down on the bench you will be able to see the bearing. This may be secured either by a cirlip or, on early dynamos, by a plate which is riveted into place. This type is very difficult to repair as it involves drilling out the rivets and hammering new ones in. If yours is this type it may be cheaper and easier to buy an exchange unit.

If your dynamo bearing is

1. Prising out the circlip from its groove

2. This bearing has a packing washer behind it

secured by a circlip, it can be carefully prised out with a screwdriver (**fig 1**) — it is brittle and may shatter or spring out of its groove, so hold a rag over it during removal.

Once the circlip is out, remove the bearing from the bracket making a note of any distance pieces or washes which may be fitted on either side of the bearing.

Push the new bearing into the front bracket, remembering to refit any washers (**fig 2**) that were removed. Push the circlip back into its groove with one or two screwdrivers.

Refit the end bracket to the armature by carefully tapping it back into place with a soft-headed hammer — use a large socket on the end bracket to protect it — or hire a press.

Reassemble the unit (see Step 6), unless you want to renew the rear bearing.

The rear bearing is a plain phosphor-bronze bush set into the end bracket. This bush is less heavily loaded than the front bearing and should not wear so quickly. However, it needs to be lubricated regularly with engine oil and if you neglect this the bearing will wear out eventually.

There are three ways to remove the bush depending on what equipment you can lay your hands on.

The first method is to use a tap

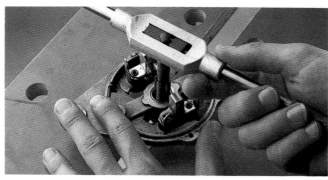

1. Using a tap (thread cutter) to remove the bush

2. Saw a slot in the bush with a hacksaw blade

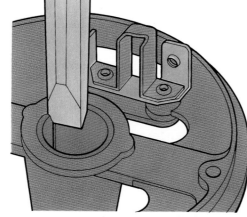

3. Use a small cold chisel to split the bush

(thread cutter) the same size as the internal diameter of the bush. Screw it into the bush as far as it will go (**fig 1**), making sure it is firmly in place. Hold the bracket tightly and try to pull out the bush. If it is tight, hammer the tap lightly until the bush comes out.

Another way to remove the bush is to use a hacksaw blade to saw down the length of the bush (**fig 2**). Then, with a small cold chisel and a hammer, split the bush (**fig 3**) very carefully until it collapses — then pull it out with a pair of pliers.

A third method is to use an internal bearing puller. This will remove the bush in one piece — it is an expensive tool but you may be able to hire one if you are lucky.

Take great care not to damage the end bracket while you are working on it. If you do break it you cannot exchange the dynamo for another one and you will have to buy a new unit.

Before you fit the new bush soak it in engine oil for at least 24 hours. Then tap it into place in the end bracket with a socket used as a drift (**fig 4**). Hammer lightly and make sure the bush goes in square.

4. Hammering the new bush in, using a socket as a drift

A better method which avoids the risk of damaging the bush is to press it into place in a vice. Place the end bracket in the vice and position the bush. Using a socket of the right size between the bush and the jaw of the vice, tighten the vice up slowly. Again make sure the bush goes in squarely. Finally, reassemble the unit (see Step 6) and refit it (see Step 10) but do not lubricate the bearing yet or you may over-oil it.

Hold the generator in position and fit the mounting bolts and adjuster bar.

Refit and adjust the drive belt (see Fact File — Generator drive belt adjustment, page 217) and tighten up all the mounting bolts. If you did not fit a new rear bearing then oil it through the small hole in the rear end bracket (**fig 1**).

Before you refit the electrical connections to the dynamo it will have to be repolarized to suit the car's electrical system. Do not avoid doing this — or not only may the dynamo burn out, but, in extreme cases, you can set the car on fire.

1. Lubricating the rear bearing with engine oil

With the battery terminals connected, attach one end of a long piece of wire to the live battery terminal. Then touch the other end to the field (F) terminal on the dynamo (**fig 2**). Do not worry if this causes a small spark — just hold the wire on to the terminal for about three seconds to make sure the dynamo is repolarized. This gives the field coils a slight permanent magnetism which is enough to make the dynamo start working properly. Disconnect the wire and refit the dynamo connections checking that they are clean and tight.

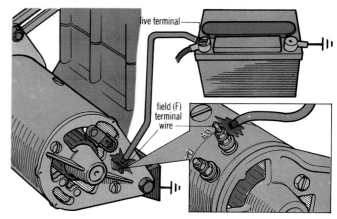

2. Repolarizing the dynamo: Inset shows alternative terminals

STEP 1A — REMOVE THE ALTERNATOR

The alternator is bolted to the side of the engine and is driven by the drive belt. Most alternators are quite easy to remove but on some transverse engines it is fitted at the back close to the bulkhead where it is tricky to reach.

Before attempting to remove the alternator first undo the battery earth strap. Then locate the electrical connector which is usually a plastic multi-connector plug that pushes into the rear casing of the alternator (**fig 1**). The connector should pull straight out but it is often tight and will need a firm tug. Some connectors are also held by a metal spring clip — so look closely before using too much force and if one is fitted lever it to one side with a small screwdriver and then carefully pull out the plug.

Some alternators have bolt-on connections (**fig 2**) — before you remove them make a note of their positions and then undo the bolts and pull the connections out of the way.

The alternator will be held by two or three bolts, depending on the type. Sometimes the

1. Pulling out the multiplug

alternator pivots on one or two bolts from the bottom, whereas others pivot from the top. In all cases there is a slotted bar which allows for adjustment of the generator drive belt and this needs to be undone together with the pivot bolts.

Loosen the bolts but do not take them out just yet. Pull the drive belt off (see Fact File — Generator drive belt adjustment, Page 217) and

supporting the alternator with one hand, take out the fixing bolts one at a time, making a note of any washers or spacers which are fitted. With all the bolts removed, lift the alternator out of the car. To avoid losing the fixing bolts put them back in to their holes on the fixing brackets.

Before you do any work on the unit clean off any road dirt with a meths soaked rag.

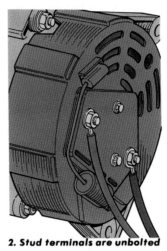

2. Stud terminals are unbolted

HOW IT WORKS

The alternator

The alternator, like the dynamo, is driven by a belt from the engine. Because of its design which uses solid state electronics it produces electricity at idling speed.

The alternator is less prone to overheating than the dynamo because the electricity is generated in the stationary *stator windings*, not in the moving central *rotor*. As the rotor — made up of two end pieces with interlocking magnetic fingers sandwiched around a single winding – turns, it is fed with electricity from the battery via the *slip ring(s)* and the two fixed *carbon brushes*. This turns it into a rotating electro-magnet turning inside the stator coils. The fast moving magnetic field generates an alternating electric current (AC) in the *stator* which is then turned into direct current (DC) to charge the battery and operate the other electrical circuits. This is done by the *diode pack* or *rectifier* which consists of a number of diodes which allow the current through them in one direction only.

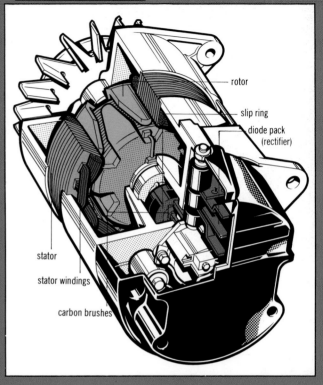

rotor
slip ring
diode pack (rectifier)
stator
stator windings
carbon brushes

STEP 2A — REPLACE EXTERNAL BRUSHES

Most alternators have brushes fitted into a plastic brush holder, held to the rear casing of the alternator by two or three screws or bolts (**figs 1-4**).

With a screwdriver or spanner, undo the securing screws or bolts and lift out the brush holder (**fig 5**). Remove the brushes and check them for wear. A few types of brush simply push out of the holder — on others you have to remove the screw holding the brush lead and then remove the brush. If you have a Bosch alternator, the brush leads have to be unsoldered to remove the brushes. If you do not want to do this part of the job take the brush holder to an auto electrician

who will fit new ones for you.

If the brushes are less than ¼ in. (7 mm) in length you should renew them. Some

manufacturers supply the new brushes complete with the brush holder so renewal is simply a case of removing the

old holder and replacing it with the new one. Fit the new brushes to the holder, soldering them if necessary.

Finally, replace the brush holder, making sure the brushes are seated on the slip rings, and tighten the screws.

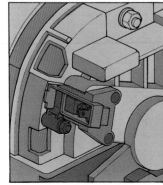

1. Ducellier brush holder

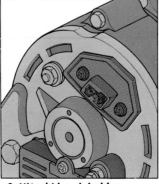

2. Hitachi brush holder

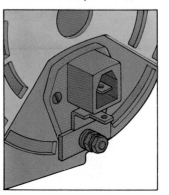

3. Lucas 10/11 AC type

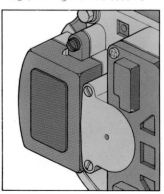

4. Motorola brush cover

5. Bosch brush holder

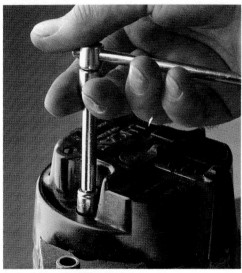

1. Undoing the slip ring cover

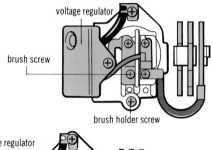

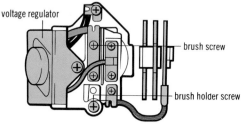

2. Two types of voltage regulator connections

voltage regulator
brush screw
brush holder screw

voltage regulator
brush screw
brush holder screw

Except for the Lucas ACR series, most alternators with internal brushes are difficult to dismantle and can only be repaired by an auto electrician.

On ACR types, use a socket spanner to undo the two recessed bolts which hold the black slip ring cover (**fig 1**). Make a note or draw a diagram of the wiring (**fig 2**) and then disconnect the connection from the brush holder to the diode pack. Then undo the screws which hold the brush holder and the surge diode to the alternator casing (**fig 3**) — some ACR models also have a screw holding the voltage regulator to the casing — and lift the brush holder away (**fig 4**).

3. Unscrewing the brush holder

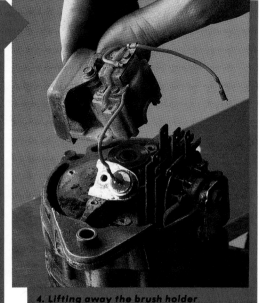

4. Lifting away the brush holder

Undo the small bolts holding the brushes to the brush holder making a note of the positions of the wires to the regulator (**fig 2**). Pull the brushes out of the holder (**fig 5**) — the brush nearest the centre should have a small flat spring fitted alongside it. Check the length of the brushes (**fig 6**) and if they are less than 3/16 in. (5 mm) in length buy some new ones.

Clean the holder with meths and then fit the new brushes into place, remembering to fit the flat spring supplied with the brushes (**fig 7**). Replace the small bolts that hold the brushes, together with any wires that were under them. Now reassemble the unit.

5. Pulling out the brushes

6. Compare new and old

7. Remember the spring

The only alternator with an internal regulator which can be easily dismantled is the Lucas ACR type. The regulator is a sealed transistorized unit so it cannot be repaired — if it is faulty you will need a new one. There are several different types of regulator and it is best to take the old one to your dealer to make sure you get the right one. If the original type of regulator is not available your dealer will be able to offer an alternative type which will fit.

To remove the regulator, first undo the slip ring cover (see Step 3) and find the regulator screws. Some models have two screws — one to the alternator body and one to the brush holder (**fig 1**) — others are held by one screw on to the brush holder (**fig 1**). Draw a diagram of the regulator connections (for the most common ones see Alternative Step 2) and then remove them. Undo the screws and lift the regulator away. Fit the new regulator into place and reconnect all the leads. Finally refit the slip ring cover.

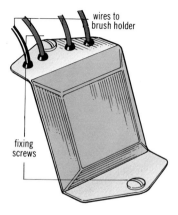

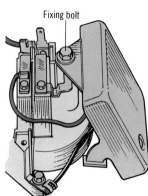

wires to brush holder

fixing screws

Fixing bolt

1. Voltage regulators are held by one — or two — bolts

Check the surface of the slip ring for glazing or wear. If the copper surface of the slip ring looks dull — as if coated with varnish — you should clean it with abrasive paper. Take care not to allow grit or dust to fall inside the unit. When the copper slip ring is smooth and bright give it a wipe with a rag soaked in meths.

If the slip ring is badly worn, scored or holed it should be replaced as it will wear out the brushes very quickly. With the brush holder removed, undo the three bolts which hold the front and rear casings of the alternator together (**fig 1**). Carefully pull the two brackets apart — the rotor and slip ring come off with the front bracket and the diode pack and stator windings come off with the rear bracket.

1. Removing the alternator through-bolts

Slip ring saver

If your slip ring is lightly scored it may be possible to make the surface smooth again to restore maximum efficiency. Lay a piece of very fine glass paper (not emery paper) on a sheet of glass and carefully rub the face of the slip ring on it. Take care to rub lightly and not to rub off too much of the copper facing as it is thin.

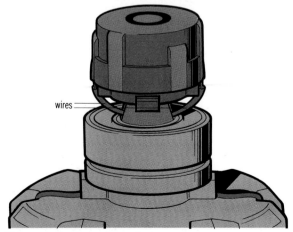

2. These are the two wires which need to be unsoldered

wires

Support the alternator firmly and then unsolder the two wires on the side of the slip ring (**fig 2**). These are firmly attached so you may have to apply the soldering iron for some time before the solder starts to melt. The slip ring will heat up while unsoldering so use a rag to pull it off the top of the rotor shaft, or you may burn yourself. If you do not want to do this part of the job, strip the alternator yourself and take it to an auto electrician.

Push the new slip ring on to the rotor shaft making sure that the small spring clip is in place and that the pip inside the slip ring hole locates in the groove on the end of the rotor shaft. Solder the wires into their grooves on the slip ring but do not use too much solder on the join — it may foul on the diode pack when you reassemble the alternator.

When reassembling the unit make sure the ventilation slots in the slip ring cover are clear and then refit it to the alternator. Now refit the unit (see Step 10).

The rotor has to be removed before the front bearing can be changed. To remove it, hold the rotor tightly and undo the nut on the end of the shaft (**fig 1**). This is often very tight — use rags or wear a pair of rubber gloves to get some extra grip. Take off the spring washer and put it safely to one side.

Using two flat-bladed screwdrivers lever the pulley off the shaft (**fig 2**). If it is tight do not be tempted to use a lot of force — you may crack or bend the pulley. If it will not budge you will have to use a puller on it.

Once the pulley is off you can remove the cooling fan. Rotate the fan until the cut-out slot lines up with the Woodruff key and then pull it off. Use a pair of pliers to remove the Woodruff key — if it is stuck, carefully prise it out with a screwdriver (**fig 3**) — and put it somewhere safe. Take off the spacer ring (**fig 4**) which holds the fan clear of the front bracket and put it safely with the Woodruff key.

Position the front bracket on the edge of a sturdy table or workbench. Make sure the rotor is not fouling on the edge of

1. Undoing the rotor nut

2. Levering off the pulley

3. Prising out Woodruff key

4. Do not forget this spacer

1. Prising out the circlip with a screwdriver

The front bearing in an alternator is a ball bearing race very similar to the ones used in dynamos. These are sealed-for-life units so once dirt has entered the bearing it will wear out quickly. Apart from an over-tightened drive belt, the main cause of bearing failure is dirt getting past a damaged seal.

The bearing is held in by a circlip which locates in a groove in the front bracket. Hold a rag over the circlip and prise it out with a long, flat-bladed screwdriver (**fig 1**). Do this carefully as the circlip is very springy.

With the circlip removed the bearing is simply pushed out —

5. Tapping the rotor out with a mallet

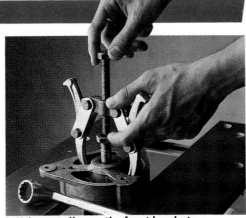

6. Using a puller on the front bracket

the bench and then put the pulley nut back on the end of the shaft. With a copper or hide-headed mallet drive the rotor out of the front bracket (**fig 5**). If the rotor shows no sign of moving do not carry on hitting the end of the shaft — all you will do is damage the nut and threads. Instead, use a two- or three-legged puller on the end of the shaft to pull the front bracket from the rotor assembly (**fig 6**).

With the legs of the puller in place, hold on to the rotor and tighten up the nuts or bolts on the puller, making sure it does not slip off.

TIP

Pulley nut removal

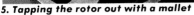

If the pulley nut is very tight, and rags do not give you enough grip on the rotor, try using a strong screwdriver to stop the rotor turning. Brace the screwdriver in one of the front brackets slots and carefully engage it in one of the slots in the rotor, making sure it does not bear on the central windings. You should then be able to undo the nut, but be careful not to damage the rotor.

if it sticks use a socket and hammer to tap it out. Make a note of the position of washers, spacers or seals (**fig 2**).

Reassembly is quite straight-forward. Fit the new seal and bearing into the front bracket, gently tapping them into place if necessary. Once the bearing is properly seated push the circlip back into its groove with two screwdrivers. This requires patience as it is a fiddly job but it will go in eventually.

Refit the bracket to the rotor by tapping the front bracket with a soft-headed mallet. Alternatively, use a press to fit the rotor into the bracket.

2. The new bearing with spacers, washers and seals

STEP 7A — RENEW THE ACR DIODE PACK

The diode pack, or rectifier, is bolted to the rear bracket of the alternator. It is connected to the stator windings by three wires which are soldered in place, so to change the pack the wires must be unsoldered. If you do not want to solder, save money by stripping the unit yourself and the taking it to an auto electrician to have the soldering done. Make a note of where the three wires go (**fig 1**) and then unsolder each one — use a pair of long-nosed pliers to grip the wire as close to the diode pack as possible.

Apply the soldering iron to the terminals for a few seconds until the wire comes loose and quickly pull the wire outwards away from the terminal.

With all three wires removed undo the nut holding the diode pack to the alternator (**fig 1**). Some types are also held inside the casing by an extra nut and bracket, so remove this, if fitted.

As you lift the pack out notice the position of the washers and the small, black rubber cap. These must be transferred to

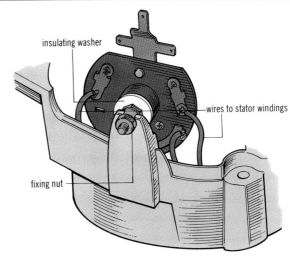

insulating washer

wires to stator windings

fixing nut

1. The diode pack is held by a nut and has three wires

the new pack before fitting it.

Place the new diode pack into position and tighten up the securing nut. Fit the three wires to their terminals, and solder them into position. Do not keep the soldering iron on the terminal for more than a few seconds at a time — the diode pack has delicate components that are easily damaged. Again, use the long-nosed pliers to grip the wires as this will help conduct the heat away.

STEP 8A — REFIT THE ALTERNATOR

Support the alternator and fit all the mounting bolts and the adjuster bar finger tight. Some alternators have an adjustable spacer tube in the rear mounting brackets (**fig 1**) which must be tapped to the correct position before you tighten up the bolts. If you do not do this you can snap the mounting bracket as you tighten up the fixing bolts.

Once you have checked the drive belt is not frayed or damaged refit it and adjust the tension (see Fact File — Generator drive belt adjustment, page 217). Finally, refit all the electrical connections to the alternator, making sure that they are clean and tight, then refit the battery leads.

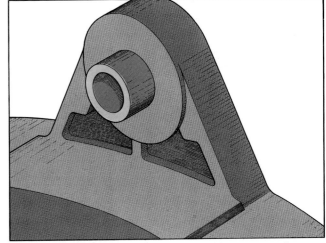

1. This spacer tube needs positioning to suit your mounting

Replacing disc brake pads

Checking and changing your disc brake pads is a straightforward job which will keep your car's brakes at peak form

Most modern cars have disc brakes on the front wheels. Because the front brakes have to do most of the work when you bring the car to a stop you should make sure that they are able to do their job.

The brake mechanism itself is very reliable and needs little maintenance. But the brake pads which rub against the metal disc are softer than metal and so they gradually wear away. A regular check on your brake pads will tell you when they should be renewed.

There is a variety of disc brake designs in use but they all work on the same basic principle. Renewing the brake pads is an essential part of routine maintenance and doing this job yourself will not only ensure that your brakes are kept in tip-top condition but save you money too.

Work on one brake at a time so that if you get into a jam you can use the other complete brake as a guide — but always renew pads on both wheels to do the job properly.

When to do this job
Check pads every 6000 miles (10,000 km) or every six months; renew them when they reach limits

What this job involves
Removing front wheels
Checking and removing brake pads
Fitting new brake pads

Related jobs in this handbook
Curing unbalanced braking
Bleeding the brakes
Renewing drum brake shoes
Handbrake adjustment
Please see Index for page numbers

To do this job
Tools: Jack; wheelbrace; screwdriver; pliers; G-clamp (maybe); hammer and drift (maybe)
Materials: New brake pads; hydraulic fluid; brake grease (maybe)
Time: Up to 2 hours
Degree of difficulty: Easy, unless the old pads are jammed

If you have the job professionally done . . .
Do brakes stop the car quickly and smoothly without squealing? Does car stop straight without brakes pulling to one side? Does brake pedal feel firm rather than spongy?

FACT FILE
Jacking up the car

Many jobs around the car begin with the task of jacking it up off the ground. The jack usually supplied with the car is simple to use — just push its shaft into a jacking point, then turn the handle to lift the side of the car. But there are drawbacks with this type, as they are not designed for anything other than the occasional wheel changing. What's more, the jacking points themselves often weaken on older cars, and can be dangerous.

It is worthwhile buying a sturdier jack for home repairs, which will last longer and allow you to use more substantial parts of the car's framework as jacking points.

One of the most simple but useful replacement jacks is the scissor jack. This is a mechanical

Axle stand

Scissor jack

device which expands upwards in a scissor movement as you turn the shaft with a handle. These jacks are relatively inexpensive and you will probably find that even a small one will be sufficient for most jobs you are likely to do.

Hydraulic jacks are extremely efficient and will lift up even a

heavy vehicle with a minimum of effort. If you expect to do a lot of DIY car repairs, a small hydraulic jack will prove a very useful item.

There are many other types of jacks, such as the hydraulic trolley jack which is ideal for more serious repairs, but which is usually too bulky and expensive to be suitable for roadside repairs or occasional DIY jobs. More recently, air jacks have become available — these use the car's exhaust gases to inflate a bag placed underneath the car and are designed primarily for emergency use.

Jacking points
Regardless of the jack you are using it is very important to give careful thought to positioning it under the car. The area you choose must be capable of standing up to the large force that is exerted on a relatively small area. Avoid areas which are rusty — the jack might just put a hole in the floor instead of lifting the car. Do not use parts of the car such as the engine sump or

cylinder block, the gearbox, rear axle, steering assembly or the thin metal that forms the floor.

Jacking tips
• Never get under a car supported only by a jack. Always support the car with axle stands if you intend to do anything more than just change a wheel.
• Use a level, firm surface, wherever possible.
• Use a warning triangle and hazard lights if you have been forced to stop on a public road.
• Turn the engine off before jacking up the car.

Hydraulic jack

• Keep the car stationary by chocking the wheels with blocks as well as by applying the handbrake.
• Loosen the wheel nuts or bolts before you raise the car and tighten them after lowering it again. Always double check that the bolts or nuts are tight before driving away.
• If you have trouble undoing the nuts you will find that a cross-shaped wheel brace makes the job much easier.
• Use a block of wood as a cushion between the jack and the car but never stack several blocks to extend the height of the jack.
• Avoid using a jack under rusted sills or under the thin metal of the car floor. A piece of sturdy wood between the jack and the car will spread the load over the area you are using as a jacking point.
• The areas of the car most suitable for jacking are the reinforced body members (coloured orange, left). These areas have ample strength to bear the weight of the car.

Safe jacking areas

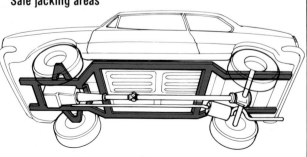

STEP 1　CHECK THE PADS

Jack up one side of the car (see Fact File box) and remove the wheel. You will see the disc, with an assembly covering it. This is the caliper — the device which presses the pads on to the

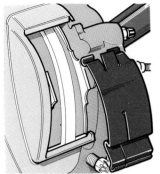

1. Clip found on some Datsuns

disc to slow it down.

On most cars you can already see the edges of the pads, made of dark coloured material, virtually touching the disc on either side of it.

On a few cars, notably later Austin Rover 1100s and 1300s, you have to dismantle a covering to see the pads. In this case you need to remove a cover held in place by split pins. On some cars, such as some Datsun models, you remove the anti-rattle clip so that you can see the pads (**fig 1**).

When you have found the pads, the next thing to decide is how worn they are. When it is new each pad consists of about 3/8 in. (10 mm) thickness of pad material bonded to a metal backing. When the pad mater-

2. New pad and worn pad (top)

ial has worn down to 1/8 in. (3 mm) — some manufacturers specify half this thickness — the pads need renewing (**fig 2**).

The pad and the metal make different sounds when tapped with a screwdriver. Pads with grooves need renewing when they wear down to the bottom of the groove.

TIP
Chock the wheels

When you jack up the car, make sure that at least one wheel is securely chocked so that the car cannot roll. You can buy wheel chocks from accessory shops but it is quite easy to make your own from wood. A piece of timber about 18 in. (450 mm) long and 3 in. (75 mm) square will make a substantial pair

of chocks if you saw it through at 45 degrees.

People often use bricks as chocks. This is not really recommended but if you do use bricks, push the end of the brick, not the side, against the tyre.

You should put chocks both in front of the wheel and behind it.

STEP 2　FIND THE HYDRAULIC RESERVOIR

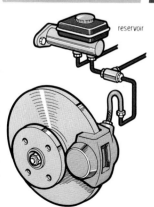

1. Locating hydraulic reservoir

Before doing any work on the brakes, you should open the bonnet, find the brake fluid reservoir, and take off the cap.

On most cars this is directly over the place where the brake pedal enters the engine compartment, as it is operated directly by the brake pedal. In a few cars, the reservoir is elsewhere and is connected by pipes or by a mechanical linkage (**fig 1**).

If the car also has a hydraulically operated clutch there will usually be a similar, but smaller, reservoir nearby linked to the

clutch pedal, so make certain which is which.

The reservoir is a metal or plastic container with a removable cap, inside which you should see the greenish or brownish hydraulic fluid.

The level of hydraulic fluid in the reservoir will rise while you are working on the brakes as you push the pistons back. So put an absorbent rag around the neck of the reservoir to catch any fluid that overflows. Do not let any hydraulic fluid run on to the car's paintwork as it can damage the paint.

HOW IT WORKS
Discs and calipers

Disc brakes consist of a metal disc attached to the wheel hub. When the driver pushes the brake pedal, pads of high-friction material are pressed against the disc to slow it down and bring the car to a halt. Four types of disc brake design are commonly used on cars. The diagrams show the different designs and numbers show the

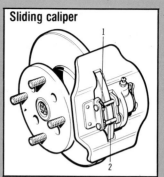
Sliding caliper

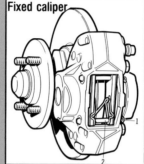
Fixed caliper

by clips. There may be an anti-rattle clip and anti-squeal shims. To remove the pads, you need to pull out the clips so that the pins will slide out. The pads will then be free

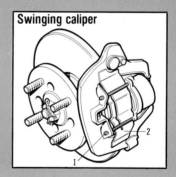
Swinging caliper

order in which you take off the assemblies that hold the pads in place.

Fixed caliper brakes have one hydraulic piston on either side of the brake disc. The pads are held in place by pins which are fastened

to come out. Then you lever with a screwdriver between the pad and the disc to push the pistons back into their housings so that there will be room to put in the new, thicker pads.

Sliding caliper brakes also have pins, held by clips, which hold the pads in place, and are dismantled in a similar way.

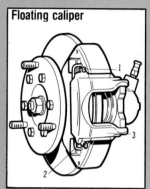
Floating caliper

Swinging caliper brakes work slightly differently. Pull out the pins and take off the pad retaining plate to expose the pads.

Floating caliper brakes have a caliper by which wedges are fastened by clips. Take out the wedges then you can lift away the caliper to expose the pads.

HOW IT WORKS
The hydraulics

Brakes off The diagram shows a simplified system on just one wheel. In practice, the pipe divides into four, with one or two slave cylinders on each wheel. A reservoir keeps the system full of fluid at all times.

Brakes on Foot pressure forces fluid from the master cylinder through the pipes. Since fluid cannot be compressed, the slave cylinders are forced on to the disc. Fluid pressure is the same throughout the system, so each cylinder has the same force on it.

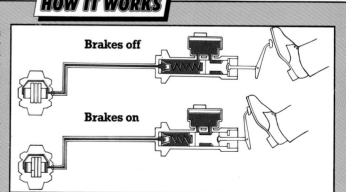
Brakes off

Brakes on

Basically, this step consists of removing whatever holds the pads in place — usually the brake caliper or, in other designs, metal pins — and pulling out the old pads.

In one common type of brake, the pads are held in place by metal pins which are in turn held in place by a variety of systems. The most common method uses springy wire clips.

To take these off, simply pull them off by hand (**fig 1**), or with a pair of pliers, preferably long-nosed ones, or yank them out with the end of a screwdriver. Sometimes they will have worked their way round so that you can see the open end of the clip. If so, prod them round with a screwdriver until you can get at the closed end.

Now you can push out the main pins, either by using your fingers or by drifting them out (see Fact File — The gentle art of drifting, and **fig 2**).

In another system the pins are what are known as roll pins — actually cleft cylinders of springy steel, slightly larger than the holes they fit in so that the spring pressure holds them in place. These can be difficult to remove. Again you must drift them out, but the drifting tool must not be so small as to get stuck in the roll pin. You will need a piece of rod slightly smaller than the hole which holds the roll pin. A nail with the point filed off may be suitable.

Another method of holding in the main pins is by using split pins. Split pins have open ends which are splayed out to hold them in place. To remove a split pin, close the splayed ends with pliers, squeeze the halves together to straighten them and then pull the closed end to remove the pin. You should always renew a split pin rather than use the old one. Makers of replacement brake pads often supply new pins with new pads.

Some brake calipers have a segment carrying the pistons which must be lifted clear of the disc before the pads can be removed. In this case, you must remove the wire clips or pull out the pins, then knock out a couple of wedges (**fig 3**).

The caliper should now simply lift away leaving the pads behind in place (**fig 4**). Hang the caliper from some suitable point to avoid straining the flexible hose, or else rest it on the drive shaft or steering arm — do not just let it swing.

Whatever type of calipers you have, take out the pins and prise away any dust cover or anti-rattle spring that you might find, making a note of how the whole assembly fits together.

You can now set about removing the old pads. It is quite safe to remove both pads from one disc at a time, but do not remove the pads from both wheels together, or you will probably allow air into the hydraulic system.

Before you can take them out, you must relieve the hydraulic pressure on the pads (except on the type where you have already removed the caliper). Do this by prising the pads away from the disc, using a wide screwdriver or a flat bar of metal (**fig 5**). Now you should be able to pull the pads out, either by hand (**fig 6**) or by using a pair of pliers.

If there is an electric wire attached to a pad, trace it along until you come to its connector and disconnect it at that point.

There may be an anti-squeal shim — a flat piece of metal or plastic — between the pad and the piston. See how the shim fits so that you can put it back in the same way.

Once either pad has been removed, you must not put your foot on the brake pedal. This will push the operating piston out of its housing in the caliper, and will probably result in air getting into the system.

TIP
Hammer it out

Sometimes the pin that holds the brake pads in place is very stiff and cannot be pulled out with pliers. If you can see that there is a hole in the caliper at the end of the pin opposite to the head, you should be able to knock this end of the pin with a drift and push it far enough out for you to be able to get hold of it with a pair of pliers.

Make sure that the end of the drift is firmly against the end of the pin before you hit the drift or else the drift may slip. A sturdy nail often makes a suitable drift.

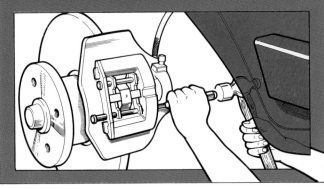

1. Pulling out the clips that retain the pins

2. Using pliers to pull out the main pins

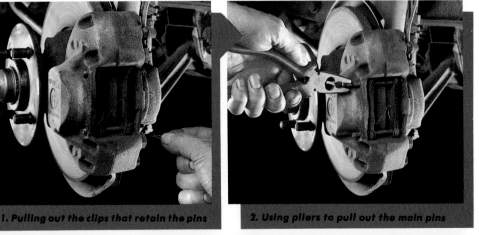

3. Removing wedges that hold the caliper

4. Lifting the caliper away from the disc

5. Levering pads against hydraulic pressure

6. Lifting pads out of caliper housing

STEP 4 — CLEAN THE BRAKES

Before you fit new pads you must clean away all the accumulated dirt in the area of the brake disc and caliper. Turn the disc against a screwdriver to scrape the dirt off the rim (taking care not to score the disc) and use a brush to remove dirt from the calipers (**fig 1**). Bear in mind that most brake pads, and therefore the dust from them, contain asbestos, so make sure that the dust does not fly up in the air. Never blow the dust away — use a damp cloth to remove it.

Also look at the condition of the disc. It does not have a mirror finish, and usually has fine concentric rings, but there should be no grooves deep enough for you to catch them with your fingernail. If a disc is badly scored, either you will need a new one or you should get the old one skimmed smooth by a specialist brake firm.

If one side of the disc is not shiny, but looks dirty or rusty, then the piston on that side is seized. (You will probably have noticed in this case that the car pulls to one side on braking.) Repairing and renewing faulty pistons is a possibility, but if you do not wish to tackle this job yourself reassemble the brake, test that it works properly, and limp off slowly to a garage.

1. Brushing dirt from caliper   **2. Most discs have fine grooves**

STEP 5 — FIT THE NEW PADS

If one or both pads are too worn to be serviceable, renew both — not just one. Similarly, if the pads on one wheel need to be renewed, you should renew the pads on the other wheel as well.

Unless new shims or anti-rattle devices are supplied with the new pads, use the old ones but clean them up. Disc brakes are notorious for squealing, so many people use a brake grease such as Copaslip on the shims (**fig 1**) or the pad backing. But you must make absolutely sure that no grease gets on to the surface of the pads or on the disc itself.

The new pads will be much thicker than the old ones, so you may need to push the pistons back against the hydraulic pressure to make room for them. If you have removed the caliper from the disc, use a G-clamp to push the piston back into the cylinder inside the caliper (**fig 2**). If you have the fixed caliper type of brake, lever the pistons back into their housings with a large screwdriver or flat metal bar (**fig 3**). Sometimes the opposite piston in the same caliper will start to move out as you push the other piston in. If this happens, slip the old brake pad back into place to prevent the piston from moving.

3. Levering the pistons back with a screwdriver   **4. Fitting new pad — wash your hands first**

Before you start to put the brakes together again (**fig 4**), make sure your hands are clean and free of grease. You can now put the new pads, shims and clips into place. If you are not sure how the brake components go together again, look at the brake on the other wheel as a check.

When you have finished reassembling the brakes, check the level of the fluid in the reservoir. If the level has dropped, add some fluid to bring it up to the level recommended in your handbook — usually about ½ in. (13 mm) below the cap — and tighten the cap.

Finally, and most importantly, after lowering the car to the ground pump the brake pedal a few times to make sure that the pads move up to the disc.

1. Smearing brake grease on the shim   **2. Pushing the piston back into the caliper**

Replacing drum brake shoes

Drum brakes must be inspected regularly to give maximum life and smooth, safe braking

Most cars still have drum brakes fitted to the rear wheels and a few small cars have them on the front too. They usually wear out more slowly than disc brakes, so they are often neglected until they wear dangerously low.

When to do this job
When linings are worn beyond adjustment limit
When linings are contaminated by oil, grease or brake fluid. Lining thickness should be checked every 5-10,000 miles (8-16,000 km)

What this job involves
Removing the wheels
Removing the brake drums
Changing brake shoes
Adjusting brakes

Related jobs in this handbook
Bleeding brakes
Replacing disc brake pads
Adjusting handbrake
Please see Index for page numbers

To do this job
Tools: Jack; axle stands; wheel chocks; wheelbrace; pliers; screwdriver (straight or crosshead); you may also need a brake adjusting spanner; hide mallet; puller; large socket; torque wrench
Materials: Relined brake shoes; brake grease; masking tape; string or wire; split pin (maybe); lockwasher (maybe)
Time: Up to 1 hour per wheel
Degree of difficulty: Drums may be hard to remove; springs and automatic adjusters may be fiddly to refit. Some strength may be needed

If you have the job professionally done...
Are brakes efficient (allowing for bedding in)? Do they operate without noise and stop the car in a straight line? Are footbrake and handbrake adjusted correctly? Are the wheels balanced?

Slacken the nuts or bolts of the wheel you are going to deal with, then jack up the car and support it on axle stands so that both wheels are clear of the ground. It is better to work on either both front wheels or both rear wheels at the same time so that you handle assemblies of the same type one after the other. But dismantle only one wheel at a time so that you can use the other complete brake as a guide if you want to check your work. Remember, though, that the brake on one side will be a mirror image of the one on the other side.

If you are working on the front wheels, apply the handbrake and chock the rear wheels. If the rear wheels are raised, the handbrake will not hold the car, so chock the front wheels securely and, if your car has front wheel drive, engage first or reverse gear.

Take off the wheel nuts or bolts and remove the wheels. If you are working on the rear wheels, release the handbrake.

Correctly adjusted brake shoes fit close to the drum face — the clearance is so small that it can be difficult to remove the drum. So if your car has manual brake adjustment, turn back the brake adjuster nuts fully to move the linings as far away from the drum as possible. Front brakes usually have two adjusters, and rear brakes only one, either behind the backplate or accessible through holes in the drum.

Automatic adjusters do not need to be backed off — but look in your owner's handbook to check whether any special procedures are necessary in order to remove the drum.

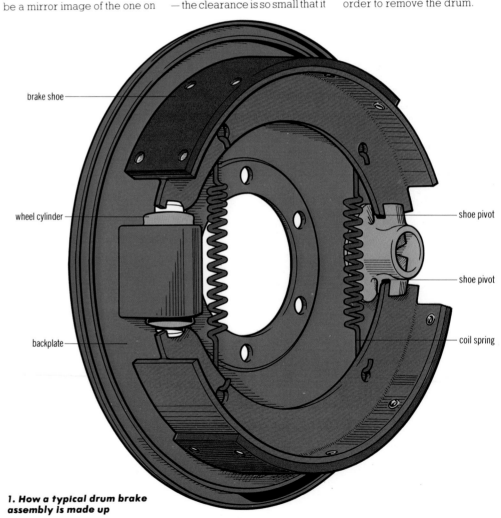

1. How a typical drum brake assembly is made up

brake shoe
wheel cylinder
backplate
shoe pivot
shoe pivot
coil spring

STEP 2 — REMOVE BRAKE DRUM

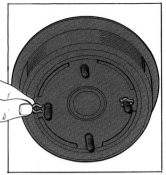

1. Drum held by clips

2. Screw locates drum

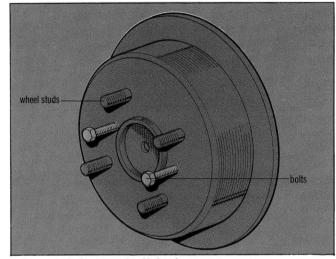

wheel studs

bolts

3. Screw in bolts to push off the drum

The drum is usually held on the hub by one or two countersunk screws or by spring clips on the wheel studs (**fig 1**), but on some models the drum and hub are made as one piece, in which case see Alternative Step 2.

Remove the screws or spring clips and pull off the drum. The drum is a tight fit, and you may find it helpful to rock the drum a little from side to side while you pull. If the drum doesn't move, hit it fairly hard around the edge with a hide mallet, or use an ordinary hammer with a piece of wood between it and the drum. Make sure you do not damage the wheel studs or the hub centre.

If hitting the front of the drum doesn't free it, tap carefully round the back of the drum edge, taking care not to hit the backplate or the hydraulic or handbrake connections, but do not use a screwdriver as a lever between the drum and the backplate or you will bend the backplate.

Alternatively, look for threaded holes in the drum through which you can see the hub face — if these are present, insert bolts and tighten them alternately. This will push the drum away from the hub and backplate assembly.

TIP

Heat the drum

If the brake drum refuses to shift and you do not have access to a proper drum puller to get it off, you may be able to loosen it with heat. Using a naked flame on a brake unit is a bit risky, but you can still heat the drum up by pouring boiling water over it. After a few more blows from the hammer and block of wood it will move.

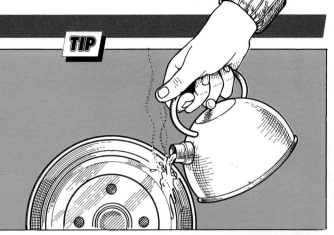

4. Jarring the drum free

5. Knocking drum off from behind

ALTERNATIVE 2 — REMOVE THE DRUM AND HUB

On some cars the drum and the hub are one piece (**fig 1**) and have to be taken off together. Taking off this kind of drum involves removing all or part of the hub bearing as well.

Sometimes the drum is very tight and you may need to use a hub puller — a special tool which exerts a strong pull on to the drum — to do the job. Hub pullers can be hired or you may be able to borrow one from a garage.

With the hub cap removed you should be able to see the hub nut which is either self-

locking or held in place by a tab washer or a split pin. Remove the split pin or knock back the tab washer so that you can unscrew and remove the hub nut.

On some cars, the nearside wheel nut has a left-hand thread and you have to turn it clockwise to loosen it.

Note carefully the order in which any washers or bearings are fitted, so that you can put them back correctly.

If the drum will not pull off, fasten the roadwheel back on to the drum and pull on the wheel.

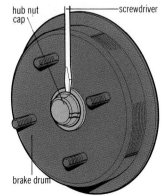

hub nut cap

screwdriver

brake drum

1. Prise off the hub cap

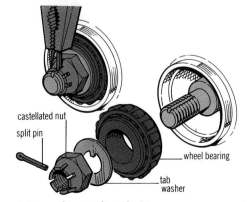

castellated nut

split pin

wheel bearing

tab washer

2. Normal type of nut locking

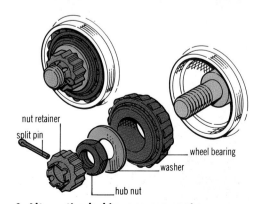

nut retainer

split pin

wheel bearing

washer

hub nut

3. Alternative locking arrangement

167

STEP 3 — CHECK THE BRAKE SHOES

Remove the dust from the drum and backplate assembly, preferably with a vacuum cleaner. Alternatively, use a slightly damp clean cloth and clean off the dust. Take care not to breathe in the dust.

Examine the inner surface of the drum — it should be smooth and shiny. If it is badly ridged the drum will need to be reground or renewed; if there are any cracks renew it.

Check the linings for wear and for contamination by grease or brake fluid. Do not touch the lining surface of the shoes unless you are going to renew them. Riveted linings must be renewed before the rivet heads are level with the lining surface (**fig 2**), and bonded linings must be renewed when they are worn down within 1/16 in. (1.5 mm) of the shoe (**fig 2**). If the linings are oily the source of the leak must be dealt with before the linings are renewed.

If everything is in order, including lining thickness, examine the brake on the other side of the same axle before refitting the first drum, because if you renew the shoes on one side, you must renew them on the other to maintain even braking.

1. A drum needing replacement

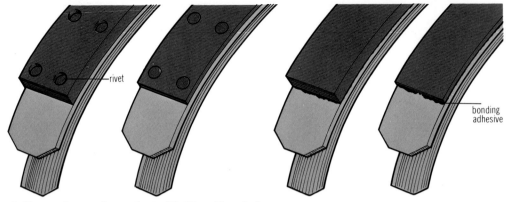

2. New and worn shoes: riveted (left) and bonded

STEP 4 — REMOVE BRAKE SHOES

Before you start taking the shoes off the backplate hold the replacements against them to make sure they match those already fitted. Make a note of how the parts fit together ready for reassembly.

The shoes are held in position by coil springs which fit between the two shoes. Steady springs hold the shoes against the brake backplate.

Before you can remove the brake shoes, you will probably have to slacken the handbrake cable and remove it from its operating lever (**fig 2**).

Most types of brake have steady springs, which can take several forms. To remove the flat spring clip type, grip the end of the spring retainer with pliers and push on the open end of the spring so that the spring slides off the retainer. If the steady springs have a coil spring and the retainer sits on a disc with a slot in it, hold the retainer with pliers and turn the disc to line up the slot with the crosspiece of the retainer.

Some earlier Lockheed brakes have a 'beehive' spring hooked into an eye on the backplate. You can remove this type by gripping the turned in end of the spring with pliers then pushing to compress the spring, and twisting it to disconnect the spring from the eye.

On Bendix brakes fitted to some Ford models the steady spring is located behind the brake shoe. To unhook this spring you may need to make up a special tool by cutting a short slot, wide enough to go over the spring wire, into the end of an old screwdriver.

Some Lockheed self-adjusting brakes have short coil springs holding the wheel cylinder and piston in contact with the shoes. If these springs are fitted, you will need to unhook them.

Note which way round the coil springs holding the shoes are fitted and which holes in the shoes they occupy.

Lever the end of one brake shoe out of the slot that it fits into and then lift the shoe towards you so that the tension on the spring is released. Now lever the opposite shoe out of its slot. You should be able to slip the coil springs out of their holes quite easily and then pull the other ends of the shoes free.

Note how any automatic adjusting mechanism is assembled, as some parts of it will probably be held by the shoes or fitted to the shoes.

TIP

Rubber band trick

When you take the brake shoes off, the pistons may come out of the wheel cylinder and let air into the system. To avoid this, fasten a strong rubber band around the cylinder.

3. Different types of steady springs

1. Removing shoe steady springs

2. Disconnecting handbrake linkage

4. Using slotted tool to unhook spring

5. Removing spring with pliers

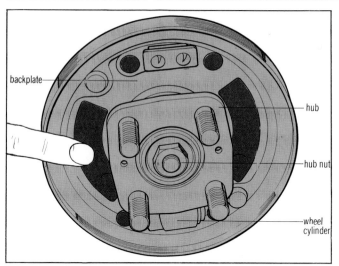

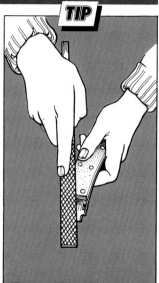

backplate

hub

hub nut

wheel cylinder

1. You can give the areas shown in red a thin smear of grease

Clean the backplate of the brake with a stiff brush and apply a very light smear of high melting point brake grease such as Copaslip to the points on the backplate where the edges of the shoes rub (**fig 1**).

Before refitting shoes with automatic adjusters, fully slacken the mechanism and transfer any parts not supplied with the new shoes. The pivots of automatic adjusters can be lubricated lightly with brake grease, as well as the shoe ends where they fit into the abutments. Do not lubricate any ratchets or screw threads.

Fit the coil springs to both shoes, making sure they are positioned exactly as before. Remove the rubber bands from the wheel cylinders.

Locate one shoe in position at each end and then place the wheel cylinder end of the other shoe in position. Now lever the remaining shoe end into place, making sure that if pins are fitted to manual adjusters they are located correctly.

If the steady spring retainers are loose in the backplate, feed them through the holes in the backplate and refit their springs.

Chamfer the shoes

Brake shoes take some time to bed in but you can start the process off by removing the sharp corner on the leading edge of the shoe with a coarse file or rasp. If you are not sure which is the leading edge, chamfer both ends of each shoe. The brakes should now be smoother and bed in faster.

If you had to disconnect the handbrake linkage, reconnect it now.

Refit the brake drum in the same position as before and secure it with its screws or clips. If the drum is secured by one central nut, reassemble any bearings and washers exactly as they came off and replace the central nut. The central nut may need to be tightened by an exact amount and you need a torque wrench for this — a type of spanner which shows you exactly how much force you exert on a nut or bolt. Look in your manual to find the figure. Do not forget to fit the split pin or tab washer, or to refit the hub cap when you have finished.

Fit the road wheels back into place and adjust the brakes.

Shoe shines

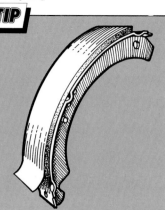

You will probably get dirt and grease on your hands when you are changing the brake shoes. The rubbing faces of the brake shoes need to be kept spotlessly clean if they are to do their job properly, so cover the shoe surfaces with adhesive tape before you fit them. When you have finished the job, peel off the tape and the surfaces will still be clean underneath the tape.

2. Take care not to damage rubber seals

3. Tightening the wheel bearing

The right end

When you lever the old shoes out or fit new ones, avoid levering against the side of the wheel cylinder that has a rubber cover.

If there is only one wheel cylinder, take the other ends of the shoes out first so that the shoe end nearest to the rubber seal can be lifted out by hand. If there are two wheel cylinders, lever the shoe end opposite to the rubber first.

When you fit the new shoes, try to put the ends against the rubber seals first before you lever the other ends into place.

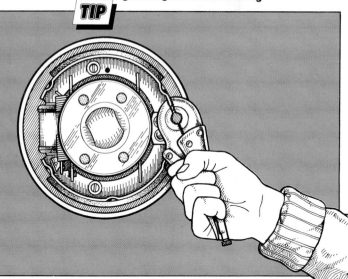

When you have dealt with both wheels on one axle you can adjust the brakes for peak braking performance. If you have manual adjusters tighten the adjusters until the brake binds, then slacken off just enough to allow the wheel to turn freely. Work the brake a few times and repeat.

If your brakes have automatic adjusters the system may operate from either the foot brake or the handbrake. Start by pumping the foot brake several times, then pause and push it again. If the pedal travel has not decreased, pull the handbrake several times and check again — the travel should

now be correct. Finally, tighten the wheel fixings.

Try the car on the road, using the brakes gently at first. You will not get full braking efficiency until the new linings have bedded in, and if you have manual adjusters you may have to adjust the brakes again after 200 or 300 miles.

Checking and replacing dampers

Car's handling not as good as it used to be? Does it dip and wallow on corners and under braking? Try checking your dampers

Dampers, also known as shock absorbers, are a vital but often ignored part of the car's suspension system. Because they are hidden from view and go without maintenance for a number of years, dampers tend to be forgotten completely. Dampers wear out slowly over a long period of time and because of this it is very difficult to notice any change in their performance, but if they are worn you will certainly be able to tell the difference when you fit a new set. The car will be much more stable in cornering and will give a better ride.

When to do this job
When the car's ride and handling becomes noticeably bouncy
If the suspension makes strange noises

What this job involves
Checking the dampers visually
Carrying out damper tests
Removing and replacing telescopic and lever arm dampers

Related jobs in this handbook
Checking a car's roadworthiness
Please see Index for page numbers

To do this job
Tools: Spanners or sockets to fit damper mounting nuts or bolts; soft mallet or hammer and block of wood; jack; ramps or large blocks of wood; screwdriver (maybe); coil spring compressors (maybe)
Materials: Penetrating oil; new dampers (maybe); new rubber bushes (maybe); damper fluid (maybe)
Time: 10 minutes to do the bounce test — half a day to replace all four dampers
Degree of difficulty: Difficulty varies from car to car but is generally awkward rather than difficult

If you have the job professionally done . . .
Does the car handle and ride better? Do the dampers look clean and new?

A good test for worn dampers is to take the car for a ride down a bumpy road with sharp bends. Do not have the car too heavily loaded or it will be difficult to tell if the dampers are worn or not.

When you go round a corner, the car should not tilt to one side, or 'roll', excessively. Nor should it feel as if it is floating, or 'wallowing' when driven over bumps. If either rolling or wallowing occurs, the steering will also tend to feel vague at the same time and both are indications that the suspension is not doing its job.

If driving over a large bump or pothole causes the car to crash down on to its bump stops with a resounding thump and a 'graunching' noise you can be sure that the dampers are worn and require attention.

If a road test is not possible, or is not conclusive, lean on the front wing and push it down as far as you can. You should be able to feel the dampers firmly resisting your efforts. Faulty dampers will either allow you to bounce the car or resist all movement completely. For comparison, try this test on a

TIP

The Bounce Test
A quick and easy damper test is to rock the car violently up and down and then let go. The car should bounce up and then down just once or twice before it settles to rest. Do the test at each corner — if the car bounces up and down repeatedly the damper at that wheel needs changing.

newer car of the same model.

Even if the dampers seem to be performing properly it is well worth carrying out a further visual check for worn bushes and fluid leaks, as described in Step 3. This will enable you to spot a damper that is about to fail and which can be repaired before the car's handling begins to suffer.

Dampers should, ideally, always be replaced in pairs — one on each side of the car. Unbalanced dampers will affect a car's handling as adversely as a damper which is worn out. But if your car is relatively new, or has only recently had its dampers replaced, fitting a single new unit may not cause any problems. If in doubt, try fitting a single replacement and then test drive the car very carefully. You may find that the new unit simply highlights the poor performance of the remaining old damper and results in handling as imprecise as that previously caused by the failed unit. If so, fit another new unit as soon as possible.

1. Carrying out the bounce test with the dampers on the car

To find and identify the dampers used on your car, first check your car's manual. But you should find that with the car jacked up and wheel removed they are easy to spot. Even if you want to work on more than one damper it is best to tackle them one at a time. Not only does this make the job easier but it leaves you a handy reference when you come to reassembly. So jack up the car at the appropriate corner and support it safely on axle stands placed under the chassis.

Take off the road wheel and

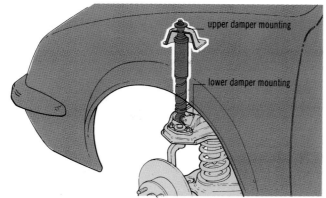

1. Typical location for a front telescopic damper

upper damper mounting

lower damper mounting

look into the wheel arch. You should see the damper mounted close to the wheel hub and fitted between the car's body and suspension.

Some older Austin Rover cars have the lever arm damper forming the top link of the front suspension, while telescopic dampers will be inside or near the coil springs, if fitted. To get a good look at the rear dampers, either telescopic or lever arm type, you may find it easier to work from underneath the car so make absolutely sure it is safely supported first.

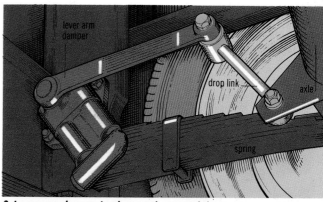

lever arm damper

drop link

axle

spring

2. Lever arm damper in place at the rear of the car

To check for wear, hold the damper firmly near its mounting and try to move it. The forces acting on the suspension are huge so pull the damper hard. But do not confuse worn mounting bushes with wear in the damper itself. If there is any free play at either end between the two parts of the damper it must be renewed as soon as possible. This is very important with lever arm dampers which form part of the suspension linkage because free play in the damper will impair steering.

If you can move the damper as a whole away from the body or suspension then the rubber mounting bushes are worn or the mounting bolts are loose. If the mounting bolts are tight and the damper is in otherwise good condition you may find that you

rubber bush

1. Testing bush for play

can renew the rubber bushes — so find out if your local accessory shop will sell you the bushes separately.

While you are looking at the damper mounts also check the suspension links and bodywork to which the dampers are attached. If you find any serious rusting here you should have the car checked by a garage as new mounts may need to be welded into place.

Finally, inspect the damper closely for any signs of a leak. If a telescopic damper is leaking it must be replaced, but in the case of lever arm dampers first make sure that the leak is not coming from the filler plug.

If the filler plug is leaking renew the washer and top up the fluid level in the dampers (**fig 5**). To do this you will need a suitable damper fluid which you can get from your dealer or accessory shop, though it is becoming a little hard to find. The dampers are filled through a hole near the top of the body of the unit. This hole is sealed by a hexagon headed plug which you have to remove with a spanner.

You can top up most lever arm dampers without removing them from the car but with some types, such as the rear units on

leaking piston seal

leaking filler washer

3. Leaking dampers — both types

the Morris Minor, you have to take them off the car to do the job (see Step 6).

Before you start refilling, ensure that the damper unit and filler plug are absolutely clean and that no dirt can enter the damper.

Take out the filler plug and pour the fluid into the damper until the level is at the bottom of the threaded hole or, if a level plug is fitted, until fluid is level with the hole.

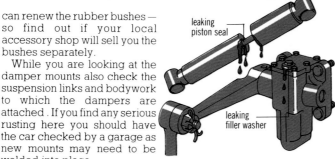

2. Perished rubber bush

The fluid should come in a plastic bottle with a tube attached which makes it easy to fill the damper, but if not use a length of rubber hose attached to a funnel. As you fill the damper pump the lever arm to get any air bubbles out of the fluid. If the damper is still on the car get someone to push gently up and down on the wing — but do not do this with someone under the car.

If you have to unbolt the damper, you will find it easy to fill the unit with one hand and pump it with the other.

When the unit is full, fit the

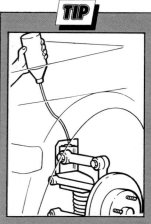

5. Topping up lever damper

plug tightly and bolt the dampers back to the car if you removed them (see Step 6).

Now repeat the bounce test. If the dampers do not perform properly or if they still leak they will have to be renewed.

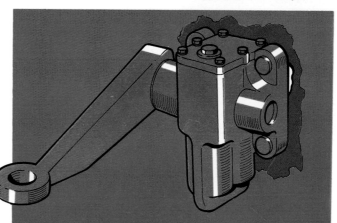

4. Rusted mounting behind lever arm damper

TIP

Squeeze it

If you find that it is difficult to get to the filler hole on a lever arm damper, put the new fluid into a clean plastic bottle. Fit a length of plastic or rubber tube to the nozzle and you will be able to pump in the fluid easily.

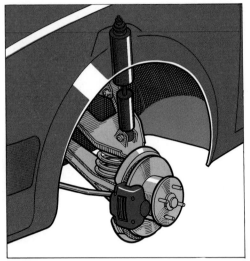

1. With the wheel off, the suspension drops

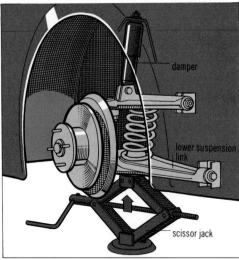

2. Compressing suspension with a jack

damper

lower suspension link

scissor jack

Telescopic dampers may be mounted within a coil spring or separately. If the spring and damper look as though they are one unit, remove them together and then separate them as described in Alternative 5.

Begin the job by removing the large nut and bolt holding the damper at each end. Take note of any washers or spacers and remember their positions for reassembly. Then take off the damper using a pulling and twisting action to ease it off. If the damper is particularly difficult to remove you may find it necessary to take the load off the suspension by using a jack to raise the lower suspension link by a small amount (**fig 2**).

The rubber bushes can also prove rather stubborn, and you may find that the metal inner bushes have corroded on to the bolt or stud. If the bush pulls away leaving the metal sleeve behind, soak the sleeve with penetrating oil and then try to twist it off using Mole grips.

You will probably find a large washer behind the damper on the other side of the rubber bush. It is essential that you replace this correctly and that you do not use one of a smaller

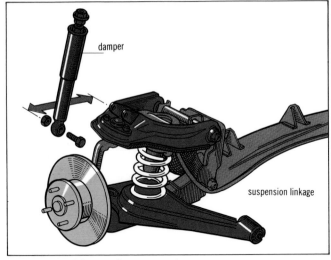

damper

suspension linkage

3. One type of damper lower mounting

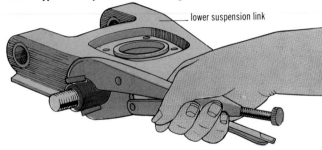

lower suspension link

4. If a sleeve sticks to the mounting, remove it with grips

size, as the washer stops the 'eye' of the damper from slipping over the rubber bush.

Telescopic dampers, which are fitted to the majority of family cars, are not designed to be serviced or overhauled. When they are worn or damaged you must replace them with new units. It is, however, worth shopping around as replacement dampers are often heavily discounted. But buy a well known brand and beware of reconditioned units.

rubber bush

chassis member

washer

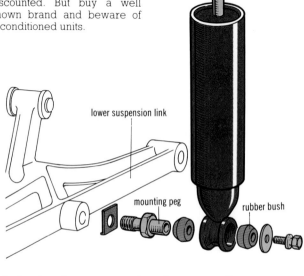

lower suspension link

mounting peg

rubber bush

6. Bush and washer arrangements on damper mountings

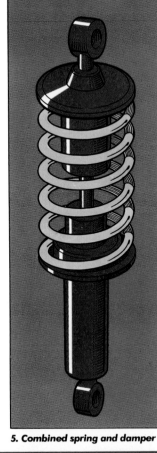

5. Combined spring and damper

STEP 5 — REPLACE THE TELESCOPIC DAMPERS

Replacing a telescopic damper is basically a reversal of the removal procedure. But before fitting a new damper it is worth operating the unit a few times by hand to check that it is working properly. To do this compress and extend the damper by hand. The damper should work smoothly and stiffly when operated slowly — but it should resist any attempt to compress or extend it rapidly.

Having established that the replacement damper is operating correctly, apply a little soap to the bushes to help them slide on, then fit it on to its mounting

studs or bolts. Make sure that you fit all the washers and spacers in the same order that they were removed. If you are unsure of the way the unit fits back on, simply take a look at the damper on the other side of the car.

HOW IT WORKS

Shock absorber

Most modern cars are fitted with telescopic dampers which consist of two tubes which contain oil. When the car goes over a bump the oil is forced slowly from one tube to the other through small holes. This means that the damper cannot be compressed or extended rapidly and counteracts the tendency for the car to bounce on its springs.

Lever arm dampers work in the same way as telescopic ones but instead of comprising two oil-filled tubes, the damping fluid is contained in a chassis-mounted square-shaped reservoir which has an arm that pivots up and down, forming the top link of the front suspension.

On some cars the suspension coil spring is mounted on the damper body and the whole unit comes off together. However, care must be taken when you dismantle this type because the spring is under tension and must be released gently.

Unfortunately you will have to use proper spring compressors to get the spring off — you can hire these quite cheaply from tool hire and larger accessory shops. You may be able to compress and remove the spring by hand but this is tricky, dangerous and needs at least two people — furthermore, replacing the spring is harder.

Put the compressors on to the spring (you need at least two), hooking them over the top and bottom coils. The idea is to try and compress as many coils as possible (**fig 2**).

Screw the compressors up until the spring is pulled away from the top of the damper unit. You should now be able to see how the top of the spring is held down. If there is a split collet, flick this out with a screwdriver and save the pieces for later. If there is a nut, unscrew it. With other types the entire cap assembly will unscrew.

Take off the cap (**fig 3**) and its washers, making sure that you keep them in the right order. You can now carefully slacken off the compressors and release the tension on the spring. With the spring removed you can now treat the damper as a normal telescopic one.

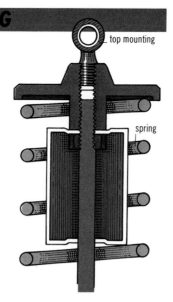
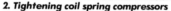

1. Section through top mounting

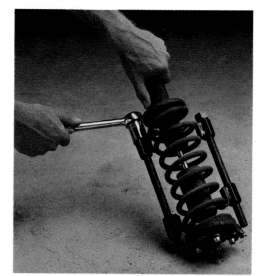

2. Tightening coil spring compressors

3. Lifting off the spring retaining cap

Because lever arm dampers sometimes form part of the load-bearing suspension linkage, more care must be taken when removing them. Whether you are taking them from the front or rear of the car, the suspension must not be at the limit of its travel when you take them off.

With the car's chassis supported on axle stands or ramps, load the suspension slightly at the back by jacking up the rear axle an inch or so, or at the front by lifting the lower link of the suspension in the same way by about the same amount. But take care to load the suspension slowly or you could jack the car off its stands.

Next, disconnect the lever arm. The nut which holds it to the suspension will probably have a split-pin through it. If so, straighten this out and pull it from the nut with a pair of pliers. If the arm is difficult to remove from the suspension, try jacking the lower link up and down while you keep pulling. If it is stuck, you can jar the arm with a soft mallet or use a hammer and block of wood. You may find that the arm will rise up to its fullest extent when you have disconnected it. This is due to fluid pressure inside the unit and is quite normal.

With the arm disconnected, undo the bolts holding the damper body to the car (**fig 2**) and lift it away. It is best to leave the lower suspension arm supported on the jack while you do the rest of the job. This will prevent the suspension upright falling outwards and straining the brake hose.

When rear lever arm dampers are fitted the dampers are held to the underside of the car by three or four bolts. The lever arm is bolted to a link which is attached to the rear axle. Undo either end of this link — whichever you find easier — then unbolt the unit from the car and lift it away.

As with telescopic dampers, it is worth shopping around for replacements for the lever arm types but note that you can get reconditioned lever arm dampers quite cheaply.

When fitting the new unit, bolt the damper to the car's body first, then make sure that the lever arm is working smoothly. Attach the end of the arm to the suspension but make sure that you use a new split-pin on the nut when you fit it. When everything is tight, lower the car to the ground and test drive the car.

1. Pulling out the old split pin with pliers

2. Undoing damper mounting bolt

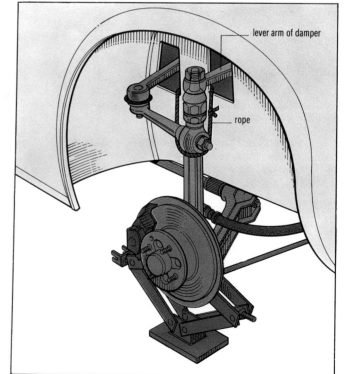

3. Supporting suspension before removing damper

Replacing a clutch cable

Driving with a faulty clutch cable is not only tiresome but is dangerous if the cable breaks. However, most clutch cable problems are quite straightforward to solve

The clutch linkage comes under a lot of strain due to the high pressure required to operate it. Because of this, cable operated systems, which are found on a large number of cars, often give trouble and require maintenance. Hydraulic systems, which are better able to deal with the pressures involved, are dealt with in a separate article.

The most common fault with clutch cables is one of incorrect adjustment, only rarely do cables snap or seize. A cable which has stretched and has too much free play will not release the clutch properly, causing clutch drag, while a cable which is too tight will cause the clutch to slip.

When to do this job
If the clutch is stiff and the car's progress is jerky when it is in use
If it is very difficult to engage the gears

What this job involves
Removing and replacing the clutch cable
Adjusting the clutch

Related jobs in this handbook
Adjusting the handbrake
Throttle linkage overhaul
All round lubrication
Please see Index for page numbers

To do this job
Tools: Two spanners the same size for the adjusting nut and lock nut; pliers; ramps or axle stands
Materials: New cable (maybe); engine oil
Time: Half to one hour
Degree of difficulty: Straightforward but you have to work under the car

If you have the job professionally done . . .
Does the clutch work more smoothly? Does the cable look new? Is there no excessive free play at the pedal?

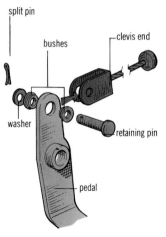

1. Clevis end and pin fixing

split pin · bushes · clevis end · washer · retaining pin · pedal

Having traced the cable run, the next step is to inspect the cable for damage or wear. Begin at the pedal end. You will have to get your head right under the dashboard to be able to see the top of the pedal. Make sure that the cable is firm where it attaches to the pedal (**figs 1 to 3**) and that neither the retaining pin nor the cable eye is distorted. At this point you will

TIP
Smooth operation

If the cable end or the clutch fork are worn unevenly the clutch will operate jerkily as the cable end pivots inside the end of the clutch fork. To check for this, get a friend to sit in the car and operate the clutch pedal while you watch the clutch fork. Any jerkiness will immediately show up. To cure it, simply smooth out the mating surfaces with a fine file and relubricate them.

be able to see a few inches of the inner cable coming out of the outer cable. No part of the cable should show any fraying or wear, as this will cause sticking, poor clutch operation and eventual cable breakage.

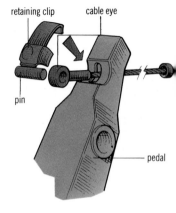

cable retaining clip · cable eye · inner cable · pin on pedal

2. Eye and pin with clip

Check especially the part of the cable where it passes through the bulkhead into the engine compartment. It should be protected by a plastic or rubber grommet. This may be perished or broken, or even missing altogether, and the cable may be fraying against the sharp metal edges of the hole in the bulkhead. A temporary measure to stop this getting any worse is to wind some electrical insulating tape around the area of the cable that is exposed. This will help protect it until you can carry out the more permanent repair of changing the cable.

Make sure that the cable is not rubbing against any other part of the car, such as the exhaust, as this could also cause damage and eventual failure. Then go back to the gearbox and ensure that the end of the cable where it connects to the clutch fork is not

damaged in any way. Again, part of the inner cable will be visible and you will be able to see what condition it is in. If it is frayed you will have to replace it, but if it is rusty, lubrication may be all that is needed.

As a general rule, however, if you find that there is any kind of distortion of or damage to the inner or outer cable you should renew it as it is unlikely that it will work properly.

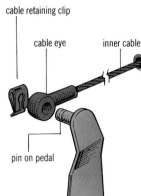

retaining clip · cable eye · pin · pedal

3. Alternative retaining clip

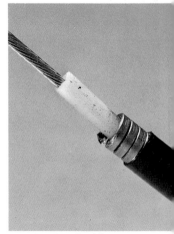

4. Nylon lined cable

To remove the clutch cable you will first have to disconnect it from the clutch engagement lever (also known as the clutch fork), at the gearbox. This takes the tension off the cable and allows you to remove it from the pedal.

If the cable follows a tortuous path it may be worth drawing a sketch of its route before removing it. Then undo the lock nut and adjuster nut and take the end of the cable from the clutch fork (**fig 1**). You may find

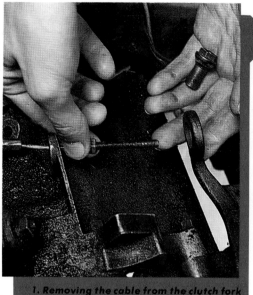

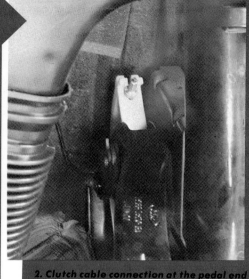

1. Removing the cable from the clutch fork

2. Clutch cable connection at the pedal end

that you do not need to completely remove the nuts to do this as the cable might lift out of the end of the clutch fork without having to pass right through it. Take great care not to let the clutch fork move around too much after you have removed the cable or it could be dislodged from the release bearing. This would mean that the gearbox might have to be removed to replace the fork and release bearing.

Next, disconnect the cable from the clutch pedal. It will be attached by an eye or a nipple on the end (**fig 2**), which is sometimes held in place by a retaining pin. If the pin becomes bent or damaged when you remove it, don't try to repair it, fit a new one.

Pull the cable away from the pedal end, through the bulkhead and out of the engine compartment. Alternatively, depending on what make of car you have, the cable may have to be pulled from inside the car.

With the cable out of the car,

3. Lubricating a nylon lined cable with a silicon based oil

check it carefully. If there are any kinks in it you should be able to straighten them out. Check the operation of the cable by hand — the inner cable should move smoothly inside the outer one. If the cable does not work smoothly, try lubricating it. If this does not improve matters it is best to buy a new cable as the old one is probably damaged or frayed inside and its operation will only get worse with time.

1. Using pliers to get the cable eye on to the pedal pin

Refitting the existing cable, if it is undamaged, or fitting a new cable if it is necessary, is basically a reverse of removal. It is a good idea to lubricate the cable thoroughly with ordinary engine oil before refitting it. However, remember that if you have a nylon lined cable you must only use a silicon based lubricant.

When you have lubricated the cable, pass the pedal end through the engine compartment bulkhead into the car or, depending on the make of car, from the inside of the car into the engine compartment, and attach it to the pedal (**fig 1**), putting a small amount of grease on the cable eye or nipple and pin. While you are in the car it is a good idea to lubricate the pedal mechanism.

2. Pushing the cable through the front bulkhead into the car

It is important to attach the cable to the pedal end first, while there is no tension on it, as this is the fiddly bit and has to be done while the cable is slack.

Now remove or slacken off the two nuts on the threaded end of the cable and pass it over or through the clutch operating fork. Screw both the lock nut

and adjuster nuts loosely on to the threaded end of the cable if you removed them. At this point smear some grease on the threads as well, to stop corrosion and make the cable easier to remove next time you do the job.

Check the route of the cable again before you adjust it. It should follow the same route as that on the diagram you made before you removed it. Again, make sure that the cable is not touching any other component of the car. Make sure also that any curves it follows are smooth, avoiding sharp corners that might stop it from working effectively. If the cable is hanging loose it is a good idea to attach it to a fixed part of the car, which will ensure that the cable stays in place.

Adjusting the cable is quite simple but it is best done from underneath the car. Cable adjustment is given in terms of clearance usually measured at either the pedal or the clutch fork. The actual clearance after adjustment is crucial so it is important to be precise how and where you set it. Check with a dealer or the car's handbook to find out the right clearance for your car and exactly where you measure it (also see **fig 5**).

Where the clearance is measured at the clutch fork, unhook the clutch fork return spring (**fig 1**), if fitted, from between the fork and the bell housing. Then move the fork backwards and forwards a few times to see how much free play there is between the flat surface of the adjuster nut and the fork itself. Ideally you should measure this with a feeler gauge, but you are unlikely to have any thick enough so use a ruler instead (**fig 2**). If you have a drill bit of the correct diameter you can use the plain shank to measure the gap in the same way as you would use a feeler gauge (**fig 4**).

If the amount of free play is not exactly right, screw the adjuster nut one way or the

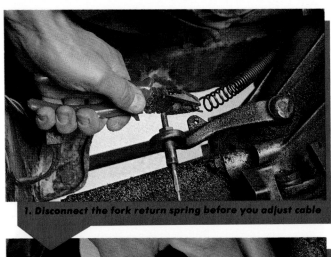

1. Disconnect the fork return spring before you adjust cable

2. Measuring the free play at the fork

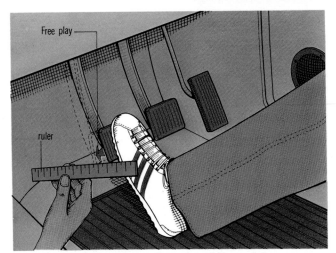

3. On some cars you measure free play at the pedal

other to increase or reduce the clearance. Measure the gap again and tighten the locknut against the adjuster nut.

Make sure that when you do this you do not move the adjuster nut at all or you will have to check the gap again.

On some cars, with constant contact release bearings, there should be no free play at the clutch fork. Instead, the clearance is measured at the clutch pedal. This means that you have to use a slightly different method of adjustment. Place a ruler by the side of the pedal, following the line it takes as it is being depressed (**fig 3**). Press the pedal gently until the free play is taken up and it gets

harder to move the pedal any further. Measure this amount of free play and compare it with the measurement given by the manufacturer — if the two measurements are different then you will have to adjust the cable. Adjust it by turning the nuts at the clutch fork on the gearbox as above.

The Mk III and Mk IV Ford Cortinas have yet another different method of adjustment. This is because the clutch fork on the Ford gearbox lies underneath a rubber gaiter and is not accessible. The threaded part of the cable with the adjuster nut screws into the bell housing of the gearbox.

First undo the locknut, then get someone to pull the clutch pedal up as far as it will go. Pull on the cable where it comes out of the bell housing and measure

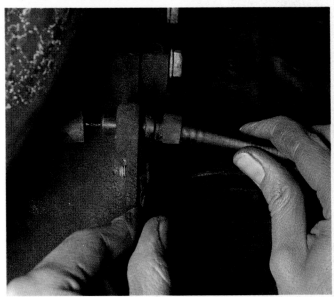

4. You can use a drill of the correct diameter as a feeler gauge

the distance between the bell housing and the adjuster nut on the cable. The distance should be 3 to 3.5 mm which will give about 25 mm of back play at the pedal. Adjust this in the same way as the other types.

A further variation, as found

on the Datsun Cherry and the Vauxhall Astra, involves measuring the total amount of pedal travel from the normal position down to the floor. Adjustment is, however, still carried out at the gearbox end of the cable in the same way as for the other types.

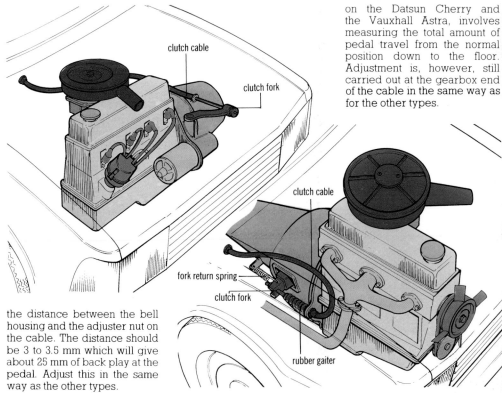

clutch cable

clutch fork

clutch cable

fork return spring

clutch fork

rubber gaiter

5. Where to find the adjusters. FWD, (left), and RWD, (right)

Curing fuel flow problems

Poor, jerky running could be caused by a simple fuel line fault — the cure is regular servicing and cleaning of the pump and filters

The car's engine needs a constant supply of clean petrol if it is to run smoothly. All cars have a fuel pump which moves petrol from the petrol tank towards the engine. Some pumps are electric but most modern cars have mechanical fuel pumps which are driven by the engine. Your car's handbook will tell you which type of pump you have and where it is mounted.

Fuel pumps are generally reliable units but they do occasionally need attention. For some pumps you can buy overhaul kits which contain the parts which are most likely to wear out or go wrong.

When to do this job
When engine splutters intermittently
When starting is difficult
When car will not develop full power or reach high revs

What this job involves
Cleaning in-line filter
Fitting new in-line filter
Cleaning filter in pump
Overhauling fuel pump

Other possible causes and related jobs
Tackling excessive fuel consumption
Dealing with a smoky exhaust
Carburettor problems
Please see Index for page numbers

To do this job
Tools: Spanners; screwdriver; hacksaw (maybe)
Materials: New in-line filter (maybe); fuel pump overhaul kit (maybe)
Time: Up to two hours
Degree of difficulty: Renewing components inside fuel pump can be fiddly

If you have the job professionally done . . .
Does car start without difficulty? Does engine run smoothly and develop full power? Are there signs of fuel leaks?

Tracking down any fault when the car is not running well can be a difficult job but there is one difference between fuel supply problems and electrical faults which will often point you in the right direction.

If the fault causes the engine to stop dead, it is likely to be electrical. If the car splutters to a halt, it may be the fuel.

To see whether any petrol is reaching the engine, take off the end of the fuel line where it joins the carburettor. It will either be held on by a hose clip or else clamped in place with a nut.

If your car has an electric fuel pump, hold the end of the fuel pipe in a jar and ask a friend to turn on the ignition but not to operate the starter. If the fuel supply system is working properly you will hear the fuel pump ticking rapidly and petrol will pour into the jar.

If you have a mechanical fuel pump, hold the end of the fuel pipe in a jar and ask a friend to turn the engine over with the starter. Petrol should pour out of the pipe.

If no petrol comes out or if only a trickle comes through, the problem is likely to be a blocked fuel filter or a faulty fuel pump.

This petrol flow test has obvious potential for danger, since the battery cannot be disconnected, but provided there is no way the fuel can be accidentally ignited and you take sensible precautions you should be in no danger. Any spilt fuel will soon evaporate, but do not take any risks while there is still a smell of petrol.

2. Test flow like this

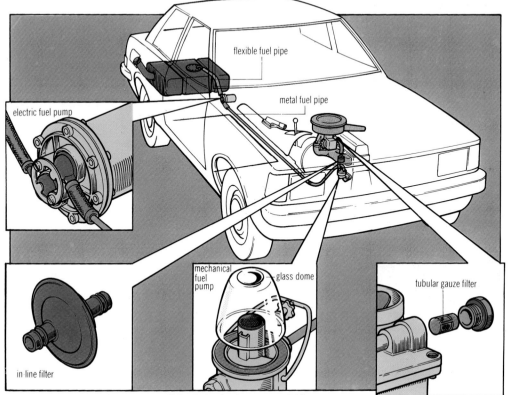

flexible fuel pipe

metal fuel pipe

electric fuel pump

mechanical fuel pump — glass dome

tubular gauze filter

in line filter

1. The most likely places you will find the fuel pump and filter

Many cars are fitted with an in-line fuel filter, fitted under the bonnet between the fuel pump and the carburettor. There are different shapes of filter, but common types include disc and barrel shaped ones (**fig 1**).

Note which way round the filter is fitted before you take it off. Some filters have arrows in the direction that the fuel flows and others are marked 'Inlet' and 'Outlet'.

Slide the filter out of the fuel line. Usually they are held in place by two clips which you need to loosen (**fig 2**). If your filter can be opened up, take it

2. Inserting an in-line filter

apart and wash the filter element in petrol. Make sure that there is no loose dirt inside the filter housing and then put the assembly back together again. Fasten the filter back into the fuel line and check that no petrol seeps out of the filter when you start the engine.

If you find that your filter does not come to pieces it is probably

paper element filter

glass dome

1. Some types of in-line filter. The arrow points towards the carburettor

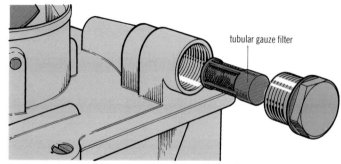

tubular gauze filter

3. A rarer type of filter housed within the carburettor

not worth trying to clean it out as you can buy a new in-line filter quite cheaply. Take the old filter with you to your car spares shop so that you can buy another one of the same type.

Some cars have in-line fuel filters which look rather like mechanical fuel pumps. They have glass domes which hold the filter element itself. This type of filter is usually mounted on the inside of the car's wing.

Unscrew the nut that holds the dome in place and lift off the

dome. There may be a spring inside that holds the filter element in place. Take out the element and wash it thoroughly in petrol. Wipe out any dirt inside the filter housing and then fasten the filter together again. Make sure that petrol does not leak out of the filter when you run the engine.

Some types of carburettor have a filter fitted into the carburettor assembly. Look for a hexagonal nut beside the carburettor body or near the

top of the carburettor. Take off the nut and inside the recess behind the nut you will find a thimble-shaped piece of gauze which is the filter element. Wash the filter in petrol and then fasten it back into place.

4. Removing the thimble filter

If your car does not already have an in-line filter in the fuel system, it may be worth fitting one to make sure that no dirt can get through to the carburettor. You can buy a kit which has a filter, some lengths of fuel pipe and some hose clips.

Find a suitable place in the fuel line to fit a filter. Trace the fuel line away from the carburettor until you find a part of the line where there is room to fit one. The extra bulk and weight of the filter must not cause the filter or the fuel line to touch any hot parts of the engine.

If your fuel line is not made of metal, cut out enough of its length to make room for the filter. Slide the ends of the filter into the fuel line and then fasten the line on to the ends with the hose clips.

If your fuel line consists of

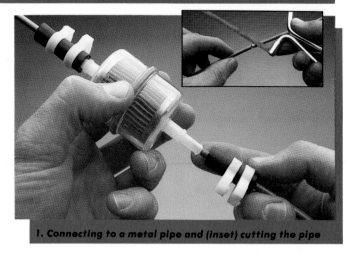

1. Connecting to a metal pipe and (inset) cutting the pipe

metal pipe, use a hacksaw to cut away a length of pipe slightly longer than the complete in-line filter assembly. Then slide a length of the pipe in the filter kit

over one end of the filter and over one end of the metal fuel line. Fit the other pipe to the other end of the filter and fasten up the connections.

The mechanical pump has a domed top which is held in place by screws or a nut. Unfasten the nut or screws and take off the pump top. Inside you will find a round disc of fine gauze. This is the fuel filter. Take out the filter and wash it in petrol to remove any dirt.

Sediment may have settled in the space underneath the domed cover. Brush out any grime in this area and wipe it clean. Check the sealing ring where the pump top meets the body. It should be in perfect condition to stop petrol from leaking out. Renew the sealing ring if it is damaged taking care to seat it correctly.

Put back the clean filter and fasten the pump together again. Check that no petrol seeps out of the pump when the engine is running.

1. Removing the gauze filter from the pump

You will need to take the fuel pump off the car to get at the filter. But first, disconnect the car's battery so that there is no danger of sparks.

Next, undo the clamp which holds the pump to the car and lift the pump clear. Then take off the two wires from the pump.

You now need to make some preparations because a lot of petrol may try to run out of the fuel pipes when you pull the pipes off the pump. Have ready two suitable tapered objects such as Biro tops to stop up the fuel pipes.

These pipes are held on to the pump by hose clips or spring

1. Stop up the pipes with anything handy

2. This electric pump has a tubular filter

clips. Loosen the clips and slide the pipes off the pump, stopping them up quickly.

There are two common locations for the filter on electric fuel pumps. In one type, the filter is inside a housing at the thicker end of the pump. Look for a six-sided nut or socket on the side of the base of the pump. Unscrew the nut and draw out the filter element, which is a thimble shaped gauze tube. Wash the filter in petrol and fasten the pump together again. Check that petrol does not come out of the filter housing when you start the engine.

In the other common design of

electric fuel pump, the filter is fitted next to the inlet valve. At the wider end of the pump you will see two black plastic domes, each with a tube sticking out to one side. The metal base of the pump is marked 'Inlet' and 'Outlet' Between the two domes is a metal plate held by two screws. Take out one of these screws and loosen the other one so that you can move the metal plate away from the 'Inlet' valve.

Carefully lift away the black dome and you will see the gauze filter underneath. Wash the filter in petrol and then reassemble the pump.

3. Newer types of pump have circular gauze filters

If cleaning the filter does not improve the fuel flow, you may need to overhaul the pump. The parts of a mechanical fuel pump which can be easily overhauled are the diaphragm and the valves. When you buy an overhaul kit it will also contain new gaskets for the joint where the pump fastens to the engine and a new sealing ring to fit around the base of the glass or metal dome.

Take off the fuel pipes at the two sides of the pump. They are either a push fit with securing clips or are clamped up with a nut at the end of the pipe. Some petrol will run out of the pipe which leads to the carburettor.

Undo the two bolts which hold the pump to the engine and lift the pump away.

The two halves of the pump are held together by bolts around the central flange Take out these bolts and any washers that go with them.

Tap the pump gently with the wooden end of a hammer to get the two halves apart. When you feel that the two parts have come free they may still be stuck together by the diaphragm between them. Pull the rubber tab on the diaphragm so that you can separate the halves completely.

The diaphragm is fastened to

1. Separating the pump halves

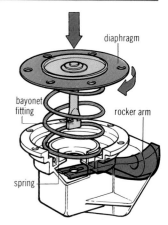

2. How to fit the diaphragm

the bottom part of the pump by a bayonet type of fixing. Push the diaphragm down and turn it through a quarter of a turn. The spring should then push the diaphragm out. Clean the inside of the diaphragm housing with petrol.

On the underside of the top of the pump you should be able to see two circular components. These are the valves. Note which way up they go so that you can fit the new valves the same way.

Lever the old valves out of their seats with a screwdriver and take out the gaskets which sit under the valves. Now fit the

new gaskets from the kit and tap the new valves into place.

Fasten the pump back together again and check that the rubber sealing ring around the base of the filter bowl is in good condition. If it is not perfect, fit the new ring from the kit to be on the safe side.

Now fasten the pump back in to place on the engine, using a new gasket between the pump and the engine. Lift the rocker arm as far as you can when you insert the pump into its housing. This will make sure that the arm stays correctly positioned above the eccentric cam which moves it up and down.

3. Make sure you fit the valves correctly   **4. Prising out a metal valve**

There are three parts of the electric fuel pump which you can easily renew. These are the valves, diaphragm and points.

The valves, in common types of pump, are located at the base of the pump, inside the plastic domes that the fuel pipes are connected to. Loosen the two screws on the metal disc that holds the plastic domes in place. Then take one of the screws out and swing the metal disc to one side. Take off the plastic domes and then take out the washers, filter and metal valves inside the housings.

Note carefully which way up the valves are fitted. If you get them upside down, the pump will not work.

Fit the new valves in place and then refit the filter, rubber sealing rings and plastic domes. Make sure the sealing rings are not trapped before you tighten up the metal disc.

The diaphragm is fitted between the two halves of the fuel pump. Take out the screws around the lip in the body of the pump. Then separate the two halves of the pump body.

You may need to tap the pump around the lip with a hammer to free the two halves. When the two parts come free, separate them carefully so that you do not damage the pump.

The diaphragm is the circular component with a metal centre which covers the end of the metal body of the pump. Make sure that the diaphragm is not stuck to the pump by running a thin screwdriver around the edge of the diaphragm. When the diaphragm is free you should be able to turn the diaphragm anticlockwise. Just turn the diaphragm a few degrees to check that this is possible.

The other end of the diaphragm assembly is held in place by the points. These are fitted underneath a cap at the top of the pump. There may be a broad rubber band or a length

1. A typical electric pump

2. Separating the diaphragm from the end cap assembly

3. The points cover removed — this one has a drain spout

of tape around the cap.

Undo the cap by sliding it up over the screw thread that the electric wire was attached to. Under the cap are the points.

Take great care at this stage. It can be rather fiddly getting the new points into place so that you can fasten the diaphragm. Note exactly how the points are assembled so that you can fit the new points correctly.

Unscrew the diaphragm and take out the spring between the diaphragm and the pump.

Then unscrew the bolt which holds the wire that is attached to the points. The points are now held only by the pin which anchors them to the pillars on the top of the pump body. Pull out the pin and you can then take out the points assembly.

When you have fitted the new points in place, screw in the new diaphragm. The collar in the points assembly that the diaphragm screws into tends to turn over, so hold the collar in position with a screwdriver while you fasten the diaphragm.

Do not screw the new diaphragm in too far or it will not be able to do its job. Hold the pump and press firmly on the metal centre of the diaphragm. You should be able to feel the diaphragm moving and to see

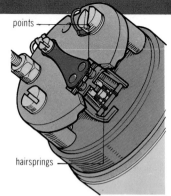

4. How the points are held

the points moving.

Now replace the part of the points assembly that sits on top of the plastic points housing. Take out the screw that holds the wire, fit the new part and reassemble the pump.

Refit the pump to the car, connect the battery again and check your work. The pump should tick vigorously for a second or two then settle down to slower, regular ticking, and soon stop. If the pump continues there could be a fuel leak.

5. Withdraw the pin to free the moving half of the points

6. Holding the collar with a screwdriver

7. Removing the stationary contact

When your choke sticks

Car difficult to start in the morning or refuses to run properly when hot? Either way, a quick choke check could solve your problems

If your choke sticks on it will cause poor running when hot and an increase in fuel consumption at the very least. If it sticks off, or the cable breaks, you will have great difficulty in starting the car and driving away — all good reasons for getting to the bottom of the problem as soon as possible.

Other, more major problems can give you similar symptoms as a sticking choke, but the choke is the most likely and is also the easiest to locate, check and put right.

When to do this job
When black smoke comes from the exhaust during normal driving with the engine warm
If the car uses too much fuel
When the car is very difficult to start and will not pull from cold
When the car starts easily from cold yet seems underpowered or misfires when hot

What this job involves
Checking the choke cable
Checking the choke linkage
Removing and replacing choke cable
Adjusting the choke cable and linkage

Related jobs in this handbook
Tackling excessive fuel consumption
Please see Index for page numbers

To do this job
Tools: Spanners; screwdriver; pliers (maybe);
Materials: Oil (maybe); new cable (maybe); new return springs (maybe)
Time: Up to two hours
Difficulty of job: Very straightforward

If you have the job professionally done
Is the car easier to start from cold? Is the fuel consumption better? Has the black smoke stopped coming from the exhaust? Has misfiring when warm stopped?

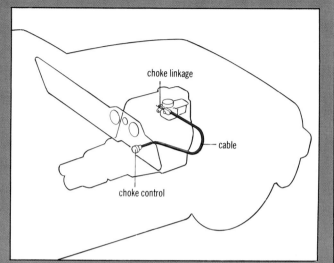

Manual chokes

There are several types of manual choke systems, but most work in roughly the same way — by pulling a dashboard mounted knob. The knob is attached to a metal rod and then to a cable as a one-piece unit.

The inner cable is attached at the other end to an operating linkage on the carburettor. The actual linkage varies according to the type of carburettor fitted but it is usually a simple spring-loaded lever. The outer cable is attached to the dash panel at one end and to the carburettor at the other. This outer cable restricts the movement of the inner cable to a forward and backward direction allowing the choke mechanism to be pulled on and pushed off.

choke linkage

cable

choke control

STEP 1 — DIAGNOSE THE FAULT

It may not always be clear that the choke is sticking — the control knob may appear to work normally without actually doing anything. However, you may notice some symptoms which will give you a clue that there is something wrong and whether it is sticking on or off.

If the choke sticks in the 'on' position, the engine will start very easily from cold. However if the knob is not stiff to push back this gives you a clue that something is wrong. You may notice uneven or high tickover, a spluttering engine when hot, high fuel consumption and bad starting when hot. If the choke sticks in the 'off' position and yet the choke tends to come out normally the engine will show signs of being extremely difficult to start from cold. If it does start, it will not pick up or pull away until it has warmed up. The engine may also misfire and spit or pop back through the carburettor when you press the throttle on starting.

Before starting to track down the cause of a sticking choke it is a good idea to check the air filter first. A clogged air filter can give almost exactly the same symptoms as a sticking choke. Air filter removal is covered on page 81. If the air filter is clean, or if it is obvious that there is a problem because the choke knob control is excessively stiff or slack then check each part of the system until you find the fault.

1. A dirty filter gives similar symptoms to a sticking choke

STEP 2 — CHECK CARBURETTOR CONNECTION

If you have not removed the air filter to check it, remove it now to allow better access to the choke linkage at the carburettor. There are usually two cables fixed to control mechanisms on the carburettor — one for the throttle and one for the choke. If you are unsure which is which, get an assistant to sit in the car and press the accelerator pedal a few times. This operates the levers on the carburettor — the one that does not move is the choke.

Now ask the assistant to pull and push the choke knob a few times. While this happens look carefully at the cable attachment on the carburettor. There are several different types (**fig 1**). Make sure that both the inner and outer cables are firmly attached to the linkage and that the operating arm moves freely when the assistant pulls and pushes the knob.

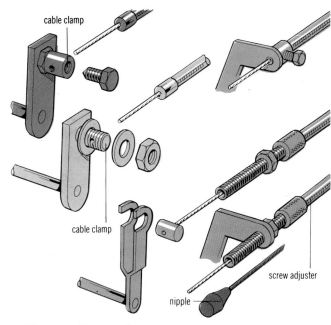

1. Different cable-to-carburettor connections

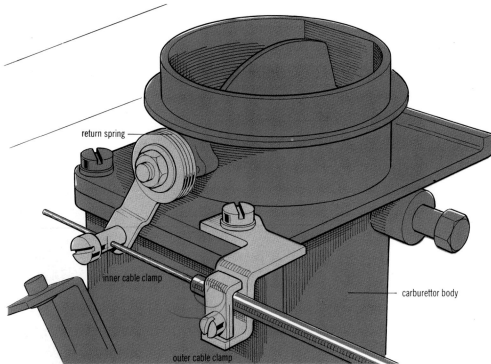

2. A typical choke cable clamp and operating arm

If the outer cable moves in its clamp, tighten up the clamp (**fig 2**). If the inner cable has frayed between the clamp and where it is fixed to the lever, the stray strands may prevent the full movement of the choke. In this case the strands need to be cut off with pliers, or, if this fails to work, the cable needs to be renewed (see Step 7).

If your cable has a sleeve on the outer that fits into a housing bracket make sure it is seated properly in place.

Next check that the inner cable is firmly clamped to the lever on the carburettor. If it is loose it will simply slide in and out of the clamp screw and the lever will not move. If this is the case you will have to readjust the cable to give the correct movement (see Step 7).

If the cable appears to move the end of the lever correctly but the choke is still not working, check that the lever or linkage is not loose where it joins the carburettor. If so, tighten the nuts which hold the lever.

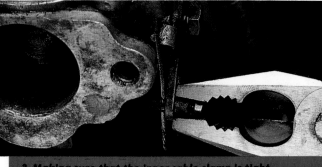

3. Making sure that the inner cable clamp is tight

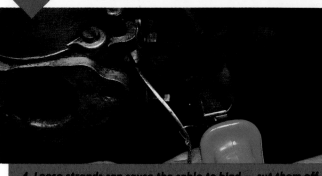

4. Loose strands can cause the cable to bind — cut them off

STEP 3 — CHECK THE LINKAGE

While you have the choke cable removed it is a good idea to check the operation of the choke lever at the carburettor.

Put your finger against the lever to which the inner cable fits and push the linkage to 'on' — when you release it it should return by itself to the 'off' position. If you cannot remember which way is 'on', an easy way to make sure is to push the linkage towards the outer cable mounting. If the choke linkage does not return by itself the return spring may have become disconnected or is broken.

If the lever fails to work properly after you have reconnected the spring you may have to remove and partly dismantle the carburettor to find the cause. A spindle problem is likely.

1. Make sure the choke returns to fully off

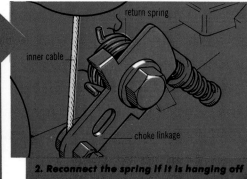

2. Reconnect the spring if it is hanging off

If the cable is kinked, twisted or damaged in any way between the dashboard mounted knob and the carburettor it will probably jam the choke or at least make it stick.

Follow the run of the cable backwards from the carburettor towards the dashboard or steering column, keeping track of it as it passes through the bulkhead. If the cable is snagged or bends sharply around a component, free it and try to straighten it out with your hands as best you can.

You can only see fraying on a cable at the carburettor end where the inner cable comes out of the outer one. However, if the choke control feels springy this is a sign that the inner cable is frayed inside at some point along its length (**fig 2**) and must be renewed (see Step 7).

If the cable run is smooth and free as far as the dash or steering column, check the large locking ring or nut securing the cable outer behind the dash panel or steering column. This should be tight up against the panel or its mounting bracket.

The choke control knob is actually attached to a short piece of metal rod which is then attached to the inner cable. If this is bent it will make the choke stiff or impossible to operate. You should be able to straighten this by hand or with a pair of pliers. If you have made the rod as straight as you can you might be able to make it work smoothly by finishing with a fine file.

The metal rod also forms the choke locking mechanism. If this is faulty there is nothing you can do to repair it — at least if it is loose the choke will not remain on unnecessarily as it will tend to self return all the time. However, if you cannot put up with holding the choke out until the engine is warm you have no alternative but to renew it. Cable replacement is covered in Step 7.

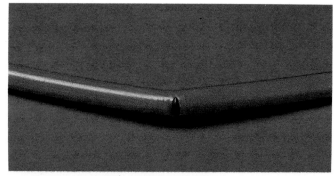

1. A kinked outer cable will cause binding

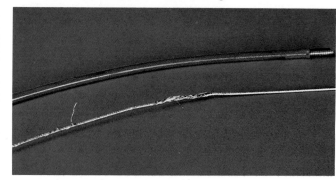

2. A badly frayed inner cable will stick in the outer

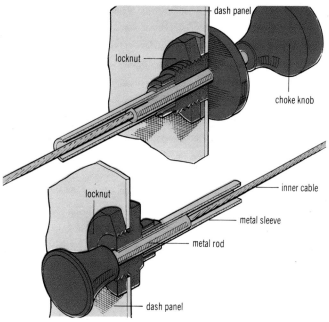

3. Two types of choke-to-dash mounting

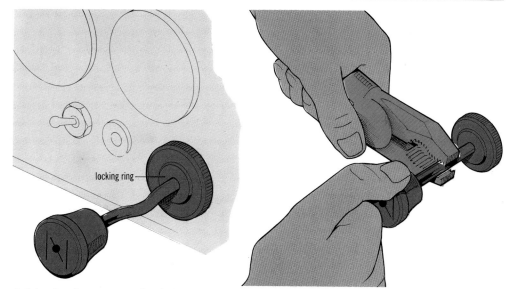

4. A bent rod may cause the choke to stick. Straighten it with pliers

You cannot normally buy a separate inner or outer cable — they are sold as a unit so removal for replacement oiling or further checking involves disconnecting the entire cable system. Disconnect the cable from the carburettor end first. Keep the locknuts or nipple clips with it to avoid losing them. At the back of the dashboard or inside the steering column undo the large locking ring or nut to free the outer cable. You will probably have to use pliers or grips. The cable can then be pulled out from inside the car. If you have to loosen or remove part or all of the steering column shroud to gain access to the back of the choke knob you will find that it is held in place by a number of self-tapping screws. You might also find a couple of small bolts holding the shroud to the dash panel. If you have to remove an awkwardly routed cable, disconnect the carburettor end and tie a piece of string to it. Withdraw the cable from inside the car in the normal way, leaving the string in place when the cable is pulled out.

When you come to refit the cable, tie the string back on and pull it back through from the carburettor end. The cable will slide along the right route quickly and easily. You should even be able to get the cable through grommets like this.

1. Pulling out the cable with string attached

STEP 6 — LUBRICATE THE CABLE

With the cable removed try moving the outer cable over the inner one to see how free it is. If it is stiff or moves roughly, yet there is nothing else wrong with the cable, it may only need oiling to make it work perfectly. This is worth trying before you buy a new cable.

By far the best method of lubrication is to use a cable oiler but if you do not have access to one of these, soak engine oil into the cable overnight through a funnel (see Tip — Drip feed).

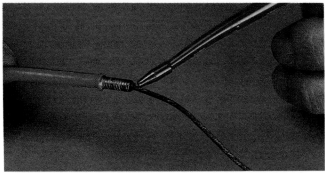

1. Oiling the cable by hand

If you do not have time to hang the cable overnight, hold the cable by hand and put a few drops of engine oil between the inner and outer cable. Slide the inner cable in and out of the outer one until the drops disappear. Repeat the process until oil appears at the other end of the cable. You might find it easier to stretch out the cable and clamp both ends of the inner to a bench while you slide the outer one over the inner with both hands.

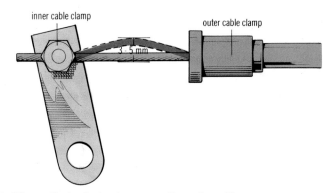

TIP

Drip feed
If you do not have a cable oiler, the next best way to fully lubricate the cable is to run oil through it for several hours. One way to do this is to make a funnel from greaseproof paper and tape it around the top of the outer cable. Fill the funnel with oil and hang up the cable overnight.

STEP 7 — REFIT THE CABLE

If you are refitting the old cable it will already be well lubricated, but if you are fitting a new one it is a wise move to oil it first (see Step 6).

Hold the locking ring or nut behind the dash panel and feed the cable through it at the same time. When the cable is pulled right through, screw the locking ring on to the outer cable and tighten it up. Push the cable through the grommet in the bulkhead, or pull it through with string, making sure that it

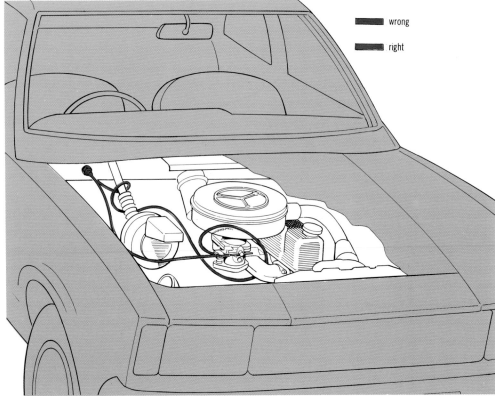

▬▬ wrong

▬▬ right

1. Make sure the choke cable follows a smooth path

does not foul the steering column or wiper gear and that it is well away from any electrical component. Route the cable to the carburettor, trying to get as smooth a cable run as possible without any kinks or bends. If the cable seems to be too short you may have routed it wrongly or wrapped it around something — feed it back around the other side of the obstruction if necessary.

Pull the inner cable as far out of the outer one as you can before you fit it to the carburettor. This will make sure that you do not have any slack in the cable when you fit it and you will be able to adjust it correctly at the end of the job.

If the cable has a nipple on the end this must be fitted first, but if the cable also has a threaded adjuster you must first pass the inner cable through the hole in the outer cable mounting bracket. If the cable has no nipple, pass the inner cable through the hole in the outer cable mounting as before. Push the outer cable into its housing and tighten the locking screw, if one is fitted.

Push the choke knob fully in at the dashboard and make sure that the choke linkage is set to 'off' at the carburettor, (linkage pushed away from the outer cable mounting).

2. Allow a little slack when you adjust the cable

inner cable clamp   3-5 mm   outer cable clamp

If the outer cable is held by a clip, pull it back until there is just a small amount of slack in the inner cable. Fit the clip to the outer cable and its mounting bracket, making sure that it is held firmly in place.

If the outer cable has a threaded adjuster, screw it into its mounting bracket until the inner cable is in the same adjustment as above and tighten up the locknuts.

If the cable has no nipple, pass it through the hole on the clamping screw. Leave a small amount of slack in the inner cable and screw up the locknut.

To check whether or not you have the right cable adjustment, try and push the choke linkage at the carburettor further off by hand. If it does go much further

off, the cable is too tight and will have to be readjusted. As a final check, operate the choke control knob a few times. It should work smoothly without any springiness. If the knob seems to come out easily for the first inch or so before tightening slightly the chances are that it is too slack and, again, the cable will have to be readjusted.

If you have lubricated and refitted the original cable and you find that the symptoms of a sticking choke are still present, try fitting a new cable as a last resort. If this still makes no improvement the chances are that something is wrong with the choke mechanism inside the carburettor although there may also be possible return spring and spindle problems.

Dealing with a smoking exhaust

A smoking exhaust may simply be due to a badly adjusted carburettor, but it could be a sign of something more serious

Smoke coming from the exhaust of your car is always a sign that something is wrong and you should try to find the cause as soon as possible.

The smoke may simply be due to a rich mixture, which can normally be corrected easily; but it may also be caused by engine wear, which may need a major overhaul to put right. So the first step is to find out just what the problem is so you can decide how to deal with it.

When an engine has run over 60,000 miles the most probable cause of a smoking exhaust is valve guide problems or worn piston rings. If these checks don't reveal a cause, seek advice.

When to do this job
If black or blue smoke comes almost continually from the exhaust when the engine is warm

What this job involves
Tracing the fault
Checking the air filter
Checking the choke controls
Setting the mixture
Testing the engine condition

Other possible causes and related jobs
When your choke sticks
Plugs get oiled up
Please see Index for page numbers

To do this job
Tools: Spanners; sockets; screwdrivers; Colortune; plug spanner; compression tester
Materials: Upper cylinder lubricant; white card
Time: Allow an hour to find the fault
Degree of difficulty: Generally straightforward though some carburettors are hard to adjust

If you have the job professionally done . . .
Is the exhaust gas now colourless? Does the car start easily and run smoothly with no signs of pinking?

You can get a good idea of the probable cause of a smoking exhaust simply by looking at the smoke, making a note of when it is worst and smelling it. Any diagnosis can then often be confirmed by checking the spark plugs.

If the smoke is present all the time and has a black appearance, it is probably due to an over-rich fuel mixture. The excess petrol is not being burned properly and comes out of the exhaust as fine black carbon particles.

To check for this, run the engine until it is warm and the choke is off, then hold a piece of white card just behind the exhaust tail pipe (**fig 1**). Any carbon in the exhaust will cover the card with a fairly dry black film. Then smell the exhaust — but do not breathe it in too deeply as it is poisonous. A rich fuel-air mixture produces exhaust gases which have a characteristically sweet smell. Finally, check the spark plugs, a soft black carbon coating on the plug tips is confirmation of a rich mixture (**fig 2**). But only do this test after taking the car for a run since such deposits are common when a car has been run on the choke after starting.

One of the most common causes of a continuing problem of enriched mixture is a sticking choke or faulty automatic choke mechanism. The choke — automatic or manual — is designed to enrich the petrol/air mixture during engine start-up. It should not be in use for much more than a minute on the coldest of days.

Also check the cleanliness of the air filter. Clogged air filters will artificially cause more fuel to be drawn into a carburettor, richen the mixture and create the poor combustion conditions that lead to black smoke fumes.

A very rich mixture can also result in the engine lacking power and running unevenly

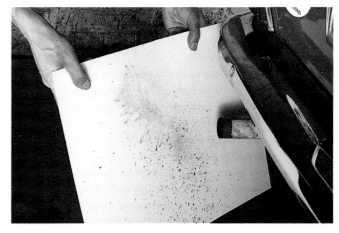

1. Using a white card to check exhaust emissions

with an erratic idle speed. Other symptoms include a tendency to stall, difficult hot starting and, of course, excessive fuel consumption.

If the smoke has more of a blue colour, has a choking smell and the deposits on your test card are oily, the smoke is probably due to engine oil finding its way into the combustion chambers and being burnt. Oily spark plugs are a symptom, although you may find that oil is only present in one cylinder. A further sign will be excessive oil consumption without any serious leaks being apparent.

2. Carbon and oily deposits

Oil can enter the combustion chambers in two ways. It can creep up a worn cylinder and past the rings or it can slide down worn valve guides. In either case, the first tell-tale sign is a puff of blue smoke when you release the accelerator pedal and change down a gear — although the only way you will know that this is happening is if someone follows you on a drive. This level of oil burning is common on most cars which have covered around 30,000 miles. However a car which burns oil and smokes constantly is probably in need of an overhaul (see Step 5), or even a completely new half or 'short' engine replacement.

One type of smoke that you need not worry about is the white steamy type that you get when you first start the car — it is just water vapour produced by the burning petrol. Although if the exhaust continues to steam even after the engine and exhaust system has warmed up, or an excessive amount of water is coming out of the pipe, then it is likely that you have blown a head gasket. Head gasket failure can also allow oil into the combustion chamber and produce excessive smoke.

1. Adjusting mixture on an SU

2. Lifting piston

3. Adjusting mixture

4. Testing the float

If the exhaust only smokes while the car is idling or being driven slowly, and the problem disappears when the car is driven at higher speeds, the problem could be due to poor setting of the idling mixture.

On a variable jet carburettor the mixture is set by moving the jet assembly up and down with an adjusting nut or screw underneath the carburettor (**fig 1**). If you are trying to correct a rich fuel–air mixture the nut has to be screwed up to reduce the gap between the jet and the metering needle.

Checking the setting is simple. If you have an SU, lift the carburettor piston a fraction (**fig 2**); if you have a Stromberg, lift the air valve a fraction — use the special lifting pin built in to the carburettor or the tip of a small screwdriver.

If the mixture is too rich, the engine will speed up, if it is too lean, the engine will stall, but if it is right the speed will increase slightly and then stabilize.

On a fixed jet carburettor the mixture is normally controlled by an adjusting screw located near the base of the carburettor (**fig 3**). To set the mixture, first set the idle to the specified speed — see your manual — then turn the mixture screw in and out to give the fastest smooth idle. Then reset the idle speed to the correct value. Uneven idling, with engine speed fluctuating, shows that the mixture is too rich and the control should be screwed in to give a leaner mixture until the engine idles smoothly and evenly.

Another way of setting the mixture is to use a Colortune unit. This is screwed into the cylinder head in place of one of the sparking plugs and lets you see the colour of the flame as the cylinder fires. The mixture control is adjusted to give a sharp blue flame, which shows that the fuel-air mixture is correct.

If you are unable to adjust the carburettor idling mixture control to give a proper setting — or the exhaust gives off black smoke all the time — there is probable something wrong with the carburettor itself. Mixture variations are more likely to occur with variable jet carburettors where wear can occur, but blockage of the bleed air passages in a fixed jet carburettor can also cause the engine to run rich.

With both types of carburettor the solution is to remove the unit from the car and give it a full service, replacing any worn parts as needed. The way you go about this varies from carburettor to carburettor so check service, overhaul and adjust the type of carburettor fitted to your car.

Flooding of the carburettor due to a faulty float or float chamber valve will also result in the engine receiving an excessively rich mixture.

In severe cases, this sort of flooding shows up as a petrol leak from the carburettor and there will be a strong smell of petrol. A slight degree of flooding, however, is so not so easy to identify.

Follow the service instructions for your carburettor and remove the float. Test the float by shaking it while listening to hear if there is any petrol inside or immersing it in water (**fig 4**) and looking for bubbles. In either case, the float is punctured and will have to be replaced.

Next, test the fuel valve by holding it shut while you get an assistant to switch on the ignition or operate the starter motor, so the petrol pump works. There should be no fuel leakage past the valve.

If the valve leaks, it could possibly be jammed by a bit of dirt getting between the valve needle and its seating, so try blowing sharply through the valve to clear it. If this does not work, you will have to fit a new valve assembly.

Once you have established that your engine is burning oil, the next step is to find out whether the oil is coming down from the cylinder head along the valve stems, or up from the crankcase past the piston rings. To do this you need to use a compression tester.

Start by warming up the engine. Then stop the engine and remove all of the spark plugs. According to the type of compression tester you are using, either screw the gauge into the plug threads (**fig 1**), or hold the gauge's pipe or adapter hard against the plug hole of the first cylinder you are going to test. Next get an assistant to operate the starter and spin the engine for six to eight full revolutions. Make a note of the pressure obtained, and the number of the cylinder. Then reset the compression gauge to

1. Using a compression tester

2. Adding cylinder lubricant

3. Checking valve guides

zero — normally by pushing in the valve pin in the nose of the gauge — and go on to repeat the test on the other cylinders.

Compare the figures you obtained for each cylinder, if the value for any one cylinder is markedly lower than that of the others, there is something wrong with that cylinder. With a worn engine, it is possible for all of the cylinders to give similar readings, though. So check with your manual (or dealer) to find out what the readings should be. If you cannot find the specified values for your car a typical compression reading for an engine in good condition would be 120 psi.

If you find that the reading is low on one or more cylinders there is a further test that you can carry out to find the reason for the poor compression. Using an oil can or a funnel, pour about 25 ml of upper cylinder lubricant, such as Redex, into the suspect cylinder (**fig 2**) and repeat the compression test. If you now get a satisfactory compression reading, the problem is that the piston rings are no longer providing a good seal to the cylinder. On the other hand if the compression pressure remains low the problem lies with the valves.

A poor seal between the piston rings and the cylinder will allow oil to get into the cylinder and the solution is to strip the engine and fit new piston rings. However, it is possible for the rings to fail to seal because they have become stuck in the piston by carbon deposits. Sometimes you can free them by pouring in a quantity of upper cylinder lubricant and leaving it to soak in overnight. Then spin the engine with a cloth over the plug holes to catch any excess lubricant, fit the plugs and start the engine. There will be a lot of white smoke as the oil burns off but run the engine for a while and then repeat your compression test. If the readings are still low, you will have to fit new rings but you may be lucky to find that the problem has been cleared up.

Faulty valve seatings will not in themselves allow oil to get into the engine, but they are often associated with worn valve guides and oil seals that do let oil get into the engine. A puff of smoke coming from the engine on the overrun is normally due to oil being sucked down the valve stems.

If this is the problem, the solution is to remove the cylinder head and check the valve stems and guides (**fig 3**). In many cases the problem will simply be that the oil seals fitted to the valve stems are worn. Replacement is a simple matter and can be carried out alone with a general head service at a garage.

Worn valve guides are a more serious matter with the fitting of replacement guides best being left to a specialist.

Internal engine faults can also produce unpleasant exhaust and they can be as difficult to confirm as they are expensive to repair. Cylinder head and block faults will often result in poor or uneven firing, mimicking an ignition fault. These causes can be confirmed with a compression tester (see — Checking engine compression).

The most common cylinder head fault is a blown gasket. If the hole is between a water gallery and the cylinder excessive steam may be produced in the exhaust but it is a fault most usually noticed by bubbles of exhaust gas appearing in the radiator. A leak between an oil gallery and a cylinder can result in very smoky exhaust. A compression test will confirm both problems. Note that, in the case of an oil leak the affected cylinder may show an unusually high reading.

If the compression test fails to show any problems and you have checked everything else, then the fault may be in the main or big end bearings. If these are worn they can produce a rumbling or knocking noise together with vibration while under load. Although on a few cars it is possible to replace these parts with the engine in situ, these faults usually indicate that the engine is badly worn and a replacement unit may be a better bet.

FACT FILE

What's in exhaust gases

Exhaust gases emitted by petrol engines are a complex mix of chemicals that are both produced by the combustion process and drawn in from the air by the engine.

By far the largest component is the nitrogen that forms about 80 percent of the air around us. Drawn into the engine, only a very small proportion of this element is effected by the extreme pressures and temperatures of combustion. The fraction that does change — by oxidation to a number of gases — is important as these nitrogen oxides are implicated in atmospheric pollution and the phenomenon of acid rain. Modern lean burn engines can produce a higher percentage of nitrogen oxides if the ignition process is not carefully regulated and properly adjusted.

The second largest gas component of exhaust is the oxides of carbon created by the burning of the petrol (a hydrocarbon) fuel. In a correctly adjusted engine it is carbon dioxide that is in the larger proportion. Emission of carbon dioxide, a naturally occurring gas, creates other components of acid rain (although cars contribute an insignificant proportion of this pollutant compared to other combustion processes).

Carbon monoxide is the other gas, a lethal poison which, in a well-tuned engine, is produced at levels of only 0.3 – 0.5 per cent. Higher levels of carbon monoxide — which can be detected by tuning equipment used at most garages — indicate inefficient combustion usually caused by poor carburettor (or injection system) adjustment. Carbon monoxide in the atmosphere very quickly becomes oxidised to carbon dioxide.

The other major constituent of exhaust is water vapour, the most visible component, especially on cold mornings when it rapidly condenses into tiny water particles. Water vapour also condenses inside exhaust systems and, in conjunction with dissolved oxides of nitrogen, sulphur (in petrol at very low levels) and carbon, corrodes silencer boxes from the inside.

Inefficient engines (badly tuned or with ignition faults) also expel unburnt fuel as well as a black soot of pure carbon. This carbon, in very finely dispersed form, together with fumes of excess oil creates the blue-black tint to exhaust smoke which betrays engine problems. Some of this mixture condenses inside the exhaust tail-pipe and can easily be examined. Fine dry carbon powder will normally show an engine that only needs a thorough tune-up. If oil is present and the deposit has a very greasy feel and appearance suspect other more drastic faults.

Among the many other very minor components of exhaust gas are lead compounds produced by reaction of a fuel additive used to minimise combustion 'knock'. It is these that are slowly being eradicated by regulation of the amount of lead that can be added to petrol and provision of lead-free fuels.

The most likely reasons for the mixture becoming too rich are the air filter becoming blocked or the choke mechanism sticking.

Start by checking the air filter (**fig 1**). A blocked air filter will restrict the flow of air to the carburettor. This leads to increased suction on the fuel jets and so to a rich mixture. On many cars, the filter is a paper element type fitted in a housing on or alongside the carburettor and you just have to unbolt or unclip the housing cover to remove the filter.

To check if the filter was the cause of a rich mixture, run the car with the filter off. If it no longer smokes you have solved the problem. Unfortunately, it is not easy to tell if a filter is blocked simply by looking at it, so your best move is to fit a new filter, especially if you know that you have covered a high mileage since the filter was last changed. Metal or plastic mesh filters need not be replaced — simply wash the element in paraffin and, where appropriate, lightly coat it in clean oil.

With the filter element removed you can go on to check the action of the choke control. Start by getting a friend to sit in the car and operate the choke while you watch the cable action at the carburettor. Make sure that

1. Checking air filter

the control moves freely and returns fully home and that both the inner and outer cables at the carburettor end are securely fixed (**fig 2**). Sometimes, if the inner cable is too long, the extra cable sticking out past the linkage will catch on the carburettor body or some other part of the engine and stop the linkage returning fully. If this is the case trim off the excess cable.

With many fixed jet carburettors, you can watch the action of the choke control as it closes the choke flap at the top of the carburettor. The flap should lie across the carburettor bore when the control is on, and return to a vertical position when the choke is off (**fig 3**).

In another arrangement the choke operates a rotary valve on the side of the carburettor to feed an extra rich mixture to the engine. Wear in this valve can cause rich running even through the choke control is working properly. You can check if this is the fault by unbolting the valve unit — once the engine has warmed up — and blocking off the connected bores in the carburettor body with masking tape. Then restart the engine and see if the mixture is still too rich.

If removing the choke valve cures the problem, you may be able to fit a replacement valve unit, but in most cases you will have to replace the carburettor. Do not run the engine for too long with the tape in place and make sure that you remove all traces of the tape when you refit the choke unit.

On variable jet carburettors the rich starting mixture is normally obtained by moving the single jet down in the carburettor body. Make sure that the jet can move freely and that it returns to its normal working position — moving up into the carburettor body — when the choke control is off.

In some cars, the choke operation is automatic with the choke action being controlled by a temperature unit.

2. Tightening choke cable

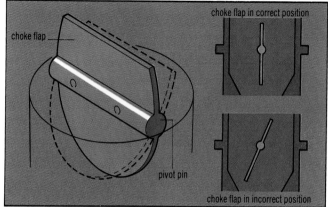

choke flap

pivot pin

choke flap in correct position

choke flap in incorrect position

3. Choke flap showing correct and incorrect adjustment

How to repair faulty gauges

The car's instruments are its early warning system. If they stop working you may not learn about an engine fault until it is too late

Faulty gauges are not only a nuisance but they may prevent you from recognizing a more serious fault until it is too late.

Many faults within the gauges themselves can be repaired and if you have a little patience and are willing to improvise you will often be able to save money.

When to do this job
If any of the dashboard instruments fail or behave erratically

What this job involves
Removing the dashboard and instruments
Checking for faulty sensors and circuits
Checking for loose or boken wires and connections
Repairing faulty gauges

Other possible causes and related jobs
Dealing with battery problems
Tracking down electrical faults
Replacing light bulbs
Replacing instrument gauges
Please see Index for page numbers

To do this job
Tools: Spanners; screwdriver (large and small); small sockets; test lamp; pliers; circuit tester; simple voltmeter; fine-pointed electrical soldering iron; blowlamp
Materials: Fine emery paper; 5 amp electrical fuse wire; replacements as required: new voltage stabiliser; new sender units; new gauge units
Time: About an hour if dashboard removal is straightforward, otherwise allow 4 to 5 hours
Degree of difficulty: Some patience required since gauge mechanisms are small

If you have the job professionally done . . .
Does the faulty gauge operate and give the correct reading? Has the dashboard been refitted properly?

The way a faulty instrument gauge behaves will often give a clue to the nature of the problem.

If you notice that more than one gauge fails to register at the same time then the fault is probably common to all the circuits and not in the gauges themselves. First check the fuse serving the instruments. But if the fuses are intact you will have to remove the dashboard to get at the instrument circuitry rear connections.

Good visibility is essential to fault finding in electrical circuits so you will need to pull the dash out as far as possible. To do this you will probably have to disconnect the speedo cable and block connectors.

If both fuel and temperature gauges fail to register or consistently read high (or low) then check the Instrument Voltage Stabilizer (IVS) unit behind the panel. This is usually a small rectangular device resembling a flasher unit, and is commonly fitted on to the instrument circuit board or sometimes located on the bulkhead.

If only one of the instrument gauges is faulty then you can assume that the IVS is working and that the fault lies in the sender unit, its related wiring or the gauge itself.

Most gauges can be tested without taking them out of the instrument cluster or circuit board. First locate the gauge connections. This is easy on instruments which are individually housed — simply pull off the connectors. In most cars, however, the instruments are secured and connected to a circuit board by small nuts on threaded connector posts.

Next, identify which of the connections is the power feed to the gauge. Do this by refitting the connector blocks and switching on the ignition. Alternatively, remove the

1. Disconnecting black connector behind instruments

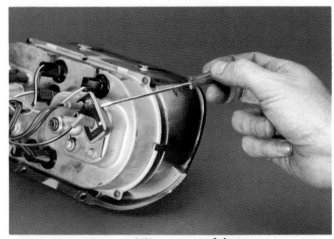

2. Instrument voltage stabiliser at rear of cluster

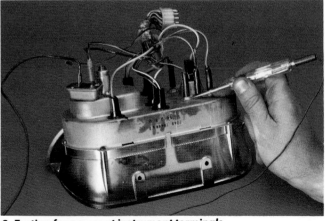

3. Testing for power at instrument terminals

4. Checking that gauge is in working order

instrument pad completely and connect the battery to the IVS (**fig 1**).

Now connect one of the leads from a test lamp to a good earth point on the dash unit — there is usually one specific earth terminal or you will see that one band of a printed circuit is common to all gauges. This will be the earth. For the following tests, this must be connected to the car's earth, either by the usual connector block or by a separate wire. Now test each of the gauge terminal posts in turn. The test lamp will glow brighter on one of the posts, indicating the power feed, and dimmer on the other which will be the sensor connection.

If the test lamp does not glow on either terminal there is a fault in the power feed to the gauge. Check that the retaining nuts or screws on the terminal posts are not loose or corroded. Clean these with fine emery paper and retighten, then check again that power is reaching the gauge.

Next, check the gauges themselves. With the test lamp connected between earth and the sensor terminal, observe what happens to the gauge from the front. If the pointer moves across the scale, disconnect the gauge immediately — the gauge is in working order and the fault must lie in the wiring from the sensor to the gauge, or in the sensor itself. If there is no movement of the pointer then the gauge is faulty.

STEP 2   REMOVE GAUGE FROM PANEL

When you have identified that a gauge is faulty, the next step is to remove it from the circuit board or cluster. With most modern cars the instruments are housed under a single perspex cover which allows you to reach the front of the individual gauges. Pull off any knobs attached to clocks and trip meters and remove the retaining screws from the panel front.

On older cars, the speedometer and other gauges may be housed in separate cowls, each with their own glass covers. These covers will come off once you have prised off the metal retaining clips. There is usually a further metal plate with gauge identify markings, to be taken out before you can see inside the gauges (**fig 1**).

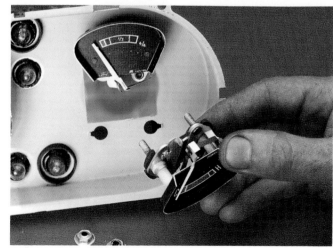

1. Removing gauge from instrument cluster

Finally disconnect the faulty gauge by unscrewing the retaining nuts or screws and corresponding washers from the circuit board (**fig 2**). Carefully withdraw the gauge.

After you have taken out the faulty gauge, give it a final test before delving into the works. In the case of the more common bimetallic type connect one of the terminals to a known live such as the battery and the other to a good earth (**fig 1**). This type of gauge is not affected by polarity so it can be connected up either way.

If the gauge responds and the needle deflects, you may have missed a bad connection in some of the earlier tests. But if there is still no response, disconnect and carefully examine the working parts. A magnifying glass or a reading aid can be useful here.

Most bimetallic gauges are not normally enclosed but consist of a metal front plate and a mica back plate riveted on to spacing posts. Access to the inide is, therefore, not a problem.

Some cars, however, do have individually housed units. To get at the inside of these gauges first remove the glass cover by carefully prising back the retaining lugs on the chromed rim. Next rotate the calibrated face plate and lift it clear of the pointer. Finally, unscrew the retaining nuts on the threaded connector posts and withdraw the mechanism from the housing (**fig 2**).

If the instrument is riveted together you may have to drill the rivets out. First flatten the rivet head with a file and dent the centre of the head with a punch. Then drill through the rivet using a bit slightly larger than the rivet.

When you have opened up the gauge, examine the heat resistant insulating material on the coil wire. Check for breaks in the insulator and in the wire itself. Do this by connecting one of the gauge terminals to the battery and probing the other terminal with a test lamp connected to earth. If the test lamp does not light, the gauge

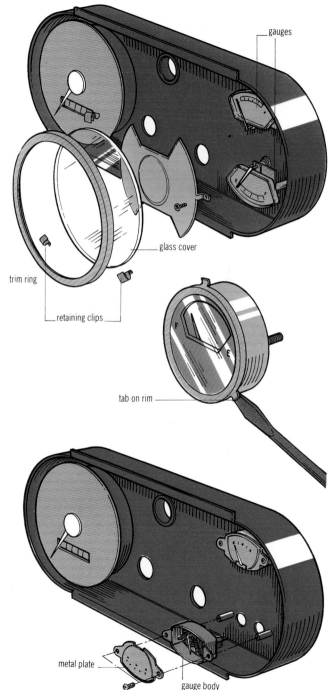

gauges

glass cover

trim ring

retaining clips

tab on rim

metal plate

gauge body

1. How instrument clusters and gauges come apart

189

2. Drilling through rivets in gauge

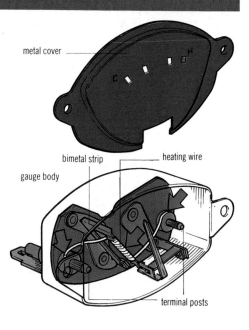

metal cover

bimetal strip

heating wire

gauge body

terminal posts

3. Removable metal cover over components

is faulty.

Each end of the coil is welded to a terminal — check that these connections have not come away. If the welds are suspect they can be repaired using 5 amp electrical fuse wire. Bend the loose end of the coil and about 3 in. (75 mm) of 5 amp fuse wire into opposing hooks. Twist the wires together

but avoid overtightening as this will break the wires. Wrap the remaining end of the fuse wire around the terminal post to make a good electrical contact. Now twist the loose ends tight and finally trim off any excess wire with a pair of cutters.

If you have a fine-pointed soldering iron, clean around the terminal post with emery

paper and run some solder on to the fuse wire connections. Do not rely on solder alone to secure the connections as the wire will get hot in normal operation and may loosen the solder. Twisting the wire around the terminal will keep it secure.

If a break has been traced in the coil itself, unwrap one or two turns carefully from each side of the break. Using a sharp knife or razor blade, cut away some of the insulation from both ends of the wire and twist them together to secure a

good electrical connection. Do not unravel too much of the coil if you can avoid doing so, otherwise the pointer may not give the right amount of deflection.

Make sure that any repair work does not leave any bare wire touching any other part of the mechanism or interfering with the pointer movement. If you have disturbed the mechanism at all, check that the pointer is seated properly on the return spring and that it is not scraping the gauge face as it deflects. It is a good idea to have a working gauge to look at as a guide. Check the repaired gauge by connecting it to the battery as before.

In cases where the coil or insulation is damaged beyond repair, there is no alternative but to renew the gauge. But since the fuel and temperature gauges are usually identical in operation you can, as a temporary measure, swap a faulty fuel gauge with a working temperature gauge. Remember that the gauges may not deflect in the same direction so you may also have to simply read the gauge backwards or temporarily alter the calibration markings by sticking a strip of paper over the front of gauge and marking the readings on it.

Faults in the electromagnetic types (identified by having three connectors) are unlikely to be in the windings as these do not heat up when the gauge is working. It is more likely that there is a loose or broken connection at the terminals. Identify the power feed (usually marked with +), connect it to a known live point and check each of the other two terminals with a test lamp connection to earth. The bulb will glow dimly (the coils have a high resistance) if the connections are good.

A faulty connection will have to be resoldered. Unravel one

turn of the wire from the winding to give more play. Hold the end of the wire to the terminal and trim off any excess wire. Clean the end to be soldered by scraping the resinous paint coating off with a sharp penknife or razor blade before you apply the solder. You may need to hold the wire

in place with a pair of tweezers whilst soldering (**fig 4**).

Replacing gauges into their respective housings is the reverse of the removal procedure. If you had to drill out rivets to remove a gauge from its housing, refit them by using self-tapping screws and washers to bridge the holes.

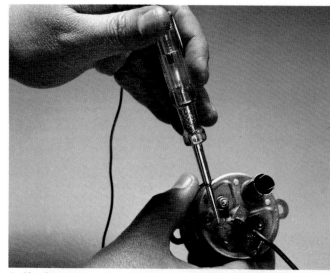

5. Checking connection inside electromechanical gauge

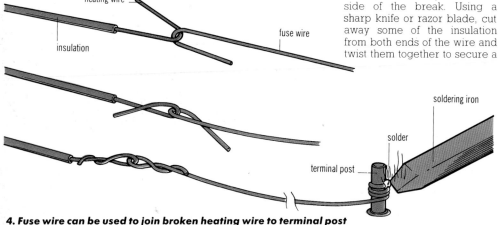

heating wire

insulation

fuse wire

soldering iron

solder

terminal post

4. Fuse wire can be used to join broken heating wire to terminal post

6. Soldering end of heating wire to terminal post

If your car is fitted with an electrical oil gauge check that the sender unit is working properly and that there is no break in the sender wire. Follow the procedure outlined in Step 3 if the gauge is faulty.

With mechanical oil gauges there are only two possible causes of a failure, a blockage in the system preventing oil reaching the gauge or a leak which drastically reduces the pressure on the gauge. Check for leaks at the engine block by wiping the area clean and then running the engine for a few minutes to see if any oil appears around the joints. Do the same for the connector at the back of the gauge. If you find a leak, first try tightening the connections with a spanner But if the leak persists you will have to undo the joint and wind plumber's PTFE tape around the threads before you refit the connection.

1. Cleaning gauge inlet

If there are no obvious leaks, check that oil is reaching the gauge. Unscrew the connector at the gauge, cover the end with a rag and run the engine for a few seconds. If no oil appears, there could be a blockage in the feed pipe or connectors. Disconnect the pipe at the engine, flush it through with petrol and blow dry using an air line. Check that the gauge inlet is not blocked and clean it using a lint-free cloth soaked in petrol. If these tests have revealed no faults, open up the gauge.

Since mechanical oil gauges are usually individually housed you can follow the same general procedure for opening them as individually housed electrical gauges (see Step 3). The mechanism is held on to the housing by a locking ring or nut on the threaded connector.

If there is oil inside the gauge it means that a solder joint has fractured. Flush the gauge out with petrol and locate the leak. A fracture in the solder can be repaired by running fresh solder on to it but you will need to use a large soldering iron since a small electric one will not give out sufficient heat. Remove the plastic pointer from the pivot and grip the mechanism in a vice whilst you are soldering.

FACT FILE

Oil gauges

There are two main types of oil gauges used in cars — electrical and mechanical. An electrical gauge, whether of bimetallic or electromagnetic type, can be identified by its two or more electrical connections at the back of the unit. One connection leads to the ignition and another to the sensor unit on the engine block. These sensors are larger than the type connected to trigger warning lights and can sometimes be joined to a common connector on the engine block which serves the gauge and the warning light. They can be resistance types or bimetallic devices which give different current pulses according to changes in oil pressure. The gauges work in the same way as other electromagnetic or bimetallic types.

The mechanical type of oil gauge is connected to the

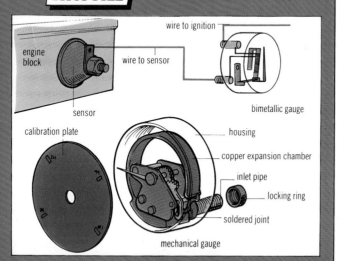

engine block by a narrow bore metal or plastic pipe. The oil is forced through a metal filter and into a hollow copper chamber bent to an arc. Pressure forces the chamber to straighten out which in turn moves a pivoted pointer. Mechanical oil gauges also have an electrical connection to the circuit board or wiring loom to power the illumination bulb.

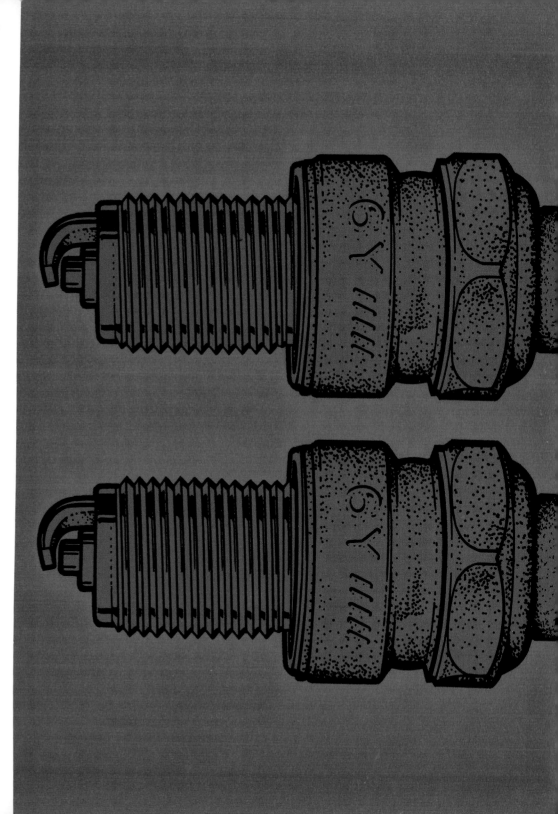

Chapter FOUR

WHAT'S WRONG?

Tracking down electrical faults

Tracking down almost any electrical fault simply requires a little basic knowledge and a methodical checking procedure — here demonstrated on a faulty number plate lamp

Electrical equipment may fail to work for several reasons. The component itself may be faulty or worn, a wiring connection may be loose or dirty, the metal around the earth wire might be rusty, causing a bad earth, the core of the wire could be broken from being bent too often, or the plastic insulation of the wire could be damaged or worn resulting in the current escaping to earth and creating a short circuit.

The type of fault can sometimes give you an idea as to its cause. For instance, dim lights are often caused by a bad earth, a blown fuse is often the sign of a short circuit and a light or other component that flickers or works only intermittently suggests a loose connection.

But whatever the problem, a few quick checks will often help you to find it — without

When to do this job
If an electrical system fails or works only intermittently
If a fuse blows

What this job involves
Using test equipment
Systematic testing of an electric circuit

Related jobs in this handbook
Pertrol gauge not working
Lights work intermittently
Horn won't work
Fuses keep blowing
Faulty wipers
Indicators fail to flash
Engine won't start
Please see index for page numbers

To do this job
Tools: Test lamp; circuit tester; length of wire
Materials: New fuses (maybe); insulation tape (maybe)
Degree of difficulty: Needs patient and methodical approach

If you have the job professionally done . . .
Does electrical component now work properly?
Have fuses stopped blowing?

even getting out your tool box.

For instance, if one sidelight is not working but the other three are, the switch must be working and the fault is likely to be in the bulb or its holder or the wiring to that bulb. Or if you notice that, for example, both the horn and the interior light have stopped working, check whether they share the same fuse. If they do, a blown or loose fuse is likely to be to blame.

If you have recently had the boot heavily laden and then notice that a rear light has stopped working, see whether you have accidentally pulled off a wire in the boot.

When only one brake light bulb works, it cannot be the switch that is faulty. But if neither brake light works, the switch could be the culprit — or, just possibly, both bulbs have failed at the same time. If

the same fuse keeps on blowing, see which components work through that fuse and turn them on one at a time. Then you can tell which one is making the fuse blow. When you know which component is at fault, you can check that component and its wiring to find the fault. If the fuse only blows when all the components are turned on, check the fuse rating.

FACT FILE

Car wiring basics

An electrical device will work only if a complete electric circuit is made. Batteries have two terminals, one positive (+) and one negative (—). To make a circuit a wire must run from one terminal to the electrical device; this is the *live* wire. Another wire must take the current back to the other battery terminal; in cars, this is called the *earth* wire. Some materials, usually metals like copper and steel, allow electricity to flow through them and are called *conductors*. Other materials like plastics and glass will not let electricity pass and are called *insulators*.

To save wiring in a car, the steel car body itself is used as one of the conductors in the circuit. One battery terminal has a braided metal strap or cable which is

bolted to the body nearby. In almost every modern car, this is the negative (—) terminal. The car body is thus used as the negative conductor, and the electrical system is described as *negative-earthed*.

In this system, many electrical devices have short wires (usually black) which are attached to the car's body. These are the earth wires which pass the current to the body and thus back to the earthed terminal of the battery. Other electrical components are bolted directly to the car body, so do not need a separate wire connecting them to the body.

In a few older cars, it is the positive (+) terminal of the battery which is connected by a strap to the car body. This system is described as *positive-earthed*.

In the tests described here, it makes no difference whether your car is negative-earthed or positive-earthed. This only becomes important when fitting radios or alternators.

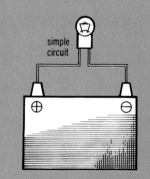

simple circuit

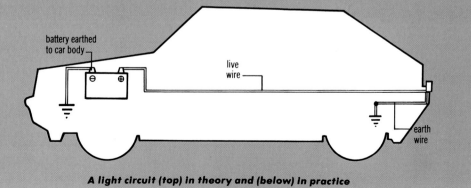

battery earthed to car body

live wire

earth wire

A light circuit (top) in theory and (below) in practice

Some cars have two number plate lights, others have one. In a two bulb system, if one bulb is lit but not the other, the fault is probably a blown bulb. For both systems, look also to see if all four sidelights, as well

as the number plate lights, have stopped working. If this is the case then the fault is probably in the sidelight switch or the fuse — all these lights are almost always served by the same switch and fuse circuit.

1. First check for a blown bulb

FACT FILE

Cheap test equipment

You can make a test lamp for use on a car quite easily from a 12-volt light bulb. You will also need a bulbholder (available from an accessory shop or car breaker) and a 3 ft or 1 m length of insulated electrical wire.

Cut the wire in half, bare the ends of insulation, and connect the two pieces to the terminals of the bulbholder. Some bulbholders have screw terminals; if not, solder the connections. On the end of one wire, screw or solder a crocodile clip. On the other wire solder a sharp point, such as a heavy pin or dart.

If the clip is connected to a live

terminal while the point is touched against bare metal on any part of the car body, the lamp will light.

Alternatively, you can buy a test lamp quite inexpensively at an accessory shop. This can look like a screwdriver with a clear handle containing a light bulb. At the end of the 'screwdriver' there is a probe which can be used to scratch through dirt or rust to make a good electrical contact. It can also be pushed through the insulation around a wire to touch the wire inside. Attached to the handle is a wire with a crocodile clip at the end.

A circuit tester (or continuity tester) is similar to a test lamp, but has its own battery. This allows it to be used to test items which have been removed from the car, or to test for breaks in a circuit without having to leave the equipment switched on.

A circuit tester also has a sharp testing probe and a wire with a crocodile clip, but its body is fatter than a screwdriver's to make room for a battery.

Test lamps are sometimes referred to as circuit testers but, for clarity, this handbook uses 'circuit tester' only to refer to the type with its own battery.

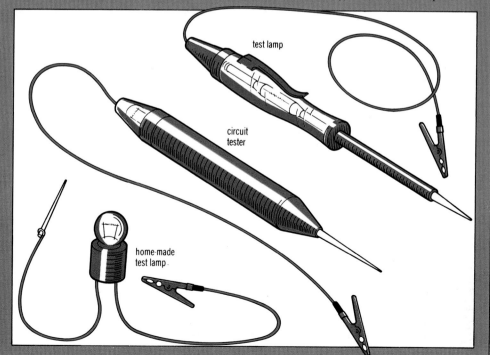

test lamp

circuit tester

home-made test lamp

CHECK THE FUSE

The fuseholder is a small box, usually with an easily detachable cover, with the fuses mounted side by side inside (**fig 1**). It is usually fairly close to the battery, on the engine side of the bulkhead or the passenger side. Since locations vary, check in your manual if it is not immediately obvious.

Look in the manual to see which fuse serves the number plate lamp. Sometimes the fuseholder itself has this information printed on it.

If there is another fuse marked with the same rating in the fuseholder, do a quick test by changing the two fuses over. If the new fuse makes the component work again, you will know that either the old fuse needs to be replaced, or it was making a bad connection in the holder.

You can test a fuse where it is by using the test lamp. Fasten the crocodile clip to earth and turn the sidelight switch on to feed power into the circuit.

Then touch the test lamp probe, in turn, to both of the clips which hold each end of the fuse (**fig 2**). If the test lamp lights when the probe is in both these

1. A typical fuseholder

2. Checking with test lamp

positions, the fuse works and is in good contact with the fuseholder clips. If the lamp lights only when touched on one end of the fuse, make sure the fuse is firmly held in its clip at the opposite end — the fuse may be intact but is not making electrical contact with its metal holder. Clean the holder terminal clips and the fuse itself, make sure the fuse is a good tight fit in the holder and try again.

If you are still not sure whether the fuse is working, take it out to test it. This time, use the circuit tester. Fasten the clip to one end of the fuse and touch

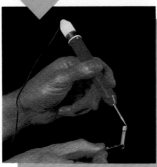

3. Using a circuit tester

the probe to the other end (**fig 3**). If the fuse is working, the circuit tester will light.

CHECK THE BULB

Remove the bulb (see Fact File — Types of bulb) and look at it against the sky — you may be able to see whether the filament has broken. If you cannot tell, test it with a length of insulated wire. Hold one end of the wire to

one battery terminal and the other end to the metal body of the bulb. Touch the base terminal of the bulb to the other battery terminal (**fig 1**). If the bulb does not light you will have to renew it.

1. Testing a bulb at the battery with a length of insulated wire

---

FACT FILE

Using test equipment

When using a test lamp, the circuit or component you are testing must be turned **on**.

If you are testing a **live** terminal or live wire, first fix the crocodile clip to earth. You can use the earth terminal of the battery, or any part of the car body where the clip can make a firm connection with clean, bright metal.

Now touch the probe to the terminal or wire you want to test. The bulb in the test lamp should light up.

Usually you will have to test at more than one place — for example, at both ends of a suspect wire — to find the fault.

To test an **earth** connection, first fasten the crocodile clip to a live point. This can be either the

live terminal of the battery, or any live connection in the car's wiring such as the live terminal of a light unit or a live point in the fuse holder.

Now touch the probe to the component you want to test. The lamp should light up.

Again, you will probably have to test at more than one point to see where the break in continuity is.

Circuit tester

When using a circuit tester, the circuit you are working on must be switched **off** — otherwise power from the car's battery will burn out the bulb of the circuit tester.

You can use the circuit tester for testing components away from the car. For example, to test

a fuse you simply clip the tester to one end of the fuse and touch the probe to the other. The bulb will light up if the fuse is working.

Another use of the circuit tester is to check that there is good electrical contact — for example, between a lightbulb and its holder. Clip the circuit tester to the metal of the bulbholder and then touch the probe to the metal body of the bulb. If the bulb is making good electrical contact with the holder the circuit tester will light up.

Similarly, to check whether there is a break in an electrical wire, fix the crocodile clip to one end of the wire and touch the probe to the other. The bulb will light if the wire is unbroken.

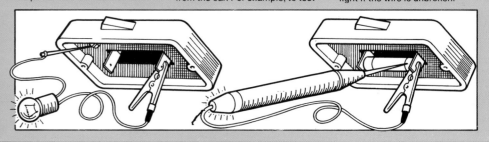

TIP

Easy way out

Sometimes a bulb which is recessed in the bulbholder can be difficult to turn when you are trying to take it out because there is not enough bulb to get hold of. A piece of Blu-Tack or a loop of sticky tape pressed on to the bulb will help you to get a grip on the glass envelope of the bulb. If your hands are oily you will find it more difficult to get a firm hold of an awkward bulb.

FACT FILE

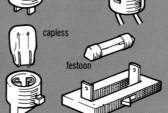

Types of bulb

There are four types of bulb commonly used in car lights. Your car may use a different type of light fixing in the sidelights and number plate light, for instance.

Some bulbs screw into the bulbholder and can be removed by turning them anticlockwise.

The capless type of bulb is a push fit in the bulbholder. To take it out, do not try to turn the bulb but just pull it.

The bayonet type can be taken out by pushing it in slightly and then turning it anticlockwise. Spring pressure will then push the bulb outwards.

Festoon bulbs are tubular in shape with pointed ends and are held in the bulbholder by a spring clip at each end. To take out a festoon bulb, pull one spring clip gently away from that end, then ease the bulb in the other direction with your other hand.

Whatever the type, there will be two contacts or terminals. One will be live, the other earth. It is usually clear which is which. With festoon bulbs the earth is the terminal connected to the metal holder, while bayonet and screw bulbs are earthed through their metal casing.

STEP 4 — CHECK THE CONNECTIONS

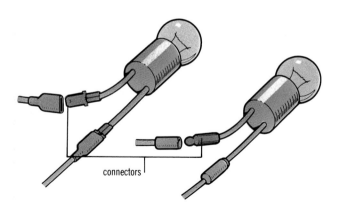

connectors

1. Often connectors look tight but are not making good contact

The light may have stopped working because the wires to it have worked loose. To test for this, turn on the sidelight switch. Check that all the connectors between wires and bulbholder are tight. (See **fig 1** for various types you might encounter.) Do this by pulling the connectors apart then pushing them firmly back again. While disconnected make sure the terminals are clean and free from corrosion — rub them lightly with emery paper. Dirty connectors may fit tightly together but may not make electrical contact. If poor contact was the problem the number plate light will now come on.

STEP 5 — CHECK THE BULB IS FIRMLY HELD

A bulb may seem to be tight in the bulbholder but, like wiring connections, electrical contact may not be made. To check this, leave the sidelight switch on. Try wobbling the bulb with a fingertip to see if it lights up.

If it does, the bulbholder is faulty. Cleaning off any corrosion may fix it; otherwise it will have to be renewed.

If the bulb does not light up, the fault may still be in the bulbholder. To make sure, you will need to check both whether power is reaching it (see Step 7) and whether it is properly earthed (see Step 6). If these connections are both in order, then the bulbholder is at fault.

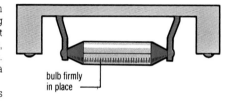

bulb firmly in place

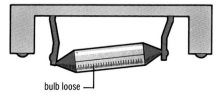

bulb loose

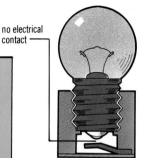

no electrical contact

1. Bulbs which are not tight in their holders may not work at all or may flicker

Avoiding damage

Some electrical components — windscreen wipers, for example — work only when the ignition is switched on. If you are testing one of these components (or its switch, or the fuse in the circuit concerned) make sure that the ignition is on. But do not leave the ignition on for more than a few minutes while you are testing because the ignition coil can be damaged if the ignition switch is in the 'on' position for too long without the engine running.

STEP 6 — CHECK THE EARTH

With the number plate bulb removed and the power off, clip one end of the circuit tester to a good earth. Then touch the probe of the tester to the inside of the bulbholder, which grips the bulb and earths it (**fig 1**). (In the case of a festoon bulb, touch the metal body of the bulbholder.) If the tester lights, the bulbholder is properly earthed. If the tester does not light, the earthing of the bulbholder is faulty.

Make sure you have cleaned all rust and dirt off the earth terminal of the bulbholder.

As **fig 2** shows, you may be able to fasten one end of a length of wire to the earth terminal of the bulbholder and the other end to an earth point, such as a nearby bolt, on the body of the car. Then test the bulbholder again to see if it is now earthed. If the bulbholder is properly earthed but the number plate lamp still fails to light, the fault is probably in the power supply wire.

1. Testing earth terminal

2. Fixing extra earth wire

STEP 7 — CHECK THE POWER SUPPLY

Turn on the sidelight switch. Clip the test lamp to an earth point. Touch the probe to the live terminal of the number plate light bulbholder (**fig 1**). If the test lamp lights, current is reaching the bulbholder and you should check again that the bulb is firmly held and that the wiring connections are tight, since there is no other reason why it should not work.

If the test lamp does not light, current is not reaching the bulbholder. So you will need to check the power feed wire (see Step 9).

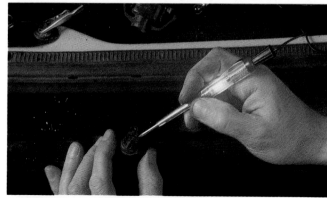

1. Using the test lamp to check the power supply wire

STEP 8 — CHECK THE SWITCH

If you can reach the back of the switch which operates the number plate light and the sidelights, use the test lamp to check whether there is current at both terminals of the switch when the switch is turned on (**fig 1**). If one terminal is live but not the other, the switch is faulty and must be renewed. If neither terminal is live, current is not reaching the switch and you should check the supply wire that comes from the fuseholder.

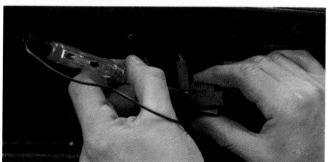

1. Testing the terminals at the back of the switch

FACT FILE

Switches and fuses

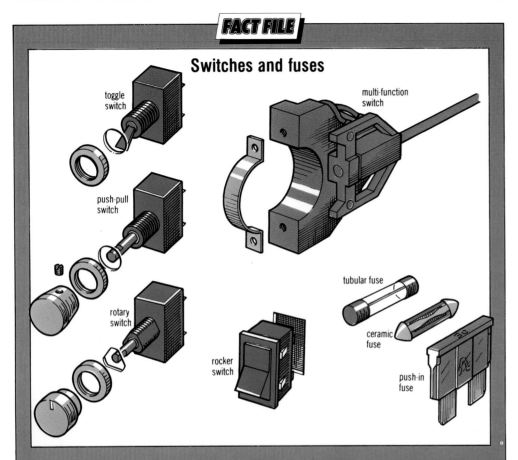

toggle switch

push-pull switch

rotary switch

multi-function switch

tubular fuse

ceramic fuse

rocker switch

push-in fuse

Switches

A switch is a device which breaks a circuit to prevent electricity from flowing. Not all switches are on the instrument panel for the driver to operate. An electric radiator fan, for instance, has a thermostatic switch in the cooling system which turns the fan on when the engine gets too hot. The brake lights are operated either by a mechanical switch underneath the brake pedal or by a hydraulic switch somewhere in the brake line.

There are various kinds of switches which can be operated by hand. They include toggle switches, rocker switches, rotary switches, and multi-function switches which control more than one piece of equipment, such as the lights and the horn.

Fuses

A fuse is deliberately designed to be the weakest link in a circuit. It often consists of a glass tube with a metal contact at each end containing a very thin wire which runs from one contact to the other. Fuses are designed to burn out or blow when they are asked to carry too much current. So, if a fault somewhere overloads the circuit, what you get is a blown fuse — not a car fire. Different ratings of fuses are used, depending on the number and type of electrical components in the circuit.

When a fuse blows, it usually means that there is a fault in the circuit which should be mended before a new fuse is fitted. Often, for example, blown fuses are caused by a live wire or a live connector touching the car's

body and making a short circuit. (You can put this right by using insulation tape to cover the bare wire.) If no fault is found, a new fuse can be fitted because fuses do sometimes wear out. But if a newly fitted fuse blows there is definitely something wrong.

Your driver's handbook will show you where to find the main fuseholder, which fuse serves which components and what ratings the fuses are. Some components may have their own fuses fitted somewhere along their supply wires and not in the fuseholder; your manual will tell you this, too.

If you renew a fuse, always use one of the same rating as the original. A higher-rated fuse will not cure a circuit fault — in fact, it might worsen it.

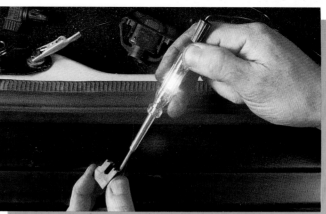

1. Testing that current is reaching the connector

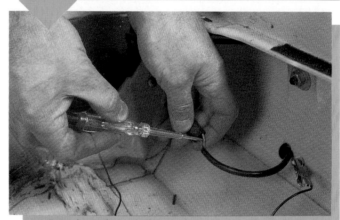

2. Probing through the insulation to test the wire inside

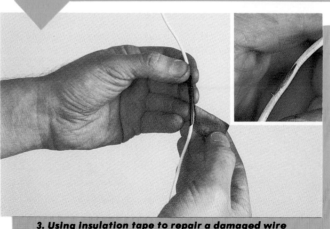

3. Using insulation tape to repair a damaged wire

When you know that the switch and fuse are working and live, the fault must be a break or short circuit somewhere along the power feed wire leading to the number plate lamp.

Make sure that any connectors in the wire are tight. Turn on the sidelight switch and clip the test lamp to earth. Then use the probe to test along the wire until you find a point in the length of wire where there is current and the test lamp lights.

The car's wiring is colour-coded, so this will help you to trace wires. Often a wire disappears through the bulkhead or into a large cluster of wires which are bundled together. Generally, a wire stays the same colour along its whole length, so you should be able to identify the wire even though you may have lost sight of it at some stage.

Test any connectors in the line either by peeling back the insulating cover and touching the probe to the metal inside (**fig 1**), or by pulling the connector apart and touching the probe to the connector terminal on the end of the wire which feeds the number plate light. Test the wire itself by clipping the test lamp to earth and pushing the probe through the insulation of the wire to touch the wire inside (**fig 2**).

Remember never to let any live connector touch the bare metal of the car — the short circuit could burn you.

When you find that there is current in one part of the wire but not at the next point along the wire, the fault must lie between those two points.

Gradually track down the exact location, then examine the wire. If its insulation has worn, causing a short circuit, you can patch it with insulating tape (**fig 3**). If it has broken, you will have to cut out the damaged length and renew it — ideally, with another length of the same colour.

Dealing with battery problems

If your car will not turn over properly when you try to start it, or the battery is a few years old, it is time to make a full check of the battery and its connections

Although it is a vital part of the car the battery is all too often overlooked until the car refuses to start one cold winter's morning. By following a simple maintenance programme such inconvenient failures can be prevented and the battery life extended.

But remember that most car batteries contain a considerable amount of sulphuric acid so always take great care to make sure that none gets spilled. If you do get any on yourself wash it off immediately with plenty of cold water — and if you are unlucky enough to get a splash in your eye seek medical advice just to make sure. Do not get too worried, though — such accidents are most unlikely if you take due care.

When to do this job
When the engine fails to turn over normally on starting, especially on cold mornings. On a regular basis every six months

What this job involves
Checking battery mountings and connections
Checking battery electrolyte level and strength
Cleaning terminals and checking connections
Charging the battery
Tracing current leakage

Related jobs in this handbook
Tracing electrical faults
Curing starting problems
Checking a used car
Please see Index for page numbers

To do this job
Tools: Screwdrivers; spanners; wire brush or emery paper; hydrometer; battery charger; junior hacksaw (maybe); file (maybe)
Time: Half an hour to two hours
Degree of difficulty: General maintenance is easy but tracing current leakage can be tedious

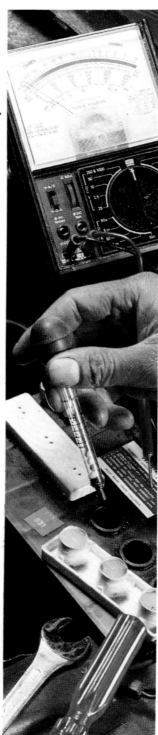

EXTEND BATTERY LIFE

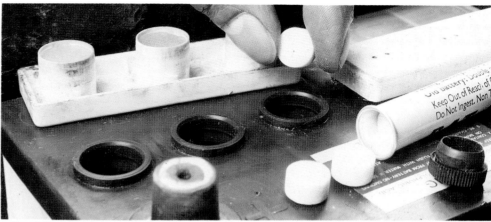

1. Special acid tablets may help revive a tired battery

Batteries do not last forever, and eventually their capacity for charging and discharging does deteriorate. Even when charged with a battery charger it may be that it will not hold that charge for any length of time because of chemical changes within the battery. Eventually, the answer has got to be replacement — but there are certain things you can do to help your battery last longer.

Try to make life for your battery as easy as possible — a cold engine is much harder to turn over than one which is only slightly warmer. If you have a garage put your car it as

soon as you come home, if not, try putting newspapers under the bonnet on top of the engine, especially during very cold weather — remember to remove them before starting in the morning. Using a thinner oil during winter can help a lot.

It will help your morning starts if you charge your battery overnight, particularly if you charge it in the warm.

Certain battery additives (**fig 1**) are available which may help extend the life of yourr battery by counteracting the chemical changes which happen to the internal plates but again they are only a

temporary measure.

Occasionally the case of a battery may become damaged — by overtightening of the clamp for example — and providing the resulting crack is not too large, a satisfactory repair can be made using one of the products designed for this purpose (**figs 2/3**). If you are carrying out a repair like this do not forget that some spillage of acid is likely to have occurred. You should wash the entire area with large quantities of water to dilute the acid further. A solution of washing soda to neutralize the acid is also a good idea.

2. Clean up damaged area around battery post

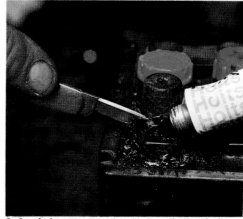

3. Apply battery repair paste and smooth down

STEP 1   CHECK THE MOUNTINGS

You should always make sure that the battery mountings are secure so that the battery is held firmly. There are two common methods of mounting the battery (**fig 1**). The first is by means of a metal strip which runs along one edge of the top of the battery and is secured to the car bodywork by hooked rods which are threaded at their upper ends and fixed with wing nuts. The second method uses two brackets at the base of the battery, one fixed and one movable, which engage with two lugs moulded into the case

of the battery.

Whichever sort of mounting is used on your car you should check the nuts periodically and tighten them if necessary, as even the smallest vibration of the battery can result in acid being spilled. However, be careful not to overtighten the nuts, as you could crack the case of your battery. Do not fasten wing nuts more than finger tight and only use a short spanner on hexagonal nuts. Keep the battery area clean and dry, as even slight spillage can be highly corrosive.

TIP

Lift with care

Batteries are heavy and can be badly damaged if dropped so carry them properly with both hands underneath. Do not try and lift a battery by its top lip or the clamping points, or you may pull them away from the casing. As a precaution against acid burn it is a good idea to wear rubber gloves.

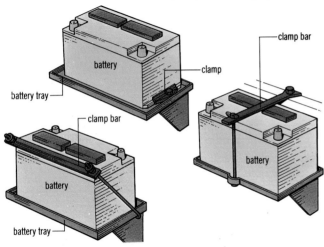

1. Common methods of holding the battery in place

STEP 2   TOP UP THE ELECTROLYTE

Unless your car is fitted with a 'no maintenance' battery which is sealed for life, you should make a regular weekly check on the level of the electolyte. This is the dilute sulphuric acid which is contained in each of the cells of the battery.

Depending on the type of case material used in your battery there are two methods of making this check. If your battery has a translucent plastic case, the levels in the individual cells can be seen by looking at the side of the

battery, and they can be compared with the 'full' mark on the outside of the casing. If the battery. is not translucent, you should remove the single trough cover, or separate cell caps if these are fitted, and then make sure that the fluid level is just above the metal plates which are visible in each cell. If your battery is not easy to get at, it may be helpful to use a mirror to look down into each cell.

If the levels of any of the cells are low you should bring them

up to the correct level by adding distilled or deionised water. This is available on most garage forecourts free of charge although you often have to ask where it is. If necessary a possible source of suitable water in the home is to collect the water which is produced when your refrigerator is defrosted. Most tap water is unsuitable because of the large number of minerals and other chemicals it contains which will shorten the working life of the battery.

STEP 3   CHECK BATTERY CONDITION

1. Hydrometers are used to check battery electrolyte strength

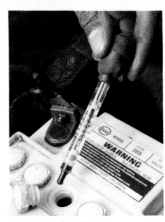

2. Test each cell in turn

The strength of the acid electrolyte in the battery depends on the state of charge or condition of the battery. An inexpensive instrument called a hydrometer (**fig 1**) can be used to measure this strength. This is a useful check as it can show the relative performance of the cells, and gives an early warning of a fault.

The specific gravity, as the strength of the acid is also known, is found by drawing a sample of electrolyte into the body of the hydrometer. Make sure you draw enough of the liquid into the hydrometer so that the float clears the bottom, or you will get a false reading.

The level at which the scale on the float settles shows the strength. The scale may be calibrated in terms of specific gravity, or may have segments labelled 'fully charged', 'half charged' and 'flat'.

Some hydrometers contain a

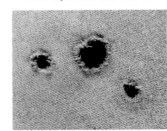

3. Beware of acid burns

number of balls, in which case the strength of the electrolyte is measured by counting the number of balls that float. For a hydrometer with a float marked with the specific gravity, a reading of 1.260-1.200 means fully charged, and one below 1.100 means that the cell has no charge. Make a note of the reading for the first cell, squeeze the electrolyte back and go on to the next cell (**fig 2**). When you have completed all the readings compare them; the readings in terms of specific gravity should be within 0.050 of each other. If they are not, one cell may be defective.

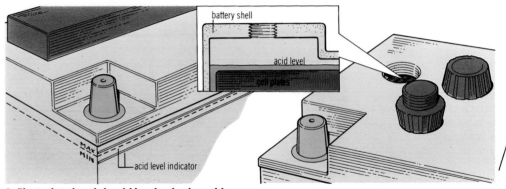

1. Electrolyte level should be checked weekly

Under normal conditions the charging system on your car keeps the battery in a good state of charge. However, if you are only using your car for short journeys, the demands put upon the battery by the starter motor may mean that the battery cannot recover fully. This is particularly true when the engine is harder to turn over and takes more current than usual, and components like headlights, windscreen wipers and rear window heaters are in frequent use.

If possible, take your car for a daytime run, and turn on as few electrical loads as possible. This should enable your battery to recover its charge.

Alternatively, you can use an external mains powered charger (**fig 1**). Most battery chargers available for home use are trickle chargers, which provide only low currents, and take a number of hours to bring a battery back to full charge. Booster chargers are also available, which are capable of charging more quickly, but

using these may damage your battery as the plates can be buckled by the high current.

If you have a suitable mains socket, you will probably find it easiest to recharge the battery

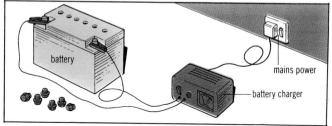

1. Home chargers can keep your battery in top condition

while it is still in your car. In all cases it is wise to disconnect the battery earth lead (**fig 2**), as otherwise damage can occur to the rectifier used on some earlier alternator-equipped

2. Disconnect earth lead

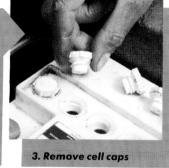

3. Remove cell caps

vehicles. Pay attention to the polarity of the battery when connecting the charger leads, making sure you put the positive (red) lead to the positive (+) terminal of the battery, and the negative lead to the negative terminal.

Once you have connected the leads you should take off the cell caps, or make sure any air vents in them are clear. You can now turn on the mains. Nearly all chargers are fitted with an ammeter to show the rate of charge. This will now be showing a reading, the bigger the deflection of the needle, the

higher the rate of charge, shown in amps. You should allow the needle to settle down to a steady reading — a few seconds is normally enough. The flatter the battery, the higher the initial reading will be. You should leave the battery charging until the charging rate is down to below 1 amp, or alternatively until all the cells are bubbling. This can be done overnight.

Always make sure that there is adequate ventilation wherever you are charging your battery, and never smoke or use flame anywhere near

the top of the battery. This is because the bubbling which you can see in the cells includes hydrogen gas, given off during the charging process, and which when mixed with air can be highly explosive. For the same reason you should always turn the charger off at the mains before unclipping the leads to the battery or sparks may occur again with possibly disastrous results.

If you are not using your car for any length of time, leave it with the battery well charged, to insure it keeps in good condition.

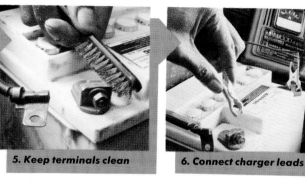

4. Top up electrolyte   **5. Keep terminals clean**   **6. Connect charger leads**

The electrical system of the car relies on good connections to the battery itself. The heavy cables to the battery terminals are needed because of the very heavy currents drawn by the starter motor. It is possible that either of the battery connections can break down totally, or deteriorate to a state where the battery gives all the appearances of being flat.

This is particularly true of the cap type found mainly on older cars. These connectors fasten to the circular battery post with a central screw, and rely on a good fit between this tapered post and the connector. If there is not a good fit you can improve things temporarily by filing a small amount away from

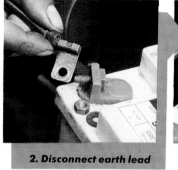

1. File post gently

the top of the post (**fig 1**) so the cap fits further down the taper.

More permanently it is a good idea to replace the cap terminals with clamp type connectors which ensure a much more reliable contact.

These are normally held to the battery cables by two screws, and are very simple to fit. Just cut through the battery leads close to the connector, peel back the insulation on the cables and screw the new connectors to the cable ends (**fig 2**).

Before buying new clamps, measure the terminal posts to make sure you get the right size clamps and check you have a proper positive (+) and negative (−) pair.

Whatever type of connectors are fitted to your car, it is a good ideal to periodically unfasten them from the battery, wipe away any vaseline and clean up the battery posts with emery paper. You should also

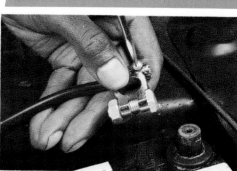

2. Screw new clamp

3. Ensure the engine earth is clean

look at the earth strap connection to the car bodywork at this stage, as this is also somewhere that corrosion can go undetected until a fault occurs. If there are signs of any rusting around this

area remove the strap which is usually connected to a bolt, and clean all around the bolt hole and the earth strap terminal with emery paper and refit.

Whenever you remove and replace your battery

connections always make sure they are tightened properly and smeared with vaseline. Keep the top of the battery clean and dry, especially after topping up, to prevent current leakage.

What if your battery still appears below par even though you have made sure that the connections are in good order, the electrolyte level is right and there are no adverse weather conditions to be taken into account? Before deciding that the battery is at fault, unless there is already some evidence such as a low hydrometer reading on one cell for example, it is a good idea to check that there is no slight current leakage somewhere in the car.

The easiest way of checking for current leakage is to use a multimeter — if you have one. Switch the meter to an ammeter (amps) range — the least sensitive if more than one is available — and connect the meter in series with the battery. To do this disconnect the live lead from the battery and connect the meter between the battery terminal and the lead (**fig 1**). When doing this make sure that you get the polarity right — that is, the positive lead from the meter should go to the positive terminal of the battery, or negative to negative if you have a positive earth car.

Make sure that nothing electrical in the car is turned on — the ignition is off and all doors are shut if courtesy switches are fitted. Take the bulb out of the under-bonnet inspection light if there is one fitted. Disconnecting your car's electric clock may be more of a problem. Some types are clockwork but are electrically wound every few minutes so they too need to be disconnected. There may be a multi-pin plug behind the clock which you can pull out or you may need to trace the wiring back until you reach a connector.

Also, pull the wiring plug out of the back of the alternator as some current may leak away here at a slow rate. Any deflection on the meter now is

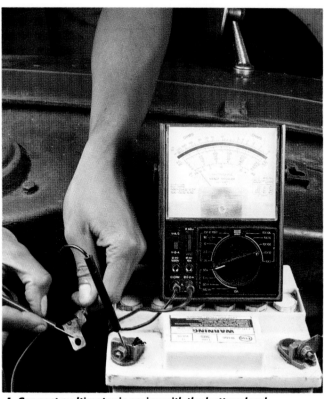

1. Connect multimeter in series with the battery lead

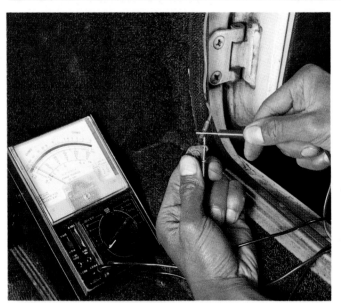

2. Checking courtesy light switch

3. Spark shows current leakage

4. Disconnect the clock at a connector if possible

due to current leakage. Switch carefully to more sensitive scales, making sure you do not exceed the maximum deflection on any scale. You can safely ignore leakages of a few milliamps.

Without a multimeter it is still possible to detect current leakage, but it is a little harder. The procedure is the same as that used with the multimeter, but here you rely on the small sparks which are made when you make and break a circuit. Again remove one battery terminal, and ensure all electrical equipment is turned off. Now bring back the connector into contact with the battery post and move it to and fro to make and break the contact. If there is any current leakage you should be able to see and possibly hear the very

slight sparking which will be occurring (**fig 3**). You will see it more easily if you cut out as much light as possible by doing this in a garage for example.

Having established that there is some current leakage the next problem is to find where it is occurring. By removing the fuses one at a time and checking the effect that this has on either the meter deflection or the sparking it is possible to identify the circuit where the trouble lies. If the sparking stops or there is no meter deflection the fault was in the circuit protected by whichever fuse was removed. By looking at either the wiring diagram in your car handbook, or sometimes the description given on the fuse box cover, check all the components (in particular the switches) on the

circuit you have identified.

Replace the fuse and reconnect the live lead to the battery terminal. Now work your way around the circuit served by that fuse, checking all the components and switches in turn. In the majority of cases the problem will lie in a switch and these can be checked in a simple manner. With the switch off, disconnect the load lead from the switch (this is the lead that goes to whatever is operated by the switch) and connect the meter

between the load terminal and earth. With the meter set to a voltage scale — with a maximum scale reading of at least 12 V — there should be no reading when the switch is off. If there is a reading the switch is faulty.

Door courtesy light switches are particularly vulnerable since they can get damp. These earth the light to the door, so test between the casing and earth while holding the switch itself closed (**fig 2**).

If you do not have a meter a

simple circuit tester consisting of a sidelight bulb in a holder with a couple of leads can be used instead. Just connect the bulb between the switch terminal and earth, and if the switch is faulty the bulb will light with the courtesy light switch off.

If the leakage cannot be traced to a fused circuit, it must be unfused — the starter, solenoid, or alternator. Again, check by disconnecting each in turn. The alternator diode pack is a prime suspect.

Curing starting problems

When your car is slow to start from cold, even though it turns over normally, it's time to check over the ignition system

Bad starting is one of the most annoying car faults. Nine times out of ten the ignition system is the culprit, so check this before looking further.

The ignition system provides the sparks that ignite the fuel in the cylinders. Power from the battery to the coil is interrupted by a contact breaker in the distributor. This makes the coil act as a transformer — changing the battery's 12 volts to a high voltage pulse which is sent to each cylinder, producing a spark at the spark plug.

When to do this job
When the car is slow or difficult to start, even though the engine appears to turn over normally

Other possible causes and related jobs
Servicing spark plugs
Carburettor: Remedying a defective choke
Repairing/renewing the distributor
Ignition timing
When the engine won't turn
Curing fuel flow problems
Please see Index for page numbers

To do this job
Tools: Screwdriver(s); spanner; wire brush or emery paper; nail file; feeler gauge (see text)
Materials: Petroleum jelly; set of points to suit your distributor (see text); sticky tape; clean rag or tissue; engine oil
Time: ½ hour – 2 hours
Degree of difficulty: Easy, though changing the points can be fiddly

If you have the job professionally done ...
Has starting problem been cured? If bill includes replacement parts (such as points) have old components been returned to you?

The distributor cap is a major potential cause of starting problems, but is is a very simple component to check. You can easily find it because all the HT leads meet at the cap (**fig 1**). It is usually held on to the distributor by two steel spring clips — use a screwdriver to prise them away so that the cap is released. Some caps use screws instead of clips (**fig 3**). These just need to be loosened — you do not have to remove them.

As you remove the cap, with the HT leads still attached, notice the way the cap fits on to the distributor. Usually there is a locating tab which makes errors impossible, but sometimes it is possible to fit the cap back into place 180° from the correct position. If you are in doubt, make a paint mark down the side of the cap and on to the distributor body so you can align them.

Now turn the cap upside down so you can see inside and use a clean, dry cloth or tissue to wipe the interior. Check for hairline cracks or tracking — scorched trails of carbon caused by the HT current short circuiting across any damp inside the cap. Sometimes these signs are barely visible, but if you are in any doubt, you should get a new cap — they do not cost very much. When fitting a new one, unplug or unscrew the leads from the old cap and fit them to the replacement one at a time to make sure each is fitted in the correct place. Also make sure

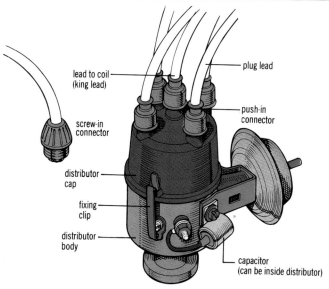

1. Distributor with clip-on distributor cap

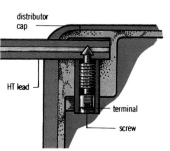

2. Screw-in connector

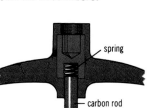

3. Screwed-on distributor cap

5. Spring-loaded rod type

6. Fixed carbon stud type

4. Locating the central stud

they are pushed fully home — or the car may not start at all.

While checking the distributor cap, have a close look at the centre connector (**fig 4**). Sometimes this is a spring loaded carbon rod (**fig 5**), which should protrude far enough to make contact with the rotor arm in the centre of the distributor. An alternative type is a carbon stud (**fig 6**), in which case the rotor arm has a springy arm on it. This carbon stud should not be completely worn away; if it is, you will need a new cap. Badly pitted brass terminals on either the distributor cap or the rotor arm also mean that you need new components

STEP 2 — CHECK THE BATTERY

As long as the engine turns over happily you need not worry that the battery is poor. If it has enough power to spin the starter motor properly there is generally enough left to provide the spark. But you should still carry out some simple checks on the wiring to make sure that you are getting as much power as possible from the battery.

Begin with the two electrical terminals on the top of the battery (**fig 1**). Corrosion that builds up here is often green and crumbly and can prevent the battery's full power from getting through to the starter. Even if the terminals look in good condition, undo the clamps and clean the metal surfaces

with emery paper or a wire brush and smear them with petroleum jelly (such as Vaseline) before you connect up again.

Also use a spanner to make sure that the earth lead is securely anchored to its

screw-on

clamp-on

bolt-through

1. Screw-on, clamp-on and bolt-through battery terminals

earthing point on the engine or the car's bodywork. If there is an earth strap between the bodywork and the engine then clean the connections and make sure that they are tight.

Other battery faults are dealt with on pages 197–200.

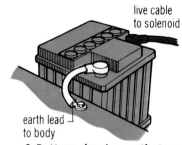

live cable to solenoid

earth lead to body

2. Battery, showing earth strap

Other battery faults are dealt with on pages 197–200.

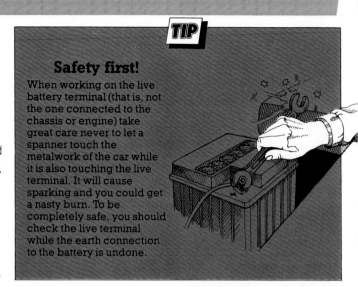

TIP

Safety first!
When working on the live battery terminal (that is, not the one connected to the chassis or engine) take great care never to let a spanner touch the metalwork of the car while it is also touching the live terminal. It will cause sparking and you could get a nasty burn. To be completely safe, you should check the live terminal while the earth connection to the battery is undone.

STEP 3 — CHECK THE HT LEADS

The high tension (HT) leads are the thick cables which carry high voltage from the coil to the distributor and on to each spark plug. Any weak spot in these leads will cause problems because the current will jump across any gap it can find. If there is a crack in the insulation, for example, the current can soon burn a hole for itself, causing some of the power to leak away. So HT leads which are damaged internally or externally should be renewed.

To check the outsides, first use a dry cloth to wipe all traces of oil and dirt from the leads and examine them for cracking. Next, check the connectors at

both ends. At the spark plug end, the connectors (**fig 1**) are usually just pushed on to the plugs; number them (**fig 3**) as you pull them off. At the distributor end, it is usually easier to remove the leads when you have removed the cap from the distributor (see Step 1). Some HT leads simply pull out of the cap, while some are held in place by small screws visible inside each contact; loosen these with a small screwdriver before pulling out the leads. Others are held by a knurled plastic knob which screws into the distributor; if you unscrew this, the lead will pull off.

However they are fixed,

copper core

insulated covering

carbon core

2. Copper and carbon leads

either remove and check the leads one at a time or draw a diagram showing which spark plug is connected to which terminal on the distributor cap. If you muddle the leads, the car will not start.

If the insides of the connectors are dirty, wipe them with a dry rag or emery cloth. If they are clean, and seem to be firmly attached to their leads, do not meddle further — although they are often just screwed or crimped on, they can be difficult to repair.

Now you can check whether there is an internal break in one or more of the HT leads. There are two types of lead — copper cored and carbon cored (**fig 2**). Copper cored leads are quite stiff, with no markings. Carbon cored leads are fairly flexible, and often have their resistance (in ohms) marked on the outside. Those with copper cores rarely fail internally, but carbon cored ones have a reputation for doing so, particularly on older cars. This is usually the result of mechanics removing the plug leads by pulling the leads rather than the connectors.

How can you check whether a carbon cored lead is working properly? If you have access to an electrical multimeter which will measure resistance, you can check whether the actual resistance corresponds with that marked on the outside, about 15,000 ohms per foot (300 mm) of cable. If you have no multimeter, you should be able to get them tested by an auto electrical specialist. Alternatively, you can replace a suspected cable, strictly temporarily, with ordinary house-

hold flex. This works, but its insulation is quite inadequate for continued use.

Unless they are cracked or broken internally, do not renew any leads until you have checked all the other components of the system. Though carbon cored leads can fail, they are often replaced unnecessarily.

3. Numbering the plug leads as they are removed

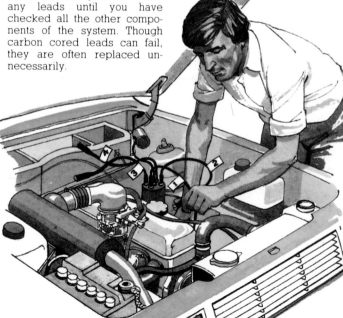

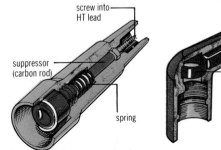

screw into HT lead

suppressor (carbon rod)

spring

HT lead

copper loop

1. Push-on and clip-on spark plug connectors

The next step in your systematic check of the ignition components is to examine the coil and its leads. On one end of the coil — in the centre — you will see the HT lead which runs to the distributor. On either side of this lead you will see the thinner wires which make the LT connections.

Begin by removing the HT lead from the coil (**fig 1**). Look at the metal terminal on the lead. Is it securely attached and clean, or is it loose and corroded? While metal connectors do go dull after a while, this does not affect their performance. But white or green crumbly corrosion definitely interferes with the current — and this lead, the *king lead*, supplies all the high tension current for the engine. Make sure that both this

to see if the lead to the distributor is secure. Sometimes a poor connection causes an intermittent fault.

If the leads are held on to their terminals by small nuts, use a spanner or a pair of pliers to check that these are tight.

Another type of connector pushes on to the bare screw threads There should be a spring clip inside the connector cap — if this does not make firm contact you need a new lead.

Sometimes the LT terminals on the coil consist of male spade connectors held in place by rivets. Check that these are tight — you may find that the rivets have worked loose. This fault can be repaired by gently tapping the top of the rivet with a hammer and a punch or a large

1. Removing the HT lead

nail — but take care not to hit the rivet any harder than necessary otherwise you may crack the insulation. Also check the female spade connector is tight and free from corrosion.

Could the coil itself be the cause of your bad starting? It is possible, but coils usually fail altogether or produce bad running at speed.

If you do suspect the coil, get hold of another one — a garage may lend you an old one — and fit it temporarily to the car.

If the car now starts properly you should renew the coil, fitting all the connections correctly.

spade connector push-on connector bolt-on connector

2. LT leads are connected to the coil in any of these three ways

and the connector at the distributor end are in a healthy state. Also look at the HT contact inside the coil itself and make sure that it is clean. If there is any sign of corrosion, clean it by rolling up a small piece of sandpaper or emery cloth and sliding it round the inside of the hole. Once the HT connection is clean, check the insulation material on the top of the coil for hairline cracks — any sign of these means that you will have to buy a new coil.

Next check the LT connections to the coil (**fig 2**) — and also look

TIP

Demon damp

People often blame damp for poor starting. Moisture inside the distributor, around the top of the coil or on the ends of the HT leads is more likely to prevent the car from starting at all rather than just making it slow to fire. If you suspect damp, wipe the vulnerable areas with a clean, dry cloth or use a proprietary damp repellent spray such as WD-40.

Starting problems can also be caused by the spark plugs. After a few thousand miles the electrodes — the electrical contacts — wear so that it is harder to create a spark. Carbon can also build up causing a weak spark.

across which the spark jumps — wear so that it is harder to create a spark. Carbon can also build up causing a weak spark.

Full details of cleaning and gapping the plugs and deciding when to fit new ones are covered on pages 82-84.

1. Removing the rotor arm

The contact breaker points are more likely to cause starting problems than any other component in the ignition system, so check these thoroughly. With the distributor cap removed (see Step 1) begin the job of checking the points by pulling away the rotor arm attached to the upper end of the distributor shaft. As **fig 1** shows, usually it is a push fit, but some distributors

use two screws to hold it in place. After removing the rotor arm you may find a dust cover fitted to protect the points — if you have one of these, simply lift it away and store it with the rotor arm.

Some distributors have the weights for the ignition timing fitted just below the rotor arm. These weights do not need to be removed to get at the points — there are usually holes or cutouts in the weights which allow you to get a screwdriver on to the points' screw(s).

After a period of use the gap between the points is likely to alter. This is hardly surprising when you consider that the points will have opened and closed around 10,000 times for every mile you drive. Have a close look at the faces of the contacts, checking for signs of pitting. The surface can be seen if you use a screwdriver to

separate the points, pushing against the pressure of the spring. Slight pitting can be smoothed with a fine file — a nail file will do (**fig 2**).

If you find that there is a distinct high spot on one contact and a corresponding pit in the other, it is no good trying to file them — the points must be replaced (see Step 7).

2. Filing the points faces

FACT FILE

Turning the engine over by hand

You will need to find a way of rotating the engine — whether you are checking the gap between the contact points, setting the static ignition timing or adjusting the valve clearances. There are several ways of doing this, depending on the job you are doing and whether your car has a manual gearbox or an automatic transmission.

With all these methods make sure that the ignition is switched off before you begin. Take the key out just to be sure.

Moving the car while in gear
This is the simplest method but it will only work with manual gearboxes. Engage third or fourth gear and, with the handbrake released, push the car forwards (not backwards) to rotate the engine until it reaches the position you want. Do this a little at a time, checking the position of the engine after each movement. Move the car either by pushing the body itself or by turning one of the front tyres with your hands. (This method is not suitable for valve adjustment.)

Rotating the fan belt
Another way of changing the position of the engine to check the points is to move the fan belt so that it turns the crankshaft pulley. The car must be in neutral so this method can also be used with automatic cars.

Remove the spark plugs as this makes the engine easier to turn. Tension one side of the belt by pressing your fingers against it while you simultaneously pull another part of the belt. Take care not to trap your fingers in the pulley.

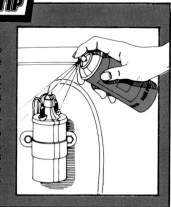

Rotating the crankshaft pulley
With this method the crankshaft pulley has to be moved directly. Once again with the car in neutral, use a large socket spanner to rotate the nut or bolt in the middle of the pulley. In some instances you may come across a pulley with four smaller nuts or bolts protruding from the front. These will enable you to fit a screwdriver or similar tool between two and lever the pulley around.

Turning the pulley itself gives you much more precise control over the position of the engine and is an ideal method if you have to turn the engine over several times — for instance when you are adjusting the valves.

Remote starter switch
The final method involves a special remote starter button. This can only be fitted to cars with the pre-engaged type of starter, with a solenoid assembly on top of the starter motor. This allows the starter to be used for long or short bursts to turn the engine to any position.

To avoid accidents, remove the LT lead from the coil.

1. Checking that the new points will fit

2. Disconnecting the LT connection

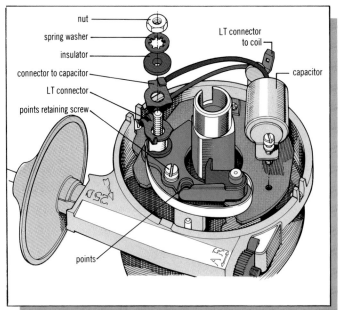

3. How the LT lead and capacitor lead fit on to the points

4. A distributor with weights fitted below the rotor arm

5. One-piece (top) and two-piece points

6. Removing the old points from distributor

If your contact breaker points are not in good condition, it is time to replace them. They are relatively inexpensive items and it is false economy to try and make them last as long as possible. There are several types of points so the procedure varies according to the distributor used in your particular engine. Generally speaking, the following basic approach applies to all cases.

Before you remove the points, compare them with the new ones which you have bought as replacements and make sure that they will fit, even if they are not identical (**fig 1**). Pay particular attention to the LT connections and the screw holes, but do not let the shape of the moulding or the colour of the plastic parts worry you.

Begin by disconnecting the LT lead from the contact points (**fig 2**). Sometimes this is held by a small nut so use a spanner or pliers to remove it from the terminal post and lift away the washer, insulator, LT lead and capacitor wire (**fig 3**). Make a careful note of the way these are fitted so you can avoid confusion later on. Some models use a simple push-fit terminal for the

capacitor wire which makes this job easier.

Choose a screwdriver that best fits the screw or screws which attach the points assembly to the baseplate of the distributor and lift away the points (**fig 6**). Most modern contact breaker sets are one-piece components, but you may find that yours consists of two separate parts (**fig 5**). This should present no problems as long as you make a careful note of their original positions – if you have any doubts, make a sketch to help you reassemble the new parts correctly.

Removing the screws which attach the points to the distributor sounds simple enough but it can turn out to be one of the most fiddly jobs you may come across on your car. The screws are often overtightened by zealous mechanics, so you must use a screwdriver which is right for the task. Never even try it if the tool you have is blunt or undersized — you may just burr the screw and make it even harder to remove. Use the widest screwdriver you can fit into the slots. Replacement points do not provide you with these screws and the originals may well have

been chewed up by previous ham-fisted attempts to undo them.

The screws are often not very long — less than ¼ in. (6 mm) so be prepared for the screw to come loose quickly. Use your fingers for the last turns or put your fingers around the tip of the screwdriver. There is always the risk that you will allow one of the screws to drop down inside the distributor. For this reason many professional mechanics use a magnetic screwdriver so that the loosened screw remains attached to the tip of the tool. In the event that you do actually drop a screw down inside the distributor, it is absolutely vital that you retrieve it — leaving it there is likely to cause expensive damage (see Tip, page 205).

Before fitting the replacement part, use a clean cloth to wipe the faces of the contacts clean of any preservative that may have been applied by the manufacturer and then wipe the baseplate. Now install the new points, making sure that the screws and wires are refitted correctly. Some baseplates are fitted with a locating post which enables you to position the points correctly by simply sliding the

points over this post and then refitting the screws (see **fig 3**). Always make sure that any insulators or washers are refitted correctly.

On two-piece units there is often a nylon sleeve that acts as both insulator and washer. Be particularly careful if you have to deal with one of these. Its job is

to make sure that the LT and capacitor connectors do not touch the metal post they are secured to since this is earthed to the car body. If you get this wrong, the car simply will not start.

Once you have replaced the points, the gap must be set (see Step 7). Now start the car and see

how well it runs. Replacing points often alters the timing of the ignition slightly — which, by chance, could either be an improvement or a disadvantage. If you are now happy with the engine's performance there is no need to touch the timing.

Timing adjustment is covered on pages 85 to 88.

Having cleaned the contacts, you can now check the gap between them. This also needs to be done when you fit new points, and as part of a normal service.

With the distributor cap and rotor still removed, begin by rotating the engine (see Fact File box) until one of the lobes on the distributor cam has pushed against the block on the contact points so that the points have opened fully (**fig 1**).

With one of the cams opening the contact points to the maximum extent, the next step is to measure the gap (see Fact File – Using a feeler gauge). Most manufacturers specify an acceptable clearance range such as 0.017 to 0.021 in.

To make an adjustment, loosen the contact breaker retaining screw, or screws (**fig 2**). Now move the position of the points in relation to the baseplate by pushing a screwdriver between the adjustment notches and turning it (**fig 3**). (In a few cases, you turn an eccentric screw instead.) As you make this adjustment, keep sliding the feeler gauge between the contacts until the gap seems to be correct. After tightening the retaining screws, check the gap again because sometimes you can disturb the setting while you are locking the contact breaker assembly in place.

Finally, refit the rotor arm and the distributor cap.

FACT FILE

Using a feeler gauge

A feeler gauge has a number of thin stainless steel blades, each one of a stated thickness. The figures printed on the blades refer to the thickness in either thousandths of an inch ('thou'), or hundredths of a millimetre. You can tell which is which by looking at the range of numbers: 1 to 25 means thousandths of an inch, while 05 to 80 means hundredths of a millimetre. When written as decimals, 25 thou is 0.025 in, and 15 on the metric scale is 0.15 mm.

The thicknesses of the blades are chosen so you can make up any thickness you need by combining no more than three blades.

As the surfaces of the blades can never touch perfectly, because of microscopic surface grime, there is bound to be a small error when combining thicknesses. Only when you combine more than three does the error become significant, however.

A feeler blade or blades should be a sliding fit in a gap of the same thickness. To find out what tolerance there is, try measuring a gap as accurately as you can. You will soon get a feel for the difference an extra thousandth of an inch makes. If the gauge is unwilling to go into the gap, try a size down till you have it just right.

cam lobe
points closed

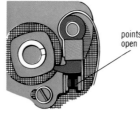

points open

1. How cam opens the points

2. Loosening the contact breaker retaining screw

3. Measuring the points' gap with a feeler gauge

Having replaced the points, you should lubricate the cam which opens and closes the contacts. Smear a small amount of grease on the faces of the cam (**fig 1**), making sure you do not get any on the points themselves. Check your manual to see if you have a lubrication point on the top of the shaft where the rotor sits. A few drops of engine oil (**fig 2**) is all that is needed to take care of this. Some distributors have a felt block which rubs against the cam. Do not oil this; its job is to wipe away excess grease from the cam.

1. Lubricating the cam lobes with grease

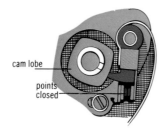

2. Oiling the points cam spindle

Capacitors usually last for a very long time and are generally best left alone if they appear to be working correctly — there is no practical way of testing these components. However, if the contact points have worn out very quickly you should replace the capacitor as well as the points. This is a simple task — just undo the retaining screw which attaches the capacitor to either the baseplate or the side of the distributor, release the wire connecting it to the contact points and lift the capacitor away. Make sure that you refit the wire correctly when you are installing the new capacitor.

1. Lifting out the capacitor

TIP

Retrieval systems

How can you recover a screw or nut if it drops down inside the distributor baseplate? Not everybody has a magnetic screwdriver — but an ordinary one will do if you attach a magnet anywhere along its shaft, thus temporarily magnetizing it.

You may not have a magnet around the place — but remember that every loudspeaker has a magnet. If all else fails you might be able to take the back off an old transistor radio and use its speaker as a magnet.

Another possibility is to use a blob of grease or Blu-Tack on the end of a long, thin tool to pick up a screw.

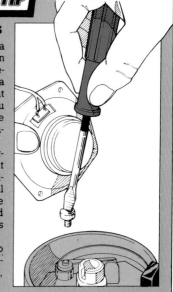

Engine turns but won't fire

If the engine refuses to fire although the starter is fine you can save time and temper by following a logical series of checks

Just turning an engine on the starter motor is frustrating and will only serve to flatten the battery. The following steps can be used both when the car has suddenly refused to catch

and if the car is usually slow to start. If your car is fitted with electronic ignition only follow Step 1. If the starter motor does not function refer to pages 203 to 206.

When to do this job
When the car turns over normally on the starter motor but refuses to fire

What this job involves
Locating the fault
Checking the low tension circuit
Checking the high tension circuit
Checking the carburettor
Testing the petrol supply
Checking linkages
Looking for air leaks
Checking for mechanical failure

Other possible causes and related jobs
Curing starting problems
Starter won't turn engine
Servicing a distributor
Ignition system problems
Tracking down electrical faults
Curing fuel flow problems
Simple spark plug service
Please see Index for page numbers

To do this job
Tools: Screwdrivers; socket set spanners; wire brush; test lamp
Materials: Contact set (possibly); HT lead; cleaning rag; Water-repellent spray
Time: Five minutes to two hours
Degree of difficulty: Fairly straightforward but can be tedious

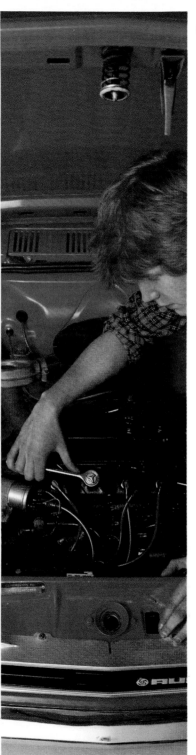

Before you start a step-by-step check of potential trouble points it is a good idea to make a quick overall assessment. The fact that the starter motor turns the engine over shows that the battery and its associated cables are in good order. A working starter motor also shows that power is getting through to the combined ignition/starter switch and if the ignition warning light comes on you can be pretty sure that the switch itself is OK (a different set of switch contacts activates the starter solenoid). As well as the ignition light the instruments should be working so you can check that there is petrol in the tank.

If your car has a security cut-out in the ignition circuit or fuel line check that it is set to the 'run' position, then move on under the bonnet and make sure that the low-tension (LT) connections — the thin wires to the coil and distributor are firmly in place with no signs of damage or corrosion (**fig 1**). Also make sure that the thick high tension (HT) leads from the coil to the distributor and from the distributor to the spark plugs are in place with no obvious damage, and that the distributor cap is clamped firmly home. Finally, take a good look round the carburettor to make sure that there are no signs of petrol leakage, if so see Step 4, and that the air intake is clear. It is possible that a loose rag or paper has been sucked in.

If the engine still does not fire the trouble lies a bit deeper, probably in either the ignition circuit or the fuel system. A very common fault is that the points close up — so you may prefer to start your checks in the distributor (see Step 2).

You can decide where to check first by taking out one of the spark plugs. If the tip of the plug is wet with petrol the engine has flooded — see Step

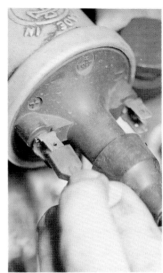

1. Checking LT connections to coil

2. Spraying distributor with water repellent

3. Checking plug for spark

need someone to help do this by operating the ignition switch — and see if there is a sharp blue-white spark across the plug points (**fig 3**). If there is a spark you can assume that the ignition system is in working order and turn your attention to the fuel system. Step 4. If there is no spark make sure that it is not the plug that is at fault by holding the HT lead about ¼ in. (6 mm) from the engine block and again checking for a spark. If there is no spark try another plug. You may need to turn back the plug cover or remove the suppressor cap from the HT lead to carry out this test. If there is still no sign of a spark there is a fault in the ignition circuit, go on to Step 2.

When the weather is damp a film of condensation can form on the coil, distributor and HT leads so providing a path for the ignition spark to divert down instead of travelling to the spark plug as intended. If you think that damp could be a problem it is worth just wiping these areas dry or applying a spray of one of the water repellents before you try to start the car again (**fig 2**). But more often than not damp is unfairly blamed, so make sure there is no other fault.

4 — but carry on with this test to make sure sure that there are no other problems. A dirty plug will not work properly so if necessary clean the top with a soft wire brush (and remove the other plugs to clean then too). Then reconnect the HT lead to the plug and hold the plug in contact with a metal part of the engine. Turn the engine over on the starter — you will probably

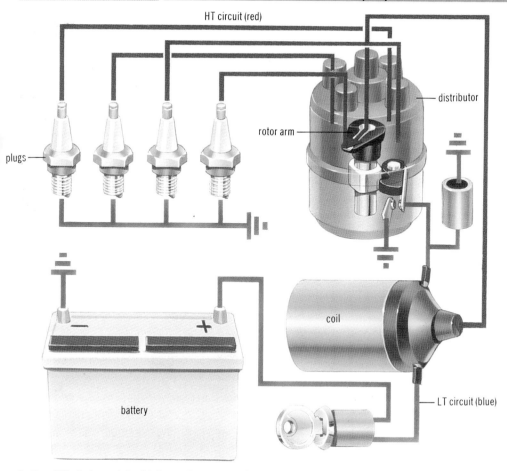

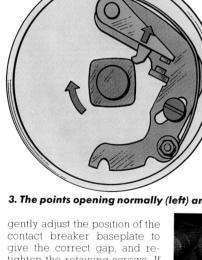

plugs

HT circuit (red)

distributor

rotor arm

coil

battery

LT circuit (blue)

1. Simplified view of the high tension (HT) and low tension (LT) circuits

3. The points opening normally (left) and staying closed (right) through baseplate slip

4. Use a test lamp to check coil

2. How to turn engine over

Probably the most common cause of ignition troubles is incorrect setting of the contact points so this is the first check you should make. Remove the distributor cap by unclipping the spring clips or undoing the retaining screws — note how the cap fits on the distributor so that you can replace it the correct way round. Pull off the rotor arm and turn the engine over by hand (**fig 2**), so that one of the lobes of the distributor cam pushes against the contact set cam follower and opens the points.

If there is no gap, or virtually none, you have probably found the fault. If there is a noticeable gap, the fault probably lies elsewhere but you should make sure that you have the correct gap before going any further (**fig 3**).

Using feeler gauges measure the gap between the points. The required measurement is given when the feeler blade (or combination of blades) just slides into the gap. Compare the measured gap to the one specified for your car, if you do not know the specified value work to a figure of 0.015 in (0.4 mm). To adjust the gap, if necessary, slacken off the contact breaker retaining screw (or screws) and gently adjust the position of the contact breaker baseplate to give the correct gap, and retighten the retaining screws. If the contact points are slightly pitted they can be cleaned up with a fine file or emery paper but if there is severe pitting a replacement set of points should be fitted, as described on pages 195 and 196.

Turn the engine over so that the points close and switch on the ignition. Now just flick the points open with your fingertip while watching to see if there is a spark between the points. If there is a small blue/white spark the LT circuit is working and you can go on to check the high tension circuit, Step 3. If there is no spark — or a large yellow spark — the low tension circuit needs further checking, as follows.

Identify the thin low tension lead between the coil and the distributor and disconnect it at the coil end. Connect a test lamp between the coil terminal and an earth on the car body. If the lamp lights the wiring to the coil and the primary winding of the coil are all right (**fig 4**).

Should the lamp not light connect it between the other coil terminal, without removing the leads to that terminal, and earth. If the lamp now lights the coil is faulty and you should replace it, while if the lamp does not light the wiring between the ignition switch and the coil is faulty and you will have to check back along the wiring looking for short circuits or faulty connectors.

Assuming that the test lamp lights at the distributor terminal on the coil connect the test lamp between this terminal and the lead to the distributor. The lamp should now light but go out when you push the contact points open with your finger. Should the light not go out check the coil-to-distributor lead and the correct breaker arm for short circuits, paying particular attention to the connection between the lead and the points. If there is no fault here the problem lies in the ignition capacitor which should be replaced. Another sign that the capacitor is faulty is a yellow spark between the contact points when you open them and excessive pitting of the faces of the contacts.

Once you have made sure that the LT circuit is working properly reconnect the coil to the distributor and move on to Step 3 to check the HT circuit.

Remove the thick HT lead which runs from the coil to the centre of the distributor, from the cap — it may be held in place by a fixing screw inside the cap, be a push fit or be held in place by a screwed cap on the outside. Hold the end of the lead about 1/4 in. (6 mm) from a suitable earth, such as the engine block, and flick the points open with an insulated screwdriver. You should see a spark jump from the end of the lead to earth, showing that the coil and lead are in good condition. If there is no spark, or a very weak one, either the coil itself is faulty and you will have to replace it or there is an internal fault in the lead. Check by substituting a new length of lead — any kind of wire will do — and retesting, or use a test meter to check the continuity of the lead, see page

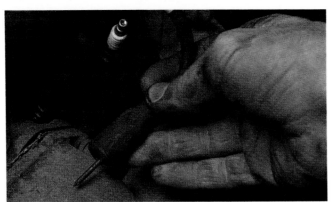

1. Use a nail to check shrouded HT lead for sparks

202 for more details.

If the spark is satisfactory replace the distributor rotor arm and hold the coil HT lead about 1/4 in. (6 mm) from the central metal contact on the rotor. Again flick the contact

points open and look for a spark. If there is a spark, there is a fault in the rotor arm allowing the HT spark to go to earth and the arm needs to be replaced.

Take a close look at the inside and outside of the cap and see if

there are any fine cracks or track marks between the HT connections. These marks are caused by the HT current short-circuiting across the surface of the cap and if any are present the cap should be replaced. Also check the centre contact inside the cap (**fig 2**). In some cases this consists of a spring-mounted carbon rod which presses against the contact plate on the rotor arm. With this type of contact check that the rod moves freely in the cap against the spring pressure. The second type of contact consists of a carbon stud which is pushed against by a spring lever on the rotor arm. This type should be checked to ensure that the stud has not been worn away, you should also check that there is spring in the rotor arm contact. Finally if the brass

2. Checking cap contacts

internal contacts in the cap show signs of severe corrosion or pitting you should replace the cap.

Now replace the central HT lead in the distributor cap and refit the cap to the distributor, making sure that it is correctly aligned. Remove the leads from the plugs and check for a spark at the lead (**fig 1**). If there is one remove each plug from the engine, connect its lead and check that the plug itself sparks as described in Step 2. Now make sure that they are clean and set to the correct gap (see pages 82-84). If you are not sure of the correct gap a setting of 0.025 in. (0.6 mm) should be satisfactory. Taking one plug at a time check the plug and associated HT lead as described in Step 1. All should now work properly.

When you remove the spark plugs take a good look at the tips. If they are wet with petrol the engine has been flooding. This happens when too much petrol is supplied to the engine when trying to start. The excess petrol builds up in the intake manifold and is carried through into the engine cylinders in the form of droplets instead of being properly atomised to form a vapour. These droplets can prevent the engine firing in two ways, first by making the mixture so rich that it will not fire, and secondly by physically wetting the tip of the sparking plug and stopping the spark from jumping the gap.

Often flooding is simply due to a poor starting technique — see page 209 — Starting your car — and the cure is to dry off the plugs by wiping them, heating with a lighter flame, or simply waiting for a short while before you replace them and try to start again using choke but no throttle. If the engine still does

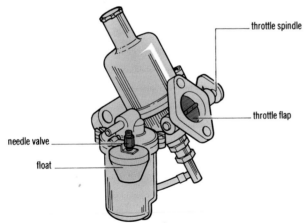

1. Cutaway of basic SU type carburettor

needle valve

float

throttle spindle

throttle flap

not fire recheck a plug, if it is wet again the problem probably lies in the carburettor itself. Remove the air filter and look into the carburettor body (**fig 3**) — you may have to push the choke flap out of the way — and try to see if there are any signs of petrol seeping from the jets. Should this be the case the

problem is most probably due to a jammed needle valve in the float chamber or a damaged float (**figs 1** and **2**). Another sign of problems in this area is petrol leakage on the outside of the carburettor.

Remove the screws from the carburettor cover, take it off and check that the needle valve

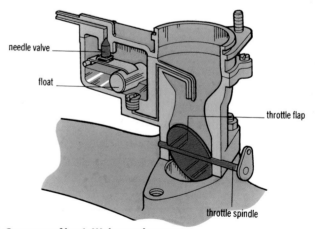

2. Cutaway of basic Weber carburettor

needle valve

float

throttle flap

throttle spindle

on the petrol inlet moves freely. You can check that it is working properly by getting someone to operate the starter while you are holding the valve in the closed position (pushed into the housing). No petrol should be pumped past the valve. If petrol does spurt out the valve is probably jammed by a bit of dirt

and must be dismantled and cleaned. Also take a close look at the float in the flat chamber. If it is a free floating type make sure that it moves up and down easily in the chamber and try lifting it out and shaking it (you can also try shaking floats mounted on the carburettor cover). If there is any sign of

3. Removing air filter

petrol inside the float it is damaged and will have to be replaced. All air pipes to carburettor from engine should be checked for leaks and if necessary replaced. When everything is in order the float and cover can be replaced the plugs dried if necessary and the car started.

If there is no sign, or smell, of petrol on the plugs when you remove them look into the carburettor while the engine is being turned over on the starter and see if there are any signs of petrol being drawn out of the jets. If there is no sign of petrol there is probably a blockage in the fuel supply. Check the supply by disconnecting the petrol pipe from the carburettor and turning the engine over briefly. On cars with electric petrol pumps all that is necessary is to turn the ignition on. Petrol should spurt out from the pipe.

When there is no sign of fuel reaching the carburettor you will have to work your way back down the fuel line checking for obvious faults such as a kinked or squashed pipe (**fig 1**). Problems can be caused by inline filters between the pump and carburettor becoming blocked. Undo the connections and test for flow by turning the engine over, any blocked filter should be replaced. Most mechanical fuel pumps have a built-in filter (**fig 2**) and you can

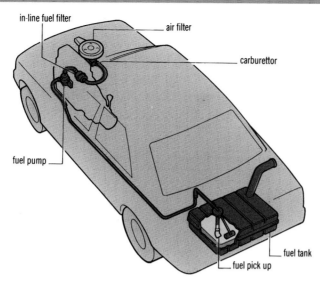

in-line fuel filter · air filter · carburettor · fuel pump · fuel tank · fuel pick up

1. A conventional petrol supply system

clean this by undoing the retaining clip or screws and removing the cover. Wash the filter element in clean petrol, clean out the filter chamber and refit.

You can check if a mechanical pump is working by undoing the inlet pipe and placing your finger over the inlet while the engine is turned over a couple of times (**fig 2**). You should feel a definite suction on the end of your finger and hear a hiss when you pull your finger away. Some pumps have a hand priming lever on them and this can be used instead of turning the

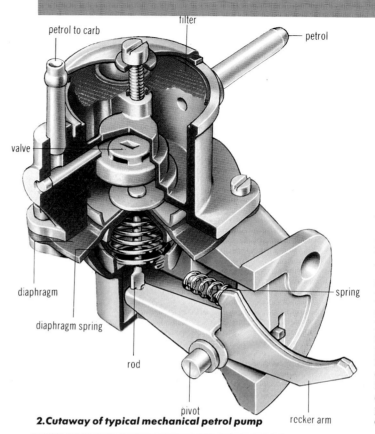

petrol to carb · filter · petrol · valve · diaphragm · diaphragm spring · rod · spring · pivot · rocker arm

2. Cutaway of typical mechanical petrol pump

engine over. If there is no suction, the pump needs overhauling. See pages 177 to 180 for how to check and overhaul the fuel pump.

Assuming that the pump is in good working order but will not deliver petrol a possible cause is blockage of the feed pipe by an accumulation of dirt in the petrol tank. This can be checked, and often cleared, by blowing hard back along the fuel pipe — you should be able to hear and feel the air bubbling up through the petrol in the tank. Repeated blockage of the fuel pipe is a sign of a badly contaminated fuel tank which you will have to remove and clean. An associated problem is a blockage of the breather pipe that allows air into the petrol tank as the fuel is pumped out. Blockage here will lead to the formation of a vacuum in the tank which will prevent further fuel flow — it can easily be checked for by removing the filler cap. If the pump now delivers petrol the breather pipe is blocked and must be cleaned.

When starting from cold an engine needs a richer mixture than for normal running and this is supplied by the choke, with proper operation of the choke mechanism being needed for easy starting. Checking this operation is straightforward on cable actuated manual chokes — get an assistant to pull the choke control out while you watch the action on the carburettor. Make sure that the outer portion of the choke cable is firmly held by its clamp and that the choke lever on the carburettor moves freely over its whole travel. With most fixed choke carburettors by removing the air filter it is possible to check that the choke flap is properly closed when the choke is

1. Checking the carburettor choke butterfly valve

applied.

Where an automatic choke is fitted it is more difficult to check the action. However, as with the manual choke it is normally possible to make a visual check that the choke flap is closed — remember that it is often necessary to depress the accelerator to set the choke flap to the closed position.

With both tyres of choke you should also check that the fast idle lever is actuated by the choke control and that the throttle linkage is working properly, paying attention to the closure of the throttle. See pages 181 to 185 for details of ways to prevent a sticking choke flap and freeing linkages.

The way that you try to start your car can make a lot of difference to the ease with which it starts. Different techniques suit different cars and it is worth experimenting to find the best method for your car — remember that the method used will vary according to whether the engine is cold or hot. Whatever technique you use it is as well to give the system as much of a chance as you can, so when starting try to keep the drain on the battery as small as possible by switching off all other electrical equipment — such as lights and defrosters.

With a cold engine the first method to try is the simplest, apply full choke and operate the starter with no throttle, though automatic chokes may need to be set by depressing the throttle pedal fully. When the engine fires apply a little throttle to rev the engine up. In some cases the engine will start more readily when part throttle is applied, while other engines respond well to a quick 'blip' on the accelerator before turning the engine over. Where this applies the 'blip' operates the carburettor accelerator pump and squirts a little petrol into the intake manifold where it helps to provide a rich starting mixture. In all cases as the engine warms up the choke should be gradually returned to the off position as soon as the engine is warm enough to tick over freely.

With a warm engine you should not use any choke and normally the best method is to apply a little throttle and turn the engine over, although here too some cars will respond better to a preliminary movement of the throttle pedal. Use of the choke or too much throttle on a hot engine can result in flooding which will stop the car from starting. Normal remedy in this case is to remove the plugs and dry them (with a cloth or a lighter flame). However, before

FACT FILE

Emergency starts

If you are unable to start your car because the battery is flat and you are sure that there is no other reason you can try a push or tow start or make use of the fully charged battery in another car by means of jump leads.

Push starts can only be used on cars with manual transmissions and you will need the help of at least a couple of willing (or at least able) pushers. The driver should sit in the car, apply full choke (with a cold engine) switch on the ignition and disengage the clutch before selecting second or third gear. Then the handbrake can be released and the pushing started. When the car has reached a speed of around 10 mph (15 kmh) the clutch should be gently engaged to turn the engine over. As soon as the engine fires the clutch should be disengaged and the engine kept running with gentle use of the accelerator while the car is stopped on the handbrake.

Jump leads can be used on both manual gearbox and automatic cars provided that a second car with a fully charged battery is available. Park the second car as close as possible to your car, positioning it so as to bring the two batteries as close together as possible. Set the ignition switches of both cars to the off position and make sure that the bodies of the two cars are not touching anywhere. Connect the first jump lead (normally coloured red) from the positive (+) terminal of the good battery to the positive (+) terminal of the other, making sure that the jump lead clamps make a good firm contact on the battery terminals. Similarly connect the second lead (normally coloured black) between the negative (−) terminals of the batteries. While connecting the batteries take care to avoid touching any part of either car with the jump lead terminals since this could lead to a short.

With the cables connected, start your car in the normal manner and run your engine for a couple of minutes until it will tick over at, or just above, normal idling speed and then carefully remove the jump leads one at a time. Removing the leads when your engine is running at a higher speed could cause damage to the charging system of either car. If your car will not start using the jump leads do not carry on until you have run down the battery of the donor car. Check your engine as described here.

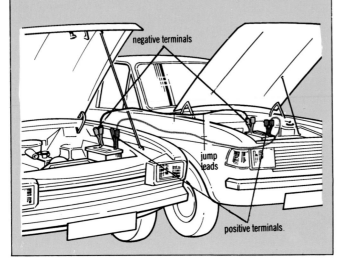

negative terminals

jump leads

positive terminals.

1. Checking insulating points on the HT leads are secure

resorting to this expedient it is worth just flooring the throttle gently — to avoid squirting too much petrol in — and operating the starter to turn the engine over (make sure that the choke is fully off). This has the effect of pumping air through the cylinders, which may disperse the excess petrol and allow you to start the engine.

Particular starting problems may be encountered with a car that has been laid up for a few months without the engine being run. To begin with you will often have to pump fuel through to fill the carburettor. Where there is a manual priming lever on the petrol pump you should use this but otherwise the best technique is to minimise the load on the battery by flooring the throttle and spinning the engine on the starter (with the choke fully off). When the carburettor is fully primed your usual starting technique can be used but problems may still arise even though both the ignition and fuel systems are in good working

2. Remove and examine rotor arm

order. This is because petrol that has been standing in a petrol tank for some months may lose some of its more volatile (and so more inflammable) fractions which are particularly important when starting. One possible solution is to drain off the old petrol and refill with fresh fuel, and another is to use a special starting aerosol. These aerosols contain a highly inflammable mixture which is sprayed directly into the air intake either during, or immediately before, starting to provide an especially rich mixture. Note that this type of starting aid should not be confused with the other type of spray which you use on the ignition system to reduce the effects of damp.

Assuming that both the ignition and fuel systems are working properly and your car still not start there is some sort of mechanical failure.

Starter won't turn engine

Starter problems can be frustrating — especially if they persist after you've renewed the unit. Here's how to fix them

When the starter motor gives trouble or refuses to turn the engine, there are always some clues which indicate where the problem lies. Luckily, the starter motor circuit is fairly straightforward, and so most faults can be traced quickly.

The majority of faults are caused by poor connections in the electrical system, but in the case of the motor itself, there may be mechanical fault. But if the checks are approached in a logical sequence, and you have a good 'ear' for mechanical sounds, then you should quickly pinpoint the problem.

When to do this job
The moment you have problems getting the engine to turn over — even if the problem is intermittent
When the starter becomes noisy

What this job involves
Checking the battery and all electrical connections in the starter circuit
Testing the ignition switch, the starter solenoid, and the motor itself
Removing and cleaning a Bendix drive
Possible fitting a new solenoid
Possibly overhauling a starter motor

Other possible causes and related jobs
Curing battery problems
Tracking down electrical faults
Please see Index for page numbers

To do this job
Tools: Test lamp; large insulated screwdriver; spanner; hydrometer
Materials: Emery paper; replacement parts as required
Time: To check the starter system about an hour
Degree of difficulty: Checks straightforward

If you have the job professionally done . . .
Does the starter work first time every time without any excessive noise?

When all else fails towing may be the only answer. To start a car which otherwise will not respond to the processes opposite you will need a rope of some 3 to 5 metres length. The means of attachment here are of paramount importance. A badly placed rope can damage body work.

If your car has towing eyes and the towing car has rear towing eyes or a tow bar, no problems should be encountered. If neither car has towing provision either at front or rear some thought has to be given to where you attach the rope. Certain suspension components should be strong enough to take the strain (**fig 2**). Some cars with spoilers cannot be towed without the spoilers being removed. Do not tow with the rope tied to independent rear suspension.

The driver of the tow car should take every precaution to avoid jerking the tow rope. Never tow an automatic car unless it is totally necessary and then always consult your maker's handbook for the correct towing procedure.

When starting the car arrange a signal with the driver of the tow car to tell him when the engine has started. Select second or third gear and when you have reached a speed of about twenty miles per hour engage the clutch. Once the engine fires disengage the clutch and take the car out of gear keeping the engine running by use of the accelerator. The towing driver can then slow down gradually bearing in mind that you will probably have to stop on the handbrake. But always be ready with the footbrake in case he stops too quickly.

For longer distance towing you will need a sign displayed at the rear of the car saying 'on tow' and giving the number of the towing vehicle (**fig 1**). Tie a rag to the centre of the tow rope to act as a warning to pedestrians and arrange a system of signals, such as too fast, too close or stop.

Disconnect the coil on the car being towed so that the ignition can remain switched on without draining the battery. Warn other road users by turning on lights but do not turn on the hazard flashers as these should only be used when stationary.

Ideally the towed car should do the majority of the braking and the brakes should be used to help you keep the tow rope taut. Always leave plenty of space on corners as a tight line could lead to the rope being dragged over the pavement, an obvious pedestrian hazard.

1. Make up 'ON TOW' sign with tow car number

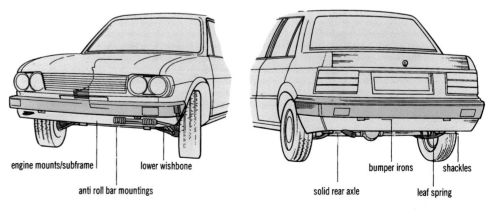

engine mounts/subframe | lower wishbone | bumper irons | shackles
anti roll bar mountings | solid rear axle | leaf spring

2. The tow rope may be attached to any of these points

If nothing at all happens when you turn the key to the start position, and neither the horn nor the lights work, then the battery is probably flat and should be checked.

If the battery has a charge, then check the battery leads and terminals. The leads should be tightly clamped, and the terminals and earth should be clean. It is quite possible for the lights to work yet for an apparently sound connection to fail when the starter tries to draw its heavy current.

If the battery and its connections are all sound (see Step 3), but there is still no power, when the ignition is switched on, then suspect the ignition switch or the connections between it and the solenoid.

The starter solenoid rarely gives any trouble, and should click when you start the engine. The click indicates that power is reaching the solenoid and that it is working.

If there is no click at the solenoid, then check all connections to it and then check the solenoid itself (see Step 5). If the solenoid is not faulty, then the problem must lie in the starter motor or in the connections to it through in rare cases the fault could be in the ring gear. Seek professional advice if you suspect this problem.

TIP

Quick action

If ever you hear strange noises coming from your starter motor — whether it is of the inertia type or pre-engaged — investigate as soon as you can. This is very important as prompt action could save the motor from the scrap heap. If the motor or the gear teeth wear, the flywheel ring gear will get chewed up very quickly, and to replace this you have to remove the engine or gearbox first.

HOW IT WORKS

The starter circuit

There are two types of starter motor; the Bendix type and the pre-engaged type. The pre-engaged type can be recognized by the fact that its solenoid — an activating switch — is situated directly on top of the motor. The solenoid for the Bendix type is located separately, usually on the bulkhead or inner wing in the engine compartment.

The Bendix type is more prone to trouble as the pinion is made to rotate and move inwards to engage with the flywheel. Because of this movement, the pinion can stick on its shaft and can also suffer from problems caused by worn teeth.

The pinion on the pre-engaged type is moved outwards from the motor to engage with the flywheel by a lever connected to the solenoid.

Power to the starter motor arrives through a simple circuit. A cable goes directly from the battery to the starter solenoid. A cable then passes from the solenoid to the starter motor — this is the power cable. A wire passes from the battery to the ignition switch, and from there passes to the solenoid. This wire closes the circuit allowing current to pass to the field coils in the motor.

The battery, ignition switch, solenoid and starter motor are all earthed and a bad earth in the circuit is a common cause of starter motor problems.

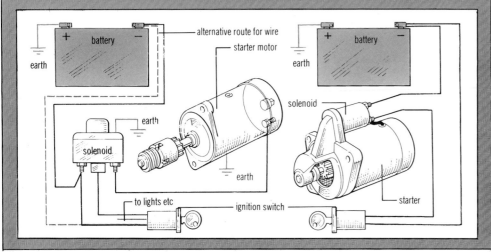

If the car seems to be electrically 'dead', check the battery terminals first. If you notice that the positive terminal is hot after trying to start the car, this is a sure sign that it is not making a proper connection. Instead of just examining the terminals, clean them first (**fig 1**), then use a spanner or screwdriver to loosen the clamps from their posts and disconnect both leads. Clean the connecting surfaces with emery paper before reconnecting and make sure that the clamps and cable are all in good condition, (see pages 197-200).

Try starting the car again. If you still have no response, follow the positive cable from

1. Cleaning up the terminal clamps — inside and out

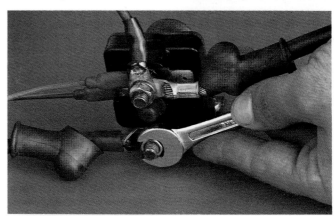

2. Checking that the battery lead is tight at the solenoid

3. Checking earth lead

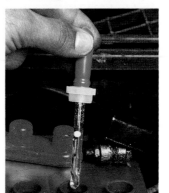

4. Checking the battery

the starter solenoid and make sure that the nut holding it in place is tight (**fig 2**). Use a spanner or socket spanner to do this, but be careful not to over-tighten it and be sure not to let the spanner touch any other part of the car or you may receive a nasty shock.

Next, examine the earth strap and its connection to the car's bodywork (**fig 3**). If there is corrosion here you should disconnect the strap and clean the area with a wire brush or sandpaper until at least some bright metal is showing through. Refit the earth strap but fit a new one

if you are in any doubt about the old one's condition.

If the car is still electrically dead, the battery must be flat. Assuming that you have not left the lights on and that the car has been in regular use, a flat battery means that either there is a drain on the electrical system caused by a short circuit or that the battery is faulty. Recharge it and then test each cell with a hydrometer (**fig 4**). If the battery will not accept a charge, not even a trickle charge overnight, then you have no alternative but to fit a new one.

STEP 4 — CHECK POWER TO SOLENOID

If you find that the battery has power but the starter still fails to turn, try switching on the headlamps while you turn the ignition key to the 'start' position. The lights should dim — if they do not it means that the starter is not drawing any current, so part of the circuit is at fault.

To make a more detailed check you will need to use a test lamp (see page 194). First locate the solenoid. This will be on top of the starter motor if you car has a pre-engaged starter motor or on one side of the engine compartment or on the bulkhead if you have a Bendix starter. If the solenoid is not immediately obvious, simply follow the wires running from the starter until you find it. Look for a thin wire connected to its own terminal on the solenoid. This carries the power from the ignition switch and it is usually a simple push-fit

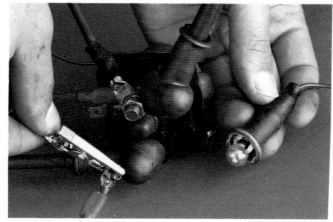

1. Make sure that power is reaching the solenoid

on to the solenoid. Pull the wire from its terminal and, with one lead of the test lamp earthed touch the other against the lead to the ignition switch **(fig 1)**. When the ignition key is turned

to operate the starter lamp should light up. If it does, it means that the ignition switch and the wire are working properly but that the starter or solenoid is faulty.

2. Where to check for power — both types of starter

If you find that there is no power reading at the solenoid, there must be a faulty electrical connection. Make sure that the switch lead is in good condition at the solenoid end and check that the push-fit connector is firmly crimped to the end of the wire and that the wire itself is undamaged. It will probably disappear into a large wiring harness so you will not be able to follow it all the way to the ignition switch. Next look at the fusebox — sometimes the wire passes through a fuse so check that the fuses are all unbroken and are making good tight connections.

The only other possibility is that the ignition switch is faulty or that there is a loose connection into the switch. Check the switch connections, if the fault persists, replace the switch with a new unit.

STEP 5 — CHECK THE STARTER SOLENOID

If there is power reaching the solenoid, but still nothing happens when you turn the ignition key, either the motor or solenoid must be faulty.

With Bendix starters where the solenoid is mounted separately from the starter motor, you will usually find a button which overrides the

solenoid to activate the starter; it sits between the two large electrical connections. Make sure the car is in neutral and the ignition key is 'off' and then press the button **(fig 3)**. The starter should work, indicating that the solenoid is faulty. A starter solenoid cannot be dismantled for repair, but it is fairly

easy to fit a new replacement. With pre-engaged starters this is a little more difficult since the starter motor itself has to be removed first. The solenoid is an integral part of the motor with internal electrical connections. Seek professional advice if you suspect a problem.

Some Bendix starter sole-

noids do not have such a button, nor do any pre-engaged starters. To check the solenoid on these types, bridge the two large electrical connections with a test lamp. Turn the ignition key to 'start' — if the lamp lights the solenoid is working. On a pre-engaged starter, connect the test lamp

between the large terminals on the solenoid **(fig 2)**. If the lamp lights, the solenoid is fine, and the starter motor is either jammed or has an internal fault (see Step 6). If the lamp does not light, the solenoid is faulty and you must replace it.

With Bendix starter solenoids, first disconnect the battery,

then make a note of the position of the electrical connections. Now disconnect the wires and undo the bolts or screws which hold the assembly inside the engine compartment **(fig 4)**. When you are fitting the new solenoid, make certain that you fit the wires back the right way round.

1. If the solenoid is working, power will reach the starter

2. Check pre-engaged type

3. Override the solenoid as a final check

4. If solenoid is faulty, renew it

A fault in the starter motor can be mechanical or electrical.

A mechanical fault is usually indicated by some form of noise, but where the motor appears to be 'dead' — that is the motor does not turn and makes no noise — the fault could be either mechanical or electrical (see Step 6).

To check whether the motor is jammed turn on the headlights — if the solenoid clicks and the lights dim but the motor fails to turn when you turn the ignition key, then the motor is jammed.

With Bendix starters, the

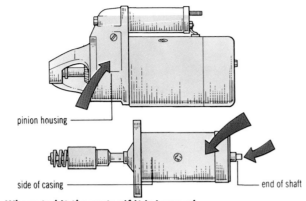

1. Where to hit the motor if it is jammed

2. If motor has a square-ended shaft, turn that instead

3. Tapping pre-engaged starter motor housing to free pinion

pinion can jam in mesh with the flywheel. To free it, look on the end of the starter motor where you will see a square peg. Use a spanner to turn it clockwise (**fig 2**) or put the car in top gear and rock it back and forth.

The same problem can occur with pre-engaged starters, but in this case, it is the operating lever linking the pinion to the solenoid which sticks. Rocking the car in gear can disengage it as can hitting the motor casing with a soft hammer (**fig 1**).

A motor which jams more than once is probably faulty so you should remove the motor and clean the components or fit a reconditioned starter motor unit — under guarantee.

With a noisy motor that fails to turn over the engine, first check that the motor mounting bolts are all tight. These bolts can work loose and so prevent the pinion from engaging properly with the flywheel.

If the Bendix motor makes a high pitched whine then the pinion has become jammed on its shaft. This is caused by wear or dirt on either the helix thread or the Bendix. Sometimes, you can encourage the Bendix to move by shocking it free with a firm hit from a soft hammer (**fig 1**). If this does not work the Bendix is faulty and you should seek professional advice.

A more serious fault is where

4. Pinion gear in good condition

5. A chewed and badly damaged pinion

the pinion on the Bendix has stripped its teeth (**fig 5**). This will be indicated by a loud mechanical chattering from the motor as it occasionally engages with the flywheel. This fault occurs only on the Bendix motor as the pinion is already rotating slightly before it engages with the flywheel. Again, the motor should be removed and stripped for inspection.

If it shows bad signs of wear you should also examine the condition of the flywheel ring gear. Usually you will be able to see the teeth of the ring gear through the hole which houses the starter motor, but there may also be an access hole in the bell housing which will give you a better view (**fig 6**). It may be covered by a metal plate or a large rubber grommet. If the ring gear teeth are worn, the only solution is to remove the flywheel to renew the ring gear or the entire flywheel and ring gear assembly — a job for professionals.

6. Checking ring gear

An electrical fault in the starter motor can be recognised by the motor being electrically 'dead' — that is it draws no power from the battery. If the test in Step 5 has shown that the starter motor is not jammed, then the fault must be electrical. This is caused by either worn out brushes, a dirty commutator, or burnt out windings.

To investigate the problem (**fig 1**) you must first remove the starter and then strip it down to discover the probable causes of the problems. Seek advice on repairs at this stage. A burnt out motor can be quickly diagnosed by the smell; as the windings short out, the protective lacquer is burnt, producing an unpleasant smell.

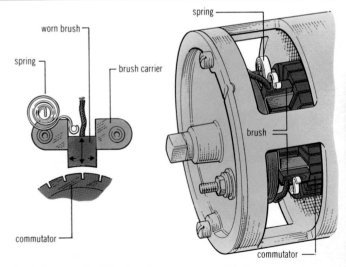

1. Make sure that the brushes are still contacting commutator

When the engine overheats

When the car overheats it's usually the radiator that gets the blame. But there's more to engine cooling than this, so check before spending money on a new one

When to do this job
When the engine overheats — especially on a long or fast run

What this job involves
Checking the cooling system for leaks
Changing the drive belt
Flushing the cooling system
Removing and refitting the radiator

Other possible causes and related jobs
Faulty electric cooling fan or switch
Faulty thermostat
Incorrect ignition timing
Incorrect fuel mixture
Blown cylinder head gasket
Leaking heater radiator
Binding brakes
Please see Index for page numbers

To do this job
Tools: Spanners to fit radiator bolts and drain plugs; screwdrivers; container for coolant; hosepipe and nylon brush
Materials: New antifreeze/soft water mixture; new thermostat (maybe); new hoses and clips (maybe); new radiator (maybe); new drive belt (maybe); flushing cleaner; leak sealer; new radiator cap
Time: Several hours
Degree of difficulty: Ease of radiator removal varies from car to car but is seldom difficult. Finding leaks and flushing the radiator is easy

If you have the job professionally done . . .
Is the overheating cured? If the car lost water, has the water loss been cured? Does the coolant look clean and has it got antifreeze in it? Is the drive belt (if changed) correctly tensioned?

Most cars use liquid to keep the engine at the correct temperature. But, occasionally, something goes wrong which prevents the cooling liquid from doing its job. Leaks and blockages are the most common causes of overheating only rarely does a key component break down.

The coolant is circulated around the engine by a water pump which is driven from the engine by a flexible drive belt.

When the engine is cold the thermostat stops coolant from getting to the radiator.

As the engine warms up, the thermostat opens and allows the hot coolant through to the radiator where it is cooled by the airflow. If the car is stationary or moving only slowly, the airflow through the radiator is increased by a mechanical or electrical fan. Connecting the parts of the system are rubber hoses.

There are, therefore, many areas where a fault could arise. But often there are tell-tale symptoms which will help pinpoint the exact cause. If the car is sluggish or pinks for example, as well as overheating, then the timing may be wrong — so if you already have a clue follow the step which tells you how to check it. If you have no idea what the problem is, follow the steps in sequence until you find the fault.

STEP 1 — CHECK THE COOLANT LEVEL

The first check to make if your car overheats is that the cooling system is full. How you check the coolant level will depend on the type of cooling system your car has. An increasing number of cars have sealed cooling systems with an expansion tank or bottle connected to the radiator by a thin pipe. You can usually see the level in the expansion tank from the outside and it should be near to the maximum mark (**fig 1**) — otherwise remove the cap and check that it is half full. If the level is correct go to Step 3.

If your car has an unsealed cooling system you simply have to remove the radiator cap to check the level. If the engine is still warm, put a cloth over the cap and unscrew it slowly, allowing any steam to escape. The cooling system is pressurized — so you should not try to remove the cap when the engine is hot or the coolant will boil and gush out. The coolant level should be about ½ in. (13 mm) below the radiator filler neck (**fig 2**). If the level is correct go to Step 3.

The coolant may be blue, green or pink depending on the antifreeze used, but if it looks rusty and there are bits of solid matter in it, then the system needs flushing (see Step 7).

If the level is low then top it up with a mixture of 2 parts water to 1 part antifreeze, taking care not to spill any as it will damage the paint. If the cause of the overheating is simply due to a low coolant level then topping up the system may cure the problem, but check the level again after a few days in case there is a leak. If the level has fallen proceed to Step 2.

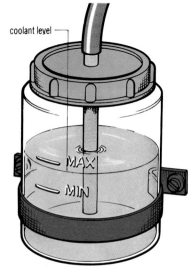

1. Correct level in sealed system expansion tank

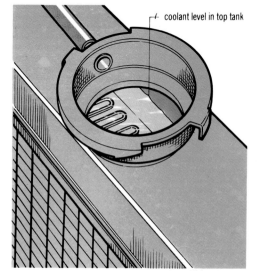

2. Correct coolant level in unsealed radiator

1. This leak probably means a new radiator

2. A split hose like this needs replacing

A badly leaking hose or radiator is usually quite easy to spot, either by telltale drips on the ground or by water stains in the surrounding area. But if the leak is only a small one the best way to find it is to start the engine and run it until the temperature gauge shows a normal running temperature. Then rev the engine hard for about ten seconds to make sure the system is properly pressurized. Any leaks should then show up as tiny jets of steam (**fig 1**).

Make a visual check of the radiator — including where the pipes join the top and bottom tanks — the water pump, the thermostat housing and the engine block itself, taking care not to get too close to any moving parts. Check all the hoses, including the ones to the heater. If you find what appears to be a leak then switch off the engine and check the area for signs of water with your hand or a rag. Keep clear of parts such as the exhaust which will still be hot. The radiator hoses will feel hot, but should not burn you.

Small leaks in the radiator or heater can be fixed with a sealing compound such as Bars Leaks or Radweld which is poured into the radiator while the engine is running. The sealant is then forced out through any small cracks or holes by the pressure inside the system, sealing the leak as it dries. A leak much larger than a pinhole cannot be effectively fixed by this method and the only cure is to replace the radiator or to have the leak fixed by a radiator specialist.

Leaks from the hoses are often caused by loose hose clips, and tightening them will cure the problem, but a hose which is split or swollen (**fig 2**) should be renewed rather than temporarily repaired.

On a car with an Austin Rover A-series engine, such as a Mini, you should also check out the small transfer hose tucked away under the thermostat casting (**fig 3**). Changing this pipe is difficult because of the lack of space to work in, but it is possible to do the job without taking off the cylinder head or water pump if you buy a new

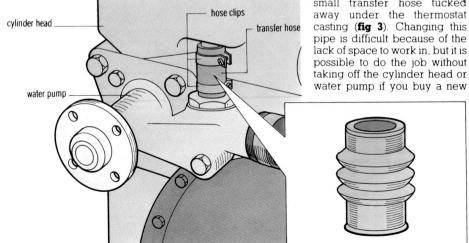

cylinder head — hose clips — transfer hose — water pump

3. A transfer hose can be replaced, without dismantling, with concertina type (inset)

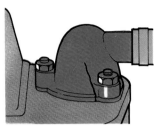

4. Cracked thermostat housing

that the pipe does not leak.

If the thermostat housing is made of aluminium it may have corroded or cracked (**fig 4**) so check it carefully and renew it if necessary.

While the engine is running another check to make is for water leaking from the radiator or overflow pipe. A steady stream of coolant from the overflow means that the radiator cap is faulty and the system is losing pressure. Check the rubber sealing ring. If it is perished buy a new cap.

If your engine continues to lose water, but no leaks can be found, you may have a blown head gasket (see Step 10).

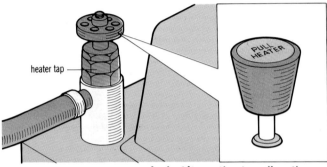

heater tap | PULL HEATER

5. Heater tap on engine may leak. Alternative type (inset)

hose of the concertina type which can be squashed up and slipped into place.

Undo the two small hose clips and cut the old hose off. Fit the clips to the new hose and then squeeze it on to the two small pipes. This is a fiddly job and requires a lot of patience but the pipe will go on if given time. Tighten up the clips and check

A radiator cannot work properly if it is covered with leaves, mud or squashed flies which block off the airflow through the core. Use a soft nylon brush to remove loose dirt, but take care as the radiator cooling fins are easily damaged.

If the spaces between the cooling fins are blocked then you will have to use a hose to try to dislodge the blockage. But before turning on the water, cover any exposed electrical components such as the generator or the distributor with plastic bags. Spray the water through the radiator in the opposite direction to the normal airflow (**fig 1**) and use the brush to carefully scrub off any loosened dirt. Be prepared to get very wet as the water will go everywhere.

If the radiator is particularly dirty it is easier to remove it (see Step 8) and clean it more thoroughly with a degreaser like Gunk or Flak (**fig 2**).

With the radiator removed you will also be able to give it a closer examination for damage.

1. Cleaning radiator with a hosepipe

2. Degreasing blocked radiator fins

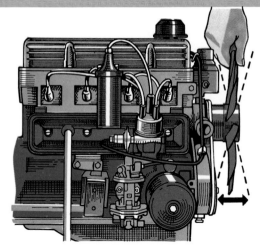

With the engine off, carefully check that the drive belt is correctly tensioned and not cracked or frayed (**fig 1**). If the belt is slack it may not be driving the fan or water pump fast enough (see Fact File).

To test the water pump bearings, first loosen the drive belt and then grasp the fan blades — or the water pump pulley if your car has an electric fan — and try to rock them from side to side (**fig 2**). Slight movement or play in the bearings is normal, but if the pump is very slack, leaking (see Step 2) or noisy then you should renew it — quite an easy job on most makes of cars.

To check that the pump is working remove the radiator cap — or the filler plug (**fig 3**) if your car has a sealed system — and then run the engine until it is warm. Check the water movement in the top of the radiator, using a torch if necessary. Now get someone to rev the engine while you watch for an increase in water flow. If it does not increase with engine speed then the water pump is faulty and needs renewing. If, while you are doing this test, the water overflows from the radiator filler then there is a blockage in the system, either in the radiator or the engine block, and it will have to be flushed (see Step 7).

If you see a stream of bubbles rising in the radiator, with blobs of oil forming on the surface of the coolant, the head gasket has probably blown (see Step 10).

1. Damaged drive belts

2. How to check for play in the water pump

3. Two types of filler plug

FACT FILE

Generator drive belt adjustment

The drive belt — often called the fan belt — is a vital part of the cooling system as it drives the water pump. To do its job properly it must be correctly tensioned. If it is too loose it will slip and the engine may overheat. If the belt is too tight then it can cause damage to the water pump bearings.

Check the belt tension
Drive belt tension should be checked at the centre of its longest run — usually this is between the fan pulley and the crankshaft pulley. Grip the belt between forefinger and thumb and try to move it from side to side. The belt should deflect about ½ in. (13 mm) if you have an alternator, or ¾ in. (19 mm) if your car has a dynamo fitted. If the belt is incorrectly adjusted or damaged you should adjust or renew it.

Renew drive belt —
Adjustable pulley type
The drive belt tension is normally adjusted by moving one of the pulleys in or out. Usually it is the generator pulley which moves, but on some cars it is the pulley on the power steering pump housing. In both cases the unit is fixed to the engine on one side by pivot bolt(s) and on the other by a slotted

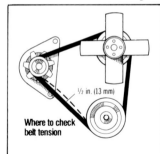

Where to check belt tension

½ in. (13 mm)

adjuster bar. This allows the unit to pivot — altering the belt tension.

To remove the drive belt slacken the pivot bolt(s) and the adjuster bar. Swing the generator towards the engine until you can pull the belt off the pulleys. Then carefully feed the belt over the fan blades taking care not to bend them. Check the belt closely and replace it if it is cracked or worn.

Before fitting a new belt, check that the pulleys are not split or cracked as this will quickly damage the belt. Feed the belt over the fan blades and on to the fan and crankshaft pulleys. Push the generator towards the engine and pull the belt on to the pulley — it may be a tight fit so some force may be needed. Then do up the

fixing bolts until they are finger tight and stick a strong wooden lever between the body of the generator and the engine. Check that you have not trapped any wires and then lever the generator away from the engine until there is the right amount of play in the belt.

Keeping the belt tensioned, tighten the bolt which goes through the adjuster bar. Once you are sure the tension is correct you can fully tighten all the bolts.

If you have fitted a new belt check the tension after 300 miles (or 500 km) and then every 6000 miles (or 10,000 km).

Fitting a drive belt on a cowled radiator

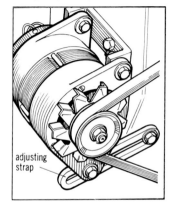

adjusting strap

Renew drive belt —
Split pulley type
On both the VW Beetle and Fiat 126 the drive belt tension is adjusted by a split pulley. The V of the pulley is narrowed or widened by the number of shims (washers) between the pulley halves. To tighten the belt you take out some shims — this narrows the V shape and makes the belt run higher up the pulley and tightens it. Putting more shims between the pulley halves slackens the belt.

To remove a worn belt, undo the nuts on the generator pulley and remove the front half. Pull the old belt off the pulleys and check the pulley flanges for damage.

Put the new belt over the crank-

shaft pulley and then over the dynamo shaft. Fit the front half of the pulley and then tighten up the securing nut(s). Check the belt tension — if it needs adjustment undo the nut(s) again and take off the pulley front. Remove or insert a shim depending on whether the belt needs to be tightened or loosened and refit the pulley front.

To avoid losing the shims, fit them on the dynamo shaft on the outside of the pulley. Tighten the nut(s) and turn the engine over to settle the belt. Check the belt tension again, retensioning it if necessary. If you have fitted a new belt you should check the tension after 300 miles (500 km) and every 6000 miles (10,000 km) after that.

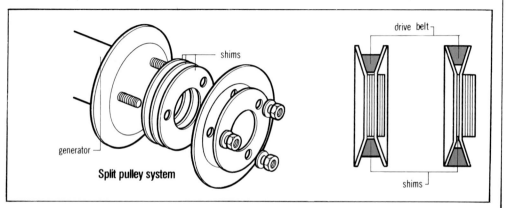

drive belt

shims

generator

Split pulley system

shims

STEP 5 — CHECK THE THERMOSTAT

To check the thermostat start with the engine cold, set the heater control in the car to hot and if there is a separate heater valve on the engine, open it too. Take off the radiator cap — or filler plug on a sealed system — and then start the engine and run it at fast idling speed.

Keeping well clear of any moving parts, watch the water flow in the top of the radiator. At first there will not be much water movement and the top hose will feel cold. But, as the thermostat opens, the hose will warm up (**fig 1**) and you should be able to see the water flowing into the top tank. If there is no marked increase in flow then the thermostat is not opening properly and should be replaced with a new one.

After the engine has run for ten minutes, the whole of the radiator surface should feel warm. If it is, this confirms that the thermostat is working.

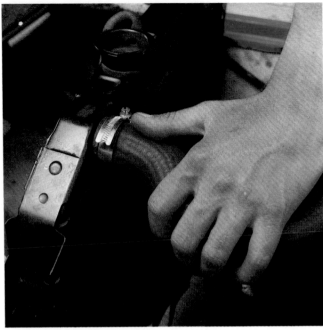

1. *Checking that the thermostat is opening*

STEP 6 — CHECK FOR INTERNAL BLOCKAGE

If you suspect a blocked radiator use a large syringe or a piece of tubing as a siphon to drain off just enough coolant so that you can see the radiator tubes in the top tank. Look for any tubes which are furred up with a hard scale (**fig 1**) — like the scale in a kettle in hard water areas. This scale is caused by using hard water in the cooling system and it can eventually block the radiator tubes. If the tubes are blocked or there is heavy coating of scale then the radiator will have to be flushed (see Step 7) or in severe cases it will need to be replaced (see Step 8). Even if the radiator tubes appear clean a thorough reverse flushing is worth doing to prevent even minor blockages occuring and causing overheating later.

1. *This radiator is clogged up with hard water scale and needs to be flushed*

STEP 7 — FLUSH THE RADIATOR

If the radiator or the water passages in the engine are blocked internally then it is often possible to clear the obstruction by flushing the system. You can flush the radiator while it is still in the car although it is much better to remove it (see Step 9) and flush it off the car. This is because to be effective the radiator must be flushed in the opposite direction to the normal water flow, and this is more easily done with the radiator turned upside down.

If you decide to flush the radiator in place, drain the cooling system by taking off the bottom hose and then remove the thermostat. Jam a garden hose into the thermostat housing and make it a tight fit in there with some rags. Then turn the water on at as high a pressure as possible. Any loose rust or sludge should be flushed out of the top stub of the radiator.

An alternative method is to use a cooling system cleaner such as Radflush which dissolves the scale and loosens sludge deposits in the radiator. Drain the cooling system completely, then refill it and add the cleaner, allowing it to circulate with the coolant. After the cleaner has been given time to work put in the neutralizing agent and then drain and flush the system.

If you take the radiator off the car to flush it then all you need to do is put the hose into the bottom hose stub with the radiator upside down (**fig 2**) and run the water for five or ten minutes.

After flushing refit the radiator to the car and refill the system. Try to use soft water or rainwater to refill the system as it will avoid the hard scale forming again. If you have a sealed system, bleed it as shown in your manual.

Because not all internal blockages are detectable or removable even a thorough flushing may not cure the problem. But if your car still overheats do not go out and buy a new radiator yet. First check all the other possible causes.

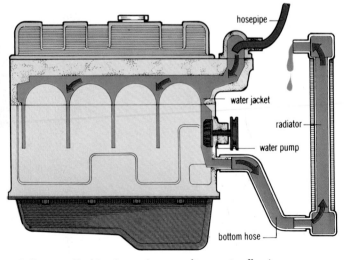

1. *Reverse flushing in car (arrows show water flow)*

hosepipe

water jacket

radiator

water pump

bottom hose

2. *Reverse flushing with the radiator removed*

STEP 8 — REMOVE AND REFIT THE RADIATOR

Before removing the radiator, find all the bolts or screws which attach it to the car or engine and soak them in penetrating oil. Disconnect the battery earth lead, as this will avoid accidentally short circuiting the electric fan (if fitted). Drain the cooling system through the tap on the bottom if one is fitted and take off the top and bottom hoses plus the overflow pipe at the filler neck.

If the temperature gauge sender or switch for an electric fan (**fig 1**) is fitted in the radiator then disconnect it.

The radiator is relatively heavy and you may have difficulty removing the fixing bolts and supporting the radiator at the same time. If you are doing the job on your own arrange several pieces of wood which will wedge the radiator in position as you remove the bolts. Alternatively ask some one to take the weight of the radiator and then slacken off all the bolts (**fig 2**).

Remove them one at a time, noting the position of any washers, spacers or bolts of dif-

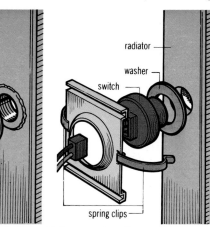
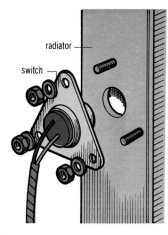

1. Three types of electric fan switch: screw-in, clip-in and bolt-on

2. Undoing the fixing bolts

3. Lifting out the radiator

ferent lengths. Once all the bolts are undone lift the radiator out of the car (**fig 3**), taking care not to catch it on the fan (see Tip). The exchange radiator may not have all the fittings which were on the old unit so you will have to remove things like the electric fan switch, or temperature sender unit and fit them to the new unit.

Refit the radiator to the car, again being careful not to damage it on the fan blades. Replace all the bolts or screws finger tight and check that you have not trapped any wires behind the radiator. Fully tighten all the bolts and refit the cooling hoses and any electrical connections. Finally refill the system with a water-antifreeze mixture and bleed the air out if you have a sealed system.

STEP 9 — CHECK MIXTURE AND TIMING

If, as well as overheating, the engine seems sluggish and runs better with the choke out even when warm, then it is likely that the problem is due to incorrect fuel mixture. Check by revving the engine hard for a few minutes and then looking at the inside of the exhaust tailpipe (**fig 1**). Also remove the spark plugs and look at their electrodes (**fig 2**). If both tailpipe and plugs appear to be coated with a white powder then the fuel mixture is weak so adjust the carburettor.

Over advanced ignition timing can also cause overheating and is usually accompanied by severe pinking which is a loud rattling sound from the engine when accelerating hard. If you suspect this fault, re-set the timing immediately.

1. White deposits indicate a weak mixture

2. This spark plug shows that the mixture is weak

STEP 10 — CHECK FOR BLOWN HEAD GASKET

A blown cylinder gasket can be diagnosed by bubbles and a smell of petrol or exhaust fumes in the coolant. Further indications are wet spark plugs, emulsified oil (**fig 1**), and moisture dripping from the exhaust even when the engine

2. Water leaking from exhaust

is hot (**fig 2**). You can confirm this with a compression test though this is not really necessary as the symptoms are unmistakeable. Do not be tempted to run the engine with the gasket blown as it may warp the cylinder head or even the cylinder block itself.

1. Emulsified oil or 'mayonnaise' on the oil filler cap

Curing running on

If the engine fails to stop when you switch off, the fault is called running on. It should be dealt with at the earliest opportunity

There are various degrees of running on. It can vary from a few hiccups to sustained slow revolutions that can only be stopped by stalling the car. A series of systematic checks is required to eliminate the problem — left too long it will eventually cause damage to your engine.

When to do this job
When the engine continues to fire after the ignition has been switched off

What this job involves
Checking the cooling system
Checking the spark plugs
Setting the ignition timing and idle speed
Checking valve clearances
Checking for inlet leaks

Other possible causes and related jobs
Servicing spark plugs
Getting your timing right
Setting valve clearances
Professional adjustment of the carburettor
Professional overhauling of the cylinder head
Please see Index for page numbers

To do this job
Tools: Screwdrivers; spanners; plug spanner; feeler gauges; stroboscopic timing light; test lamp
Materials: New parts where necessary; upper cylinder lubricant
Time: Up to two hours unless extensive cylinder head work is required
Degree of difficulty: Routine running on easy to cure but wear faults can be more difficult to track down

If you have the job professionally done...
Has running on disappeared under all conditions? Does the engine idle smoothly? Has fuel economy improved?

How running on occurs

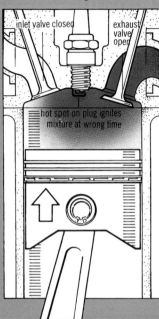

inlet valve closed   exhaust valve open

hot spot on plug ignites mixture at wrong time

Although it is normally the spark produced by the ignition system that triggers the combustion of fuel and air in a cylinder, engine faults can create other conditions under which the fuel mixture will burn. Even when the ignition system is turned off the engine continues to turn, drawing fresh charges of fuel and air into the cylinders. These charges are compressed to a pressure and temperature only a little below the point at which they spontaneously ignite. It only takes a small additional temperature rise in a tiny part of the compressed gas volume for combustion to take place.

There are several ways in which parts of the combustion chamber — the cylinder head, the valve faces or the piston crown — can become hotter than usual. One of the most common is the buildup of carbon and mineral deposits on the spark plug tip. Deposits elsewhere in the combustion chamber have the same effect. Buildup of these materials can arise from an overrich carburettor mixture setting, or using the wrong type of spark plug, or the wrong grade of petrol.

Running conditions where too much heat passes from the burning gases to the combustion chamber surfaces will lead to local hot spots and hence cause running on. Many well adjusted engines run on after hard driving or long, hot journeys. If the mixture is too weak because of air leaks into the induction system or faulty carburettor adjustment, the combustion will be too fast and too hot. Pre-ignition, due to over-advanced ignition timing or petrol of low octane rating, results in more heat passing to the combustion chamber surfaces. Incorrect valve clearance adjustment and cooling system faults can also lead to local high temperature conditions and cause running on.

STEP 1 — CHECK COOLING SYSTEM AND PLUGS

If persistent topping up of your radiator is needed this could be the cause of your running on problem — see pages 215 to 219 for curing cooling system faults.

If the problem persists, next check the spark plugs.

Fouling of the plug tip by sooty deposits (**fig 1**) is usually a sign of an over rich carburettor mixture. Refer to the manual for your car or seek specialist tuning advice for all carburettor adjustment problems.

A plug which appears very pale brown, almost white, is a sign of a weak mixture (**fig 2**). Brown deposits baked on to the tip of the plug (**fig 3**) indicate that you have been running on a low grade of petrol and may mean a decoke. Seek professional tuning advice if a decoke appears unavoidable as this is a skilled job.

1. Plug with sooty deposits

2. Signs of a weak mixture

Even if you can adjust the carburettor easily to give a stronger mixture, this may not be the complete answer. You may simply be compensating for an air leak which could get worse. So check for air leaks as described in Step 4 before adjusting the mixture.

If the plugs are otherwise in good condition clean and check the gaps — see pages 82-84.

3. Low octane fuel causes this

Next check the valve clearances — for an OHV engine, see pages 89 to 93 for OHC engines, see pages 93-96. If running on has been caused by incorrect valve clearances, the valves or valve seatings may be damaged and the fault will not be cured by resetting the clearances. You will have to replace or reseat the valves — a job for a garage.

Idle speed is often a cause of running on because it is common to set the tickover too high.

The only accurate way to set the idle speed is to adjust it in conjunction with a rev counter. The correct idle speed is usually given in your workshop manual. If you do not have a rev counter, set the idle speed sufficiently low that the engine runs happily without risk of stalling.

The adjuster is generally a screw on the side of the carburettor near the throttle linkage (**fig 1**).

High idle speeds waste fuel as well as causing running on, and you should track down the cause of the idling unevenness by following the other steps.

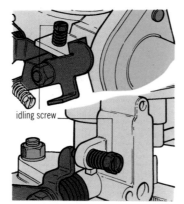

1. Two idle screw positions

Leaks in the carburettor and induction manifold plus any associated vacuum pipework will cause uneven idling as well as running on.

You will hear a hissing noise if there is a serious leak. But even if you cannot hear a hiss, look for signs that a gasket has failed. Run a thin bead of oil — used engine oil will do — along the lines of the gasket or joint (**fig 1**) to see if any is sucked in when the engine is running.

The main places to check are the manifold-to-block flange bolts (**fig 2**) (your manual will give the correct torque figures to which they should be tightened), the bolts securing the carburettor to the manifold and any vacuum connections made to the distributor, the crankcase ventilation system and the brake servo.

Thoroughly inspect the gaskets at each end of the manifold by dismantling them if you have to. Thick, flexible anti-vibration gaskets used for carburettor mounting can distort and may need additional silicon rubber sealant to be completely airtight. Check along the length of all plastic or rubber tubing in the vacuum system for cracking, burn or wear spots.

On an older car (over 50,000

1. Running oil along inlet joint

2. Tightening manifold bolts

miles or 80,000 km) it is possible that the carburettor butterfly spindle bearings or bushes have worn to the extent that air can leak past the throttle. There should be no appreciable play if the main spindle is shaken in its bearings. Consult a manual for your car on carburettor repair or take garage advice.

Once you are satisfied that the inlet system is completely airtight, run the engine to see if the problem persists. If it does the engine may need decarbonizing — more commonly known as a decoke.

TIP
Curing air leaks

Many car vacuum system joints are only push fit connections which loosen as the tube material expands with heat and age. To tighten the joints use PTFE plumbers' jointing tape. Wind a little tape on to the connection before pushing the vacuum pipe home. The tape is resistant to high temperatures and should be leakproof.

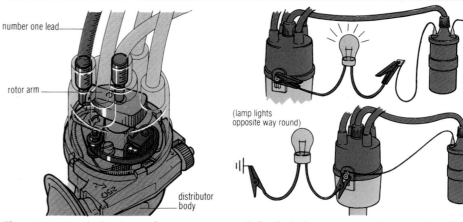

number one lead

rotor arm

distributor body

1. The rotor arm pointing to number one contact

(lamp lights opposite way round)

2. Static timing: two ways to connect test lamp

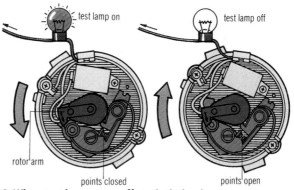

test lamp on

test lamp off

rotor arm

points closed

points open

3. When test lamp goes off static timing is set

Running on can be one of the consequences of faulty timing. Other signs that the timing may be wrongly set include overheating, poor performance and fuel economy, erratic idling and unwillingness to start. Preignition, caused by overadvanced timing, leads to spark plug overheating and electrode erosion, while retarded ignition results in a build up of carbon deposits. Both these conditions can lead to running on.

If you have a stroboscopic light, check and set the ignition timing dynamically, as described on page 88.

Alternatively, on most cars you can use static timing to set the ignition. To do this, first locate the timing marks on the flywheel or crankshaft pulley (see page 86). Label each of the HT leads, disconnect them and remove the plugs.

Remove the distributor cap and note the direction of rotation of the rotor arm. Normally this is marked by an arrow, but if you are not sure, put the car in fourth gear and note the direction of rotation as you edge the car forwards.

Place the distributor cap in its normal position and note where the HT lead for the No. 1 cylinder is attached — your manual should tell you which this is. Now turn the engine by hand (see Fact File — Turning the engine over by hand, page 203) until the rotor arm points in the direction of the No. 1 terminal (**fig 1**). The timing marks should be close together — turn the engine a few degrees until the mark on the flywheel or pulley is exactly opposite the notch or pointer. Loosen, but do not remove, the pinch bolt holding the distributor in place. If a Vernier screw gauge is fitted, set it in its midway position.

Remove the LT leads from the coil and connect a test lamp between them. Alternatives are shown in **fig 2**. Switch on the ignition. Slowly turn the body of the distributor one way and then the other — you should see the lamp go on and off as the points open and close. First move the distributor slowly in the direction of the arm's rotation until the light just comes on (**fig 3**). Then turn it in the opposite direction to the arm's rotation and the light should go off. At this point, the ignition is correctly set. Retighten the pinch bolts, but only enough to hold the distributor securely. Check the adjustment by turning the engine once or twice by hand to make sure that the advance timing mark is exactly in line with the stationary marker when the light goes off. Make any final adjustments with the Vernier gauge if your distributor has one.

If the engine runs badly even when the static timing is correct, the distributor itself may need a thorough overhaul — see pages 149 to 152.

Curing excessive fuel consumption

If your car seems to be using too much fuel, find out why. You may only have faulty gauges, but there could be a dangerous leak

You should always keep an eye on your fuel consumption, not only because of the cost but because a sudden, sharp reduction in your car's fuel economy shows that something is wrong.

If you notice that your car is using more petrol, check the possible causes of excessive fuel consumption before considering the many economy devices on the market. Generally, keeping your car in tune is the best way to fuel economy.

One of the greatest effects on fuel economy is exerted by the driver. Minimising time spent running with the choke out, moving slickly into a higher gear as soon as possible and accelerating very gently are ways to save a lot of fuel.

When to do this job
When the car is using too much petrol

What this job involves
Checking instruments
Measuring fuel consumption
Servicing the car
Checking the engine temperature

Other possible causes and related jobs
Look after your tyres
Cooling system faults
Get your timing right
Please see Index for page numbers

To do this job
Tools: Spanners; screwdrivers
Materials: Oil; spares as required
Time: Allow a morning to do the service and general checks
Degree of difficulty: Straightforward

If you have the job professionally done . . .
Try to give the garage as much information about how and where you drive the car, and how it performs. Make it clear that you want all the simple, quick checks done first and that you do not necessarily wish to pay for new parts which do not solve the problem

FACT FILE

Tread lightly for fuel economy

Assuming that your car is in perfect tune, the greatest effect is exerted on fuel consumption by the way in which you drive. While general tuning faults can add as much as 10-15% to a fuel bill, poor driving technique can increase fuel usage by a factor of 20% or more. And it isn't just a question of breaking bad driving habits that will put pounds back in your pocket. There are some easy and completely safe driving techniques that, once learned and regularly used, make a really worthwhile contribution to the motoring budget.

First, look over your car. In the boot there could be many items which are adding extra weight and costing fuel. Clear out the boot and interior regularly — carry the minimum of heavier items such as tools. Never leave a roof rack in place if it is not in use — it adds air resistance that costs up to 5% extra fuel use at higher speeds (the same goes for caravan towing aerofoils). When it is in use pack it carefully with smaller items at the front and larger ones to the rear to create a wedged profile. Then secure it with a heavy duty plastic or fabric luggage cover and a strong elastic spider so nothing flaps.

The warmer the car engine is kept, the more economical it will be, particularly during those first critical moments of choked running. Garaging the car at any time makes sense, even if you know you're going to use it again within a short time, just to preserve a little heat in the engine.

Never set out on a journey, or start the engine, without a firm idea of how to get to your destination. If the route is unfamiliar, prepare a route card and have a good map ready — maps aren't just a convenience, they really can save fuel. Listen to traffic information on the radio — or view it on Oracle, Ceefax or Prestel — to spot obstacles on your route and navigate around them.

Always try to park the car in a position where a straight drive off is possible — time spent manoeuvring a cold, choked car is money thrown away. Do all the manoeuvring while the car is warm at the end of the previous journey. If garage doors must be closed, try to get someone else to do it. An idling engine is a petrol waster.

Greatest fuel saving comes from gentle use of the throttle. Never accelerate by jamming the accelerator to the floor. Feed the pedal in a tiny amount at a time until you reach the required speed and then back off a fraction. You'll be surprised how far you can release the pedal and still maintain speed. Move into the highest possible gear at any speed as soon as it is possible to do so — and if the car has a fifth gear use it as often as possible.

Be acutely aware of the traffic situation ahead and back off the throttle as soon as there's any likelihood of slowing or stopping. Keen anticipation is essential to fuel economy driving as well as general safety for you and your family.

Apply brakes as gently as possible to come to rest smoothly. For corners and bends judge your speed carefully to avoid the need to brake. Select a steering radius that will carry the car smoothly round the bend without rapid mid-course corrections and the scrubbing off of speed that makes extra acceleration necessary. Take hills with the minimum of extra accelerator pressure, if possible holding your foot steady on the pedal. Coast down the other side, always staying in gear for safety.

Get caught in a traffic jam; then turn off the engine for as long as you can without impeding other cars' progress. And turn off electrical accessories for as long as safety and convenience allows. Headlamps and the heated rear window are a formidable electrical load on the generator which requires more engine power to turn it and that means more fuel squandered.

Finally, there are false economies. The biggest of these is the use of most fuel economy devices. Even if they work, the tiny savings of fuel to be made on modern engines mean that their cost can rarely be recovered within a reasonable time scale. There aren't so many of these devices on the market nowadays. Obviously drivers are becoming that much more fuel economy wise.

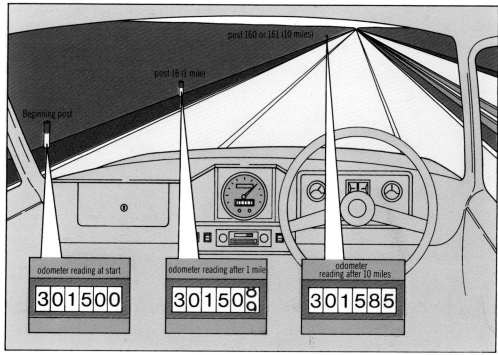

1. Distance measured by motorway posts show milometer is under reading by 15 per cent

The high cost of petrol and frequent advertisers' claims of exceptionally low fuel consumption for new cars might make you think your own car is using far too much fuel. The chances are that this suspicion will be confirmed if you check the official figures for your car, but be careful that you are comparing wisely. It is no good complaining, for example, that your high performance automatic used around town gives only 14 miles to the gallon when a neighbour's small family saloon returns 40 to the gallon on a run. On the other hand, two cars in the same class might give widely different figures for fuel consumption, due to a combination of factors.

The most basic of these factors is the design of the car. Some of the latest models in the small car range, for example, do in fact use more fuel than earlier models. To find out why,

you must look at whether the cars were built purely for economy, or with some degree of luxury and performance. And you must consider how legal requirements to reduce noise and poisonous exhaust emissions can limit the performance of later models.

If you use your car mostly out of town on flat, uncrowded roads and your average journey length is over five miles then you should achieve optimum economy. Excessive fuel consumption under such circumstances is a clear indication of a fault. On the other hand, you will not fail to notice the greater demand for fuel if you do frequent stop-start journeys in town traffic (**fig 2**) or over long distances in hilly regions (**fig 3**).

Your driving technique can also have a tremendous effect on your car's economy. Frequent use of lower gears, hard acceleration and high average

speeds will all increase fuel consumption — particularly on smaller engined cars. But if after taking all these factors into account, and after comparing notes with other owners you still suspect that your car's fuel consumption is excessive, the next step is to check that your figures are accurate.

The way you measure fuel consumption is also crucially important to how you assess fuel economy. The milometer, or *odometer*, incorporated in the speedometer, is a convenient instrument by which you can measure distance travelled (**fig 1**), but do not assume it is invariably accurate. The distance checks on motorways, such as 'services seven miles', are usually accurate to within 0.2 of a mile over distances of about 10 miles. Fairly accurate, too, are the location markers on UK motorways that let you specify your position to a breakdown or

emergency service. These are small posts, about 1 foot tall placed at intervals of 1/16 mile on old motorways and 100 metres on newer ones. Using any such reference, check the accuracy of your milometer. A fault may have developed so you may need a new instrument but remember that if you fit non-standard or incorrectly inflated tyres, or fit a non-standard gearbox the milometer reading will be inaccurate. If, for example, your milometer under-reads by 15 per cent (**fig 1**) your car will in fact be doing 15 per cent more miles per gallon than is indicated.

You will also need to measure how much petrol the car uses over a set distance, but the petrol gauge is not intended for such precise measurements. Instead, try to fill your petrol tank to the same level — ideally to the brim or to the nozzle cut-off level using the same garage pump — note the distance between refills, and note how many gallons you need to bring the level back to your reference mark. Then all you have to do is total the number of miles travelled and gallons used; divide the one by the other and you will have your car's average fuel consumption in miles per gallon. Alternatively, you could fit a flow meter in the fuel line to measure the amount of fuel used over a given measured distance.

If after you have checked your instruments and taken readings you discover your fuel consumption is excessive then give the fuel line a quick look over. Your petrol economy problem might be due simply to leakage. Petrol evaporates rapidly, however, often leaving no trace so if you have smelled petrol inside the car but can find no leak start the engine and check again. Check the fuel tank, pump and pipes for leaks and the carburettor for any signs of flooding.

2. Fast getaways mean poor economy

3. Hills requiring low gears will increase fuel consumption

Having established that your car is actually using too much petrol, and that there are no leaks, the next step is to check the engine. A badly tuned engine can use up to 25 per cent more fuel, so regular servicing is well worthwhile. But before tuning the engine, first remove the spark plugs and check their colour. Dry, black sooty deposits indicate a rich mixture probably due to a carburettor fault.

It is quite common for carburettors to waste petrol because the mixture they deliver is too rich. Often, the first sign of this fault is that the choke is needed for only a short time after the engine has been started. Such a setting may be good for driving on cold morning, but as soon as the engine has warmed up, it will be wasting petrol.

The rich mixture may be due to several faults. First check that the air filter is clean and not blocked (see page 81). Next check that the choke is not sticking (see pages 132 to 135). If the mixture is still too rich, the fault must be in the carburettor. On fixed jet carburettors the problem is likely to be a blocked air jet or an incorrect float level. To cure these faults you will have to strip the carburettor down. Do not try to simply adjust the mixture screw as this only affects the idle mixture and is unlikely to be the cause of the trouble.

If you have a variable jet carburettor the problem is much more likely to be one of adjustment. To weaken the mixture on Stromberg and SU carburettors raise the fuel jet about half a turn, then test the car again to see if the plugs show that the mixture is normal. You can weaken the mixture until the spark plugs are a biscuity colour. When the mixture is correct, you should notice that the fuel consumption has improved, and that the engine runs more smoothly during ac-

celeration, even though you need more choke for a longer duration when starting from cold.

If you do the job carefully, fuel consumption should improve immediately. If it does not, and the car has done more than about 50,000 miles, the most likely reason for a rich mixture is mechanical wear. This occurs most usually where the throttle spindle pivots in the carburettor body. Check this by rocking the spindle up and down and side to side (**fig 4**). On very old carburettors, there can be as much as 1/8 in. of play. Wear also occurs in the jets and petrol passages. You cannot measure it or see it,

but you can see the effect if you try to reduce the mixture strength and find that the spark plugs get covered in carbon whatever you do to the settings. If this is the case, you can either accept the poor performance and fuel consumption or fit a replacement carburettor (see below).

Another course of action is to re-build the carburettor (see a manual for details) but if the wear on the spindle is bad, there is no alternative but to fit a new unit. Manufacturers such as Weber and Solex offer a wide range of replacement carburettors jetted to suit most popular cars and which fit directly on to the

original manifold.

Yet another solution is to fit a completely different carburettor to achieve better fuel consumption. For example, the early HC Vivas were fitted with a poor carburettor, which was soon replaced with a much better Stromberg one. You could buy the complete assembly cheaply from a scrapyard or buy a new Stromberg and have it adjusted.

Similarly, Leyland A series engines with 1¼ in. SU carburettors give better fuel consumption if you replace the standard manifold with a later one to which a 1½ in. or 1¾ in. carburettor can be fitted. Pro-

vided you search out a secondhand carburettor in good condition, you can fit a new jet and needle cheaply, and it will reduce the fuel consumption. There are many other similar possibilities. Study the different ways in which the manufacturers have used the basic engine and work out how best to use the later modifications.

Although a rich mixture is the most common cause of excessive fuel consumption, a weak mixture can have exactly the same effect. The reasons for this are twofold. First the choke will be required much longer than is normal and fuel consumption with the choke out can increase

by 60 per cent. Second, because the engine will not be running efficiently, more fuel will be required to achieve any given speed.

Apart from requiring the choke for longer, you can also check if your car's fuel mixture is weak by inspecting the spark plugs for the characteristic white deposit (see Simple spark plug service detailed on pages 82 and 84). In order to set the mixture a little richer on an SU or Stromberg carburettor, lower the jet about half a turn.

To enrich the mixture on a fixed jet carburettor is more difficult, as it is set by the design and cannot be adjusted. The only reason for these carburettors delivering a weak mixture, however, is that the internal passages or the jets are blocked. If you are certain that the mixture is weak, dismantle the unit and clean all the jets and passages.

With twin carburettors, most drivers seems to accept excessive fuel consumption as the price for better performance. However, if properly tuned and balanced, twin carburettors should give reasonable economy.

Having checked and, if necessary, tuned the carburettor you should next examine the ignition system. Visually check the condition of all the major parts (see pages 201-205), fitting new plugs and points as necessary. Check the ignition timing (see page 65). If the timing proves to be way out, after adjusting it you should recheck the carburettor adjustments as further fine tuning may be required. If the fuel and ignition systems required only fine tuning, then it is likely that the cause of the excessive fuel consumption may be due to the engine not reaching the correct temperature (see Step 3) or some less obvious cause such as drivetrain drag or overloading (see Step 4).

1. Carry out the service before making checks

2. Checking the points and condenser

3. Adjusting the carburettor

4. Checking the throttle spindle for wear

Engines work best when they are running hot, but not over-heating and when they are receiving a warm fuel–air mixture. For best fuel consumption, the engine should heat up quickly and stay at about 100°C, whatever the conditions. This is particularly important on short journeys, because a quick warm-up will enable you to push the choke in soon after starting.

If you have a temperature gauge, note the reading during a few days typical running. If the gauge is working well, it should ideally indicate that the temperature climbs quickly after a cold start and reaches the warm or 70°C sector of the gauge after about a mile and a half. By the time you have driven five miles, the gauge should be indicating that the engine has reached its normal operating temperature.

On some cars, the reading might increase at different rates, partly because of the speed and loading on the engine. On many cars, the temperature needle seldom reaches half way up the gauge and, even if your car is fitted with an electric fan controlled by a thermostat, you will probably find that it takes a while in heavy traffic before the fan switches on.

After the engine has run for a few minutes, you should also be able to feel a difference in temperature between the top and the bottom radiator hoses. If both of the hoses feel cool, the thermostat in the cooling system is probably not working. If the top hose is noticeably hotter than the bottom one, the thermostat is probably working correctly. Nevertheless, the list of thermostats at your local spares shop should indicate whether there is a choice of thermostat opening temperatures.

Where there is a choice, and you do not put the car to any abnormal strain, fit the higher temperature thermostat (see page 218). At the same time, check the hoses to make sure that they can withstand a higher temperature. In any event, fit new cooling system components (**fig 1**) every two years.

Study the temperature gauge again for a few days to make sure that the engine does not overheat. You might have to fit a new radiator cap if the existing washer or the spring is suspect. If your engine still fails to warm up correctly and you have an electric cooling fan, it is possible that the fan is faulty. A faulty fan thermostat, for example, could result in the fan overcooling the engine.

If the engine still takes a long time to warm up, you can blank off the radiator to reduce its cooling effect. During the winter, all you need do is place a piece of cardboard or aluminium foil in front of the radiator and fasten it with adhesive tape. With care, you can adjust the size of the blanking sheet so that there is just sufficient cooling to prevent overheating.

For summer use or if your driving pattern is varied, either fit an electric radiator fan as an extra or a radiator blind. The radiator blind does the same job as a piece of cardboard but it can be raised and lowered from the driver's seat to vary the amount of cooling.

On air-cooled engines, manufacturers always supply an air-intake blind as an accessory. This is designed for use in particularly cold weather and it restricts the amount of air drawn in by the cooling fan. On some cars, the blind has small flaps to allow even finer control over the cooling air, but these blinds are no substitute for a correctly adjusted thermostat.

As well as a warm engine, a warmed fuel–air mixture is also essential to good economy. This can be achieved in two ways: either by angling the air intake close to the exhaust manifold, or by fitting a water heated manifold. So first check the air intake is correctly positioned. On many of the latest cars, there is no adjustable intake. Instead, there is a flap, controlled by temperature or by vacuum, in the air intake. This flap blends hot and cold air to produce the optimum temperature. You will probably be able to spot these by the vacuum pipes running to the end of the air intake pipe away from the carburettor or by the two different air intakes with a flap between them.

If the flap is vacuum controlled by pipes from the bottom of the air cleaner, pull the pipe off the bottom of the air cleaner, wipe it and suck it. You should be able to feel the resistance of the flap opening and closing, and you may even be able to see it moving. Fit a new air cleaner assembly (**fig 2**) if necessary.

You should also be able to detect the operation of a thermostatically controlled air intake if you put your hand lightly over the cold air intake. As the engine warms up, you should feel the flow of air increase over your hand.

To check a water heated manifold, run the car until warm and then touch the manifold. If it is not warm, there must be a blockage or air lock in the cooling system (see page 215).

1. Cooling system components

2. Renewing the air cleaner element

If after checking the engine you still have not found problem you will have to widen your search.

Binding brakes are fairly common and can increase fuel consumption by around 15 per cent. Note whether the car will roll freely on a slope, or better still, jack up each wheel and check that it can be turned freely by hand. A wheel which cannot be turned by hand will probably have faulty brakes. However the fault could also be in the wheel bearings, the driveshaft or even the differential so if the brakes have not seized, check these components.

If all the wheels turn freely, the fault may still lie in the transmission but be due to a slipping clutch, out of adjustment or worn or automatic gearbox internal problems. Loss of drive will waste fuel as the engine will be revving higher for any given road speed.

While you are checking around the car have a close look at the tyres and exhaust. Low tyre pressures and a leaking exhaust — particularly on flat and V-engines — can both increase fuel consumption.

If the car is mechanically sound finally check that you have not missed anything obvious. A roof rack, for example, can play havoc with your car's aerodynamics — even when unloaded. In tests carried out on a 3.5 Rover an unloaded roof rack caused an increase in average fuel consumption of 3 per cent. Similarly, check that you are not carrying around any unnecessary weight. Extra load may not increase your fuel consumption much on a long run, but in stop-start city traffic, it will.

1. A roof rack will increase consumption

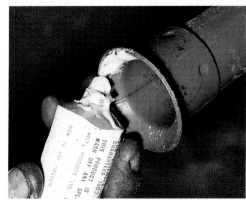
2. Applying sealing compound to exhaust joint

Faulty gear linkages

If the linkage between the gear lever and gearbox is worn or badly adjusted it can be difficult to find the gear you want. So don't blame the gearbox — a remedy is at hand

The play caused by a slack or badly adjusted gearchange linkage can also cause parts inside the gearbox to wear, since the gears may not be allowed to engage correctly. Often only a couple of minor parts are at fault, so the cure is usually quite cheap.

However, before you begin to investigate, you would be wise to check the clutch to make sure that it is letting the gears engage and disengage. A clutch which does not disengage fully will not 'let go' of the gears. Check also that the engine and gearbox mountings and the linkage stabilizer bar, if fitted, are sound. Weak or worn mountings will allow excessive movement between gearbox and gear lever, possibly knocking the car out of gear.

When to do this job
If the gear change feels sloppy and vague
If there is a buzzing sound from the gear lever when you decelerate or drive at high speed

What this job involves
Tracing gear linkage and locating wear
Fitting new parts where required

Other possible causes and related jobs
Fitting a new clutch
Replacing engine mountings and stabilizer rubbers
Bad clutch adjustment

To do this job
Tools: Long-nosed pliers; file; pin punch; vice; screwdrivers; spanners; hammer; tape measure
Materials: Graphited grease; heavy oil (gearbox oil will do); selection of washers and split pins; spares as required
Time: Two to three hours
Degree of difficulty: Getting at the area can be tiresome

If you have the job professionally done . . .
Has the whole linkage been overhauled or just the faulty part? Is gear changing more precise now?

Several faults can crop up with gear linkages, but they must not be confused with problems actually inside the gearbox. Although a faulty gear linkage can make it difficult to find the gears, and will give a sloppy, unpleasant gearchange, it will rarely prevent you from engaging a gear at all.

Crashing from the gearbox as you change down is usually caused by worn synchromesh or even a clutch problem — if the gearchange becomes easier when you double declutch and push the pedal right down to the floor, then the gear linkage cannot be at fault.

If the car jumps out of gear, particularly on the overrun, this may be caused by a very badly adjusted linkage, although this problem is usually caused by worn selector forks inside the gearbox (see Fact File — Rod gear linkages). Gearbox overhaul is covered in a subsequent article.

The gear linkage problems which are usually encountered are more trivial but still annoying; lots of slack at the gear lever, or the lever buzzing and rattling, especially at high engine speeds or when you decelerate. These faults are often caused by wear in the large ball joint on which the lever pivots, although excessive play usually indicates wear throughout the linkage.

Bear in mind, however, that some cars have a very imprecise gearchange even when new. There is nothing which can be done to improve the imprecision of this kind of gearchange.

HOW IT WORKS

Rod gear linkages

Every car must have some sort of linkage between the gear lever and the gear selectors — the parts which actually move the gears and dogs into engagement inside the gear box.

A front engined, rear wheel drive car has the simplest form of remote gearchange. The gear lever is mounted on one end of an alloy housing which is bolted to the top of the gearbox. This housing, containing one or more selector rods, can extend up to a foot (300 mm) behind the gearbox. When the gear lever is moved it pushes on a selector rod which in turn moves the appropriate selector in the gearbox, engaging the gear.

Where three selector rods are fitted, one is for first and second gear, another for third and fourth gear, the other for reverse. When only one selector rod is fitted it can be thought of as a straight-forward extension of the gear lever. A fork on the end of the selector rod engages with one of the selectors in the gearbox when the gear lever is moved.

Occasionally, with a front engined, rear wheel drive car, the bottom of the gear lever operators directly on the ends of the selector forks. However, to keep the gear lever short and to bring it closer to the driver's hand, extra rods and links are fitted between the gear lever and the gear box. In the case of front wheel drive cars these rods and links are quite long as the gearboxes are often mounted some distance from the bottom of the gear lever.

Front wheel drive cars have longer linkages, often involving only one main rod between the bottom of the gear lever and the gearbox, but with more complicated joints and more links. Unfortunately the joints are usually exposed, which leads to accelerated wear. A stabilizer bar is often fitted alongside the gearchange rod, attached at one end to the gear lever housing, and at the other end near to the gearbox. This minimizes the amount of movement between the housing and the gearbox to avoid selector problems.

Another common type of front wheel drive linkage has several rods, links and bellcranks, although still attached to a single shaft which enters the gearbox. Part of the linkage twists the shaft and the lever attached to it from side to side and the rest of the linkage pushes the shaft back and forth. These types of linkage are quite involved as each bellcrank has to have a separate unmoving support for its pivot. The bellcranks are often bolted to such unlikely places as the steering rack.

Probably the simplest form of front engine front wheel drive gear linkage is the one used by some French cars which have the gearbox mounted in front of the engine. A horizontal gear lever with a hook at one end sticks out from the dashboard, its other end reaching over the engine. The lever slides in bushes and connects to a plain steel gear lever sticking from the top of the gearbox. Some rear wheel drive cars also use this kind of system, only they run under the car and are operated by a floor mounted gear lever, although some do use a linkage similar to the single rod front wheel drive type linkage, except that they point in the opposite direction.

With all these systems, the problems which arise most often are caused by wear in the joints.

To work on the linkage of a front engined rear wheel drive (FERWD) car you will need to work inside the car so it will often be worth taking the front passenger seat out to give you more room to work in. Lift the adjustment lever under the seat and pull it forward until it comes off the runners. Sometimes the best way to get the seat off is to tie the adjustment lever up and push the seat out from side to side while you are in the rear seat. Now wipe the slides as they are usually smeared with grease.

Sit in the driver's seat and unscrew the gear lever knob or pull it off if it is rubber-mounted. Now work out how the gear lever gaiter is held in place. Sometimes there is a chrome bezel fastened to the transmission tunnel with crosshead screws. On other models the rubber gaiter tucks around the gear lever or into the trim and it can just be pulled away. Finally, some gaiters can only be taken off by removing the console on the transmission tunnel. Remove the console, at the back and at the top front where the console meets the dashboard. You may need to prise parts of the console out to reach the screws.

With the gaiter removed you will be able to see the base of the gear lever and its round housing. Below the housing a rod or tube will run forward and disappear out of sight in the direction of the engine and gearbox. Almost all the wear in the linkage occurs in the circular housing which you can now inspect.

Sometimes the gear lever itself is in two parts, held together by a rubber bush (**fig 1**). If a circlip is fitted inside the belled-out section of the upper lever, close it up and remove it with a pair of long-nosed pliers then pull the gear lever off; otherwise a strong pull in a straight line is all that is needed

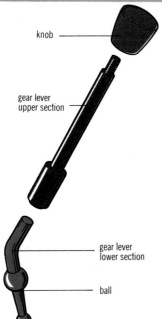

1. Two piece gear lever

knob

gear lever upper section

gear lever lower section

ball

to separate the two parts of the lever. Note whether the bush has softened with age — renewal is cheap and easy and will contribute to improving the precision of the gear change.

Next, check that the ball further down the gear lever is held firmly in the circular housing. Sometimes a large dome nut is screwed down over the stub on the housing to hold the ball and is locked with a tab washer (**fig 2**). This type does not often give trouble provided

that the tab washer is in good condition. A more common alternative is the bayonet fitting where pins or pegs project from the side of the circular housing. These engage in slots in the side of the domed ball retainer. You remove it just like a light bulb. Some gear lever retainers are held by bolts which also allow for adjustment.

If there is any noticeable slackness of the ball in its housing, then you can expect to have to renew some of the parts. If your car is fitted with a domed nut retainer, undo it with a self-locking wrench or a large adjustable spanner. Otherwise push down the ball-shaped retainer at the bottom of the lever and turn it anticlockwise — the pressure of the spring will push the lever and the other components out. This will also happen as you undo the bolts where a gate type retainer plate is fitted.

On some cars, the fork at the bottom of the gear lever is pinned to a rod which operates one of three control levers linked to the gearbox. To remove the gear lever you will first have to drive out this pin from underneath the car.

Withdraw the lever and the minor components from the housing and lay them out in order on a flat surface (**fig 3**). Watch carefully as you withdraw the lever in case there are

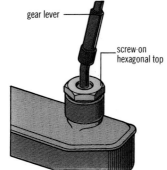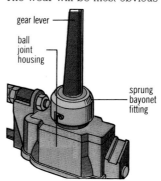

2. Three ways of retaining gear lever to remote control housing

gear lever

domed screw-on retainer

gear lever

screw-on hexagonal top

any spring-loaded plungers which press on the ball from the side to take up slackness.

Next, examine the components in turn. The gear lever itself will have a ball-shaped section lower down where it fits into the housing with another smaller ball or a fork right at the bottom where it connects with the slots in the gear change selector rods or the selector rod extension. The ball or fork should be complete and unworn; pay particular attention to the bottom end and smooth out any burrs or ridges on these parts with a light file. Make sure that all the surfaces and edges of the fork are smooth. Fit a new lever if the old one has a chunk worn out of it.

The other components usually comprise an upper and lower nylon housing and a spring with spacers, a plate and washers. The wear will be most obvious

gear lever

ball joint housing

sprung bayonet fitting

on the nylon components so you should be prepared to renew these any time that you strip or service the gear linkage. Renew the spring as well if it is broken, but you will only be able to check an old spring for slackness by comparing it with a new one.

If your gearbox has a bayonet fitting for the ball retainer, examine the pin or pins which project through the side of the housing. These can get very loose and eventually may

disappear into the gearbox or remote control housing altogether. If there is any sign at all of this happening, set the pin into the housing with an epoxy resin adhesive and make doubly sure of its security by fitting a large worm-drive clip around the housing once you have reassembled it. In extreme cases the pin or pins can fall out with the rather unnerving result of the gear lever coming off in your hand while you are driving.

When you have checked all the parts and bought replacements for any that are showing signs of wear, place all the components in order on the gear lever and lightly grease all the moving parts. Grease the

3. Gear lever assembly

recess where the bottom end of the gear lever fits and make sure that you insert the fork or the ball into the gear change rod correctly. Refit the retainer at the top and pin the lower fork back to the transverse rod if your car has the external multi-lever type linkage (**fig 4**). The bushes in these levers will probably need renewing before you adjust the rods as described in your manual. Grease the joints before you use the car. Before you drive the car though, check that you can find all the gears — including reverse.

If you can still detect a buzzing noise from the gearbox on the overrun, look in your handbook to see if any anti-noise dampers are fitted to the gear change rod. Try packing the anti-noise springs with a ball bearing of the same diameter to compress them slightly to see if that will stop the noise.

All that remains is to reassemble the console, refit the gaiter and check the gearbox oil level with the car on level ground, if you have not done this for some time.

gear lever

boot

pin

drop links

selector rods

transverse rod

4. With some linkages the lever is pinned to a transverse rod

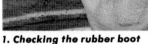
1. Checking the rubber boot

2. Checking the control rod for wear

3. Most FWD linkages have some form of universal joint

Car designers have tried many different ways to overcome the problem of linking the gear lever to the gearbox in a front wheel drive (FWD) car, and certain models are prone to gear linkage faults.

First, check and overhaul the ball joint which supports the lever, as described in Step 2.

Next, examine the condition of the rubber boot that usually fits around the base of the gear lever, underneath the car (**fig 1**). If the boot is torn or hanging off, the bushes inside have probably become worn. The bushes are usually plastic so

they wear quite quickly. Undo the retaining bolts or screws, if any, which hold the boot in place and clean up the joint with some degreasing fluid such as Gunk.

Whether or not the boot has been damaged, ask an assistant to hold the gear lever still from inside the car while you locate the main control rod that runs forward towards the engine. Do not confuse the control rod with the stabilizer bar, sometimes fitted alongside the gear linkage. Move the control rod around with a reasonable amount of force (**fig 2**) and try to

work out if the slack occurs at the bottom of the gear lever or at the other end of the control rod.

Now work forward underneath the car and trace the route of the main control rod. There is often a ball and socket or universal joint arrangement somewhere in the linkage. The ball and socket joint normally has two spherical eyes held inside a sleeve by steel pins. These joints do not normally give any trouble but try to pull the two halves apart to see if there is any wear present (**fig 3**). There should be no play in the joint. If there is, drive out the pins and press in new ones. Check any other joints that are fitted in the same way and replace them if you detect even a slight amount of wear.

If a part of the linkage is covered with a rubber boot, peel back the boot carefully and check the condition of the parts inside. Look especially for the small roll pins that are often used to join the different parts of the linkage together (**fig 4**). Do not be satisfied with an external examination in this case; drive the pin out — renew it if it is showing any sign of wear whatsoever. If the pin is reluctant to

come out you will have to drill it out, using a drill bit just slightly smaller in diameter than the pin. Tap the new pin in with a hammer.

The rest of the linkage is often bolted to the front of the control rod or held by splined joints. Check the bolts for tightness and ask your assistant to go through the gears while you check to see if any of the links are loose. If the pinch bolt or a splined joint is loose, tighten it, but if the threads are damaged, replace the pinch bolt with an ordinary nut and bolt. Other designs sometimes use linkages made of light steel rod and strip joined together quite crudely with spring clips or split pins. Wear in these parts is often quite severe as they are difficult to lubricate. Shake each part of the linkage and move it around with your hand — there should always be a little free movement so that the linkage does not bind but if movement is noticeable, then some attention is needed.

This type of linkage is often combined with relay levers joined with a vertical or horizontal shaft. Make sure that the relay levers do not move in relation to each other by watching them while your assistant goes through the gears once again. If they do move in

relation to each other, try oiling them.

Plastic ball joints and bushes are often held together by small spring clips. Prise off the clip, unscrew the ball joint body from the rod and screw on a new one. Leave the locknut in position so you get the new joint in the right place. The ball, attached to the other part of the joint, will not wear as it is made of steel: the plastic body always wears first. Snap the joint back together and refit the spring clip.

To prevent noise being transmitted along the gear linkage, a

rubber block is sometimes fitted somewhere along the control rod to insulate the engine from the gear lever. Like all rubber items it can deteriorate with age and if it is at all soft when you examine it, consider renewing it.

Finally check all the plastic or nylon bushes in the linkage. While you are going to the bother of dismantling the linkage, you might as well renew all the bushes as a matter of course because they are invariably quite cheap and it will only take a few minutes.

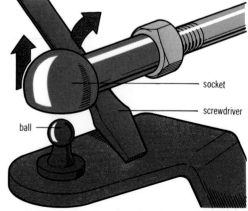

4. Many linkages are held together with roll pins

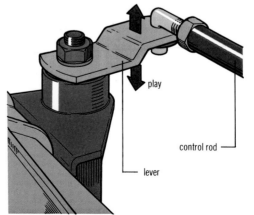

5. Check steel levers for play

6. Remove clips and snap joints apart

During your examination of the linkage, you may well find that the slackness is not due to wear at any one point but that it is produced by play at a lot of minor points. When you have made the repairs indicated in the manual for your model, work through this step making whatever adjustments you can.

If you have located some of the wear in the joint at the base of the gear lever, it can either be in the ball joint housings or in the clevis arrangement that is usually found at the bottom of the gear lever. Take off the rubber boot — this is usually fitted underneath the car but can be found inside the car on some models. Pull out the R-clip or split pin which secures the clevis pin and examine the clevis pin. You must renew a badly worn pin but in some cases the best solution will be to first flatten it slightly with a hammer if possible, so that the resulting oval section takes up some of the wear. This will not work if the pin is of the type which is clamped in the bottom of the lever (**fig 1**).

Another idea is to use one or more washers fitted on to the clevis pin between the clevis

1. Undo the grub screw to release a clamped clevis pin

and the spherical joint, so that the clevis itself is held more tightly. This will not provide a complete solution but it will take up a lot of the side to side wear. Inspect the ball joint housings to see if the surface of the plastic has been indented at all by long use. If there are any signs of wear, renew these parts. Grease all the parts lightly with general purpose grease or graphited grease as you reassemble the gear lever and

fit an undamaged boot so that the mechanism is protected from grit and the elements (Step 2).

If you have to renew a threaded ball joint anywhere in the linkage (**fig 2**), count the number of turns required to take it off and fit the new one with just the same adjustment to start with. Grease all the joints slightly as you go and where there are rubber boots fitted to the linkage, pack them lightly with grease.

Before you fit any of the roll pins, fit each part of the joint on to its respective shaft or rod and check to see that they are a tight fit. If not, try flattening the joint slightly by squeezing it in a vice or with grips. You cannot expect a small roll pin to make up for a loose joint. If you do not tighten the fit, the new pin will fail in the same way as the old one. If you find you can get slightly larger roll pins than those originally fitted, try drilling out the hole to take the larger pin. This should eliminate some of the play.

Spline fittings (**fig 3**) or bolt connections that cannot be tightened enough to stop them moving on their shafts must be taken off the car. Use a vice to

flatten the outer part of a splined sleeve and do not worry if you have to tap it back on gently with a hammer. If you find that the gap has closed up after the slight flattening, use a thin file to widen the slot while the outer part of the spline is still in the vice (**fig 4**). Sometimes a new and undamaged bolt will enable you to nip up a connection properly, but if the worst comes to the worst, replace it with a nut and bolt. If this does not work, renew the parts that are worn.

Where a bent rod is held into a link or a lever by a spring clip or a split pin, you can eliminate slop by packing out the joint with some washers of suitable thickness. Refit a spring clip in such a way that the rod is pulled into contact with the link, or use a new split pin that fits tightly into its hole in the link.

Finally look in your handbook to see if it gives any adjustment procedures for your car. Sometimes distances in millimetres are quoted for clearance between various parts and sometimes you just have to set the gear lever and selector rods to a certain position before

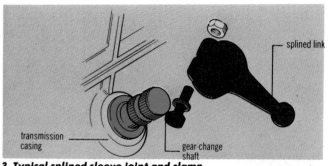

3. Typical splined sleeve joint and clamp

4. Enlarging slot in joint will enable you to clamp it tighter

finally tightening all the joints, and the linkage is automatically adjusted. On many cars, however, there is nothing to adjust and if the gearchange is still not

right the selectors inside the gearbox must need attention.

Dashboard gear changes do not wear much but they do become lighter if you smear some graphited grease or oil where the rod slides in its bushes over the engine. Try to grease the bush that supports the gear lever as it goes through the dashboard. Where access is difficult, just put some grease on the polished portion of the rod that you can get at, and give it time to work its way down to the bush. Wipe off the excess grease immediately and again after a few days use. Fit a new spring on to the rod if it has become difficult to find your way through the gears. Where the long gear change rod joins the long rod sticking vertically from the gearbox there will be a flexible bush. This will be just about the only source of wear on this type of gear linkage, so renew the bush if it is still slack or sloppy (**fig 5**).

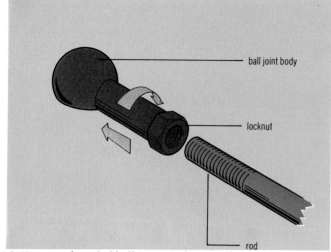

2. Unscrew threaded ball joints and renew if worn

- ball joint body
- locknut
- rod

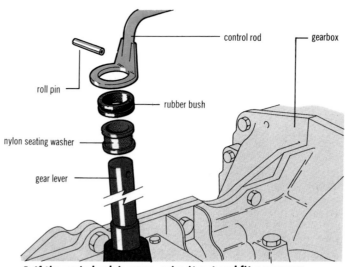

- control rod
- gearbox
- roll pin
- rubber bush
- nylon seating washer
- gear lever

5. If the main bush is worn, prise it out and fit a new one

Tyres wear unevenly

If one or both of your front tyres are showing signs of uneven wear, a simple adjustment may be all you need

The tyres are your car's only contact with the road which is perhaps why they are subject to more regulations than almost any other part of a car. You should regularly inspect them for wear and tear — at least once a month and particularly prior to the annual MOT test. Bear in mind that it is illegal and that tread patterns should be visible across the whole tread width and circumference.

General tyre care is dealt with on pages 40 to 43, but if one or both of your front tyres show signs of wear after only a few hundred miles the problem is not going to be one of the normal deterioration. You will need to check whether the wheels are correctly aligned (toe-out or toe-in), whether their camber angle is right and whether the track rod ball joints need some attention or complete renewal.

Traditionally these checks and adjustments are done professionally because they involve precise measurements and specialist equipment.

However, provided you approach each job with care there is no reason why you cannot tackle most of them yourself at home.

If you feel at all unhappy at the outcome of your work, however, or feel that you have discovered a major fault, have it checked by a specialist.

When to do this job
When front tyres show signs of uneven wear

What this job involves
Checking front tyres
Checking toe-out/toe-in
Adjusting toe-out/toe-in
Checking camber
Checking track rod ball joints

Other possible causes and related jobs
Suspension fault
Shock absorber fault
Worn wheel bearings
Please see Index for page numbers

To do this job
Tools: wheel brace; axle stands; Mole wrench; spanners; screwdrivers
Materials: Chalk, offcut or hardboard or plywood; ruler; screws; offcuts of wood
Time: Checks take less than half an hour; adjustment may take up to an hour
Degree of difficulty: Can be fiddly

If you have the job professionally done . . .
Do the steering and suspension feel more precise?
Do the tyres wear normally?

HOW IT WORKS

Steering geometry

Two aspects of the steering geometry — toe-in/toe-out and camber — directly affect tyre wear.

On most cars the front wheels are not exactly parallel to each other. Instead they are set at a small angle either pointing outwards (toe-out) or inwards (toe-in). Front wheel drive cars normally have tow-out, rear wheel drive cars toe-in. The wheels are arranged in this way to counteract the tendency for the wheels to converge or spread apart as the car's speed increases.

The steering swivels which support the front wheels are slightly to one side of the wheel — so they are subject to considerable stress. To reduce this strain, the wheels are angled slightly. This angle is known as the camber of the wheel. Some cars have their wheels angled wider apart at the bottom than the top (negative camber); others have their wheels wider apart at the top (positive camber).

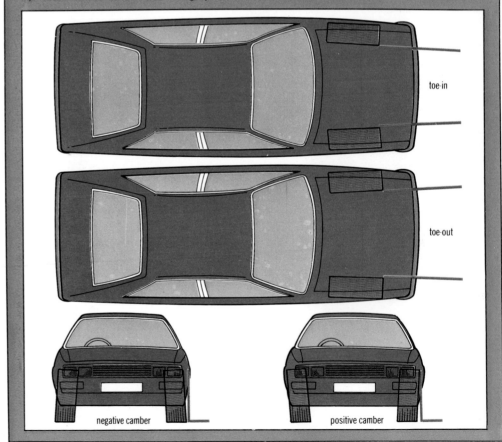

toe-in

toe-out

negative camber

positive camber

STEP 1 — CHECK FRONT TYRES

You should check the front tyres regularly for signs of uneven wear. The easiest way to do this is to look at the front of each tyre while the car is sitting on the road. You should then roll the car forward — or backward — a quarter turn of the tyre so that a new section of the tyre comes into view and can be closely examined. Make a point of comparing the two front tyres to see if the tyres are wearing in roughly the same way.

If you want a closer look, jack up the car, place it on axle stands and spin each tyre around slowly by hand while you examine the tread pattern (see Fact File — Jacking up the car, page 162). This method is more thorough as it allows you to see whether the wear pattern is consistent all the way around the tyre.

A consistent pattern of wear or damage to one side of the tyre (**fig 1**) is usually caused by one of the critical angles of steering geometry being out of line — particularly toe-out/toe-in or camber (see How it Works — Steering geometry).

Alternatively, the track rod ball joints or some part of the steering or suspension may be worn or damaged. The result is that the outer edge of the tread pattern of one or both tyres becomes worn, usually leaving a characteristic feathered pattern to the rubber (**fig 2**).

1. **Wear on one side of tyre**   2. **Feathered pattern of wear**

If you recognize this type of wear when you examine the front tyres, you should check and rectify the fault at once — before the tyre becomes dangerous.

If the wear pattern is not consistent then this would indicate a possible fault elsewhere. The tyre and the wheel should then be checked by a specialist for possible faults in the tyre itself or for wheel imbalance or damage.

STEP 2 — CHECK TOE-OUT/TOE-IN

The correct toe-out/toe-in adjustment listed in your car handbook or workshop manual is often given as an angle. However many handbooks also list the distances between the two wheel rims when toe-out or toe-in is set correctly. This is generally given as two figures,

seconds at small cost. However, you can do the job yourself by measuring the two distances and subtracting the difference. Ideally you would use a flexible steel rule held absolutely taut, but in practice this is not possible as inside wheel arches and the engine are likely to get

Then place the car on level ground with the wheels pointing straight ahead. Use the homemade device to measure the distance between the two inner wheel rims at hub height at the front of the wheel (**fig 2**). In case the rims are buckled it is best to take three separate measure-

ments — spread at, roughly 120° around the rim. Make three chalk marks on both wheels and measure the distance between each one when it is exactly level with the axle. Then roll the car forward (or backward) so that the chalk marks move through 180°.

Place the device on the inner rims on each chalk mark (again at hub height, at the rear of the wheels). Note the difference between each set of measurements. If your wheels are not buckled they should all be the same. If they vary, one or both of your wheels is buckled and the

three figures you get should be averaged.

If they correspond to the maker's recommended toe-out/toe-in figures (see Steps 4 and 5) the problem lies elsewhere. If the readings are out of true the toe-out/toe-in angle will have to be adjusted.

1. **Measuring toe-out/toe-in with homemade jig**

one measured in front of the axle and the other behind, alternatively a single figure is given for the difference between the two measurements.

Measuring the toe-out/toe-in is generally a job best left to your garage or local tyre specialist. He will have equipment that can give an accurate measurement in a matter of

in the way.

The best way is to make a measuring device from offcuts of wood, designed to fit the dimensions of your wheels (**fig 1**). Bolts are screwed to both ends and are then adjusted so that each touches a wheel rim.

First take out heavy items, such as the tool box, which could affect suspension height.

TIP
Tyre change

Whenever you have new tyres fitted to your car, its always a good idea to have the toe-out/toe-in checked at the same time. Most garages will do this for you at little extra cost.

2. **Turning in screw to wheel rim**

3. **Gap at front for toe-out measurement**

Adjustment of toe-out/toe-in is made by changing the lengths of the track rods. This is normally done by a garage or tyre fitter using specialized measuring equipment but you can make adjustments yourself — although it is always best to have these checked.

To allow for adjustment, the track rods are threaded into a sleeve or into the track ball joint with a clamp or locknut to maintain the setting. On most cars both track rods have to be adjusted, on others, only one of the track rods has an adjuster.

It is best to make adjustments with the car on the ground. This way you can take toe-out/toe-in measurements and check the adjustment as you progress. But if the track rod adjusters are difficult to get at, you should jack the car up and place it or axle stands or run the car up on ramps (see Fact File — Jacking up the car, page 162). You will then have to lower the car to the

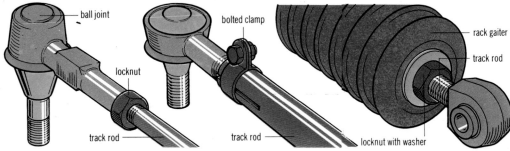

1. **Three main types of adjustable track rod end**

ground to check the measurements once the track rods have been adjusted.

As **fig 1** shows, there are three main types of adjustable track rod. Some are covered by a rubber gaiter secured at each end by a locknut and clip. Undo these to remove the gaiter.

If the track rods screw into a thread on the ball joint adjust the length of the rod by turning the track rod using a Mole wrench (**fig 2**). You may find that threads on each side of the car

turn in opposite directions.

If the track rod is screwed into a sleeve, there will be a right hand internal thread at one end and a left hand thread at the other. Undo the pinch bolts at each end of the sleeve (**fig 3**) and adjust the rod by turning the track rod sleeve.

If the car is fitted with a two-piece track rod, separate the outer from the inner rod — which is threaded into the end of the steering rack — by undoing the locknut that locks the outer

TIP

Make it easy

If you are adjusting the toe-out/toe-in with the car on the ground, put glossy magazines (of the same thickness) under each of the front wheels. When you need to move the wheels they will turn much more easily.

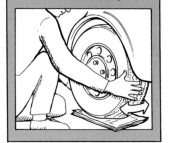

track rod in place. Use a Mole wrench on the exposed part of the inner rod to adjust accordingly. Alternatively, take the ball joint out of the steering arm (**fig 4**) and screw the outer track rod in or out as required.

When you alter the length of the track rod, turn the adjuster on each side by only half a turn at a time. After each turn, measure the toe-out/toe-in angle as described in Step 2 do not forget to roll the car back and forth first or you may get a false reading. Continue this process until the adjustment is correct, then retighten the locknuts or pinch bolts. Finally, replace the gaiter and tighten the fixing clips, if necessary.

3. **Releasing pinch bolts on track rod sleeve**

4. **Removing ball joint from steering arm**

2. **Adjusting track rod length by turning track rod**

1. Using homemade tool to measure camber

True camber measurement requires sophisticated gauges, but you can make a rough check using a homemade tool of your own made from an offcut of hardboard or thin plywood.

To make the tool you need a triangle of wood long enough to reach the top wheel rim when it is standing flat on the ground. Make absolutely sure that the right angle corner is true or your readings will not be accurate.

Cut sections of wood away so that a vertical straight edge of the wood will just touch both the top and bottom of the shoulder of the wheel rim. You may have to cut out a section in the middle to allow for a protruding hub or trim. The distance between top and bottom measuring points is the same as the wheel diameter.

Set the car on level ground as described in Step 2. Hold the tool up against the shoulder of

	10"	12"	13"	15"
0°30'	2·2mm	2·7mm	2·9mm	3·3mm
1°	4·4	5·3	5·8	6·7
1°30"	6·7	8·0	8·6	10·0
2°	8·9	10·6	11·5	13·3
2°30"	11·1	13·3	14·4	16·6
3°	13·3	16·0	17·3	20·0

2. Chart converts camber angle to measurment in mm

the wheel rim with its bottom edge flat against the ground. The vertical edge of the tool will touch the same point on the rim at the top — called positive camber, or bottom — negative camber.

To convert the camber angle quoted in your handbook for your wheel rim size, use the table given in **fig 2**. For example, on a 13 in. wheel a negative camber angle of 1°30' (1½°) will produce a gap of 8.6 mm at the top wheel rim. Estimate intermediate values.

Measure the gap between the bottom or top of the vertical side of the tool and the wheel rim (**fig 1**). Repeat this procedure on both sides of the car. The measurement should be the same. If there are consistent variations get a garage to carry out a check on the camber and make any appropriate adjustments.

A possible cause of uneven tyre wear could be worn or damaged track rod ball joints. To check the joints, jack up the car and place it on stands (see Fact File — Jacking up the car, page 162).

Clean off dirt from around the rubber seal — which is fitted over the exposed part of the joint — with a brush or a rag and examine it closely for signs of damage. If the seal is split, it is likely that dirt and water will have entered the joint and corrosion will have set in. If so, the joint should be renewed and a new seal fitted to retain the lubricant.

If the seals are undamaged, check the joint for free play. Get a helper to turn the steering wheel slowly from side to side while you grip the joint and feel for any undue slackness as the wheels are turned from lock to lock (**fig 1**). Then push the track rod up and down to see if there is any vertical play. If any of the tests reveal movement, the joint should be renewed.

You should also check for wear between the track rod and the steering rack. To do this first split the ball joint and disconnect the rod from the steering arm completely. Then grip the track rod and push and pull it towards and away from the gaiter. If any play can be felt the rack should be changed or serviced.

1. Checking ball joint for play as wheels are turned by helper

2. Checking for wear between track rod and steering rack

When the bolt won't budge

Almost every car has a few nuts and bolts which are difficult to shift, but with a little care you can free even the most stubborn of them

Even the simplest job can turn into a nightmare when a nut, bolt or screw refuses to undo. And once you have burred the metal it becomes progressively harder to deal with, until it is virtually a lost cause and you have drawn blood.

The main reason why professional mechanics do not have to spend hours trying to undo stubborn nuts is that they use the right tool for the job in the first place, and use it properly.

This means, for example, using ring or socket spanners wherever possible (see Fact File — Tools for the job), and also not simply reaching for a pair of grips or any spanner that seems to fit. They give a better grip on the nut or bolt head than the cheaper open-ended spanners.

The answer is to know how to undo nuts, bolts and screws properly. If one proves awkward, use these professional methods to make the job easier.

Clean the fastener

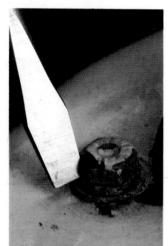

1. Scraping paint from bolt head

2. Using oil from the dipstick

Before attempting to undo any nut, bolt or screw, clean off dirt, rust or paint. Use an old screwdriver blade to chip off paint or thick layers of dirt and give a rusty fastening a good cleaning with a wire brush. If a nut or bolt head is covered with oil and dirt clean it with a paintbrush soaked in paraffin (kerosene).

Releasing fluid

If you try to turn the fastening and find that it will not move, it is worth spraying around it with a releasing fluid, such as WD-40, or a penetrating oil, such as Plus-Gas. Leave the fastening for a few minutes to allow the fluid to soak in to the threaded section. If you have neither type of fluid or any other oil to hand, a little oil dropped on to the fastening from the engine dipstick may help to release it.

If you anticipate trouble with a rusty-looking fastening, spray a little releasing fluid on it each day for three or four days before attempting the job. This allows the fluid plenty of time to work and should release the component with a minimum of struggling.

Jarring the threads

Tapping any tight nut or bolt before you try to unscrew it will jar the threads and may loosen them slightly. Use a hammer to hit the bolt squarely on its head or use a hammer together with a soft metal bar (made of copper or brass) to hit the nut or bolt on one of its flats (**fig 1**). Be careful not to damage any exposed thread. Where you have to jar a nut on the exposed end of a bolt or stud, put a block or wood between the hammer and nut to protect the threads (**fig 2**).

You can loosen screws in the same way by tapping the screwdriver handle, with the blade securely in the slot on the screw. Hold the screwdriver blade tightly, making sure that it is in line with the screw when you do this.

Beware of damaging the screwdriver handle when you hit it — whenever possible use a screwdriver with a wooden handle or one with a metal shaft which goes right through the handle.

TIP

Open-ended technique

When undoing nuts and bolts with an open-ended spanner always make sure the longer of the two jaws is behind the nut or bolt head in the direction of leverage. This gives you maximum leverage from the spanner and makes it less likely to slip off the head.

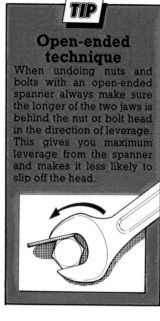

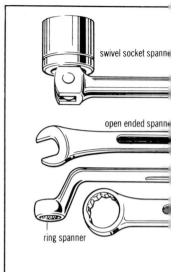

swivel socket spanner

open ended spanner

ring spanner

There are four types of spanners that you are likely to use time and time again for dismantling and reassembling jobs. Depending on how much work you intend to do, you may build up a tool kit containing some or all types. These are — open-ended; ring; combination and socket spanners (see above). No single type is suited to every application and each has its advantages and disadvantages.

An open-ended spanner can be used to reach the head of a bolt that is inaccessible with any other type. However, it grips only part of the bolt or nut head and may slip under heavy pressure (see Tip — Open-ended technique).

1. Trying to jar nut around

2. Hitting end of bolt threads

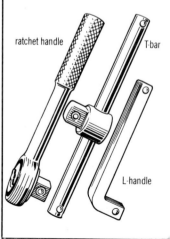

ratchet handle

T-bar

L-handle

Tools for the job

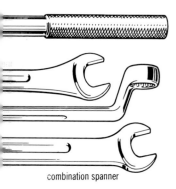

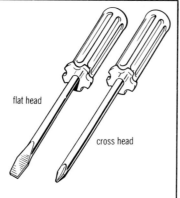

flat head

cross head

combination spanner

Ring spanners encircle the whole of the nut head and are less likely to slip off than open-enders, so a great deal of pressure can be exerted with this type.

Combination spanners have open-ended jaws at one end and a ring of the same size at the other and offer the convenience of both spanner types in a single tool.

Socket spanners are similar to ring spanners in the way that they grip the whole nut or bolt. Sockets are fitted to one of a range of jointed levers such as a T-bar, knuckle bar or two-way ratchet. Sockets give more leverage on a tight fastening than any other type of spanner and, when used with a knuckle joint, can be turned from an angle. But the bulky body of a socket may prevent it fitting on a nut or bolt where space around the head is limited.

There are other kinds of spanners with more specialized uses. Among those you may need to use are box spanners and socket wrenches (Allen keys). A box spanner is like a tubular socket with a hexagonal end section. It is particularly useful for reaching deep recesses. The spanner is turned by a steel bar inserted through holes in the tube section. Socket wrenches are used on socket-headed screws — that is, screws which have hexagon shaped recesses in the top of the screw head.

Most modern cars have metric nuts and bolts made in millimetre sizes — though older UK produced cars may have Imperial sizes or a mixture of the two. Generally, though, a small range of spanner sizes should be sufficient to shift most nuts and bolts. You may even find that some metric sizes fit Imperial fitting and vice versa (see Fact File — Spanner equivalents).

When you cannot find the right size spanner you may be tempted to use an adjustable type, either one with flat jaws or the self-locking grip type with serrated jaws — such as Mole grips. These frequently prove useful when all else fails, but use them with care as the jaws may slip under heavy pressure and cause damage to the nut or bolt head.

Screwdrivers are made in a great variety of sizes and types. The blade ends are of two basic shapes, either flat blade or crosshead shape. They are not interchangeable and you should not try to use, for example, a flat blade driver in a crosshead screw.

The important thing to remember whenever you use a screwdriver is to choose a blade size that either completely fills, or is wider than, the screw head and to keep the blade well down in the slot. A correctly fitting screwdriver will

box spanner

socket wrench

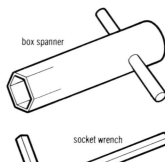

impact driver

give maximum leverage on the screw with the least risk of slipping and damaging the head.

Before using a flat blade screwdriver always check that the blade is in good condition. The blade should be absolutely flat on each side and squared off at the end. If the screwdriver is damaged discard it, or file it flat on the sides and square off the tip.

Screwdriver handles vary considerably in size and shape. Generally, the larger and fatter the handle the easier it is to grip and the more turning power you can exert with it.

You can buy short screwdrivers which are intended for use on screws in positions where it is difficult to use a long screwdriver.

Screws which cannot be undone by any other means can often be removed with an impact screwdriver. This is a tool with interchangeable blades which, when put in a screw head and struck with a hammer, turns the blade automatically at the same time. Some types also accept socket heads as well as screwdriver blades. Though relatively expensive to buy, an impact screwdriver may pay for itself in terms of time and effort saved if you own an older car with many corroded or stubborn nuts, bolts and screws.

Get more leverage

A nut, bolt or screw which was overtightened, rather than one that has rusted in place, can usually be released by adding more leverage to the normal spanner or screwdriver. Before you try this, though, try to further tighten the fastening with your spanner or screwdriver. Quite often this is actually easier than trying to turn it the other way. If the nut or bolt turns, it will help release the grip between the threads and then makes the fastening easy to undo.

Gain more leverage on a spanner by slipping a length of metal tubing over the spanner shank to extend it (**fig 1**) Do not try this on rusted fastenings as the extra force you can exert may simply shear off the head. However, if all else has failed it may be the only way to shift a very stubborn bolt or nut. If you shear the head off a bolt or a nut off a stud, remove the rest of it later with mole grips.

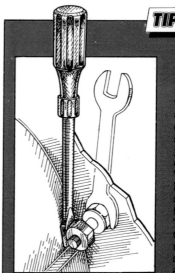

1. Extend spanner with tubing

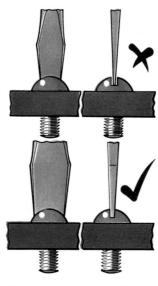

2. Correct screwdriver fitting

3. Extra leverage using grips

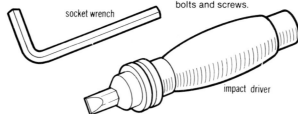

TIP

Wedge it

If a bolt head or nut spins without undoing when turned from the other end and you cannot fit a spanner on it, it may be possible to stop it from turning by jamming it with the tip of an old flat-bladed screwdriver. Try to wedge the flat of the blade between a close-by solid object or surface and a flat on the bolt head or nut. This stops the head from turning and enables you to undo the nut normally. Make sure that you do not wedge against anything fragile.

4. Spanner on square shank

You can gain more leverage with a screwdriver by using it together with self-locking grips, pliers or a spanner. First tap the screwdriver in to the screw slot to locate it securely, then apply pressure to make sure it does not jump out. Clip the grips tightly to the metal (**fig 3**) and turn. Alternatively, grip the flat

5. Using pliers on screwdriver

blade end of a screwdriver with pliers (**fig 5**) and turn — or get an assistant to help you. Some screwdrivers are made with a square shank — if you have one of these, use a spanner on the flats for extra turning power while you push hard on the end of the screwdriver (**fig 4**). Take care not to let it slip.

IMPERIAL – METRIC SPANNER EQUIVALENTS

When And How To Use This Table

Quite often you have to undo a nut or bolt but you do not have the right spanner. What other spanners will fit? Measure the distance across the flats of the nut or bolt in millimetres, then look at the table to find Imperial sizes that are close. You may have to tap some of the equivalents on to the head. Some may be a loose fit, these are indicated by the sizes shown in italics.

Example A nut measures 15 mm across. You can use a 19/32" AF spanner — which actually measures 15.09 mm across the flats, virtually a perfect fit. Alternatively, a 5/16" Whitworth spanner or a 3/8" BSF spanner will be a rather loose fit, as shown in italics. Strictly, you should not use them — they could round off the nuts — but they may do in an emergency.

ISO Metric (Stamped figure is size in mm)	Unified (Stamped 'A/F')	Whitworth (Stamped 'W' or 'BSW')	British Standard Fine (Stamped 'BSF')
6mm	1/4" (6.35mm)		
7mm			
8mm	5/16" (7.95mm)		
9mm	11/32" (8.71mm)	1/8" (8.71mm)	
10mm	3/8" (9.53mm)		
11mm	7/16" (11.13mm)	3/16" (11.30mm)	1/4" (11.30mm)
12mm			
13mm	1/2" (12.70mm)	1/4" (13.34mm)	5/16" (13.34mm)
14mm	9/16" (14.30mm)		
15mm	19/32" (15.09mm)	5/16" (15.24mm)	3/8" (15.24mm)
16mm	5/8" (15.88mm)		
17mm	11/16" (17.48mm)		
18mm	11/16" (17.48mm)	3/8" (18.03mm)	7/16" (18.03mm)
19mm	3/4" (19.05mm)		
20mm	25/32" (19.84mm)		
21mm	13/16" (20.65mm)	·7/16" (20.83mm)	1/2" (20.83mm)
22mm	7/8" (22.23mm)		
23mm			
24mm	15/16" (23.83mm)		
25mm	1" (25.40mm)	9/16" (25.65mm)	5/8" (25.65mm)
26mm	1" (25.40mm)	9/16" (25.65mm)	5/8" (25.65mm)
27mm	1 1/16" (26.99mm)		
28mm	1 1/8" (28.58mm)	5/8" (27.94mm)	11/16" (27.94mm)
29mm	1 1/8" (28.58mm)		
30mm	none	none	none

Removing studs

Studs are headless bolts threaded at both ends with plain metal between, or threaded along their whole length. On the type with a thread at both ends, clamp self-locking grips on the plain section to undo the stud section. Where there is no threadless section, screw a pair of nuts on the stud and tighten them to lock against each other (**fig 1**). You can then use a spanner on the lower nut to extract the stud in the same way as undoing a bolt.

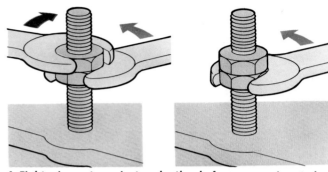

1. Tightening nuts against each other before unscrewing stud

Using heat

If all else fails to move a nut, bolt or screw, heating it up may help to release it. You can do this with direct heat, from a blowtorch, for example, or indirect heat from boiling water. Only a gentle warming is needed — so if using a blowtorch do not play a hot flame on the nut or bolt for too long. Remember, also, if heating something below the car that heat may pass through the floor and set fire to carpets

or damage wiring on the other side. Remove anything flammable, therefore, before you start. Also ensure that naked flames are kept well away from fuel lines, tank and carburettor and any rubber, plastic or wiring insulation. If this is difficult, make up a heat shield from a tin can and place it between the flame and fastening (**fig 3**).

Boiling water can be poured directly over a fastening if it is accessible from above, but make sure none enters electri-

1. Making a heat shield

2. After cutting to shape

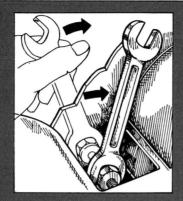

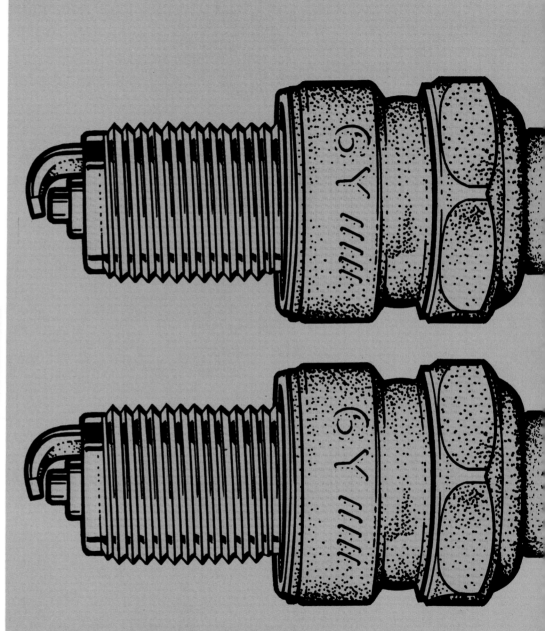

TIP

Nuts and through-bolts

Remember when undoing a nut and through-bolt that you need to hold both with spanners. However, it is often impossible to hold both spanners at the same time because space is tight or you cannot reach. Depending on the location, the solution to this problem is to put both spanners in position on the heads and turn one spanner until the other becomes jammed against surrounding body-work or another component. Make sure though, that the surface against which the spanner jams is quite solid. Do not jam a spanner against flexible hoses, pipes, paint-work, thin metal plate or any other surface which could be damaged.

cal components. If you want to heat up bolt heads or nuts accessible only from below, hold a container of boiling water close to them so they remain immersed for a minute or two (**fig 4**).

After you have heated the fastenings, spray them with releasing fluid and they should come undone more easily. Do not worry if the releasing fluid just turns to steam when it hits the bolt or stud — some of it will reach the threads.

4. Using boiling water to expand screw threads

3. Heating bolt with a blowtorch

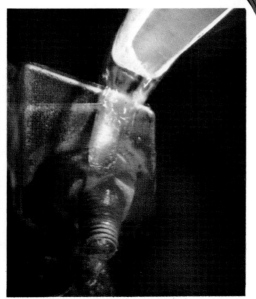

5. Pouring hot water over threads

INDEX

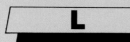

INDEX